SECOND EDITION

Programming WPF

Chris Sells and Ian Griffiths

D1354872

O'REILLY®

Beijing · Cambridge · Farnham · Köln · Paris · Sebastopol · Taipei · Tokyo

Programming WPF, Second Edition
by Chris Sells and Ian Griffiths

Copyright © 2007, 2005 O'Reilly Media, Inc. All rights reserved.
Printed in the United States of America.

Published by O'Reilly Media, Inc., 1005 Gravenstein Highway North, Sebastopol, CA 95472.

O'Reilly books may be purchased for educational, business, or sales promotional use. Online editions are also available for most titles (*safari.oreilly.com*). For more information, contact our corporate/institutional sales department: (800) 998-9938 or *corporate@oreilly.com*.

Editor: John Osborn
Production Editor: Rachel Monaghan
Copyeditor: Audrey Doyle
Proofreader: Rachel Monaghan

Indexer: John Bickelhaupt
Cover Designer: Karen Montgomery
Interior Designer: David Futato
Illustrators: Robert Romano and Jessamyn Read

Printing History:

August 2007:	Second Edition.
September 2005:	First Edition.

 This book uses RepKover™, a durable and flexible lay-flat binding.

ISBN-13: 978-0-596-51037-4
[C]   [4/08]

Table of Contents

Forewords . . . . **xi**

Preface . . . . **xv**

1. Hello, WPF **1**

    WPF from Scratch   1

    XAML Browser Applications (XBAPs)   14

    Content Models   16

    Layout   19

    Controls   22

    Data Binding   22

    Dependency Properties   27

    Resources   28

    Styles   30

    Animation   31

    Control Templates   32

    Graphics   33

    3D   34

    Documents and Printing   34

2. Applications and Settings **36**

    Application Lifetime   36

    Application Deployment   48

    Settings   55

3. Layout **61**
   Layout Basics   61
   StackPanel   62
   WrapPanel   65
   DockPanel   66
   Grid   69
   Canvas   84
   Viewbox   86
   Common Layout Properties   89
   When Content Doesn't Fit   99
   ScrollViewer   101
   Custom Layout   105

4. Input **109**
   Routed Events   109
   Mouse Input   117
   Keyboard Input   120
   Ink Input   122
   Commands   124
   Code-Based Input Handling Versus Triggers   137

5. Controls **139**
   What Are Controls?   139
   Buttons   141
   Slider and Scroll Controls   144
   ProgressBar   145
   Text Controls   146
   ToolTip   149
   GroupBox and Expander   150
   List Controls   152
   Menus   160
   Toolbars   164
   GridSplitter   166

6. Simple Data Binding **168**
   Without Data Binding   168
   Data Binding   177
   Debugging Data Binding   198

7. Binding to List Data **200**

Binding to List Data   200

Data Source Providers   228

Master-Detail Binding   245

Hierarchical Binding   252

8. Styles **257**

Without Styles   257

Inline Styles   261

Named Styles   262

Element-Typed Styles   268

Data Templates and Styles   271

Triggers   275

9. Control Templates **284**

Beyond Styles   284

Logical and Visual Trees   305

Data-Driven UI   308

10. Windows and Dialogs **314**

Window   314

Dialogs   322

11. Navigation **341**

NavigationWindow   341

Pages   342

Frames   359

XBAPs   361

Navigation to HTML   363

12. Resources **365**

Creating and Using Resources   365

Resources and Styles   378

Binary Resources   383

Global Applications   389

13. Graphics **395**

Graphics Fundamentals   395

Shapes   406

Bitmaps   429

Brushes and Pens 439
Transformations 461
Visual Layer Programming 463

14. Text and Flow Documents **468**
Fonts and Text Styles 468
Text and the User Interface 478
Text Object Model 493
Typography 519

15. Printing and XPS **522**
XPS 522
XPS Document Classes 524
Generating XPS Output 533
XPS File Generation Features 543
System.Printing 555
Displaying Fixed Documents 561

16. Animation and Media **563**
Animation Fundamentals 563
Timelines 579
Keyframe Animations 593
Path Animations 598
Clocks and Control 601
Transition Animations 605
Audio and Video 608

17. 3D Graphics **612**
3D Content in a 2D World 612
Cameras 613
Models 618
Lights 629
Textures 635
Transforms 637
3D Data Visualization 642
Hit Testing 648

18. Custom Controls **651**

Custom Control Basics   651

Choosing a Base Class   652

Custom Functionality   655

Supporting Templates in Custom Controls   668

Default Styles   674

UserControl   676

Adorners   678

A. XAML **683**

B. Interoperability **715**

C. Asynchronous and Multithreaded WPF Programming **738**

D. WPF Base Types **750**

E. Silverlight **766**

Index **821**

Forewords

First Edition

Over the past two-plus years, my day job has involved XAML-izing various parts of the Microsoft universe. My standard refrain when encountering XAML newbies has been "read the XAML appendix from Chris and Ian's book." That appendix (originally printed in the beta edition of this book) was easily the most direct and to-the-point treatment of the topic I've seen, and several dozen of my coworkers got their first taste of XAML from Ian's excellent writing. (Ian wrote the XAML appendix.) Over the past year, as I've started to make the transition from runtime plumber to pixel pusher, the chapters on WPF proper were super-efficient in getting me off the ground (things have changed a lot since I wrote my last WndProc).

At the time this edition hits the shelves, there are numerous books dedicated to WPF, written by some pretty notable folks. This book is unique in that Ian has been telling the story on the road for a couple of years getting the right balance of conceptual understanding and pragmatic "everyone screws this up" experience. I know from personal experience that there's nothing like teaching to hone a story to perfection—this book is evidence of that.

Ian's co-author should thank his lucky stars that Ian was willing to travel the planet trying out the material rather than taking a cushy job in Windows.

Now that they've gotten this book out, maybe Ian should take a cushy job, too.

He's certainly earned it.

Second Edition

Wow, I can't believe that after all that time in the chute, .NET 3.0 and Windows Vista have finally shipped.

I vividly remember scrambling backstage at PDC 2003 with Chris trying to ready the first live demonstration of .NET 3.0 (then called WinFX) for the keynote speaker,

Jim Allchin. It was an especially stressful keynote because Los Angeles was plagued with brush fires at the time and Chris Anderson's flight had been canceled; fortunately Chris Sells had already arrived and was ready to pinch-hit both in preparation and presentation if Chris, in fact, couldn't make it to L.A. in time. At the time, Chris' job at Microsoft was to make sure that Vista—including WPF—was a smashing success. Little did he know it would take almost four years until the product actually shipped (which of course is a prerequisite for success).

So, what's the big deal with WPF?

Like its sister .NET 3.0 technology, Windows Workflow Foundation (WF), WPF embraces the "it takes a village" approach to software development and uses XAML to allow people with different skill sets to collaborate in the development process. In the case of WF, XAML lets high-level process and rule descriptions integrate with imperative code written in C# or Visual Basic. In the case of WPF, XAML is the bridge between us code monkeys and the beret-wearing, black-turtleneck set who design visuals that look like they weren't designed by, well, us code monkeys.

WPF really is an impressive piece of technology: documents, forms, and multimedia all wrapped up nicely in a markup- and code-friendly package.

What I find even more impressive is the fact that Chris found the time outside his day job to pull together the book you're holding in your hands right now, capturing those four-plus years of experience with WPF (including screenshots!) into a digestible and portable form.

I've had the good fortune of having many conversations with Chris over the years about the nuances of WPF—sometimes on the phone, sometimes in his office (it's across the hall from mine), and sometimes at the poker table.

This book has taught me a whole lot more.

Now that it's all shipped, let the light blinking begin!

—Don Box
Architect, Microsoft

When I joined Microsoft 11 years ago, I first worked in the IT group, building applications to help the Microsoft sales force analyze data. I developed using Visual Basic 4.0 on early versions of Windows 95 and Windows NT 3.51 before moving over to work on the development team for Visual Basic 5.0, and later, 6.0. As time went on, I worked on Visual J++, Windows Foundation Classes, .NET, Windows Forms, ASP.NET, and eventually the Windows Presentation Foundation (WPF).

When I learned to program Windows, I read the book that was considered the "bible" of Windows programming at the time, *Programming Windows 3.1* by Charles Petzold (Microsoft Press). After helping to build the next-generation programming platform for Microsoft—the .NET Framework—I was first introduced to Chris Sells because he'd written the "bible" of programming .NET client applications: *Windows Forms Programming* (Addison-Wesley). Later, while I was building WPF, Chris and Ian were already writing the first book for that technology, too. As part of his work, Chris provided feedback on early versions of WPF, drawing on his extensive experience as a preeminent author and educator for programming client applications for Windows. In fact, based on his sensibilities, we actually refer to a customer-focused style of system design used in my group as the "Sellsian" approach.

Of course, Chris didn't write this book all by himself. Ian Griffiths is a tremendously gifted technologist with a pedigree that includes working with Develop-Mentor and now Pluralsight as a consultant, developer, speaker, and author (his works include *.NET Windows Forms in a Nutshell* [O'Reilly]), focusing on a wide range of technologies including Windows Forms and WPF. I've had less opportunity to spend time with Ian; however, in every interaction with him, I have been amazed!

Chris and Ian have both followed client technology since the early days of Windows. While I have spent my career building platforms, Chris and Ian have spent their careers making them accessible to a broad range of developers. As Chris puts it, they've been "following along behind [me] with a broom and a dustpan, cleaning up [my] messes for years."

This book is a thorough and comprehensive dive into WPF. Chris and Ian's unique approach to explaining and building software illuminates the corners and open vistas of the platform. When they bump into its limitations, they don't just explain them, but they show you how to work around them and solve real-world problems.

If you are looking for an exhaustive treatment of how to build applications using the Windows Presentation Foundation, this book deserves a spot on your shelf.

—Chris Anderson
Former architect of Windows Presentation Foundation

Preface

It's been a long road to the Windows Presentation Foundation.

I learned to program Windows from *Programming Windows 3.1*, by Charles Petzold (Microsoft Press). In those days, programming for Windows was about windows, menus, dialogs, and child controls. To make it all work, we had WndProcs (window procedure functions) and messages. We dealt with the keyboard and the mouse. If we got fancy, we would do some nonclient work. Oh, and there was the stuff in the big blank space in the middle that I could fill however I wanted with the graphics device interface (GDI), but my 2D geometry had better be strong to get it to look right, let alone perform adequately.

Later I moved to the Microsoft Foundation Classes (MFC), where we had this thing called a "document," which was separate from the "view." The document could be any old data I wanted it to be and the view, well, the view was the big blank space in the middle that I could fill however I wanted with the MFC wrappers around GDI.

Later there was this thing called DirectX, which was finally about providing tools for filling in the space with hardware-accelerated 3D polygons, but DirectX was built for writing full-screen games, so using it to build content visualization and management applications just made my head hurt.

Windows Forms, on the other hand, was such a huge productivity boost and I loved it so much that I wrote a book about it (as did my coauthor). Windows Forms was built on top of .NET, a managed environment that took a lot of programming minutiae off my hands so that I could concentrate on the content. Plus, Windows Forms itself gave me all kinds of great tools for laying out my windows, menus, dialogs, and child controls. And the inside of the windows where I showed my content? Well, if the controls weren't already there to do what I wanted, I could draw the content however I wanted using the GDI+ wrappers in System.Drawing, which was essentially the same drawing model Windows programmers had been using for the past 20 years, before even hardware graphics acceleration in 2D, let alone 3D.

In the meantime, a whole other way of interacting with content came along: HTML. HTML was great at letting me arrange my content, both text and graphics, and it would flow it and reflow it according to the preferences of the user. Further, with the recent emergence of AJAX (Asynchronous JavaScript and XML), this environment gets even more capable. Still, HTML isn't so great if you want to control more of the user experience than just the content, or if you want to do anything Windows-specific, both things that even Windows 3.1 programmers took for granted.

More recently, the Windows Presentation Foundation (WPF) happened. Initially it felt like another way to create my windows, menus, dialogs, and child controls. However, WPF shares a much deeper love for content than has yet been provided by any other Windows programming framework.

To support content at the lowest levels, WPF merges controls, text, and graphics into one programming model; all three are placed into the same element tree in the same way. And although these primitives are built on top of DirectX to leverage the 3D hardware acceleration that is dormant when you're not running the latest twitch game, they're also built into .NET, providing the same productivity boost to WPF programmers that Windows Forms programmers enjoy.

One level up, WPF provides its "content model," which allows any control to host any group of other controls. You don't have to build special `BitmapButton` or `IconComboBox` classes; you put as many images, shapes, videos, 3D models, or whatever into a `Button` (or a `ComboBox`, `ListBox`, etc.) as suit your fancy.

To help you arrange the content, whether in fixed or flow layout, WPF provides container elements that implement various layout algorithms in a way that is completely independent of the content they're holding.

To help you visualize the content, WPF provides data binding, control templates, and animation. Data binding produces and synchronizes visual elements on the fly based on your content. Control templates allow you to replace the complete look of a control while maintaining its behavior. Animation brings your user interface control to life, giving your users immediate feedback as they interact with it. These features give you the power to produce data visualizations so far beyond the capabilities of the data grid, the pinnacle most applications aspire to, that even Edward Tufte would be proud.

Combine these features with ClickOnce for the deployment and update of your WPF applications, both as standalone clients and as blended with your web site inside the browser, and you've got the foundation of the next generation of Windows applications.

The next generation of applications is going to blaze a trail into the unknown. WPF represents the best of the control-based Windows and content-based web worlds, combined with the performance of DirectX and the deployment capabilities of Click-Once, building for us a vehicle just itching to be taken for a spin. And like the introduction of fonts to the PC, which produced "ransom note" office memos, and the invention of HTML, which produced blinking online brochures, WPF is going to produce its own accidents along the road. Before we learn just what we've got in WPF, we're going to see a lot of strange and wonderful sights. I can't tell you where we're going to end up, but with this book, I hope to fill your luggage rack so that you can make the journey.

The good news is that you will not be traveling alone. In the period between the first and second editions of this book, a large user base has sprung up, providing all kinds of information and real-world applications to inspire you. A tiny sampling of the best of this information is listed here:

- Tim Sneath's big list of great WPF applications: *http://blogs.msdn.com/tims/ search.aspx?q=%22great+wpf+applications%22* (*http://tinysells.com/114*)
- Tim Sneath's big list of WPF blogs: *http://blogs.msdn.com/tims/articles/475132.aspx* (*http://tinysells.com/115*)
- Karsten Januszewski's Five-Day Course for Hitting the WPF Curve/Cliff: *http:// blogs.msdn.com/karstenj/archive/2006/06/15/632639.aspx* (*http://tinysells.com/116*)
- Microsoft's WPF community site: *http://wpf.netfx3.com*
- The MSDN WPF home page: *http://msdn2.microsoft.com/en-us/netframework/ aa663326.aspx* (*http://tinysells.com/117*)
- CodeProject's WPF section: *http://www.codeproject.com/WPF* (*http://tinysells.com/ 118*)
- thirteen23's inspirational set of WPF lab experiments: *http://www.thirteen23.com/ labs.html* (*http://tinysells.com/119*)
- Lee Brimelow's set of WPF designer tutorials: *http://contentpresenter.com*

—Chris Sells

Who This Book Is For

As much as I love the designers of the world, who are going to go gaga over WPF, this book is aimed squarely at my people: developers. We're not teaching programming here, so having experience with some sort of programming environment is a must before you read this book. Programming in .NET and C# is pretty much required; Windows Forms, XML, and HTML are all recommended.

How This Book Is Organized

Here's what each chapter of this book will cover:

Chapter 1, *Hello, WPF*

This chapter introduces the basics of WPF. It then provides a whirlwind tour of the features that we will cover in the following chapters, so you can see how everything fits together before we delve into the details.

Chapter 2, *Applications and Settings*

In this chapter, we show how WPF manages application-wide concerns, such as the lifetime of your process, keeping track of open windows, and storing application-wide states and settings. We also show your options for deploying applications to end users' machines using ClickOnce.

Chapter 3, *Layout*

WPF provides a powerful set of tools for managing the visual layout of your applications. This chapter shows how to use this toolkit, and how to extend it.

Chapter 4, *Input*

This chapter shows how to make your WPF application respond to user input. We illustrate low-level input event handling, and the higher-level command system.

Chapter 5, *Controls*

Controls are the building blocks of a user interface. This chapter describes the controls built into the WPF framework.

Chapter 6, *Simple Data Binding*

All applications need to present information to the user. This chapter shows how to use WPF's data binding features to connect the user interface to your underlying data.

Chapter 7, *Binding to List Data*

This chapter builds on the preceding one, showing how data binding works with lists of items. It also shows how to bind to hierarchical data.

Chapter 8, *Styles*

WPF's styling mechanism provides a powerful way to control your application's appearance while ensuring its consistency.

Chapter 9, *Control Templates*

WPF provides an astonishing level of flexibility in how you can customize the appearance of your user interface and the controls it contains. This chapter examines these facilities, showing how you can modify the appearance of built-in controls.

Chapter 10, *Windows and Dialogs*

WPF's Window class is the basis for your main application windows. It also provides the facilities necessary to build dialog windows.

Chapter 11, *Navigation*

As well as supporting traditional single window and cascading window applications, WPF offers support for a web-like navigation style of user interface. This chapter shows how to use these services either for your whole application, or within a nested frame as part of a window. It also shows the "XBAP" deployment model, which allows a WPF application to be hosted in a web browser.

Chapter 12, *Resources*

This chapter describes WPF's resource handling mechanisms, which are used for managing styles, themes, and binary resources such as graphics.

Chapter 13, *Graphics*

WPF offers a powerful set of drawing primitives. It also offers an object model for manipulating drawings once you have created them.

Chapter 14, *Text and Flow Documents*

WPF offers support for high-quality rendering of formatted text throughout the user interface. This chapter explains the text services available wherever text is used, and the text object model that defines how text is formatted. It also describes how to use FlowDocuments to present large volumes of mixed text and graphics, in a way that is optimized for on-screen viewing.

Chapter 15, *Printing and XPS*

This chapter describes WPF's printing services. Printing in WPF is very closely tied to XPS—the XML Paper Specification. This fixed-format document format allows printable output to be written into a file. The chapter explores both the XPS file format, and the APIs for printing and generating XPS documents.

Chapter 16, *Animation and Media*

This chapter describes WPF's animation facilities, which allow most visible aspects of a user interface, such as size, shape, color, and position, to be animated. It also describes the media playback services, which allow video and audio to be synchronized with animations.

Chapter 17, *3D Graphics*

WPF applications can host 3D models in their user interface. Two-dimensional graphics and user interfaces can also be projected onto 3D surfaces. This chapter describes the 3D API, and shows how the worlds of 2D and 3D come together in WPF.

Chapter 18, *Custom Controls*

This chapter shows how to write custom controls and other custom element types. It shows how to take full advantage of the WPF framework to build controls as powerful and flexible as those that are built-in.

Appendix A, *XAML*

The eXtensible Application Markup Language (XAML) is an XML-based language that can be used to represent the structure of a WPF user interface. This appendix describes how XAML is used to create graphs of objects.

Appendix B, *Interoperability*

WPF is able to coexist with old user interface technologies, enabling developers to take advantage of WPF without rewriting their existing applications. This appendix describes the interoperability features that make this possible.

Appendix C, *Asynchronous and Multithreaded WPF Programming*

Multithreaded code and asynchronous programming are important techniques for making sure your application remains responsive to user input at all times. This appendix explains WPF's threading model, and shows how to make sure your threads coexist peacefully with a WPF UI.

Appendix D, *WPF Base Types*

WPF has a large and complex class inheritance hierarchy. Understanding the roles of all these types and the relationships between them can be very daunting when you first approach WPF. This appendix singles out the most important types, and explains how they fit into WPF.

Appendix E, *Silverlight*

Although WPF's XBAP model allows WPF applications to run inside a web browser, this requires that .NET 3.0 be installed on an end user's machine. This makes WPF unsuitable for applications that need to be accessible from platforms other than Windows. However, WPF's cousin, Silverlight, is a cross-platform solution, offering a subset of the services available in WPF. This appendix provides a quick introduction to Silverlight from Shawn Wildermuth, Microsoft MVP.

What You Need to Use This Book

This book targets Visual Studio 2005 and the .NET Framework 3.0, which includes WPF (among other things). You'll also want the Visual Studio 2005 extensions that provide WPF templates that are mentioned in this book. You can download all of this for free* (even Visual Studio 2005, if you're willing to limit yourself to Visual C# 2005 Express Edition†).

WPF itself is supported on Windows XP, Windows Server 2003, and Windows Vista (and will be supported on future versions of Windows, of course).

---

* You can find the links to download the .NET Framework 3.0 and the WPF extensions to Visual Studio at *http://sellsbrothers.com/news/showTopic.aspx?ixTopic=2053* (*http://tinysells.com/104*).

† You can download Visual C# Express from *http://msdn.microsoft.com/vstudio/express/downloads* (*http://tinysells.com/105*).

Conventions Used in This Book

The following typographical conventions are used in this book:

Italic
> Indicates new terms.

`Constant width`
> Indicates code, commands, options, switches, variables, attributes, keys, functions, types, classes, namespaces, methods, modules, properties, parameters, values, objects, events, event handlers, XML tags, HTML tags, macros, the contents of files, or the output from commands.

`Constant width bold`
> Shows code or other text that should be noted by the reader.

`Constant width italic`
> Indicates code that should be replaced with user-supplied values.

`Constant width ellipses (...)`
> Shows code or other text not relevant to the current discussion.

 This icon signifies a tip, suggestion, or general note.

 This icon signifies a warning or caution.

Using Code Examples

This book is here to help you get your job done. In general, you may use the code in this book in your programs and documentation. You do not need to contact us for permission unless you're reproducing a significant portion of the code. For example, writing a program that uses several chunks of code from this book does not require permission. Selling or distributing a CD-ROM of examples from O'Reilly books *does* require permission. Answering a question by citing this book and quoting example code does not require permission. Incorporating a significant amount of example code from this book into your product's documentation *does* require permission.

We appreciate, but do not require, attribution. An attribution usually includes the title, author, publisher, and ISBN. For example: "*Programming WPF*, Second Edition, by Chris Sells and Ian Griffiths. Copyright 2007 O'Reilly Media Inc., 978-0-596-51037-4."

If you feel your use of code examples falls outside fair use or the permission given above, feel free to contact us at *permissions@oreilly.com*.

How to Contact Us

Please address comments and questions concerning this book to the publisher:

O'Reilly Media, Inc.
1005 Gravenstein Highway North
Sebastopol, CA 95472
800-998-9938 (in the United States or Canada)
707-829-0515 (international or local)
707-829-0104 (fax)

For the code samples associated with this book and for errata, visit the web site maintained by the authors at:

http://sellsbrothers.com/writing/wpbook

To contact Ian Griffiths, visit:

http://www.interact-sw.co.uk/iangblog/

To contact Chris Sells, visit:

http://sellsbrothers.com

The publisher maintains a web page for this book at:

http://www.oreilly.com/catalog/9780596510374

To comment or ask technical questions about this book, send email to:

bookquestions@oreilly.com

For more information about our books, conferences, Resource Centers, and the O'Reilly Network, see our web site at:

http://www.oreilly.com

Safari® Books Online

When you see a Safari® Books Online icon on the cover of your favorite technology book, that means the book is available online through the O'Reilly Network Safari Bookshelf.

Safari offers a solution that's better than e-books. It's a virtual library that lets you easily search thousands of top tech books, cut and paste code samples, download chapters, and find quick answers when you need the most accurate, current information. Try it for free at *http://safari.oreilly.com*.

Ian's Acknowledgments

Writing this book wouldn't have been possible without the support and feedback generously provided by a great many people. I would like to thank the following:

The readers, without whom this book would have a rather sad, lonely, and pointless existence.

My coauthor, Chris Sells, both for getting me involved in writing about WPF in the first place, and for his superb feedback and assistance.

Shawn Wildermuth, for contributing the Silverlight appendix, and enduring Chris's and my uncompromising approach to technical review.

Tim Sneath, both for his feedback and for providing me with the opportunity to meet and work with many members of the WPF team.

Microsoft employees and contractors, for producing a technology I like so much that I just had to write a book about it. And in particular, thank you to those people at Microsoft who gave their time to answer my questions or review draft chapters, including Chris Anderson, Marjan Badiei, Jeff Bogdan, Mark Boulter, Ben Carter, Dennis Cheng, Karen Corby, Vivek Dalvi, Nathan Dunlap, Ifeanyi Echeruo, Pablo Fernicola, Filipe Fortes, Kevin Gjerstad, Aaron Goldfeder, John Gossman, Mark Grinols, Namita Gupta, Henry Hahn, Robert Ingebretson, Kurt Jacob, David Jenni, Michael Kallay, Amir Khella, Adam Kinney, Nick Kramer, Lauren Lavoie, Daniel Lehenbauer, Kevin Moore, Elizabeth Nelson, Seema Ramchandani, Rob Relyea, Chris Sano, Greg Schechter, Eli Schleifer, Ashish Shetty, Adam Smith, Michael Stokes, Zhanbo Sun, David Teitlebaum, Stephen Turner, and Dawn Wood.

The following non-Microsoft people for their direct or indirect contributions to the quality of this book: Matthew Adams, Craig Andera, Richard Blewett, Keith Brown, Ryan Dawson, Kirk Fertitta, Kenny Kerr, Drew Marsh, Dave Minter, Brian Noyes, Fritz Onion, Aaron Skonnard, Dan Sullivan, Bill Williams, and Zhou Yong.

John Osborn and Caitrin McCullough at O'Reilly for their support throughout the writing process.

The technical review team: Chris Anderson, Elsa Bartley, Patrick Cauldwell, Dennis Cheng, Arik Cohen, Beatriz de Oliveira Costa, Glyn Griffiths, Scott Hanselman, Karsten Januszewski, Nikola Mihaylov, Mark Miller, Eric Stollnitz, and Jeff Tentschert. And particular thanks to Mike Weinhardt for his extensive and thoughtful feedback.

Finally, I especially want to thank Abi Sawyer for all her support, and for putting up with me while I wrote this book—thank you!

Chris's Acknowledgments

I'd like to thank the following people, without whom I wouldn't have been able to write either the first or second edition of this book:

The readers. When you've got a story to tell, you've got to have someone to tell it to. I've been writing about WPF in various forums for almost four years and the readers have always pushed and encouraged me further.

My coauthor, Ian Griffiths. Ian has an extensive background in all things graphical and video-related, including technologies so deep I can't understand him half the time. This, in addition to his vast experience teaching the WPF course and writing real-world WPF applications, along with his wonderful writing style, made him the perfect coauthor on this book. I couldn't have asked for better.

Shawn Wildermuth, for the cutting-edge Silverlight appendix. Shawn's been doing a bunch of advanced Silverlight work, so when I asked him to add his knowledge to this book, he graciously agreed, completely unaware of the buzz saw that is the Griffith/Sells reviewing process. Sorry, Shawn, and thanks!

Kenny Kerr, for his most excellent Window Clippings tool. His tool, plus the features he added at my request, saved me countless hours of work and produced much higher-quality screenshots than I would've normally had the patience to capture.

Chango Valtchev and Michael Weinhardt, for their huge help on navigation and the pitfalls thereof. The material in Chapter 11 was influenced very much by Chango and Michael.

Microsoft employees and contractors (in the order in which I found them in my WPF email folder): Mark Lawrence, Robert Wlodarczyk, Hua Wang, Worachai Chaoweeraprasit, Preeda Ola, Varsha Mahadevan, Larry Golding, Benjamin Westbrook, Ben Constable, Brian Chapman, Niklas Borson, Ryan Molden, Hamid Mahmood, Lauren Lavoie, Lars Bergstrom, Amir Khella, Kevin Kennedy, David Jenni, Elizabeth Nelson, Beatriz de Oliveira Costa, Nick Kramer, Allen Wagner, Chris Sano, Tim Sneath, Steve White, Matthew Adams, Eli Schleifer, Karsten Januszewski, Rob Relyea, Mark Boulter, Namita Gupta, John Gossman, Kiran Kumar, Filipe Fortes, Guy Smith, Zhanbo Sun, Ben Carter, Joe Marini, Dwayne Need, Brad Abrams, Feng Yuan, Dawn Wood, Vivek Dalvi, Jeff Bogdan, Steve Makofsky, Kenny Lim, Dmitry Titov, Joe Laughlin, Arik Cohen, Eric Stollnitz, Pablo Fernicola, Henry Hahn, Jamie Cool, Sameer Bhangar, and Brent Rector. I regularly spammed a wide range of my Microsoft brethren and instead of snubbing me, they answered my email questions, helped me make things work, gave me feedback on the chapters, sent me additional information without an explicit request, and in the case of John Gossman, forwarded the chapters along to folks with special knowledge so that they could give me feedback. This is the first book I've written "inside," and with the wealth of information and conscientious people available, it'd be very, very hard to go back to writing "outside."

The external technical reviewers, who provide an extremely important mainstream point of view that Microsoft insiders can't: Craig Andera, Chris Anderson, Elsa Bartley, Patrick Cauldwell, Dennis Cheng, Arik Cohen, Beatriz de Oliveira Costa, Ryan Dawson, Glyn Griffiths, Scott Hanselman, Karsten Januszewski, Adam Kinney, Drew Marsh, Nikola Mihaylov, Mark Miller, Dave Minter, Brian Noyes, Eric Stollnitz, and Jeff Tentschert.

Glyn Griffiths, not just for raising Ian right, but also for his eagle eye as the last reviewer of what we thought was the "final" manuscript. Not only did he catch a frightening number of grammatical errors, but he also pointed out the copyedits from the first edition of the book that we'd failed to reverse-integrate into our Word documents for the second edition. He literally did a three-way diff for us, which was impressive and spooky at the same time...

Caitrin McCullough and John Osborn from O'Reilly Media, for supporting me in breaking a bunch of the normal ORA procedures and guidelines to publish the book I wanted.

Shawn Morrissey, for letting me make writing a part of my first two years at Microsoft, and even giving me permission to use some of that material to seed this book. Shawn put up with me, trusting me to do my job remotely when very few Microsoft managers would.

Don Box, for setting my initial writing quality bar and hitting me squarely between the eyes until I could clear it. Of course, thank you for the foreword and for acting as my soundboard on this preface. You're an invaluable resource and a dear friend.

Barbara Box, for putting me up in the Chez Box clubhouse while I balance work and family in a way that wouldn't be possible without you.

Chris Anderson, architect on WPF, for his foreword and a ton of illuminating conversations even after he wrote a competing book. Chris is a very generous man. After I'd reviewed the first chapter of his book and realized that reading it was giving me insights that would affect my own writing, he wouldn't let me stop. He cared most about getting the right story out there, and not at all about into which book it went.

Michael Weinhardt, as the primary developmental editor on both editions of this book. His feedback is probably the single biggest factor in whatever quality we've been able to cram in. As if that wasn't enough, he produced many of the figures in my chapters. (Ian, as a rule, is far more industrious than I.)

Tim Ewald, for that critical eye at the most important spots in the first edition.

My wife and sons. The first edition was the first book I've ever written while holding a full-time job and, worse than that, while I was learning a completely new job. Frankly, I neglected my family pretty thoroughly for about three solid months on the first edition and nearly six months on the second, but they understood and supported me, like they have all of my endeavors over the years. I am very much looking forward to getting back to them (again).

CHAPTER 1

Hello, WPF

WPF is a completely new presentation framework, integrating the capabilities of many frameworks that have come before it, including User, GDI, GDI+, and HTML, as well as being heavily influenced by toolkits targeted at the Web, such as Adobe Flash, and popular Windows applications like Microsoft Word. This chapter will give you the basics of WPF from scratch, and then a whirlwind tour of the things you'll read about in detail in the chapters that follow.

WPF from Scratch

Example 1-1 is pretty much the smallest WPF "application" you can write in C#.

Example 1-1. Minimal C# WPF application

```
// MyApp.cs
using System;
using System.Windows; // the root WPF namespace

namespace MyFirstWpfApp {
  class MyApp {
    [STAThread]
    static void Main() {
      // the WPF message box
      MessageBox.Show("Hello, WPF");
    }
  }
}
```

The STAThread attribute signals .NET to make sure that when COM is initialized on the application's main thread, it's initialized to be compatible with single-threaded UI work, as required by WPF applications.

In fact, this is such a lame WPF application that it doesn't even use any of the services of WPF; the call to `MessageBox.Show` is just an interop call to Win32. However, it does require the same infrastructure required of other WPF applications, so it serves as a useful starting point for our explorations.

Building Applications

Building this application (Example 1-2) is a matter of firing off the C# compiler from a command shell with the appropriate environment variables.[*] (The command line here has been spread across multiple lines for readability, but you need to put it all on one line.)

Example 1-2. Building a WPF application manually

```
C:\1st> csc /target:winexe /out:.\1st.exe
  /r:System.dll
  /r:"C:\Program Files\Reference Assemblies\Microsoft\Framework\v3.0\WindowsBase.dll"
  /r:"C:\Program Files\Reference Assemblies\Microsoft\Framework\v3.0\PresentationCore.dll"
  /r:"C:\Program Files\Reference Assemblies\Microsoft\Framework\v3.0\
PresentationFramework.dll"
  MyApp.cs

Microsoft (R) Visual C# 2005 Compiler version 8.00.50727.312
for Microsoft (R) Windows (R) 2005 Framework version 2.0.50727
Copyright (C) Microsoft Corporation 2001-2005. All rights reserved.
```

Here, we're telling the C# compiler that we'd like to create a Windows application (instead of a Console application, which we get by default), putting the result, *1st.exe*, into the current folder, referencing the three main WPF assemblies (`WindowsBase`, `PresentationCore`, and `PresentationFramework`), along with the core .NET `System` assembly, and compiling the *MyApp.cs* source file.

Running the resulting *1st.exe* produces the world's lamest WPF application, as shown in Figure 1-1.

Figure 1-1. A lame WPF application

---

[*] Start → All Programs → Microsoft Windows SDK → CMD Shell.

In anticipation of less lame WPF applications with more source files and more compilation options, let's refactor the compilation command line into an msbuild project file (Example 1-3).

Example 1-3. A minimal msbuild project file

```
<!-- 1st.csproj -->
<Project
  DefaultTargets="Build"
  xmlns="http://schemas.microsoft.com/developer/msbuild/2003">
  <PropertyGroup>
    <OutputType>winexe</OutputType>
    <OutputPath>.\</OutputPath>
    <Assembly>1st.exe</Assembly>
  </PropertyGroup>
  <ItemGroup>
    <Compile Include="MyApp.cs" />
    <Reference Include="System" />
    <Reference Include="WindowsBase" />
    <Reference Include="PresentationCore" />
    <Reference Include="PresentationFramework" />
  </ItemGroup>
  <Import Project="$(MsbuildBinPath)\Microsoft.CSharp.targets" />
</Project>
```

The msbuild tool is a .NET 2.0 command-line application that understands XML files in the form shown in Example 1-3. The file format is shared between msbuild and Visual Studio 2005 so that you can use the same project files for both command-line and integrated development environment (IDE) builds. In this *.csproj* file (which stands for "C# Project"), we're saying the same things we said to the C# compiler—in other words, we'd like a Windows application, we'd like the output to be *1st.exe* in the current folder, and we'd like to reference the System assembly and the main WPF assemblies while compiling the *MyApp.cs* file. The actual smarts of how to turn these minimal settings into a compiled .NET application are contained in the .NET 2.0 *Microsoft.CSharp.targets* file that's imported at the bottom of the file.

Executing *msbuild.exe* on the *1st.csproj* file looks like Example 1-4.

Example 1-4. Building using msbuild

```
C:\1st>msbuild 1st.csproj
Microsoft (R) Build Engine Version 2.0.50727.312
[Microsoft .NET Framework, Version 2.0.50727.312]
Copyright (C) Microsoft Corporation 2005. All rights reserved.

Build started 2/4/2007 2:24:46 PM.
_____
Project "C:\1st\1st.csproj" (default targets):

Target PrepareForBuild:
    Creating directory "obj\Debug\".
```

Example 1-4. Building using msbuild (continued)

```
Target CoreCompile:
    C:\Windows\Microsoft.NET\Framework\v2.0.50727\Csc.exe /noconfig /nowarn:1701
,1702 /reference:"C:\Program Files\Reference Assemblies\Microsoft\Framework\v3.0
\PresentationCore.dll" /reference:"C:\Program Files\Reference Assemblies\Microso
ft\Framework\v3.0\PresentationFramework.dll" /reference:C:\Windows\Microsoft.NET
\Framework\v2.0.50727\System.dll /reference:"C:\Program Files\Reference Assembli
es\Microsoft\Framework\v3.0\WindowsBase.dll" /debug+ /out:obj\Debug\1st.exe /tar
get:winexe MyApp.cs
Target _CopyFilesMarkedCopyLocal:
    Copying file from "C:\Program Files\Reference Assemblies\Microsoft\Framework
\v3.0\PresentationCore.dll" to ".\PresentationCore.dll".
    Copying file from "C:\Program Files\Reference Assemblies\Microsoft\Framework
\v3.0\System.Printing.dll" to ".\System.Printing.dll".
    Copying file from "C:\Program Files\Reference Assemblies\Microsoft\Framework
\v3.0\PresentationCore.xml" to ".\PresentationCore.xml".
    Copying file from "C:\Program Files\Reference Assemblies\Microsoft\Framework
\v3.0\System.Printing.xml" to ".\System.Printing.xml".
Target CopyFilesToOutputDirectory:
    Copying file from "obj\Debug\1st.exe" to ".\1st.exe".
    1st -> C:\1st\1st.exe
    Copying file from "obj\Debug\1st.pdb" to ".\1st.pdb".

Build succeeded.
    0 Warning(s)
    0 Error(s)

Time Elapsed 00:00:04.15
```

As I mentioned, msbuild and Visual Studio 2005 share a project file format, so loading the project file into Visual Studio is as easy as double-clicking on *1st.csproj* (as shown in Figure 1-2).

Unfortunately, as nice as the project file makes building our WPF application, the application itself is still lame.

WPF Applications

A real WPF application is going to need more than a message box. WPF applications have an instance of the Application class from the System.Windows namespace. The Application class provides methods like Run for starting the application, events like Startup and SessionEnding for tracking lifetime, and properties like Current, ShutdownMode, and MainWindow for finding the global application object, choosing when it shuts down, and getting the application's main window. Typically, the Application class serves as a base for custom application-wide data and behavior (Example 1-5).

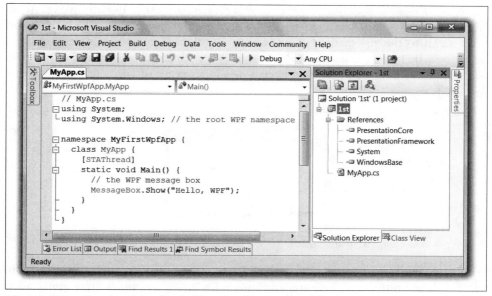

Figure 1-2. Loading the minimal msbuild project file into Visual Studio

Example 1-5. A less minimal WPF application

```
// MyApp.cs
using System;
using System.Windows;

namespace MyFirstWpfApp {
  class MyApp : Application {
    [STAThread]
    static void Main() {
      MyApp app = new MyApp();
      app.Startup += app.AppStartup;
      app.Run();
    }

    void AppStartup(object sender, StartupEventArgs e) {
      // By default, when all top level windows
      // are closed, the app shuts down
      Window window = new Window();
      window.Title = "Hello, WPF";
      window.Show();
    }
  }
}
```

Here, our MyApp class derives from the Application base class. In Main, we create an instance of the MyApp class, add a handler to the Startup event, and kick things off with a call to the Run method. Our Startup handler creates our sample's top-level window, which is an instance of the built-in WPF Window class, making our sample WPF application more interesting from a developer point of view, although visually less so, as shown in Figure 1-3.

Figure 1-3. A less lame WPF application

Although we can create instances of the built-in classes of WPF, such as Window, populating them and wiring them up from the application, it's much more encapsulating (not to mention abstracting) to create custom classes for such things, like the Window1 class (Example 1-6).

Example 1-6. Window class declaring its own controls

```
// Window1.cs
using System;
using System.Windows;
using System.Windows.Controls; // Button et al

namespace MyFirstWpfApp {
  class Window1 : Window {
    public Window1( ) {
      this.Title = "Hello, WPF";

      // Do something interesting (sorta...)
      Button button = new Button( );
      button.Content = "Click me, baby, one more time!";
      button.Width = 200;
      button.Height = 25;
      button.Click += button_Click;

      this.Content = button;
    }

    void button_Click(object sender, RoutedEventArgs e) {
      MessageBox.Show(
        "You've done that before, haven't you...",
        "Nice!");
    }
  }
}
```

In addition to setting its caption text, an instance of our `Window1` class will include a button with its `Content`, `Width`, and `Height` properties set, and its `Click` event handled. With this initialization handled in the `Window1` class itself, our app's startup code looks a bit simpler (even though the application behavior itself has gotten "richer"; see Example 1-7).

Example 1-7. Simplified Application instance

```
// MyApp.cs
using System;
using System.Windows;

namespace MyFirstWpfApp {
  class MyApp : Application {
    [STAThread]
    static void Main(string[] args) {
      MyApp app = new MyApp();
      app.Startup += app.AppStartup;
      app.Run();
    }

    void AppStartup(object sender, StartupEventArgs e) {
      // Let the Window1 initialize itself
      Window window = new Window1();
      window.Show();
    }
  }
}
```

The results (after updating the *.csproj* file appropriately) are shown in Figure 1-4 and are unlikely to surprise you much.

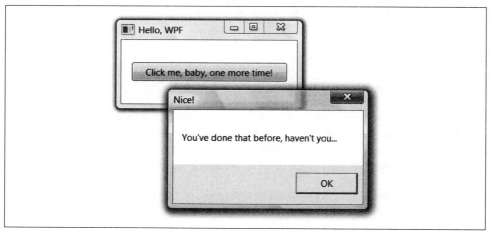

Figure 1-4. A slightly more interesting WPF application

As the `Window1` class gets more interesting, we're mixing two very separate kinds of code: the "look," represented by the initialization code that sets the window and child window properties, and the "behavior," represented by the event handling code. As the look is something that you're likely to want handled by someone with artistic sensibilities (a.k.a. turtleneck-wearing designer types) whereas the behavior is something you'll want to leave to the coders (a.k.a. pocket-protector-wearing engineer types), separating the former from the latter would be a good idea. Ideally, we'd like to move the imperative "look" code into a declarative format suitable for tools to create with some drag-and-drop magic. For WPF, that format is XAML.

XAML

XAML is an XML-based language for creating and initializing .NET objects. It's used in WPF as a human-authorable way of describing the UI, although you can use it for a much larger range of CLR types than just those in WPF. Example 1-8 shows how we declare the UI of our `Window`-derived class using XAML.

Example 1-8. Declaring a Window in XAML

```
<!-- Window1.xaml -->
<Window
  x:Class="MyFirstWpfApp.Window1"
  xmlns="http://schemas.microsoft.com/winfx/2006/xaml/presentation"
  xmlns:x="http://schemas.microsoft.com/winfx/2006/xaml"
  Title="Hello, WPF">

  <Button
    x:Name="button"
    Width="200"
    Height="25"
    Click="button_Click">Click me, baby, one more time!</Button>

</Window>
```

The root element, `Window`, is used to declare a portion of a class, the name of which is contained in the `Class` attribute from the XAML XML namespace (declared with a prefix of "x" using the "xmlns" XML namespace syntax). The two XML namespace declarations pull in two commonly used namespaces for XAML work, the one for XAML itself (the one with the "x" prefix) and the one for WPF (which we've declared as the default for this XML file). You can think of the XAML in Example 1-8 as creating the partial class definition in Example 1-9.

Example 1-9. C# equivalent of XAML from Example 1-8

```
namespace MyFirstWpfApp {
  partial class Window1 : Window {
    Button button;
```

Example 1-9. C# equivalent of XAML from Example 1-8 (continued)

```
    void InitializeComponent( ) {
      // Initialize Window1
      this.Title = "Hello, WPF";

      // Initialize button
      button = new Button( );
      button.Width = 200;
      button.Height = 25;
      button.Click += button_Click;

      this.AddChild(button);
    }
  }
}
```

XAML was built to be as direct a mapping from XML to .NET as possible. Generally, a XAML element is a .NET class name and a XAML attribute is the name of a property or an event on that class. This makes XAML useful for more than just WPF classes; pretty much any old .NET class that exposes a default constructor can be initialized in a XAML file.

Notice that we don't have the definition of the click event handler in this generated class. For event handlers and other initializations and helpers, a XAML file is meant to be matched with a corresponding *code-behind* file, which is a .NET language code file that implements behavior in code "behind" the look defined in the XAML. Traditionally, this file is named with a *.xaml.cs* extension and contains only the things not defined in the XAML. With the XAML from Example 1-8 in place, we can reduce our single-buttoned main window code-behind file to the code in Example 1-10.

Example 1-10. C# code-behind file

```
// Window1.xaml.cs
using System;
using System.Windows;
using System.Windows.Controls;

namespace MyFirstWpfApp {
  public partial class Window1 : Window {
    public Window1( ) {
      InitializeComponent( );
    }

    void button_Click(object sender, RoutedEventArgs e) {
      MessageBox.Show(...);
    }
  }
}
```

Notice the partial keyword modifying the Window1 class, which signals to the compiler that the XAML-generated class is to be paired with this human-generated class to form one complete class, each depending on the other. The partial Window1 class defined in XAML depends on the code-behind partial class to call the InitializeComponent method and to handle the click event. The code-behind class depends on the partial Window1 class defined in XAML to implement InitializeComponent, thereby providing the look of the main window (and related child controls).

Further, as mentioned, XAML is not just for visuals. For example, nothing is stopping us from moving most of the definition of our custom MyApp class into a XAML file (Example 1-11).

Example 1-11. Declaring an application in XAML

```
<!-- MyApp.xaml -->
<Application
  x:Class="MyFirstWpfApp.MyApp"
  xmlns="http://schemas.microsoft.com/winfx/2006/xaml/presentation"
  xmlns:x="http://schemas.microsoft.com/winfx/2006/xaml"
  Startup="AppStartup">
</Application>
```

This reduces the MyApp code-behind file to the event handler in Example 1-12.

Example 1-12. Application code-behind file

```
// MyApp.xaml.cs
using System;
using System.Windows;

namespace MyFirstWpfApp {
  public partial class MyApp : Application {
    void AppStartup(object sender, StartupEventArgs e) {
      Window window = new Window1();
      window.Show();
    }
  }
}
```

You may have noticed that we no longer have a Main entry point to create the instance of the application-derived class and call its Run method. That's because WPF has a special project setting to specify the XAML file that defines the application class, which appears in the msbuild project file (Example 1-13).

Example 1-13. Specifying the application's XAML in the project file

```
<!-- MyFirstWpfApp.csproj -->
<Project ...>
  <PropertyGroup>
    <OutputType>winexe</OutputType>
    <OutputPath>.\</OutputPath>
    <Assembly>1st.exe</Assembly>
  </PropertyGroup>
```

Example 1-13. Specifying the application's XAML in the project file (continued)

```
  <ItemGroup>
    <ApplicationDefinition Include="MyApp.xaml" />
    <Page Include="Window1.xaml" />
    <Compile Include="Window1.xaml.cs">
      <DependentUpon>Window1.xaml</DependentUpon>
    </Compile>
    <Compile Include="MyApp.xaml.cs" />
      <DependentUpon>MyApp.xaml</DependentUpon>
    </Compile>
    <Reference Include="System" />
    <Reference Include="WindowsBase" />
    <Reference Include="PresentationCore" />
    <Reference Include="PresentationFramework" />
  </ItemGroup>
  <Import Project="$(MsbuildBinPath)\Microsoft.CSharp.targets" />
  <Import Project="$(MSBuildBinPath)\Microsoft.WinFX.targets" />
</Project>
```

The combination of the `ApplicationDefinition` element and the .NET 3.0-specific *Microsoft.WinFX.targets* file produces an application entry point that will create our application for us. Also notice in Example 1-13 that we've replaced the *MyApp.cs* file with the *MyApp.xaml.cs* file, added the *Window1.xaml.cs* file, and included the window's corresponding XAML file as a `Page` element (we don't do the same thing for the application's XAML file, as it's already referenced in the `ApplicationDefinition` element). The XAML files will be compiled into partial class definitions using the instructions in the *Microsoft.WinFX.targets* file. The `DependentUpon` element is there to associate a code-behind file with its XAML file. This isn't necessary for the build process, but it's useful for tools that want to show the association. For example, Visual Studio uses `DependentUpon` to show the code-behind file nested under the XAML file.

This basic arrangement of artifacts (i.e., application and main windows each split into a XAML and a code-behind file) is such a desirable starting point for a WPF application that creating a new project using the "Windows Application (WPF)" project template from within Visual Studio 2005 gives you the same initial configuration, as shown in Figure 1-5.

Editing XAML

Now that we've seen the wonder that is declarative UI description in XAML, you may wonder, "Do I get all the fun of editing the raw XML, or are there some tools that can join in the fun, too?" The answer is "sort of." For example, if you've got the .NET Framework 3.0 extensions for Visual Studio 2005 (the same extensions that give you the WPF project templates in VS05), you will have a visual editor for XAML files that works very similarly to the built-in Windows Forms Designer. It will trigger by default when you double-click a file in the Solution Explorer, or you can right-click on

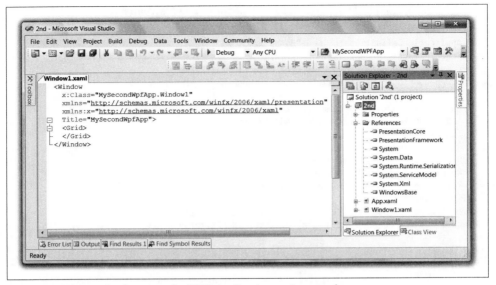

Figure 1-5. The result of running the WPF Application project template

a XAML file in the Solution Expression and choose Open With. One of the options offered will be "WPF Designer (Cider)" (where "Cider" is the codename for the WPF Designer still under development). The WPF Designer allows for drag-and-drop-style construction of XAML files with elements from the Toolbox and setting properties in the property browser. In addition, you can see the XAML as the designer makes changes, and in fact, you can make changes in the XAML view itself and see those reflected in the designer. Figure 1-6 shows the WPF Designer in action.

Unfortunately, as of the writing of this book, the WPF Designer is still very much under development and such basic features as visually adding event handlers, let alone more advanced features like data binding, styles, control templates, and animation, are not supported, which is why you're unlikely to do much with it. If you're following along with the Visual Studio "Orcas" beta, you'll get more current (and more full-featured) versions of the WPF Designer, but if you can't wait, you have other choices, including two XAML designer tools (Microsoft Expression Blend and Microsoft Expression Design), a third-party XAML 3D editor (ZAM 3D), and several conversion tools from other popular vector drawing formats (e.g., Adobe Illustrator and Flash), all of which are currently downloadable at the time of this writing.*

---

* Michael Swanson, the general manager of the Microsoft Platform Evangelist team, maintains a wonderful list of WPF-related first- and third-party tools and controls for your development enjoyment at *http://blogs.msdn.com/ mswanson/articles/WPFToolsAndControls.aspx* (*http://tinysells.com/88*).

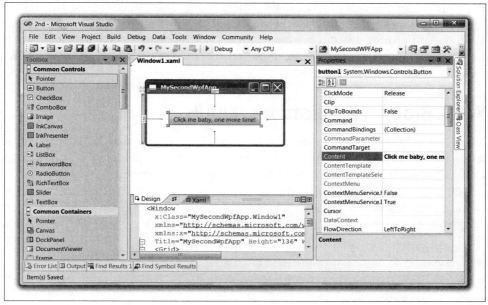

Figure 1-6. The WPF Designer in action

Another very useful tool for playing with XAML is the XamlPad tool that comes with the Windows SDK. It actually shows the visual representation of your XAML as you type it, as shown in Figure 1-7.

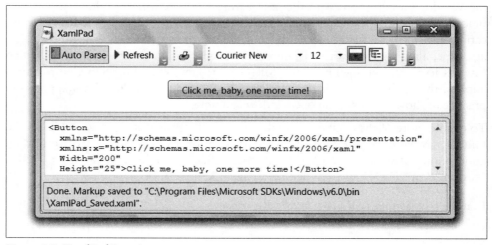

Figure 1-7. XamlPad in action

XamlPad has some limitations; the most important is that it doesn't allow code (e.g., x:Class or event handler declarations), but as instant gratification, it can't be beat.

WPF provides a number of services for applications that we haven't covered, including lifetime management and ClickOnce-based deployment. In addition, although WPF doesn't provide any direct support for application instance management or settings, the .NET 2.0 support for both of these features integrates with WPF. Chapter 2 covers all of these topics.

XAML Browser Applications (XBAPs)

While we're talking about Visual Studio tools for WPF, you may notice that a few icons away from the "Windows Application (WPF)" project template is another one called "XAML Browser Application (WPF)," as shown in Figure 1-8.

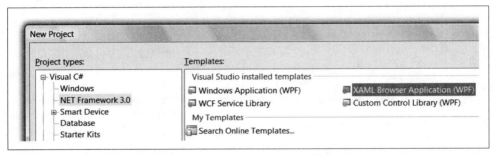

Figure 1-8. The WPF XAML Browser Application project template in VS05

WPF itself was created as a unified presentation framework, meant to enable building Windows applications with the best features from existing Windows application practice and existing web application practice. One of the nice things that web applications provide is a single window showing the user one page of content/functionality at a time, allowing for navigation among the pages. For some applications, including Internet Explorer, the shell Explorer, Microsoft Money, and a bunch of Control Panel applets, this is thought to be preferable to the more common Windows application practice of showing more than one window at a time.

To enable more of these kinds of applications, WPF provides the *page*, which is the unit of navigation in an XML Browser Application (XBAP). Instead of setting an application's `StartupUri` to a XAML file that defines a window, we point an XBAP's `StartupUri` at a XAML file that defines a page (Example 1-14).

Example 1-14. Starting with a Page instead of a Window

```
<!-- App.xaml -->
<Application
  x:Class="MyFirstXbapApp.App"
  xmlns="http://schemas.microsoft.com/winfx/2006/xaml/presentation"
  xmlns:x="http://schemas.microsoft.com/winfx/2006/xaml"
  StartupUri="Page1.xaml" />
```

A WPF page is a class that derives from the `Page` class, as shown in Example 1-15.

Example 1-15. A sample page

```xml
<!-- Page1.xaml -->
<Page
  x:Class="MyFirstXbapApp.Page1"
  xmlns="http://schemas.microsoft.com/winfx/2006/xaml/presentation"
  xmlns:x="http://schemas.microsoft.com/winfx/2006/xaml"
  WindowTitle="Page1">
  <TextBlock FontSize="36">
    Check out <Hyperlink NavigateUri="page2.xaml">page 2</Hyperlink>, too.
  </TextBlock>
</Page>
```

```csharp
    // Page1.xaml.cs
    ...
    namespace MyFirstXbapApp {
      public partial class Page1 : System.Windows.Controls.Page {
        public Page1() {
          InitializeComponent();
        }
      }
    }
```

The primary way to allow the user to navigate in an XBAP is via the `Hyperlink` element, setting the `NavigateUri` to a relative URL of another XAML page in the project. The first page of our sample XBAP looks like Figure 1-9.

Figure 1-9. A simple XBAP hosted in Internet Explorer 7

In Figure 1-9, the hyperlinked text is underlined in blue, and if you were to move your mouse cursor over the hyperlink, it would show up as red. Further, the page's `WindowTitle` property is set as the window caption. Of course, the most obvious thing to notice is that the XBAP is hosted inside the browser—Internet Explorer 7 to be exact. The reason for this is simple: XBAPs are meant to be deployed via the Web (which we'll talk about later in this chapter) and to blend seamlessly with web pages. As you navigate among the pages in an XBAP, those pages are added to the navigation history just as web pages would be, and you're allowed to use the Internet Explorer toolbar to go backward and forward, as you're used to doing.

For example, let's define *page2.xaml* as shown in Example 1-16.

Example 1-16. Another simple page

```
<!-- Page2.xaml -->
<Page ... WindowTitle="Page2">
  <TextBlock FontSize="36">
    Hello and welcome to page 2.
  </TextBlock>
</Page>
```

Clicking on the hyperlink on page 1 navigates to page 2, as shown in Figure 1-10.

Figure 1-10. XBAP and navigation history

Notice in Figure 1-10 that the history for the back button is showing page 1, which is where we were just before getting to page 2.

As you might imagine, there are many more topics to discuss to make your XBAPs integrate with the browser and still provide the rich functionality we expect from WPF applications. In addition, you can have any number of navigation windows in your standalone WPF applications. We cover these topics and more in Chapter 11.

Content Models

Although the different kinds of WPF application types are useful, the core of any presentation framework is in the presentation elements themselves. In presentation systems of old, fundamentally we had "chunks of look and behavior" (often called *controls*) and "containers of chunks of look and behavior." In WPF, this characterization doesn't really hold up very well. Many elements that provide their own content and behavior can also be containers of elements (and so on). As an example, let's take a look at a Button.

The first thing that may surprise you about a WPF Button object is that you don't need to use a string as the content; it will take any .NET object. You've already seen a string as a button's content (see Example 1-17).

Example 1-17. A button with string content

```
<Window ...>
  <Button Width="100" Height="100">Hi</Button>
</Window>
```

However, as Example 1-18 shows, you can also use an image (see Figure 1-11).

Example 1-18. A button with image content

```
<Window ...>
  <Button Width="100" Height="100">
    <Image Source="tom.png" />
  </Button>
</Window>
```

Figure 1-11. A button with image content

You can even use an arbitrary control, like a TextBox, as shown in Example 1-19 and Figure 1-12.

Example 1-19. A button with control content

```
<Window ...>
  <Button Width="100" Height="100">
    <TextBox Width="75">edit me</TextBox>
  </Button>
</Window>
```

Further, as you'll see in Chapters 3 and 6, you can get fancy and show a collection of nested elements in a Button or even nonvisual objects as the content of a Button. The Button can take any object as content because it's derived ultimately from a class called ContentControl, as are many other WPF classes (e.g., Label, ListBoxItem, ToolTip, CheckBox, RadioButton, and, in fact, Window itself).

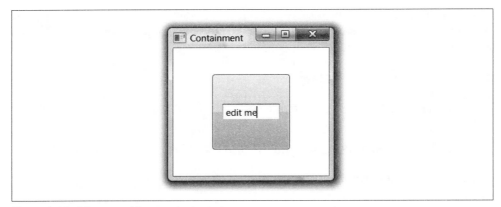

Figure 1-12. A button with control content

A `ContentControl` knows how to hold anything that's able to be rendered, not just a string. A `ContentControl` gets its content from the `Content` property, so you could specify a `Button`'s content like so (this is the longhand version of Example 1-17):

```
<Button Width="100" Height="100" Content="Hi" />
```

`ContentControl`s are especially useful because you get all the behavior of the "thing" (e.g., `Button`, `Window`, `ListBoxItem`), but you can display whatever you like in it without having to build yourself a special class (e.g., `ImageButton`, `TextBoxListBoxItem`, etc.).

The content model is not relegated to just the `ContentControl`. For example, the `HeaderedContentControl` is like a `ContentControl`, except it has two spots for content, the header and the content. The `GroupBox` and `TabItem` controls both derive from the `HeaderedContentControl` and both provide a header (i.e., the group title and the tab), as well as content (i.e., the group contents and the tab contents). By using the content model, `HeaderedContentControl`s allow any kind of content in either content spot, allowing for much greater flexibility still within a simple model.

XAML Property Element Syntax

Although setting the `Content` property as an XML attribute works just fine for specifying a string as a property, it doesn't work at all well for specifying a subelement, like the image example. For this reason, XAML defines the *property element* syntax, which uses nested *Element.Property* elements for specifying objects as property values. For instance, Example 1-20 shows the property element syntax for the string setting of a button's content.

Example 1-20. Property element syntax with a string

```
<Button Width="100" Height="100">
  <Button.Content>Hi</Button.Content>
</Button>
```

Example 1-21 shows the property element syntax using an image.

Example 1-21. Property element syntax with an image

```
<Button Width="100" Height="100">
  <Button.Content>
    <Image Source="tom.png" />
  </Button.Content>
</Button>
```

Because XML attributes can contain only one thing, property element syntax is especially useful when you've got more than one thing to specify. For example, you might imagine a button with a string and an image defined, as in Example 1-22.

Example 1-22. You can't have multiple things in a ContentControl

```
<Button Width="100" Height="100">
  <!-- WARNING: doesn't work! -->
  <Button.Content>
    <TextBlock>Tom: </TextBlock>
    <Image Source="tom.png" />
  </Button.Content>
</Button>
```

Although the property element syntax can be useful for this kind of thing, in this particular case it doesn't work at all. This brings us to the second thing that may surprise you about content containment in WPF: many content containers can take only a single piece of content. For example, whereas a Button can take any old thing as content, it can take only a single thing which, without additional instructions, it will center and cause to fill up its entire client area. For more than one content element or a richer layout policy, you'll need a panel.

Layout

Taking another look at Example 1-22 with the TextBlock and the Image as content for the Button, we don't really have enough information to place them inside the area of the button. Should they be stacked left to right or top to bottom? Should one be docked on one edge and one docked to the other? How will things be stretched or arranged if the button resizes? These are questions best answered with a *panel*.

A panel is a control that knows how to arrange its content. WPF comes with the following general-purpose panel controls:

Canvas
> Arranges content by position and size with no automatic rearrangement when the Canvas is resized

DockPanel
> Arranges content according to the edge that each piece of content "docks" to, except for the last, which fills the remaining area

Grid
> Arranges content in rows and columns as specified by the developer

StackPanel
  Arranges content top to bottom or left to right according to the orientation of
  the panel

UniformGrid
  Arranges content in a grid with the same number of rows and columns generated as needed to display the content

WrapPanel
  Arranges things in a horizontal row until the next item won't fit, in which case it
  wraps to the next row

Grid Layout

The most flexible panel by far is the grid, which arranges content elements in rows
and columns, including the ability to span multiple rows and/or multiple columns,
as shown in Example 1-23.

Example 1-23. A sample usage of the Grid panel

```
<Window ...>
  <Grid>
    <Grid.RowDefinitions>
      <RowDefinition />
      <RowDefinition />
      <RowDefinition />
    </Grid.RowDefinitions>
    <Grid.ColumnDefinitions>
      <ColumnDefinition />
      <ColumnDefinition />
      <ColumnDefinition />
    </Grid.ColumnDefinitions>
    <Button Grid.Row="0" Grid.Column="0" Grid.ColumnSpan="2">A</Button>
    <Button Grid.Row="0" Grid.Column="2">C</Button>
    <Button Grid.Row="1" Grid.Column="0" Grid.RowSpan="2">D</Button>
    <Button Grid.Row="1" Grid.Column="1">E</Button>
    <Button Grid.Row="1" Grid.Column="2">F</Button>
    <Button Grid.Row="2" Grid.Column="1">H</Button>
    <Button Grid.Row="2" Grid.Column="2">I</Button>
  </Grid>
</Window>
```

Example 1-23 used the XAML property element syntax to define a grid with three
rows and three columns inside the RowDefinition and ColumnDefinition elements.
On each element, we've specified the Grid.Row and Grid.Column properties so that the
grid knows which elements go where (the grid can have multiple elements in the same
cell). One of the elements spans two rows and one spans two columns, as shown in
Figure 1-13.

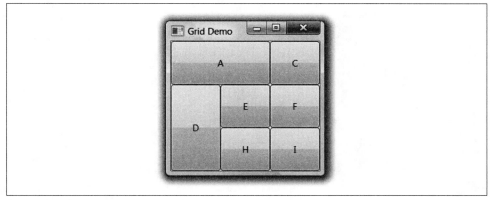

Figure 1-13. An example Grid panel in action

Using the grid, we can be explicit about how we want to arrange an image with a text caption (Example 1-24).

Example 1-24. Arranging an image and text in a grid

```
<Button Width="100" Height="100">
  <Button.Content>
    <Grid>
      <Grid.RowDefinitions>
        <RowDefinition />
        <RowDefinition Height="Auto" />
      </Grid.RowDefinitions>
      <Image Grid.Row="0" Source="tom.png" />
      <TextBlock
        Grid.Row="1"
        HorizontalAlignment="Center">Tom</TextBlock>
    </Grid>
  </Button.Content>
</Button>
```

Figure 1-14 shows how the grid arranges the image and text for us.

Because we're just stacking one element on top of another, we could've used the stack panel, but the grid is so general-purpose that many WPF programmers find themselves using it for most layout configurations.

XAML Attached Property Syntax

You may have noticed that in setting up the Grid.Row and Grid.Panel attributes of the Button elements, we used another dotted syntax, similar to the property element syntax, but this time on the attribute instead of on the element. This is the *attached property* syntax, and it is used to set a property as associated with the particular element (e.g., a Button), but as defined by another element (e.g., a Grid).

Figure 1-14. A grid arranging an image and a text block

The attached property syntax is used in WPF as an extensibility mechanism. We don't want the Button class to have to know that it's being arranged in a Grid, but we do want to specify Grid-specific attributes on it. If the Button was being hosted in a Canvas, the Grid properties wouldn't make any sense, so building Row and Column properties into the Button class isn't such a great idea. Further, when we define our own custom panel that the WPF team never considered (e.g., HandOfCards), we want to be able to apply the HandOfCards-related attached properties to arbitrary elements it contains.

This kind of extensibility is what the attached property syntax was designed for and it is common when arranging content on a panel.

For the nitty-gritty of layout, including the other panels that I didn't show, you'll want to read Chapter 3.

Controls

Although the layout panels provide the container, the controls are the important things you'll be arranging. So far, you've seen how to create instances of controls, set properties, and handle events. You've also seen the basics of the content models that make controls in WPF special. However, for the details of event routing, command handling, mouse/keyboard input, and an enumeration of the controls in WPF, you'll want to check out Chapters 4 and 5. Further, for information about packaging up custom UI and behavior, you'll want to read Chapter 18.

Data Binding

Once we've got a set of controls and a way to lay them out, we still need to fill them with data and keep that data in sync with wherever the data actually lives. (Controls are a great way to show data but a poor place to keep it.) For example, imagine that we'd like to build a WPF application for keeping track of people's nicknames. Something like Figure 1-15 would do the trick.

Figure 1-15. Data binding to a collection of custom types

In Figure 1-15, we've got two TextBox controls, one for the name and one for the nickname. We've also got the actual nickname entries in a ListBox in the middle and a Button to add new entries. We could easily build the core data of such an application with a class, as shown in Example 1-25.

Example 1-25. A custom type with data binding support

```
public class Nickname : INotifyPropertyChanged {
  // INotifyPropertyChanged Member
  public event PropertyChangedEventHandler PropertyChanged;
  void Notify(string propName) {
    if( PropertyChanged != null ) {
      PropertyChanged(this, new PropertyChangedEventArgs(propName));
    }
  }

  string name;
  public string Name {
    get { return name; }
    set {
      name = value;
      Notify("Name"); // notify consumers
    }
  }

  string nick;
  public string Nick {
    get { return nick; }
    set {
      nick = value;
      Notify("Nick"); // notify consumers
    }
  }

  public Nickname() : this("name", "nick") { }
  public Nickname(string name, string nick) {
    this.name = name;
    this.nick = nick;
  }
}
```

This class knows nothing about data binding, but it does have two public properties that expose the data, and it implements the standard INotifyPropertyChanged interface to let consumers of this data know when it has changed.

In the same way that we have a standard interface for notifying consumers of objects when they change, we also have a standard way to notify consumers of collections of changes, called INotifyCollectionChanged. WPF provides an implementation of this interface, called ObservableCollection, which we'll use so that appropriate events are fired when Nickname objects are added or removed (Example 1-26).

Example 1-26. A custom collection type with data binding support

```
// Notify consumers
public class Nicknames : ObservableCollection<Nickname> { }
```

Around these classes, we could build nickname management logic that looks like Example 1-27.

Example 1-27. Making ready for data binding

```
// Window1.xaml.cs
...
namespace DataBindingDemo {
  public class Nickname : INotifyPropertyChanged {...}
  public class Nicknames : ObservableCollection<Nickname> { }

  public partial class Window1 : Window {
    Nicknames names;

    public Window1() {
      InitializeComponent();
      this.addButton.Click += addButton_Click;

      // create a nickname collection
      this.names = new Nicknames();

      // make data available for binding
      dockPanel.DataContext = this.names;
    }

    void addButton_Click(object sender, RoutedEventArgs e) {
      this.names.Add(new Nickname());
    }
  }
}
```

Notice that the window's class constructor adds a click event handler to add a new nickname and creates the initial collection of nicknames. However, the most useful thing that the Window1 constructor does is set its DataContext property so as to make the nickname data available for data binding.

In WPF, *data binding* is about keeping object properties and collections of objects synchronized with one or more controls' views of the data. The goal of data binding is to save you the time required to write the code to update the controls when the data in the objects changes, and to update the data when the user edits the data in the controls. The synchronization of the data to the controls depends on the INotifyPropertyChanged and INotifyCollectionChanged interfaces that we've been careful to use in our data and data collection implementations.

For example, because the collection of our example nickname data and the nickname data itself both notify consumers when there are changes, we can hook up controls using WPF data binding, as shown in Example 1-28.

Example 1-28. An example data binding usage

```
<!-- Window1.xaml -->
<Window ...>
  <DockPanel x:Name="dockPanel">
    <TextBlock DockPanel.Dock="Top">
      <TextBlock VerticalAlignment="Center">Name: </TextBlock>
      <TextBox Text="{Binding Path=Name}" />
      <TextBlock VerticalAlignment="Center">Nick: </TextBlock>
      <TextBox Text="{Binding Path=Nick}" />
    </TextBlock>
    <Button DockPanel.Dock="Bottom" x:Name="addButton">Add</Button>
    <ListBox
      ItemsSource="{Binding}"
      IsSynchronizedWithCurrentItem="True" />
  </DockPanel>
</Window>
```

This XAML lays out the controls as shown in Figure 1-15 using a dock panel to arrange things top to bottom and a text block to contain the editing controls. The secret sauce that takes advantage of data binding is the {Binding} values in the control attributes instead of hardcoded values. By setting the Text property of the TextBox to {Binding Path=Name}, we're telling the TextBox to use data binding to peek at the Name property out of the current Nickname object. Further, if the data changes in the Name TextBox, the Path is used to poke the new value back in.

The current Nickname object is determined by the ListBox because of the IsSynchronizedWithCurrentItem property, which keeps the TextBox controls showing the same Nickname object as the one that's currently selected in the ListBox. The ListBox is bound to its data by setting the ItemsSource attribute to {Binding} without a Path statement. In the ListBox, we're not interested in showing a single property on a single object, but rather all of the objects at once.

But how do we know that both the ListBox and the TextBox controls are sharing the same data? That's where setting the dock panel's DataContext comes in (back in Example 1-27). In the absence of other instructions, when a control's property is set using data binding, it looks at its own DataContext property for data. If it doesn't find any, it looks at its parent and then *its* parent, and so on, all the way up the tree. Because the ListBox and the TextBox controls have a common parent that has a DataContext property set (the DockPanel), all of the data bound controls will share the same data.

XAML Markup Extensions

Before we take a look at the results of our data binding, let's take a moment to discuss XAML *markup extensions*, which is what you're using when you set an attribute to something inside of curly braces (e.g., Text="{Binding Path=Name}"). Markup extensions add special processing to XAML attribute values. For example, this:

```
<TextBox Text="{Binding Path=Name}" />
```

is just a shortcut for this (which you'll recognize as the property element syntax):

```
<TextBox.Text>
  <Binding Path="Name" />
</TextBox.Text>
```

For a complete discussion of markup extensions, as well as the rest of the XAML syntax, read Appendix A.

Data Templates

With the data binding markup syntax explained, let's turn back to our example data binding application, which so far doesn't look quite like what we had in mind, as seen in Figure 1-16.

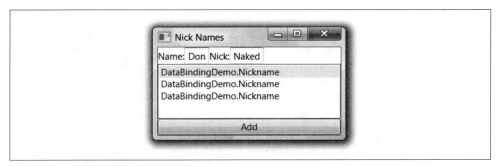

Figure 1-16. ListBox showing objects of a custom type without special instructions

It's clear that the data is making its way into the application, because the currently selected name and nickname are shown for editing. The problem is that, unlike the TextBox controls, which were each given a specific field of the Nickname object to show, the ListBox is expected to show the whole thing. Lacking special instructions, it's calling the ToString method of each object, which results in only the name of the type. To show the data, we need to compose a data template, like the one in Example 1-29.

Example 1-29. Using a data template

```
<ListBox
  ItemsSource="{Binding}"
  IsSynchronizedWithCurrentItem="True">

  <ListBox.ItemTemplate>
    <DataTemplate>
      <TextBlock>
        <TextBlock Text="{Binding Path=Name}" />:
        <TextBlock Text="{Binding Path=Nick}" />
      </TextBlock>
    </DataTemplate>
  </ListBox.ItemTemplate>

</ListBox>
```

A *data template* is a set of elements that should be inserted somewhere. In our case, we are specifying a data template to be inserted for each listbox item by setting the ItemTemplate property. In Example 1-29, we've composed a data template from a text block that flows together two other text blocks, each bound to a property on a Nickname object separated by a colon, as shown back in Figure 1-15.

At this point, we've got a completely data-bound application. As data in the collection or the individual objects changes, the UI will be updated, and vice versa. However, there is a great deal more to say on this topic, including binding to XML and relational data, master-detail binding, and hierarchical binding, which you'll see in Chapters 6 and 7.

Dependency Properties

Although our data source Nickname object made its data available via standard .NET properties, we need something special to support data binding on the target element. Even though the TextContent property of the TextBlock element is exposed with a standard property wrapper, in order for it to integrate with WPF services like data binding, styling, and animation, it also needs to be a *dependency property*. A dependency property provides several features not present in .NET properties, including the ability to inherit its value from a container element, provide for object-independent storage (providing a potentially huge memory savings), and change tracking.

Most of the time, you won't have to worry about dependency properties versus .NET properties, but when you need the details, you can read about them in Chapter 18.

Resources

Resources are named chunks of data defined separately from code and bundled with your application or component. .NET provides a great deal of support for resources, a bit of which we already used when we referenced *tom.png* from our XAML button earlier in this chapter. WPF also provides special support for resources scoped to elements defined in the tree.

As an example, let's declare some default instances of our custom `Nickname` objects in XAML (see Example 1-30).

Example 1-30. Declaring objects in XAML

```
<!-- Window1.xaml -->
<Window ... xmlns:local="clr-namespace:DataBindingDemo" />

  <Window.Resources>
    <local:Nicknames x:Key="names">
      <local:Nickname Name="Don" Nick="Naked" />
      <local:Nickname Name="Martin" Nick="Gudge" />
      <local:Nickname Name="Tim" Nick="Stinky" />
    </local:Nicknames>
  </Window.Resources>

  <DockPanel DataContext="{StaticResource names}">
    <TextBlock DockPanel.Dock="Top" Orientation="Horizontal">
      <TextBlock VerticalAlignment="Center">Name: </TextBlock>
      <TextBox Text="{Binding Path=Name}" />
      <TextBlock VerticalAlignment="Center">Nick: </TextBlock>
      <TextBox Text="{Binding Path=Nick}" />
    </TextBlock>
    ...
  </DockPanel>
</Window>
```

Notice the `Window.Resources`, which is property element syntax to set the `Resources` property of the `Window1` class. Here we can add as many named objects as we like, with the name coming from the `Key` attribute and the object coming from the XAML elements (remember that a XAML element is just a mapping to .NET class names). In this example, we're creating a `Nicknames` collection named `names` to hold three `Nickname` objects, each constructed with the default constructor, and then setting each of the `Name` and `Nick` properties.

Also notice the use of the `StaticResource` markup extension to reference the `names` resource as the collection to use for data binding. With this XAML in place, our window construction reduces to the code shown in Example 1-31.

Example 1-31. Finding a resource in code

```
public partial class Window1 : Window {
  Nicknames names;

  public Window1( ) {
    InitializeComponent( );
    this.addButton.Click += addButton_Click;

    // get names collection from resources
    this.names = (Nicknames)this.FindResource("names");

    // no need to make data available for binding here
    //dockPanel.DataContext = this.names;
  }

  void addButton_Click(object sender, RoutedEventArgs e) {
    this.names.Add(new Nickname( ));
  }
}
```

Now instead of creating the collection of names, we can pull it from the resources with the FindResource method. Just because this collection was created in XAML doesn't mean that we need to treat it any differently than we treated it before, which is why the Add button event handler is the exact same code. Also, there's no need to set the data context on the dock panel because that property was set in the XAML.

For the full scoop on resources, including resource scoping and lookup, static and dynamic binding to resources, and using resources for theming and skinning, read Chapter 12.

XAML Namespace Mapping Syntax

Before we go on with resource applications, we need to discuss a new XAML syntax that's come up: the *mapping syntax*. This provides the ability to bring in types not already known by the XAML compiler (in fact, the XAML compiler knows about only a couple of types). Our use of the mapping syntax looks like Example 1-32.

Example 1-32. XAML mapping syntax

```
<Window ... xmlns:local="clr-namespace:DataBindingDemo" />

  <Window.Resources>
    <local:Nicknames x:Key="names">
      <local:Nickname Name="Don" Nick="Naked" />
      ...
    </local:Nicknames>
  </Window.Resources>
  ...
</Window>
```

When bringing a new CLR namespace into XAML, we use the XML namespace prefix mapping syntax. If we've got control of the CLR assembly in question, we can add an attribute to tag it with any URI we like. Otherwise, we have to use a specific format:

```
xmlns:myPrefix="clr-namespace:MyNamespace[;assembly=MyAssembly]"
```

The XML prefix is how we access the CLR namespace when referring to a CLR type in a XAML document (e.g., local:Nickname). I've chosen the XML namespace local in this case because the CLR namespace to which I'm referring must be part of the assembly being compiled along with the XAML in question. You can import CLR namespaces for another assembly by specifying the optional assembly attribute as part of the mapping. For a more thorough discussion of the namespace mapping syntax, including the attribute you can use to tag your CLR assemblies with URIs for more seamless mapping into XAML, read Appendix A.

Styles

One of the major uses for resources is to specify styles. A *style* is a set of property/value pairs to be applied to one or more elements. For example, recall the two TextBlock controls from our Nickname sample, each of which was set to the same VerticalAlignment (Example 1-33).

Example 1-33. Multiple TextBlock controls with the same settings

```
<!-- Window1.xaml -->
<Window ...>
  <DockPanel ...>
    <TextBlock ...>
      <TextBlock VerticalAlignment="Center">Name: </TextBlock>
      <TextBox Text="{Binding Path=Name}" />
      <TextBlock VerticalAlignment="Center">Nick: </TextBlock>
      <TextBox Text="{Binding Path=Nick}" />
    </TextBlock>
    ...
  </DockPanel>
</Window>
```

If we wanted to bundle the VerticalAlignment setting into a style, we could do this with a Style element in a Resources block (Example 1-34).

Example 1-34. An example TextBlock style

```
<Window ...>
  <Window.Resources>
    ...
    <Style x:Key="myStyle" TargetType="{x:Type TextBlock}">
      <Setter Property="VerticalAlignment" Value="Center" />
      <Setter Property="Margin" Value="2" />
```

Example 1-34. An example TextBlock style (continued)

```
    <Setter Property="FontWeight" Value="Bold" />
    <Setter Property="FontStyle" Value="Italic" />
  </Style>
</Window.Resources>
<DockPanel ...>
  <TextBlock ...>
    <TextBlock Style="{StaticResource myStyle}">Name: </TextBlock>
    <TextBox Text="{Binding Path=Name}" />
    <TextBlock Style="{StaticResource myStyle}">Nick: </TextBlock>
    <TextBox Text="{Binding Path=Nick}" />
  </TextBlock>
  ...
</DockPanel>
</Window>
```

The Style element is really just a named collection of Setter elements for a specific target type (and specified with the Type markup extension). The new TextBlock style centers the vertical alignment property and, just for fun, sets the margin, font width, and font style. With the style in place, you can use it to set the Style property of any TextBlock that references the style resource. Figure 1-17 illustrates the use to which we've put this style.

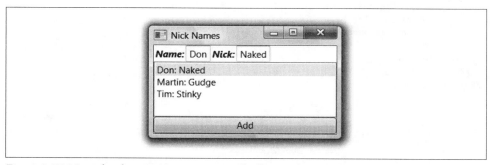

Figure 1-17. Named style in action on two TextBlock controls

Styles provide one great way to set the look of a control without building a custom control, by merely setting properties. There's much more on this topic in Chapter 8.

Animation

If you'd like to apply property changes to a control (or other visual element) over time, you can do so with styles that include animation information, which is discussed in Chapter 16 (although Figure 1-18 is a small taste of what WPF animations can produce).

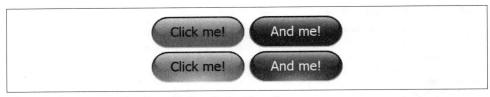

Figure 1-18. Buttons with animated glow (Color Plate 1)

Control Templates

In addition to changing a control's look by manipulating properties, you can replace it with something completely different by setting a control's Template property.

In Example 1-35, we've decided that our Add button is a yellow ellipse, as shown in Figure 1-19.

Example 1-35. Replacing a control's look completely with a control template

```
<Button DockPanel.Dock="Bottom" x:Name="addButton" Content="Add">
  <Button.Template>
    <ControlTemplate TargetType="{x:Type Button}">
      <Grid>
        <Ellipse Width="128" Height="32" Fill="Yellow" Stroke="Black" />
        <ContentPresenter
          VerticalAlignment="Center" HorizontalAlignment="Center" />
      </Grid>
    </ControlTemplate>
  </Button.Template>
</Button>
```

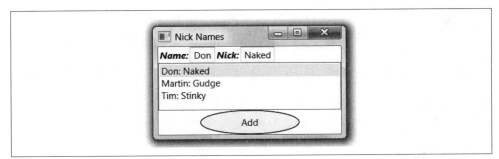

Figure 1-19. A yellow ellipse button

The *template* of a control in WPF is what defines the look, whereas the code defines the behavior. The default template comes from the system-scope resources (as described in Chapter 12), but if you don't like that one, you can replace it with whatever you like, using a content presenter to drop in the content provided by the developer using your control. However, the behavior remains the same (e.g., if you click on the ellipse-shaped button in Figure 1-19, a Click event is still fired). We explore in detail the power of replacing the look of a control in Chapter 9.

Graphics

When building up a control's template, you'll likely build it with a set of graphics primitives that WPF provides, including rectangles, polygons, lines, ellipses, and so on. WPF also lets you affect the way it renders graphics in any element, offering facilities that include bordering, rotating, or scaling another shape or control. WPF's support for graphics is engineered to fit right into the content model we're already familiar with, as shown in Example 1-36, from Chapter 13.

Example 1-36. Adding graphics to a Button

```
<Button>
  <Button.LayoutTransform>
    <ScaleTransform ScaleX="3" ScaleY="3" />
  </Button.LayoutTransform>
  <StackPanel Orientation="Horizontal">
    <Canvas Width="20" Height="18" VerticalAlignment="Center">
      <Ellipse Canvas.Left="1" Canvas.Top="1" Width="16" Height="16"
               Fill="Yellow" Stroke="Black" />
      <Ellipse Canvas.Left="4.5" Canvas.Top="5" Width="2.5" Height="3"
               Fill="Black" />
      <Ellipse Canvas.Left="11" Canvas.Top="5" Width="2.5" Height="3"
               Fill="Black" />
      <Path Data="M 5,10 A 3,3 0 0 0 13,10" Stroke="Black" />
    </Canvas>
    <TextBlock VerticalAlignment="Center">Click!</TextBlock>
  </StackPanel>
</Button>
```

Here we've got three ellipses and a path composed inside a canvas that is hosted inside a stack panel with a text block that, when scaled via the LayoutTransform property on the button, produces Figure 1-20.

Figure 1-20. A scaled button with a collection of graphics primitives

Notice that there's nothing special about the graphics primitives in XAML; they're declared and integrated as content just like any of the other WPF elements we've discussed. The graphics and the transformation are integrated into the same presentation stack as the rest of WPF, which is a bit of a difference for experienced User/GDI programmers.

For a complete discussion of how graphics primitives, retained drawings, color, lines, brushes, and transformations happen in WPF, both declaratively and in code, and for an introduction to 3D and video, read Chapter 13.

3D

Graphics in WPF are not limited to 2D; Figure 1-21 shows an example of a figure that was defined using WPF's 3D capabilities.

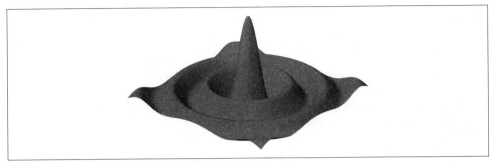

Figure 1-21. 3D plot of data (Color Plate 2)

For an introduction to 3D and how it integrates with your WPF applications, you'll want to read Chapter 17.

Documents and Printing

The document support in WPF is about flowing all the different content types you've seen in the rest of this chapter, along with special text-specific content types, into a seamless whole, a small sample of which is shown in Figure 1-22.

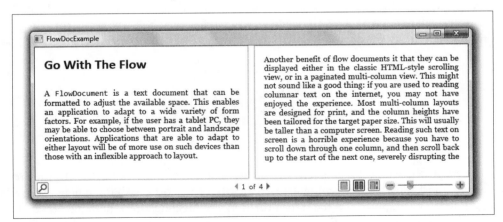

Figure 1-22. A flowing document

The text-specific content support is provided with the flow document and related elements that provide advanced typography; adaptive, flow-based layout; spellchecking; hyphenation; and more, as described in Chapter 14.

In addition, the base of the flow document supports printing, as do the rest of the WPF visual elements, via the XML Paper Specification (XPS), as covered in Chapter 15.

Where Are We?

WPF applications have a great deal of power, at which this chapter can only hint. The base services of the application aren't too surprising, but the support for page-based navigation and browser hosting certainly adds a new capability for Windows applications, further enhanced with .NET 2.0 ClickOnce support.

Building your application is a matter of grouping controls in containers—either single content containers, like windows or buttons, or multiple content containers that provide layout capabilities, like the canvas and the grid.

When bringing your controls together, you'll want to populate them with data that's synchronized with the in-memory home of the data, which is what data binding is for, and keep them pretty, which is what styles are for. If you want to declare data or styles in your XAML, you can do so using resources, which are just arbitrarily named objects that aren't used to render the WPF UI directly.

If no amount of data or style property settings makes you satisfied with the look of your control, you can replace it completely with control templates, which can comprise other controls or graphics primitives. In addition, you can apply graphics operations, like rotating, scaling, or animation, to 2D or 3D graphics primitives or controls in WPF's integrated way. These elements can further be gathered into documents for viewing or printing.

CHAPTER 2
Applications and Settings

A WPF application is a Windows process in which you have an instance of the WPF Application object. The Application object provides lifetime services and integration with ClickOnce deployment. Between application sessions, you'll want to be able to keep application and user settings in a way that integrates well with WPF applications. All of these topics are the focus of this chapter.

On the other hand, if you're interested in XML Browser Applications (XBAPs)—applications hosted in the browser and deployed over the Web—read Chapter 11.

Application Lifetime

In the Windows sense, an "application" is an address space and at least one thread of execution (a.k.a. a "process"). In the WPF sense, an *application* is a singleton object that provides services for UI components and UI programmers in the creation and execution of a WPF program. More specifically, in WPF, an application is an instance of the Application class from the System.Windows namespace.

Explicit Application Creation

Example 2-1 shows code for creating an instance of the Application class.

Example 2-1. Creating an application explicitly

```
using System;
using System.Windows; // the home of the Application class

class Program {
    [STAThread]
    static void Main() {
        Application app = new System.Windows.Application();
        Window1 window = new Window1();
        window.Show();
        app.Run();
    }
}
```

Here, we're creating an application inside an STA thread,[*] creating a window and showing it, and then running the application. While the application is running, WPF processes Windows messages and routes events to WPF UI objects as necessary. When the Run method returns, messages have stopped being routed and generally don't start again (unless you show a modal window after the Run method returns, but that's not something you'll usually do). During its lifetime, the application provides various services.

Application Access

One of the services the Application class provides is access to the current instance. Once an instance of the Application class is created,[†] it's available via the Current static property of the Application class. For example, the code in Example 2-1 is equivalent to the code in Example 2-2.

Example 2-2. Implicitly filling in the Application.Current property

```
using System;
using System.Windows;

class Program {
    [STAThread]
    static void Main( ) {
        // Fills in Application.Current
        Application app = new System.Windows.Application( );

        Window1 window = new Window1( );
        window.Show( );

        Application.Current.Run(); // same as app.Run( )
    }
}
```

Here, in the process's entry point, we're creating an application, creating and showing the main window, and then running the application. Creation of the Application object fills the static Application.Current property. Access to the current application is very handy in other parts of your program where you don't create the application or when you let WPF create the application for you itself.

---

[*] The "Single Threaded Apartment" (STA) was invented as part of the native Component Object Model (COM) to govern the serialization of incoming COM calls. All Microsoft presentation frameworks, native or managed, require that they be run on a thread initialized as an STA thread so that they can integrate with one another and with COM services (e.g., drag-and-drop).

[†] WPF makes sure that, at most, one Application object is created per application domain. For a discussion of .NET application domains, I recommend *Essential .NET*, by Don Box with Chris Sells (Addison-Wesley Professional).

Implicit Application Creation

Because a `Main` method that creates and runs an application is pretty darn common, WPF can provide the process's entry point for you. WPF projects generally designate one XAML file that defines the application. For example, if we had defined our application in a XAML file with code behind, it would look like Example 2-3.

Example 2-3. Declaring an application in XAML

```
<!-- App.xaml -->
<Application
  x:Class="ImplicitAppSample.App"
  xmlns="http://schemas.microsoft.com/winfx/2006/xaml/presentation"
  xmlns:x="http://schemas.microsoft.com/winfx/2006/xaml" />


// App.xaml.cs
using System;
using System.Windows;

namespace ImplicitAppSample {
  public partial class App : System.Windows.Application {
    protected override void OnStartup(StartupEventArgs e) {
      // let the base class have a crack
      base.OnStartup(e);

      // WPF itself is providing the Main that creates an
      // Application and calls the Run method; all we have
      // to do is create a window and show it
      Window1 window = new Window1();
      window.Show();
    }
  }
}
```

Notice that Example 2-3 is defining a custom application class in this code (`ImplicitAppSample.App`) that derives from the `Application` class. In the `OnStartup` override, we're only creating a window and showing it, assuming WPF is going to create the `Main` for us that creates the instance of the `App` class and calls the `Run` method (which calls the `OnStartup` method). The way that WPF knows which XAML file contains the definition of the `Application` class is that the Build Action is set to `ApplicationDefinition`, as shown in Figure 2-1.

The `ApplicationDefinition` Build Action lets WPF know which class is our application and hooks it up appropriately in a `Main` method it generates for us, which saves us from writing several lines of boilerplate code.

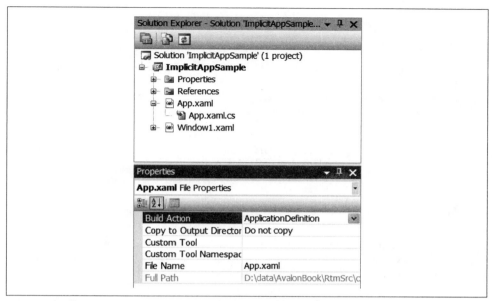

Figure 2-1. Setting the Build Action for the application definition XAML file

For msbuild aficionados, the standard XAML Build Action setting of Page looks like this in the *.csproj* file:

```
<Project ...>
  ...
  <ItemGroup>
    <Page Include="App.xaml" />
    <Compile Include="App.xaml.cs">
      <DependentUpon>App.xaml</DependentUpon>
      <SubType>Code</SubType>
    </Compile>
    ...
  </ItemGroup>
  ...
</Project>
```

When we switch the Build Action to ApplicationDefinition, it looks like this:

```
<Project ...>
  ...
  <ItemGroup>
    <ApplicationDefinition Include="App.xaml" />
    <Compile Include="App.xaml.cs">
      <DependentUpon>App.xaml</DependentUpon>
      <SubType>Code</SubType>
    </Compile>
```

```
    ...
  </ItemGroup>
  ...
</Project>
```

This setting causes the WPF build tasks to generate the following code:

```
namespace ImplicitAppSample {
  public partial class App : Application {
    [System.STAThreadAttribute()]
    [DebuggerNonUserCodeAttribute()]
    public static void Main() {
      ImplicitAppSample.App app =
        new ImplicitAppSample.App();
      app.Run();
    }
  }
}
```

Except for the debugger attribute (which stops Visual Studio from stepping into this method when debugging), this is equivalent to what we were writing by hand a few code samples ago.

If our window class is defined in a XAML file itself (as most likely it will be), we can save ourselves from overriding the OnStartup method by setting the StartupUri property in the application's XAML file (see Example 2-4).

Example 2-4. Setting the StartupUri on the application

```
<!-- App.xaml -->
<Application
  x:Class="ImplicitAppSample.App"
  xmlns="http://schemas.microsoft.com/winfx/2006/xaml/presentation"
  xmlns:x="http://schemas.microsoft.com/winfx/2006/xaml"
  StartupUri="Window1.xaml" />
```

The combination of setting the Build Action of the application's XAML file to ApplicationDefinition and the StartupUri property provides the following features:

- Creating an instance of the Application object and setting it as the value of the Application.Current property
- Creating and showing an instance of the UI defined in the XAML designated in the StartupUri property
- Setting the Application object's MainWindow property
- Calling the Application object's Run method, keeping the application running until the main window is closed

This set of features makes more sense when we get a handle on what the "main window" is.

Top-Level Windows

A *top-level* window is a window that is not contained within or owned by another window (window ownership is discussed in more detail later). A WPF application's *main window* is the top-level window that is set in the MainWindow property of the Application object. This property is set by default when the first instance of the Window class is created and the Application.Current property is set. In other words, by default, the main window is the top-level window that's created first after the application itself has been created. If you like, you can override this default by setting the MainWindow property manually.

In addition to the main window, the Application class provides a list of top-level windows from the Windows property. This is useful if you'd like to implement a Window menu, like the one in Figure 2-2.

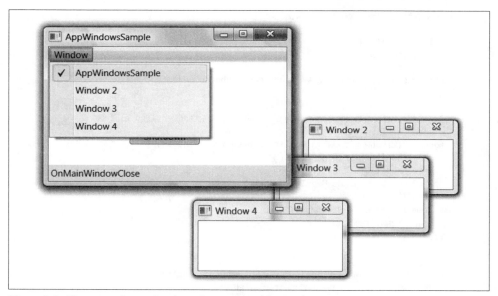

Figure 2-2. Managing the top-level windows exposed by Application

To implement the Window menu, we first start with a MenuItem element:

```
<!-- Window1.xaml -->
<Window ...>
  <Grid>
    <Grid.RowDefinitions>
      <RowDefinition Height="auto" />
      <RowDefinition />
      <RowDefinition Height="auto" />
    </Grid.RowDefinitions>
```

```
<Menu>
  <MenuItem Header="Window" x:Name="windowMenu">
    <MenuItem Header="dummy item" />
  </MenuItem>
</Menu>
    </Grid>
  </Window>
```

MenuItem is a HeaderedItemControl (as described in Chapter 5), which means that it has header content that we'll use to hold the name of the menu item ("Window"), and subcontent that we'll use to hold the menu items for each top-level window. Notice the use of a dummy subitem to start with. Without this dummy item, you won't be able to get notification that the user has asked to show the menu items (whether via mouse or via keyboard).

To populate the Window menu, we'll handle the menu item's SubmenuOpened event:

```
public partial class Window1 : Window {
  ...
  public Window1() {
    InitializeComponent();

    windowMenu.SubmenuOpened += windowMenu_SubmenuOpened;
  }

  void windowMenu_SubmenuOpened(object sender, RoutedEventArgs e) {
    windowMenu.Items.Clear();
    foreach (Window window in Application.Current.Windows) {
      MenuItem item = new MenuItem();
      item.Header = window.Title;
      item.Click += windowMenuItem_Click;
      item.Tag = window;
      item.IsChecked = window.IsActive;
      windowMenu.Items.Add(item);
    }
  }

  void windowMenuItem_Click(object sender, RoutedEventArgs e) {
    Window window = (Window)((MenuItem)sender).Tag;
    window.Activate();
  }
}
```

When the SubmenuOpened event is triggered, we use the Application object's Windows property to get a list of each top-level Window, creating a corresponding MenuItem for each Window.

> For those of you already steeped in data binding and data templates who are wondering why we're populating the Window menu manually, it's because the WindowCollection class that the Windows property returns doesn't provide notifications when it changes, so once the Window menu is populated initially, there's no way to keep it up-to-date. Maybe next version...

Application Shutdown Modes

Some applications work naturally with the idea of a single main window. For example, many applications (drawing programs, IDEs, Notepad, etc.) have a single top-level window that controls the lifetime of the application itself (i.e., when the main window goes away, the application shuts down). On the other hand, some applications have multiple top-level windows or some other kind of lifetime control that's independent of a single main window.* You can specify when your application shuts down by setting the application's ShutdownMode property to one of the values of the ShutdownMode enumeration:

```
namespace System.Windows {
  public enum ShutdownMode {
    OnLastWindowClose = 0, // default
    OnMainWindowClose = 1,
    OnExplicitShutdown = 2,
  }
}
```

The OnMainWindowClose value is useful when you've got a single top-level window, and the OnLastWindowClose value is useful for multiple top-level windows (and is the default). In either of these cases, in addition to the automatic application shutdown the ShutdownMode policy describes, an application can also be shut down manually by calling the Application object's Shutdown method. However, in the case of OnExplicitShutdown, the only way to stop a WPF application is by calling Shutdown:

```
public partial class Window1 : System.Windows.Window {
  ...
  void shutdownButton_Click(object sender, RoutedEventArgs e) {
    Application.Current.Shutdown( );
  }
}
```

You can change the shutdown mode in code whenever you like, or you can set it in the application definition XAML:

```
<Application
  x:Class="AppWindowsSample.App"
  xmlns="http://schemas.microsoft.com/winfx/2006/xaml/presentation"
  xmlns:x="http://schemas.microsoft.com/winfx/2006/xaml"
  StartupUri="Window1.xaml"
  ShutdownMode="OnExplicitShutdown" />
```

 Of course, there are a number of ways to shut down a Windows process. The Application.Shutdown method is a *nice* way of doing it by closing the top-level windows and returning from the Run method. This lets the windows involved get their Closing and Closed notifications, although canceling the shutdown in the Closing event doesn't actually stop the application shutdown process.

---

* For example, if an Office application is serving OLE objects, closing the windows will not cause the process to stop until those OLE objects are no longer needed.

Application Events

You can best see the life cycle of a standard application in the set of events that it exposes:*

- Startup
- Activated
- Deactivated
- DispatcherUnhandledException
- SessionEnding
- Exit

Startup event

The Application object's Startup event is fired when the application's Run method is called, and it is a useful place to do application-wide initialization, including the handling of command-line arguments, which are passed in the StartupEventArgs:

```
void App_Startup(object sender, StartupEventArgs e) {
  for (int i = 0; i != e.Args.Length; ++i) {
    // do something useful with each e.Args[i]
    ...
  }
}
```

Activated and Deactivated events

The Activated event is called when one of the application's top-level windows is activated (e.g., via a mouse click or Alt-Tab). Deactivated is called when your application is active and another application's top-level window is activated. These events are handy when you want to stop or start some interactive part of your application:

```
void App_Activated(object sender, EventArgs e) {
  ResumeGame();
}

void App_Deactivated(object sender, EventArgs e) {
  PauseGame();
}
```

DispatcherUnhandledException event

The application's *dispatcher* is an object that routes events to the correct place, including unhandled exceptions. In the event that you'd like to handle an exception otherwise unhandled in your application—maybe to give the user a chance to save his current document and exit—you can handle the DispatcherUnhandledException event:

---

* Navigation events aren't listed here, but are discussed in Chapter 11.

```
void App_DispatcherUnhandledException(
   object sender, DispatcherUnhandledExceptionEventArgs e) {

   string err = "Oops: " + e.Exception.Message);

   MessageBox.Show(err, "Exception", MessageBoxButton.OK);

   // Only useful if you've got some way of guaranteeing that
   // your app can continue reliably in the face of an exception
   // without leaving this AppDomain in an unreliable state...
   //e.Handled = true; // stop exception from bringing down the app
}
```

The Exception property of the DispatcherUnhandledExceptionEventArgs event argument is useful to communicate to your users what happened, whereas the Handled property is useful to stop the exception from actually bringing down the application (although this is a dangerous thing to do and can easily result in data loss).

SessionEnding event

The SessionEnding event is called when the Windows session itself is ending (e.g., in the event of a shutdown, logoff, or restart):

```
void App_SessionEnding(object sender, SessionEndingCancelEventArgs e) {
   if (MessageBox.Show(
         e.ReasonSessionEnding.ToString(),
         "Session Ending",
         MessageBoxButton.OKCancel) == MessageBoxResult.Cancel) {
      e.Cancel = true; // stop the session from ending
   }
}
```

The ReasonSessionEnding property of the SessionEndingCancelEventArgs event argument is one value in the ReasonSessionEnding enumeration:

```
namespace System.Windows {
   public enum ReasonSessionEnding {
      Logoff = 0,
      Shutdown = 1,
   }
}
```

The Cancel property is useful if you'd like to stop the session from ending, although this is considered rude, and more progressive versions of Windows (like Vista) may not let you change its decision to end a session at all.

Exit event

The Exit event is called when the application is actually exiting, whether the last window has gone away, the Application.Shutdown method is called, or the session is ending. One of the overloads of the Shutdown method allows the programmer to pass an integer exit code, which is ultimately exposed by the process for use by your favorite Win32 process examination APIs. By default, this value is zero, but you can observe or override it in the handlers for this event:

```
void App_Exit(object sender, ExitEventArgs e) {
  e.ApplicationExitCode = 452; // keep 'em guessing...
}
```

Application Instancing

While we've just been talking about the lifetime of an application, things get a bit more interesting when you take into account that multiple instances of a single application can be running at any one time simply because the user can double-click on the same EXE multiple times. In fact, the default behavior in Windows and WPF does nothing to hamper or support multiple instances of the same application. For example, if we double-click on the *AppWindowsSample.exe* from Figure 2-2 more than once, we get more than one instance, as Figure 2-3 shows.

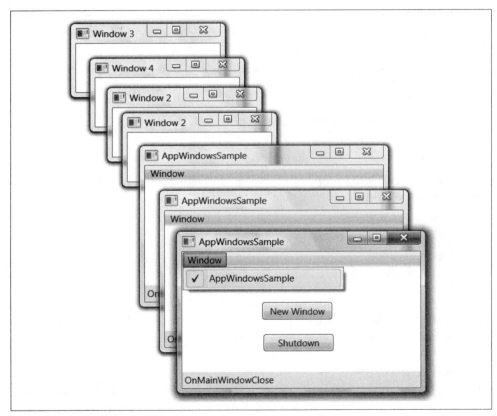

Figure 2-3. Multiple instance applications

In Figure 2-3, we've got several top-level windows, some associated with each of three instances of the application. Sometimes more than one instance of a single application is a good thing. However, sometimes it just confuses users. For example, in Figure 2-3, even though we've got a Window menu, only the windows associated with each instance of the application are shown, which can be confusing as heck to the poor user faced with such an application.

Single instance applications

If you'd like your application to be single instance, it's easy to detect an existing instance and shut down any subsequent instances (see Example 2-5).

Example 2-5. Very simple existing instance detection

```
public partial class App : System.Windows.Application {
  Mutex mutex;
  protected override void OnStartup(StartupEventArgs e) {
    base.OnStartup(e);

    // Check for existing instance
    string mutexName = "MyCompanyName.MyAppName";
    bool createdNew;
    mutex = new Mutex(true, mutexName, out createdNew);

    // If there is an existing instance, shut down this one
    if( !createdNew ) { Shutdown(); }
  }
}
```

In Example 2-5, the key is to access a Windows mutex with a session-wide unique name so that we can tell whether it was already created by an initial instance or whether we're the initial instance. The mutex name we're using is one we pick to be sufficiently unique for our needs. Once the mutex has been created, it'll live for the life of the WPF Application object itself, which will live for the life of the process, so if we're not the first one to create the mutex, we shut down our application, causing our process to exit.

However, it's at this point that we realize that single instance detection isn't the only feature we want; we also want the following:

- Passing command-line arguments to the initial instance (e.g., in case a subsequent instance was passed a filename that the user would like opened)
- Activating the main window of the initial instance
- Dealing properly with multiple users logging into a single computer (even the same user logged in multiple times), giving each login an instance of the application

These are services that are not trivial to implement and we'd really love it if .NET provided this functionality for us. The good news is that it does. The bad news is that it's provided only as part of the .NET 2.0 Visual Basic support for Windows Forms.

If you'd like to take advantage of robust single instance management, you have to load the `Microsoft.VisualBasic` assembly, and you have an interesting integration challenge ahead of you, as both Visual Basic's support for single instance management and WPF want to be "the" application. However, it *is* possible and you get to leverage Other People's Code (OPC), of which I'm a big fan, especially when the "other people" are a multibillion-dollar corporation with a record of framework maintenance and upgrades.* For an example of how to integrate single instance detection from Visual Basic into WPF, check out the "Single Instance Detection" sample in the Windows Platform SDK.†

Other Application Services

In addition to what we've already discussed, the `Application` class provides access to app-level resources and navigation services. Chapter 12 discusses resources and Chapter 11 discusses navigation. The other major service that WPF applications support is ClickOnce deployment, which we'll discuss right now.

Application Deployment

For the purposes of demonstration, let's build something vital for procrastinators the world over: an application to generate excuses. The application was started with the "Windows Application (WPF)" project template in Visual Studio 2005 and was implemented with some very simple code. When you run it, it gives you an excuse from its vast database, as shown in Figure 2-4.

Figure 2-4. A WPF excuse-generation application

---

* Whether Microsoft has a "good" record of framework maintenance and updates, I'll leave to you to decide....

† Available online at *http://msdn2.microsoft.com/en-us/library/ms771662.aspx* (*http://tinysells.com/85*).

Simple Publishing

For anyone to use this wonderful application, it must be published. The simplest way to publish your WPF application is by right-clicking on the project in the Solution Explorer and choosing the Publish option, which will bring up the first page of the Publish Wizard (shown in Figure 2-5).

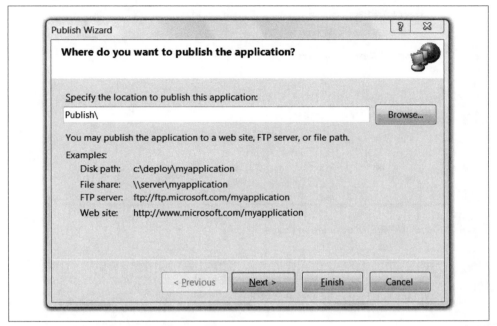

Figure 2-5. Publish Wizard publish location

Figure 2-5 asks you to choose where you'd like to deploy your application, including to the disk, to a network share, to an FTP server, or to a web site. By default, the Publish Wizard will assume you want to publish to the Publish subdirectory of your project directory. Clicking the Next button yields Figure 2-6.

Because we've chosen to publish to something besides a web site, the Publish Wizard wants to know how users will access your published application—in other words, from a URL, from a UNC path, or from some optical media. (If you choose to publish to a web site, the only way to access the application is from a URL, so it won't bother to ask.) We'd like to test web deployment, so we pick that option and leave the default URL alone. Clicking Next yields Figure 2-7.

For WPF applications, Figure 2-7 lets us choose whether we'd like this application to be made available *online* (when the computer is able to connect to the application's URL) as well as *offline* (when the computer can't connect to the URL), or whether you'd like the application to be only available online. These two options correspond to the ClickOnce terms *locally installed* and *online only*, respectively.

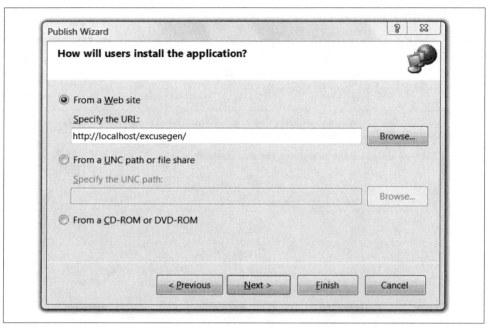

Figure 2-6. Publish Wizard installation options

Figure 2-7. Install mode in the Publish Wizard

The job of the Publish Wizard is to bundle up the files needed to deploy an application using ClickOnce, including the manifest files that ClickOnce needs to deploy the application to a client machine after it's been published.

 This example assumes a standalone application, which provides its own host window. WPF also supports the XBAP application type, which is an application composed of one or more pages and hosted in Internet Explorer 6+. You can also publish an XBAP via ClickOnce from within Visual Studio, but the options are different. Chapter 11 discusses XBAP creation, publication, and deployment details.

Leaving the default "online or offline" option and clicking the Finish button yields Figure 2-8.

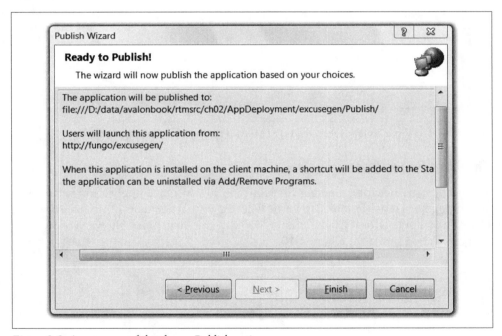

Figure 2-8. A summary of the chosen Publish options

Figure 2-8 reminds us what we get with a locally installed ClickOnce application (i.e., the application will appear in the Start menu and in the Add or Remove Programs Control Panel). Clicking Finish causes Visual Studio to publish the application to the filesystem, including a *publish.htm* file that you can use to test deployment. If you happen to have an IIS application set up in the same folder to which Visual Studio publishes, it will launch the *publish.htm* file for you, as shown in Figure 2-9.

For simple needs, this is the complete experience for publishing a WPF ClickOnce locally installed application.

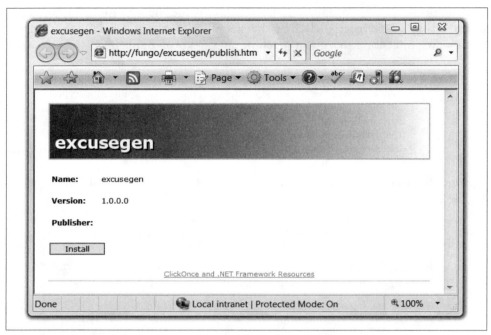

Figure 2-9. The Visual Studio-generated HTML file for testing ClickOnce applications

The User Experience

The user experience for running a ClickOnce locally installed application begins with a web page, such as the one shown in Figure 2-9, that includes a link to install the ClickOnce application. Clicking the link for the first time shows a download progress dialog similar to Figure 2-10.

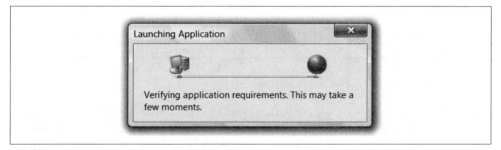

Figure 2-10. Progress dialog for checking the application manifest

Once the metadata file describing the application deployment settings has been downloaded (this file is called the *application manifest*), it will be checked for a *certificate*, which is extra information attached to the application that identifies a validated publisher name. ClickOnce requires all published applications to be signed, so Visual Studio will generate a certificate file for you as part of the initial publication process if you haven't already provided one.

If the certificate used to sign the application manifest identifies a publisher that is already approved to install the application on the user's machine (such as from a previous version or a IT-administered group policy), the application will be run without further ado, as shown at the beginning of this chapter in Figure 2-4.

If, on the other hand, the publisher's certificate cannot be verified or is not yet trusted to run the application in question, a dialog similar to Figure 2-11 will be presented.

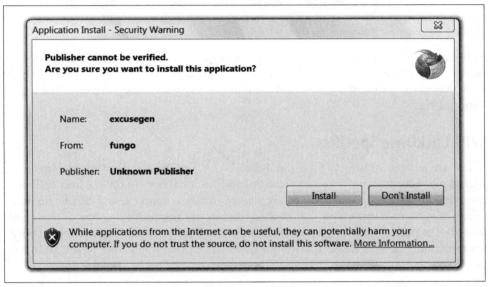

Figure 2-11. The Application Install dialog with an unknown publisher

Figure 2-11 displays the name of the application, the source of the application, and the publisher of the application according to the certificate (or "Unknown Publisher" if the certificate could not be verified). It also lists a summary of the reasons this dialog is being shown, along with a link to more detailed warning information. However, such information will likely be ignored by the user choosing between the Install and Don't Install buttons, from which the user will choose depending on the level of trust she has for the publisher she sees in the Security Warning dialog.

If the user chooses Don't Install, no application code will be downloaded or executed. If she chooses Install, the application is downloaded, added to the Start menu, and added to the Add or Remove Programs Control Panel, all under the umbrella of the progress dialog shown in Figure 2-12, after which the application is executed.

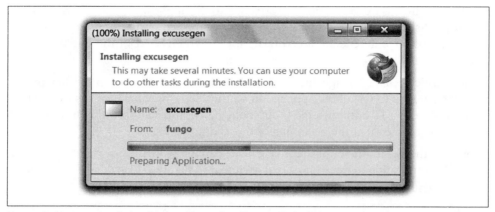

Figure 2-12. Progress dialog for installing a locally installed ClickOnce application

Subsequent runs of the same version of the application, as launched from either a web site or the Start menu, will not ask for any additional user input (although they may show a dialog if checking for updates), but will launch the installed application directly.

WPF ClickOnce Specifics

There are a great number of additional details to ClickOnce application deployment, including security considerations, command-line handling, updating and rollback, prerequisite installation, access to external information sources, and certificate management, just to name a few. All of these details are beyond the scope of this book and are covered in great detail by other sources.* However, following are some specifics to standalone and XBAP ClickOnce deployment you might like to see all in one place.

Standalone WPF applications deployed using ClickOnce:

- Can implement the main window with `Window` or `NavigationWindow` (although only the former has a project template in Visual Studio—the "Windows Application [WPF]" template)
- Can be online-only or online/offline
- If installed online/offline, can integrate with the Start menu, and can be rolled back and uninstalled
- Must set "full trust" in the project's Security settings (the `Window` class demands this)

---

* The SDK does a pretty good job, as does *Smart Client Deployment with ClickOnce: Deploying Windows Forms Applications with ClickOnce*, by Brian Noyes (Addison-Wesley Professional).

XBAP applications deployed using ClickOnce:

- Provide their content with one or more Page objects to be hosted in the browser
- Must be online-only to deploy with ClickOnce
- There can be no "Security Warning" dialog, so must not attempt to elevate permissions beyond what is provided already on the client's machine
- No custom pop-up windows are allowed (e.g., no dialogs); can use standard page navigation, page functions, and message boxes instead
- Designated as XBAP by setting the HostInBrowser property to True in the project file (will be set by the "XAML Browser Application (WPF)" project template in Visual Studio)

For the details of navigation-based applications and XBAP browser hosting and deployment, read Chapter 11.

Settings

WPF applications gain access to all the same application and user setting options that any other .NET application can use (e.g., the Registry, *.config* files, special folders, isolated storage, etc.).

Designing Settings

The preferred settings mechanism for WPF applications is the one provided by .NET 2.0 and Visual Studio 2005: the ApplicationSettingsBase class from the System.Configuration namespace with the built-in designer. To access the settings for your application, click on the Settings tab in your project settings. This will bring up the Settings Designer shown in Figure 2-13.

Here we've defined two settings: a user setting of type System.String, called LastExcuse; and an application setting of type System.Boolean, called ExcludeAnimalExcuses with a default value of True. These two settings will be loaded automatically when I run my application, pulled from the application's configuration file (named *MyApplication.exe.config*) and the user settings file saved from the application's last session.

The Settings Designer manages a settings file and generates a class that allows you to program against the settings. For instance, our settings example will result in the class in Example 2-6 being generated (roughly).

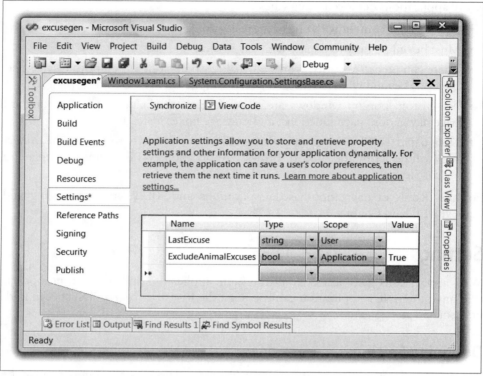

Figure 2-13. The Settings Designer

Example 2-6. The Settings Designer-generated class

```csharp
using namespace System.Configuration;

namespace excusegen.Properties {
  sealed partial class Settings : ApplicationSettingsBase {
    static Settings defaultInstance =
      ((Settings)(ApplicationSettingsBase.Synchronized(new Settings())));

    public static Settings Default {
      get { return defaultInstance; }
    }

    [UserScopedSettingAttribute()]
    [DefaultSettingValueAttribute("")]
    public string LastExcuse {
      get { return ((string)(this["LastExcuse"])); }
      set { this["LastExcuse"] = value; }
    }

    [ApplicationScopedSettingAttribute()]
    [DefaultSettingValueAttribute("True")]
    public bool ExcludeAnimalExcuses {
```

Example 2-6. The Settings Designer-generated class (continued)

```
    get { return ((bool)(this["ExcludeAnimalExcuses"])); }
  }
 }
}
```

There are several interesting things to notice about Example 2-6. The first is the defaultInstance member, which is initialized with an instance of the generated Settings class that's been synchronized to allow for safe multithreaded access. Second, notice that this defaultInstance member is static and exposed from the Default static property, which makes it very easy to get to our settings, as we'll soon see. Finally, notice the two properties exposed from the Settings class, one property for each of our settings in the Settings Designer. You can see that the mode of each property, user versus application, the default value, and the type all match. Further, although a user setting is read-write (it has a getter and a setter), because it can change during an application session, the application setting is read-only (it has only a getter). The implementations of the properties are just type-safe wrappers around calls to the ApplicationSettingsBase base class, which does the work of reading and writing your settings to the associated settings storage.

Using Settings

With these typed properties in place and the Default static property to expose an instance of our generated Settings class, usage is no different from any other CLR object, as you can see in Example 2-7.

Example 2-7. Using the Settings Designer-generated class

```
public partial class Window1 : Window {
  string[] excuses = {...};

  public Window1() {
    InitializeComponent();
    this.newExcuseButton.Click += newExcuseButton_Click;

    // If there is no "last excuse," show a random excuse
    if( string.IsNullOrEmpty(Properties.Settings.Default.LastExcuse) ) {
      ShowNextExcuse();
    }
    // Show the excuse from the last session
    else {
      excuseTextBlock.Text = Properties.Settings.Default.LastExcuse;
    }
  }

  void newExcuseButton_Click(object sender, RoutedEventArgs e) {
    ShowNextExcuse();
  }
```

Example 2-7. Using the Settings Designer-generated class (continued)

```
Random rnd = new Random( );
void ShowNextExcuse( ) {
  // Pick a random excuse, saving it for the next session
  // and checking for animals
  do {
    Properties.Settings.Default.LastExcuse =
      excuses[rnd.Next(excuses.Length - 1)];
  }
  while( Properties.Settings.Default.ExcludeAnimalExcuses &&
         HasAnimal(Properties.Settings.Default.LastExcuse) );

  // Show the current excuse
  excuseTextBlock.Text = Properties.Settings.Default.LastExcuse;
}

bool HasAnimal(string excuse) {...}

protected override void OnClosed(EventArgs e) {
  base.OnClosed(e);

  // Save user settings between sessions
  Properties.Settings.Default.Save( );
}

}
```

In Example 2-7, we're using the LastExcuse user setting to restore the last excuse the user saw when running the application previously, changing it each time a new excuse is generated. The ExcludeAnimalExcuses application setting is checked to exclude animal-based excuses, but it is never set.* To store user settings that change during an application's session, we're calling the Save method on the Settings object from the ApplicationSettingsBase base class. This class does the magic of not only keeping the settings in memory and notifying you when a setting changes (if you choose to care), but also automatically loading the settings when the application is loaded, saving on demand.

To help with the loading and saving, the ApplicationSettingsBase uses a *settings provider*, which is a pluggable class that knows how to read/write application settings (e.g., from the local filesystem, from the Registry, from a network server, etc.). The only settings provider that comes out of the box in .NET 2.0 is the one that writes to disk in a way that's safe to use from even partial trust applications (like an XBAP), but it's not hard to plug in your own settings provider if you need other behavior.†

---

* There is no configuration API to set an application setting.

† The SDK comes with custom settings provider samples that use a web service and the Registry. I didn't like the one based on the Registry, so I updated it and wrote a little article about the experience of writing and using a custom settings provider. It's available at *http://www.sellsbrothers.com/writing/default. aspx?content=dotnet2customsettingsprovider.htm* (*http://tinysells.com/86*).

Integrating Settings with WPF

None of the basics of the `ApplicationSettingsBase`-inspired support for settings, or any of the other mechanisms for doing settings in .NET, is specific to WPF. However, because the `ApplicationSettingsBase` class supports data change notifications (specifically, it implements `INotifyPropertyChanged`), we can bind to settings data just like any other data (for the details of data binding, see Chapters 6 and 7). For example, instead of manually keeping the `TextBlock` that shows the excuse up-to-date, we can just bind the `Text` property to the `LastExcuse` property, as shown in Example 2-8.

Example 2-8. Data binding to a settings class

```
<Window ... xmlns:local="clr-namespace:excusegen">
  ...
  <TextBlock ...
    Text="{Binding
            Path=LastExcuse,
            Source={x:Static local:Properties.Settings.Default}}" />
  ...
</Window>
```

Example 2-8 shows a bit of an advanced use of the binding syntax, but basically it says that we're binding the `Text` property of the `TextBlock` to the `LastExcuse` property of the `excusegen.Properties.Settings.Default` object. As the `LastExcuse` property changes, so does the `Text` property, so we no longer need to keep the `Text` property manually up-to-date; all we need to do is manage the `LastExcuse` property and the `Text` property will follow. For example:

```
Random rnd = new Random();

void ShowNextExcuse() {
  // Pick a random excuse, saving it for the next session
  // and checking for animals
  do {
    // This updates the Text property on the TextBlock, too
    Properties.Settings.Default.LastExcuse =
      excuses[rnd.Next(excuses.Length - 1)];
  }
  while( Properties.Settings.Default.ExcludeAnimalExcuses &&
         HasAnimal(Properties.Settings.Default.LastExcuse) );

  // No longer any need to manually update the TextBlock
  //excuseTextBlock.Text = Properties.Settings.Default.LastExcuse;
}
```

The ability to use settings to drive a WPF UI makes the new .NET 2.0 `ApplicationSettingsBase` and Settings Designer the preferred means for managing settings in a WPF application.

Where Are We?

In WPF, the application contains an instance of the Application object. This object provides management services that let you control the lifetime of your application, as well as resource management and navigation, covered in Chapter 12, Appendix C, and Chapter 11, respectively. In this chapter, we also discussed deploying standalone applications using ClickOnce. (XBAP deployment can be found in Chapter 11.) Finally, to manage user and application settings between application sessions, we briefly discussed the ApplicationSettingsBase-related settings services provided by .NET 2.0 and Visual Studio 2005.

CHAPTER 3

Layout

WPF provides a powerful and flexible array of tools for controlling the layout of the user interface. These tools enable applications to present information to users in a clear and logical way.

There is a fine line between giving developers or designers enough control over the user interface's layout, and leaving them to do all the work. A good layout system should be able to automate common scenarios such as resizing, scaling, and adaptation to localization, but should allow manual intervention where necessary. In this chapter, we will look at how WPF's layout system helps fulfill these goals.

Layout Basics

WPF provides a set of *panels*—special-purpose user interface elements whose job is to arrange the elements they contain. Each individual panel type offers a straightforward and easily understood layout mechanism. As with all WPF elements, layout objects can be composed in any number of different ways, so although each individual panel type is fairly simple, the flexible way in which they can be combined makes for a very powerful layout system. And you can even create your own layout element types should the built-in ones not meet your needs.

Table 3-1 describes the main panel types built into WPF.* Whichever panel you use, the same basic rule always applies: an element's position is always determined by the containing panel. Most panels also manage the size of their children.

---

* A frequently asked question is "why do some of these type names end in 'Panel' when some do not? The naming seems to be inconsistent." The pattern appears to be that the names should be, unambiguously, nouns. Stack, Wrap, and Dock can all be used as verbs, which is why "Panel" is appended. Grid and Canvas are both nouns, so they don't get "Panel" tacked on the end.

Table 3-1. Main panel types

Panel type	Usage
StackPanel	Lays children out in a vertical or horizontal stack; extremely simple, useful for managing small-scale aspects of layout.
WrapPanel	Lays children out from left to right, moving onto a new line each time it fills the available width.
DockPanel	Allocates an entire edge of the panel area to each child; useful for defining the rough layout of simple applications at a coarse scale.
Grid	Arranges children within a grid; useful for aligning items without resorting to fixed sizes and positions. The most powerful of the built-in panels.
Canvas	Performs no layout logic—puts children where you tell it to; allows you to take complete control of the layout process.
UniformGrid	Arranges children in a grid where every cell is the same size.

 By default, panels have no appearance of their own, the only visible effect of their presence being how they size and position their children. However, they can be made visible by setting their Background property.

We'll start with one of the most basic panels, StackPanel.

StackPanel

StackPanel is a very simple panel that arranges its children in a row or a column. You will not normally use StackPanel to lay out your whole user interface. It is most useful for arranging small subsections. Example 3-1 shows how to build a simple search user interface.

Example 3-1. StackPanel search layout

```
<StackPanel Background="#ECE9D8">
  <TextBlock Margin="3">Look for:</TextBlock>
  <ComboBox  Margin="3"/>
  <TextBlock Margin="3">Filtered by:</TextBlock>
  <ComboBox  Margin="3"/>
  <Button    Margin="3,5">Search</Button>
  <CheckBox  Margin="3">Search in titles only</CheckBox>
  <CheckBox  Margin="3">Match related words</CheckBox>
  <CheckBox  Margin="3">Search in previous results</CheckBox>
  <CheckBox  Margin="3">Highlight search hits (in topics)</CheckBox>
</StackPanel>
```

Figure 3-1 shows the results. As you can see, the UI elements have simply been stacked vertically one after another. This example used the Margin property to space the elements out a little. Most elements use a single number, indicating a uniform margin all around. The Button uses a pair of numbers to specify different vertical and horizontal margins. This is one of several standard layout properties available on all WPF elements, which are all described in the "Common Layout Properties" section, later in this chapter.

 Many of the examples in this book represent typical snippets of XAML, rather than complete self-contained programs. You can download runnable versions of the examples from the book's web site at *http://sellsbrothers.com/writing/wpfbook*. If you would prefer to type in the examples, you can do that using the XamlPad tool that ships with the Windows SDK, but because the examples are only snippets, you will need to host them in a suitable root element such as a Page.

Figure 3-1. Search StackPanel with Margin

There is one problem with this layout: the Search button is much wider than you would normally expect a button to look. The default behavior of a vertical StackPanel is to make all of the controls the same width as the panel. Likewise, a horizontal StackPanel will make all of the controls the same height. For the ComboBox controls, this is exactly what we want. For the TextBlock and CheckBox controls, it doesn't show that the controls have been stretched to be as wide as the panel, because they look only as wide as their text makes them look. However, a Button's visuals always fill its entire logical width, which is why the button in Figure 3-1 is unusually wide. (See the upcoming "Fixed Size Versus Size to Content" sidebar for more details on how this process works.)

When an element has been given a fixed amount of space that is greater than required by its content, the way in which the extra space gets used is determined by the HorizontalAlignment and VerticalAlignment properties.

We can prevent the button from being stretched across the panel's whole width by setting its HorizontalAlignment property to Left:

```
<Button Margin="3,5" HorizontalAlignment="Left">Search</Button>
```

Fixed Size Versus Size to Content

WPF can tackle the layout of an element in one of two ways. The strategy is determined by whether or not the amount of space available is fixed. For example, if the user resizes a window, the size of the window's content is whatever the user wants it to be. From the point of view of the layout system, the size is fixed—it is imposed on the layout system by the user. In such a case, the job of the layout system is to arrange the contents as best it can in the space available.

On the other hand, if the available space is not predetermined, WPF uses a "size to content" approach, where the size is not dictated upfront, but is instead calculated based on the content to be displayed. The most straightforward example of this is when a Window whose SizeToContent property is set to WidthAndHeight is first displayed—although the user may resize the window after it opens, its initial size is determined by measuring the content.

A mixture of these two styles may be used—one in each direction. For example, if a window's SizeToContent is set to Height, the window height will be determined by measuring the content, but the width will be fixed, as specified by the Width property.

A panel subject to fixed layout does not necessarily pass this layout style on to its children. For example, suppose the user resizes a window that contains a vertical StackPanel. The window will impose a fixed size on the StackPanel, but although the StackPanel will pass the fixed width on to its children, it will use the size to content approach to determine each element's height.

The converse can also apply—unconstrained elements may constrain their children. For example, if a vertical StackPanel is unconstrained (i.e., its parent asks it to size to content), it must choose a width for itself. It does this by measuring each child's preferred width, but it then picks the width of the widest child. This is then passed on as a fixed width to every child in the panel. (This is exactly what's happening in Figure 3-1—the panel has made itself wide enough for the widest child, and has fixed every child to that width. It might not look that way with the checkboxes, as they look only as wide as their text. However, if they acquired the focus, the focus rectangle would illustrate their full width.)

HorizontalAlignment determines an element's horizontal position and width in situations where the containing panel gives it more space than it needs. The default is Stretch, meaning that if more space is available than the child requires, it will be stretched to fill that space. The alternatives—Left, Right, and Center—do not attempt to stretch the element; these determine where the element will be placed within the excess space, allowing the element to use its natural width. Here we are using Left, meaning that the control will have its preferred width, and will be aligned to the left of the available space (see Figure 3-2).

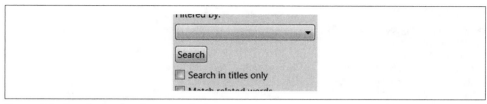

Figure 3-2. Search panel with unstretched Button

The preceding example used the default vertical orientation. StackPanel also supports horizontal layout. Example 3-2 shows a StackPanel with its Orientation property set to Horizontal.

Example 3-2. Horizontal StackPanel layout

```
<StackPanel Orientation="Horizontal">
  <TextBlock>This is some text</TextBlock>
  <Button>Button</Button>
  <Button>Button (different one)</Button>
  <CheckBox>Check it out</CheckBox>
  <TextBlock>More text</TextBlock>
</StackPanel>
```

These elements will be arranged in a horizontal line, as shown in Figure 3-3.

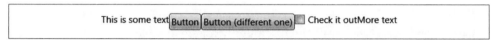

Figure 3-3. Horizontal StackPanel layout

StackPanel is not very smart when it runs out of space. If you give it more elements than will fit, it will just truncate the content. However, its close relative, the WrapPanel, copes rather better.

WrapPanel

WrapPanel works just like a StackPanel until it runs out of space. If you provide a horizontal WrapPanel with more children than will fit in the available width, it will arrange its content in a way similar to how a word processor lays out words on a line. It puts the children in a row from left to right until it runs out of space, at which point it starts on the next line.

WrapPanel is very simple to use. Just as with a StackPanel, you add a sequence of children, as Example 3-3 shows.

Example 3-3. WrapPanel

```
<WrapPanel Background="Beige">
  <Button>One</Button>
  <Button>Two</Button>
  <Button>Three</Button>
  <Button>Four</Button>
  <Button>Five</Button>
  <Button>Six</Button>
  <Button>Seven</Button>
  <Button>Eight</Button>
</WrapPanel>
```

As Figure 3-4 shows, the items are arranged from left to right. As you can see from the panel's filled-in background, it is not wide enough to accommodate all the items, so the last three have been wrapped onto the next line.

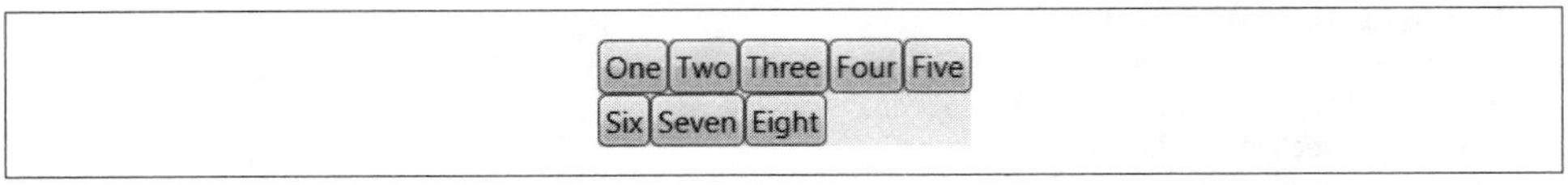

Figure 3-4. WrapPanel

WrapPanel also offers an Orientation property. Setting this to Vertical will arrange the children in a sequence of vertical stacks, a layout style very similar to Windows Explorer's "List" view.

WrapPanel and StackPanel really are useful only for small-scale layout. You will need to use a more powerful panel to define the overall layout of your application, such as DockPanel.

DockPanel

DockPanel is useful for describing the overall layout of a simple user interface. You can carve up the basic structure of your window using a DockPanel, and then use the other panels to manage the details.

A DockPanel arranges each child element so that it fills a particular edge of the panel. If multiple children are docked to the same edge, they simply stack up against that edge in order. By default, the final child fills any remaining space not occupied by controls docked to the panel's edges.

Example 3-4 shows a simple DockPanel-based layout. Five buttons have been added to illustrate each option. Notice that four of them have a DockPanel.Dock attribute applied. This property is defined by DockPanel to allow elements inside a DockPanel to specify their position. DockPanel.Dock is an *attached property* (as described in the upcoming sidebar, "Attached Properties and Layout").

Example 3-4. Simple DockPanel layout

```
<DockPanel>
  <Button DockPanel.Dock="Top">Top</Button>
  <Button DockPanel.Dock="Bottom">Bottom</Button>
  <Button DockPanel.Dock="Left">Left</Button>
  <Button DockPanel.Dock="Right">Right</Button>
  <Button>Fill</Button>
</DockPanel>
```

Attached Properties and Layout

Most WPF panels allow child elements to specify their layout requirements. For example, a child of a DockPanel needs to be able to specify to which edge it would like to dock.

The obvious solution would be for a base class such as FrameworkElement to define a Dock property—all WPF user interface elements derive from FrameworkElement, so this would enable anything to specify its dock position. However, DockPanel is not the only panel type, so we would need to add properties for the benefit of other panels, too. This would add a lot of clutter. Worse, it would also be inflexible—what if you want to design a custom panel that implements some new layout mechanism? It might need to define new attributes for its children to use.

Attached properties solve this problem. They allow one element to define properties that can be "attached" to some other element. DockPanel defines a Dock property that can be attached to any child. In XAML, the dotted attribute syntax (DockPanel.Dock) signifies that an attached property is being used. Example 3-4 uses this technique. See Appendix A for more detailed information about XAML and attached properties.

Figure 3-5 shows how the UI built in Example 3-4 looks on-screen. Notice how the Top and Bottom buttons have filled the entire top and bottom edges of the window, and yet the Left and Right buttons do not fill their edges—the Top and Bottom buttons have taken control of the corners. This is because Top and Bottom were added to the panel first.

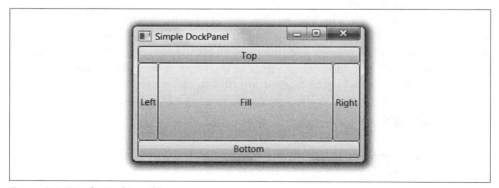

Figure 3-5. Simple DockPanel layout

If you swapped these over so that the Left and Right buttons came first in the markup, as shown in Example 3-5, they would fill their whole edges, including the corners, leaving the Top and Bottom buttons with just the remaining space. Figure 3-6 shows the results.

Example 3-5. Docking Left and Right before Top and Bottom

```
<DockPanel>
  <Button DockPanel.Dock="Left">Left</Button>
  <Button DockPanel.Dock="Right">Right</Button>
  <Button DockPanel.Dock="Top">Top</Button>
  <Button DockPanel.Dock="Bottom">Bottom</Button>
  <Button>Fill</Button>
</DockPanel>
```

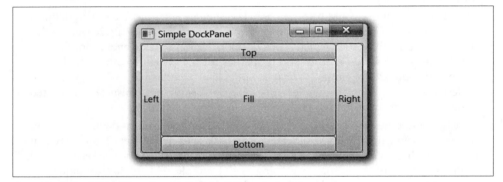

Figure 3-6. DockPanel layout, with Left and Right docked first

Elements never overlap in a DockPanel, so each successive child only gets to use space not already used by the previous children. By default, the final child takes all of the remaining space, but if you would prefer to leave a blank space in the middle, you can set the LastChildFill attribute of the DockPanel to False. (It defaults to True.) The final child will dock to the left by default, leaving the center empty.

For items docked to the top or bottom, DockPanel sets the width to fill the space available, but for the height, it sizes to content—as described in the earlier sidebar. Likewise, items docked to the left or right have their heights fixed to fill the available space, but size to content horizontally. In Figures 3-5 and 3-6, the buttons at the top and bottom are just tall enough to contain their text. Likewise, the buttons docked to the left and right are just wide enough to hold their text. If we put a lot more text into one of the buttons, it will try to expand in order to make the text fit. We can see in Figure 3-7 that the DockPanel is letting the button be exactly as wide as it wants to be.

The DockPanel is good for creating the top-level structure of a basic user interface. For example, you could use it to position a menu and a toolbar at the top of the window, with other content filling the remaining space. However, if you have lots of controls to arrange, it can be helpful to have table-like layout functionality. For this, we turn to the powerful Grid panel.

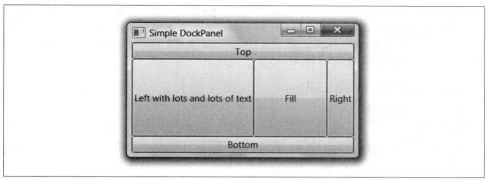

Figure 3-7. DockPanel layout, with an unusually wide button

Grid

Consider the document Properties dialog from Internet Explorer shown in Figure 3-8. Notice how the main area of the form is arranged as two columns. The column on the left contains labels, and the column in the middle contains information.

Figure 3-8. Document Properties dialog

Achieving this kind of layout with any of the panels we've looked at so far is difficult, because they are not designed with two-dimensional alignment in mind. We could try to use nesting—Example 3-6 shows a vertical StackPanel with three rows, each with a horizontal StackPanel.

Example 3-6. Ineffective use of StackPanel

```
<StackPanel Orientation="Vertical" Background="Beige">
  <StackPanel Orientation="Horizontal">
    <TextBlock>Protocol:</TextBlock>
    <TextBlock>HyperText Transfer Protocol</TextBlock>
  </StackPanel>
  <StackPanel Orientation="Horizontal">
      <TextBlock>Type:</TextBlock>
    <TextBlock>HTML Document</TextBlock>
  </StackPanel>
  <StackPanel Orientation="Horizontal">
    <TextBlock>Connection:</TextBlock>
   <TextBlock>Not Encrypted</TextBlock>
  </StackPanel>
</StackPanel>
```

The result, shown in Figure 3-9, is not what we want at all. Each row has been arranged independently, so we don't get the two columns we were hoping for.

Protocol:HyperText Transfer Protocol
Type:HTML Document
Connection:Not Encrypted

Figure 3-9. Inappropriate use of StackPanel

The Grid panel solves this problem. Rather than working a single row or a single column at a time, it aligns all elements into a grid that covers the whole area of the panel. This allows consistent positioning from one row to the next. Example 3-7 shows the same elements as Example 3-6, but arranged with a Grid rather than nested StackPanel elements.

Example 3-7. Grid layout

```
<Grid Background="Beige"
      ShowGridLines="True"> <!-- ShowGridLines for testing only -->
  <Grid.ColumnDefinitions>
    <ColumnDefinition />
    <ColumnDefinition />
  </Grid.ColumnDefinitions>
  <Grid.RowDefinitions>
    <RowDefinition />
    <RowDefinition />
    <RowDefinition />
  </Grid.RowDefinitions>
```

Example 3-7. Grid layout (continued)

```
<TextBlock Grid.Column="0" Grid.Row="0">Protocol:</TextBlock>
<TextBlock Grid.Column="1" Grid.Row="0">HyperText Transfer Protocol</TextBlock>
<TextBlock Grid.Column="0" Grid.Row="1">Type:</TextBlock>
<TextBlock Grid.Column="1" Grid.Row="1">HTML Document</TextBlock>
<TextBlock Grid.Column="0" Grid.Row="2">Connection:</TextBlock>
<TextBlock Grid.Column="1" Grid.Row="2">Not encrypted</TextBlock>
```

```
</Grid>
```

The Grid needs to know how many columns and rows we require, and we indicate this by specifying a series of ColumnDefinition and RowDefinition elements at the start. This may seem rather verbose—a simple pair of properties on the Grid itself might seem like a simpler solution. However, you will often need to control the characteristics of each column and row independently, so in practice, it makes sense to have elements representing them.

Notice that each element in the grid has its column and row specified explicitly using attached properties. This is mandatory—without these, everything ends up in column 0, row 0. (Grid uses a zero-based numbering scheme, so 0,0 corresponds to the top-left corner.)

Grid, Element Order, and Z Order

You might be wondering why the Grid doesn't simply put items into the grid in the order in which they appear; this would remove the need for the Grid.Row and Grid.Column attached properties. However, grids do not necessarily have exactly one element per cell.

Grid cells can be empty. If the grid's children simply filled the cells in order, you would need to provide placeholders of some kind to indicate blank cells. But because elements indicate their grid position, you can leave cells empty simply by providing no content for those cells.

Elements may span multiple cells, by using the Grid.RowSpan and Grid.ColumnSpan attached properties.

Cells can also contain multiple elements. In this case, the order in which the relevant elements are listed in the markup determines which appears "on top." Elements that appear later in the document are drawn over those that appear earlier. The order in which overlapping elements are drawn is usually referred to as the Z *order*. This is because the x- and y-axes are traditionally the ones used for drawing on-screen, so the z-axis, representing the third dimension, "sticks out" of the screen. This makes it the logical axis to represent how overlapping elements stack up on top of one another.

In general, panels that allow their children to overlap (e.g., Grid and Canvas) rely on the order in which elements appear in the XAML to determine the Z order. However, you can override this: the attached Panel.ZIndex property allows the Z order to be specified explicitly.

Figure 3-10 shows the result of Example 3-7. This figure has lines showing the grid outline, because we enabled the ShowGridLines property. You would not normally do this on a finalized design—this feature is intended to make it easy to see how the Grid has divided up the available space. With grid lines displayed, it is clear that the Grid has made all the columns the same width, and all the rows the same height.

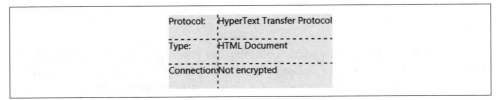

Figure 3-10. Grid layout

 What may not be obvious from Figure 3-10 is that each element has been given the full available cell space. It doesn't show here because a TextBlock looks only as large as the text it shows. But the behavior is somewhat similar to a StackPanel—each element's width is as wide as its containing column, and its height is that of its containing row. As always, you can use HorizontalAlignment and VerticalAlignment to determine what elements do with excess space.

This default "one size fits all" behavior is useful when you want all the items in the grid to be the same size, but it's not what we want here. It would make more sense for the column on the left to be wide enough to contain the labels, and for the column on the right to be allocated the remaining space. Fortunately, the Grid provides a variety of options for managing column width and row height.

Column Widths and Row Heights

You configure the column widths and row heights in a Grid using the ColumnDefinition and RowDefinition elements. There are three sizing options: fixed, automatic, and proportional.

Fixed sizing is the simplest to understand, but often requires the most effort to use, as you end up having to do all of the work yourself. You can specify the Width of a column or the Height of a row in *device-independent pixels*. (These are 1/96th of an inch. WPF's coordinate system is described in Chapter 13.) Example 3-8 shows a modified version of the column definitions in Example 3-7, specifying a fixed width for the first column.

Example 3-8. Fixed column width

```
...
<Grid.ColumnDefinitions>
  <ColumnDefinition Width="50" />
```

Example 3-8. Fixed column width (continued)

```
  <ColumnDefinition />
</Grid.ColumnDefinitions>
...
```

Figure 3-11 illustrates the main problem with using fixed column widths. If you make the column too narrow, the contents will simply be cropped. Fixed widths and heights may seem to be an attractive idea because they give you complete control, but in practice they tend to be inconvenient. If you change the text or the font, you will need to modify the sizes to match. You will need to be flexible on layout if you want your application to fit in with the system look and feel, because the default font is not the same on all versions of Windows. Localization of strings will also require the sizes to be changed. (See Chapter 12 for more information about localization.) So in practice, fixed widths and heights are not what you will normally want to use. This is true not only with grids and text blocks. In general, you should try to avoid fixed sizes in WPF—the more you let the layout system do for you, the easier it is to adapt to localization, different screen sizes, and display orientations.

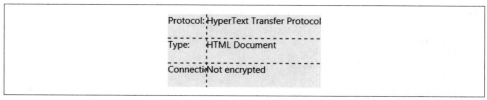

Figure 3-11. Fixed-width column truncation

The most appropriate sizing strategy for our label column will be automatic sizing. This tells the Grid to make the column wide enough to contain the widest element (i.e., to size to content). Example 3-9 shows a modified version of the column and row definitions from Example 3-7, specifying automatic width for the first column, and automatic heights for all of the rows.

Example 3-9. Automatic width and height

```
...
<Grid.ColumnDefinitions>
  <ColumnDefinition Width="Auto" />
  <ColumnDefinition />
</Grid.ColumnDefinitions>

<Grid.RowDefinitions>
  <RowDefinition Height="Auto" />
  <RowDefinition Height="Auto" />
  <RowDefinition Height="Auto" />
</Grid.RowDefinitions>
...
```

This is not quite right yet—as you can see from Figure 3-12, the Grid has not left any space around the text, so the results seem rather cramped. The solution is exactly the same as it was for the StackPanel—we simply use the Margin property on the TextBlock elements in the Grid to indicate that we want some breathing room around the text. The Grid will honor this, giving us the layout we require.

Figure 3-12. Automatic width and height

If the idea of adding a Margin attribute to every single element sounds tedious, don't worry. We can give all of the TextBlock elements the same margin by defining a *style*. Styles are discussed in Chapter 8. Example 3-10 does this to set a horizontal margin of five device-independent pixels, and a vertical margin of three.

Example 3-10. Applying a consistent margin with a style

```
<Grid Background="Beige"
      ShowGridLines="True">
  <Grid.Resources>
    <Style TargetType="TextBlock">
      <Setter Property="Margin" Value="5,3" />
    </Style>
  </Grid.Resources>
  <Grid.ColumnDefinitions>
    <ColumnDefinition Width="Auto" />
... as before
```

As Figure 3-13 shows, this provides the better-spaced layout we require.

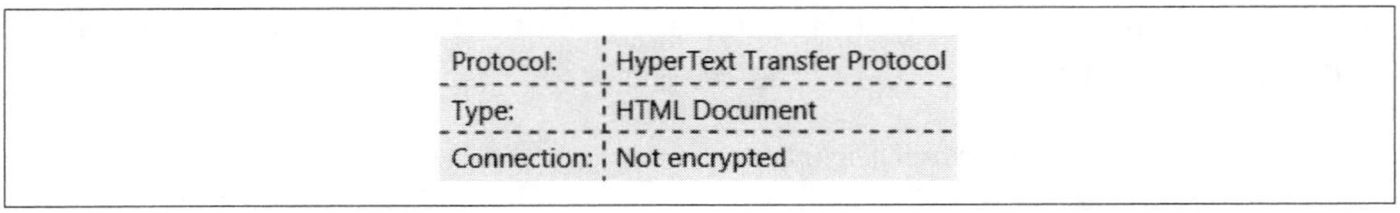

Figure 3-13. Using margins

The final mechanism for specifying width and height in a Grid is the proportional method. This is sometimes called "star" sizing because of the corresponding XAML syntax. If you set the width or height of a column or row to be *, this tells the Grid that it should fill all the space left over after any fixed and automatic items have taken their share. If you have multiple items set to *, the space is shared evenly among them.

The default value for column width and row height is *, so you have already seen the effect of this. As Figure 3-10 shows, when we don't specify column widths or row heights, each cell ends up with exactly the same amount of space.

The star syntax is a little more flexible than this. Rather than dividing up space evenly among all the rows or columns marked with a star, we can choose a proportional distribution. Consider the set of row definitions in Example 3-11.

Example 3-11. Mixing row height styles

```
<Grid.RowDefinitions>
  <RowDefinition Height="Auto" />
  <RowDefinition Height="2*" />
  <RowDefinition Height="1*" />
</Grid.RowDefinitions>
```

Here, the first row has been set to size automatically, and the other two rows both use proportional sizing. However, the middle row has been marked as 2*. This indicates that it wants to be given twice as much of the available space as the row marked with 1*. For example, if the grid's total height was 350, and the first row's automatic height came out as 50, this would leave 300 for the other rows. The second row's height would be 200, and the third row's height would be 100. Figure 3-14 shows how this grid looks for a couple of different heights; the filled-in background shows the size of the grid in each case. As you can see, the row with Auto height is the same in both cases. The two star-sized rows share out the remaining space, with the 2* row getting twice the height of the 1* row.

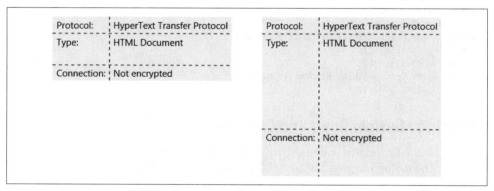

Figure 3-14. Proportional Grid sizing

The numbers before the * specify relative sizes, not absolute sizes. If you modified the preceding example to use 6* and 3* instead of 2* and 1*, the result would be exactly the same. It's equivalent to saying that you want the rows to use six-ninths and three-ninths of the available space, instead of saying that you want them to use two-thirds and one-third—it's just two ways of expressing the same ratio.

These numbers are floating point, so you can specify noninteger sizes such as 2.5*. And if you specify just * without a number, this is equivalent to 1*.

 If you are familiar with HTML, you may have been wondering whether you can use percentage sizes. You can't, but the star mechanism lets you achieve similar effects.

You may have noticed that for all three grid-sizing strategies, we used the Width and Height properties each time, although the property values looked quite different in each case. Width and Height are both of type GridLength. The GridLength type holds a number and a unit type. The number is stored as a Double and the unit type is represented by the GridUnitType enumeration.

For a fixed size, the unit type is Pixel. (As mentioned previously, in WPF *pixel* is really a device-independent unit, meaning 1/96th of an inch.) In XAML, this is indicated by providing just a number.[*] For automatic sizing, the unit type is Auto and no number is required. In XAML, this is indicated by the string "Auto". For proportional sizing, the unit type is Star. In XAML, this is indicated either by just * or a number and a star (e.g., 3.5*). Example 3-12 shows the C# equivalent of the row settings shown in XAML in Example 3-11.

Example 3-12. Setting row heights in code

```
Grid g = new Grid( );
RowDefinition r = new RowDefinition( );
r.Height = new GridLength(0, GridUnitType.Auto);
g.RowDefinitions.Add(r);
r = new RowDefinition( );
r.Height = new GridLength(2, GridUnitType.Star);
g.RowDefinitions.Add(r);
r = new RowDefinition( );
r.Height = new GridLength(1, GridUnitType.Star);
g.RowDefinitions.Add(r);
```

Spanning Multiple Rows and Columns

Looking at the Properties dialog shown earlier in Figure 3-8, there is a feature we have left out. The dialog has two horizontal lines dividing the UI into three sections. However, the aligned columns span the whole window, straddling these dividing lines.

It would be inconvenient to try to achieve a layout like this with multiple grids. If you used one for each section of the window, you could keep the columns aligned in all the grids by using fixed column widths. As discussed earlier, use of fixed widths is inconvenient because it tends to require manual adjustment of the widths whenever

---

[*] In XAML, you can also use the suffix *in*, *cm*, or *pt* to specify inches, centimeters, or points. These will all be converted to device-independent pixels, and the unit type will be Pixel. Sometimes these units don't map neatly into pixels (e.g., a value of 1pt will be converted into 1.3333 pixels).

anything changes. With this layout, it becomes triply inconvenient—you would have to change all three grids every time anything changed.

Fortunately, it is possible to add these dividing lines without splitting the UI into separate grids. The way to do this is to put the dividing lines into cells that span across all of the columns in the grid. An element indicates to its parent `Grid` that it would like to span multiple columns by using the attached `Grid.ColumnSpan` property.

Example 3-13 uses a single `Grid` to show three sets of properties. These sets are separated by thin `Rectangle` elements, using `Grid.ColumnSpan` to fill the whole width of the `Grid`. Because a single `Grid` is used for all three sections, the columns remain aligned across all three sections, as you can see in Figure 3-15. If we had used three separate grids with the leftmost column set to use automatic width, each would have chosen its own width, causing the righthand columns to be misaligned.

Example 3-13. Using Grid.ColumnSpan

```
<Grid Background="Beige">
  <Grid.Resources>
    <Style TargetType="TextBlock">
      <Setter Property="Margin" Value="5,3" />
    </Style>
  </Grid.Resources>

  <Grid.ColumnDefinitions>
    <ColumnDefinition Width="Auto" />
    <ColumnDefinition />
  </Grid.ColumnDefinitions>
  <Grid.RowDefinitions>
    <RowDefinition Height="Auto" />
    <RowDefinition Height="Auto" />
    <RowDefinition Height="Auto" />
    <RowDefinition Height="Auto" />
    <RowDefinition Height="Auto" />
    <RowDefinition Height="Auto" />
    <RowDefinition Height="Auto" />
    <RowDefinition Height="Auto" />
  </Grid.RowDefinitions>


  <TextBlock Grid.Column="0" Grid.Row="0">Title:</TextBlock>
  <TextBlock Grid.Column="1" Grid.Row="0">Information Overload</TextBlock>

  <Rectangle Grid.Row="1" Grid.ColumnSpan="2" Margin="5"
             Height="1" Fill="Black" />

  <TextBlock Grid.Column="0" Grid.Row="2">Protocol:</TextBlock>
  <TextBlock Grid.Column="1" Grid.Row="2">Unknown Protocol</TextBlock>
  <TextBlock Grid.Column="0" Grid.Row="3">Type:</TextBlock>
  <TextBlock Grid.Column="1" Grid.Row="3">Not available</TextBlock>
  <TextBlock Grid.Column="0" Grid.Row="4">Connection:</TextBlock>
  <TextBlock Grid.Column="1" Grid.Row="4">Not encrypted</TextBlock>
```

Example 3-13. Using Grid.ColumnSpan (continued)

```
<Rectangle Grid.Row="5" Grid.ColumnSpan="2" Margin="5"
           Height="1" Fill="Black" />

<TextBlock Grid.Column="0" Grid.Row="6">Created:</TextBlock>
<TextBlock Grid.Column="1" Grid.Row="6">Not available</TextBlock>
<TextBlock Grid.Column="0" Grid.Row="7">Modified:</TextBlock>
<TextBlock Grid.Column="1" Grid.Row="7">Not available</TextBlock>

</Grid>
```

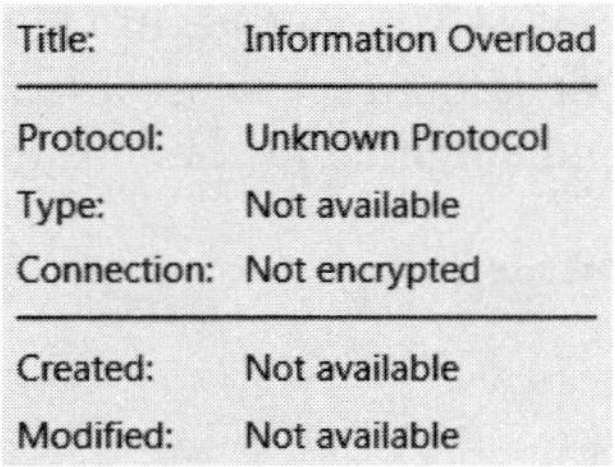

Title:	Information Overload
Protocol:	Unknown Protocol
Type:	Not available
Connection:	Not encrypted
Created:	Not available
Modified:	Not available

Figure 3-15. Dividing lines spanning multiple columns

The Grid class also defines a Grid.RowSpan attached property. This works in exactly the same way as Grid.ColumnSpan, but vertically.

You are free to use both Grid.RowSpan and Grid.ColumnSpan on the same element—any element may occupy as many grid cells as it likes. Also, note that you are free to put multiple overlapping items into each cell.

Example 3-14 illustrates both of these techniques. It adds two Rectangle elements to color in areas of the grid. The first spans multiple rows, and the second spans both multiple rows and columns. Both Rectangle elements occupy cells in the Grid that are also occupied by text.

Example 3-14. Multiple items in a Grid cell

```
<Rectangle Grid.Column="1" Grid.Row="2" Grid.RowSpan="3"
       Margin="5,3" Fill="White" />
<Rectangle Grid.Column="0" Grid.Row="6" Grid.ColumnSpan="2" Grid.RowSpan="2"
       Margin="5,3" Fill="White" />

<TextBlock Grid.Column="0" Grid.Row="0">Title:</TextBlock>
...as before
```

Figure 3-16 shows the results. Note that, in the absence of a Panel.ZIndex property, the order in which the elements appear in the markup is crucial, as it determines the Z order for overlapping elements. In Example 3-14 the Rectangle elements were added before the TextBlock items whose cells they share. This means that the colored rectangles appear behind the text, rather than obscuring them. If the rectangles had been added at the end of the Grid, after the text, they would have been drawn over the text.

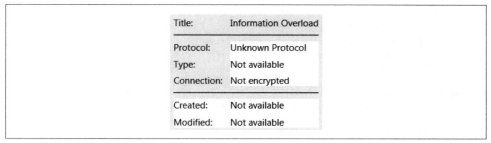

Figure 3-16. Overlapping Grid items

This example illustrates why the `Grid` requires the row and column of each item to be specified explicitly, rather than being implied by the order of the elements. Cells can be shared by multiple elements. Elements can span multiple cells. This makes it impossible for the `Grid` to guess which element goes in which cell.

Consistency Across Multiple Grids

Although the row and column spanning features described in the preceding section often make it possible to arrange your UI as you need, it will not always be possible to put all of the information you wish to present into a single `Grid` element. For example, consider a scrollable `Grid` with headings.* You could just put headings and contents into a single `Grid` and then place that `Grid` in a `ScrollViewer` to make it scrollable, but this suffers from a problem, which Example 3-15 illustrates.

Example 3-15. Grid in ScrollViewer

```
<ScrollViewer>
  <Grid>
    <Grid.Resources>
      <Style TargetType="TextBlock">
        <Setter Property="Margin" Value="5,3" />
      </Style>
    </Grid.Resources>

    <Grid.ColumnDefinitions>
      <ColumnDefinition Width="*" />
      <ColumnDefinition Width="Auto" />
      <ColumnDefinition Width="Auto" />
    </Grid.ColumnDefinitions>
    <Grid.RowDefinitions>
      <RowDefinition Height="Auto" />
      <RowDefinition Height="Auto" />
      <RowDefinition Height="Auto" />
    </Grid.RowDefinitions>
```

---

* The `ListView` control provides just such a thing, so you don't necessarily have to build your own. However, it also entails certain interactive behaviors that you may not want in your application. For example, `ListView` requires you to use data binding, whereas the alternative presented here does not.

Example 3-15. Grid in ScrollViewer (continued)

```
    <Border Grid.Column="0" Grid.Row="0"
            Background="LightGray" BorderBrush="Gray"
            BorderThickness="1">
      <TextBlock>Title</TextBlock>
    </Border>
    <Border Grid.Column="1" Grid.Row="0"
            Background="LightGray" BorderBrush="Gray"
            BorderThickness="1">
        <TextBlock>Location</TextBlock>
    </Border>
    <Border Grid.Column="2" Grid.Row="0" Background="LightGray"
            BorderBrush="Gray" BorderThickness="1">
      <TextBlock>Rank</TextBlock>
    </Border>

    <TextBlock Grid.Column="0" Grid.Row="1" Text="Programming WPF" />
    <TextBlock Grid.Column="1" Grid.Row="1" Text="O'Reilly Media, Inc." />
    <TextBlock Grid.Column="2" Grid.Row="1" Text="1" />

    <TextBlock Grid.Column="0" Grid.Row="2" Text="IanG on Tap" />
    <TextBlock Grid.Column="1" Grid.Row="2" Text="The Internet" />
    <TextBlock Grid.Column="2" Grid.Row="2" Text="2" />
  </Grid>
</ScrollViewer>
```

Figure 3-17 shows the results. If you look at the righthand side, you can see that the scroll bar runs the entire height of the Grid, including the header line with the titles. This means that as soon as you scroll down, the headings will disappear. This is not particularly helpful.

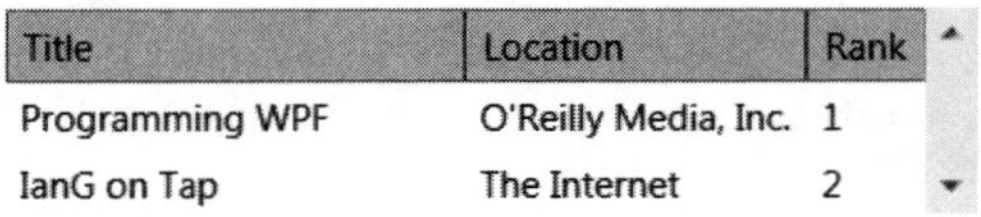

Figure 3-17. Grid in ScrollViewer

We could solve this by using two grids, one for the header and one for the main results area. Only the second grid would be placed inside a ScrollViewer. Figure 3-18 shows the results.

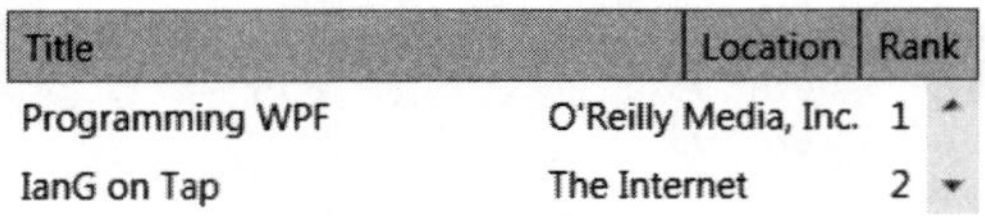

Figure 3-18. Separate Grid for headers

The scroll bar is now applied just to the part that needs to be scrollable, but the alignment is all wrong. Each Grid has arranged its columns independently, so the headings no longer line up with the main contents.

The Grid supports *shared size groups* to solve this problem. A shared size group is simply a named group of columns, all of which will have the same width, even if they are in different grids.

 You can use shared size groups either across multiple grids or within a single grid.

We can use a shared size group to keep the headings Grid consistent with the scrollable contents Grid. Example 3-16 illustrates the use of shared size groups.

Example 3-16. Shared size groups

```
<DockPanel Grid.IsSharedSizeScope="True">
  <DockPanel.Resources>
    <Style TargetType="TextBlock">
      <Setter Property="Margin" Value="5,3" />
    </Style>
  </DockPanel.Resources>
  <Grid DockPanel.Dock="Top">
    <Grid.ColumnDefinitions>
      <ColumnDefinition Width="*" />
      <ColumnDefinition Width="Auto" SharedSizeGroup="Location" />
      <ColumnDefinition Width="Auto" SharedSizeGroup="Rank" />
      <ColumnDefinition Width="Auto" />
    </Grid.ColumnDefinitions>
    <Grid.RowDefinitions>
      <RowDefinition Height="Auto" />
    </Grid.RowDefinitions>

    <Border Grid.Column="0" Grid.Row="0" BorderThickness="1"
            Background="LightGray" BorderBrush="Gray">
      <TextBlock>Title</TextBlock>
    </Border>
    <Border Grid.Column="1" Grid.Row="0" BorderThickness="1"
            Background="LightGray" BorderBrush="Gray">
      <TextBlock>Location</TextBlock>
    </Border>
    <Border Grid.Column="2" Grid.Row="0" BorderThickness="1"
            Grid.ColumnSpan="2"
            Background="LightGray" BorderBrush="Gray">
    </Border>
    <TextBlock Grid.Column="2" Grid.Row="0">Rank</TextBlock>
```

Example 3-16. Shared size groups (continued)

```
    <FrameworkElement Grid.Column="3"
      Width="{DynamicResource
                  {x:Static SystemParameters.VerticalScrollBarWidthKey}}" />

  </Grid>
  <ScrollViewer>
    <Grid>
      <Grid.ColumnDefinitions>
        <ColumnDefinition Width="*" />
        <ColumnDefinition Width="Auto" SharedSizeGroup="Location" />
        <ColumnDefinition Width="Auto" SharedSizeGroup="Rank" />
      </Grid.ColumnDefinitions>
      <Grid.RowDefinitions>
        <RowDefinition Height="Auto" />
        <RowDefinition Height="Auto" />
      </Grid.RowDefinitions>

      <TextBlock Grid.Column="0" Grid.Row="0" Text="Programming WPF" />
      <TextBlock Grid.Column="1" Grid.Row="0" Text="O'Reilly Media, Inc." />
      <TextBlock Grid.Column="2" Grid.Row="0">1</TextBlock>

      <TextBlock Grid.Column="0" Grid.Row="1">IanG on Tap</TextBlock>
      <TextBlock Grid.Column="1" Grid.Row="1">The Internet</TextBlock>
      <TextBlock Grid.Column="2" Grid.Row="1">2</TextBlock>
    </Grid>
  </ScrollViewer>
</DockPanel>
```

In this example, the overall layout is defined by a DockPanel, using the attached Dock.Top property to position the header Grid at the top, and allowing the ScrollViewer to fill the remaining space.

Shared size groups are identified by strings. Strings are prone to name collisions—it's quite possible that two developers independently working on different parts of the user interface might end up choosing the same name for their shared size groups, inadvertently causing unrelated columns to have the same size. To avoid this problem, Example 3-16 sets the Grid.IsSharedSizeScope attached property on the DockPanel. This indicates that the DockPanel is the common ancestor, and prevents the groups defined inside the DockPanel from being associated with any groups of the same name defined elsewhere in the UI.

 Grid.IsSharedSizeScope is not optional. If you do not specify a shared size scope, WPF will ignore your shared size groups.

Having defined the scope of the names, using shared size groups is very straightforward. We just apply the SharedSizeGroup attribute to the "Location" and "Rank" ColumnDefinition, and this ensures that the columns are sized consistently across the two grids. Figure 3-19 shows the results.

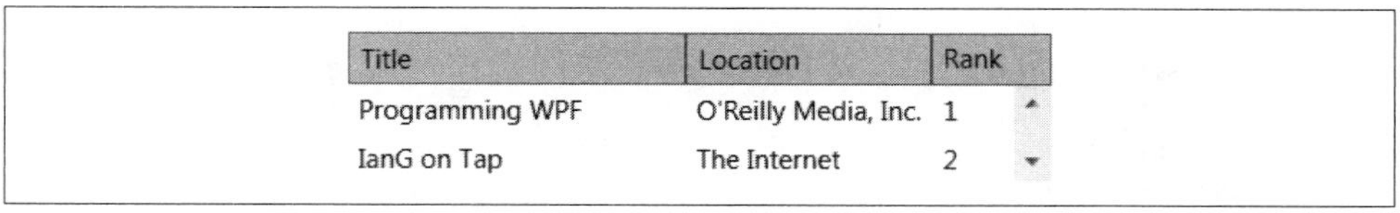

Title	Location	Rank
Programming WPF	O'Reilly Media, Inc.	1
IanG on Tap	The Internet	2

Figure 3-19. Shared size groups

The ScrollViewer adds a scroll bar to the display, and this means that a small hack is required to get this layout to work correctly. This scroll bar takes away some space from the main Grid, making it slightly narrower than the header Grid. Remember that the "Title" column's size is set to *, meaning that it should fill all available space. The ScrollViewer's scroll bar eats into this space, making the "Title" column in the main Grid slightly narrower than the one in the header Grid, destroying the alignment.

You might think that we could fix this by adding a shared size group for the "Title" column. Unfortunately, specifying a shared size group disables the * behavior—the column reverts to automatic sizing.

The fix for this is to add an extra column to the header row. This row needs to be exactly the same width as the scroll bar added by the ScrollViewer. So we have added a fourth column, containing a FrameworkElement, with its Width set to the system scroll width metric in order to make sure that it is exactly the same width as a scroll bar. (We are using a DynamicResource reference to retrieve this system parameter. This technique is described in Chapter 12.) It's unusual to use a FrameworkElement directly, but because we just need something that takes up space but has no appearance, it makes a good lightweight filler object. Its presence keeps all of the columns perfectly aligned across the two grids.

> The Grid is the most powerful of the built-in panels. You can get the Grid to do anything that DockPanel and StackPanel can do—those simpler elements are provided for convenience. For nontrivial user interfaces, the Grid is likely to be the best choice for your top-level GUI layout, as well as being useful for detailed internal layout.

UniformGrid

Powerful though the Grid is, it's occasionally a little cumbersome to use. There's a simplified version worth knowing about, called UniformGrid. All its cells are the same size, so you don't need to provide collections of row and column descriptions—just set the Rows and Columns properties to indicate the size. In fact, you don't even need to set these—by default, it creates rows and columns automatically. It always keeps the number of rows and columns equal to each other, adding as many as are required to make space for the children. Each cell contains just one child, so you do not need to add attached properties indicating which child belongs in which cell—you just add children. This means you can use something as simple as Example 3-17.

Example 3-17. UniformGrid

```
<UniformGrid TextBlock.TextAlignment="Center">
  <TextBlock Text="X" />
  <TextBlock Text="O"/>
  <TextBlock Text="X"/>
  <TextBlock Text="X"/>
  <TextBlock Text="X"/>
  <TextBlock Text="O"/>
  <TextBlock Text="O"/>
  <TextBlock Text="O"/>
  <TextBlock Text="X"/>
</UniformGrid>
```

This contains nine elements, so the UniformGrid will create three rows and three columns. Figure 3-20 shows the result.

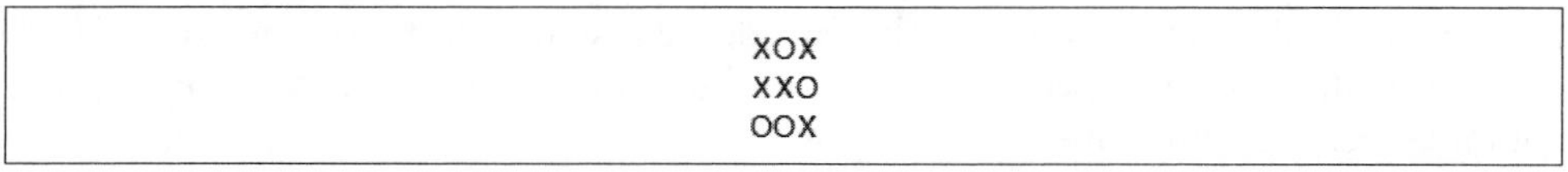

```
                            XOX
                            XXO
                            OOX
```

Figure 3-20. UniformGrid

Canvas

Occasionally, it can be necessary to take complete control of the precise positioning of every element. For example, when you want to build an image out of graphical elements, the positioning of the elements is dictated by the picture you are creating, not by any set of automated layout rules. For these scenarios, you can use a Canvas.

Canvas is the simplest of the panels. It allows the location of child elements to be specified precisely relative to the edges of the canvas. The Canvas doesn't really do any layout at all; it simply puts things where you tell it to. Also, Canvas will not size elements to fill the available space—all its children are sized to content.

If you are accustomed to working with fixed layout systems such as those offered by Visual Basic 6, MFC, and the most basic way of using Windows Forms, the Canvas will seem familiar and natural. However, it is strongly recommended that you avoid it unless you really need this absolute control. The automatic layout provided by the other panels will make your life much easier because they can adapt to changes in text and font. They also make it far simpler to produce resizable user interfaces. Moreover, localization tends to be much easier with resizable user interfaces, because different languages tend to produce strings with substantially different lengths. Don't opt for the Canvas simply because it seems familiar.

When using a Canvas, you must specify the location of each child element. If you don't, all of your elements will end up at the top-left corner. Canvas defines four attached properties for setting the position of child elements. Vertical position is set with either the Top or Bottom property, and horizontal position is determined by either the Left or Right property.

Example 3-18 shows a Canvas containing two TextBlock elements. The first has been positioned relative to the top-left corner of the Canvas: the text will always appear 10 pixels in from the left and 20 pixels down from the top. (As always, these are device-independent pixels.) Figure 3-21 shows the result.

Example 3-18. Positioning on a Canvas

```
<Canvas Background="Yellow" Width="150" Height="100">
  <TextBlock Canvas.Left="10" Canvas.Top="20">Hello</TextBlock>
  <TextBlock Canvas.Right="10" Canvas.Bottom="20">world!</TextBlock>
</Canvas>
```

Figure 3-21. Simple Canvas layout

The second text element is more interesting. It has been positioned relative to the bottom right of the form, which means that if the canvas gets resized, the element will move with that corner of the canvas. For example, if the Canvas were the main element of a window, the second TextBlock element would move with the bottom-right corner of the window if the user resized it.

If you have used Windows Forms, you may be wondering whether setting both the Top and Bottom properties (or both Left and Right properties) will cause the element to resize automatically when the containing canvas is resized. But unlike with anchoring in Windows Forms, this technique does not work. If you specify both Left and Right, or both Top and Bottom, one of the properties will simply be ignored. (Top takes precedence over Bottom, and Left takes precedence over Right.)

Fortunately, it is easy to get this kind of behavior with a single-cell Grid and the Margin property. If you put an element into a grid with a margin of, say, "10,10,30,40", its top-left corner will be at (10,10) relative to the top left of the grid, its righthand side will always be 30 pixels from the right edge of the grid, and its bottom edge will always be 40 pixels from the bottom of the grid. This is another reason to prefer Grid over Canvas.

The main use for Canvas is to arrange drawings. If you employ graphical elements such as Ellipse and Path, which are discussed in Chapter 13, you will typically need precise control over their location, in which case the Canvas is ideal.

When child elements are larger than their parent panel, most panels crop them, but the Canvas does not by default, allowing elements to be partially or entirely outside of its bounds. You can even use negative coordinates. The noncropping behavior is sometimes useful because it means you do not need to specify the size of the canvas— a zero-size canvas works perfectly well. However, if you want to clip the content, set ClipToBounds to True.

The price you pay for the precise control offered by the Canvas is that it is inflexible. However, there is one common scenario in which you can mitigate this rigidity. If you've used a Canvas to arrange a drawing and you would like that drawing to be automatically resizable, you can use a Viewbox in conjunction with the Canvas.

Viewbox

The Viewbox element automatically scales its content to fill the space available. Strictly speaking, Viewbox is not a panel—it derives from Decorator. This means that unlike most panels, it can have only one child. However, its capability to adjust the size of its content in order to adapt to its surroundings makes it a useful layout tool.

Figure 3-22 shows a window that doesn't use a Viewbox but probably should. The window's content is a Canvas containing a rather small drawing. Example 3-19 shows the markup.

Figure 3-22. Canvas without Viewbox

Example 3-19. Canvas without Viewbox

```
<Window xmlns="http://schemas.microsoft.com/winfx/2006/xaml/presentation">

  <Canvas Width="18" Height="18" VerticalAlignment="Center">
```

Example 3-19. Canvas without Viewbox (continued)

```
    <Ellipse Canvas.Left="1" Canvas.Top="1" Width="16" Height="16"
            Fill="Yellow" Stroke="Black" />
    <Ellipse Canvas.Left="4.5" Canvas.Top="5" Width="2.5" Height="3"
                        Fill="Black" />
    <Ellipse Canvas.Left="11" Canvas.Top="5" Width="2.5" Height="3"
                        Fill="Black" />
    <Path Data="M 5,10 A 3,3 90 0 0 13,10" Stroke="Black" />
  </Canvas>

</Window>
```

We can use a Viewbox to resize the content automatically. It will expand it to be large enough to fill the space, as shown in Figure 3-23. (If you're wondering why the drawing doesn't touch the edges of the window, it's because the Canvas is slightly larger than the drawing it contains.)

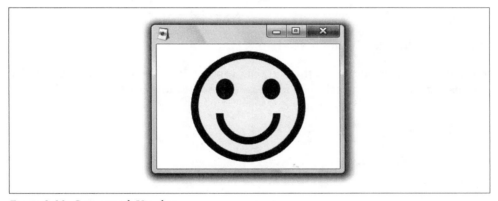

Figure 3-23. Canvas with Viewbox

All we had to do to get this automatic resizing was wrap the Canvas element in a Viewbox element, as shown in Example 3-20.

Example 3-20. Using Viewbox

```
<Window xmlns="http://schemas.microsoft.com/winfx/2006/xaml/presentation">

  <Viewbox>
    <Canvas Width="18" Height="18" VerticalAlignment="Center">

        ...as before...

    </Canvas>
  </Viewbox>

</Window>
```

Notice how in Figure 3-23 the Canvas has been made tall enough to fill the window, but not wide enough. This is because by default, the Viewbox preserves the aspect ratio of its child. If you want, you can disable this so that it fills all the space, as Figure 3-24 shows.

Figure 3-24. Viewbox with Stretch

To enable this behavior we set the Stretch property. Its default value is Uniform. We can make the Viewbox stretch the Canvas to fill the whole space by setting the property to Fill, as Example 3-21 shows.

Example 3-21. Specifying a Stretch

```
...
  <Viewbox Stretch="Fill">
...
```

You can also set the Stretch property to None to disable stretching. That might seem pointless, because the effect is exactly the same as not using a Viewbox at all. However, you might do this from code to flip between scaled and normal-size views of a drawing. There is also a UniformToFill setting, which preserves the aspect ratio but fills the space, clipping the source in one dimension, if necessary (see Figure 3-25).

 The Viewbox can scale any child element—it's not just for Canvas. However, you would rarely use it to size anything other than a drawing. If you were to use a Viewbox to resize some nongraphical part of your UI, it would resize any text in there as well, making it look inconsistent with the rest of your UI. For a resizable user interface, you are best off relying on the resizable panels shown in this chapter.

Figure 3-25. UniformToFill

Common Layout Properties

All user interface elements have a standard set of layout properties, mostly inherited from the FrameworkElement base class. These properties are shown in Table 3-2. We saw a few of these in passing in the preceding section, but we will now look at them all in a little more detail.

Table 3-2. Common layout properties

Property	Usage
Width	Specifies a fixed width
Height	Specifies a fixed height
MinWidth	The minimum permissible width
MaxWidth	The maximum permissible width
MinHeight	The minimum permissible height
MaxHeight	The maximum permissible height
HorizontalAlignment	Horizontal position if element is smaller than available space
VerticalAlignment	Vertical position if element is smaller than available space
Margin	Space around outside of element
Padding	Space between element border and content
Visibility	Allows the element to be made invisible to the layout system where necessary
FlowDirection	Text direction
Panel.ZIndex	Controls which elements are on top or underneath
RenderTransform	Applies a transform without modifying the layout
LayoutTransform	Applies a transform that affects layout

A couple of these properties are not from `FrameworkElement`. `Padding` is defined in several places: `Control`, `Border`, and `TextBlock` each define this property. It has the same meaning in all cases. It is not quite ubiquitous because padding is meaningful only on elements that have content. `Panel.ZIndex` may be applied to any element, but it's not strictly inherited from `FrameworkElement`—it is an attached property.

Width and Height

You can set these properties to specify an exact width and height for your element. You should try to avoid using these—in general it is preferable to let elements determine their own size where possible. It will take less effort to change your user interface if you allow elements to "size to content." It can also simplify localization. However, you will occasionally need to provide a specific size.

If you specify a `Width` or `Height`, the layout system will always attempt to honor your choices. Of course, if you make an element wider than the screen, WPF can't make the screen any wider, but as long as what you request is possible, it will be done.

MinWidth, MaxWidth, MinHeight, and MaxHeight

These properties allow you to specify upper and lower limits on the size of an element. If you need to constrain your user interface's layout, it is usually better to use these than `Width` and `Height` where possible. By specifying upper and lower limits, you can still allow WPF some latitude to automate the layout.

It is possible to mandate limits that simply cannot be fulfilled. For example, if you request a `MinWidth` of `"10000"`, WPF won't be able to honor that request unless you have some very exotic display hardware. In these cases, your element will be truncated to fit the space available.

HorizontalAlignment and VerticalAlignment

These properties control how an element is placed inside a parent when more room is available than is necessary. For example, a vertical `StackPanel` will normally be as wide as the widest element, meaning that any narrower elements are given excess space. Alignment is for these sorts of scenarios, enabling you to determine what the child element does with the extra space.

The default setting for both of these properties is `Stretch`—when excess space is available, the element will be enlarged to fill that space. The alternatives are `Left`, `Center`, and `Right` for `HorizontalAlignment`, and `Top`, `Center`, and `Bottom` for `VerticalAlignment`. If you choose any of these, the element will not be stretched—it will use its natural height or width, and will then be positioned to one side or in the center.

Margin

This property determines the amount of space that should be left around the element during layout.

You can specify Margin as a single number, a pair of numbers, or a list of four numbers. When one number is used, this indicates that the same amount of space should be left on all sides. With two numbers, the first indicates the space to the left and right and the second indicates the space above and below. When four numbers are specified, they indicate the amount of space on the left, top, right, and bottom sides, respectively.

You can use the Margin property to control an element's position. For example, although Grid does not define attached properties to control the exact positioning of an element, it will honor the Margin property relative to the element's cell. Example 3-22 shows a simple single-cell grid that uses this technique.

Example 3-22. Controlling an element's position with Margin

```
<Border BorderBrush="Black" BorderThickness="1">
  <Grid>
    <Rectangle Margin="20, 10, 0, 0" Fill="Green"
        Width="80" Height="30"
        HorizontalAlignment="Left" VerticalAlignment="Top" />
  </Grid>
</Border>
```

The rectangle it contains will be 20 device-independent pixels in from the left and 10 down from the top, as Figure 3-26 shows. Note that we've left the last two values of the Margin property—the right and bottom margins—at zero. That's because we only want to use the margin to specify the position of the top left of the rectangle. The position of the bottom right is determined by the rectangle's size in this case.

Figure 3-26. Margin

Padding

Whereas Margin indicates how much space should be left around the outside of an element, Padding specifies how much should be left between a control's outside and its internal content.

Padding is not present on all WPF elements, because not all elements have internal content. It is defined by the `Control` base class, and the `Border` and `TextBlock` classes, as well as some of the text elements described in Chapter 14.

Example 3-23 shows three buttons, one with just a margin, one with both a margin and padding, and one with just padding. It also fills the area behind the buttons with color so that the effects of the margin can be seen.

Example 3-23. Margin versus Padding

```
<Grid ShowGridLines="True" Background="Cyan">
  <Grid.ColumnDefinitions>
    <ColumnDefinition Width="Auto" />
    <ColumnDefinition Width="Auto" />
    <ColumnDefinition Width="Auto" />
  </Grid.ColumnDefinitions>
  <Grid.RowDefinitions>
    <RowDefinition Height="Auto" />
  </Grid.RowDefinitions>

  <Button Grid.Column="0" Margin="20" Padding="0">Click me!</Button>
  <Button Grid.Column="1" Margin="10" Padding="10">Click me!</Button>
  <Button Grid.Column="2" Margin="0"  Padding="20">Click me!</Button>

</Grid>
```

Figure 3-27 shows the results. The button with a margin but no padding has appeared at its normal size, but has space around it. The middle button is larger, because the padding causes space to be added around its content. The third button is larger still because it has more padding, but it has no space around it because it has no margin.

Figure 3-27. Buttons with a margin and padding

Visibility

The `Visibility` property determines whether an element is visible. It has an impact on layout, because if you set it to `Collapsed`, the preferred size of the element will become zero. This is different from `Hidden`—this indicates that although the element is not visible, the layout system should treat it in the same way as it would if it were `Visible`.

FlowDirection

The FlowDirection property controls how text flows; the default is based on the system locale. For example, in English-speaking locales, it will be left to right, but many cultures use the alternative right-to-left style. Setting the FlowDirection property to RightToLeft affects the flow direction of all text, and of any WrapPanel elements contained within that element. This is an *inherited property*, meaning that it applies to all its descendants—setting this on a window implicitly sets it for all elements in the window. Example 3-24 shows this property applied to a WrapPanel.

Example 3-24. FlowDirection

```
<StackPanel>
  <WrapPanel Orientation="Horizontal">
    <Button>One</Button>
    <Button>Two</Button>
    <Button>Three</Button>
  </WrapPanel>
  <WrapPanel Orientation="Horizontal" FlowDirection="RightToLeft">
    <Button>One</Button>
    <Button>Two</Button>
    <Button>Three</Button>
  </WrapPanel>
</StackPanel>
```

Figure 3-28 shows the results.

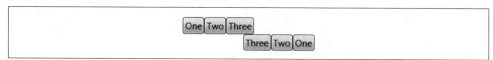

Figure 3-28. FlowDirection

Although the WrapPanel offers the most straightforward way of illustrating FlowDirection, the property's main purpose is to control how text is arranged—its impact on WrapPanel is of secondary importance. On the face of it, a property for controlling text flow direction may seem to be unnecessary, because Unicode defines the directionality of each codepoint. If a string contains, say, Hebrew letters, these have an intrinsic right-to-left direction, and will be rendered in that direction regardless of the FlowDirection setting. Example 3-25 shows three Hebrew letters: Alef (א), Bet (ב), and Gimel (ג).

Example 3-25. Intrinsic character direction

```
<TextBlock>
  &#x05d0;&#x05d1;&#x05d2;
</TextBlock>
```

This will appear as shown in Figure 3-29. Notice that the first character has appeared on the right, with the second and third appearing to the left. This illustrates that WPF doesn't need to be told the flow direction for text with intrinsic directionality. And even if we explicitly set the text block's flow direction to LeftToRight, the directionality of these characters would override this setting.

Figure 3-29. Right-to-left characters

However, problems emerge when using characters that do not have a strong directionality. Example 3-26 makes a subtle change.

Example 3-26. Mixed character directions

```
<TextBlock>
  &#x05d0;&#x05d1;&#x05d2;:
</TextBlock>
```

This adds a colon to the end of the second line, after the Hebrew characters, and the results will appear as shown in Figure 3-30. Although the three Hebrew characters have been displayed from right to left as before, the colon has been shown to the right. This is because the colon is not a right-to-left character. (Strictly speaking, Unicode considers its directionality to be "weak.") But because the TextBlock doesn't have an explicit FlowDirection, the default flow direction applies—left to right, on the authors' machines. So the colon has appeared where it normally would with left-to-right text, which is inconsistent with the right-to-left text it appears next to here.

Figure 3-30. Mixed directions

To make the colon appear in a location consistent with the directionality of the remaining text, we need to tell WPF that we would like right-to-left text flow here. This won't affect any text with an intrinsic directionality, but it will determine where the colon appears. Example 3-27 contains a mixture of Hebrew and Latin characters to illustrate this.

Example 3-27. FlowDirection

```
<TextBlock FlowDirection="RightToLeft">
  &#x05d0;&#x05d1;&#x05d2;: Foo
</TextBlock>
```

The sequence of characters here is three Hebrew letters, a colon, a space, and then three Latin letters. As Figure 3-31 illustrates, the Hebrew letters have been shown from right to left as they were before. But this time, the colon has been shown to the left of these letters rather than to the right, because of the FlowDirection setting. The three Latin letters appear to the left of the other letters in accordance with the RightToLeft flow direction, but because these letters all have an intrinsic left-to-right directionality, this block of Latin letters has been displayed from left to right.

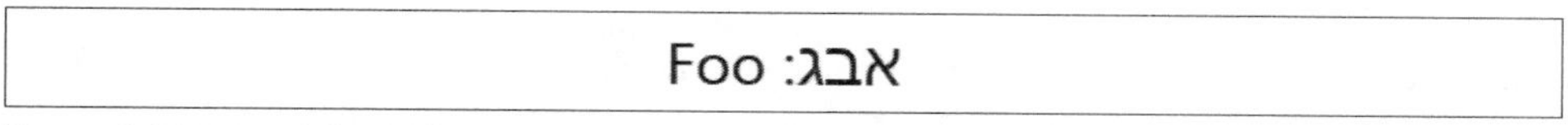

Foo :אבג

Figure 3-31. Mixed directions with RightToLeft FlowDirection

The full details of the algorithm used for bidirectional layout of Unicode text is given in Annex 9 of the Unicode specification. It is too complex to describe in full detail here, but you can find it at *http://www.unicode.org/reports/tr9* (*http://tinysells.com/99*).

Panel.ZIndex

Panel defines an attached property, ZIndex, that determines which element appears on top when two of them overlap. By default, the Z order of elements is determined by the order in which they are defined. Of the elements inside a particular panel, they will typically be rendered in the order in which they appear, causing the last one to appear to be "on top." Panel.ZIndex lets you control the rendering order independently of the document order.

Elements with a higher Panel.ZIndex appear on top of those with a lower Panel.ZIndex. The default value is 0, so elements with a positive Panel.ZIndex will appear on top of those that do not specify one. Example 3-28 does not use Panel.ZIndex, so the element overlapping order is determined by the order in which the elements appear.

Example 3-28. Without Panel.ZIndex

```
<Grid>
  <Button Width="75" Height="23" Margin="0,0"
      HorizontalAlignment="Left" VerticalAlignment="Top">
    One
  </Button>
  <Button Width="75" Height="23" Margin="15,15"
      HorizontalAlignment="Left" VerticalAlignment="Top">
    Two
  </Button>
  <Button Width="75" Height="23" Margin="30,30"
      HorizontalAlignment="Left" VerticalAlignment="Top">
    Three
  </Button>
</Grid>
```

This is shown on the left of Figure 3-32. The version on the right comes from Example 3-29.

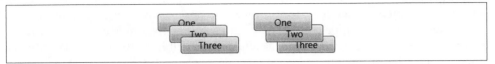

Figure 3-32. Panel.ZIndex

Example 3-29 uses `Panel.ZIndex` to reverse the overlap.

Example 3-29. With Panel.ZIndex

```
<Grid>
  <Button Width="75" Height="23" Margin="0,0" Panel.ZIndex="3"
      HorizontalAlignment="Left" VerticalAlignment="Top">
    One
  </Button>
  <Button Width="75" Height="23" Margin="15,15" Panel.ZIndex="2"
      HorizontalAlignment="Left" VerticalAlignment="Top">
    Two
  </Button>
  <Button Width="75" Height="23" Margin="30,30" Panel.ZIndex="1"
      HorizontalAlignment="Left" VerticalAlignment="Top">
    Three
  </Button>
</Grid>
```

RenderTransform and LayoutTransform

You can use both the RenderTransform and LayoutTransform properties to apply a transform, such as scaling or rotation, to an element and all of its children. Transforms are described in Chapter 13, but it is useful to understand their impact on layout.

If you apply a transform that doubles the size of an element, the element will appear to be twice as large on-screen. You would normally want the layout system to take this into account—if a Rectangle with a Width of 100 is scaled up to twice its size, it will normally make sense for the layout system to treat it as having an effective width of 200. However, you might sometimes want the transformation to be ignored for layout purposes. For example, if you are using a transform in a short animation designed to draw attention to a particular part of the UI, you probably don't want the entire UI's layout to be changed as a result of that animation.

You can apply a transform to an object using either LayoutTransform or RenderTransform. The former causes the transform to be taken into account by the layout system, and the latter causes it to be ignored. Example 3-30 shows three buttons, one containing untransformed content, and the other two containing content transformed with these two properties.

Example 3-30. RenderTransform and LayoutTransform

```
<StackPanel>
  <Button>
    <TextBlock>
      Foo bar
    </TextBlock>
  </Button>
  <Button>
    <TextBlock>
      <TextBlock.RenderTransform>
        <ScaleTransform ScaleX="3" ScaleY="3" />
      </TextBlock.RenderTransform>
      Foo bar
    </TextBlock>
  </Button>
  <Button>
    <TextBlock>
      <TextBlock.LayoutTransform>
        <ScaleTransform ScaleX="3" ScaleY="3" />
      </TextBlock.LayoutTransform>
      Foo bar
    </TextBlock>
  </Button>
</StackPanel>
```

Figure 3-33 shows the results. As you can see, the button with content scaled by RenderTransform has the same size border as the unscaled one. The presence of the transform has had no effect on layout, and the content no longer fits inside the space allocated for it. However, the LayoutTransform has been taken into account by the layout system—the third button has been enlarged in order for the scaled content to fit.

Figure 3-33. RenderTransform and LayoutTransform

The layout system deals with LayoutTransform in a straightforward manner for simple scaling transforms. The size allocated for the content is scaled up accordingly. But what about rotations? Figure 3-34 shows a button whose content has a LayoutTransform that rotates the content by 30 degrees. This is not a scaling transform, but notice that the button has grown to accommodate the content—it is taller than a normal button.

Figure 3-34. LayoutTransform and rotation

When it encounters a LayoutTransform, the layout system simply applies that transform to the bounding box, and makes sure that it provides enough space to hold the transformed bounding box. This can occasionally lead to surprising results. Consider the two buttons in Example 3-31.

Example 3-31. Rotation of content

```
<StackPanel>
  <Button HorizontalAlignment="Left">
    <Line Stroke="Blue" Y1="30" X2="100" />
  </Button>
  <Button HorizontalAlignment="Left">
    <Line Stroke="Blue" Y1="30" X2="100">
      <Line.LayoutTransform>
        <RotateTransform Angle="50" />
      </Line.LayoutTransform>
    </Line>
  </Button>
</StackPanel>
```

These are shown in Figure 3-35. The top button looks as you would expect—the button is large enough to contain the graphical content. But the bottom one is rather surprising—the button appears to be taller than necessary.

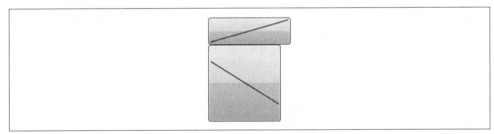

Figure 3-35. Rotated content

This result makes sense only when you consider the bounding box—remember that the layout system decides how much space to allocate by applying the LayoutTransform to the bounding box. So let's look at it again, this time with the bounding boxes shown. Example 3-32 is a modified version of Example 3-31, with Border elements added to show the bounding box of the lines.

Example 3-32. Rotation showing bounding box

```
<StackPanel>
  <Button HorizontalAlignment="Left">
    <Border BorderBrush="Black" BorderThickness="1">
      <Line Stroke="Blue" Y1="30" X2="100" />
    </Border>
  </Button>
  <Button HorizontalAlignment="Left">
```

Example 3-32. Rotation showing bounding box (continued)

```
  <Border BorderBrush="Black" BorderThickness="1">
    <Border.LayoutTransform>
      <RotateTransform Angle="50" />
    </Border.LayoutTransform>
    <Line Stroke="Blue" Y1="30" X2="100" />
  </Border>
</Button>
</StackPanel>
```

In Figure 3-36, we can now see the bounding box of the content. The button on the bottom shows this bounding box with the same 50 degree rotation as has been applied to the line. This makes it clear that the button is exactly large enough to hold this rotated bounding box.

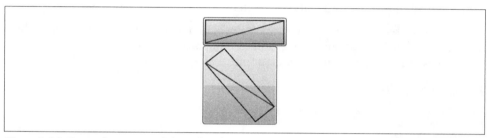

Figure 3-36. Rotated content with bounding boxes

You might be wondering why WPF doesn't simply calculate a new bounding box for the transformed content instead of transforming the existing one. The reason is that calculating a new bounding box may not be possible. Some elements, such as Canvas, can declare a width and height that do not directly reflect their apparent size. The only sensible way in which the layout system can deal with such elements is to treat their logical shape as being rectangular. Using this approach of transforming the bounding box everywhere ensures consistent behavior.

When Content Doesn't Fit

Sometimes WPF will not be able to honor your requests because you have asked the impossible. Example 3-33 creates a StackPanel with a Height of 100, which contains a Button with a Height of 195.

Example 3-33. Asking the impossible

```
<StackPanel Height="100" Background="Yellow" Orientation="Horizontal">
  <Button>Foo</Button>
  <Button Height="30">Bar</Button>
  <Button Height="195">Quux</Button>
</StackPanel>
```

Clearly that last button is too big to fit—it is taller than its containing panel. Figure 3-37 shows how WPF deals with this.

Figure 3-37. Truncation when content is too large

The `StackPanel` has dealt with the anomaly by truncating the element that was too large. When confronted with contradictory hardcoded sizes like these, most panels take a similar approach, and will crop content where it simply cannot fit.

There is some variation in the way that panels handle overflow in situations where sizes are not hardcoded, but there is still too much content to fit. Example 3-34 puts two copies of a `TextBlock` and its content into a `StackPanel` and a `Grid` cell.

Example 3-34. Handling overflow

```
<Grid Background="Yellow" ShowGridLines="True">
  <Grid.RowDefinitions>
    <RowDefinition />
    <RowDefinition />
  </Grid.RowDefinitions>

  <StackPanel Height="100" Orientation="Horizontal">
    <TextBlock TextWrapping="Wrap" FontSize="20">
      This is some text that is too long to fit.
    </TextBlock>
  </StackPanel>

  <TextBlock Grid.Row="1" TextWrapping="Wrap" FontSize="20">
    This is some text that is too long to fit.
  </TextBlock>
</Grid>
```

Figure 3-38 shows what happens when the available space is too narrow to hold the `TextBlock` at its natural length.

The `StackPanel` has simply truncated the `TextBlock`. The `Grid` has been slightly more intelligent. It has exploited the fact that the `TextBlock` had wrapping enabled, and was able to flow the text into the narrow space available.* `WrapPanel` and `DockPanel` both show the same behavior. Even this technique has its limits, of course—sometimes you really will have more content than fits in the space available. In that case, it may be appropriate to use a `ScrollViewer`, discussed presently.

---

* The reason for the difference in behavior is that `StackPanel` uses a very simple layout mechanism. A horizontal `StackPanel` always sizes its children to content horizontally, regardless of whether there is sufficient space.

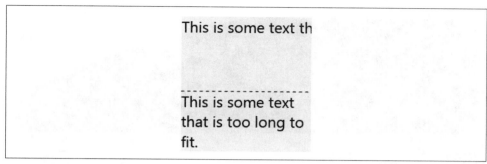

Figure 3-38. Overflow handling

The reason StackPanel doesn't result in wrapped text is that it does not attempt to constrain its children in the stacking direction: a horizontal StackPanel lets each child choose its preferred width, whether or not it fits. In effect, it pretends there is an infinite amount of space, which is why the child TextBlock didn't attempt to wrap. StackPanel will constrain children in the other direction, though, so a vertical StackPanel would pass on the horizontal constraint, causing the TextBlock in this example to wrap. Canvas allows its children to determine both their width and their height regardless of available space, so a Canvas would fail to wrap, just like the StackPanel in this example.

ScrollViewer

The ScrollViewer control allows oversized content to be displayed by putting it into a scrollable area. A ScrollViewer element has a single child. Example 3-35 uses an Ellipse element, but it could be anything. If you want to put multiple elements into a scrollable view, you would nest them inside a panel.

Example 3-35. ScrollViewer

```
<ScrollViewer HorizontalScrollBarVisibility="Auto">
  <Ellipse Fill="Green" Height="1000" Width="2000" />
</ScrollViewer>
```

If the content of a ScrollViewer is larger than the space available, the ScrollViewer can provide scroll bars to allow the user to scroll around the content, as Figure 3-39 shows. By default, a ScrollViewer provides a vertical scroll bar, but not a horizontal one. In Example 3-35, the HorizontalScrollBarVisibility property has been set to Auto, indicating that a horizontal scroll bar should be added if required.

This Auto visibility we've chosen for the horizontal scroll bar is different from the default vertical behavior. The VerticalScrollBarVisibility defaults to Visible, meaning that the scroll bar is present whether it is required or not.

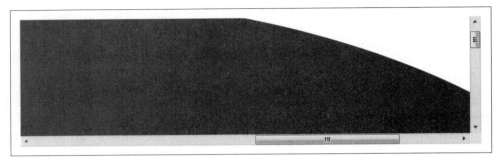

Figure 3-39. ScrollViewer

There are two ways to make sure a scroll bar does not appear. You can set its visibility either to Disabled (the default for horizontal scroll bars) or to Hidden. The distinction is that Disabled constrains the logical size of the ScrollViewer's contents to be the same as the available space. Hidden allows the logical size to be unconstrained, even though the user has no way of scrolling into the excess space. This can change the behavior of certain layout styles.

To examine how these settings affect the behavior of a ScrollViewer, we'll start with the code shown in Example 3-36, and then show what happens as we change the ScrollViewer properties.

Example 3-36. A resizable layout

```
<ScrollViewer ...>
  <Grid>
    <Grid.ColumnDefinitions>
      <ColumnDefinition />
      <ColumnDefinition />
      <ColumnDefinition />
    </Grid.ColumnDefinitions>
    <Grid.RowDefinitions>
      <RowDefinition Height="Auto" />
    </Grid.RowDefinitions>

    <Button Grid.Column="0">Stretched</Button>
    <Button Grid.Column="1">Stretched</Button>
    <Button Grid.Column="2">Stretched</Button>
  </Grid>
</ScrollViewer>
```

This example shows a Grid containing three Button elements in a row. If the Grid is given more space than it requires, it will stretch the buttons to be wider than necessary. If it is given insufficient space, it will crop the buttons. If it is placed inside a ScrollViewer, it will be possible for the ScrollViewer to provide enough virtual, scrollable space for it, even if the space on-screen is insufficient.

Figure 3-40 shows how the Grid in Example 3-36 appears in a ScrollViewer when there is more than enough space. All four options for HorizontalScrollBarVisibility are shown, and in all four cases, the buttons have been stretched to fill the space.

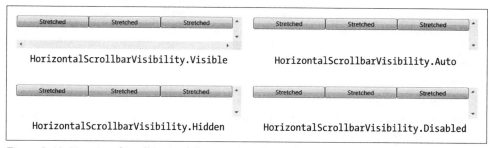

Figure 3-40. HorizontalScrollBarVisibility settings with enough space

Figure 3-41 shows the same four arrangements, but with insufficient horizontal space. The top two ScrollViewer elements have horizontal scrolling enabled, with Visible and Auto, respectively. As you would expect, the ScrollViewer has provided enough space to hold all of the content, and allows the user to scroll the hidden part into view. At the bottom left, where the horizontal scroll bar is set to Hidden, the layout behavior is the same—it has arranged the elements as though there were enough space to hold all of them. The only difference is that it has not shown a scroll bar. (Scrolling will still occur if the user uses keyboard navigation to move the focus into the hidden area.) At the bottom right, we can see that the behavior resulting from Disabled is different. Here, not only is a scroll bar not shown, but also horizontal scrolling is disabled completely. The Grid has therefore been forced to crop the buttons to fit into the available space.

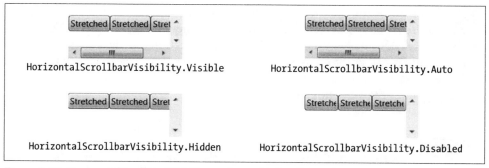

Figure 3-41. HorizontalScrollBarVisibility settings with insufficient space

Scrollable Region and IScrollInfo

If you place a panel or any other ordinary element inside a ScrollViewer, the ScrollViewer will measure its size in the normal way: the scrollable area essentially sizes to content (unless the available area is surplus to requirements, in which case the ScrollViewer gives the child all of the available space). It keeps track of the currently visible region, and moves the child content around as required. Most of the time, this is exactly the behavior you require. However, occasionally you might need to take a bit more control.

For example, if you have a large scrollable area containing lots of items, it might not be very efficient to create all of the items upfront. You might be able to improve performance significantly by creating items on demand only as they scroll into view. Such tricks require you to get more deeply involved in the scrolling process.

If you want to take control of how scrolling functions, you must write a user interface element that implements IScrollInfo. ScrollViewer looks for this interface on its child element. If the child implements the interface, the ScrollViewer will no longer pretend that the child has all the space it requires—instead, it will tell the child exactly how much space is available on-screen for the viewport, and will defer to the child for all scrolling operations. In this case, the ScrollViewer's role is reduced to showing scroll bars and notifying the child when the user attempts to scroll.

This is not a step to be taken lightly. IScrollInfo has 24 members, and requires you to do most of the work that ScrollViewer would otherwise have done for you.[*] Fortunately, for the very common scenario of scrolling through a list, we can use the built-in IScrollInfo implementation provided by VirtualizingStackPanel. The VirtualizingStackPanel implements IScrollInfo so that it can show scroll feedback for all of the data, even though it only generates UI elements to represent those items currently visible, "virtualizing" the view of the data. You don't need to take any special steps to enable virtualization—a data-bound ListBox automatically displays its items using a VirtualizingStackPanel. You would need to implement IScrollInfo only if you are not using data binding, or if you need something other than a simple linear stack of items.

 If you customize the appearance of an ItemsControl using the template techniques described in Chapters 8 and 9, you might end up disabling virtualization. To avoid this, you should ensure that if you change the Template or ItemsPanelTemplate property of an ItemsControl, your replacement template contains a VirtualizingStackPanel.

---

[*] For a full example of how to implement IScrollInfo, see a series of three articles on this subject, written by a Microsoft developer, at *http://blogs.msdn.com/bencon/archive/2006/01.aspx* (*http://tinysells.com/64*).

We have now looked at all of the built-in mechanisms for helping you manage your application's layout. But what if you have unusual requirements that are not met by the built-in panels? Sometimes it is necessary to customize the layout process by writing your own panel.

Custom Layout

Although WPF supplies a flexible set of layout elements, you might decide that none of them suits your requirements. Fortunately, the layout system is extensible, and it is fairly straightforward to implement your own custom panel. To write a panel, you need to understand how the layout system works.

Layout occurs in two phases: *measure* and *arrange*. Your custom panel will first be asked how much space it would like to have—that's the measure phase. The panel should measure each of its children to find out how much space they require, and use this information to calculate how much space the panel needs in total.

Of course, you can't always get what you want. If your panel's measure phase decides it needs an area twice the size of the screen, it won't get that unless its parent happens to be a ScrollViewer. Moreover, even when there is enough space on-screen, your panel's parent could still choose not to give it to you. For example, if your custom panel is nested inside a Grid, the Grid may have been set up with a hardcoded width for the column your panel occupies, in which case that's the width you'll get regardless of what you asked for during the measure phase.

It is only in the "arrange" phase that we find out how much space we have. During this phase, we must decide where to put all of our children as best we can in the space available.

 You might be wondering why the layout system bothers with the measure phase when the amount of space we get during the arrange phase may be different. The reason for having both is that most panels try to take the measured size of their children into account during the arrange phase. You can think of the measure phase as asking every element in the tree what it would like, and the arrange phase as honoring those measurements where possible, compromising only where physical or configured constraints come into play.

Let's create a new panel type to see how the measure and arrange phases work in practice. We'll call this new panel DiagonalPanel, and it will arrange elements diagonally from the top left of the panel down to the bottom right, as Figure 3-42 shows. Each element's top-left corner will be placed where the preceding element's bottom-right corner went.

You don't really need to write a new panel type to achieve this layout—you could get the same effect with a Grid, setting every row and column's size to Auto. However, you could make the same argument for StackPanel and DockPanel—neither of those does anything that you couldn't do with the Grid. It's just convenient to have a simple single-purpose panel, as the Grid equivalent is a little more verbose.

Figure 3-42. Custom DiagonalPanel in action

To implement this custom layout, we must write a class that derives from Panel, and that implements the measure and arrange phases. As Example 3-37 shows, we do this by overriding the MeasureOverride and ArrangeOverride methods.

Example 3-37. Custom DiagonalPanel

```
using System;
using System.Windows.Controls;
using System.Windows;

namespace CustomPanel {
    public class DiagonalPanel : Panel {

        protected override Size MeasureOverride( Size availableSize ) {
            double totalWidth = 0;
            double totalHeight = 0;

            foreach( UIElement child in Children ) {
                child.Measure( new Size( double.PositiveInfinity,
                                         double.PositiveInfinity ) );
                Size childSize = child.DesiredSize;
                totalWidth += childSize.Width;
                totalHeight += childSize.Height;
            }

            return new Size( totalWidth, totalHeight );
        }

        protected override Size ArrangeOverride( Size finalSize ) {
            Point currentPosition = new Point( );

            foreach( UIElement child in Children ) {
                Rect childRect = new Rect( currentPosition, child.DesiredSize );
                child.Arrange( childRect );
                currentPosition.Offset( childRect.Width, childRect.Height );
```

Example 3-37. Custom DiagonalPanel (continued)

```
        }

        return new Size( currentPosition.X, currentPosition.Y );
    }
  }
}
```

Notice that the MeasureOverride method is passed a Size parameter. If the parent is aware of size constraints that will need to be applied during the arrange phase, it passes them here during the measure phase. For example, if this panel's parent was a Window with a specified size, the Window would pass in the size of its client area during the measure phase. However, not all panels will do this. You may find the available size is specified as being Double.PositiveInfinity in both dimensions, indicating that the parent is not informing us of any fixed constraints at this stage. An infinite available size indicates that we should simply pick whatever size is appropriate for our content. You must pick a finite size—returning an infinite size from your MeasureOverride will cause an exception to be thrown.

Some elements ignore the available size, because their size is always determined by their contents. For example, our panel's simple layout is driven entirely by the natural size of its children, so it ignores the available size. Our MeasureOverride simply loops through all of the children, adding their widths and heights. We pass in an infinite size when calling Measure on each child in order to use its preferred size.

> You must call Measure on all of your panel's children. If your MeasureOverride fails to measure all of its children, the layout process may not function correctly. All elements expect to be measured before they are arranged. Their arrange logic might rely on the results of calculations performed during the measure phase. When you write a custom panel, it is your responsibility to ensure that child elements are measured and arranged at the appropriate times.

In our ArrangeOverride, we loop through all of the child elements, setting them to their preferred size, basing the position on the bottom-righthand corner of the preceding element. Because this very simple layout scheme cannot adapt, it ignores the amount of space it has been given. Any child elements that do not fit will be cropped, as happens with StackPanel.

This measure and arrange sequence traverses the entire user interface tree—all elements use this mechanism, not just panels. A custom panel is the most appropriate place to write custom layout logic for managing the arrangement of controls. However, there is one other situation in which you might want to override the MeasureOverride and ArrangeOverride methods. If you are writing a graphical element that uses the low-level visual APIs described in Chapter 13, you may want to override these methods in order for the layout system to work with your element.

The code will typically be simpler than for a panel, because you will not have child elements to arrange. Your MeasureOverride will simply need to report how much space it needs, and ArrangeOverride tells you how much space you have been given.

Where Are We?

WPF provides a wide range of options for layout. Many panel types are available, each offering its own layout style. You can then compose these into a single application in any number of ways, supporting many different user interface styles. The top-level layout will usually be set with either a Grid or a DockPanel. The other panels are typically used to manage the details. You can use the common layout properties on child elements to control how they are arranged—these properties work consistently across all panel types. And if none of the built-in layout mechanisms meets your requirements, you can write your own custom panel.

CHAPTER 4

Input

A user interface wouldn't be much use if it couldn't respond to user input. In this chapter, we will examine the input handling mechanisms available in WPF. There are three main kinds of user input for a Windows application: mouse, keyboard, and ink.* Any user interface element can receive input—not just controls. This is not surprising, because controls rely entirely on the services of lower-level elements like `Rectangle` and `TextBlock` in order to provide visuals. All of the input mechanisms described in the following sections are, therefore, available on all user interface element types.

Raw user input is delivered to your code through WPF's *routed event* mechanism. There is also a higher-level concept of a *command*—a particular action that might be accessible through several different inputs such as keyboard shortcuts, toolbar buttons, and menu items.

Routed Events

The .NET Framework defines a standard mechanism for managing events. A class may expose several events, and each event may have any number of subscribers. WPF augments this standard mechanism to overcome a limitation: if a normal .NET event has no registered handlers, it is effectively ignored.

Consider what this would mean for a typical WPF control. Most controls are made up of multiple visual components. For example, suppose you give a button a very plain appearance consisting of a single `Rectangle`, and provide a simple piece of text as the content. (Chapter 9 describes how to customize a control's appearance.) Even with such basic visuals, there are still two elements present: the text and the rectangle. The button should respond to a mouse click whether the mouse is over the text or the rectangle. In the standard .NET event handling model, this would mean registering a `MouseLeftButtonUp` event handler for both elements.

---

* Ink is input written with a stylus, whether on a Tablet PC or a hand-held device, although the mouse can be used in a pinch.

This problem would get much worse when taking advantage of WPF's content model. A Button is not restricted to having plain text as a caption—it can contain any object as content. The example in Figure 4-1 is not especially ambitious, but even this has six visible elements: the yellow outlined circle, the two dots for the eyes, the curve for the mouth, the text, and the button background itself. Attaching event handlers for every single element would be tedious and inefficient. Fortunately, it's not necessary.

Figure 4-1. A button with nested content

WPF uses *routed events*, which are rather more thorough than normal events. Instead of just calling handlers attached to the element that raised the event, WPF walks the tree of user interface elements, calling all handlers for the routed event attached to any node from the originating element right up to the root of the user interface tree. This behavior is the defining feature of routed events, and is at the heart of event handling in WPF.

Example 4-1 shows markup for the button in Figure 4-1. If one of the Ellipse elements inside the Canvas were to receive input, event routing would enable the Button, Grid, Canvas, and Ellipse to receive the event, as Figure 4-2 shows.

Example 4-1. Handling events in a user interface tree

```
<Button PreviewMouseDown="PreviewMouseDownButton"
        MouseDown="MouseDownButton">

    <Grid PreviewMouseDown="PreviewMouseDownGrid"
          MouseDown="MouseDownGrid">
        <Grid.ColumnDefinitions>
            <ColumnDefinition />
            <ColumnDefinition />
        </Grid.ColumnDefinitions>

        <Canvas PreviewMouseDown="PreviewMouseDownCanvas"
                MouseDown="MouseDownCanvas"
                Width="20" Height="18" VerticalAlignment="Center">

            <Ellipse PreviewMouseDown="PreviewMouseDownEllipse"
                     MouseDown="MouseDownEllipse"
                     x:Name="myEllipse"
                     Canvas.Left="1" Canvas.Top="1" Width="16" Height="16"
                     Fill="Yellow" Stroke="Black" />
```

Example 4-1. Handling events in a user interface tree (continued)

```
            <Ellipse Canvas.Left="4.5" Canvas.Top="5" Width="2.5" Height="3"
                    Fill="Black" />
            <Ellipse Canvas.Left="11" Canvas.Top="5" Width="2.5" Height="3"
                    Fill="Black" />
            <Path Data="M 5,10 A 3,3 0 0 0 13,10" Stroke="Black" />
        </Canvas>

        <TextBlock Grid.Column="1">Click!</TextBlock>
    </Grid>
</Button>
```

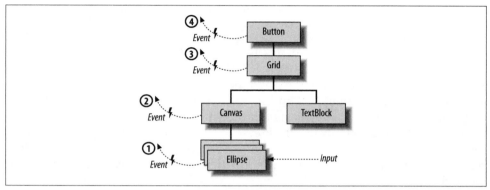

Figure 4-2. Routed events

A routed event can either be *bubbling*, *tunneling*, or *direct*. A bubbling event starts by looking for event handlers attached to the target element that raised the event, and then looks at its parent and then its parent's parent, and so on until it reaches the root of the tree; this order is indicated by the numbers in Figure 4-2. A tunneling event works in reverse—it looks for handlers at the root of the tree first and works its way down, finishing with the originating element.

Direct events work like normal .NET events: only handlers attached directly to the originating element are notified—no real routing occurs. This is typically used for events that make sense only in the context of their target element. For example, it would be unhelpful if mouse enter and leave events were bubbled or tunneled—the parent element is unlikely to care about when the mouse moves from one child element to another. At the parent element, you would expect "mouse leave" to mean "the mouse has left the parent element," and because direct event routing is used, that's exactly what it does mean. If bubbling were used, the event would effectively mean "the mouse has left an element that is inside the parent, and is now inside another element that may or may not be inside the parent," which would be less useful.

You may be wondering whether there is a meaningful difference between a direct routed event and an ordinary CLR event—after all, a direct event isn't really routed anywhere. The main difference is that with a direct routed event, WPF provides the underlying implementation, whereas if you were to use the normal C# event syntax to declare an event, the C# compiler would provide the implementation. The C# compiler would generate a hidden private field to hold the event handler, meaning that you pay a per-object overhead for each event whether or not any handlers are attached. With WPF's event implementation, event handlers are managed in such a way that you pay an overhead only for events to which handlers are attached. In a UI with thousands of elements each offering tens of events, most of which don't have handlers attached, this starts to add up. Also, WPF's event implementation offers something not available with ordinary C# events: attached events, which are described later.

With the exception of direct events, WPF defines most routed events in pairs—one bubbling and one tunneling. The tunneling event name always begins with Preview and is raised first. This gives parents of the target element the chance to see the event before it reaches the child (hence the Preview prefix). The tunneling preview event is followed directly by a bubbling event. In most cases, you will handle only the bubbling event—the preview would usually be used only if you wanted to be able to block the event, or if you needed a parent to do something in advance of normal handling of the event.

In Example 4-1, most of the elements have event handlers specified for the PreviewMouseDown and MouseDown events—the bubbling and tunneling events, respectively. Example 4-2 shows the corresponding code-behind file.

Example 4-2. Handling events

```
using System;
using System.Windows;
using System.Diagnostics;


namespace EventRouting {
    public partial class Window1 : Window {
        public Window1() {
            InitializeComponent();
        }

        void PreviewMouseDownButton(object sender, RoutedEventArgs e)
        { Debug.WriteLine("PreviewMouseDownButton"); }

        void MouseDownButton(object sender, RoutedEventArgs e)
        { Debug.WriteLine("MouseDownButton"); }
```

Example 4-2. Handling events (continued)

```
        void PreviewMouseDownGrid(
          object sender, RoutedEventArgs e)
        { Debug.WriteLine("PreviewMouseDownGrid"); }

        void MouseDownGrid(object sender, RoutedEventArgs e)
        { Debug.WriteLine("MouseDownGrid"); }


        void PreviewMouseDownCanvas(object sender, RoutedEventArgs e)
        { Debug.WriteLine("PreviewMouseDownCanvas"); }

        void MouseDownCanvas(object sender, RoutedEventArgs e)
        { Debug.WriteLine("MouseDownCanvas"); }


        void PreviewMouseDownEllipse(object sender, RoutedEventArgs e)
        { Debug.WriteLine("PreviewMouseDownEllipse"); }

        void MouseDownEllipse(object sender, RoutedEventArgs e)
        { Debug.WriteLine("MouseDownEllipse"); }

    }
}
```

Each handler prints out a debug message. Here is the debug output we get when clicking on the Ellipse inside the Canvas:

```
PreviewMouseDownButton
PreviewMouseDownGrid
PreviewMouseDownCanvas
PreviewMouseDownEllipse
MouseDownEllipse
MouseDownCanvas
MouseDownGrid
```

This confirms that the preview event is raised first. It also shows that it starts from the Button element and works down, as we would expect with a tunneling event. The bubbling event that follows starts from the Ellipse element and works up. (Interestingly, it doesn't appear to get as far as the Button. We'll look at why this is shortly.)

This bubbling routing offered for most events means that you can register a single event handler on a control, and it will receive events for any of the elements nested inside the control. You do not need any special handling to deal with nested content, or controls whose appearance has been customized with templates—events simply bubble up to the control and can all be handled there.

Halting Event Routing

There are some situations in which you might not want events to bubble up. For example, you may wish to convert the event into something else—the Button element effectively converts a MouseDown event followed by a MouseUp event into a single Click event. It suppresses the more primitive mouse button events so that only the Click event bubbles up out of the control. (This is why the event bubbling stopped at the button in the previous example.)

Any handler can prevent further processing of a routed event by setting the Handled property of the RoutedEventArgs, as shown in Example 4-3.

Example 4-3. Halting event routing with Handled

```
void ButtonDownCanvas(object sender, RoutedEventArgs e) {
    Debug.WriteLine("ButtonDownCanvas");
    e.Handled = true;
}
```

If you set the Handled flag in a Preview handler, not only will the tunneling of the Preview event stop, but also the corresponding bubbling event that would normally follow will not be raised at all. This provides a way of stopping the normal handling of an event.

Determining the Target

Although it is convenient to be able to handle events from a group of elements in a single place, your handler might need to know which element caused the event to be raised. You might think that this is the purpose of the sender parameter of your handler. In fact, the sender always refers to the object to which you attached the event handler. In the case of bubbled and tunneled events, this often isn't the element that caused the event to be raised. In Example 4-1, the MouseDownGrid handler's sender will always be the Grid itself, regardless of which element in the grid was clicked.

Fortunately, it's easy to find out which element was the underlying cause of the event. The handler has a RoutedEventArgs parameter, which offers a Source property for this purpose. This is particularly useful if you need to handle events from several different sources in the same way. For example, suppose you create a window that contains a number of graphical elements, and you'd like each to change shape when clicked. Instead of attaching a MouseDown event handler to each individual shape, you could attach a single handler to the window. All the events would bubble up from any shape to this single handler, and you could use the Source property to work out which shape you need to change. (Shapes are discussed in Chapter 13. Example 13-5 uses exactly this trick.)

Routed Events and Normal Events

Normal .NET events (or, as they are often called, CLR events) offer one advantage over routed events: many .NET languages have built-in support for handling CLR events. Because of this, WPF provides wrappers for routed events, making them look just like normal CLR events.* This provides the best of both worlds: you can use your favorite language's event handling syntax while taking advantage of the extra functionality offered by routed events.

 This is possible thanks to the flexible design of the CLR event mechanism. Though a standard simple behavior is associated with CLR events, CLR designers had the foresight to realize that some applications would require more sophisticated behavior. Classes are therefore free to implement events however they like. WPF reaps the benefits of this design by defining CLR events that are implemented internally as routed events.

Examples 4-1 and 4-2 arranged for the event handlers to be connected by using attributes in the markup. But we could have used the normal C# event handling syntax to attach handlers in the constructor instead. For example, you could remove the `MouseDown` and `PreviewMouseDown` attributes from the `Ellipse` in Example 4-1, and then modify the constructor from Example 4-2, as shown here in Example 4-4.

Example 4-4. Attaching event handlers in code

```
...
public Window1( ) {
    InitializeComponent( );

    myEllipse.MouseDown += MouseDownEllipse;
    myEllipse.PreviewMouseDown += PreviewMouseDownEllipse;
}
...
```

When you use these CLR event wrappers, WPF uses the routed event system on your behalf. The code in Example 4-5 is equivalent to that in Example 4-4.

Example 4-5. Attaching event handlers the long-winded way

```
...
public Window1( ) {
    InitializeComponent( );

    myEllipse.AddHandler(Ellipse.MouseDownEvent,
        new MouseButtonEventHandler(MouseDownEllipse));
    myEllipse.AddHandler(Ellipse.PreviewMouseDownEvent,
        new MouseButtonEventHandler(PreviewMouseDownEllipse));
}
...
```

---

* If you write custom elements, you should do the same. Chapter 18 describes how to do this.

Example 4-5 is more verbose and offers no benefit—we show it here only so that you can see what's going on under the covers. The style shown in Example 4-4 is preferred.

The code behind is usually the best place to attach event handlers. If your user interface has unusual and creative visuals, there's a good chance that the XAML file will effectively be owned by a graphic designer. A designer shouldn't have to know what events a developer needs to handle, or what the handler functions are called. Ideally, the designer will give elements names in the XAML and the developer will attach handlers in the code behind.

Attached Events

It is possible to define an *attached event*. This is the routed-event equivalent of an attached property: an event defined by a different class than the one from which the event will be raised. This keeps the input system open to extension. If a new kind of input device is invented, it could define new events as attached events, enabling them to be raised from any UI element.

In fact, the WPF input system already works this way. The mouse, stylus, and keyboard events examined in this chapter are just wrappers for underlying attached events defined by the Mouse, Keyboard, and Stylus classes in the System.Windows.Input namespace. This means we could change the Grid element in Example 4-1 to use the attached events defined by the Mouse class, as shown in Example 4-6.

Example 4-6. Attached event handling

```
<Grid Mouse.PreviewMouseDown="PreviewMouseDownGrid"
    Mouse.MouseDown="MouseDownGrid">
```

This would have no effect on the behavior, because the names Example 4-1 used for these events are aliases for the attached events used in this example.

Handling attached events from code looks a little different. Normal CLR events don't support this notion of attached events, so we can't use the ordinary C# event syntax like we did in Example 4-4. Instead, we have to call the AddHandler method, passing in the RoutedEvent object representing the attached event (see Example 4-7).

Example 4-7. Explicit attached event handling

```
myEllipse.AddHandler(Mouse.PreviewMouseDownEvent,
    new MouseButtonEventHandler(PreviewMouseDownEllipse));
myEllipse.AddHandler(Mouse.MouseDownEvent,
    new MouseButtonEventHandler(MouseDownEllipse));
```

Alternatively, we can use the helper functions provided by the Mouse class. Example 4-8 uses this to perform exactly the same job as the preceding two examples.

Example 4-8. Attached event handling with helper function

```
Mouse.AddPreviewMouseDownHandler(myEllipse, PreviewMouseDownEllipse);
Mouse.AddMouseDownHandler(myEllipse, MouseDownEllipse);
```

Example 4-8 is more compact than Example 4-7 because we were able to omit the explicit construction of the delegate, relying instead on C# delegate type inference. Example 4-7 cannot do this because AddHandler can attach a handler for any kind of event, so in its function signature the second parameter is of the base Delegate type. By convention, classes that define attached events usually provide corresponding helper methods like these to let you use this slightly neater style of code.

Mouse Input

Mouse input is directed to whichever element is directly under the mouse cursor. All user interface elements derive from the UIElement base class, which defines a number of mouse input events. These are listed in Table 4-1.

Table 4-1. Mouse input events

Event	Routing	Meaning
GotMouseCapture	Bubble	Element captured the mouse.
LostMouseCapture	Bubble	Element lost mouse capture.
MouseEnter	Direct	Mouse pointer moved into element.
MouseLeave	Direct	Mouse pointer moved out of element.
PreviewMouseLeftButtonDown, MouseLeftButtonDown	Tunnel, Bubble	Left mouse button pressed while pointer inside element.
PreviewMouseLeftButtonUp, MouseLeftButtonUp	Tunnel, Bubble	Left mouse button released while pointer inside element.
PreviewMouseRightButtonDown, MouseRightButtonDown	Tunnel, Bubble	Right mouse button pressed while pointer inside element.
PreviewMouseRightButtonUp, MouseRightButtonUp	Tunnel, Bubble	Right mouse button released while pointer inside element.
PreviewMouseDown, MouseDown	Tunnel, Bubble	Mouse button pressed while pointer inside element (raised for any mouse button).
PreviewMouseUp, MouseUp	Tunnel, Bubble	Mouse button released while pointer inside element (raised for any mouse button).
PreviewMouseMove, MouseMove	Tunnel, Bubble	Mouse pointer moved while pointer inside element.
PreviewMouseWheel, MouseWheel	Tunnel, Bubble	Mouse wheel moved while pointer inside element.
QueryCursor	Bubble	Mouse cursor shape to be determined while pointer inside element.

In addition to the mouse-related events, UIElement also defines a pair of properties that indicate whether the mouse pointer is currently over the element: IsMouseOver and IsMouseDirectlyOver. The distinction between these two properties is that the former will be true if the cursor is over the element in question or over any of its child elements, but the latter will be true only if the cursor is over the element in question but not one of its children.

Note that the basic set of mouse events shown in Table 4-1 does not include a Click event. This is because clicks are a higher-level concept than basic mouse input—a button can be "clicked" with the mouse, the stylus, the keyboard, or through the Windows accessibility API. Moreover, clicking doesn't necessarily correspond directly to a single mouse event—usually, the user has to press and release the mouse button while the mouse is over the control to register as a click. Accordingly, these higher-level events are provided by more specialized element types. The Control class adds a PreviewMouseDoubleClick and MouseDoubleClick event pair. Likewise, ButtonBase—the base class of Button, CheckBox, and RadioButton—goes on to add a Click event.

Mouse Input and Hit Testing

WPF always takes the shapes of your elements into account when handling mouse input. Many graphical systems just use the rectangular bounding box of elements to perform *hit testing* (i.e., testing to see which element the mouse input "hit"). WPF does not employ this shortcut, no matter what shapes your elements may be. For example, if you create a donut-shaped control and click on the hole in the middle, the click will be delivered to whatever was visible behind your control through the hole.

Occasionally it is useful to subvert the standard hit testing behavior. You might wish to create a donut-shaped control with a visible hole, but which doesn't let clicks pass through it. Alternatively, you might want to create an element that is visible to the user, but transparent to the mouse. WPF lets you do both of these things.

To achieve the first trick—transparent to the eye but opaque to the mouse—you can paint an object with a transparent brush. For example, an Ellipse with its Fill set to Transparent will be invisible to the eye, but not to the mouse. Alternatively, you can use a nontransparent brush, but make the whole element transparent by setting its Opacity property to 0. If a donut-shaped control paints such an ellipse over the hole, this enables it to receive any clicks on the hole. As far as the mouse is concerned, an element is a valid mouse target as long as it is painted with some kind of brush. The mouse doesn't even look at the level of transparency on the brush, so it treats a completely transparent brush in exactly the same way as a completely opaque brush.

 If you want a shape with a transparent fill that does not receive mouse input, simply supply no Fill at all. For example, you might want the shape to have an outline but no fill. If the Fill is null, as opposed to being a completely transparent brush, the shape will not act as an input target.

WPF supports the second trick—creating a visible object that is transparent to the mouse—with the IsHitTestVisible property, which can be applied to any element. Setting this to false ensures that the element will not receive mouse input; instead, input will be delivered to whatever is under the element. For example, suppose you had written code to make some sort of graphical embellishment follow the mouse around, such as a semi-transparent ellipse to act as a halo for the pointer. Setting IsHitTestVisible to false would ensure that this visual effect had no impact on the interactive behavior.

 If you are using 3D (as described in Chapter 17), hit testing can be an expensive process. If you don't require hit testing for your 3D content, making it invisible to hit testing can offer a useful performance boost.

Mouse State

As well as defining events, the Mouse class defines some static properties and methods that you can use to discover information about the mouse or modify its state.

The GetPosition method lets you discover the position of the mouse. As Example 4-9 shows, you must pass in a user interface element. It will return the mouse position relative to the specified element, taking into account any transformations that may be in effect.

Example 4-9. Retrieving the mouse position

```
Point positionRelativeToEllipse = Mouse.GetPosition(myEllipse);
```

The Capture method allows an element to capture the mouse. Mouse capture means that all mouse input events are sent to the capturing element, even if the mouse is currently outside of that element.* Example 4-10 captures the mouse to an ellipse when a mouse button is pressed, enabling it to track the movement of the mouse even if it moves outside of the ellipse. In fact, it will continue to receive MouseMove events even if the mouse moves outside of the window. This is useful for drag operations, as the user will expect an item being dragged to follow the mouse for as long as the mouse button is pressed. The capture is released by passing null to the Capture method.

Example 4-10. Mouse capture

```
public Window1( ) {
    InitializeComponent( );

    myEllipse.MouseDown += myEllipse_MouseDown;
    myEllipse.MouseMove += myEllipse_MouseMove;
    myEllipse.MouseUp += myEllipse_MouseUp;
}
```

---

* Capturing the mouse does not constrain its movement. It merely controls where mouse events are delivered.

Example 4-10. Mouse capture (continued)

```
void myEllipse_MouseDown(object sender, MouseButtonEventArgs e) {
    Mouse.Capture(myEllipse);
}

void myEllipse_MouseUp(object sender, MouseButtonEventArgs e) {
    Mouse.Capture(null);
}

void myEllipse_MouseMove(object sender, MouseEventArgs e) {
    Debug.WriteLine(Mouse.GetPosition(myEllipse));
}
```

The Mouse class provides a Captured property that returns the element that has currently captured the mouse; it returns null if the mouse is not captured. You can also discover which element in your application, if any, the mouse is currently over, by using the static Mouse.DirectlyOver property.

Mouse provides five properties that reflect the current button state. Each returns a MouseButtonState enumeration value, which can be either Pressed or Released. Three of these properties—LeftButton, MiddleButton, and RightButton—are self-explanatory. The other two—XButton1 and XButton2—are perhaps less obvious. These are for the extra buttons provided on some mice, typically found on the side. The locations of these so-called *extended buttons* are not wholly consistent—one of the authors' mice has these two buttons on the lefthand side, and another has one on each side. This explains the somewhat abstract property names.

Mouse also provides an OverrideCursor property that lets you set a mouse cursor to be shown throughout your whole application, as shown in Example 4-11. This overrides any element-specific mouse cursor settings. You could use this to temporarily show an hourglass cursor when performing some slow work.

Example 4-11. Temporary mouse cursor override

```
private void StartSlowWork() {
    Mouse.OverrideCursor = Cursors.AppStarting;
    ...
}

private void SlowWorkCompleted() {
    Mouse.OverrideCursor = null;
}
```

Keyboard Input

The target for mouse input is always the element currently under the mouse, or the element that has currently captured the mouse. This doesn't work so well for keyboard input—the user cannot move the keyboard, and it would be inconvenient to need to keep the mouse directly over a text field while typing. Windows therefore uses a different mechanism for directing keyboard input. At any given moment, a particular element is designated as having the *focus*, meaning that it acts as the target for keyboard input. The user sets the focus by clicking the control in question with the mouse or stylus, or by using navigation keys such as the Tab and arrow keys.

 The UIElement base class defines an IsFocused property, so in principle, any user interface element can receive the focus. However, the Focusable property determines whether this feature is enabled on any particular element. By default, this is true for controls, and false for other elements.

Table 4-2 shows the keyboard input events offered by user interface elements. Most of these items use tunnel and bubble routing for the preview and main events, respectively.

Table 4-2. Keyboard input events

Event	Routing	Meaning
PreviewGotKeyboardFocus, GotKeyboardFocus	Tunnel, Bubble	Element received the keyboard focus.
PreviewLostKeyboardFocus, LostKeyboardFocus	Tunnel, Bubble	Element lost the keyboard focus.
GotFocus	Bubble	Element received the logical focus.
LostFocus	Bubble	Element lost the logical focus.
PreviewKeyDown, KeyDown	Tunnel, Bubble	Key pressed.
PreviewKeyUp, KeyUp	Tunnel, Bubble	Key released.
PreviewTextInput, TextInput	Tunnel, Bubble	Element received text input.

Strictly speaking, the TextInput event is not caused exclusively by keyboard input. It represents textual input in a device-independent way, so this event can also be raised as a result of ink input from a stylus.

As Table 4-2 shows, WPF makes a distinction between logical focus and keyboard focus. Only one element can have the keyboard focus at any given instant. Often, the focus will not even be in your application—the user may switch to another application. However, applications typically remember where the focus was so that if the user switches back, the focus returns to the same place as before. WPF defines the *logical focus* concept to keep track of this: when an application loses the keyboard focus, the last element that had the keyboard focus retains the logical focus. When the application regains the keyboard focus, WPF ensures that the focus is put back into the element with the logical focus.

Keyboard State

The Keyboard class provides a static property called Modifiers. You can read this at any time to find out which modifier keys, such as the Alt, Shift, and Ctrl keys, are pressed. Example 4-12 shows how you might use this in code that needs to decide whether to copy or move an item according to whether the Ctrl key is pressed.

Example 4-12. Reading keyboard modifiers

```
if (Keyboard.Modifiers & ModifierKeys.Control) != 0) {
    isCopy = true;
}
```

Keyboard also provides the IsKeyDown and IsKeyUp methods, which let you query the state of any individual key, as shown in Example 4-13.

Example 4-13. Reading individual key state

```
bool homeKeyPressed = Keyboard.IsKeyDown(Key.Home);
```

You can also discover which element has the keyboard focus, using the static FocusedElement property, or set the focus into a particular element by calling the Focus method.

The state information returned by Keyboard does not represent the current state. It represents a snapshot of the state for the event currently being processed. This means that if for some reason, your application gets bogged down and gets slightly behind in processing messages, the keyboard state will remain consistent.

As an example of why this is important, consider a drag operation where the Ctrl key determines whether the operation is a move or a copy. To behave correctly, your mouse up handler needs to know the state the Ctrl key had when the mouse button was released, rather than the state that it's in now. If the user releases the Ctrl key after letting go of the mouse button, but before your application has processed the mouse up event, the user will expect a copy operation to be performed, and he will be unhappy if the application performs a move simply because your code couldn't keep up. By returning a snapshot of the keyboard state rather than its immediate state, the Keyboard class saves you from this problem.

Ink Input

The stylus used on Tablet PCs and other ink-enabled systems has its own set of events. Table 4-3 shows the ink input events offered by user interface elements.

Table 4-3. Stylus and ink events

Event	Routing	Meaning
GotStylusCapture	Bubble	Element captured stylus.
LostStylusCapture	Bubble	Element lost stylus capture.
PreviewStylusButtonDown, StylusButtonDown	Tunnel, Bubble	Stylus button pressed while over element.
PreviewStylusButtonUp, StylusButtonUp	Tunnel, Bubble	Stylus button released while over element.
PreviewStylusDown, StylusDown	Tunnel, Bubble	Stylus touched screen while over element.
PreviewStylusUp, StylusUp	Tunnel, Bubble	Stylus left screen while over element.
StylusEnter	Direct	Stylus moved into element.
StylusLeave	Direct	Stylus left element.
PreviewStylusInRange, StylusInRange	Tunnel, Bubble	Stylus moved close enough to screen to be detected.
PreviewStylusOutOfRange, StylusOutOfRange	Tunnel, Bubble	Stylus moved out of detection range.
PreviewStylusMove, StylusMove	Tunnel, Bubble	Stylus moved while over element.
PreviewStylusInAirMove, StylusInAirMove	Tunnel, Bubble	Stylus moved while over element but not in contact with screen.
PreviewStylusSystemGesture, StylusSystemGesture	Tunnel, Bubble	Stylus performed a gesture.
PreviewTextInput, TextInput	Tunnel, Bubble	Element received text input.

The Stylus class provides a static Capture method that works exactly the same as the Mouse.Capture method described earlier. It also offers Captured and DirectlyOver properties that do the same for the stylus as the matching properties of the Mouse class do for the mouse.

There is an alternative way of dealing with stylus input. Instead of handling all of these low-level events yourself, you can use WPF's high-level ink handling element, InkCanvas. Example 4-14 shows how little is required to add an ink input area to a WPF application.

Example 4-14. InkCanvas

```
<InkCanvas />
```

The `InkCanvas` accepts free-form ink input. Figure 4-3 shows the `InkCanvas` in action. (It also demonstrates that I should probably stick to using the keyboard.) `InkCanvas` makes all of the ink input available to your program through its `Strokes` property. It is possible to connect this data to the handwriting recognition APIs in Windows, but that is beyond the scope of this book.

Figure 4-3. InkCanvas

Commands

The input events we've examined give us a detailed view of user input directed at individual elements. However, it is often helpful to focus on what the user wants our application to do, rather than how she asked us to do it. WPF supports this through the *command* abstraction—a command is an action the application performs at the user's request.

The way in which a command is invoked isn't usually important. Whether the user presses Ctrl-C, selects the Edit → Copy menu item, or clicks the Copy button on the toolbar, the application's response should be the same in each case: it should copy the current selection to the clipboard. The event system we examined earlier in this chapter regards these three types of input as being unrelated, but WPF's command system lets you treat them as different expressions of the same command.

The command system lets a UI element provide a single handler for a command, reducing clutter and improving the clarity of your code. It enables a more declarative style for UI elements; by associating a `MenuItem` or `Button` with a particular command, you are making a clearer statement of the intended behavior than you would by wiring up `Click` event handlers. Example 4-15 illustrates how commands can simplify things.

Example 4-15. Commands with a menu and text box

```
<DockPanel>
  <Menu DockPanel.Dock="Top">
    <MenuItem Header="_Edit">
```

Example 4-15. Commands with a menu and text box (continued)

```
    <MenuItem Header="Cu_t"    Command="ApplicationCommands.Cut" />
    <MenuItem Header="_Copy"   Command="ApplicationCommands.Copy" />
    <MenuItem Header="_Paste"  Command="ApplicationCommands.Paste" />
  </MenuItem>
</Menu>
<ToolBarTray DockPanel.Dock="Top">
  <ToolBar>
    <Button Command="Cut" Content="Cut" />
    <Button Command="Copy" Content="Copy" />
    <Button Command="Paste" Content="Paste" />
  </ToolBar>
</ToolBarTray>

<TextBox />
</DockPanel>
```

Each menu item is associated with a command. This is all that's required to invoke these clipboard operations on the text box; we don't need any code or event handlers because the TextBox class has built-in handling for these commands. More subtly, keyboard shortcuts also work in this example: the built-in cut, copy, and paste commands are automatically associated with their standard keyboard shortcuts, so these work wherever you use a text box. WPF's command system ensures that when commands are invoked, they are delivered to the appropriate target, which in this case is the text box.

You are not obliged to use commands. You may already have classes to represent this idea in your own frameworks, and if WPF's command abstraction does not suit your needs, you can just handle the routed events offered by menu items, buttons, and toolbars instead. But for most applications, commands simplify the way your application deals with user input.

There are five concepts at the heart of the command system:

Command object

An object identifying a particular command, such as copy or paste

Input binding

An association between a particular input (e.g., Ctrl-C) and a command (e.g., Copy)

Command source

The object that invoked the command, such as a Button, or an input binding

Command target

The UI element that will be asked to execute the command—typically the control that had the keyboard focus when the command was invoked

Command binding

A declaration that a particular UI element knows how to handle a particular command

Not all of these features are explicitly visible in Example 4-15—the command bindings are buried inside the text box's implementation, and although input bindings are in use (Ctrl-C will work just fine, for example), they've been set up implicitly by WPF. To make it a bit easier to see all of the pieces, let's look at a slightly more complex example that uses all five concepts explicitly (see Example 4-16).

Example 4-16. Basic command handling

```
<!-- XAML -->
<Window ...>
  <Grid>
    <Button Command="ApplicationCommands.Properties"
            Content="_Properties"/>
  </Grid>
</Window>

// Codebehind
public partial class Window1 : Window {

    public Window1() {
        InitializeComponent();

        InputBinding ib = new InputBinding(
            ApplicationCommands.Properties,
            new KeyGesture(Key.Enter, ModifierKeys.Alt));
        this.InputBindings.Add(ib);

        CommandBinding cb = new CommandBinding(ApplicationCommands.Properties);
        cb.Executed += new ExecutedRoutedEventHandler(cb_Executed);
        this.CommandBindings.Add(cb);
    }

    void cb_Executed(object sender, ExecutedRoutedEventArgs e) {
        MessageBox.Show("Properties");
    }

}
```

This example uses the standard `ApplicationCommands.Properties` *command object*. Applications that support this command would typically open a property panel or window for the selected item. The XAML in this example associates a button with this command object; clicking the button will invoke the command. The code behind establishes an *input binding* so that the Alt-Enter shortcut may also be used to invoke the command. Our example, therefore, has two potential *command sources*: the button and the input binding. The *command target* in this particular example will be the button; this is true even if the command is invoked with a keyboard shortcut, because the button is the only element in the window capable of having the keyboard focus. However, the button doesn't know how to handle this command, so it will bubble up to the window, much like an input event. The window does know how to handle the command; it has declared this by creating a *command binding* with a handler attached to the binding's Executed event. This handler will be called when the user invokes the command.

Now that we've seen all five features in use, we'll examine each one in more detail.

Command Objects

A command object identifies a particular command. It does not know how to handle a command—as we've seen, that's the job of a command binding. Command objects are typically made available through static properties, such as ApplicationCommands.Properties.

There are several places from which you can get hold of a command object. Some controls define commands. For example, the ScrollBar control defines one for each of its actions, and makes these available in static fields, such as LineUpCommand and PageDownCommand. However, most commands are not unique to a particular control. Some correspond to application-level actions such as "new file" or "open." Others represent actions that could be implemented by several different controls. For example, TextBox and RichTextBox can both handle clipboard operations.

WPF provides a set of classes that define standard commands. These classes are shown in Table 4-4. This means you don't need to create your own command objects to represent the most common operations. Moreover, built-in controls understand many of these commands.

Table 4-4. Standard command classes

Class	Command types
ApplicationCommands	Commands common to almost all applications. Includes clipboard commands, undo and redo, and document-level operations (open, close, print, etc.).
ComponentCommands	Operations for moving through information, such as scroll up and down, move to end, and text selection.
EditingCommands	Text editing commands such as bold, italic, center, and justify.
MediaCommands	Media-playing operations such as transport (play, pause, etc.), volume control, and track selection.
NavigationCommands	Browser-like navigation commands such as Back, Forward, and Refresh.

Although the standard commands cover a lot of the common features found in many applications, applications usually have functionality of their own not addressed by the standard commands. You can use the command system for application-specific actions by defining custom commands.

Defining commands

Example 4-17 shows how to define a custom command. WPF uses object instances to establish the identity of commands—if you were to create a second command of the same name, it would not be treated as the same command. Because commands are identified by their command objects rather than their names, commands are usually put in public static fields or properties.

Example 4-17. Creating a custom command

```
...
using System.Windows.Input;

namespace MyNamespace {

    public class MyAppCommands {
    public static RoutedUICommand AddToBasketCommand;

    static MyAppCommands() {
        InputGestureCollection addToBasketInputs =
                new InputGestureCollection();
        addToBasketInputs.Add(new KeyGesture(
            Key.B, ModifierKeys.Control|ModifierKeys.Shift));
        AddToBasketCommand = new RoutedUICommand(
            "Add to Basket", "AddToBasket",
            typeof(MyAppCommands), addToBasketInputs);
        }
    }
}
```

The first RoutedUICommand constructor parameter is the name as it should appear in the user interface. In a localizable application, you would use a mechanism such as the .NET class library's ResourceManager to retrieve a localized string rather than hardcoding it. The second constructor parameter is the internal name of the command as used from code—this should match the name of the field in which the command is stored, with the command suffix removed.

As with the built-in commands, your application command doesn't do anything on its own. It's just an identifier. You will need to supply command bindings to implement the functionality. You will also typically want to associate the command with menu items or buttons.

Using commands in XAML

Example 4-18 shows a Button associated with the standard Copy command.

Example 4-18. Invoking a command with a Button

```
<Button Command="Copy">Copy</Button>
```

Because this example uses a standard command from the ApplicationCommands class, we can use this short form syntax, specifying nothing but the command name.

However, for commands not defined by the classes in Table 4-4, a little more information is required. The full syntax for a command attribute in XAML is:

```
[[xmlNamespacePrefix:]ClassName.]EventName
```

If only the event name is present, the event is presumed to be one of the standard ones. For example, Undo is shorthand for ApplicationCommands.Undo. Otherwise, you must also supply a class name and possibly a namespace prefix. The namespace prefix is required if you are using either custom commands, or commands defined by some third-party component. This is used in conjunction with a suitable XML namespace declaration to make external types available in a XAML file. (See Appendix A for more information on clr-namespace XML namespaces.)

Example 4-19 shows the use of the command-name syntax with all the parts present. The value of m:MyAppCommands.AddToBasketCommand means that the command in question is defined in the MyNamespace.MyAppCommands class in the MyLib component, and is stored in a field called AddToBasketCommand.

Example 4-19. Using a custom command in XAML

```
<Window xmlns:m="clr-namespace:MyNamespace;assembly=MyLib" ...>
    ...
    <Button Command="m:MyAppCommands.AddToBasketCommand">Add to Basket</Button>
    ...
```

Because commands represent the actions performed at the user's request, it's likely that some commands will be invoked very frequently. It is helpful to provide keyboard shortcuts for these commands in order to streamline your application for expert users. For this, we turn to input bindings.

Input Bindings

An input binding associates a particular form of *input gesture*, such as a keyboard shortcut, with a command. Two input gesture types are currently supported: a MouseGesture is a particular mouse input such as a Shift-left-click, or a right-double-click; a KeyGesture, as used in Example 4-16, is a particular keyboard shortcut. Many of the built-in commands are associated with standard gestures. For example, ApplicationCommands.Copy is associated with the standard keyboard shortcut for copying (Ctrl-C in most locales).

Although a command can be associated with a set of gestures when it is created, as Example 4-17 showed, you may wish to assign additional shortcuts for the command in the context of a particular window or element. To allow this, user interface elements have an InputBindings property. This collection contains InputBinding objects that associate input gestures with commands. These augment the default gestures associated with the command. Example 4-16 illustrated this technique—it bound the Alt-Enter shortcut to the built-in Properties command.

Occasionally, it can be useful to disable the default input bindings. A common reason for doing this is that a particular application may have a history of using certain nonstandard keyboard shortcuts, and you wish to continue this to avoid disorienting users. For example, email software has traditionally used Ctrl-F to mean "Forward," even though this is more commonly associated with "Find" in other applications.

In most cases, you can just add a new input binding to your window, and that will override the existing binding. But what if you simply want to disassociate a particular shortcut from any command? You can do this by binding it to the special `ApplicationCommands.NotACommand` object. Establishing an input binding to this pseudocommand effectively disables the binding.

Command Source

The command source is the object that was used to invoke the command. It might be a user interface element, such as a button, hyperlink, or menu item. But it can also be an input gesture. Command sources all implement the `ICommandSource` interface, as shown in Example 4-20.

Example 4-20. ICommandSource

```
public interface ICommandSource {
    ICommand Command { get; }
    object CommandParameter { get; }
    IInputElement CommandTarget { get; }
}
```

If you set the `Command` property to a command object, the source will invoke this command when clicked, or in the case of an input gesture, when the user performs the relevant gesture.

The `CommandParameter` property allows us to pass information to a command when it is invoked. For example, we could tell our hypothetical `AddToBasket` command what we would like to add to the basket, as shown in Example 4-21.

Example 4-21. Passing a command parameter

```
<MenuItem Command="m:MyAppCommands.AddToBasketCommand"
          CommandParameter="productId4823"
          Header="Add to basket" />
```

The command handler can retrieve the parameter from the `Parameter` property of the `ExecutedRoutedEventArgs`, as Example 4-22 shows. (This example is a command handler for our hypothetical `AddToBasketCommand`. The handler would be attached with a command binding as was shown in Example 4-16.)

Example 4-22. Retrieving a command parameter

```
void AddToBasketHandler(object sender, ExecutedRoutedEventArgs e) {
    string productId = (string) e.Parameter;
    ...
}
```

Command parameters are slightly less useful if you plan to associate commands with keyboard shortcuts. Input bindings are command sources, so they also offer a `CommandParameter` property, but Example 4-23 shows the problem with this.

Example 4-23. Associating a command parameter with a shortcut

```
public Window1( ) {
    InitializeComponent( );

    KeyBinding kb = new KeyBinding(MyAppCommands.AddToBasketCommand, Key.B,
                        ModifierKeys.Shift|ModifierKeys.Control);
    kb.CommandParameter = "productId4299";
    this.InputBindings.Add(kb);
}
```

This adds an input binding, associating the Ctrl-Shift-B shortcut with our `AddToBasketCommand`. The `CommandParameter` property of the binding will be passed to the command handler just as it is when the input source is a button or menu item. But of course, it will pass the same parameter every time, which limits the utility—you might just as well hardcode the value into the command handler. So in practice, you would normally use command parameters only for commands without a keyboard shortcut.

If you were building a real application with shopping-basket functionality, it would probably make more sense to use data binding rather than command parameters. If you arrange for the control that invokes the command to have its data context set to the data you require, the command handler can retrieve the `DataContext` of the command target, as Example 4-24 shows.

Example 4-24. Commands and data

```
void AddToBasketHandler(object sender, ExecutedRoutedEventArgs e) {
    FrameworkElement source = (FrameworkElement) e.Source;
    ProductInfo product = (ProductInfo) source.DataContext;
    ...
}
```

This technique has the benefit of working even when a keyboard shortcut is used. Chapter 6 explains data contexts.

The `ICommandSource` interface also offers a `CommandTarget` property. Although the interface defines this as a read-only property, all of the classes that implement this interface in WPF add a setter, enabling you to set the target explicitly. If you don't set this, the command target will typically be the element with the input focus (although, as we'll see later, there are some subtle exceptions). CommandTarget lets you ensure that a particular command source directs the command to a specific target, regardless of where the input focus may be. As an example of where you might use this, consider an application that uses a RichTextBox as part of a data template (introduced in Chapter 1)—you might use this to allow the user to add annotations to data items in a list. If you provided a set of buttons right next to the RichTextBox to invoke commands such as ToggleBold or ToggleItalic, you would want these to be applicable only to the RichTextBox they are next to. It would be confusing to the user if she clicked on one of these while the focus happened to be elsewhere in her application. By specifying a command target, you ensure that the command only ever goes where it is meant to go.

Command Bindings

For a command to be of any use, something must respond when it is invoked. Some controls automatically handle certain commands—the TextBox and RichTextBox handle the copy and paste commands for us, for example. But what if we want to provide our own logic to handle a particular command?

Command handling is slightly more involved than simply attaching a CLR event handler to a UI element. The classes in Table 4-4 define 144 commands, so if FrameworkElement defined CLR events for each distinct command, that would require 288 events once you include previews. Besides being unwieldy, this wouldn't even be a complete solution—many applications define their own custom commands as well as using standard ones.

The obvious alternative would be for the command object itself to raise events. However, each command is a singleton—there is only one ApplicationCommands.Copy object, for example. If you were able to add a handler to a command object directly, that handler would run anytime the command was invoked anywhere in your application. What if you want to handle the command only if it is executed in a particular window or within a particular element?

The CommandBinding class solves these problems. A CommandBinding object associates a specific command object with a handler function in the scope of a particular user interface element. This CommandBinding class offers PreviewExecuted and Executed events, which are raised as the command tunnels and bubbles through the UI.

Command bindings are held in the CommandBindings collection property defined by UIElement. Example 4-25 shows how to handle the ApplicationCommands.New command in the code behind for a window.

Example 4-25. Handling a command

```
public partial class Window1 : Window {
    public Window1() {
        InitializeComponent();

        CommandBinding cmdBindingNew = new CommandBinding(ApplicationCommands.New);
        cmdBindingNew.Executed += NewCommandHandler;
        CommandBindings.Add(cmdBindingNew);
    }

    void NewCommandHandler(object sender, ExecutedRoutedEventArgs e) {
        if (unsavedChanges) {
            MessageBoxResult result = MessageBox.Show(this,
                "Save changes to existing document?", "New",
                MessageBoxButton.YesNoCancel);

            if (result == MessageBoxResult.Cancel) {
                return;
            }
            if (result == MessageBoxResult.Yes) {
                SaveChanges();
            }
        }

        // Reset text box contents
        inputBox.Clear();
    }
    ...
}
```

Enabling and disabling commands

As well as supporting execution of commands, CommandBinding objects can be used to determine whether a particular command is currently enabled. The binding raises a PreviewCanExecute and CanExecute pair of events, which tunnel and bubble in the same way as the PreviewExecuted and Executed events. Example 4-26 shows how to handle this event for the system-defined Redo command.

Example 4-26. Handling QueryEnabled

```
public Window1() {
    InitializeComponent();

    CommandBinding redoCommandBinding =
        new CommandBinding(ApplicationCommands.Redo);
    redoCommandBinding.CanExecute += RedoCommandCanExecute;
    CommandBindings.Add(redoCommandBinding);
}

void RedoCommandCanExecute(object sender, CanExecuteRoutedEventArgs e) {
    e.CanExecute = myCustomUndoManager.CanRedo;
}
```

Command bindings rely on the bubbling nature of command routing—the top-level Window element is unlikely to be the target of the command, as the focus will usually belong to some child element inside the window. However, the command will bubble up to the top. This routing makes it easy to put the handling for commands in just one place. For the most part, command routing is pretty straightforward—it usually targets the element with the keyboard focus, and uses tunneling and bubbling much like normal events. However, there are certain scenarios where the behavior is a little more complex, so we will finish off with a more detailed look at how command routing works under the covers.

Command routing

All of the built-in command objects use a class called RoutedUICommand, and you will normally use this if you define application-specific commands.[*] RoutedUICommand provides the mechanism for finding the right command binding when the command is invoked. This often needs to be determined by context. Consider Example 4-27.

Example 4-27. Multiple command targets

```
<Grid>
  <Grid.RowDefinitions>
    <RowDefinition Height="Auto" />
    <RowDefinition />
    <RowDefinition />
  </Grid.RowDefinitions>

  <Menu Grid.Row="0">
    <MenuItem Header="_Edit">
      <MenuItem Header="Cu_t"   Command="ApplicationCommands.Cut" />
      <MenuItem Header="_Copy"  Command="ApplicationCommands.Copy" />
      <MenuItem Header="_Paste" Command="ApplicationCommands.Paste" />
    </MenuItem>
  </Menu>

  <TextBox Grid.Row="1" AcceptsReturn="True" />
  <ListBox Grid.Row="2">
    <TextBlock Text="One" />
    <TextBlock Text="Two" />
  </ListBox>
</Grid>
```

If the focus is in the text box when the Copy command is invoked, the text box handles the command itself as you would expect, copying the currently selected text to the clipboard. But not all controls have an obvious default Copy behavior. If the command were invoked while the focus was in the listbox, you would need to supply

---

[*] It is technically possible to provide a different class if you have special requirements. Command sources are happy to use any implementation of the ICommand interface, so you are not obliged to use the normal command routing mechanism. But most applications will use RoutedUICommand.

application-specific code in order for the command to do anything. `RoutedUICommand` supports this by providing a mechanism for identifying the command's target and locating the correct handler.

The target of the `RoutedUICommand` is determined by the way in which the command was invoked. Typically, the target will be whichever element currently has the focus, unless the command source's `CommandTarget` has been set. Figure 4-4 shows the controls and menu from Example 4-27. As you can see from the selection highlight, the `TextBox` at the top had the focus when the menu was opened, so you would expect it to be the target of the commands. This is indeed what happens, but it's not quite as straightforward as you might expect.

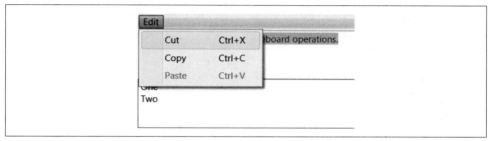

Figure 4-4. Command targets and focus

`RoutedUICommand` tries to locate a handler using a tunneling and bubbling system similar to the one used by the event system. However, command routing has an additional feature not present in normal event routing: if bubbling fails to find a handler, `RoutedUICommand` may try to retarget the command. This is designed for the scenario where commands are invoked by user interface elements such as menu or toolbar items because these present an interesting challenge.

Example 4-27 is an example of this very scenario. It has a subtle potential problem. While the menu is open, it steals the input focus away from the `TextBox`. It's unlikely that the menu item itself is the intended target for a command—it's merely the means of invoking the command. Users will expect the `Copy` menu item to copy whatever was selected in the `TextBox`, rather than copying the contents of the menu item. The menu deals with this by relinquishing the focus when the command is executed. This causes the focus to return to the `TextBox`, and so the command target is the one we expect. However, there's a problem regarding disabled commands.

A command target can choose whether the commands it supports are enabled. A `TextBox` enables copying only if there is some selected text. It enables pasting only if the item on the clipboard is text, or can be converted to text. Menus gray out disabled commands, as Figure 4-4 shows. To do this, a menu item must locate the command target. The problem is that the menu is in possession of the keyboard focus at the point at which it needs to discover whether the command is enabled; the appropriate command target is therefore not the focused item in this case.

The RoutedUICommand class relies on *focus scopes* to handle this situation. If a RoutedUICommand fails to find a command binding, it checks to see whether the initial target was in a nested focus scope. If it was, WPF finds the parent focus scope, which will typically be the window. It then retargets the command, choosing the element in the parent scope that has the *logical* focus (i.e., the last element to have the focus before the menu grabbed it). This causes a second tunneling and bubbling phase to occur. The upshot is that the command's target is whichever element had the focus before the menu was opened, or the toolbar button clicked.

If you are using menus or toolbars, you don't need to do anything to make this work, because Menu and ToolBar elements both introduce nested focus scopes automatically. However, if you want to invoke commands from other elements, such as buttons, you'll need to define the focus scope explicitly. Consider Example 4-28.

Example 4-28. Without focus scope

```
<StackPanel>
  <Button Command="ApplicationCommands.Copy"  Content="_Copy" />
  <Button Command="ApplicationCommands.Paste" Content="_Paste" />
  <TextBox />
</StackPanel>
```

This associates two buttons with commands supported by a TextBox. And yet, as Figure 4-5 shows, the buttons remain disabled even when the TextBox should be able to process at least one of the commands.

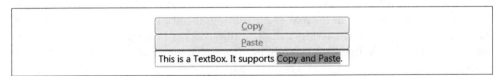

Figure 4-5. Commands disabled due to missing focus scope

We can fix this by introducing a focus scope around the buttons, as Example 4-29 shows.

Example 4-29. Focus scope

```
<StackPanel>
  <StackPanel FocusManager.IsFocusScope="True">
    <Button Command="ApplicationCommands.Copy"  Content="Copy" />
    <Button Command="ApplicationCommands.Paste" Content="Paste" />
  </StackPanel>
  <TextBox />
</StackPanel>
```

Now when the buttons attempt to locate a handler in order to choose whether they are enabled, the presence of the focus scope will cause the command routing to look for the element with the focus. If the TextBox has the logical focus, it will become the command target. As Figure 4-6 shows, this causes the buttons to reflect the availability of the commands correctly, and it means they invoke the command on the correct target when clicked.

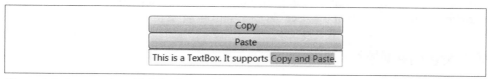

Figure 4-6. Command enabled thanks to focus scope

We don't have to use focus scopes to solve the problem in this particular example. You can use the more explicit, though slightly cumbersome, approach shown in Example 4-30.

Example 4-30. Explicit command targets

```
<StackPanel>
  <Button Command="Copy" Content="Copy"
        CommandTarget="{Binding ElementName=targetControl}" />
  <Button Command="Paste" Content="Paste"
        CommandTarget="{Binding ElementName=targetControl}" />
  <TextBox x:Name="targetControl" />
</StackPanel>
```

Here, each button specifies its command target explicitly. This makes it absolutely clear what the target will be. However, it is more verbose, so the automatic command routing is often more convenient. And even if the thought of manually specifying the command target for every item in a menu doesn't strike you as unbearable, command routing has the added benefit of working well when there are multiple potential command targets (e.g., multiple text boxes on a form) and you want the command to go to whichever one last had the focus.

Code-Based Input Handling Versus Triggers

The input handling techniques shown in this chapter all involve writing code that runs in response to some user input. If your reason for handling input is simply to provide some visible feedback to the user, be aware that writing an event handler or a custom command is likely to be overkill. It is often possible to create the visual feedback you require entirely within the user interface markup by using triggers. Triggers offer a declarative approach, where WPF does more of the work for you.

Any discussion of input handling in WPF would be incomplete without some mention of triggers. However, trigger-based input handling is radically different from the more traditional approach shown in this chapter, and it depends on aspects of WPF not yet described. Accordingly, it is dealt with later, in Chapters 8 and 9. So, for now just be aware of the two techniques and their intended usage: triggers are best suited for superficial responses, such as making a button change color when the mouse moves over it; event handling is appropriate for more substantive behavior, such as performing an action when the user clicks a button.

Where Are We?

Input is handled through events and commands, which use a routing system to allow simple uniform event handling regardless of how complex the structure of the user interface visuals might be. Input events are the lower level of these two mechanisms, reporting the exact nature of the user's input in detail. Commands allow us to work at a higher level, focusing on the actions the user would like our applications to perform, rather than the specific input mechanism used to invoke the action.

CHAPTER 5

Controls

A *control* is a user interface component that provides a particular interactive behavior. There are many familiar examples in Windows, such as text boxes, which offer text editing, and radio buttons, which let the user choose from a set of options. Controls are the building blocks of any WPF user interface.

Although controls are typically associated with a default appearance, WPF offers many ways to alter or replace a control's look. We can adjust properties to make simple alterations such as setting foreground and background colors. With controls that support the content model, we can put any mixture of graphics and text inside the control. We can even use templates to replace the whole look of the control. However, even if we replace the visuals of, say, a scroll bar, we have not changed its fundamental role as an element for performing scrolling. In WPF, it is this behavior that forms the essence of a control.

In this chapter, we will examine how to use controls to handle input, and we will explore the set of behaviors offered by the built-in controls. We will cover creation of custom controls in Chapter 18.

What Are Controls?

Whereas most popular UI frameworks offer an abstraction similar to a control, WPF takes a slightly unusual approach, in that controls are typically not directly responsible for their own appearance. Controls in WPF are all about behavior, and they defer to templates to provide their visuals. Many GUI frameworks require you to write a custom control when customizing a control's appearance, but in WPF, this is not necessary—nested content and templates offer simpler yet powerful solutions. You do not need to write a custom control unless you need interactive behavior that is different from any of the built-in controls.

Many WPF user interface elements are not controls. For example, shapes like Rectangle and Ellipse have no intrinsic behavior—they are just about appearance. Lower-level elements do not derive directly from Control. Usually they derive from FrameworkElement. See Appendix D for a detailed description of these and other important base types in WPF's class hierarchy.

Figure 5-1 shows how a control fits into a program. As you can see, the visible parts of the control are provided by its template, rather than the control itself. The control is not completely disconnected from these visuals, of course. It uses them to present information to the user. Moreover, because the visuals are all that the user can see, they will be the immediate target of any user input. This means that although visuals can be replaced, the replacement has certain responsibilities—there is a form of contract between the control and its visuals. We discuss the use of templates to replace visuals in Chapter 9.

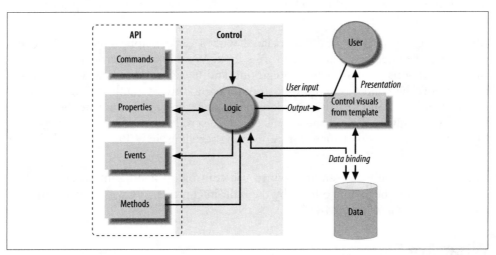

Figure 5-1. A control's relationship with its visuals and data

 You may be familiar with the Model View Controller (MVC) concept. This is a way of structuring the design of interactive systems. MVC has been interpreted in many different ways over the years, but broadly speaking, it always breaks down the design into objects representing the underlying data (the Model), objects that display that data (the View), and objects that manage input from the user and interactions between the model and the view (the Controller).

MVC is a concept that you can use at many different scales, and it is somewhat unusual to apply it at the level of an individual control. However, if you are accustomed to the MVC way of looking at things, you may find it helpful to think of data binding as a way of attaching a Model, the template as the View, and the control as the Controller.

Although the control makes itself visible to the user through its template, it makes its services available to developers mainly through an API, shown on the left side of Figure 5-1. Controls may use *commands* to represent supported operations. For example, text boxes support the cut, copy, and paste commands, among others. Controls offer *properties* to provide a means of modifying either behavior or appearance, or to manage information associated with the control, such as the text being edited in a text box. Controls raise *events* when something important happens such as receiving some form of input. Commands, properties, and events are the preferred mechanisms for exposing functionality because they can be used from markup, and they are supported by design tools. However, for features that would only ever be used from code, *methods* may be a more appropriate form of API.

WPF provides a range of built-in controls. Most of these correspond to standard Windows control types that you will already be familiar with. Note that these controls are not wrappers around old Win32 controls. Although they look like their Win32 counterparts, they are all native WPF controls.* This means that they offer all of the WPF functionality described in this book, including styling, resolution independence, data binding, composition, and fully integrated support for WPF's graphical capabilities.

Buttons

Buttons are controls that a user can click. The result of the click is up to the application developer, but there are common expectations depending on the type of button. For example, clicking on a CheckBox or RadioButton expresses a choice, and does not normally have any immediate effect beyond visually reflecting that choice. By contrast, clicking on a normal Button usually has some immediate effect.

Using buttons is straightforward. Example 5-1 shows markup for a Button element.

Example 5-1. Markup for a Button

```
<Button Click="ButtonClicked">Button</Button>
```

The contents of the element (the text "Button" in this case) are used as the button caption. An XML attribute specifies the handler for the Click event. This indicates that the code behind for the XAML must contain a method with the name specified in the markup, such as that shown in Example 5-2 (we could also attach the event handler by giving the button an x:Name and using normal C# event handling syntax).

---

* An upshot of this is that tools that know how to deal with Win32 controls will often not understand WPF controls. For example, the SDK Spy++ utility that lets you delve into the structure of a Win32 UI sees WPF applications as just one big HWND filling the entire window. (Fortunately, the UISpy SDK tool and the excellent WPF Snoop utility at *http://www.blois.us/Snoop* fills the gap left by Spy++.) However, WPF controls integrate with the accessibility features in Windows, so screen reader and automated test tools that use the automation APIs will typically continue to work.

Example 5-2. Handling a Click event

```
void ButtonClicked(object sender, RoutedEventArgs e) {
    MessageBox.Show("Button was clicked");
}
```

Alternatively, a button's `Command` property may be set, in which case the specified command will be invoked when the button is clicked. Example 5-3 shows a button that invokes the standard `ApplicationCommands.Copy` command.

Example 5-3. Invoking a command with a Button

```
<Button Command="Copy">Copy</Button>
```

Figure 5-2 shows the three button types provided by WPF, which offer the same behavior as the standard push-button, radio button, and checkbox controls with which any Windows user will be familiar. These all derive from a common base class, `ButtonBase`. This in turn derives from `ContentControl`, meaning that they all support its content model—you are not restricted to using simple text as the label for a button.

Figure 5-2. Button types

As Figure 5-3 shows, you can use whatever content you like, although you will still get the default look for the button around or alongside your chosen content. (If you wish to replace the whole appearance of the button rather than just customize its caption, you can use a control template; see Chapter 9 for more information on templates.)

Figure 5-3. Buttons with nested content

It's common practice in Windows to enable applications to be used easily from the keyboard alone. One common way of doing this is to allow buttons to be invoked by pressing the Alt key and an *access key* (also known as a *mnemonic*). The control typically provides a visual hint that you can do this by underlining the relevant key when Alt is pressed. Figure 5-4 shows an example: this button can be "clicked" by pressing Alt-B.

Figure 5-4. Button with access key

WPF supports this style of keyboard access with the `AccessText` element. You can wrap this around some text, putting an underscore in front of the letter that will act as the access key, as shown in Example 5-4. If you really want an underscore, rather than an underlined letter, just put two underscores in a row.

 Earlier Windows UI frameworks used a leading ampersand to designate an access key character. However, ampersands are awkward to use in XML because they have a special meaning. You need to use the character entity reference `&amp;` to add an ampersand to XML. Because this is rather unwieldy, WPF uses a leading underscore instead.

Example 5-4. AccessText

```
<Button Width="75">
  <AccessText>_Button</AccessText>
</Button>
```

The `AccessText` element raises the `AccessKeyPressedEvent` attached event defined by the `AccessKeyManager` class. This in turn is handled by the `Button`, which then raises a `Click` event.

In fact, you often don't need to add an `AccessText` element explicitly. If the button's content is purely text, you can put an underscore in it and WPF will automatically wrap it in an `AccessText` element for you. So in fact, Example 5-5 is all that you need. An explicit `AccessText` element is necessary only if you are exploiting the content model in order to put more than just text in a button.

Example 5-5. Access key without AccessText

```
<Button Width="75">_Button</Button>
```

 This automatic generation of an `AccessText` wrapper is available on controls for which access keys are likely to be useful.

Although the buttons derive from the common `ButtonBase` base class, `RadioButton` and `CheckBox` derive from it indirectly via the `ToggleButton` class. This defines an `IsChecked` property, indicating whether the user has checked the button. This is of type `bool?` and returns null if the button is in an indeterminate state. Figure 5-5 shows how `CheckBox` appears for each `IsChecked` value.

Figure 5-5. Checkbox IsChecked values

Radio buttons are normally used in groups in which only one button may be selected at a time. The simplest way to group radio buttons is to give them a common parent. In Example 5-6, the two radio buttons will form a group simply because they share the same parent.

Example 5-6. Grouping radio buttons by parent

```
<StackPanel>
  <RadioButton>To be</RadioButton>
  <RadioButton>Not to be</RadioButton>
</StackPanel>
```

Sometimes you may want to create multiple distinct groups with a common parent. You can do this by setting the GroupName property, as Example 5-7 shows.

Example 5-7. Grouping radio buttons by name

```
<StackPanel>
  <RadioButton GroupName="Fuel">Petrol</RadioButton>
  <RadioButton GroupName="Fuel">Diesel</RadioButton>

  <RadioButton GroupName="Induction">Unforced</RadioButton>
  <RadioButton GroupName="Induction">Mechanical supercharger</RadioButton>
  <RadioButton GroupName="Induction">Turbocharger</RadioButton>
</StackPanel>
```

This technique also works if you want to create a single group of buttons that do not share a single parent.

Slider and Scroll Controls

WPF provides controls that allow a value to be selected from a range. They all offer a similar appearance and usage: they show a track, indicating the range, and a draggable "thumb" with which the value can be adjusted. There is the Slider control, shown in Figure 5-6, and the ScrollBar control, shown in Figure 5-7. The main difference is one of convention rather than functionality—the ScrollBar control is commonly used in conjunction with some scrolling viewable area, and the Slider control is used to adjust values.

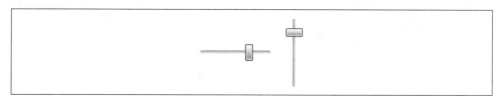

Figure 5-6. Horizontal and vertical sliders

Figure 5-7. Horizontal and vertical scroll bars

Slider and ScrollBar are very similar in use. Both controls have an Orientation property to select between vertical and horizontal modes. They both derive from a common base class, RangeBase. This provides Minimum and Maximum properties, which define the range of values the control represents, and a Value property holding the currently selected value. It also defines SmallChange and LargeChange properties, which determine by how much the Value changes when adjusted with the arrow keys, or the Page Up and Page Down keys, respectively. The LargeChange value is also used when the part of the slider track on either side of the thumb is clicked.

Whereas slider controls have a fixed-size thumb, the thumb on a scroll bar can change in size. If the scroll bar is used in conjunction with a scrollable view, the relative size of the thumb and the track is proportional to the relative size of the visible area and the total scrollable area. For example, if the thumb is about one-third the length or height of the scroll bar, this indicates that one-third of the scrollable area is currently in view.

You can control the size of a scroll bar's thumb with the ViewportSize property. The larger ViewportSize is, the larger the thumb will be. (WPF sets the ratio of the thumb and track sizes to be ViewportSize/(ViewportSize + Maximum - Minimum).)

If you want to provide a scrollable view of a larger user interface area, you would not normally use the scroll bar controls directly. It is usually easier to use the ScrollViewer control, as described in Chapter 3.

ProgressBar

The ProgressBar control indicates how much of a long-running process the application has completed. It provides the user with an indication that work is progressing, and a rough idea of how long the user will need to wait for work to complete. As Figure 5-8 shows, it is approximately rectangular, and the nearer to completion the task is, the more of the rectangle is filled in by a color bar. If an operation is likely to take much more than a second, you should consider showing a ProgressBar to let users know how long they are likely to wait.

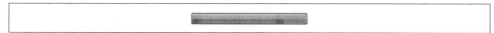

Figure 5-8. ProgressBar control

ProgressBar derives from RangeBase, the same base class as the scroll bar and slider controls discussed in the preceding section. From a developer perspective, it is very similar to these other range controls, the main difference being that it does not respond to user input—sadly, users cannot drag the progress bar indicator to the right in order to make things run faster. The progress indicator's size is based on the Value property, so it is your application's responsibility to update this as work progresses.

Text Controls

WPF provides controls for editing and displaying text. The simplest text editing control is TextBox. By default, it allows a single line of text to be edited, but by setting AcceptsReturn to true, it can edit multiple lines. It provides basic text editing facilities: selection support, system clipboard integration (cut, paste, etc.), and multilevel undo support.

Example 5-8 shows two TextBox elements, one with default settings and one in multiline mode. Figure 5-9 shows the results. (To illustrate the multiline text box, I typed "Enter" in the middle of the text before taking the screenshot.) Example 5-8 and Figure 5-9 also show PasswordBox, which is similar to TextBox, but is designed for entering passwords. As you can see, the text in the PasswordBox has been displayed as a line of identical symbols. This is common practice to prevent passwords from being visible to anyone who can see the screen. You can set the symbol with the PasswordChar property. The PasswordBox also opts out of the ability to copy its contents to the clipboard.

Example 5-8. TextBox and PasswordBox

```
<StackPanel Orientation="Horizontal">

  <TextBox Margin="5" VerticalAlignment="Center" Text="Single line textbox" />

  <TextBox AcceptsReturn="True" Margin="5" Height="50"
           VerticalScrollBarVisibility="Visible"
           VerticalAlignment="Center" Text="Multiline textbox" />

  <PasswordBox Margin="5" VerticalAlignment="Center" Password="Un5ecure" />

</StackPanel>
```

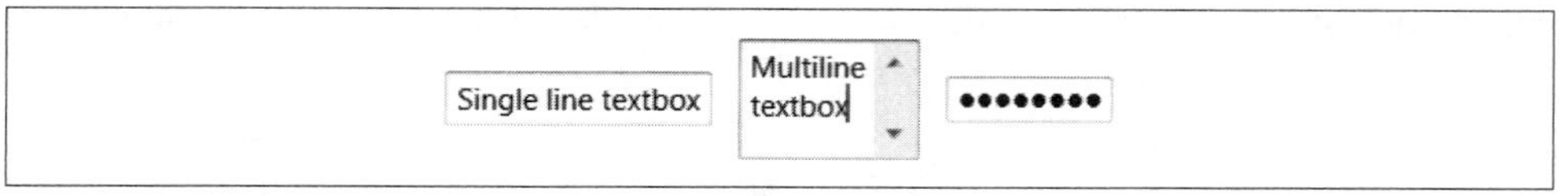

Figure 5-9. TextBox and PasswordBox

`TextBox` and `PasswordBox` support only plain text. This makes them easy to use for entering and editing simple data. `TextBox` provides a `Text` property that represents the control's contents as a `String`. `PasswordBox` has a `Password` property, also of type `String`.

The simplicity of plain text is good if you require nothing more than plain text as input. However, it is sometimes useful to allow more varied input. WPF therefore offers the `RichTextBox`. This edits a `FlowDocument`, which can contain a wide variety of content. If you want full control over the content inside a `RichTextBox`, you will need to work with the `FlowDocument` class and corresponding text object model types, which are described in Chapter 14. However, for simple formatted text support, the `RichTextBox` has some useful built-in behavior that does not require you to delve into the text object model.

`RichTextBox` supports all of the commands defined by the `EditingCommands` class. This includes support for common formatting operations such as bold, italic, and underline. These are bound to the Ctrl-B, Ctrl-I, and Ctrl-U keyboard shortcuts. Most of the editing commands have default keyboard input gestures, so you don't need to do anything special to enable keyboard access to formatting operations. You could enter the example shown in Figure 5-10 entirely with the keyboard. The control also recognizes the RTF format for data pasted from the clipboard, meaning that you can paste formatted text from Internet Explorer and Word, or syntax-colored code from Visual Studio.

Figure 5-10. RichTextBox

Both `TextBox` and `RichTextBox` offer built-in spellchecking. All you need to do is set the `SpellCheck.IsEnabled` attached property to `True`. As Figure 5-11 shows, this causes "red squiggly" underlines, similar to those in Microsoft Word, to appear under misspelled words.

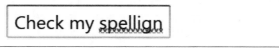

Figure 5-11. TextBox with SpellCheck.IsEnabled="True"

The dictionary used for spellchecking honors the standard `xml:lang` attribute. Example 5-9 illustrates the use of this attribute to select French. From code, setting the element's `Language` property has the same effect.

Example 5-9. Selecting a language for spellchecking

```
<TextBox xml:lang="fr-FR" SpellCheck.IsEnabled="True"
        AcceptsReturn="True" />
```

As Figure 5-12 shows, this causes correctly spelled French to be accepted. But incorrect French and correct English will be underlined.

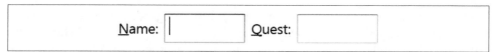

Figure 5-12. French spellchecking

Label

Some controls do not have their own built-in caption; the most widely used example is the `TextBox` control. `Label` is used to provide a caption for such controls. This might appear to be redundant, because you can achieve the same visual effect without a full control—you could just use the low-level `TextBlock` element. However, `Label` has an important focus handling responsibility.

Well-designed user interfaces should be easy to use from the keyboard. A common way of achieving this is to provide access keys. You've already seen how to add an access key to a button, using either an underscore in the text, or an explicit `AccessText` element. This is straightforward for controls with an integral caption, such as a button. The `TextBox` poses slightly more of a challenge than a `Button` when it comes to access keys. A `TextBox` does not have an intrinsic caption—the only text it displays is the text being edited. The caption is supplied by a separate element to the left of the `TextBox`, as shown in Figure 5-13.

Figure 5-13. Access key underlines

This is where the `Label` control comes in. The purpose of the `Label` control is to provide a place to put a caption with an access key. When the access key is pressed, the `Label` will redirect the focus to the relevant control, which in this case is a `TextBox`.

> Just as with a `Button`, you can denote a `Label` control's access key by preceding the letter with an underscore.

How does the `Label` know to which control it should redirect its access key? `Label` has a `Target` property, indicating the intended target of the access key. We use a binding expression to connect the label to its target. (We discuss binding expressions in detail in Chapter 6.) The expressions in Example 5-10 simply set the `Target` properties to refer to the named elements.

Example 5-10. Label controls

```
<Label Target="{Binding ElementName=nameText}">_Name:</Label>
<TextBox x:Name="nameText" Width="70" />
<Label Target="{Binding ElementName=questText}">_Quest:</Label>
<TextBox x:Name="questText" Width="70" />
```

You must supply a Target. In the absence of this property, the Label control does nothing useful. In particular, it does not choose the next element in the UI tree or the Z order. Pressing the access key for a label without a target will just cause Windows to play the alert sound, indicating that it was unable to process the input.

ToolTip

The ToolTip control allows a floating label to be displayed above some part of the user interface. It is an unusual control in that it cannot be part of the normal user interface tree—you can use it only in conjunction with another element. It becomes visible only when the mouse pointer hovers over the target element, as Figure 5-14 shows.

Figure 5-14. TextBox with ToolTip

To associate a ToolTip with its target element, you set it as the ToolTip property of its target, as shown in Example 5-11.

Example 5-11. Using ToolTip the long way

```
<TextBox Width="100">
  <TextBox.ToolTip>
    <ToolTip Content="Type something here" />
  </TextBox.ToolTip>
</TextBox>
```

In fact, you don't need to specify the ToolTip object explicitly. You can just set the ToolTip property to a string, as shown in Example 5-12.

Example 5-12. Using ToolTip the short way

```
<TextBox Width="100" ToolTip="Type something here" />
```

If you set the property to anything other than a ToolTip, WPF creates the ToolTip control for you, and sets its Content property to the value of the target element's ToolTip property. Examples 5-11 and 5-12 are therefore equivalent.

ToolTip derives from ContentControl, so its content is not restricted to simple strings—we can put anything we like in there, as shown in Example 5-13.

Example 5-13. Exploiting the content model in a tool tip

```
<TextBox Width="100">
  <TextBox.ToolTip>
    <TextBlock FontSize="25">
      <Ellipse Fill="Orange" Width="20" Height="20" />
      Plain text is <Italic>so</Italic>
      <Span FontFamily="Old English Text MT">last century</Span>
      <Ellipse Fill="Orange" Width="20" Height="20" />
    </TextBlock>
  </TextBox.ToolTip>
</TextBox>
```

Figure 5-15 shows the results. Note that the tool tip will normally close as soon as the mouse pointer moves over it. This means that although it is possible to put interactive elements such as buttons inside a tool tip, it's not typically a useful thing to do, because it's not possible to click on them. However, it is possible to subvert the auto-close behavior: you can force the tool tip to open before the user hovers over the target by setting its IsOpen property to True. This causes the tool tip to open immediately, and to remain open for as long as the target element's window has the focus. Or if you set IsOpen to True and also set StaysOpen to False, it will open immediately, and remain open until you click somewhere outside of the tool tip. In these cases, you could host interactive content inside a tool tip.

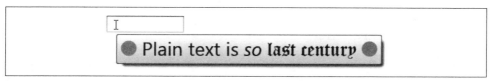

Figure 5-15. ToolTip with mixed content

 The ToolTip is shown in its own top-level window. This is useful for tool tips on elements near the edge of your window—if the tool tip is large enough that it flows outside of the main window, it won't be cropped.

GroupBox and Expander

GroupBox and Expander are very similar controls: both provide a container for arbitrary content and a place for a header on top. Figure 5-16 shows both controls. Aside from their different appearances, the main difference between these controls is that the Expander can be expanded and collapsed; the user can click on the arrow at the top left to hide and show the content. A GroupBox always shows its content.

Both controls derive from HeaderedContentControl, which in turn derives from ContentControl. So, we can place whatever content we like directly inside the control, as shown in Example 5-14.

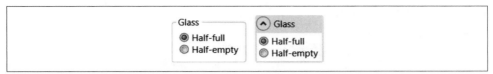

Figure 5-16. Header and Expander controls

Example 5-14. Using Header and Expander

```
<StackPanel Orientation="Horizontal">

  <GroupBox Header="Glass">
    <Border Margin="2" Background="White" Padding="3">
      <StackPanel>
        <RadioButton Content="Half-full" IsChecked="True" />
        <RadioButton Content="Half-empty" />
      </StackPanel>
    </Border>
  </GroupBox>

  <Expander Header="Glass" IsExpanded="True"
      Background="#def" VerticalAlignment="Center" MinWidth="90"
      Margin="10,0">
    <Border Margin="2" Background="White" Padding="3">
      <StackPanel>
        <RadioButton Content="Half-full" IsChecked="True" />
        <RadioButton Content="Half-empty" />
      </StackPanel>
    </Border>
  </Expander>

</StackPanel>
```

The HeaderedContentControl supports a dual form of content model: not only can the body of an Expander or GroupBox be anything you like, so can the header. Example 5-15 uses a mixture of text, video, graphics, and a control.

Example 5-15. Header with mixed content

```
<GroupBox>
  <GroupBox.Header>
    <StackPanel Orientation="Horizontal">
      <TextBlock Text="Slightly " FontStyle="Italic" VerticalAlignment="Center" />
      <MediaElement Source="C:\Users\Public\Videos\Sample Videos\Butterfly.wmv"
                Width="80" />
      <TextBlock Text=" more " VerticalAlignment="Center" />
      <Ellipse Fill="Red" Width="20" Height="60" />
      <TextBlock Text=" interesting " VerticalAlignment="Center"
             FontWeight="Bold" />
      <Button Content="_header" VerticalAlignment="Center" />
    </StackPanel>
  </GroupBox.Header>
  <TextBlock Text="Boring content" />
</GroupBox>
```

Figure 5-17 shows the results.

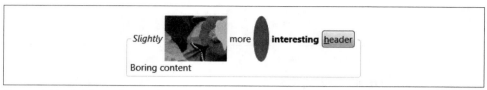

Figure 5-17. Header with mixed content

List Controls

WPF offers several controls that can present multiple items. ListBox, ComboBox, and ListView can all present a linear sequence of items. TreeView presents a hierarchy of items. The TabControl may not seem like an obvious relative of the ListBox, but it shares the basic features: it presents a sequence of items (tab pages) and lets the user choose which is the current item. All of these controls share a common base class, ItemsControl.

The simplest way to use any of these controls is to add content to their Items property. Example 5-16 shows the markup for a ComboBox with various elements added to its Items.* This example illustrates that all list controls allow any content to be used as a list item—we're not restricted to plain text. This content model makes these list controls much more powerful than their Win32 equivalents.

Example 5-16. Content in Items

```
<ComboBox>
  <Button>Click!</Button>
  <TextBlock>Hello, world</TextBlock>
  <StackPanel Orientation="Horizontal">
    <TextBlock>Ellipse:</TextBlock>
    <Ellipse Fill="Blue" Width="100" />
  </StackPanel>
</ComboBox>
```

You also can use this technique with ListBox, TabControl, and ListView. (TreeView is a little more involved, as the whole point of that control is to show a tree of items, rather than a simple list. We'll see how to do that later.) As you can see in Figure 5-18, each control presents our items in its own way. The ListBox and ComboBox generate a line in the list for each item. The ListView does something similar, although the lines it generates can display one item for each column if necessary. The TabControl puts each element in its own TabItem, in order to present it in its own tab page. (Figure 5-18 shows just the third item, but the other three are accessible through the three tab headers.)

---

* This example does not mention the Items property explicitly because children of a ComboBox element in XAML get added to its Items property automatically. Appendix A details how XAML content is assigned to properties.

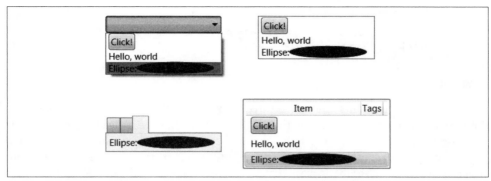

Figure 5-18. Content in list controls (left to right, top to bottom: ComboBox, ListBox, TabControl, and ListView)

All controls derived from `ItemsControl` wrap items in order to present them in a suitable way. This process is referred to as *item container generation*. Each control has a corresponding container type, such as `ComboBoxItem`, `ListBoxItem`, `TabItem`, `ListViewItem`, and `TreeViewItem`. Although the automatic container generation can be convenient, in some cases you will want a little more control. For example, the `TabControl` shown in Figure 5-18 isn't particularly useful—it has wrapped our items with tabs that have no title. To fix this, we simply provide our own `TabItem` elements instead of letting the `TabControl` generate them for us. We can then set the `Header` property in order to control the tab page caption, as Example 5-17 shows.

Example 5-17. Setting tab page headers

```
<TabControl>

  <TabItem Header="_Button">
    <Button>Click!</Button>
  </TabItem>

  <TabItem>
    <TabItem.Header>
      <TextBlock FontSize="18" FontFamily="Palatino Linotype">
        <AccessText>_Text</AccessText>
      </TextBlock>
    </TabItem.Header>

    <TextBlock>Hello, world</TextBlock>
  </TabItem>

  <TabItem>
    <TabItem.Header>
      <Ellipse Fill="Blue" Width="30" Height="20" />
    </TabItem.Header>

    <StackPanel Orientation="Horizontal">
      <TextBlock>Ellipse:</TextBlock>
```

Example 5-17. Setting tab page headers (continued)

```
    <Ellipse Fill="Blue" Width="100" />
  </StackPanel>
 </TabItem>

</TabControl>
```

This TabControl contains the same three items as before, but this time with the TabItem elements specified explicitly. In the first of these, the Header property has been set to the text "_Button". This uses the header's support of the content model: this is why we can use underscores to denote accelerators. (TabItem derives from HeaderedContentControl—the same base class as GroupBox and Expander.) The other two items exploit the content model's support for nested content—the first uses a TextBlock to control the text appearance, and the second puts an Ellipse into the header instead of text. Figure 5-19 shows the results.

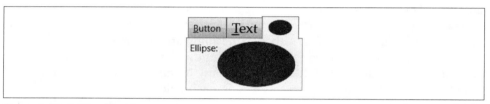

Figure 5-19. TabItem headers

Providing a fixed set of elements through the Items property makes sense for tab pages and radio buttons, where you are likely to know what elements are required when you design the user interface. But this may not be the case for combo boxes and lists. To enable you to decide what items will appear at runtime, all list controls offer an alternative means of populating the list: data binding. Instead of using Items, you can provide a data source object through the ItemsSource property, and use data templates to determine how the elements appear. These techniques are described in Chapters 6 and 8.

Regardless of whether you use a fixed set of items or a bound data source, you can always find out when the selected item changes by handling the relevant event: SelectedItemChanged for the TreeView and SelectionChanged for the other controls. You can then use either the SelectedItem property (supported by all controls), or SelectedIndex (supported by everything except TreeView) to find out which item is currently selected.

The ListView and TreeView controls have a few extra features that make them slightly different to use than the other controls in this section. So, we will now look at the differences.

List View

`ListView` derives from `ListBox`, adding support for a grid-like view. To use this, you must give the `View` property a `GridView`* object describing the columns in the list. Example 5-18 shows a simple example.

Example 5-18. Defining ListView columns

```
<ListView>
  <ListView.View>
    <GridView AllowsColumnReorder="true">
      <GridViewColumn Header="Name" />
      <GridViewColumn Header="Line Spacing" />
      <GridViewColumn Header="Sample" />
    </GridView>
  </ListView.View>
</ListView>
```

Figure 5-20 shows the result. By default, the `ListView` sets the column sizes to be as large as necessary—either as wide as the header or as wide as required by the column content. You can also specify a `Width` property if you prefer. The `Header` property supports the content model, so you are not limited to text for column headers.

 If you are using data binding, you will probably want to set the column widths manually, because virtualization makes the auto-sizing behavior slightly unpredictable. By default, a data-bound `ListView` will virtualize items (i.e., it only creates the UI elements for list rows when they become visible). This significantly improves performance for lists with large numbers of items, but it means the control cannot measure every single list item upfront—it can measure only the rows it has created. So if you use automatic sizing, the columns will be made large enough to hold the rows that are initially visible. If there are larger items further down the list and not yet in view, the columns will not be large enough to accommodate these.

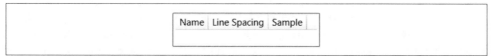

Figure 5-20. A ListView with column headers

Our `ListView` isn't very interesting yet, as it doesn't contain any items. You can add user interface elements as children, and they will be added to the `Items` property as before. However, this isn't terribly useful, because this doesn't provide a way of filling

---

* `GridView` is the only view type defined in the current version of WPF. The other view types traditionally supported by the Windows list view control can all be achieved with `ListBox`, data binding, and the `ItemsPanel` property, which is described in Chapter 9.

in each column in the list. Providing explicit ListViewItem containers doesn't help either—these don't do anything more than the basic ListBoxItem. ListView isn't designed to be used with user interface elements in its Items property: it is really intended for data binding scenarios. We will cover data binding in detail in the next two chapters, but in order to show the ListView in action, we must see a sneak preview. Example 5-19 creates a populated ListView with three columns.

Example 5-19. Populating ListView rows

```
<ListView ItemsSource="{x:Static Fonts.SystemFontFamilies}">
  <ListView.View>
    <GridView>
      <GridViewColumn Header="Name"
                      DisplayMemberBinding="{Binding Source}" />

      <GridViewColumn Header="Line Spacing"
                      DisplayMemberBinding="{Binding LineSpacing}" />

      <GridViewColumn Header="Sample">
        <GridViewColumn.CellTemplate>
          <DataTemplate>
            <TextBlock FontFamily="{Binding}" FontSize="20"
                       Text="ABCDEFGabcdefg" />
          </DataTemplate>
        </GridViewColumn.CellTemplate>
      </GridViewColumn>
    </GridView>
  </ListView.View>
</ListView>
```

The control has been data-bound to the collection of FontFamily objects returned by the static Fonts.SystemFontFamilies property. This effectively fills the control's Items collection with those FontFamily objects. The GridView then specifies three columns. The first two use the DisplayMemberBinding property to indicate what should be displayed. The binding expressions here simply extract the Source and LineSpacing properties from the FontFamily object for each row. The third column uses the alternative mechanism: the CellTemplate property. This allows you to define a DataTemplate specifying arbitrary markup to be instantiated for each row—in this case a TextBlock is used, with its FontFamily property bound to the FontFamily object for the row. This allows a preview sample of the font to be generated. Figure 5-21 shows the results.

Setting the DisplayMemberBinding property on a particular column causes the CellTemplate property to be ignored on that column, because the two are different mechanisms for controlling the same thing. DisplayMemberBinding is provided for convenience—it offers an easy way to display just a single piece of information from the source in a TextBlock without having to provide a complete template.

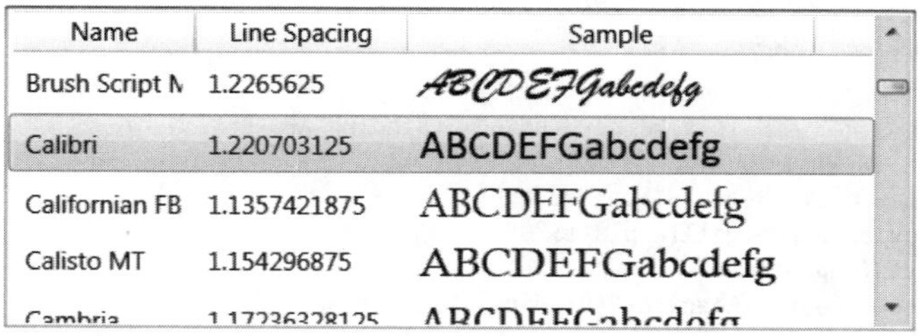

Figure 5-21. Populated ListView

Because the `CellTemplate` property lets us put arbitrary content into a column, we are not limited to displaying fixed content. As Figure 5-22 shows, we are free to create columns that contain controls such as checkboxes and text boxes.

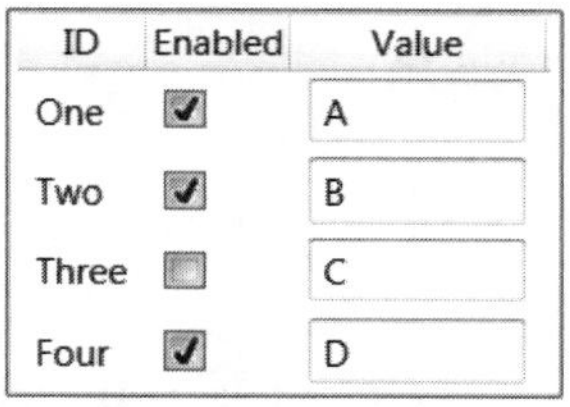

Figure 5-22. ListView with CheckBox and TextBox columns

Again, this requires the `ListView` to be bound to a data source, a technique that will be explained in the next chapter. But as a preview, the markup for Figure 5-22 is shown in Example 5-20.

Example 5-20. ListView control with controls for columns

```
<Grid HorizontalAlignment="Center" VerticalAlignment="Center">
  <Grid.Resources>
    <XmlDataProvider x:Key="src" XPath="/Root">
      <x:XData>
        <Root xmlns="">
          <Item id="One" flag="True" value="A" />
          <Item id="Two" flag="True" value="B" />
          <Item id="Three" flag="False" value="C" />
          <Item id="Four" flag="True" value="D" />
        </Root>
      </x:XData>
    </XmlDataProvider>
  </Grid.Resources>

  <ListView DataContext="{StaticResource src}"
            ItemsSource="{Binding XPath=Item}">
    <ListView.View>
```

Example 5-20. ListView control with controls for columns (continued)

```
      <GridView>
        <GridViewColumn Header="ID"
                        DisplayMemberBinding="{Binding XPath=@id}" />

        <GridViewColumn Header="Enabled">
          <GridViewColumn.CellTemplate>
            <DataTemplate>
              <CheckBox IsChecked="{Binding XPath=@flag}" />
            </DataTemplate>
          </GridViewColumn.CellTemplate>
        </GridViewColumn>

        <GridViewColumn Header="Value">
          <GridViewColumn.CellTemplate>
            <DataTemplate>
              <TextBox Text="{Binding XPath=@value}" Width="70" />
            </DataTemplate>
          </GridViewColumn.CellTemplate>
        </GridViewColumn>
      </GridView>
    </ListView.View>
  </ListView>
</Grid>
```

The data source in this case is an embedded XML data island, but any data source would work. The interesting feature of this example is the use of the CellTemplate in the GridViewColumn definitions. By providing templates with controls, we have made the ListView editable. And by the wonder of data binding, when the user makes changes with these controls, those changes will be written back into the data source. Binding expressions and data templates will be explained in detail in the next two chapters.

Tree View

The TreeView control presents a hierarchical view, instead of the simple linear sequence of items the other list controls present. This means the TreeViewItem container needs to be able to contain nested TreeViewItem elements. Example 5-21 shows how this is done.

Example 5-21. TreeView control

```
<TreeView>
  <TreeViewItem Header="First top-level item" IsExpanded="True">
    <TreeViewItem Header="Child" />
    <TreeViewItem Header="Another child" IsExpanded="True">
      <TreeViewItem Header="Grandchild" />
      <TreeViewItem Header="Grandchild 2" />
    </TreeViewItem>
    <TreeViewItem Header="A third child" />
  </TreeViewItem>
```

Example 5-21. TreeView control (continued)

```
  <TreeViewItem Header="Second top-level item">
    <TreeViewItem Header="Child a" />
    <TreeViewItem Header="Child b" />
    <TreeViewItem Header="Child c" />
  </TreeViewItem>

  <TreeViewItem IsExpanded="True">
    <TreeViewItem.Header>
      <StackPanel Orientation="Horizontal">
        <Ellipse Fill="Blue" Width="15" Height="15" />
              <TextBlock Text="Third top-level item" />
              <Ellipse Fill="Blue" Width="15" Height="15" />
          </StackPanel>
      </TreeViewItem.Header>

      <TreeViewItem Header="Child a" />
      <TreeViewItem Header="Child b" />
      <TreeViewItem Header="Child c" />
    </TreeViewItem>
</TreeView>
```

As Figure 5-23 shows, this defines a `TreeView` with nested items. Each `TreeViewItem` corresponds to a node in the tree, with the `Header` property supplying the caption for each node. This is another form of content model, allowing us to use either plain text, or, as the third of the top-level items illustrates, nested content.

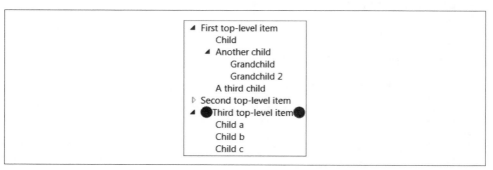

Figure 5-23. TreeView

As with the other list controls, you can discover which item is selected with the `SelectedItem` property and the `SelectedItemChanged` event. But unlike the other controls, there is no `SelectedIndex`. Such a property makes sense for controls that present a linear list of items, but it would not work so well for a tree.

Because `TreeView` derives from `ItemsControl`, it supports data binding—you can point its `ItemsSource` at a list of objects and it will generate a `TreeViewItem` for each item. Of course, the point of a tree view is to display a hierarchy of items. `TreeView` therefore supports hierarchical data binding, an extension of basic list binding that determines how child items are discovered. Hierarchical binding is described in Chapter 7.

Menus

Many windows applications provide access to their functionality through a hierarchy of menus. These are typically presented either as a main menu at the top of the window, or as a pop-up "context" menu. WPF provides two menu controls. Menu is for permanently visible menus (such as a main menu), and ContextMenu is for context menus.

 Menus in pre-WPF Windows applications are typically treated differently from other user interface elements. In Win32, menus get a distinct handle type and special event handling provisions. In Windows Forms, most visible elements derive from a Control base class, but menus do not. This means that menus tend to be somewhat inflexible—some user interface toolkits choose not to use the built-in menu handling in Windows simply to avoid the shortcomings. In WPF, menus are just normal controls, so they do not have any special features or restrictions.

Both kinds of menus are built in the same way—their contents consist of a hierarchy of MenuItem elements. Example 5-22 shows a typical example.

Example 5-22. A main menu

```
<Menu>
  <MenuItem Header="_File">
    <MenuItem Header="_New" />
    <MenuItem Header="_Open..." />
    <MenuItem Header="_Save" />
    <MenuItem Header="Sa_ve As..." />
    <Separator />
    <MenuItem Header="Page Se_tup..." />
    <MenuItem Header="_Print..." />
    <Separator />
    <MenuItem Header="E_xit" />
  </MenuItem>
  <MenuItem Header="_Edit">
    <MenuItem Header="_Undo" />
    <MenuItem Header="_Redo" />
    <Separator />
    <MenuItem Header="Cu_t" />
    <MenuItem Header="_Copy" />
    <MenuItem Header="_Paste" />
    <MenuItem Header="_Delete" />
    <Separator />
    <MenuItem Header="Select _All" />
  </MenuItem>
  <MenuItem Header="_Help">
    <MenuItem Header="Help _Topics" />
    <MenuItem Header="_About..." />
  </MenuItem>
</Menu>
```

Figure 5-24 shows the results.

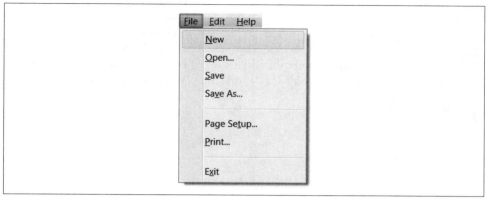

Figure 5-24. Menu

ContextMenu is used in a very similar way, although the appearance is different. The top level of a Menu appears as a horizontal bar, which you would typically put at the top of a window, but context menus do not have this bar, their top level consisting of a pop up. This means that a context menu needs a UI element from which to launch this pop up. You attach a context menu to an element by setting that element's ContextMenu property. Example 5-23 shows a Grid element with a ContextMenu.

Example 5-23. Grid with ContextMenu

```
<Grid Background="Transparent">
  <Grid.ContextMenu>
    <ContextMenu>
      <MenuItem Header="Foo" />
      <MenuItem Header="Bar" />
    </ContextMenu>
  </Grid.ContextMenu>
...
</Grid>
```

With this context menu in place, a right-click anywhere on the grid will bring up the context menu. (The grid's Background property has been set to ensure that this will work—if the Background has its default null value, the grid will effectively be invisible to the mouse unless the mouse is over one of the grid's children. Using a Transparent brush makes the grid visible to the mouse, without making it visually opaque.) Figure 5-25 shows the context menu in action.

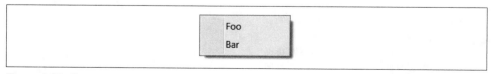

Figure 5-25. Context menu

Each `MenuItem` has a `Header` property. For children of a `Menu`, the header determines the label shown on the menu bar. For a `MenuItem` nested either in a `ContextMenu` or inside another `MenuItem`, the `Header` contains the content for that menu line. The `Header` property supports the content model, so it allows either plain text with optional underscores to denote access keys, as shown in Example 5-22, or nested content. Example 5-24 shows a modified version of one of the menu items, exploiting the ability to add structure in order to add some graphics into the menu.

Example 5-24. Nesting content inside MenuItem.Header

```
<MenuItem>
  <MenuItem.Header>
    <StackPanel Orientation="Horizontal">
      <AccessText>_New...</AccessText>
      <Ellipse Fill="Blue" Width="40" Height="15" Margin="10,0" />
    </StackPanel>
  </MenuItem.Header>
</MenuItem>
```

Note that it's now necessary to supply an `AccessText` element if we want an access key. With plain-text headers, this element was generated for us automatically, but once nested content is in use, we need to define it explicitly. Figure 5-26 shows the results.

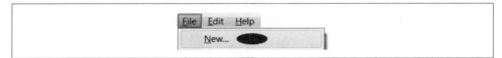

Figure 5-26. Menu with nested content

The menu in Example 5-22 doesn't do anything useful, because there are no event handlers or commands specified. There are two ways in which you can hook a `MenuItem` up to some code. You can handle its `Click` event in much the same way that you would handle a button click. Alternatively, you can set the `Command` property on the `MenuItem`, as was described in Chapter 4.

Example 5-25 shows a modified version of the Edit submenu with menu items associated with the relevant standard commands. As long as the focus is in a control such as `TextBox` or `RichTextBox` that understands these standard commands, the commands will be handled without needing any explicit coding. If the focus is not in such a control, the commands will simply bubble up. For example, the command can be handled by a command binding registered for the window. If nothing handles the command, it will be ignored.

Example 5-25. MenuItems with commands

```
<MenuItem Header="_Edit">
    <MenuItem Header="_Undo" Command="Undo" />
    <MenuItem Header="_Redo" Command="Redo"/>
```

Example 5-25. MenuItems with commands (continued)

```
    <Separator />
    <MenuItem Header="Cu_t" Command="Cut" />
    <MenuItem Header="_Copy" Command="Copy" />
    <MenuItem Header="_Paste" Command="Paste" />
    <MenuItem Header="_Delete" Command="Delete" />
    <Separator />
    <MenuItem Header="Select _All" Command="SelectAll" />
</MenuItem>
```

If you were to remove the Header properties from Example 5-25, you would find that the menu items all still appear with the correct header text for the commands. This is because RoutedUICommand knows the display name for the command it represents, and MenuItem is able to extract the name. However, there is one problem with taking advantage of this: you will lose the accelerators. RoutedUICommand cannot prescribe a particular access key, because access keys should be unique within the scope of a particular menu. If a menu assigns the same access key to more than one item in a menu, ambiguity ensues, and pressing the access key will simply highlight the menu item rather than selecting it, with further key presses alternating between the choices. This significantly reduces how effectively access keys streamline user input.

To guarantee a unique key for each menu item, a developer must coordinate access keys with knowledge of which commands are used in which menus. So, the appropriate place to assign access keys is the menu, not the command. Imagine you're writing a custom command of your own—how would you choose which access key to use? You would be able to choose only if you knew what other commands will be sharing a menu with your command. Now consider WPF's built-in commands—these will be used in all sorts of contexts in any number of applications, and because there are considerably more built-in commands than there are keys on the keyboard, Microsoft cannot possibly assign access keys in a way guaranteed to prevent ambiguity. Commands therefore don't get to specify the access key. So, in practice, you will normally want to define the Header property for menu items associated with commands, even though it may appear to be optional.

Menu items often have a shortcut key as well as an access key. The access key works only when the menu is open. A shortcut such as Ctrl-S (for save) works whether the menu is open or not. Of course, the menu isn't responsible for binding the control shortcut to the key gesture—as we saw in Chapter 4, we associate inputs with commands using input bindings. However, menus conventionally display shortcuts in order to help users discover them.

If a menu item's Command has an associated shortcut key, WPF will automatically display this in the menu. Example 5-25 uses standard clipboard and undo/redo commands, and these all have default shortcuts, so the menu reflects this, as you can see in Figure 5-27.

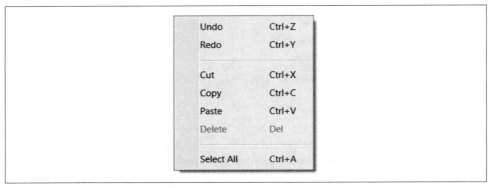

Figure 5-27. Automatic shortcut display

If, for some reason, you choose not to use WPF's command system—maybe you have an existing application framework that provides its own command abstraction—you can still display a shortcut. `MenuItem` provides an `InputGestureText` property that lets you choose the text that appears in the normal place for such shortcuts. Example 5-26 shows a menu item with both a shortcut and an access key.

Example 5-26. Menu item with shortcut and access key

```
<MenuItem Header="_New" InputGestureText="Ctrl+N" />
```

`Menu` and `ContextMenu` both derive indirectly from `ItemsControl`, the same base class as all of the list controls. This means that you can use the `ItemsSource` property to populate a menu using hierarchical data binding rather than fixed content. This could be useful if you want to make your menu structure reconfigurable. See Chapter 6 for more details on how to use data binding.

Toolbars

Most Windows applications offer toolbars as well as menus. Toolbars provide faster access for frequently used operations, because the user does not need to navigate through the menu system—the toolbar is always visible on-screen. Figure 5-28 shows a pair of typical toolbars.

Figure 5-28. Application with toolbars

WPF supports toolbars through the ToolBarTray and ToolBar controls. ToolBarTray provides a container into which you can add multiple ToolBar elements. Example 5-27 shows a simple example with two toolbars; this is the markup for the toolbars in Figure 5-28.

Example 5-27. ToolBarTray and ToolBar

```
<ToolBarTray>
  <ToolBar>
    <Button>
      <Canvas Width="16" Height="16" SnapsToDevicePixels="True">
        <Polygon Stroke="Black" StrokeThickness="0.5"
                 Points="2.5,1.5 9.5,1.5 12.5,4.5 12.5,15 2.5,15">
          <Polygon.Fill>
            <LinearGradientBrush StartPoint="1,1" EndPoint="0.2,0.7">
              <GradientStop Offset="0" Color="#AAA" />
              <GradientStop Offset="1" Color="White" />
            </LinearGradientBrush>
          </Polygon.Fill>
        </Polygon>
        <Polygon Stroke="Black" Fill="DarkGray" StrokeThickness="0.5"
                 StrokeLineJoin="Bevel"
                 Points="9.5,1.5 9.5,4.5 12.5,4.5" />
      </Canvas>
    </Button>

    <Button>
      <Canvas Width="16" Height="16" >
        <Polygon Stroke="Black" StrokeThickness="0.5" Fill="Khaki"
                 SnapsToDevicePixels="True"
                 Points="0.5,14.5 0.5,4.5 1.5,3.5 6.5,3.5 8.5,5.5
                         12.5,5.5 12.5,14.5" />
        <Polygon Stroke="Black" SnapsToDevicePixels="True"
                 StrokeThickness="0.5"
                 Points="1.5,14.5 4.5,7.5 15.5,7.5 12.5,14.5" >
          <Polygon.Fill>
            <LinearGradientBrush StartPoint="0.25,0" EndPoint="0.5,1">
              <GradientStop Offset="0" Color="#FF4" />
              <GradientStop Offset="1" Color="#CA7" />
            </LinearGradientBrush>
          </Polygon.Fill>
        </Polygon>
        <Path    Stroke="Blue" StrokeThickness="1"
                 Data="M 8,2 C 9,1 12,1 14,3"  />
        <Polygon Fill="Blue" Points="15,1 15.5,4.5 12,4" />
      </Canvas>
    </Button>
  </ToolBar>
  <ToolBar>
    <Button>Second toolbar</Button>
    <CheckBox IsChecked="True">Choice</CheckBox>
  </ToolBar>
</ToolBarTray>
```

This contains just two toolbars, with a couple of buttons each. In this example, we have used some simple vector graphics to draw the usual New and Open icons. The graphical elements used are explained in more detail in Chapter 13. In practice, you would rarely put graphics inline like this—you would usually expect drawings to be resources that are simply referred to by the buttons in the toolbar. See Chapter 12 for more details. The second toolbar just uses the default visuals for a Button and a CheckBox. As you can see, these take on a flat, plain appearance when they appear in a toolbar.

Because toolbar buttons are just normal Button or CheckBox elements with specialized visuals, there is nothing particularly special about their behavior. Toolbars just provide a particular way of arranging and presenting controls. You can also add other elements such as a TextBox or ComboBox. These will just be arranged on the toolbar along with the buttons.

GridSplitter

GridSplitter lets you offer the user a way to adjust the layout of your application, by changing the size of a column or row in a grid. This lets you provide a similar feature to Windows Explorer, where if you turn on the folder view, or one of the other panels that can appear on the lefthand side of a window, you can change the amount of space available to the panel by dragging on the vertical bar between the panel and the main area. You can use GridSplitter only to rearrange a Grid panel (see Example 5-28).

Example 5-28. GridSplitter

```
<Grid Height="100" Width="400">
  <Grid.ColumnDefinitions>
    <ColumnDefinition Width="1*" />
    <ColumnDefinition Width="6" />
    <ColumnDefinition Width="2*" />
  </Grid.ColumnDefinitions>

  <Ellipse Grid.Column="0" Fill="Red" />
  <GridSplitter Grid.Column="1" HorizontalAlignment="Stretch" />
  <Ellipse Grid.Column="2" Fill="Blue" />
</Grid>
```

This puts a GridSplitter into the middle of the three columns. As Figure 5-29 shows, if the user moves the mouse over the GridSplitter, the mouse pointer changes to the horizontal resize arrow. Dragging the slider resizes the columns on either side.

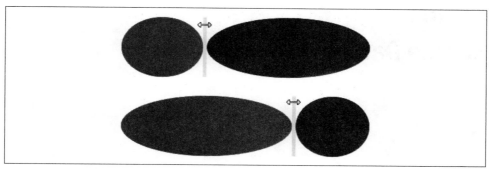

Figure 5-29. GridSplitter

Where Are We?

Controls are the building blocks of applications. They represent the features of the interface with which the user interacts. Controls provide behavior, and they rely on styling and templates to present an appearance. WPF provides a set of built-in controls based on the controls commonly used in Windows applications. WPF significantly reduces the need for custom controls. In part, this is enabled by content models, but as we will see in Chapters 8 and 9, the extent to which built-in controls can be customized means that custom controls are necessary only in the most specialized of circumstances.

CHAPTER 6
Simple Data Binding

The purpose of most applications is to display data to users and, often, to let them edit that data. Your job as the application developer is to bring the data in from a variety of sources that expose their data in object, hierarchical, or relational format. Regardless of where the data comes from or the format it's in, there are several things that you'll most likely need to do with the data, including showing it, converting it, sorting it, filtering it, grouping it, relating one part of it to another part, and, more often than not, editing it. Without some kind of engine for shuttling data back and forth between data sources and controls, you're going to be writing a great deal of code. With WPF's data binding engine, you get more features with less code, which is always a nice place to be.

Without Data Binding

Consider a very simple application for editing a single person's name and age, as shown in Figure 6-1.

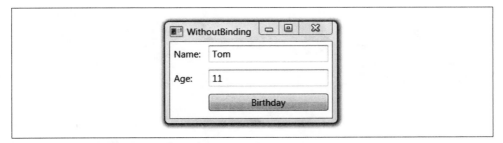

Figure 6-1. An exceedingly simple application

Figure 6-1 can be implemented with some simple XAML, as shown in Example 6-1.

Example 6-1. A simple Person editor layout

```
<!-- Window1.xaml -->
<Window ...>
  <Grid>
    ...
    <TextBlock ...>Name:</TextBlock>
    <TextBox Name="nameTextBox" ... />
    <TextBlock ...>Age:</TextBlock>
    <TextBox Name="ageTextBox" ... />
    <Button Name="birthdayButton" ...>Birthday</Button>
  </Grid>
</Window>
```

We can represent the data to be shown in our simple application in a simple class (see Example 6-2).

Example 6-2. A simple Person class

```
public class Person {
  string name;
  public string Name {
    get { return this.name; }
    set { this.name = value; }
  }

  int age;
  public int Age {
    get { return this.age; }
    set { this.age = value; }
  }

  public Person() {}
  public Person(string name, int age) {
    this.name = name;
    this.age = age;
  }
}
```

With the Person class, Example 6-3 shows a naïve implementation of the UI of our application.

Example 6-3. Naïve Person editor code

```
// Window1.xaml.cs
...
public class Person {...}

public partial class Window1 : Window {
  Person person = new Person("Tom", 11);
```

Example 6-3. Naïve Person editor code (continued)

```
public Window1( ) {
  InitializeComponent( );

  // Fill initial person fields
  this.nameTextBox.Text = person.Name;
  this.ageTextBox.Text = person.Age.ToString( );

  // Handle the birthday button click event
  this.birthdayButton.Click += birthdayButton_Click;
}

void birthdayButton_Click(object sender, RoutedEventArgs e) {
  ++person.Age;
  MessageBox.Show(
    string.Format(
      "Happy Birthday, {0}, age {1}!",
      person.Name,
      person.Age),
    "Birthday");
}
}
```

The code in Example 6-3 creates a Person object and initializes the text boxes with the Person object properties. When the Birthday button is pressed, the Person object's Age property is incremented and the updated Person data is shown in a message box, as shown in Figure 6-2.

Figure 6-2. Our simple application is too simple

Our simple application implementation is, in fact, too simple. The change in the Person Age property does show up in the message box, but it does not show up in the main window. One way to keep the application's UI up-to-date is to write code that, whenever a Person object is updated, manually updates the UI at the same time:

```
void birthdayButton_Click(object sender, RoutedEventArgs e) {
  ++person.Age;
```

```
        // Manually update the UI
        this.ageTextBox.Text = person.Age.ToString( );

        MessageBox.Show(
          string.Format(
            "Happy Birthday, {0}, age {1}!",
            person.Name,
            person.Age),
          "Birthday");
    }
```

With a single line of code, we've "fixed" our application. This is a seductive and popular road, but it does not scale as the application gets more complicated and requires more of these "single" lines of code. To get beyond the simplest of applications, we'll need something better.

Object Changes

A more robust way for the UI to track object changes is for the object to raise an event when a property changes. The right way for an object to do this is with an implementation of the INotifyPropertyChanged interface, as shown in Example 6-4.

Example 6-4. A class that supports property change notification

```
using System.ComponentModel; // INotifyPropertyChanged
...
public class Person : INotifyPropertyChanged {
  // INotifyPropertyChanged Members
  public event PropertyChangedEventHandler PropertyChanged;

  protected void Notify(string propName) {
    if( this.PropertyChanged != null ) {
      PropertyChanged(this, new PropertyChangedEventArgs(propName));
    }
  }

  string name;
  public string Name {
    get { return this.name; }
    set {
      if( this.name == value ) { return; }
      this.name = value;
      Notify("Name");
    }
  }

  int age;
  public int Age {
    get { return this.age; }
    set {
      if(this.age == value ) { return; }
      this.age = value;
```

Example 6-4. A class that supports property change notification (continued)

```
      Notify("Age");
    }
  }

  public Person() {}
  public Person(string name, int age) {
    this.name = name;
    this.age = age;
  }
}
```

In Example 6-4, when either of the Person properties changes (due to the implementation of the Birthday button Click handler), a Person object raises the PropertyChanged event. We could use this event to keep the UI synchronized with the Person properties, as shown in Example 6-5.

Example 6-5. Simple Person editor code

```
// Window1.xaml.cs
...
public class Person : INotifyPropertyChanged {...}

public partial class Window1 : Window {
  Person person = new Person("Tom", 11);

  public Window1() {
    InitializeComponent();

    // Fill initial person fields
    this.nameTextBox.Text = person.Name;
    this.ageTextBox.Text = person.Age.ToString();

    // Watch for changes in Tom's properties
    person.PropertyChanged += person_PropertyChanged;

    // Handle the birthday button click event
    this.birthdayButton.Click += birthdayButton_Click;
  }

  void person_PropertyChanged(
    object sender,
    PropertyChangedEventArgs e) {

    switch( e.PropertyName ) {
      case "Name":
      this.nameTextBox.Text = person.Name;
      break;

      case "Age":
      this.ageTextBox.Text = person.Age.ToString();
      break;
    }
```

Example 6-5. Simple Person editor code (continued)

```
    }

    void birthdayButton_Click(object sender, RoutedEventArgs e) {
        ++person.Age; // person_PropertyChanged will update ageTextBox
        MessageBox.Show(
            string.Format(
                "Happy Birthday, {0}, age {1}!",
                person.Name,
                person.Age),
            "Birthday");
    }
}
```

Example 6-5 shows an example of a single instance of the Person class that's created when the main window first comes into existence, initializing the name and age text boxes with the initial person values and then subscribing to the property change event to keep the text boxes up-to-date as the Person object changes. With this code in place, the Birthday button Click event handler doesn't have to manually update the text boxes when it updates Tom's age; instead, updating the Age property causes a cascade of events that keeps the age text box up-to-date with the Person object's changes, as shown in Figure 6-3.

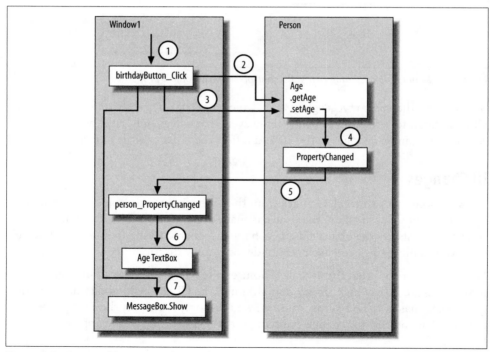

Figure 6-3. Keeping the UI up-to-date with changes in the object

The steps are as follows:

1. User clicks on button, which causes Click event to be raised.
2. Click handler gets the age (11) from the Person object.
3. Click handler sets the age (12) on the Person object.
4. Person Age property setter raises the PropertyChanged event.
5. PropertyChanged event is routed to event handler in the UI code.
6. UI code updates the age TextBox from "11" to "12."
7. Button click event handler displays a message box showing the new age ("12").

By the time the message box is shown with Tom's new age, the age text box in the window has already been updated, as shown in Figure 6-4.

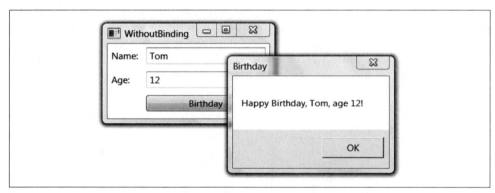

Figure 6-4. Manually populating two WPF controls with two object properties

By handling the PropertyChanged event, we ensure that when the data changes, the UI is updated to reflect that change. However, that solves only half the problem; we still need to handle changes in the UI and reflect them back to the object.

UI Changes

Without some way to track changes from the UI back into the object, we could easily end up with a case where the user has made some change (like changing the person's name), shows the object's data (as happens when clicking the Birthday button), and expects the change to have been made, only to be disappointed with Figure 6-5.

Notice in Figure 6-5 that the Name is "Thomsen Frederick" in the window, but "Tom" in the message box, which shows that although the UI has been updated, the underlying object has not. To fix this problem, we need only watch for the Text property in our TextBox object to change, updating the Person object as appropriate (see Example 6-6).

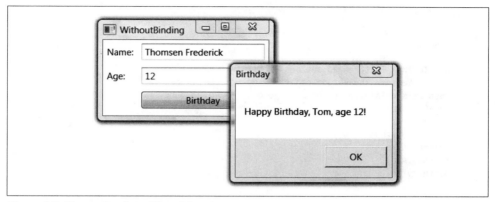

Figure 6-5. The need to keep UI and data in sync

Example 6-6. Tracking changes in the UI

```
public partial class Window1 : Window {
  Person person = new Person("Tom", 11);

  public Window1( ) {
    InitializeComponent( );

    // Fill initial person fields
    this.nameTextBox.Text = person.Name;
    this.ageTextBox.Text = person.Age.ToString( );

    // Watch for changes in Tom's properties
    person.PropertyChanged += person_PropertyChanged;

    // Watch for changes in the controls
    this.nameTextBox.TextChanged += nameTextBox_TextChanged;
    this.ageTextBox.TextChanged += ageTextBox_TextChanged;

    // Handle the birthday button click event
    this.birthdayButton.Click += birthdayButton_Click;
  }

  ...

  void nameTextBox_TextChanged(object sender, TextChangedEventArgs e) {
    person.Name = nameTextBox.Text;
  }

  void ageTextBox_TextChanged(object sender, TextChangedEventArgs e) {
    int age = 0;
    if( int.TryParse(ageTextBox.Text, out age) ) {
      person.Age = age;
    }
  }
}
```

Example 6-6. Tracking changes in the UI (continued)

```
void birthdayButton_Click(object sender, RoutedEventArgs e) {
  ++person.Age;

  // nameTextBox_TextChanged and ageTextBox_TextChanged
  // will make sure the Person object is up-to-date
  // when it's displayed in the message box
  MessageBox.Show(
    string.Format(
      "Happy Birthday, {0}, age {1}!",
      person.Name,
      person.Age),
    "Birthday");
  }
}
```

Figure 6-6 shows the name changes in the UI correctly propagating to the Person object.

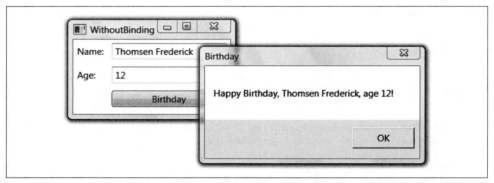

Figure 6-6. Manually keeping properties and controls in sync

Now, regardless of where the data changes, both the Person object and the UI showing the Person object are kept synchronized. And although we've gotten the functionality we wanted, we had to write quite a bit of code to make it happen:

- Window1 constructor code to set controls to initial values, converting data to strings as appropriate
- Window1 constructor code to hook up the PropertyChanged event to track the Person object's property changes
- PropertyChanged event handler to grab the updated data from the Person object, converting data to strings as appropriate
- Window1 constructor code to hook up the TextBox object's TextChanged event to track the UI changes
- TextChanged event handlers to push the updated TextBox data into the Person object, converting the data as appropriate

This code allows us to write our Birthday button Event handler safe in the knowledge that all changes are synchronized when we display the message box. However, it's easy to imagine how this code could quickly get out of hand as the number of object properties or the number of objects we're managing grows. Plus, this seems like such a common thing to want to do that someone must have already provided a simpler way to do this. And in fact, someone has; it's called data binding.

Data Binding

Our manual code to keep the data and the UI synchronized has the effect of manually binding together two pairs of properties, each pair composed of one property on the Person object and the Text property on a TextBox object. In WPF, *data binding* is the act of registering two properties with the data binding engine and letting the engine keep them synchronized, converting types as appropriate, as shown in Figure 6-7.

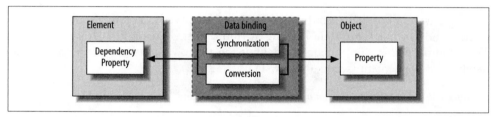

Figure 6-7. The synchronization and conversion duties of data binding

Bindings

We can register two properties to be kept in sync by the data binding engine using an instance of a Binding object, as shown in Example 6-7.

Example 6-7. Binding a UI target property to a data source property

```
<TextBox ...>
  <TextBox.Text>
    <Binding Path="Age" />
  </TextBox.Text>
</TextBox>
```

In Example 6-7, we've used the property element syntax introduced in Chapter 1 to create an instance of the Binding markup extension class and initialize its Path property to Age. This establishes the synchronization relationship with the Text property of the TextBox object. Using the binding markup extension syntax (also introduced in Chapter 1), we can shorten Example 6-7 to the code snippet shown in Example 6-8.

Example 6-8. The shortcut binding syntax

```
<TextBox Text="{Binding Path=Age}" />
```

As an even shorter cut, you can drop the Path designation altogether and the Binding will still know what you mean (see Example 6-9).

Example 6-9. The shortest cut binding syntax

```
<TextBox Text="{Binding Age}" />
```

I prefer to be more explicit, so I won't use the syntax in Example 6-9, but I won't judge if you like it. As an example of something more exotic, Example 6-10 sets more than one attribute of a binding.

Example 6-10. A more full-featured binding example, longhand

```
<TextBox ...>
  <TextBox.Foreground>
    <Binding Path="Age" Mode="OneWay" Source="{StaticResource Tom}"
             Converter="{StaticResource ageConverter}" />
  </TextBox.Foreground>
</TextBox>
```

We'll see what all of these Binding properties mean directly. You might also be interested in how to pack multiple binding attribute settings using the shortcut syntax. To accomplish this, simply comma-delimit the name-value pairs, using spaces and newlines as convenient (see Example 6-11).

Example 6-11. A more full-featured binding example, shorthand

```
<TextBox ...
  Foreground="{Binding Path=Age, Mode=OneWay, Source={StaticResource Tom},
                Converter={StaticResource ageConverter}}" />
```

Table 6-1 shows the list of available properties on a Binding object, many of which you'll see described in more detail later in this chapter.

Table 6-1. The Binding class's properties

Property	Meaning
BindsDirectlyToSource	Defaults to False. If set to True, indicates a binding to the parameters of a DataSourceProvider (like the ObjectDataProvider discussed later in this chapter), instead of to the data returned from the provider. See the BindingToMethod sample included with this book for an example.
Converter	An implementation of IValueConverter to use to convert values back and forth from the data source. Discussed later in this chapter.
ConverterCulture	Optional parameter passed to the IValueConverter methods indicating the culture to use during conversion.
ConverterParameter	Optional application-specific parameter passed to the IValueConverter methods during conversion.
ElementName	Used when the source of the data is a UI element as well as the target. Discussed later in this chapter.

Table 6-1. The Binding class's properties (continued)

Property	Meaning
FallbackValue	The value to use in case retrieving the value from the data source has failed, one of the parts of a multipart path is null, or the binding is asynchronous and the value hasn't yet been retrieved.
IsAsync	Defaults to False. When set to True, gets and sets the data on the source asynchronously. Uses the FallbackValue while the data is being retrieved.
Mode	One of the BindingMode values: TwoWay, OneWay, OneTime, OneWayToSource, or Default.
NotifyOnSourceUpdated	Defaults to False. Whether to raise the SourceUpdated event or not.
NotifyOnTargetUpdated	Defaults to False. Whether to raise the TargetUpdated event or not.
NotifyOnValidationError	Defaults to False. Whether to raise the Validation.Error attached event or not. Discussed later in this chapter.
Path	Path to the data of the data source object. Use the XPath property for XML data.
RelativeSource	Used to navigate to the data source relative to the target. Discussed later in this chapter.
Source	A reference to the data source to be used instead of the default data context.
UpdateSourceExceptionFilter	Optional delegate to handle errors raised while updating the data source. Valid only if accompanied by an ErrorValidationRule (discussed later in this chapter).
UpdateSourceTrigger	Determines when the data source is updated from the UI target. Must be one of the UpdateSourceTrigger values: PropertyChanged, LostFocus, Explicit, or Default. Discussed in Chapter 7.
ValidationRules	Zero or more derivations of the ValidationRule class. Discussed later in this chapter.
XPath	XPath to the data on the XML data source object. Use the Path property for non-XML data. Discussed in Chapter 7.

The Binding class has all kinds of interesting facilities for managing the binding between two properties, but the one that you'll most often set is the Path property.[*] For most cases, you can think of the Path as the name of the property on the object serving as the data source. So, the binding statement in Example 6-8 is creating a binding between the Text property of the TextBox and the Name property of some object to be named later, as shown in Figure 6-8.

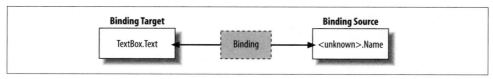

Figure 6-8. Binding targets and sources

---

[*] Or XPath property, if your data is XML, which is discussed in Chapter 7.

In this binding, the TextBox control is the *binding target*, as it acts as a consumer of changes to the *binding source*, which is the object that provides the data. The binding target can be any WPF element, but you're only allowed to bind to the element's dependency properties (described in Chapter 1).

On the other hand, you can bind to any public CLR property or dependency property on the binding source object.* The binding source is not named in this example specifically so that we can have some freedom as to where it comes from at runtime and so that it's easier to bind multiple controls to the same object (like our name and age text box controls bound to the same Person object).

Commonly, the binding source data comes from a data context.

Implicit Data Source

A *data context* is a place for bindings to look for the data source if they don't have any other special instructions (which we'll discuss later). In WPF, every FrameworkElement and every FrameworkContentElement has a DataContext property. The DataContext property is of type Object, so you can plug anything you like into it (e.g., string, Person, List<Person>, etc.). When looking for an object to use as the binding source, the binding object logically traverses up the tree from where it's defined, looking for a DataContext property that has been set.†

This traversal is handy because it means that any two controls with a common logical parent can bind to the same data source. For example, both of our text box controls are children of the grid, and they each search for a data context, as shown in Figure 6-9.

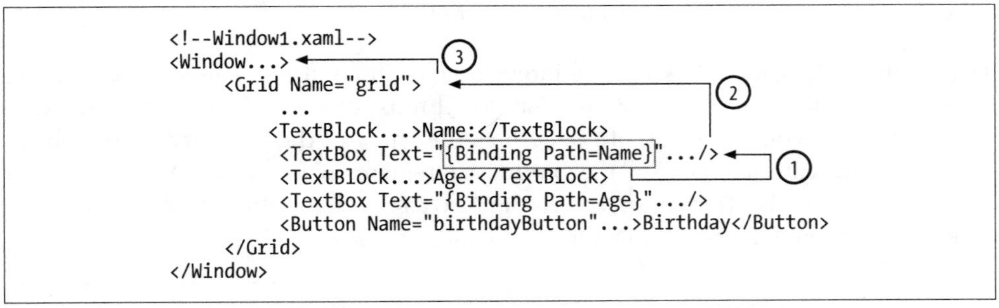

```
<!--Window1.xaml-->
<Window...>  ◄────────── ③
    <Grid Name="grid">  ◄──────────────────────── ②
        ...
        <TextBlock...>Name:</TextBlock>
        <TextBox Text="{Binding Path=Name}"...>  ◄─── ①
        <TextBlock...>Age:</TextBlock>
        <TextBox Text="{Binding Path=Age}"...>
        <Button Name="birthdayButton"...>Birthday</Button>
    </Grid>
</Window>
```

Figure 6-9. Searching the element tree for a non-null DataContext

---

* WPF data binding sources can also expose data via implementations of ICustomTypeDescriptor, which is how ADO.NET's data sources are supported.

† Actually, data binding doesn't do any searching at runtime. Instead, it relies on the fact that the DataContext property is inheritable, which means that the WPF property system itself implements the scoping/searching behavior described here. (Inheritable dependency properties are described in Chapter 18.)

The steps work like this:

1. The binding looks for a DataContext that has been set on the TextBox itself.
2. The binding looks for a DataContext that has been set on the Grid.
3. The binding looks for a DataContext that has been set on the Window.

Providing a DataContext value for both of the text box controls is a matter of setting the shared Person object as a value of the grid's DataContext property in the Window1 constructor, as shown in Example 6-12.

Example 6-12. Editor code simplified with data binding

```
// Window1.xaml.cs
using System;
using System.Windows;
using System.Windows.Controls;

namespace WithBinding {
  public partial class Window1 : Window {
    Person person = new Person("Tom", 11);

    public Window1() {
      InitializeComponent();

      // Let the grid know its data context
      grid.DataContext = person;

      this.birthdayButton.Click += birthdayButton_Click;
    }

    void birthdayButton_Click(object sender, RoutedEventArgs e) {
      // Data binding keeps person and the text boxes synchronized
      ++person.Age;
      MessageBox.Show(
        string.Format(
          "Happy Birthday, {0}, age {1}!",
          person.Name,
          person.Age),
        "Birthday");
    }
  }
}
```

So, although the functionality of our app is the same as shown in Figure 6-6, the data synchronization code has been reduced to a binding object for each property in the XAML where data is to be shown and a data context for the bindings to find the data. There is no need for the UI initialization code or the event handlers that copy and convert the data (notice that no code has been elided from Example 6-12).

To be clear, *the use of the INotifyPropertyChanged implementation is a required part of this example.* This is the interface that WPF's data binding engine uses to keep the

UI synchronized when an object's properties change. Without it, a UI change can still propagate to the object, but the binding engine will have no way of knowing when the object changes outside of the UI.

 It's not quite true that the binding engine will have *no* way of knowing when a change happens on an object that does not implement the INotifyPropertyChanged interface. Another way it can know is if the object implements the *PropertyName*Changed events as proscribed in .NET 1.x data binding (e.g., SizeChanged, TextChanged, etc.), with which WPF maintains backward compatibility. Another way is a manual call to the UpdateTarget method on the BindingExpression object associated with the Binding in question. For example:

```
BindingOperations.GetBindingExpression(
    ageTextBox, TextBox.TextProperty).UpdateTarget( );
```

Without rebinding or setting the data again manually, the call to UpdateTarget is your only option if the data source provides no notifications and you have no access to the source code. However, it's safe to say that an implementation of INotifyPropertyChanged is the recommended way to enable property change notifications in WPF data binding.

Data Islands

Although our application is attempting to simulate a more complicated application that, perhaps, loads its "person data" from some serialized form and saves it between application sessions, it's not hard to imagine cases where some data is known at compile time (e.g., sample data like our Tom).

As discussed in Chapter 1, XAML is a language for describing object graphs, so practically any type with a default constructor can be initialized in XAML (the default constructor is needed because XAML has no syntax for calling a nondefault constructor).* Luckily, as you'll recall from Example 6-4, our Person class has a default constructor, so we can create an instance of it in our application's XAML, as shown in Example 6-13.

Example 6-13. Creating an instance of a custom type in XAML

```
<Window ... xmlns:local="clr-namespace:WithBinding">
  <Window.Resources>
    <local:Person x:Key="Tom" Name="Tom" Age="11" />
  </Window.Resources>
  <Grid>...</Grid>
</Window>
```

---

* If you want to get fancy, you can create a TypeConverter that can accept a string as input or a markup extension as well, but generally the default constructor route is the easiest way to provide XAML support for your custom types.

Here we've created an "island" of data (sometimes called a *data island*) inside the window's Resources element, bringing the Person type in using the clr-namespace syntax described in Chapter 1.

With a named Person in our XAML code, we can declaratively set the grid's DataContext instead of setting it in the code behind programmatically, as shown in Example 6-14.

Example 6-14. Binding to an object declared in XAML

```
<!-- Window1.xaml -->
<Window ... xmlns:local="clr-namespace:WithBinding">
  <Window.Resources>
    <local:Person x:Key="Tom" Name="Tom" Age="11" />
  </Window.Resources>
  <Grid DataContext="{StaticResource Tom}">
    ...
    <TextBlock ...>Name:</TextBlock>
    <TextBox ... Text="{Binding Path=Name}" />
    <TextBlock ...>Age:</TextBlock>
    <TextBox ... Text="{Binding Path=Age}" />
    <Button ... Name="birthdayButton">Birthday</Button>
  </Grid>
</Window>
```

Now that we've moved the creation of the Person object to the XAML, we have to update our Birthday button Click handler from using a member variable to using the data defined in the resource (see Example 6-15).

Example 6-15. Using an object bound in XAML

```
public partial class Window1 : Window {
  ...
  void birthdayButton_Click(object sender, RoutedEventArgs e) {
    // Get the Person from the Window's resources
    Person person = (Person)this.FindResource("Tom");

    ++person.Age;
    MessageBox.Show(...);
  }
}
```

In Example 6-15, we're using the FindResource method (introduced in Chapter 1 and detailed in Chapter 12) to pull the Person object from the main window's resources. With this minor change, the result is brought again into parity with Figure 6-6.

In practice, I haven't found data islands as described here to be useful for much beyond sample data. However, the facilities of XAML that allow it to produce graphs of arbitrary objects have a great number of uses beyond WPF.

Explicit Data Source

Once you've got yourself a named source of data, you can be explicit in the XAML about the source in the binding instead of relying on implicitly binding to a DataContext property set somewhere in the tree. Being explicit is useful if you've got more than one source of data (e.g., two Person objects). Setting the source explicitly is accomplished with the Source property in the binding, as shown in Example 6-16.

Example 6-16. Data binding using the Source property

```
<!-- Window1.xaml -->
<Window ...>
  <Window.Resources>
    <local:Person x:Key="Tom" ... />
    <local:Person x:Key="John" ... />
  </Window.Resources>
  <Grid>
    ...
    <TextBox Name="tomTextBox"
      Text="
        {Binding
          Path=Name,
          Source={StaticResource Tom}}" />

    <TextBox Name="johnTextBox"
      Text="
        {Binding
          Path=Name,
          Source={StaticResource John}}" />
    ...
  </Grid>
</Window>
```

In Example 6-16, we've bound two text boxes to two different Person objects, setting the Source property of the Binding object to each person explicitly.

Binding to Other Controls

As another example of using explicit data sources, WPF provides for binding one element's property to another element's property. For instance, if we wanted to synchronize the brush used to draw the Birthday button's text with the foreground brush of the age text box (this will be handy later when we change the age text box's color based on the person's age), we can use the ElementName property of the Binding object, as shown in Example 6-17.

Example 6-17. Binding to another UI element

```
<TextBox Name="ageTextBox" Foreground="Red" ... />

<!-- keep button's foreground brush in sync w/ age text box's -->
```

Example 6-17. Binding to another UI element (continued)

```
<Button ...
  Foreground="{Binding Path=Foreground, ElementName=ageTextBox}"
  >Birthday</Button>
```

Now, no matter what means we use to change the foreground brush's color of the age text box—via binding, code, or triggers (as we'll see in Chapter 8)—the button's foreground brush will always follow.

Value Conversion

In Example 6-17, we've bound the foreground brush of the Birthday button to whatever the foreground brush is for the age text box, but our text box never changes color, so neither will the Birthday button. However, we might decide that anyone over age 25 is hot, so should be marked in the UI as red.* When someone ages at the click of the Birthday button, we want to keep the UI up-to-date, which means we've got ourselves a perfect candidate for data binding—something along the lines of Example 6-18.

Example 6-18. Binding to a non-Text property

```
<!-- Window1.xaml -->
<Window ...>
  <Grid>
    ...
    <TextBox
      Text="{Binding Path=Age}"
      Foreground="{Binding Path=Age, ...}"
      ...
    />
    ...
  </Grid>
</Window>
```

In Example 6-18, we've bound the age text box's Text property to the Person object's Age property, as we've already seen, but we're also binding the Foreground property of the text box to the same property on the Person object. As Tom's age changes, we want to update the foreground color of the age text box. However, because the Age is of type Int32 and Foreground is of type Brush, a mapping from Int32 to Brush needs to be applied to the data binding from Age to Foreground. That's the job of a value converter.

A *value converter* (or just "converter" for short) is an implementation of the IValueConverter interface, which contains two methods: Convert and ConvertBack.

---

* Or, anyone over 25 is in more danger of dying and red means "danger"—whichever makes you more likely to recommend this book to your friends...

The Convert method is called when converting from the source data to the target UI data (e.g., from Int32 to Brush). The ConvertBack method is called to convert back from the UI data to the source data. In both cases, the current value and the type wanted for the converted data are passed to the method.

To convert an Age Int32 into a Foreground Brush, we can implement whatever mapping in the Convert function we feel comfortable with (see Example 6-19).

Example 6-19. A simple value converter

```
[ValueConversion(/*sourceType*/ typeof(int), /*targetType*/ typeof(Brush))]
public class AgeToForegroundConverter : IValueConverter {

    // Called when converting the Age to a Foreground brush
    public object Convert(object value, Type targetType, ...) {
        // Only convert to brushes...
        if( targetType != typeof(Brush) ) { return null; }

        // DANGER! After 25, it's all downhill...
        int age = int.Parse(value.ToString());
        return (age > 25 ? Brushes.Red : Brushes.Black);
    }

    public object ConvertBack(object value, Type targetType, ...) {
        // Should not be called in our example
        throw new NotImplementedException();
    }
}
```

In Example 6-19, in addition to deriving from IValueConverter, we've also applied the optional ValueConversion attribute. The ValueConversion attribute is useful for documenting the expected source and target types for developers and tools, but it is not enforced by WPF, so don't expect it to catch values that don't match the source or target types. The part that is required for our example is the implementation of Convert, where we hand out the brush that's appropriate for the age being displayed. Because we haven't provided any facility to change the Foreground brush being used to display the age, there's no reason to do anything useful in the ConvertBack method—it won't be called.

> I chose the name AgeToForegroundConverter because I have specific semantics I'm building into my converter class that go above simply converting an Int32 to a Brush. Even though this converter could be plugged in anywhere that converted an Int32 to a Brush, I might have very different requirements for a HeightToBackgroundConverter, for example.

Once you've got a converter class, it's easy to create an instance of one in the XAML, just like we've been doing with our Person object (see Example 6-20).

Example 6-20. Binding with a value converter

```
<!-- Window1.xaml -->
<Window ... xmlns:local="clr-namespace:WithBinding">
  <Window.Resources>
    <local:Person x:Key="Tom" ... />
    <local:AgeToForegroundConverter x:Key="ageConverter" />
  </Window.Resources>
  <Grid DataContext="{StaticResource Tom}">
    ...
    <TextBox
      Text="{Binding Path=Age}"
      Foreground="
        {Binding
          Path=Age,
          Converter={StaticResource ageConverter}}"
      ... />
    ...
    <Button ...
      Foreground="{Binding Path=Foreground, ElementName=ageTextBox}"
      >Birthday</Button>
  </Grid>
</Window>
```

In Example 6-20, once we have a named converter object in our XAML, we establish it as the converter between the Age property and the Foreground brush by setting the Converter property of the binding object. Figure 6-10 shows the result of our conversion.

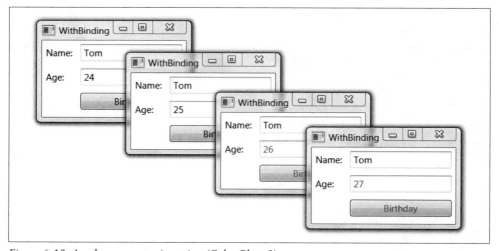

Figure 6-10. A value converter in action (Color Plate 3)

In Figure 6-10, notice that as Tom's age increases past the threshold, the converter switches the foreground brush from black to red. This change happens when the Age property changes. Because WPF detects the change, you do not need any explicit code to force the color change, just as with any other kind of data binding. Notice also that the foreground color of the Birthday button matches the age text box's color, because we're using element binding to keep them in sync.

Value Conversion Versus Type Conversion

You may have noticed that until we decided to bring brushes into the mix, we didn't need value converters at all. For example, with the Person class's Age property in an Int32, we didn't have to use a value converter even though the TextBox class's Text property is of type String. This works because the Binding class uses the type converter support that's been built into .NET since Version 1.0. Type converters work on a type basis (i.e., there's a type converter that knows how to convert from integers to strings and back [and there are many more type converters as well]). This works because there is a reasonable general-purpose way to convert strings to integers (and vice versa).

On the other hand, a value converter works on an application-specific basis. Although there is no built-in general-purpose conversion from integers to brushes, we can define an application-specific conversion to handle a certain kind of integer (e.g., ages, in our example) to brushes and apply that on a case-by-case basis.

Editable Value Conversion

In addition to value conversion from the underlying data type to some other type for display, like our age-to-foreground-brush converter, you may also use value conversion for editing convenience. For example, although the Age property is automatically converted for us between an Int32 and a String in base 10, maybe your users would prefer base 16 (who wouldn't?!). Enabling editing in base 16 is a matter of converting to and from a string in hexadecimal format, as shown in Example 6-21.

Example 6-21. A value converter for integers in base 16

```
public class Base16Converter : IValueConverter {
  public object Convert(
    object value, Type targetType, ...) {
    // Convert to base 16
    return ((int)value).ToString("x");
  }

  public object ConvertBack(
    object value, Type targetType, ...) {
    // Convert from base 16
    return int.Parse(
      (string)value, System.Globalization.NumberStyles.HexNumber);
  }
}
```

Hooking up this value converter works just like before, but this time we're converting the Text property of the TextBox instead of the Foreground property:

```
<TextBox ...
    Text="
      {Binding
        Path=Age,
        Converter={StaticResource base16Converter}}" />
```

Figure 6-11 shows the base-16 converter in action.

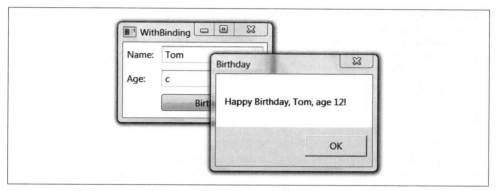

Figure 6-11. The base-16 value converter in action

One thing you'll notice in our Base16Converter implementation of IValueConverter is that we haven't guarded against a user entering something that can't be interpreted as a hexadecimal number. If he does, the resulting exception is not handled by WPF, but is instead shown to the user as an unhandled exception. Although you can spend your time writing code to catch conversion errors, what you'll really like to do is catch those errors before they ever get to the value converter, and instead communicate them to your users. For that, you'll be best served by validation rules.

Validation

A *validation rule* is some code for validating a piece of data in the target before it's used to update the source. The validation code is realized as an instance of a class that derives from the base ValidationRule class (from the System.Windows.Controls namespace) and overrides the Validate method. A built-in validation rule called ExceptionValidationRule (see Example 6-22) provides some measure of protection against a user intent on entering data outside the range supported by our age-to-foreground value converter.

Example 6-22. Hooking up a validation rule

```
<Window ... xmlns:local="clr-namespace:WithBinding">
  <Window.Resources>
    ...
```

Example 6-22. Hooking up a validation rule (continued)

```
    <local:AgeToForegroundConverter x:Key="ageConverter" />
  </Window.Resources>
...
<TextBox ...
  Foreground="
    {Binding
      Path=Age,
      Converter={StaticResource ageConverter}}">

  <TextBox.Text>
    <Binding Path="Age">
      <Binding.ValidationRules>
        <ExceptionValidationRule />
      </Binding.ValidationRules>
    </Binding>
  </TextBox.Text>

</TextBox>
```

In Example 6-22, we're using the shortcut markup extension binding syntax to bind the Foreground property to the Age (via the age-to-foreground value converter), but using the longhand syntax to bind the Text property to the Age so that we can create a list of validation rules. These validation rules will be executed in order when the target property changes. If they all succeed, the object is updated and everyone's happy. If one of the rules fails, WPF highlights the offending data to make it easy to see what to fix, as shown in Figure 6-12.

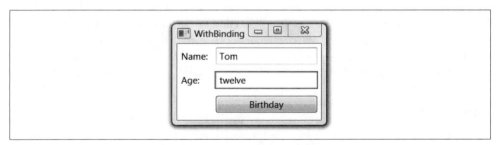

Figure 6-12. A TextBox control highlighted as invalid (Color Plate 4)

As nifty as the red outline around the offending text box is, it still doesn't let the user know what's wrong (i.e., the error message associated with the exception isn't shown). To do that, we need to look under the hood a bit.

When a validation result indicates invalid data, a ValidationError object is created that contains an object meant to describe the error, ideally for display by the UI. In the case of the ExceptionValidationRule, this "error content" object contains the

Message property of the Exception the validation rule catches. To gain access to those errors, you can listen to the ValidationError attached event, which you can set up as shown in Example 6-23.

Example 6-23. Handling the ValidationError event with a message box

```
// Window1.cs
...
public Window1( ) {
  InitializeComponent( );

  this.birthdayButton.Click += birthdayButton_Click;

  // Listen for the validation error event on the age text box
  // (you can do this in XAML by handling the Validation.Error
  //  attached event on the ageTextBox)
  Validation.AddErrorHandler(this.ageTextBox,
    ageTextBox_ValidationError);
}

void ageTextBox_ValidationError(
  object sender, ValidationErrorEventArgs e) {

  // Show the string pulled out of the exception by the
  // ExceptionValidationRule
  MessageBox.Show(
    (string)e.Error.ErrorContent, "Validation Error");
}
...

    <!-- Window1.xaml -->
    ...
    <TextBox Name="ageTextBox" ...>
      <TextBox.Text>
        <Binding Path="Age" NotifyOnValidationError="True">
          <Binding.ValidationRules>
            <ExceptionValidationRule />
          </Binding.ValidationRules>
        </Binding>
      </TextBox.Text>
    </TextBox>
    ...
```

In Example 6-23, we're calling the static AddErrorHandler method on the Validation class so that when a validation event happens on the age text box, we'll get a notification. In that event handler, we can access the Error.ErrorContent property to get to the string provided by the validation rule. This event fires, however, only if the NotifyOnValidationError property is set to True on the Binding (the default is False).

With this event handler in place, we get our message box when there's a validation error, as shown in Figure 6-13.

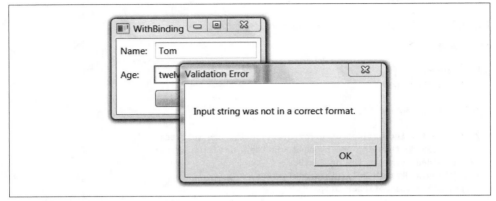

Figure 6-13. Handling the ValidationError event by showing a message box

And although "Input string was not in a correct format" is the message in the exception that the Parse method of the Int32 class throws when there's a parse error, I think we can do better—especially if we'd also like to set a range on the numbers that our users can enter for age.*

Custom validation rules

To make sure that our person's age is within a certain range, we simply derive from the ValidationRule class and override the Validate method, as shown in Example 6-24.

Example 6-24. A custom validation rule

```
public class NumberRangeRule : ValidationRule {
  int min;
  public int Min {
    get { return min; }
    set { min = value; }
  }

  int max;
  public int Max {
    get { return max; }
    set { max = value; }
  }
```

---

* On August 4, 1997, the world's oldest person so far, Jeanne Louise Calment, died at age 122, having taken up fencing at age 85 and outlived the holder of her reverse-mortgage. Although I firmly believe that Ms. Calment is showing us the way to a richer, longer life, it'll be a while yet before we need the full range supported by the Int32 class (2,147,483,647 years young).

Example 6-24. A custom validation rule (continued)

```
  public override ValidationResult Validate(
    object value, System.Globalization.CultureInfo cultureInfo) {
    int number;
    if( !int.TryParse((string)value, out number) ) {
      return new ValidationResult(
        false,
        "Invalid number format");
    }

    if( number < min || number > max ) {
      return new ValidationResult(
        false,
        string.Format("Number out of range ({0}-{1})", min, max));
    }

    //return new ValidationResult(true, null); // valid result
    return ValidationResult.ValidResult; // static valid result
                                         // to save on garbage
  }
}
```

In this case, we're creating a custom class with two public properties that describe the valid range of a number (specifically, an integer). The result of the validation is always an instance of the ValidationResult class. The most important part of the ValidationResult is the first argument to the constructor, which indicates whether the data is valid (true) or invalid (false). After that, we're free to pass whatever we want as a CLR object. In our example, we check whether the string can be parsed into an integer and is within our range, passing back False and an error string if it's not. Otherwise, we pass back True. (Because a valid result has little need for error detail, the ValidationResult class provides the static ValidResult property—a ValidationResult constructed by passing True and null—which you should use instead of creating a new ValidationResult object for a valid result.)

To hook up our validation rule, we put it to the Binding object's ValidationRules collection instead of the ExceptionValidationRule, as shown in Example 6-25.

Example 6-25. Hooking up a custom validation rule

```
<TextBox ...
  Foreground="
    {Binding
      Path=Age,
      Converter={StaticResource ageConverter}}">
  <TextBox.Text>
    <Binding Path="Age">
      <Binding.ValidationRules>
        <local:NumberRangeRule Min="0" Max="128" />
      </Binding.ValidationRules>
    </Binding>
  </TextBox.Text>
</TextBox>
```

Now, when there's a problem with the data, we get a message such as those shown in Figures 6-14 and 6-15.

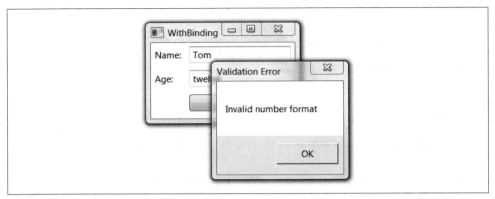

Figure 6-14. A validation error from a custom validation rule

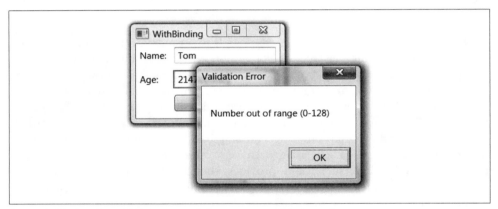

Figure 6-15. Another validation error from a custom validation rule

And so, although we now have nicer, more meaningful messages for our user when he enters invalid data, I am not a fan of the message box for validation error reporting (it stops the very activity you're trying to enable). Instead, I prefer a tool tip, as in Example 6-26.

Example 6-26. Handling the ValidationError event with a tool tip

```
void ageTextBox_ValidationError(
  object sender, ValidationErrorEventArgs e) {

  // Show the string created in NumberRangeRule.Validate
  ageTextBox.ToolTip = (string)e.Error.ErrorContent;
}
```

At first, this code works just peachy keen, as shown in Figure 6-16.

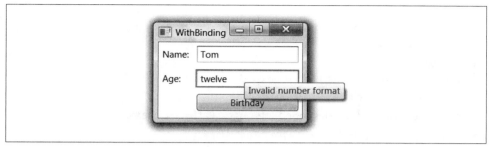

Figure 6-16. Handling the ValidationError event by setting a tool tip

When there's a validation error, the message is shown in the tool tip on the control that's holding invalid data. The problem is, once the user has corrected the data, the tool tip continues to hang around, as shown in Figure 6-17.

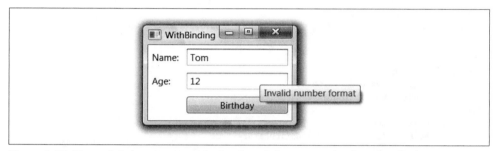

Figure 6-17. The tool tip hanging around after the validation error has been resolved

Unfortunately, there's no `ValidationSuccess` event that lets us clear the error message from the tool tip. What we really want is to update the tool tip based on the changing validation error data, whether it's in error or success, which sounds like a job for data binding. However, before we can do that, we need to take a closer look at Path syntax.

Binding Path Syntax

When you use `Path=Something` in a `Binding` statement, the *Something* can be in a number of formats, including the following commonly used variants:[*]

`Path=Property`
    Bind to the property of the current object, whether the property is a CLR property, a dependency property, or an attached property (e.g., `Path=Age`).

`Path=(OwnerType.AttachedProperty)`
    Bind to an attached dependency property (e.g., `Path=(Validation.HasError)`).

---

[*] The Windows Platform SDK has a more complete list of the WPF binding path syntax variants, including escaping rules, on a page titled "Binding Declarations Overview," available at *http://msdn2.microsoft.com/en-us/library/ms752300.aspx#Path_Syntax* (*http://tinysells.com/65*).

`Path=Property.SubProperty`

Bind to a subproperty (or a sub-subproperty, etc.) of the current object (e.g., `Path=Name.Length`).

`Path=Property[n]`

Bind to an indexer (e.g., `Path=Names[0]`).

`Path=Property/Property`

Master-detail binding, described later (e.g., `Path=Customers/Orders`).

`Path=(OwnerType.AttachedProperty)[n].SubProperty`

Bind to a mixture of properties, subproperties, and indexers (e.g., `Path=(Validation.Errors)[0].ErrorContent`).

So far, we've been using the `Path=Property` syntax, but if we want to get at an error on the validation errors collection, we'll need to use a mixed path that includes an attached property, an indexer, and a subproperty, as shown in Example 6-27.

Example 6-27. Binding the ToolTip property to the validation error message

```
<TextBox
  Name="ageTextBox" ...
  ToolTip="{Binding
            ElementName=ageTextBox,
            Path=(Validation.Errors)[0].ErrorContent}">
  <TextBox.Text>
    <Binding Path="Age">
      <!-- No need for NotifyOnValidationError="true" -->
      <Binding.ValidationRules>
        <local:NumberRangeRule Min="0" Max="128" />
      </Binding.ValidationRules>
    </Binding>
  </TextBox.Text>
</TextBox>
```

In Example 6-27, the tool tip has been bound to the first error from the attached property `Errors` collection. When there are no errors, the tool tip is empty. When there is an error, the `ErrorContent` property (which, you'll recall, we pack with an error string in `NumberRangeRule.Validate`) is used to populate the tool tip. We no longer need to set the `NotifyOnValidationError` property or handle the `ValidationError` event because as the `Errors` collection changes, the binding makes sure that the tool tip is kept up-to-date. In other words, we use data binding to the `ToolTip` property on the age text box to report a validation error on the `Text` property. When the collection of errors is null, the binding engine will automatically null out the tool tip, giving us the empty tool tip on success that we so deeply desire.

Relative Sources

One thing you may find a bit onerous in Example 6-27 is the use of the explicit `ElementName` to bind to another part of the target as the data source. Wouldn't it be nicer if you could just say, "Bind to myself, please?" And in some cases, you may not have a name for the thing to which you'd like to bind (e.g., to fulfill queries like "Bind to the Border that's the parent or grandparent [or great-grandparent] of me" or even "Bind to the *previous* bit of data in the list instead of the *current* bit of data"). All of these are available with the use of the `RelativeSource` property of a binding, shown in Example 6-28.

Example 6-28. Using a RelativeSource

```
<TextBox ...
  ToolTip="{Binding RelativeSource={RelativeSource Self},
                    Path=(Validation.Errors)[0].ErrorContent}">
```

In Example 6-28, we're using the `Self` designator to use the `TextBox` currently serving as the data binding UI target as the data source, so that we can bind to the validation errors collection associated with it to compose the tool tip. For more information about `Self` and the other relative sources—`FindAncestor`, `Previous`, and `TemplatedParent` (which is also discussed in Chapter 9)—I recommend the SDK documentation.[*]

Update Source Trigger

If you've been following along, you may have noticed that validation, and therefore the pushing of the updated data into the underlying object, doesn't happen until the age text box loses focus. On the other hand, you may decide that you'd like validation et al. to happen immediately when the control state changes, long before the focus is lost. This behavior is governed by the `UpdateSourceTrigger` property on the `Binding` object:

```
namespace System.Windows.Data {
  public enum UpdateSourceTrigger {
    Default = 0, // updates "naturally" based on the target control
    PropertyChanged = 1, // updates the source immediately
    LostFocus = 2, // updates the source when focus changes
    Explicit = 3, // must call BindingExpression.UpdateSource()
  }
}
```

The default value of `UpdateSourceTrigger` is `UpdateSourceTrigger.Default`, which means that the trigger for updating the data source is based on the target property (e.g., the trigger for the `Text` property of the `TextBox` is `LostFocus`). If you'd like to force another kind of behavior, you can set it on the `Binding`, as shown in Example 6-29.

---

[*] A good place to continue your exploration of relative sources is the "RelativeSourceMode Enumeration" page in the Windows Platform SDK, which is available at *http://msdn2.microsoft.com/en-us/library/system.windows.data.relativesourcemode.aspx* (*http://tinysells.com/66*).

Example 6-29. Changing the update source trigger

```
<TextBox ...>
  <TextBox.Text>
    <Binding Path="Age" UpdateSourceTrigger="PropertyChanged">
      ...
    </Binding>
  </TextBox.Text>
</TextBox>
```

In this case, instead of waiting for the focus to be lost to do validation, it happens on each character entered.

Debugging Data Binding

You may have noticed that our age text box's binding options have gotten fairly involved:

```
<TextBox ...
  Foreground="{Binding Path=Age,
                       Source={StaticResource Tom},
                       Converter={StaticResource ageConverter}}"
  ToolTip="{Binding RelativeSource={RelativeSource Self},
                    Path=(Validation.Errors)[0].ErrorContent}">
  <TextBox.Text>
    <Binding Path="Age" UpdateSourceTrigger="PropertyChanged">
      <Binding.ValidationRules>
        <local:NumberRangeRule Min="0" Max="128" />
      </Binding.ValidationRules>
    </Binding>
  </TextBox.Text>
</TextBox>
```

There's a lot going on here and it would be easy to get some of it wrong. For example, if we had a background in journalism, we might have used one-based indexing instead of zero-based indexing to access the first error in our list of validation errors when setting up the binding for the tool tip:

```
<TextBox ...
  ToolTip="{Binding RelativeSource={RelativeSource Self},
                    Path=(Validation.Errors)[1].ErrorContent}">
  ...
</TextBox>
```

In this case, as in most others, the WPF data binding engine will simply swallow the error so as not to disturb our user friends.[*] So, how are we to find it? Well, you need only check the debug output to see the error shown in Example 6-30, and all will be revealed.

---

[*] The swallowing of errors like these lets us declare data bindings before the data is actually available, simplifying our programming chores considerably in this area.

Example 6-30. Watch debug output for help debugging data binding problems

```
System.Windows.Data Error: 12 : Cannot get '' value (type 'ValidationError') from
'(Validation.Errors)' (type 'ReadOnlyObservableCollection`1').
BindingExpression:Path=(0).[1].ErrorContent; DataItem='TextBox'
(Name='ageTextBox'); target element is 'TextBox' (Name='ageTextBox');
target property is 'ToolTip' (type 'Object') TargetInvocationException:
'System.Reflection.TargetInvocationException: Exception has been thrown by the target of
an invocation. --->
System.ArgumentOutOfRangeException: Index was out of range. Must be non-negative and less
than the size of the collection.
Parameter name: index
```

In this case, we can see that the index is out of range, giving us a clue as to how to fix it. The data binding debug output provides all kinds of helpful hints like this, and you should check it if eyeballing your data binding expressions doesn't yield the source of the issue.[*]

Where Are We?

Data binding is about keeping two values synchronized. One value, the target, is a dependency property, typically on a UI element. The other, the source, is a CLR property—the result of an XPath expression, a dependency property, or a dynamic property used by objects like those provided by ADO.NET that don't know what the data is going to be until runtime. By default, as either the target or the source changes, the other value is updated, but you can control that with the alternate binding modes (e.g., one-way, one-time, etc.). As data changes, type conversion happens automatically if a converter is available, although you can take full control of the conversion and validation process if you so choose, doing things like restricting data ranges and converting data formats, or even automatically showing errors in tool tips. You might think that WPF data binding is powerful with these features, and you'd be right, but we've just touched on the bare essentials associated with bindings to properties on a single object. When you've got a list of objects as your data source, you've got all kinds of other facilities, which is the subject of the next chapter.

---

[*] For more on the data binding debug output, see the SDK documentation for the `PresentationTraceSources` class at *http://msdn2.microsoft.com/en-us/library/system.diagnostics.presentationtracesources.aspx* or *http://tinysells.com/79* and Mike Hillberg's most excellent blog posting on this subject at *http://blogs.msdn.com/mikehillberg/archive/2006/09/14/WpfTraceSources.aspx* or *http://tinysells.com/78*.

CHAPTER 7
Binding to List Data

In Chapter 6, we looked at the basics of data binding with respect to single objects. However, when you've got lists of objects, you've got still more flexibility and power, including managing the "current" object in a list, sorting, filtering, and grouping. Also, WPF gives you the ability to expand a single data source object into a set of target UI elements with data templates, bring in XML and relational data, and perform master-detail binding and hierarchical binding. We discuss all of these topics in this chapter.

Binding to List Data

To kick things off, recall our Person class from Chapter 6; let's add a new type for keeping track of a list of Person objects (see Example 7-1).

Example 7-1. Declaring a custom list type

```
using System.Collections.Generic; // List<T>
...
namespace PersonBinding {
  public class Person : INotifyPropertyChanged {
    // INotifyPropertyChanged Members
    public event PropertyChangedEventHandler PropertyChanged;

    protected void Notify(string propName) {
      if( this.PropertyChanged != null ) {
        PropertyChanged(this, new PropertyChangedEventArgs(propName));
      }
    }

    string name;
    public string Name {
      get { return this.name; }
      set {
        if( this.name == value ) { return; }
        this.name = value;
        Notify("Name");
      }
    }
  }
```

Example 7-1. Declaring a custom list type (continued)

```
    int age;
    public int Age {
      get { return this.age; }
      set {
        if(this.age == value ) { return; }
        this.age = value;
        Notify("Age");
      }
    }

    public Person( ) {}
    public Person(string name, int age) {
      this.name = name;
      this.age = age;
    }
  }

  // Create an alias for a generic type so that we can
  // create a list of Person objects in XAML
  class People : List<Person> {}

  ...
}
```

We can bind this new list data source in exactly the same way as if we were binding to a single object data source (see Example 7-2).

Example 7-2. Declaring a collection in XAML

```
<!-- Window1.xaml -->
<Window ... xmlns:local="clr-namespace:ListBinding">
  <Window.Resources>
    <local:People x:Key="Family">
      <local:Person Name="Tom" Age="11" />
      <local:Person Name="John" Age="12" />
      <local:Person Name="Melissa" Age="38" />
    </local:People>
    <local:AgeToForegroundConverter
      x:Key="ageConverter" />
  </Window.Resources>
  <Grid DataContext="{StaticResource Family}">
    ...
    <TextBlock ...>Name:</TextBlock>
    <TextBox Text="{Binding Path=Name}" ... />
    <TextBox
      Text="{Binding Path=Age}"
      Foreground="{Binding Path=Age, Converter=...}" ... />
    <Button ...>Birthday</Button>
  </Grid>
</Window>
```

In Example 7-2, we've created an instance of the People collection and populated it with three Person objects. Running it will look just like running the Person object version from Chapter 6 (Figure 7-1).

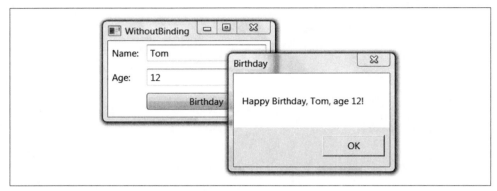

Figure 7-1. Showing one person at a time from a list

Even though we're binding to a list of Person objects, each TextBlock can be bound to a property from only a single Person object.

Current Item

While the text box properties can be bound to only a single object at a time, the binding engine is giving them the *current item* in the list of possible objects they could bind against, as illustrated in Figure 7-2.

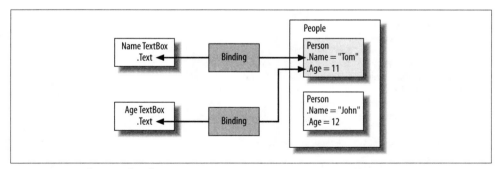

Figure 7-2. Binding to a list data source

By default, the first item in the list is the initial current item. Because the first item in our list example is the same as the only item to which we were binding before, things look and act in exactly the same way as our single Person object example, except for the Birthday button.

Getting the current item

Recall the current Birthday button click event handler from Chapter 6 (see Example 7-3).

Example 7-3. Finding a custom object declared in XAML

```
public partial class Window1 : Window {
  ...
  void birthdayButton_Click(object sender, RoutedEventArgs e) {
    Person person = (Person)this.FindResource("Tom"));
    ++person.Age;
    MessageBox.Show(...);
  }
}
```

Our Birthday button has always been about celebrating the birthday of the current person, but so far the current person has always been the same, so we could just shortcut things and go directly to a single Person object. Now that we've got a list of objects, this no longer behaves acceptably (unless you consider an unhandled exception message box acceptable behavior). Further, pulling the collection out of the resources won't tell us which Person is currently being shown in the UI, because it has no idea about such things (nor should it). For this information, we're going to have to go to the broker between the data bound control and the collection of items, the *collection view*.

The job of the collection view (or just "view") is to provide services on top of the data, including sorting, filtering, grouping, and, most important for our purposes at the moment, control of the current item. A view is an implementation of a data-specific interface which, in our case, is going to be the ICollectionView interface. We can access a view over our data with the static GetDefaultView method of the CollectionViewSource class, as shown in Example 7-4.

Example 7-4. Getting a collection's view

```
public partial class Window1 : Window {
  ...
  void birthdayButton_Click(object sender, RoutedEventArgs e) {
    // Get the current person out of the collection view
    People people = (People)this.FindResource("Family");
    ICollectionView view =
      CollectionViewSource.GetDefaultView(people);
    Person person = (Person)view.CurrentItem;

    ++person.Age;
    MessageBox.Show(...);
  }
}
```

To retrieve the view associated with the Family collection, Example 7-4 makes a call to the GetDefaultView method of CollectionViewSource, which provides us with an implementation of the ICollectionView interface associated with our bound data collection. Our collection happens to have been created in a resource, but that doesn't matter to the GetDefaultView method; it only maps a bound collection to its associated view. With the collection view, we can grab the current item, cast it into an item from our collection (the CurrentItem property returns an object), and use it for display.

Navigating between items

In addition to getting the current item, we can also change which item is current using the MoveCurrentTo methods of the ICollectionView interface, as shown in Example 7-5.

Example 7-5. Navigating between items via the view

```
public partial class Window1 : Window {
  ...
  ICollectionView GetFamilyView( ) {
    People people = (People)this.FindResource("Family");
    return CollectionViewSource.GetDefaultView(people);
  }

  void birthdayButton_Click(object sender, RoutedEventArgs e) {
    ICollectionView view = GetFamilyView( );
    Person person = (Person)view.CurrentItem;

    ++person.Age;
    MessageBox.Show(...);
  }

  void backButton_Click(object sender, RoutedEventArgs e) {
    ICollectionView view = GetFamilyView( );
    view.MoveCurrentToPrevious( );
    if( view.IsCurrentBeforeFirst ) {
      view.MoveCurrentToFirst( );
    }
  }

  void forwardButton_Click(object sender, RoutedEventArgs e) {
    ICollectionView view = GetFamilyView( );
    view.MoveCurrentToNext( );
    if( view.IsCurrentAfterLast ) {
      view.MoveCurrentToLast( );
    }
  }
}
```

The ICollectionView methods MoveCurrentToPrevious and MoveCurrentToNext change which item is currently selected by going backward and forward through the collection. If we walk off the end of the list in one direction or the other, the IsCurrentBeforeFirst or IsCurrentAfterLast property will tell us that. The MoveCurrentToFirst and MoveCurrentToLast help us recover after walking off the end of the list, and would be useful for implementing the Back and Forward buttons shown in Figure 7-3 as well as the First and Last buttons (this is an opportunity for you to apply what you've learned...).

Figure 7-3. Navigating between items in a list data source (Color Plate 5)

Figure 7-3 shows the effect of moving forward from the first Person in the collection, including the color changing based on the Person object's Age property (which still works in exactly the same way).

List Data Targets

Of course, we can push the user of list data only so far without providing him with a control that can actually show more than one item at a time—like the ListBox control, shown in Example 7-6.

Example 7-6. Binding a list element to a list data source

```
<!-- Window1.xaml -->
<Window ... xmlns:local="clr-namespace:ListBinding2">
  <Window.Resources>
    <local:People x:Key="Family">...</local:People>
    ...
  </Window.Resources>
  <Grid DataContext="{StaticResource Family}">
    ...
```

Example 7-6. Binding a list element to a list data source (continued)

```
<ListBox
  ItemsSource="{Binding}"
  IsSynchronizedWithCurrentItem="True" ... />
<TextBlock ...>Name:</TextBlock>
<TextBox Text="{Binding Path=Name}" ... />
  ...
</Window>
```

In Example 7-6, the ItemsSource property of the ListBox is a Binding with no path, which is the same as saying "bind to the entire current object." Notice that there's no source, either, so the binding works against the first data context it finds that is set. In this case, the first set data context is the one from the Grid, the same one as shared between both the name and the age text boxes. Also, we're setting the ListBox class's IsSynchronizedWithCurrentItem property to True so that as the selected item of the listbox changes, it updates the current item in the view (and vice versa).[*]

With our ItemsSource binding in place, we should expect to see all three Person objects in the listbox, as shown in Figure 7-4.

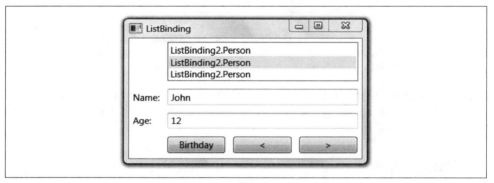

Figure 7-4. Person objects being displayed in a ListBox without help

As you might have noticed, everything is not quite perfect in Figure 7-4. When you bind against an object, data binding does its best to display it. Without special instructions, it'll use a type converter to get a string representation (falling back on the ToString method when all else fails). In the case of both the Name and Age properties, the built-in conversions give us a string representation that works well for our purposes. However, the Person object provides no special instructions, so the fallback does nothing but show the name of the type.

---

[*] By default, listboxes do not synchronize with the current item for reasons I have yet to fathom…

Because binding uses an object's ToString method if it has nothing else, you may feel tempted to add a ToString method as a way to decide how your data objects look in your WPF UIs. You should avoid this temptation, for at least the following reasons:

- It is impossible to provide a string representation of a data object that would be appropriate for every way that you might like to display it.

- You lose all kinds of flexibility in how to display a data object if all you have is the whole thing represented as a string (e.g., maybe you'd like some of it bold or some of it as the content of a Button).

- There's no way to fire a notification to WPF such that it will automatically pull in the new data object's data as it changes when ToString is used, giving you a single, static view.

Display Members, Value Members, and Look-Up Bindings

If you want to show only one of the properties, the ListBox class (and the rest of the ItemsControl-derived controls—e.g., Menu, ListBox, ListView, ComboBox, TreeView, etc.) provides the DisplayMemberPath property:

```
<ListBox ... ItemsSource="{Binding}" DisplayMemberPath="Name" />
```

This at least gives us part of the data, as you can see in Figure 7-5.

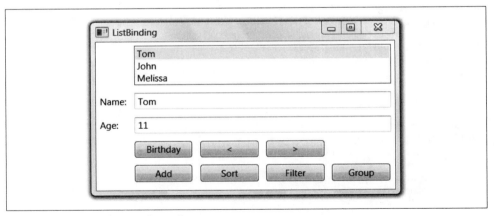

Figure 7-5. The DisplayMemberPath in action

In addition to the path describing the data to display, the ItemsControl class provides a path to describe the selected value of a piece of data:

```
<ListBox ... Name="lb" ItemsSource="{Binding}"
    DisplayMemberPath="Name" SelectedValuePath="Age" />
```

The SelectedValue is exposed from the ItemsControl as an application-defined way to separate the data from what's displayed. By default, the SelectedValue, the SelectedItem, and the object used to construct the item at that spot in the list are all the same (e.g., a Person if we hadn't changed it by setting the SelectedValuePath). This data is often used when the selection changes or an item is double-clicked:

```
void lb_MouseDoubleClick(object sender, MouseButtonEventArgs e) {
    int index = lb.SelectedIndex;
    if( index < 0 ) { return; }

    Person item = (Person)lb.SelectedItem;
    int value = (int)lb.SelectedValue; // Age

    // Do something profitable with this data
    ...
}
```

The difference between display value and selected value becomes especially interesting when you want to do something like a combo box with friendly names (e.g., salesperson name), but key off of opaque values in the real data (e.g., salesperson ID).

For example, if we wanted to provide a UI that mapped ages represented in scary numbers to soothing phrases, we could construct a NamedAge type for use in populating a look-up table, as shown in Example 7-7.

Example 7-7. A helper for populating a look-up table

```
public class NamedAge : INotifyPropertyChanged {
  // INotifyPropertyChangeIdINotifyPropertyChanged Members
  public event PropertyChangedEventHandler PropertyChanged;
  protected void Notify(string propNameForAge) {
    if( this.PropertyChanged != null ) {
      PropertyChanged(this, new PropertyChangedEventArgs(propNameForAge));
    }
  }

  string nameForAge;
  public string NameForAge {
    get { return this.nameForAge; }
    set {
      if( this.nameForAge == value ) { return; }
      this.nameForAge = value;
      Notify("NameForAge");
    }
  }

  int ageId;
  public int AgeId {
    get { return this.ageId; }
    set {
      if( this.ageId == value ) { return; }
      this.ageId = value;
      Notify("AgeId");
```

Example 7-7. A helper for populating a look-up table (continued)

```
    }
  }
}
```

```
class NamedAges : ObservableCollection<NamedAge> { }
```

Now we can populate the table for looking up an age's name from its number, as in Example 7-8.

Example 7-8. A look-up table suitable for binding

```
<local:NamedAges x:Key="NamedAgeLookup">
  <local:NamedAge NameForAge="zero" AgeId="0" />
  <local:NamedAge NameForAge="one" AgeId="1" />
  ...
</local:NamedAges>
```

This handy table is all we need to replace the TextBox for entering hard-to-format-correctly ages into an easy-to-use combo box with all of the values filled in for us, as shown in Figure 7-6.

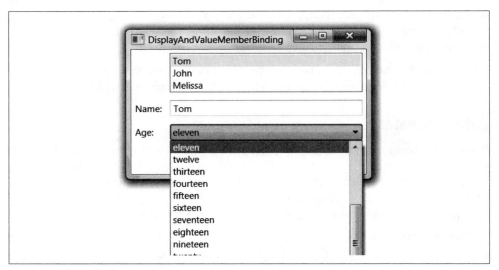

Figure 7-6. Data binding to a look-up table

OK, obviously this particular example isn't useful, but mapping IDs to names is something we want to do all the time in data binding applications. To get our combo box to show the list of available options, we need to bind the set of options to our look-up table, setting the display and value members appropriately, as in Example 7-9.

Example 7-9. Data binding to a look-up table

```
<ComboBox ...
    ItemsSource="{Binding Source={StaticResource NamedAgeLookup}}"
    DisplayMemberPath="NameForAge" SelectedValuePath="AgeId" />
```

Example 7-9 tells the combo box where the possible choices come from (the NamedAgeLookup table), which property to show the user (the NameForAge property), and which property is the real value (the AgeId property). The final step is the bit of binding that tells the combo box where to get the currently selected value (in terms that match our selected value path; in other words, Age), as in Example 7-10.

Example 7-10. Binding the look-up table to the selected value

```
<ComboBox ...
    ItemsSource="{Binding Source={StaticResource NamedAgeLookup}}"
    DisplayMemberPath="NameForAge" SelectedValuePath="AgeId"
    SelectedValue="{Binding Path=Age}" />
```

Just as before, where the TextBox object's Text property was set to bind to the Age property of the currently selected Person, so is the ComboBox object's SelectedValue property set. As the display value changes (due to interaction with the user), the selected value is updated, as is the underlying Age. Likewise, as the Age changes (like when the Birthday button is clicked), the binding synchronizes the selected value, causing the value displayed in the combo box to change.

All of this is very handy, but in our case, we don't really want to have named ages, nor do we want to display a single property in the ListBox for each Person object it displays.

Data Templates

If you want to show more than one property from a custom class or mix things up with more than just a plain TextBlock object (which is all the DisplayMemberPath gives you), you want a *data template*. A data template is a tree of elements to expand in a particular context. For example, for each Person object, you might like to be able to concatenate the name and age together in a string like the following:

> John (age:12)

We can think of this as a logical template that looks like this:

> *Name* (age:*Age*)

To define this template for items in the listbox, we create a DataTemplate element, as shown in Example 7-11.

Example 7-11. Using a data template

```
<ListBox ... ItemsSource="{Binding}">
  <ListBox.ItemTemplate>
    <DataTemplate>
```

Example 7-11. Using a data template (continued)

```
    <TextBlock>
      <TextBlock Text="{Binding Path=Name}" />
      (age: <TextBlock
        Text="{Binding Path=Age}"
        Foreground="{Binding
                      Path=Age,
                      Converter={StaticResource ageConverter}}" />)
    </TextBlock>
  </DataTemplate>
  </ListBox.ItemTemplate>
</ListBox>
```

In this case, the ListBox control has an ItemTemplate property, which accepts an instance of the DataTemplate class. The DataTemplate allows us to specify a single child element to repeat for every item that the ListBox control binds against (although that child can have any number of children of its own, and so on). In our case, we're using a TextBlock to gather together some hardcoded text and two nested TextBlock controls for text bound to properties on each Person object. Notice that we're also binding the Foreground to the Age property using the age-to-foreground value converter so that Age properties show up black or red consistently between the listbox and age text box.

With the use of the data template, our experience goes from Figure 7-4 to Figure 7-7.

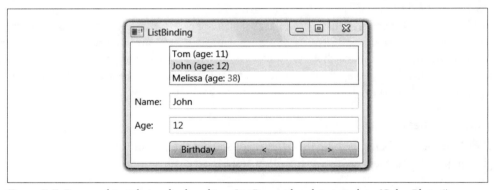

Figure 7-7. Person objects being displayed in a ListBox with a data template (Color Plate 6)

Notice that the listbox shows all the items in the collection and keeps the view's idea of the current item synchronized with it as the selection moves or the back and forward buttons are clicked (actually, you can't really "notice" this based on the screenshot, but trust me, that's what happens). In addition, as data changes on Person objects, the listbox and the text boxes are all kept in sync, including the Age color.

Typed data templates

In Example 7-11, we explicitly set the data template for items in our listbox by creating the `DataTemplate` inside the `ListBox.ItemTemplate` element. Using this technique, if a `Person` object shows up in a button or in some other element, we'd have to specify the data template for those `Person` objects separately. On the other hand, if you'd like a `Person` object to have a specific template no matter where it shows up, you can do so with a *typed data template*, as shown in Example 7-12.

Example 7-12. A typed data template

```
<Window.Resources>
  <local:People x:Key="Family">...</local:People>
  ...
  <DataTemplate DataType="{x:Type local:Person}">
    <TextBlock>
      <TextBlock Text="{Binding Path=Name}" />
      (age: <TextBlock Text="{Binding Path=Age}" ... />)
    </TextBlock>
  </DataTemplate>
  ...
</Window.Resources>
...
<!-- no need for an ItemTemplate setting -->
<ListBox ItemsSource="{Binding}" ... />
```

In Example 7-12, we've hoisted the data template definition into a resources block and tagged it with a type using the `DataType` property.[*] Now, unless told otherwise, whenever an element using the WPF content model[†] sees an instance of the `Person` object within the scope of the data template, it will apply the appropriate data template. This is a handy way to make sure that data shows in a consistent way throughout your application without worrying about just where it shows.

DataTemplates and the DataContext

You'll notice in Example 7-12 that we're not setting the `Source` property. As you saw in the preceding chapter, this means that the `Binding` object will use the `DataContext` as its source.

You should also recall (from the preceding chapter) that the `DataContext` uses the dependency property inheritance mechanism to travel the element tree to find its value if it's not set explicitly (i.e., if the element we're binding has no explicit `DataContext` set, we'll use the one from the parent or the grandparent, etc.).

---

[*] If you've skipped ahead to Chapter 12, you know that all resources, without exception, must have a Key. Certain resource types have a property that, when set, also sets the Key implicitly. In the case of the DataTemplate, setting the DataType property also sets the Key property.

[†] As you'll recall from Chapter 1, the content model of WPF allows you to put arbitrary content into most elements (e.g., Button supports the content model whereas the TextBox doesn't).

However, if you'll look at the where the binding takes place on the text blocks inside the data template in Example 7-12, you'll notice that we don't actually want the data context to be on the parent of the `DataTemplate`, but rather to be on the individual elements of the items source on the listbox where our `Person` data template is being expanded. To enable the bindings in our data template to work as we expect the template expansion engine in WPF will set the `DataContext` property of the root of each element tree that it expands. For instance, in our example, we've got three `Person` objects, so you can think of the logical expansion of the data template inside the listbox as shown in Example 7-13.

Example 7-13. Logical expansion of the Person data template

```
<ListBox ...>
  <TextBlock DataContext="Family[0]">
    <TextBlock Text="{Binding Path=Name}" />
    (age: <TextBlock Text="{Binding Path=Age}" Foreground="..." />)
  </TextBlock>

  <TextBlock DataContext="Family[1]">
    <TextBlock Text="{Binding Path=Name}" />
    (age: <TextBlock Text="{Binding Path=Age}" Foreground="..." />)
  </TextBlock>

  <TextBlock DataContext="Family[2]">
    <TextBlock Text="{Binding Path=Name}" />
    (age: <TextBlock Text="{Binding Path=Age}" Foreground="..." />)
  </TextBlock>
</ListBox>
```

As the data template is expanded for each item in the list referenced by the `ItemsSource` property, the data context is set to the individual item so that when the `Binding` objects are looking for their data sources, they find the data context of the element at the root of the expanded data template, like the top-level `TextBlock` in our example. Not only does this explain how data bindings work inside data templates, but also this is something we can use. For example, we need to use the `DataContext` property if we want to handle events on objects inside the data template and figure out which data object was used to expand the template, as shown in Example 7-14.

Example 7-14. DataTemplates and the DataContext

```
<!-- Window1.xaml.cs -->
...
<Window.Resources>
  <local:People x:Key="Family">...</local:People>
  ...
  <DataTemplate DataType="{x:Type local:Person}">
    <TextBlock>
      <TextBlock Text="{Binding Path=Name}" />
      (age: <TextBlock Text="{Binding Path=Age}" ... />)
      <Button Click="showButton_Click">Show</Button>
```

Example 7-14. DataTemplates and the DataContext (continued)

```
        </TextBlock>
    </DataTemplate>
    ...
</Window.Resources>
...

// Window1.xaml.cs
...
void showButton_Click(object sender, RoutedEventArgs e) {
    // Get the button generated by the data template expansion
    Button showButton = (Button)sender;

    // Get the person associated with the generated button via the data context
    Person person = (Person)showButton.DataContext;

    // Do something with that person...
    MessageBox.Show(string.Format("{0} is {1} years old", person.Name, person.Age));
}
...
```

In this example, we added a Button to the data template with a Click event handler. When the button is clicked, the event handler's sender argument is the Button that was generated when the template was expanded. Because of dependency property inheritance, the DataContext property on the Button gets the same value of the DataContext property on the root TextBlock in the DataTemplate for the item in the list of Person objects that was used to populate the ListBox. Figure 7-8 shows the results of clicking one of the Show buttons.

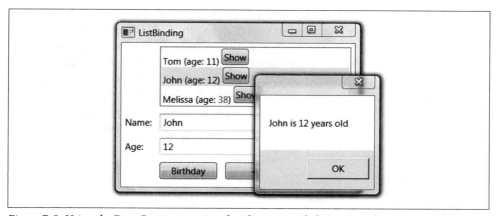

Figure 7-8. Using the DataContext associated with an expanded DataTemplate

In Figure 7-8, the Show button in the second row was clicked, which means that the same Person object in the second row of the listbox is the one that is available in the DataContext on the Show button in that row.

List Changes

Thus far, we've got a list of objects that we can edit in place and navigate among, even highlighting certain data values with ease and providing an automatic look for data that wasn't shipped with a rendering from the manufacturer. In the spirit of how far we've come, you might suspect that implementing an Add button, as in Example 7-15, would be a breeze.

Example 7-15. Adding an item to a data bound collection

```
public partial class Window1 : Window {
  ...
  void addButton_Click(object sender, RoutedEventArgs e) {
    People people = (People)this.FindResource("Family");
    people.Add(new Person("Chris", 37));
  }
}
```

The problem with this code is that although the collection view associated with our list data source can figure out the existence of a new item as you move to it, the listbox itself has no idea that something new has been added, as shown in Figure 7-9.

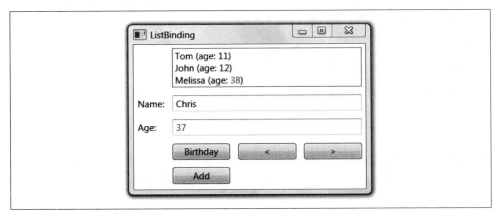

Figure 7-9. The ListBox doesn't know the collection has gotten bigger

In interacting with the state of the application shown in Figure 7-9, I ran the application, clicked the Add button, and used the Forward button to navigate to it. However, just as data bound *objects* need to implement the INotifyPropertyChanged interface, data bound *lists* need to implement the INotifyCollectionChanged interface[*] (see Example 7-16).

---

[*] Again, this is not really a requirement; WPF data works even if the collection doesn't implement INotifyCollectionChanged, although it won't know about changes to the collection. If you have to integrate with collections that don't implement this interface, or the .NET 1.x version of this interface—IBindingList (which WPF still supports)—you'll need to fall back on the manual updating technique mentioned in Chapter 6 (i.e., BindingExpression.UpdateTarget).

Example 7-16. The INotifyCollectionChanged interface

```
namespace System.Collections.Specialized {
  public interface INotifyCollectionChanged {
    event NotifyCollectionChangedEventHandler CollectionChanged;
  }
}
```

The INotifyCollectionChanged interface is used to notify the data bound control that items have been added or removed from the bound list. Although it's common to implement INotifyPropertyChanged in your custom types to enable two-way data binding on your type's properties, it's less common to implement your own collection classes, which leaves you less opportunity to implement the INotifyCollectionChanged interface. Instead, you'll most likely be relying on one of the collection classes in the .NET Framework Class Library to implement INotifyCollectionChanged for you. The number of such classes is small and unfortunately, List<T>, the collection class we're using to hold Person objects, is not among them. Although you're more than welcome to spend your evenings and weekends implementing the INotifyCollectionChanged interface, including hooking all of the methods that change whatever base collection you use as a helper, WPF provides the ObservableCollection<T> class, shown in Example 7-17, for those of us with more pressing duties.

Example 7-17. WPF's implementation of INotifyCollectionChanged

```
namespace System.Collections.ObjectModel {
  public class ObservableCollection<T> :
    Collection<T>, INotifyCollectionChanged, INotifyPropertyChanged {
    ...
  }
}
```

Because ObservableCollection<T> derives from Collection<T> and implements the INotifyCollectionChanged interface, we can use it instead of List<T> for our Person collection (see Example 7-18).

Example 7-18. ObservableCollection<T> in action

```
using System.ComponentModel; // INotifyPropertyChanged
using System.Collections.ObjectModel; // ObservableCollection<T>
...
class Person : INotifyPropertyChanged {...}
class People : ObservableCollection<Person> {}
...
```

Now, when an item is added to or removed from the Person collection, those changes will be reflected in the list data bound controls, as shown in Figure 7-10.

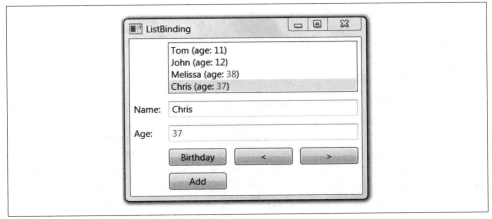

Figure 7-10. Keeping the ListBox in sync with INotifyCollectionChanged

Here, we've clicked the Add button and clicked on the new Person object that the listbox displayed for us (a newly added item in a collection does not become the selected item automatically).

Sorting

Once we have data targets showing more than one thing at a time properly, a person's fancy turns to, well, fancier things, like sorting the view of the data, filtering the data out of the view, or grouping related data. Recall that the view always sits between the data bound target and the data source. The view allows us to do a number of things to the data before it's displayed, including changing the order in which the data is shown (a.k.a. *sorting*). The simplest way to sort is by manipulating the SortDescriptions property of the view, as shown in Example 7-19.

Example 7-19. Sorting

```
public partial class Window1 : Window {
  ...
  ICollectionView GetFamilyView( ) {
    People people = (People)this.FindResource("Family");
    return CollectionViewSource.GetDefaultView(people);
  }

  void sortButton_Click(object sender, RoutedEventArgs e) {
    ICollectionView view = GetFamilyView( );
    if( view.SortDescriptions.Count == 0 ) {
      view.SortDescriptions.Add(
        new SortDescription("Name", ListSortDirection.Ascending));
      view.SortDescriptions.Add(
        new SortDescription("Age", ListSortDirection.Descending));
    }
```

Example 7-19. Sorting (continued)

```
      else {
        view.SortDescriptions.Clear();
      }
    }
  }
}
```

Here we're toggling between sorted and unsorted views by checking the SortDescriptionCollection exposed by the ICollectionView SortDescription property. If there are no sort descriptions, we sort first by the Name property in ascending order, then by the Age property in Descending order. If there are sort descriptions, we clear them, restoring the order to whatever it was before we applied our sort. While the sort descriptions are in place, any new objects added to the collection will be displayed in their proper sort position by the view, as Figure 7-11 shows.

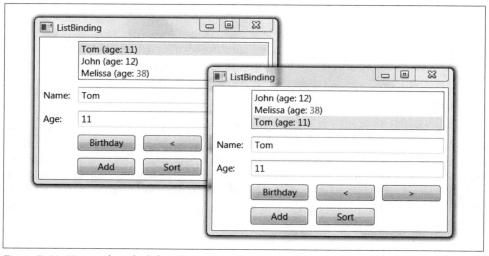

Figure 7-11. Unsorted on the left and sorted on the right

A collection of SortDescription objects should cover most cases, but if you'd like a bit more control, you can provide the view with a custom sorting object by implementing the IComparer interface from the System.Collections namespace,* as shown in Example 7-20.

Example 7-20. Custom sorting

```
class PersonSorter : IComparer {
  public int Compare(object x, object y) {
    Person lhs = (Person)x;
    Person rhs = (Person)y;
```

---

* Unfortunately, WPF doesn't use the generic IComparer<T> interface from the System.Collections.Generic namespace.

Example 7-20. Custom sorting (continued)

```
    // Sort Name ascending and Age descending
    int nameCompare = lhs.Name.CompareTo(rhs.Name);
    if( nameCompare != 0 ) return nameCompare;
    return rhs.Age - lhs.Age;
  }
}

public partial class Window1 : Window {
  ...
  ICollectionView GetFamilyView( ) {
    People people = (People)this.FindResource("Family");
    return CollectionViewSource.GetDefaultView(people);
  }

  void sortButton_Click(object sender, RoutedEventArgs e) {
    ListCollectionView view = (ListCollectionView)GetFamilyView( );
    if( view.CustomSort == null ) {
      view.CustomSort = new PersonSorter( );
    }
    else {
      view.CustomSort = null;
    }
  }
}
```

In the case of setting a custom sorter, we cast the result of GetDefaultView to a
ListCollectionView, which is what WPF wraps around an implementation of IList
(which our ObserverableCollection provides) to provide view functionality. There
are other implementations of ICollectionView that don't provide custom sorting, so
you'll want to test this code before shipping it.[*]

Default Collection Views

The SDK documentation for the individual views will tell you how each different
kind of collection data is mapped to a default view, but Table 7-1 is a handy guide to
help you along.

Table 7-1. The default views for each collection data type

Collection data	Default view
IEnumerable	CollectionView
IList	ListCollectionView
IBindingList	BindingListCollectionView

---

[*] Hopefully, you'll test the rest of your code before shipping it, too, but it never hurts to point these things out…

If you don't like the view that WPF provides, you can create your own implementation of ICollectionView and bind to that, too. In fact, this is handy for "stacking" views, that is, using one view as the input to another—when you need to implement custom views for features that WPF doesn't support out of the box (like "top *N*" functionality).

Filtering

Just because all of the objects are shown in an order that makes you happy doesn't mean that you want all of the objects to be shown. For those rogue objects that happen to be in the data but that shouldn't be displayed, we need to feed the view an implementation of the Predicate<object> delegate* that takes a single object parameter and returns a Boolean indicating whether the object should be shown (see Example 7-21).

Example 7-21. Filtering

```
public partial class Window1 : Window {
  ...
  ICollectionView GetFamilyView( ) {
    People people = (People)this.FindResource("Family");
    return CollectionViewSource.GetDefaultView(people);
  }

  void filterButton_Click(object sender, RoutedEventArgs e) {
    ICollectionView view = GetFamilyView( );
    if( view.Filter == null ) {
      view.Filter = delegate(object item) {
      // Just show the over 25-year-olds
      return ((Person)item).Age >= 25;
      };
    }
    else {
      view.Filter = null;
    }
  }
}
```

Like sorting, with a filter in place, new things are filtered appropriately, as Figure 7-12 shows.

The top window in Figure 7-12 shows no filtering, the middle window shows filtering of the initial list, and the bottom window shows adding a new adult with filtering still in place.

---

* Unlike sorting, which uses a single method interface implementation because of history, filtering uses a generic delegate because the addition of anonymous delegates and generics to C# 2.0 has made them all the rage.

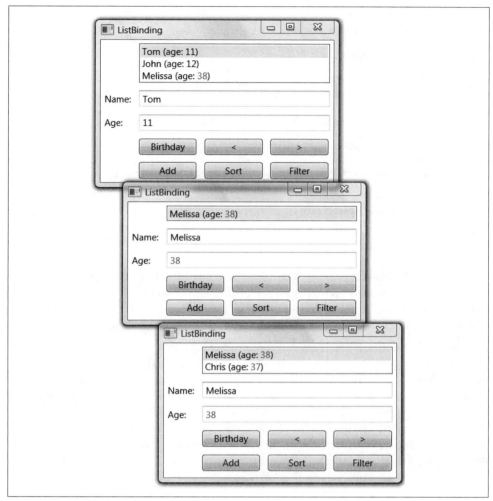

Figure 7-12. Unfiltered, filtered for adults, and adding to a filtered view

Grouping

Grouping is just what it sounds like—displaying data based on some criteria in a named group. The grouping criteria can be anything you like, but the only criterion that comes with WPF out of the box is grouping by property values. As we'll see, this one is pretty darn flexible, so you'll rarely need anything else.

You have to do two things to set up grouping. The first is to establish the groups you'd like to use, which you do by manipulating the GroupDescriptions collection on your view (see Example 7-22).

Example 7-22. Establishing data groups

```
public partial class Window1 : Window {
  ...
  ICollectionView GetFamilyView( ) {
    People people = (People)this.FindResource("Family");
    return CollectionViewSource.GetDefaultView(people);
  }

  void groupButton_Click(object sender, RoutedEventArgs e) {
    ICollectionView view = GetFamilyView( );
    if( view.GroupDescriptions.Count == 0 ) {
      // Group by age
      view.GroupDescriptions.Add(new PropertyGroupDescription("Age"));
    }
    else {
      view.GroupDescriptions.Clear( );
    }
  }
}
```

The `PropertyGroupDescription` object takes the name of the property you'd like to use for grouping. The groups themselves will be composed of all of the unique values pulled from the designated property on the items in the collection (e.g., Tom: 11, John: 12, Melissa: 38, and Penny: 38 will yield three named groups based on age: 11, 12, and 38).

All classes that derive from `ItemsControl` can display items in groups. To exploit this, we need to provide the control with a group style. A *group style* is not related to a normal style (as introduced in Chapter 1 and explored in depth in Chapter 8), but is rather a collection of group visualization-related information, like the real style for the container,[*] the data template for the header, and whether to hide empty groups. A group style is an instance of the `GroupStyle` class, and `ItemsControl` objects won't group data visually without one. Luckily, the `GroupStyle` class itself provides a static `Default` property that exposes a group style that works nicely to get us started, which we can use as shown in Example 7-23.[†]

Example 7-23. Using the default group style

```
<ListBox ... ItemsSource="{Binding}" >
  <ListBox.GroupStyle>
    <x:Static Member="GroupStyle.Default" />
  </ListBox.GroupStyle>
</ListBox>
```

---

[*] The `ItemsControl` generates containers for group items in the same way as the "item container generation" mechanism described in Chapter 5.

[†] Unfortunately, the XAML compiler won't accept the standard `<ListBox ... GroupStyle="{x:Static GroupStyle.Default}"/>` shortcut syntax, but the long syntax works just fine. For the curious, the XAML compiler is having trouble because the CLR `GroupStyle` property, defined on the `ItemsControl` base class, is defined as a read-only collection, even though the underlying dependency property is read-write.

This group style shows the name of the group above each indented group, as shown in Figure 7-13.

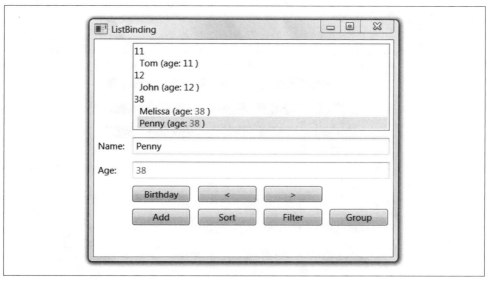

Figure 7-13. Grouping with the default group style

The data template used in the default group style shows the Name of the CollectionViewGroup constructed to reference the items in each group. If you'd like to replace that data template with one that includes custom formatting of group name data or other information from the CollectionViewGroup object (like the number of items in the group), you can do so with a custom data template, as shown in Example 7-24.

Example 7-24. A custom group style

```
<ListBox ... ItemsSource="{Binding}">
  <ListBox.GroupStyle>
    <GroupStyle>
      <GroupStyle.HeaderTemplate>
        <DataTemplate>
          <TextBlock
            Background="Black" Foreground="White" FontWeight="Bold">

            <TextBlock Text="{Binding Name}" />
            (<TextBlock Text="{Binding ItemCount}" />)

          </TextBlock>
        </DataTemplate>
      </GroupStyle.HeaderTemplate>
    </GroupStyle>
  </ListBox.GroupStyle>
</ListBox>
```

Here we've set the header template of the group style to a data template containing a TextBlock with a black background, a white foreground, and two nested TextBlock objects, one to display the name of the group and another to display the number of items, as Figure 7-14 shows.

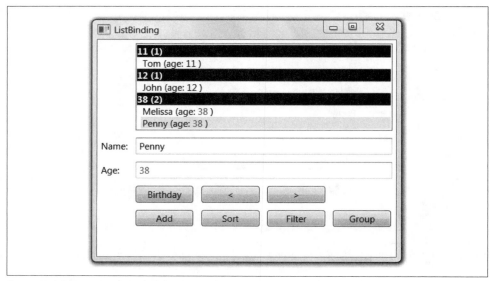

Figure 7-14. A custom group style in action

Figure 7-14 shows grouping by each possible value of the Age property in all of the data, automatically indenting the data in each group. Taking it one step further, what if we'd like to group by ranges—say, over and under 25. If we wanted, we could derive from the GroupDescription, overriding the GroupNamesFromItem method to classify items as belonging to one or more groups. (The PropertyGroupDescription class derives from GroupDescription, as do all data grouping policy implementations.) However, the PropertyGroupDescription class itself provides this flexibility by allowing for a custom IValueConverter implementation that groups items without the need for a custom GroupDescription class. Example 7-25 shows a value converter that converts values from the Age property into groups.

Example 7-25. A custom value converter for grouping

```
public class AgeToRangeConverter : IValueConverter {
  public object Convert(object value, Type targetType, ...) {
    return (int)value < 25 ? "Under the Hill" : "Over the Hill";
  }

  public object ConvertBack(object value, Type targetType, ...) {
    // should not be called in our example
    throw new NotImplementedException();
  }
}
```

This code assumes that the PropertyGroupDescription class will take each Person object and pass in the Age property, giving us the opportunity to group the data into our two buckets. We can configure the PropertyGroupDescription object to do this by passing the value converter to the constructor, as in Example 7-26.

Example 7-26. Using a custom value converter for grouping

```
void groupButton_Click(object sender, RoutedEventArgs e) {
  ICollectionView view = GetFamilyView();
  if( view.GroupDescriptions.Count == 0 ) {
    // Group by range
    view.GroupDescriptions.Add(
      new PropertyGroupDescription("Age", new AgeToRangeConverter()));
  }
  else {
    view.GroupDescriptions.Clear();
  }
}
```

Figure 7-15 shows the results.

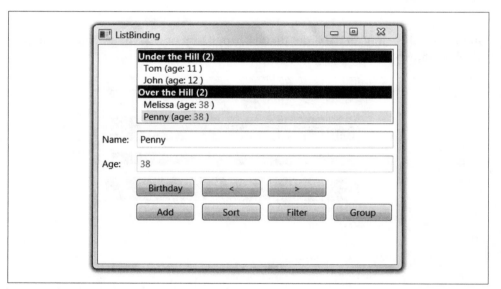

Figure 7-15. A custom value converter used for grouping

In fact, the use of the converter is so flexible that it's hard to imagine needing to implement a custom group description at all. If you want an object to belong to more than one group, you can return a collection of group names from the Convert method instead of a single name. If you want to get at all of the object's data instead of just a single property, you can construct a PropertyGroupDescriptor with null as the property name, which will pass in the entire object as the value parameter to Convert instead of just a single property's data. Finally, if you want to have control over the way string comparison is done, you can pass in a member of the `StringComparison` enumeration. The `PropertyGroupDescriptor` can almost do it all.

One thing it can't do, at least by itself, is group at multiple levels. However, if you'd like to, you can add multiple group descriptors to the view's `GroupDescriptions` list, as shown in Example 7-27.

Example 7-27. Multiple groups

```
void groupButton_Click(object sender, RoutedEventArgs e) {
  ICollectionView view = GetFamilyView( );
  if( view.GroupDescriptions.Count == 0 ) {
    // Group by range, then age
    view.GroupDescriptions.Add(
      new PropertyGroupDescription("Age", new AgeToRangeConverter( )));
    view.GroupDescriptions.Add(
      new PropertyGroupDescription("Age"));
  }
  else {
    view.GroupDescriptions.Clear( );
  }
}
```

Grouping will be done in the order that the groups are described, indenting as appropriate, as shown in Figure 7-16.

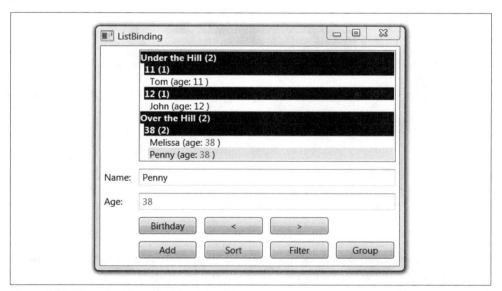

Figure 7-16. Grouping by more than one criterion

Groups are pretty darn handy. They're even handier if you'd like to combine them with sorting in your XAML.

Declarative Sorting and Grouping

Setting up sorting and grouping characteristics in code is handy if you want to flip the characteristics programmatically, as we've been doing. However, if you've got a predetermined set of data massaging you'd like to do, a CollectionViewSource is a handy place to keep those settings (see Example 7-28).

Example 7-28. Declarative sorting and grouping

```
<Window ...
  xmlns:local="clr-namespace:CollectionViewSourceBinding"
  xmlns:compModel="clr-namespace:System.ComponentModel;assembly=WindowsBase"
  xmlns:data="clr-namespace:System.Windows.Data;assembly=PresentationFramework">
  <Window.Resources>
    <local:People x:Key="Family">
      <local:Person Name="Tom" Age="11" />
      <local:Person Name="John" Age="12" />
      <local:Person Name="Melissa" Age="38" />
      <local:Person Name="Penny" Age="38" />
    </local:People>

    <local:AgeToRangeConverter x:Key="ageConverter" />

    <CollectionViewSource x:Key="SortedGroupedFamily"
                          Source="{StaticResource Family}">

      <CollectionViewSource.SortDescriptions>
        <compModel:SortDescription PropertyName="Name" Direction="Ascending" />
        <compModel:SortDescription PropertyName="Age" Direction="Descending" />
      </CollectionViewSource.SortDescriptions>

      <CollectionViewSource.GroupDescriptions>
        <data:PropertyGroupDescription PropertyName="Age"
              Converter="{StaticResource ageConverter}" />
        <data:PropertyGroupDescription PropertyName="Age" />
      </CollectionViewSource.GroupDescriptions>
    </CollectionViewSource>

  </Window.Resources>
  <Grid>
    <ListBox
      ItemsSource="{Binding Source={StaticResource SortedGroupedFamily}}"
      DisplayMemberPath="Name">

      <ListBox.GroupStyle>
        <x:Static Member="GroupStyle.Default" />
      </ListBox.GroupStyle>

    </ListBox>
  </Grid>
</Window>
```

In Example 7-28, we bring in the System.ComponentModel and System.Windows.Data namespaces first so that we can create SortDescription and PropertyGroupDescription objects. Then we create a CollectionViewSource object, which sorts and groups our data (provided via the Source property) and exposes an ICollectionView implementation.

Inside the CollectionViewSource, we set up the sorting and grouping policies we've been setting up programmatically. Notice the use of multiple group descriptors, including one that brings in a custom value converter, just like our most advanced grouping code sample.

Finally, we bind the listbox to the CollectionViewSource, so it can get the sorted and grouped data, as shown in Figure 7-17.

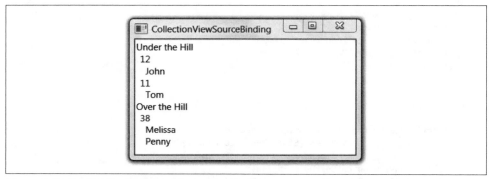

Figure 7-17. Declarative sorting and grouping in action

Unfortunately, this technique isn't quite as robust as the code-based technique; it doesn't allow custom sorting code, nor does it allow filtering of any kind. However, it lets us go quite a way without imperative code (excluding the custom value converter, of course).

Data Source Providers

So far, we've been dealing with simple, hardcoded objects. However, objects can come from long operations for which we'd prefer not to wait, like over a network connection or as translated from XML or relational data. For these cases, we'd really like a layer of indirection for pulling objects from other sources and even pushing that work off to a worker thread if said retrieval is a ponderous operation. For this indirection, we turn to *data source providers*, whose job is (as the name suggests) to provide data sources for use in binding scenarios.

Object Data Provider

WPF ships with two data source providers, both derived from the DataSourceProvider base class: ObjectDataProvider and XmlDataProvider. Data source providers create a layer of indirection for any kind of operation that produces objects against which to data-bind. For example, if we wanted to load a set of Person objects over the Web, we could encapsulate that logic into a bit of code, as shown in Example 7-29.

Example 7-29. A type to be used by ObjectDataProvider

```
...
public class Person : INotifyPropertyChanged {...}
public class People : ObservableCollection<Person> {}

public class RemotePeopleLoader {
  // ObjectDataProvider will expose results for binding
  public People LoadPeople() {
    // Load people from afar
    People people = new People();
    ...
    return people;
  }
}
...
```

In Example 7-29, the RemotePeopleLoader class exposes a method (LoadPeople) that will load people however it feels and return that data for binding. To configure the object data provider to create the RemotePeopleLoader and call the LoadPeople method is a matter of a little XAML (see Example 7-30).

Example 7-30. Using the ObjectDataProvider

```
<Window.Resources>
  ...
  <ObjectDataProvider
    x:Key="Family"
    ObjectType="{x:Type local:RemotePeopleLoader}"
    MethodName="LoadPeople" />
</Window.Resources>
<Grid DataContext="{StaticResource Family}">
  ...
  <ListBox ItemsSource="{Binding}" .../>
</Grid>
```

Here we're creating an ObjectDataProvider as a named resource so that we can use it as the data context for the grid, enabling binding at the listbox, text boxes, and so on. The ObjectType property is the type of the class to create, but you can use a pre-created object via the ObjectInstance property as well (e.g., if another resource was an object that could load data for you). The MethodName property is the name of the method to call to retrieve the data.

With an object data provider acting as an intermediary between the data and the bindings, we need to update our code to retrieve the People collection from the ObjectDataProvider resource, as shown in Example 7-31.

Example 7-31. Accessing the data held by an object data provider

```
public partial class Window1 : Window {
  ...
  ICollectionView GetFamilyView( ) {
    DataSourceProvider provider =
      (DataSourceProvider)this.FindResource("Family");
    People people = (People)provider.Data;
    return CollectionViewSource.GetDefaultView(people);
  }

  void birthdayButton_Click(object sender, RoutedEventArgs e) {
    ICollectionView view = GetFamilyView( );
    Person person = (Person)view.CurrentItem;

    ++person.Age;
    MessageBox.Show(...);
  }

  void addButton_Click(object sender, RoutedEventArgs e) {
    DataSourceProvider provider =
      (DataSourceProvider)this.FindResource("Family");
    People people = (People)provider.Data;
    people.Add(new Person("Chris", 37));
  }
  ...
}
```

Because the Family resource is now an ObjectDataProvider, itself derived from DataSourceProvider, in Example 7-31 when we need the People collection, we're casting to DataSourceProvider on the Family resource and pulling the collection out of the Data property.

 Even though the object data provider exposes its data from the Data property, this does not mean you should bind to the Data property. If you notice from Example 7-30, we're still binding the listbox as before:

```
<!-- Do not bind to Path=Data -->
<ListBox ItemsSource="{Binding}" ... />
```

This works because WPF has built-in knowledge of DataSourceProvider, so there's no need for you to do the indirection yourself.

Asynchronous data retrieval

In Example 7-30, the object data provider was retrieving the data from the remote people loader synchronously, which means that if it took a long time, the UI thread would block. Instead, we can use the IsAsynchronous property to get the most interesting piece of functionality that the object data provider gives us and that we lack when we declare objects directly in XAML:

```
<ObjectDataProvider
  x:Key="Family"
  ObjectType="{x:Type local:RemotePeopleLoader}"
  IsAsynchronous="True"
  MethodName="LoadPeople" />
```

When the IsAsynchronous property is set to True (the default is False), the task of retrieving the data is handled on a worker thread, letting the user continue to interact with the UI in the meantime and performing the binding on the UI thread only when the data has been retrieved. This is not the same as binding to the data as it's retrieved (e.g., from a stream over the network), but it's better than blocking the UI thread while a long retrieval happens.

Passing parameters

The object data provider also provides the MethodParameters property, which is a collection of objects to be passed to the method that retrieves the data. For example, if we wanted to pass in a set of URLs from which to try to retrieve the data, we could use the MethodParameters property as we do in Example 7-32.

Example 7-32. Passing method parameters via ObjectDataProvider

```
<Window ...
  xmlns:sys="clr-namespace:System"
  xmlns:local="clr-namespace:ObjectBinding">
  <Window.Resources>
    <ObjectDataProvider
      x:Key="Family"
      ObjectType="{x:Type local:RemotePeopleLoader}"
      IsAsynchronous="True"
      MethodName="LoadPeople">
      <ObjectDataProvider.MethodParameters>
        <sys:String>http://sellsbrothers.com/boys.dat</sys:String>
        <sys:String>http://sellssisters.com/girls.dat</sys:String>
      </ObjectDataProvider.MethodParameters>
    </ObjectDataProvider>
    ...
  </Window.Resources>
  ...
</Window>
```

In Example 7-32, we've added a list of two URLs, which will be translated into a call to the LoadPeople method that takes two strings (see Example 7-33).

Example 7-33. Accepting arguments passed by ObjectDataProvider

```
namespace PersonBinding {
  public class RemotePeopleLoader : People {
    public People LoadPeople(string url1, string url2) {
      // Load People from afar using two URLs
      ...
    }
  }
}
```

Using the object data provider and any method on any object that returns data, you can retrieve data asynchronously and bind to it when it's available. Although it's possible to create your own custom data source provider (just derive from DataSourceProvider and have a party), the flexibility of the object data provider means that you almost certainly won't need to.

 The object data provider allows for another way to get the data as well as from a named method. If you don't provide a MethodName, the object data provider will assume that the data is retrieved in the constructor (either the default or as described by the ConstructorParameters list, structured just like the MethodParameters list) and that the object itself is the data. The use of the constructor and optional constructor parameters is handy if you're binding to one or more collections exposed from properties on the constructed object. For example:

```
<Window ...
  <Window.Resources>
    <ObjectDataProvider
      x:Key="topLevel"
      ObjectType="{x:Type local:FinanceData}"/>
  </Window.Resources>
  ...
  <Grid DataContext="{StaticResource topLevel}">
    ...
    <ListBox ItemsSource="{Binding Path=Customers,
                           IsAsync=True}" ... />
    ...
    <ListBox ItemsSource="{Binding Path=Partners,
                           IsAsync=True}" ... />
    ...
  </Grid>
</Window>
```

In this case, you might want to use the IsAsync property on binding to the lower-level data instead of the IsAsynchronous property on the top-level data provider, as now the former is likely to take longer.

Binding to Relational Data

Although UI designer support is still being developed to help bring relational data into your WPF pages specifically, the tools we've already got can be pressed into service for WPF work without issue. For example, assume a table like the one in Figure 7-18 defined in an Access database (*family.mdb*).

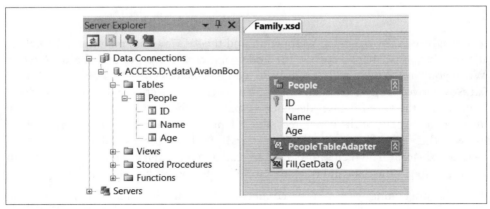

Figure 7-18. A Person table in Access (family.mdb)

Although we could write the ADO.NET code to bring this table into our project, we don't have to. Instead, we can bring in the data using the typed dataset designer, which has been in Visual Studio since .NET 1.0. Bringing a new typed data set into your project is as simple as right-clicking on your project, choosing Add → New Item → Dataset, choosing a name, and clicking Add. This brings up the typed dataset designer, onto which you can drag any number of tables, setting up relationships and specifying the way you'd like the data to be projected into your project. A ready source of data for the data set design is the Server Explorer, which you can use to connect to various databases. To connect to the Access database, *family.mdb*, I right-clicked on Data Connections and chose Add Connection, configuring things properly for Access. I then drilled in to the People table and dragged it onto the designer surface, as shown in Figure 7-19.

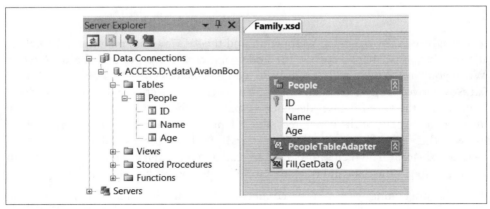

Figure 7-19. Creating a typed data set in a WPF project works just fine

All of these dragging and dropping shenanigans produced for me three interesting classes: PeopleRow, PeopleDataTable, and PeopleTableAdapter, summarized in Example 7-34 from the generated *Family.Designer.cs* file.

Example 7-34. The interesting class the typed dataset designer generates

```
namespace AdoBinding {
  ...
  public partial class Family : System.Data.DataSet {
    ...
    public partial class PeopleRow : System.Data.DataRow {
      ...
      public int ID { get {...} set {...} } }
      public string Name { get {...} set {...} } }
      public int Age { get {...} set {...} } }
      ...
    }

    public partial class PeopleDataTable :
      System.Data.DataTable, System.Collections.IEnumerable {
      ...
      public PeopleRow AddPeopleRow(string Name, int Age) {...}
      public PeopleRow FindByID(int ID) {...}
      public void RemovePeopleRow(PeopleRow row) {...}
      ...
    }
  }

  namespace FamilyTableAdapters {
    ...
    public partial class PeopleTableAdapter :
      System.ComponentModel.Component {
      ...
      public virtual Family.PeopleDataTable GetData() {...}
      ...
    }
  }
}
```

The PeopleRow class is a typed wrapper around the DataRow class built into ADO.NET. It's the thing that maps between the underlying database types and the CLR types. When you bind to relational data in WPF, you'll be binding to a DataTable full of these DataRow-derived objects. Actually, just plain DataRow objects work, too—you don't have to use the typed dataset designer to make this work. However, if you do, you also get the benefit of the generated table adapters, like our PeopleDataTable, which knows the shortest way to create and find PeopleRow objects, and the PeopleTableAdapter, which knows how to read and write data to and from Access (in our case), to get the data and track updates for pushing back to the database.

The one other thing we get is the connection string plopped into the *app.config* so that it can be maintained separately from the code, as you can see in Example 7-35.

Example 7-35. The connection string we get when we add a new data connection

```xml
<?xml version="1.0" encoding="utf-8" ?>
<configuration>
  <connectionStrings>
    <add name="AdoBinding.Properties.Settings.familyConnectionString"
      connectionString="Provider=Microsoft.Jet.OLEDB.4.0;Data Source=family.mdb"
      providerName="System.Data.OleDb" />
  </connectionStrings>
</configuration>
```

With these two wrappers in place, and the connection string all set up for us in the app's *.config* file, all we really have to do is create an instance of the PeopleTableAdapter and call GetData, binding to the results. We could do this in the main window's constructor if we wanted to, as shown in Example 7-36.

Example 7-36. Using the classes generated by the dataset designer

```csharp
public Window1() {
  InitializeComponent();

  // Get the data for binding synchronously
  DataContext = (new FamilyTableAdapters.PeopleTableAdapter()).GetData();

  ...
}
```

In Example 7-36, the GetData call is synchronous, which is fine for our simple sample. However, because in a real app we're often accessing data that is located over a network connection, synchronously retrieving the data and blocking the UI thread while we wait isn't such a good idea. This is an excellent use of the asynchronous support we've got in the object data provider (see Example 7-37).

Example 7-37. Binding to relational data declaratively

```xml
<!-- Window1.xaml -->
<Window ...
  xmlns:local="clr-namespace:AdoBinding"
  xmlns:tableAdapters="clr-namespace:AdoBinding.FamilyTableAdapters">
  <Window.Resources>
    <ObjectDataProvider
      x:Key="Family"
      ObjectType="{x:Type tableAdapters:PeopleTableAdapter}"
      IsAsynchronous="True"
      MethodName="GetData" />

    <local:AgeToForegroundConverter x:Key="ageConverter" />
  </Window.Resources>
  <Grid DataContext="{StaticResource Family}">
    ...
    <ListBox ... ItemsSource="{Binding}">
      <ListBox.ItemTemplate>
        <DataTemplate>
```

Example 7-37. Binding to relational data declaratively (continued)

```
        <TextBlock>
          <TextBlock Text="{Binding Path=Name}" />
          (age: <TextBlock Text="{Binding Path=Age}"
            Foreground="
              {Binding
                Path=Age,
                Converter=
                  {StaticResource ageConverter}}" />)
        </TextBlock>
      </DataTemplate>
    </ListBox.ItemTemplate>
  </ListBox>
  ...
  </Grid>
</Window>
```

At the top of Example 7-37, we're doing just what we did in code—that is, creating an instance of the `PeopleTableAdapter` type, calling `GetData`, and binding to the results. The difference is that we're doing it declaratively, which makes it very easy to bind asynchronously—all we have to do is set the `IsAsynchronous` property to `True` and the data retrieval happens on a worker thread, keeping the UI from freezing.

Another thing to notice is that the bindings are all the same as before, although in this case, we're using the names of the columns as properties and trusting ADO.NET and WPF to negotiate properties dynamically at runtime via the `ICustomTypeDescriptor` interface.* Finally, notice that our use of the age to foreground brush value converter remains the same.

 Example 7-37 uses a template created specifically for use by the `ListBox` object's `ItemTemplate` property instead of a typed data template to automatically share across content controls. This is because we're no longer dealing with objects of the custom `Person` class at the top level of a namespace, but objects of type `DataRowView`.

Because we've got the ADO.NET `DataRowView` type and the typed dataset designer-generated `PeopleDataTable` and `PeopleDataRow` types instead of our custom `Person` and `People` types, implementing our data management code is a little different, as you can see in Example 7-38.

---

* The `ICustomTypeDescriptor` interface has been with us since .NET 1.0 for data bound objects to expose properties not known until runtime (e.g., the dynamic results of an SQL query). In the case of ADO.NET, even though we used the typed dataset designer to get typed properties, WPF will still use the `DataRowView` class's implementation of `ICustomTypeDescriptor`, which is why typed and untyped data sets work equally well.

Example 7-38. Accessing the data held by ADO.NET

```
// Window1.xaml.cs
...
using System.Data;
using System.Data.OleDb;

public partial class Window1 : Window {

  public Window1( ) {
    InitializeComponent( );

    this.birthdayButton.Click += birthdayButton_Click;
    this.backButton.Click += backButton_Click;
    this.forwardButton.Click += forwardButton_Click;
    this.addButton.Click += addButton_Click;
    this.sortButton.Click += sortButton_Click;
    this.filterButton.Click += filterButton_Click;
    this.groupButton.Click += groupButton_Click;
  }

  ICollectionView GetFamilyView( ) {
    DataSourceProvider provider =
      (DataSourceProvider)this.FindResource("Family");
    return CollectionViewSource.GetDefaultView(provider.Data);
  }

  void birthdayButton_Click(object sender, RoutedEventArgs e) {
    ICollectionView view = GetFamilyView( );

    // Each item is a DataRowView, which we can use to access
    // the typed PersonRow
    AdoBinding.Family.PeopleRow person =
      (AdoBinding.Family.PeopleRow)((DataRowView)view.CurrentItem).Row;

    ++person.Age;
    MessageBox.Show(
      string.Format(
        "Happy Birthday, {0}, age {1}!",
        person.Name,
        person.Age),
      "Birthday");
  }

  void backButton_Click(object sender, RoutedEventArgs e) {
    ICollectionView view = GetFamilyView( );
    view.MoveCurrentToPrevious( );
    if( view.IsCurrentBeforeFirst ) {
      view.MoveCurrentToFirst( );
    }
  }

  void forwardButton_Click(object sender, RoutedEventArgs e) {
    ICollectionView view = GetFamilyView( );
```

Example 7-38. Accessing the data held by ADO.NET (continued)

```
    view.MoveCurrentToNext( );
    if( view.IsCurrentAfterLast ) {
      view.MoveCurrentToLast( );
    }
  }

  void addButton_Click(object sender, RoutedEventArgs e) {
    // Creating a new PeopleRow
    DataSourceProvider provider =
      (DataSourceProvider)this.FindResource("Family");
    AdoBinding.Family.PeopleDataTable table =
      (AdoBinding.Family.PeopleDataTable)provider.Data;
    table.AddPeopleRow("Chris", 37);
  }

  void sortButton_Click(object sender, RoutedEventArgs e) {
    ICollectionView view = GetFamilyView();
    if( view.SortDescriptions.Count == 0 ) {
      view.SortDescriptions.Add(
        new SortDescription("Name", ListSortDirection.Ascending));
      view.SortDescriptions.Add(
        new SortDescription("Age", ListSortDirection.Descending));
    }
    else {
      view.SortDescriptions.Clear( );
    }
  }

  void filterButton_Click(object sender, RoutedEventArgs e) {
    // Can't set the Filter property, but can set the
    // CustomFilter on a BindingListCollectionView
    BindingListCollectionView view =
      (BindingListCollectionView)GetFamilyView( );
    if( string.IsNullOrEmpty(view.CustomFilter) ) {
      view.CustomFilter = "Age > 25";
    }
    else {
      view.CustomFilter = null;
    }
  }

  void groupButton_Click(object sender, RoutedEventArgs e) {
    ICollectionView view = GetFamilyView();
    if( view.GroupDescriptions.Count == 0 ) {
      // Group by age
      view.GroupDescriptions.Add(new PropertyGroupDescription("Age"));
    }
    else {
      view.GroupDescriptions.Clear( );
    }
  }
}
```

In Example 7-38, you'll notice that manipulating and displaying a person is different because we're dealing with a DataRowView object's Row property to get the typed PeopleRow we want. Also, adding a new person is different because we're dealing with a PeopleDataTable. Finally, filtering is different because the BindingListCollectionView doesn't support the Filter property (setting it causes an exception at runtime). However, we set the CustomFilter string on the BindingListCollectionView using the ADO. NET filter syntax. Everything else, though—including accessing the collection view, navigating the rows, and even sorting and grouping—is the same, as shown in Figure 7-20.

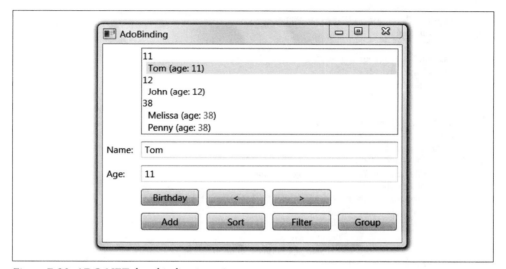

Figure 7-20. ADO.NET data binding in action

So, although there was no relational data-specific data provider, none is needed—the object data provider works just fine for data binding to relational data in WPF.

XML Data Source Provider

In addition to object and relational data, WPF also supports binding to XML data. For instance, Example 7-39 shows some family data represented in XML.

Example 7-39. A random family rendered in XML

```
<Family xmlns="http://sellsbrothers.com">
  <Person Name="Tom" Age="11" />
  <Person Name="John" Age="12" />
  <Person Name="Melissa" Age="38" />
</Family>
```

With this file available in the same folder as the executing application, we can bind to it using the XmlDataProvider, as shown in Example 7-40.

Example 7-40. An XmlDataProvider in action

```
<!-- Window1.xaml -->
<Window ...>
  <Window.Resources>
    <XmlDataProvider
      x:Key="Family"
      Source="family.xml"
      XPath="/sb:Family/sb:Person">
      <XmlDataProvider.XmlNamespaceManager>
        <XmlNamespaceMappingCollection>
          <XmlNamespaceMapping Uri="http://sellsbrothers.com" Prefix="sb" />
        </XmlNamespaceMappingCollection>
      </XmlDataProvider.XmlNamespaceManager>
    </XmlDataProvider>

    <local:AgeToForegroundConverter
      x:Key="ageConverter" />
  </Window.Resources>
  <Grid DataContext="{StaticResource Family}">
    ...
    <ListBox ... ItemsSource="{Binding}">
      <ListBox.ItemTemplate>
        <DataTemplate>
          <StackPanel Orientation="Horizontal">
            <TextBlock Text="{Binding XPath=@Name}" />
            <TextBlock Text=" (age: " />
            <TextBlock Text="{Binding XPath=@Age}"
              Foreground="{Binding
                             XPath=@Age,
                             Converter=
                               {StaticResource ageConverter}}" />
            <TextBlock Text=")" />
          </StackPanel>
        </DataTemplate>
      </ListBox.ItemTemplate>
    </ListBox>
    ...
  </Grid>
</Window>
```

The first thing I want to point out in Example 7-40 is the use of the XmlDataProvider with a relative URL that points to the *family.xml* file. The first thing you'll probably notice, though, is the large amount of XAML to deal with namespaces. Looking back at the XML file (Example 7-39), you'll notice that no prefix was used, only a default namespace of http://sellsbrothers.com. Using namespace prefixes in the XAML makes it possible to construct the XPath statement to find the set of Person elements in our sample XML. Finally, notice the use of the XPath property in the Binding objects instead of the Path property, and the @ symbol to designate binding to an XML attribute.*

---

* An explanation of the XPath syntax is beyond the scope of this book, but for a good reference, I'd start with *Essential XML Quick Reference*, by Aaron Skonnard and Martin Gudgin (Addison-Wesley Professional).

XML data islands

If you happen to know your data at compile time, the XML data provider also supports XML data islands, as shown in Example 7-41.

Example 7-41. An XML data island in XAML

```
<XmlDataProvider x:Key="Family" XPath="/sb:Family/sb:Person">
  <XmlDataProvider.XmlNamespaceManager>
    <XmlNamespaceMappingCollection>
      <XmlNamespaceMapping Uri="http://sellsbrothers.com" Prefix="sb" />
    </XmlNamespaceMappingCollection>
  </XmlDataProvider.XmlNamespaceManager>

  <x:XData>
    <Family xmlns="http://sellsbrothers.com">
      <Person Name="Tom" Age="11" />
      <Person Name="John" Age="12" />
      <Person Name="Melissa" Age="38" />
    </Family>
  </x:XData>
</XmlDataProvider>
```

In Example 7-41, we've copied the contents of *family.xml* under the XmlDataProvider element and wrapped it in an XData element to designate it as separate from the rest of how XAML is parsed (Appendix A is a good place to read up on that topic). We've also dropped the Source attribute (because the data is embedded), but left the XPath statement as it was.

And as you might expect, now that we're using XML instead of object data, some of the operations in our sample application need to be changed (see Example 7-42).

Example 7-42. Managing XML bound data

```
// Window1.xaml.cs
...
using System.Xml;

public partial class Window1 : Window {

  public Window1() {
    InitializeComponent();

    this.birthdayButton.Click += birthdayButton_Click;
    this.backButton.Click += backButton_Click;
    this.forwardButton.Click += forwardButton_Click;
    this.addButton.Click += addButton_Click;
    this.sortButton.Click += sortButton_Click;
    this.filterButton.Click += filterButton_Click;
    this.groupButton.Click += groupButton_Click;
  }
```

Example 7-42. Managing XML bound data (continued)

```csharp
ICollectionView GetFamilyView( ) {
  DataSourceProvider provider =
    (DataSourceProvider)this.FindResource("Family");
  return CollectionViewSource.GetDefaultView(provider.Data);
}

void birthdayButton_Click(object sender, RoutedEventArgs e) {
  ICollectionView view = GetFamilyView( );

  // Each "person" is an XmlElement and attribute
  // values come from a string-based indexer
  XmlElement person = (XmlElement)view.CurrentItem;
  person.SetAttribute("Age",
    (int.Parse(person.Attributes["Age"].Value) + 1).ToString( ));
  MessageBox.Show(
    string.Format(
      "Happy Birthday, {0}, age {1}!",
      person.Attributes["Name"].Value,
      person.Attributes["Age"].Value),
    "Birthday");
}

void backButton_Click(object sender, RoutedEventArgs e) {
  ICollectionView view = GetFamilyView( );
  view.MoveCurrentToPrevious( );
  if( view.IsCurrentBeforeFirst ) {
    view.MoveCurrentToFirst( );
  }
}

void forwardButton_Click(object sender, RoutedEventArgs e) {
  ICollectionView view = GetFamilyView( );
  view.MoveCurrentToNext( );
  if( view.IsCurrentAfterLast ) {
    view.MoveCurrentToLast( );
  }
}

void addButton_Click(object sender, RoutedEventArgs e) {
  // Creating a new XmlElement
  XmlDataProvider provider =
    (XmlDataProvider)this.FindResource("Family");
  XmlElement person =
    provider.Document.CreateElement("Person", "http://sellsbrothers.com");
  person.SetAttribute("Name", "Chris");
  person.SetAttribute("Age", "37");
  provider.Document.ChildNodes[0].AppendChild(person);
}
```

Example 7-42. Managing XML bound data (continued)

```
void sortButton_Click(object sender, RoutedEventArgs e) {
  ICollectionView view = GetFamilyView( );
  if( view.SortDescriptions.Count == 0 ) {
    view.SortDescriptions.Add(
      new SortDescription("@Name", ListSortDirection.Ascending));
    view.SortDescriptions.Add(
      new SortDescription("@Age", ListSortDirection.Descending));
  }
  else {
    view.SortDescriptions.Clear( );
  }
}

void filterButton_Click(object sender, RoutedEventArgs e) {
  ICollectionView view = GetFamilyView( );

  if( view.Filter == null ) {
    view.Filter = delegate(object item) {
      return
        int.Parse(((XmlElement)item).Attributes["Age"].Value) > 25;
    };
  }
  else {
    view.Filter = null;
  }
}

void groupButton_Click(object sender, RoutedEventArgs e) {
  ICollectionView view = GetFamilyView( );
  if( view.GroupDescriptions.Count == 0 ) {
    // Group by age
    view.GroupDescriptions.Add(new PropertyGroupDescription("@Age"));
  }
  else {
    view.GroupDescriptions.Clear( );
  }
}
}
```

Whereas in the ADO.NET example we used `PeopleDataTable`, `PeopleDataRow`, and `DataRowView`, in the XML example we use `XmlDocument` and `XmlElement`. For updating and accessing values, Example 7-42 uses the `XmlElement` `SetAttribute` method to change a value and the `Attributes` collection to get one. When adding a new person, we get the `XmlDocument` from the `XmlDataProvider`, ask it to create a new `XmlElement`, set the attributes, and add it to the child node collection of the document. When filtering, we simply cast to an `XmlElement` to access the attributes we need to make filtering decisions. Finally, when sorting or grouping, the descriptions include paths as XPath expressions (e.g., @Age). The results look just like Figure 7-20.

XML binding without the data source provider

If you've already got a source of XML data that isn't readily available for use by the XML data source provider,* you can programmatically bind to it instead, as shown in Example 7-43.

Example 7-43. XML binding without the data source provider

```
<!-- Window1.xaml -->
<Window ...>
  <Window.Resources>
    <!-- no XmlDataProvider -->
    <local:AgeToForegroundConverter x:Key="ageConverter" />
  </Window.Resources>

  <!-- DataContext set in code-behind -->
  <Grid Name="grid">...</Grid>
</Window>

// Window1.xaml.cs
...
public partial class Window1 : Window {
  // the family XML document
  XmlDocument doc;

  public Window1() {
    ...
    LoadFamilyXml();
  }

  void LoadFamilyXml() {
    // Load the XML using an XmlDocument
    doc = new XmlDocument();
    doc.Load("family.xml");

    // Make the namespace prefix mappings available for use in binding
    XmlNamespaceManager manager = new XmlNamespaceManager(doc.NameTable);
    manager.AddNamespace("sb", "http://sellsbrothers.com");
    Binding.SetXmlNamespaceManager(grid, manager);

    // Make the XML available for data binding. We use a binding here
    // because it will detect when the source document changes so it can
    // refresh the set of nodes returned by the XPath query
    Binding b = new Binding();
    b.XPath = "/sb:Family/sb:Person";
    b.Source = doc;
    grid.SetBinding(Grid.DataContextProperty, b);
  }
```

---

* For example, if you need to retrieve XML data via an HTTP POST, you can't use the XML data source provider, as it can only use HTTP GET.

Example 7-43. XML binding without the data source provider (continued)

```
ICollectionView GetFamilyView( ) {
  // The default view comes directly from the data
  return CollectionViewSource.GetDefaultView(grid.DataContext);
}

...

void addButton_Click(object sender, RoutedEventArgs e) {
  // Creating a new XmlElement
  XmlElement person =
    doc.CreateElement("Person", "http://sellsbrothers.com");

  person.SetAttribute("Name", "Chris");
  person.SetAttribute("Age", "37");

  doc.DocumentElement.AppendChild(person);
}
...
}
```

In Example 7-43, we're loading the XML manually from a file, but you can get access to the XML in whatever way is convenient, as long as you have an XmlNode or XmlNodeList to which to bind. Here we're creating the XmlDocument as a member variable so that we can use it again to create and add a new XmlElement in the addButton_Click event handler. Notice also that we're populating an XmlNamespaceManager and binding it to the grid so that binding knows how to translate XPath strings that use namespace prefixes. And finally, instead of setting the XML data directly as the grid's DataContext, we're actually binding it, along with the XPath to filter the set of nodes available in the XML data. The binding is there so that when the underlying XML data changes, resulting in a new set of nodes returned from the XPath expression, the grid's data context is updated appropriately. Also, as this data context changes, the view may change, so we're using the DataContext property of the grid to get the view in GetFamilyView each time we need it.

The rest of the XML-related code in this sample does not have to change, as we've just done manually what the XML data source provider was doing for us (although we did leave out support for asynchronous access to the data, if it happens to be far away).

Master-Detail Binding

We've seen binding to a single object. We've seen binding to a single list of objects. Another very popular thing to do is to bind to more than one list, especially related lists. For example, if you're showing your users a list of customers and then, when they select one, you'd like to show that customer's related orders, you'll want master-detail binding.

Master-detail binding is a form of filtering, where the selection in the master list (e.g., customer 452) sets the filtering parameters for the associated detail data (e.g., orders for customer 452).

In our discussion thus far, we don't have customers and orders, but we do have families and people, which we could further formalize as shown in Example 7-44.

Example 7-44. Master-detail data for binding

```
public class Person {
  string name;
  public string Name {
    get { return name; }
    set { name = value; }
  }

  int age;
  public int Age {
    get { return age; }
    set { age = value; }
  }
}

public class People : ObservableCollection<Person> {}

public class Family {
  string familyName;
  public string FamilyName {
    get { return familyName; }
    set { familyName = value; }
  }

  People members;
  public People Members {
    get { return members; }
    set { members = value; }
  }
}

public class Families : ObservableCollection<Family> {}
```

In Example 7-44, we've got our familiar Person class with Name and Age properties, collected into a familiar People collection. Further, we have a Family class with a FamilyName property and a Members property of type People. Finally, we have a Families collection, which collects Family objects. In other words, families have members, which consist of people with names and ages.

You could imagine instances of Families, Family, People, and Person that looked like Figure 7-21.

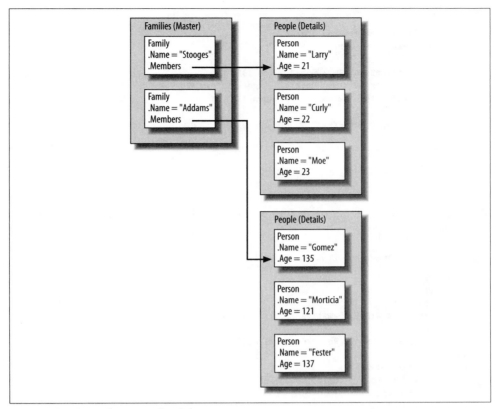

Figure 7-21. Example master-detail data

In Figure 7-21, the Families collection forms the master data, holding instances of the Family class, each of which holds a Members property of type People, which holds the detail Person data. You could populate instances of these data structures as shown in Example 7-45.

Example 7-45. Declaring example master-detail data

```
<!-- Window1.xaml -->
<Window ... xmlns:local="clr-namespace:MasterDetailBinding">
  <Window.Resources>
    <local:Families x:Key="Families">
      <local:Family FamilyName="Stooge">
        <local:Family.Members>
          <local:People>
            <local:Person Name="Larry" Age="21" />
            <local:Person Name="Curly" Age="22" />
            <local:Person Name="Moe" Age="23" />
          </local:People>
        </local:Family.Members>
      </local:Family>
```

Example 7-45. Declaring example master-detail data (continued)

```
        <local:Family FamilyName="Addams">
          <local:Family.Members>
            <local:People>
              <local:Person Name="Gomez" Age="135" />
              <local:Person Name="Morticia" Age="121" />
              <local:Person Name="Fester" Age="137" />
            </local:People>
          </local:Family.Members>
        </local:Family>
      </local:Families>
    </Window.Resources>
  ...
</Window>
```

Binding to this data at the top level (i.e., to show the family names) could look like Example 7-46.

Example 7-46. Binding to master Family data

```
<!-- Window1.xaml -->
<Window ...>
  <Window.Resources>
    <local:Families x:Key="Families">...</local:Families>
  </Window.Resources>
  <Grid DataContext="{StaticResource Families}">
    ...
    <!-- Families Column -->
    <TextBlock Grid.Row="0" Grid.Column="0">Families:</TextBlock>
    <ListBox Grid.Row="1" Grid.Column="0"
      IsSynchronizedWithCurrentItem="True"
      ItemsSource="{Binding}">
      <ListBox.ItemTemplate>
        <DataTemplate>
          <TextBlock Text="{Binding Path=FamilyName}" />
        </DataTemplate>
      </ListBox.ItemTemplate>
    </ListBox>
</Window>
```

In Example 7-46, we're setting two things in the Families column (column 0). The first is the header, which is set to the constant string Families. The second forms the body, which is a list of Family objects in the Families collection, showing each family's FamilyName property, as shown in Figure 7-22.

Figure 7-22 isn't master-detail yet, because selecting a master family doesn't show its associated details. To do that, we need to bind to the next level, as shown in Example 7-47.

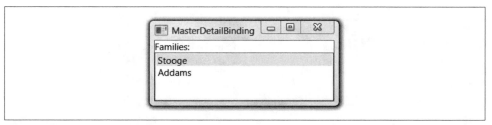

Figure 7-22. Showing family data

Example 7-47. Binding to detail Person data

```
<Grid DataContext="{StaticResource Families}">
  ...
  <!-- Families Column -->
  ...
  <!-- Members Column -->
  <StackPanel Grid.Row="0" Grid.Column="1" Orientation="Horizontal">
    <TextBlock Text="{Binding Path=FamilyName}" />
    <TextBlock Text=" Family Members:" />
  </StackPanel>
  <ListBox Grid.Row="1" Grid.Column="1"
    IsSynchronizedWithCurrentItem="True"
    ItemsSource="{Binding Path=Members}" >
    <ListBox.ItemTemplate>
      <DataTemplate>
        <StackPanel Orientation="Horizontal">
          <TextBlock Text="{Binding Path=Name}" />
          <TextBlock Text=" (age: " />
          <TextBlock Text="{Binding Path=Age}" />
          <TextBlock Text=" )" />
        </StackPanel>
      </DataTemplate>
    </ListBox.ItemTemplate>
  </ListBox>
```

In the Members column (column 1), we're also setting a header and body, but this time the header is bound to the FamilyName of the currently selected Family object.

Also, recall that in the Families column, our listbox's items source was bound to the entire collection via a Binding statement without a Path. In the details case, however, we want to tell the data binding engine that we'd like to bind to the Members property of the currently selected Family object, which is itself a collection of Person objects. Figure 7-23 shows master-detail binding in action.

But wait; there's more! Master-detail binding doesn't stop at just two levels, oh no. You can go as deep as you like, with each detail binding becoming the master binding for the next level. To see this in action, let's add one more level of detail to our data classes (see Example 7-48).

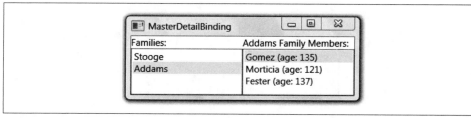

Figure 7-23. Showing master Family and detail Person data

Example 7-48. Adding a third level of detail

```
public class Person {
  string name;
  public string Name {
    get { return name; }
    set { name = value; }
  }

  int age;
  public int Age {
    get { return age; }
    set { age = value; }
  }

  Traits traits;
  public Traits Traits {
    get { return traits; }
    set { traits = value; }
  }
}

public class Traits : ObservableCollection<Trait> {}

public class Trait {
  string description;
  public string Description {
    get { return description; }
    set { description = value; }
  }
}
```

Now, not only do families have family names and members that consist of people with names and ages, but each person also has a set of traits, each with its own description. Expanding our XAML a bit to include traits would look like Example 7-49.

Example 7-49. Declaring a third level of detail

```
<local:Families x:Key="Families">
  <local:Family FamilyName="Stooge">
    <local:Family.Members>
```

Example 7-49. Declaring a third level of detail (continued)

```
      <local:People>
        <local:Person Name="Larry" Age="21">
          <local:Person.Traits>
            <local:Traits>
              <local:Trait Description="In Charge" />
              <local:Trait Description="Mean" />
              <local:Trait Description="Ugly" />
            </local:Traits>
          </local:Person.Traits>
        </local:Person>
        <local:Person Name="Curly" Age="22" >...</local:Person>
        ...
      </local:People>
    </local:Family.Members>
    ...
  </local:Family>
  ...
</local:Families>
```

With a third level of detail, we bind as shown in Example 7-50.

Example 7-50. Binding to a third level of detail data

```
<Grid DataContext="{StaticResource Families}">
  ...

  <!-- Families Column -->
  ...

  <!-- Members Column -->
  ...

  <!-- Traits Column -->
  <StackPanel Grid.Row="0" Grid.Column="2" Orientation="Horizontal">
    <TextBlock Text="{Binding Path=Members/Name}" />
    <TextBlock Text=" Traits:" />
  </StackPanel>
  <ListBox Grid.Row="1" Grid.Column="2"
    IsSynchronizedWithCurrentItem="True"
    ItemsSource="{Binding Path=Members/Traits}" >
    <ListBox.ItemTemplate>
      <DataTemplate>
        <TextBlock Text="{Binding Path=Description}" />
      </DataTemplate>
    </ListBox.ItemTemplate>
  </ListBox>
</Grid>
```

In the case of the Families column header, recall that we had no binding at all; the text was hardcoded:

```
<TextBlock ...>Families:</TextBlock>
```

In the case of the Members column header, we bound to the FamilyName of the currently selected Family object like so:

```
<TextBlock ... Text="{Binding Path=FamilyName}" />
```

Logically, you could think of that as expanding to the following:

```
<TextBlock ... Text="{Binding Path=family.FamilyName}" />
```

where family is the currently selected Family object.

Taking this one level deeper, in the case of the traits column header, we're binding to the Name property of the currently selected Person from the Members property of the currently selected Family, which binds like this:

```
<TextBlock ... Text="{Binding Path=Members/Name}" />
```

Again, logically you could think of it expanding like this:

```
<TextBlock ... Text="{Binding Path=family.Members.person.Name}" />
```

where family is the currently selected Family object and person is the currently selected Person object. The / in the binding statement acts as the separator between objects, with the object at each level assumed to be "currently selected."

The binding for the listbox's items source works the same way, except we want the Traits collection from the currently selected Person, not the Name. Our trilevel master-detail example looks like Figure 7-24.

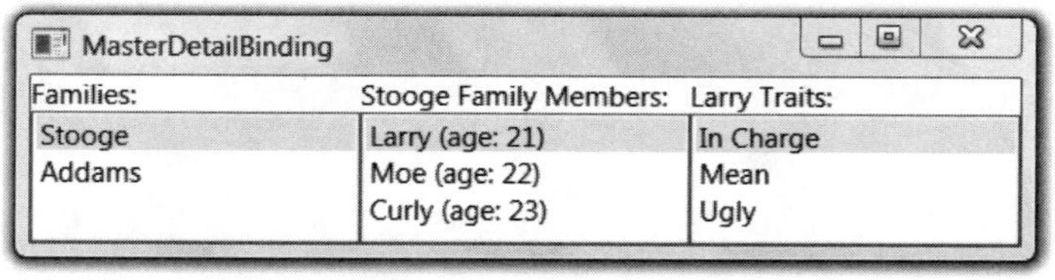

Figure 7-24. Showing master-detail–more detail data

Hierarchical Binding

Master-detail binding is one step away from true hierarchical binding in that it generally involves a known set of levels. For example, when we wanted to go from two levels to three levels, we added another column to the table and manually set up the relationship at the new level. On the other hand, *hierarchical binding* (sometimes called *tree binding*) generally involves some number of levels that aren't known until runtime and a control that can expand itself as appropriate, like a menu or a tree. WPF has built-in support for hierarchical binding using a special kind of data template that knows both how to display the current level of data and where to go for the next level. It's a bit involved, though, so let's go back to first principles with our family data (see Example 7-51).

Example 7-51. The beginnings of hierarchical data binding

```
<Window ...>
  <Window.Resources>
    <local:Families x:Key="Families">
      ...
    </local:Families>
  </Window.Resources>

  <TreeView DataContext="{StaticResource Families}">
    <TreeViewItem ItemsSource="{Binding}" Header="Families" />
  </TreeView>
</Window>
```

In Example 7-51, we're binding a `TreeView` control's root item to the top level of the families data, labeling the root "Families," as shown in Figure 7-25.

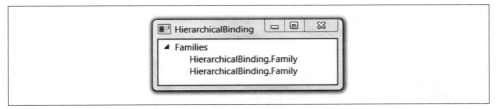

Figure 7-25. The beginnings of hierarchical data binding

Because the Families collection contains two `Family` objects, but we haven't provided a template, WPF shows them as their type. If we want to show something more meaningful, we already know to provide a data template (see Example 7-52).

Example 7-52. Slightly better hierarchical data binding

```
<Window ...>
  <Window.Resources>
    <local:Families x:Key="Families">
      ...
    </local:Families>
    <DataTemplate DataType="{x:Type local:Family}">
      <TextBlock Text="{Binding Path=FamilyName}" />
    </DataTemplate>
  </Window.Resources>

  <TreeView DataContext="{StaticResource Families}">
    <TreeViewItem ItemsSource="{Binding}" Header="Families" />
  </TreeView>
</Window>
```

The result is that we see the family name for each family in the collection, as shown in Figure 7-26.

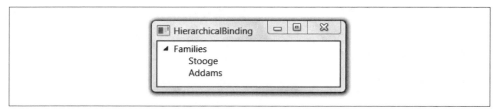

Figure 7-26. Slightly better hierarchical data binding

Figure 7-26 looks better, but now we've dead-ended our tree because the `TreeViewItem` element doesn't know where to get the next level of data. To provide this data, we have the hierarchical data template, shown in Example 7-53.

Example 7-53. The next level of hierarchical data binding

```
<Window ...>
  <Window.Resources>
    <local:Families x:Key="Families">

      ...

    </local:Families>

    <HierarchicalDataTemplate DataType="{x:Type local:Family}"
      ItemsSource="{Binding Path=Members}">
      <TextBlock Text="{Binding Path=FamilyName}" />
    </HierarchicalDataTemplate>

  </Window.Resources>

  <TreeView DataContext="{StaticResource Families}">
    <TreeViewItem ItemsSource="{Binding}" Header="Families" />
  </TreeView>
</Window>
```

In Example 7-53, the `HierarchicalDataTemplate` element is exactly the same as the normal `DataTemplate` element, except that it provides the `ItemsSource` property so that the tree can keep digging into the data, as shown in Figure 7-27.

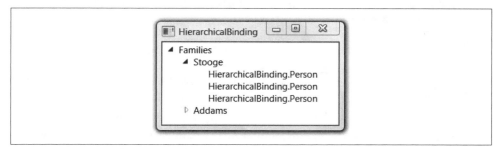

Figure 7-27. The next level of hierarchical data binding

Once again, the default behavior is to show the type name. We need to provide one last template to show something more useful for the Person objects. Because these are the leaves on our tree, we can use an ordinary data template, as shown in Example 7-54.

Example 7-54. Plumbing all of the hierarchical nodes

```
<Window ...>
  <Window.Resources>
    <local:Families x:Key="Families">
      ...
    </local:Families>

    <HierarchicalDataTemplate DataType="{x:Type local:Family}"
      ItemsSource="{Binding Path=Members}">
      <TextBlock Text="{Binding Path=FamilyName}" />
    </HierarchicalDataTemplate>

    <HierarchicalDataTemplate DataType="{x:Type local:Person}"
      ItemsSource="{Binding Path=Traits}">
      <StackPanel Orientation="Horizontal">
        <TextBlock Text="{Binding Path=Name}" />
        <TextBlock Text=" (age: " />
        <TextBlock Text="{Binding Path=Age}" />
        <TextBlock Text=")" />
      </StackPanel>
    </HierarchicalDataTemplate>

    <DataTemplate DataType="{x:Type local:Trait}">
      <TextBlock Text="{Binding Path=Description}" />
    </DataTemplate>

  </Window.Resources>

  <TreeView DataContext="{StaticResource Families}">
    <TreeViewItem ItemsSource="{Binding}" Header="Families" />
  </TreeView>
</Window>
```

Notice in Example 7-54 that we have two hierarchical data templates (one for Family, which contain Person objects, and one for Person, which contains Trait objects) and one normal data template (for the Trait object, which doesn't contain anything else). With these templates in place, we get a tree that looks like Figure 7-28.

In you take another look at Example 7-54, you'll notice that we're not describing the overall structure of the tree, but only how to get from any one object to its children. This means that wherever an object of a type that has a hierarchical data template appears in the tree, we can get to its children. For example, if you had Folder and File, where Folder had a collection that contained both Files and Folders, Folders would open to arbitrary levels in the tree given a single hierarchical data template that told WPF how to get to those children. This makes hierarchical data binding much more flexible than master-detail binding.

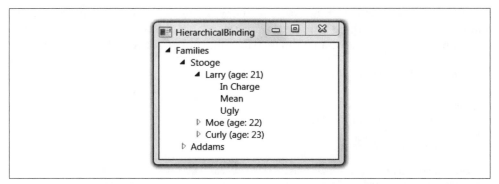

Figure 7-28. Hierarchical data binding in action

Where Are We?

Whereas the preceding chapter dealt with the fundamentals of data binding, in this chapter we discussed those topics necessary to make the most of binding to lists of data, including list data sources in object, relational, and XML data formats; managing the current item; value conversion; sorting; filtering; grouping; data templates; and even master-detail and hierarchical relationships. It may seem hard to believe, but there are things that WPF's data binding engine supports that we haven't discussed (some of which we'll get to in the next chapter, but some of which are beyond the scope of this book*).

The thorough support for data binding at every level of WPF makes it a first-class feature in a way that data binding has never been before. You'll find that it permeates pretty much every aspect of your WPF programming, including styles and control templates, which are the topics of the next two chapters.

---

* PriorityBinding and MultiBinding are the two topics that leap to mind as being uncovered in this book; for details, refer to the Windows Platform SDK documentation at *http://msdn2.microsoft.com/en-us/library/ default.aspx* (*http://tinysells.com/68*).

CHAPTER 8

Styles

In a word-processing document, a *style* is a set of properties to be applied to ranges of content (e.g., text, images, etc.). For example, the name of the style I'm using now is called *Normal,Body,b* and for this document in prepublication, that means a font family of Times, a size of 10, and full justification. Later in the document, I'll be using a style called *Code,x,s*, which will use a font family of Courier New, a size of 9, and left justification. Styles are applied to content to produce a certain look when the content is rendered.

In WPF, a *style* is also a set of properties applied to content used for visual rendering, like setting the font weight of a Button control. In addition to the features in word-processing styles, WPF styles have specific features for building applications, including the ability to apply different visual effects based on user events. All of these features come without the need to build a custom control (although that's still a useful thing to be able to do, as discussed in Chapter 18).

Without Styles

As an example of how styles can make themselves useful in WPF, let's look at a simple implementation of tic-tac-toe (see Example 8-1).

Example 8-1. A simple tic-tac-toe layout

```
<!-- Window1.xaml -->
<Window
  x:Class="TicTacToe.Window1"
  xmlns="http://schemas.microsoft.com/winfx/2006/xaml/presentation"
  xmlns:x="http://schemas.microsoft.com/winfx/2006/xaml"
  Title="TicTacToe"
  Height="300"
  Width="300">
  <!-- the black background lets the tic-tac-toe -->
  <!-- crosshatch come through on the margins -->
  <Grid Background="Black">
```

Example 8-1. A simple tic-tac-toe layout (continued)

```
    <Grid.RowDefinitions>
      <RowDefinition />
      <RowDefinition />
      <RowDefinition />
    </Grid.RowDefinitions>
    <Grid.ColumnDefinitions>
      <ColumnDefinition />
      <ColumnDefinition />
      <ColumnDefinition />
    </Grid.ColumnDefinitions>
    <Button Margin="0,0,2,2" Grid.Row="0" Grid.Column="0" Name="cell00" />
    <Button Margin="2,0,2,2" Grid.Row="0" Grid.Column="1" Name="cell01" />
    <Button Margin="2,0,0,2" Grid.Row="0" Grid.Column="2" Name="cell02" />
    <Button Margin="0,2,2,2" Grid.Row="1" Grid.Column="0" Name="cell10" />
    <Button Margin="2,2,2,2" Grid.Row="1" Grid.Column="1" Name="cell11" />
    <Button Margin="2,2,0,2" Grid.Row="1" Grid.Column="2" Name="cell12" />
    <Button Margin="0,2,2,0" Grid.Row="2" Grid.Column="0" Name="cell20" />
    <Button Margin="2,2,2,0" Grid.Row="2" Grid.Column="1" Name="cell21" />
    <Button Margin="2,2,0,0" Grid.Row="2" Grid.Column="2" Name="cell22" />
  </Grid>
</Window>
```

This grid layout arranges a set of nine buttons in a 3×3 grid of tic-tac-toe cells, using the margins on the button for the tic-tac-toe crosshatch. A simple implementation of the game logic in the XAML code-behind file looks like Example 8-2.

Example 8-2. A simple tic-tac-toe implementation

```
// Window1.xaml.cs
...
namespace TicTacToe {
  public partial class Window1 : Window {
    // Track the current player (X or O)
    string currentPlayer;

    // Track the list of cells for finding a winner, etc.
    Button[] cells;

    public Window1() {
      InitializeComponent();

      // Cache the list of buttons and handle their clicks
      this.cells = new Button[] { this.cell00, this.cell01, ... };
      foreach( Button cell in this.cells ) {
        cell.Click += cell_Click;
      }

      // Initialize a new game
      NewGame();
    }
```

Example 8-2. A simple tic-tac-toe implementation (continued)

```
    // Wrapper around the current player for future expansion,
    // e.g., updating status text with the current player
    string CurrentPlayer {
      get { return this.currentPlayer; }
      set { this.currentPlayer = value; }
    }

    // Use the buttons to track game state
    void NewGame() {
      foreach( Button cell in this.cells ) {
        cell.ClearValue(Button.ContentProperty);
      }
      CurrentPlayer = "X";
    }

    void cell_Click(object sender, RoutedEventArgs e) {
      Button button = (Button)sender;

      // Don't let multiple clicks change the player for a cell
      if( button.Content != null ) { return; }

      // Set button content
      button.Content = CurrentPlayer;

      // Check for winner or a tie
      if( HasWon(this.currentPlayer) ) {
        MessageBox.Show("Winner!", "Game Over");
        NewGame();
        return;
      }
      else if( TieGame() ) {
        MessageBox.Show("No Winner!", "Game Over");
        NewGame();
        return;
      }

      // Switch player
      if( CurrentPlayer == "X" ) {
        CurrentPlayer = "O";
      }
      else {
        CurrentPlayer = "X";
      }
    }

    // Use this.cells to find a winner or a tie
    bool HasWon(string player) {...}
    bool TieGame() {...}
  }
}
```

Our simple tic-tac-toe logic uses strings to represent the players and uses the buttons themselves to keep track of the game state. As each button is clicked, we set its content to the string indicating the current player and switch players. When the game is over, the content for each button is cleared.* The middle of a game looks like Figure 8-1.

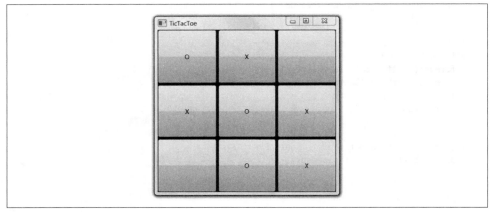

Figure 8-1. A simple tic-tac-toe game

Notice in Figure 8-1 how the grid background comes through from the margin. These spacers almost make the grid look like a drawn tic-tac-toe board (although we'll do better later). However, if we're really looking to simulate a hand-drawn game, we have to do something about the size of the font used on the buttons; it doesn't match the thickness of the lines.

One way to fix this problem is by setting the font size and weight for each `Button` object, as shown in Example 8-3.

Example 8-3. Setting control properties individually

```
<Button FontSize="32pt" FontWeight="Bold" ... Name="cell00" />
<Button FontSize="32pt" FontWeight="Bold" ... Name="cell01" />
...
<Button FontSize="32pt" FontWeight="Bold" ... Name="cell22" />
```

The results, shown in Figure 8-2, look nicer.

Setting the font size and weight properties makes the Xs and Os look better according to my visual sensibilities today. However, if I want to change it later, I've now committed myself to changing both properties in nine separate places, which is a duplication of effort that offends my coding sensibilities. I'd much prefer to refactor my decisions about the look of my tic-tac-toe cells into a common place for future maintenance. That's where styles come in handy.

---

* We clear the content of each button by using the `ClearValue` method instead of setting the CLR property to null so that setting the `Content` property in the triggers works later on.

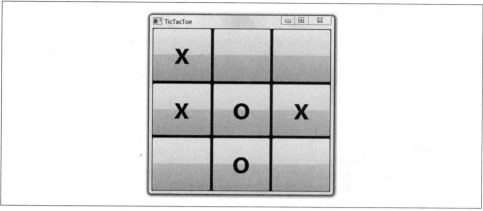

Figure 8-2. A nicer-looking tic-tac-toe board

Inline Styles

A style in WPF is expressed as zero or more `Setter` objects inside a `Style` object. Every element in WPF that derives from either `FrameworkElement` or `FrameworkContentElement` has a `Style` property, which you can set inline using standard XAML property element syntax, as shown in Example 8-4.

Example 8-4. Setting an inline style

```
<Button ... Name="cell00">
  <Button.Style>
    <Style>
      <Setter Property="Button.FontSize" Value="32pt" />
      <Setter Property="Button.FontWeight" Value="Bold" />
    </Style>
  </Button.Style>
</Button>
```

Because we want to bundle two property values into our style, we have a `Style` element with two `Setter` subelements, one for each property we want to set (i.e., `FontSize` and `FontWeight`), both with the `Button` prefix to indicate the class that contains the property. Properties suitable for styling must be dependency properties.

Due to the extra style syntax and because inline styles can't be shared across elements, inline styles actually involve more typing than just setting the properties. For this reason, inline styles aren't used nearly as often as named styles.*

---

* However, an inline style is useful if you want to add property and data triggers to an individual element. We discuss triggers later in this chapter.

Named Styles

By hoisting the same inline style into a resource (as introduced in Chapter 1), we can award it a name and use it by name in our button instances, as shown in Example 8-5.

Example 8-5. Setting a named style

```
<!-- Window1.xaml -->
<Window ...>
  <Window.Resources>
    <Style x:Key="CellTextStyle">
      <Setter Property="Control.FontSize" Value="32pt" />
      <Setter Property="Control.FontWeight" Value="Bold" />
    </Style>
  </Window.Resources>
  ...
  <Button Style="{StaticResource CellTextStyle}" ... Name="cell00" />
  ...
</Window>
```

In Example 8-5, we've used the class name as a prefix on our properties so that the style knows what dependency property we're talking about. We used Control as the prefix instead of Button to allow the style to be used more broadly, as we'll soon see.

The Target Type Attribute

As a convenience, if all of the properties can be set on a shared base class, like Control in our example, we can promote the class prefix into the TargetType attribute and remove it from the name of the property (see Example 8-6).

Example 8-6. A target-typed style

```
<Style x:Key="CellTextStyle" TargetType="{x:Type Control}">
  <Setter Property="FontSize" Value="32pt" />
  <Setter Property="FontWeight" Value="Bold" />
</Style>
```

When providing a TargetType attribute, you can only set properties available on that type. If you'd like to expand to a greater set of properties down the inheritance tree, you can do so by using a more derived type (see Example 8-7).

Example 8-7. A more derived target-typed style

```
<Style x:Key="CellTextStyle" TargetType="{x:Type Button}">
  <!-- IsCancel is a Button-specific property -->
  <Setter Property="IsCancel" Value="False" />
  <Setter Property="FontSize" Value="32pt" />
  <Setter Property="FontWeight" Value="Bold" />
</Style>
```

In this case, the IsCancel property is available only on Button, so to set it, we need to switch the target type attribute for the style.

Reusing Styles

In addition to saving you from typing out the name of the class prefix for every property name, the TargetType attribute will also confirm that all classes that have the style applied are an instance of that type (or derived type). That means that if we leave TargetType set to Control, we can apply it to a Button element, but not to a TextBlock element, as the former derives ultimately from Control but the latter does not.

However, if we'd like to define a style that contains properties not shared by every element to which we'd like to apply them, we can do that by dropping the TargetType and putting back the property prefix, as shown in Example 8-8.

Example 8-8. Styles can have properties that targets don't have

```
<Style x:Key="CellTextStyle">
  <Setter Property="TextElement.FontSize" Value="32pt" />
  <Setter Property="Button.IsCancel" Value="False" />
</Style>
...
<!-- has an IsCancel property -->
<Button Style="{StaticResource CellTextStyle}" ... />

<!-- does *not* have an IsCancel property -->
<TextBlock Style="{StaticResource CellTextStyle}" ... />
```

In Example 8-8, we've added the Button.IsCancel property to the CellTextStyle and applied it to the Button element, which has this property, and the TextBlock element, which doesn't. This is OK. At runtime, WPF will apply the dependency properties and the elements themselves will ignore those values that don't apply to them.*

 WPF's ability to apply styles to objects that don't have all of the properties defined in the style is analogous to applying the Word Normal style, which includes a font size property of its own, to both a range of text and an image. Even though Word knows that images don't have a font size, it applies the portions of the Normal style that do make sense (like the justification property), ignoring the rest.

Getting back to our sample, we can use the CellTextStyle on the Buttons to show nice Xs and Os, and on a TextBlock in a new row to show whose turn it is (see Example 8-9).

---

* The ability to set a value for a property that an element doesn't have is useful for inheritable properties, because those values will flow on through to child elements. See Chapter 18 for a description of dependency property inheritance.

Example 8-9. Applying a style to Button and TextBlock elements

```
<Window.Resources>
  <Style x:Key="CellTextStyle">
    <Setter Property="Control.FontSize" Value="32pt" />
    <Setter Property="Control.FontWeight" Value="Bold" />
  </Style>
</Window.Resources>
<Grid Background="Black">
  <Grid.RowDefinitions>
    <RowDefinition />
    <RowDefinition />
    <RowDefinition />
    <RowDefinition Height="Auto" />
  </Grid.RowDefinitions>
  <Grid.ColumnDefinitions>
    <ColumnDefinition />
    <ColumnDefinition />
    <ColumnDefinition />
  </Grid.ColumnDefinitions>
  <Button Style="{StaticResource CellTextStyle}" ... />
  ...
  <TextBlock
    Style="{StaticResource CellTextStyle}"
    Foreground="White"
    Grid.Row="3"
    Grid.ColumnSpan="3"
    Name="statusTextBlock" />
</Grid>
</Window>
```

With our new text block in place, we can inform the next player of her turn by updating the CurrentPlayer property setter:

```
string CurrentPlayer {
  get { return this.currentPlayer; }
  set {
    this.currentPlayer = value;
    this.statusTextBlock.Text =
      "It's your turn, " + this.currentPlayer;
  }
}
```

This reuse of the style across controls of different types gives us a consistent look in the application, as shown in Figure 8-3.

One thing you'll notice is that the status text in Figure 8-3 is white, whereas the text in the buttons is black. Because black is the default text color, if we want the status text to show up against a black background, we have to change the color to something else, hence the need to set the Foreground property to white on the TextBlock. Setting per-instance properties works just fine in combination with a style, and you can combine the two techniques of setting property values as you see fit.

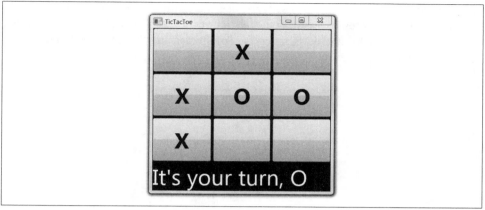

Figure 8-3. A tic-tac-toe game with style

Overriding Style Properties

Further, if we wanted to *override* a style property on a specific instance, we can do so by setting the property on the instance (see Example 8-10).

Example 8-10. Overriding the FontWeight property from the style

```
<Style x:Key="CellTextStyle">
  <Setter Property="TextElement.FontSize" Value="32pt" />
  <Setter Property="TextElement.FontWeight" Value="Bold" />
</Style>
...
<TextBlock
  Style="{StaticResource CellTextStyle}"
  FontWeight="Normal" ... />
```

In Example 8-10, the TextBlock instance property setting of FontWeight takes precedence over the style property setting of FontWeight.

Extending Styles

In addition to the abilities to reuse and override existing styles, you can also extend a style, adding new properties or overriding existing ones (see Example 8-11).

Example 8-11. Extending a style

```
<Style x:Key="CellTextStyle">
  <Setter Property="Control.FontSize" Value="32pt" />
  <Setter Property="Control.FontWeight" Value="Bold" />
</Style>
<Style x:Key="StatusTextStyle" BasedOn="{StaticResource CellTextStyle}">
  <Setter Property="TextBlock.FontWeight" Value="Normal" />
  <Setter Property="TextBlock.Foreground" Value="White" />
  <Setter Property="TextBlock.HorizontalAlignment" Value="Center" />
</Style>
```

The `BasedOn` style attribute is used to designate the style being extended. In Example 8-11, the `StatusTextStyle` style gets all of the `CellTextStyle` property setters, overrides the `FontWeight`, and adds setters for `Foreground` and `HorizontalAlignment`. Our current use of styles causes our tic-tac-toe game to look like Figure 8-4.

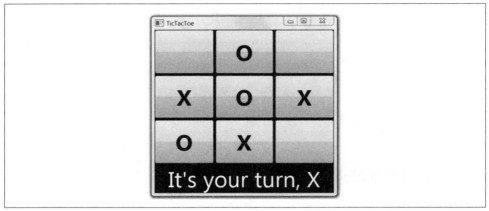

Figure 8-4. A tic-tac-toe game with more style

Our application so far is looking pretty good, but we can do better.

Setting Styles Programmatically

Once a style has a name, it's easily available from our code. For example, we might decide that we'd like each player to have his own style:

```
<Style x:Key="XStyle" BasedOn="{StaticResource CellTextStyle}">
  <Setter Property="Control.Foreground" Value="Red" />
</Style>
<Style x:Key="OStyle" BasedOn="{StaticResource CellTextStyle}">
  <Setter Property="Control.Foreground" Value="Green" />
</Style>
```

In this case, applying named styles to each button in XAML at compile time won't do the trick, because we want to set the style based on the content, and in this application, the content changes when a button is clicked at runtime. However, nothing requires us to set the `Style` property of a control statically; we can set it programmatically as well, as we do in Example 8-12.

Example 8-12. Setting styles programmatically

```
public partial class Window1 : Window {
  ...
  void cell_Click(object sender, RoutedEventArgs e) {
    Button button = (Button)sender;
    ...
```

Example 8-12. Setting styles programmatically (continued)

```
    // Set button content
    button.Content = this.CurrentPlayer;
    ...
    if( this.CurrentPlayer == "X" ) {
      button.Style = (Style)FindResource("XStyle");
      this.CurrentPlayer == "O";
    }
    else {
      button.Style = (Style)FindResource("OStyle");
      this.CurrentPlayer == "X";
    }
    ...
  }
  ...
}
```

In Example 8-12, whenever the player clicks, in addition to setting the button's content, we pull a named style out of the window's resources with the FindResource method and use that to set the button's style, as shown in Figure 8-5.

Figure 8-5. Setting styles programmatically based on an object's content (Color Plate 7)

Notice that the Xs and Os are colored according to the named player styles. In this particular case (and in many other cases, too), data triggers should be preferred to setting styles programmatically, but we'll get to that later.

 As with all XAML constructs, you are free to create styles themselves programmatically. Appendix A is a good introduction on how to think about going back and forth between XAML and code.

Element-Typed Styles

Named styles are useful when you have a set of properties to be applied to a specific element instance. However, if you'd like to apply a style uniformly to all instances of a certain type of element, set the TargetType without a Key (see Example 8-13).

Example 8-13. Element-typed styles

```
...
<!-- without a Key -->
<Style TargetType="{x:Type Button}">
  <Setter Property="FontSize" Value="32pt" />
  <Setter Property="FontWeight" Value="Bold" />
</Style>
<!-- with a Key -->
<Style x:Key="StatusTextStyle" TargetType="{x:Type TextBlock}">
  <Setter Property="FontSize" Value="32pt" />
  <Setter Property="FontWeight" Value="Normal" />
  <Setter Property="Foreground" Value="White" />
  <Setter Property="HorizontalAlignment" Value="Center" />
</Style>
...
<!-- no need to set the Style -->
<Button Grid.Row="0" Grid.Column="0" x:ID="cell00" />
...
<!-- need to set the Style -->
<TextBlock Style="{StaticResource StatusTextStyle}" ... />
...
```

In Example 8-13, we have two styles, one with a TargetType of Button and no Key, and another with a TargetType of TextBlock and a Key. The TextBlock style works just as we've seen (i.e., you have to assign a TextBlock Style property explicitly to the style using the key for it to take effect). On the other hand, when an instance of Button is created without an explicit Style attribute setting, it uses the style that matches the target type of the style to the type of the control. Our element-typed styles return our game to looking again like Figure 8-4.

Element-typed styles are handy whenever you'd like all instances of a certain element to share a look, depending on the scope. For example, we've scoped the button style in our sample thus far at the top-level Window (see Example 8-14).

Example 8-14. Style scoped to the Window

```
<!-- Window1.xaml -->
<Window ...>
  <!-- every Button in the Window is affected -->
  <Window.Resources>
    <Style TargetType="{x:Type Button}">...</Style>
  </Window.Resources>
  ...
</Window>
```

However, you may want to reduce the scope of an element-typed style. In our sample, it would work just as well to scope the button style inside the grid so that only buttons in the grid are affected (see Example 8-15).

Example 8-15. Style scoped below the Window

```
<!-- Window1.xaml -->
<Window ...>
  <Grid ...>
    <!-- only Buttons in the Grid are affected -->
    <Grid.Resources>
      <Style TargetType="{x:Type Button}">...</Style>
    </Grid.Resources>
    ...
  </Grid>
  <!-- Buttons outside the Grid are unaffected -->
  ...
</Window>
```

Alternatively, if you want to make your style have greater reach in your project, you can put it into the application scope (see Example 8-16).

Example 8-16. Style scoped to the application

```
<!-- MyApp.xaml -->
<Application ...>
  <!-- every Button in the Application is affected -->
  <Application.Resources>
    <Style TargetType="{x:Type Button}">...</Style>
  </Application.Resources>
</Application>
```

In general, it's useful to understand the scoping rules of element-typed styles so that you can judge their effect on the various pieces of your WPF object model. Chapter 12 discusses resource scoping of all kinds, including styles, in more detail.

Element-Typed Styles and Derived Types

When you define a style with only a TargetType, that style will be applied only to elements of that exact type and not to derived types. For example, if you've got a single style that you'd like to apply to both the CheckBox and the RadioButton types, you might think to create a style for their common base type (ToggleButton), as in Example 8-17.

Example 8-17. Element-typed styles aren't applied to derived types

```
<Window ...>
  <Window.Resources>
    <!-- this isn't going to be applied to RadioButton or CheckBox -->
    <Style TargetType="ToggleButton">
      <Setter Property="FontSize" Value="32" />
    </Style>
```

Example 8-17. Element-typed styles aren't applied to derived types (continued)

```
    </Window.Resources>
    <StackPanel Margin="5">
      <TextBlock FontSize="32">two toggle buttons:</TextBlock>
      <CheckBox>my checkbox</CheckBox>
      <RadioButton>my radio button</RadioButton>
    </StackPanel>
</Window>
```

As Figure 8-6 shows, the style associated with the ToggleButton type will not be applied to either the radio button or the checkbox.

Figure 8-6. Element-typed styles aren't applied to derived types

This limitation keeps styles from leaking to unknown derived types. However, if you'd like to centralize the settings for a style on a base type and apply it to known derived types, you can do so with a little extra work (see Example 8-18).

Example 8-18. Manually applying element-typed styles to derived types

```
<Window ...>
  <Window.Resources>
    <Style x:Key="toggleButtonStyle" TargetType="ToggleButton">
      <Setter Property="FontSize" Value="32" />
    </Style>
    <Style TargetType="RadioButton"
      BasedOn="{StaticResource toggleButtonStyle}" />
    <Style TargetType="CheckBox"
      BasedOn="{StaticResource toggleButtonStyle}" />
  </Window.Resources>
  ...
</Window>
```

In Example 8-18, we gave our toggle button style a key and then used it with the BasedOn property of our element-typed styles for RadioButton and CheckBox, as shown in Figure 8-7.

Using this technique, we're able to define element-typed styles and reuse settings across known derived types.

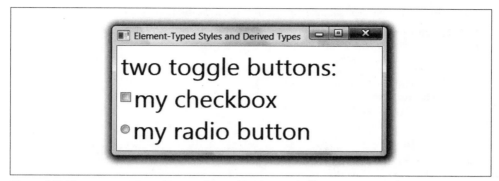

Figure 8-7. You can mix TargetType and BasedOn for good effect

Data Templates and Styles

Let's imagine that we want to implement a variant of tic-tac-toe that's more fun to play (an important feature in most games). For example, one variant of tic-tac-toe only allows players to have three of their pieces on at any one time, dropping the first move off when the fourth move is played, dropping the second move when the fifth is played, and so on. To implement this variant, we need to keep track of the sequence of moves, with each move represented by a PlayerMove object, as shown in Example 8-19.

Example 8-19. A custom type suitable for tracking tic-tac-toe moves

```
public class PlayerMove : INotifyPropertyChanged {
  string playerName;
  public string PlayerName {
    get { return playerName; }
    set {
      if( string.Compare(playerName, value) == 0 ) { return; }
      playerName = value;
      Notify("PlayerName");
    }
  }

  int moveNumber;
  public int MoveNumber {
    get { return moveNumber; }
    set {
      if( moveNumber == value ) { return; }
      moveNumber = value;
      Notify("MoveNumber");
    }
  }
```

Example 8-19. A custom type suitable for tracking tic-tac-toe moves (continued)

```
  bool isPartOfWin = false;
  public bool IsPartOfWin {
    get { return isPartOfWin; }
    set {
      if( isPartOfWin == value ) { return; }
      isPartOfWin = value;
      Notify("IsPartOfWin");
    }
  }

  public PlayerMove(string playerName, int moveNumber) {
    this.playerName = playerName;
    this.moveNumber = moveNumber;
  }

  // INotifyPropertyChanged Members
  public event PropertyChangedEventHandler PropertyChanged;
  void Notify(string propName) {
    if( PropertyChanged != null ) {
      PropertyChanged(this, new PropertyChangedEventArgs(propName));
    }
  }
}
```

Now, instead of using a simple string for each button object's content, we'll use an instance of PlayerMove, as shown in Example 8-20.

Example 8-20. Adding the PlayerMove as Button content

```
namespace TicTacToe {
  public partial class Window1 : Window {
    ...
    int moveNumber;

    void NewGame( ) {
      ...
      this.moveNumber = 0;
    }

    void cell_Click(object sender, RoutedEventArgs e) {
      ...
      // Set button content
      //button.Content = this.CurrentPlayer;
      button.Content =
        new PlayerMove(this.CurrentPlayer, ++this.moveNumber);
      ...
    }
    ...
  }
}
```

Figure 8-8 shows the brilliance of such a change (after turning off the button style so that the text isn't too large to read).

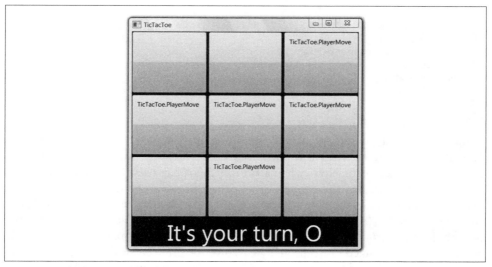

Figure 8-8. PlayerMove objects displayed without any special instructions

As you'll recall from Chapter 6, in Figure 8-8 the button doesn't have enough information to render a `PlayerMove` object, but we can fix that with a data template.

Data Templates Redux

As you already know from Chapter 7, WPF allows you to define a data template, which is a tree of elements to expand in a particular context. We use data templates to provide an application with the capability to render nonvisual objects (see Example 8-21).

Example 8-21. Setting a PlayerMove data template without styles

```
<Window ... xmlns:local="clr-namespace:TicTacToe">
  <Window.Resources>
    ...
    <Style TargetType="{x:Type Button}">
      <Setter Property="HorizontalContentAlignment" Value="Stretch" />
      <Setter Property="VerticalContentAlignment" Value="Stretch" />
      <Setter Property="Padding" Value="8" />
    </Style>
    <DataTemplate DataType="{x:Type local:PlayerMove}">
      <Grid>
        <TextBlock
          Text="{Binding Path=PlayerName}"
          FontSize ="32pt"
          FontWeight="Bold"
          VerticalAlignment="Center"
          HorizontalAlignment="Center" />
```

Example 8-21. Setting a PlayerMove data template without styles (continued)

```
      <TextBlock
        Text="{Binding Path=MoveNumber}"
        FontSize="16pt"
        FontStyle="Italic"
        VerticalAlignment="Bottom"
        HorizontalAlignment="Right" />
    </Grid>
  </DataTemplate>
 </Window.Resources>
 ...
</Window>
```

Using the XAML mapping syntax described in Chapter 1, we've mapped the PlayerMove type into the XAML with the xmlns attribute, which we've used as the data type of the data template. Now, when a WPF element that uses the content model sees a PlayerMove object, like the content of all of our buttons, the data template will be expanded.* In our case, the template consists of a grid to arrange two text blocks, one showing the player name in the middle of the button and one showing the move number in the bottom right, along with some other settings to make things pretty. In addition, we've changed our button style to give the grid the entire space of the content area, less some padding around the edge (otherwise, things get a little cramped). Figure 8-9 shows the result.

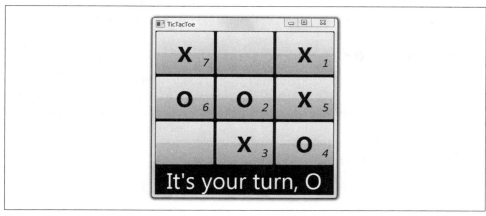

Figure 8-9. Showing objects of a custom type using data templates and styles

---

* Controls that use the content model in WPF are those with control templates that use a ContentPresenter, as discussed in Chapter 9.

Data Templates with Style

Just as it's a good idea to take "magic numbers" out of your code, pulling them out and giving them names for easy maintenance, it's a good idea to move groups of settings into styles,* as shown in Example 8-22.

Example 8-22. Setting a PlayerMove data template with styles

```
<Window.Resources>
  ...
  <Style x:Key="CellTextStyle" TargetType="{x:Type TextBlock}">
    <Setter Property="FontSize" Value="32pt" />
    <Setter Property="FontWeight" Value="Bold" />
    <Setter Property="VerticalAlignment" Value="Center" />
    <Setter Property="HorizontalAlignment" Value="Center" />
  </Style>
  <Style x:Key="MoveNumberStyle" TargetType="{x:Type TextBlock}">
    <Setter Property="FontSize" Value="16pt" />
    <Setter Property="FontStyle" Value="Italic" />
    <Setter Property="VerticalAlignment" Value="Bottom" />
    <Setter Property="HorizontalAlignment" Value="Right" />
  </Style>
  <DataTemplate DataType="{x:Type local:PlayerMove}">
    <Grid>
      <TextBlock
        Text="{Binding Path=PlayerName}"
        Style="{StaticResource CellTextStyle}" />
      <TextBlock
        Text="{Binding Path=MoveNumber}"
        Style="{StaticResource MoveNumberStyle}" />
    </Grid>
  </DataTemplate>
</Window.Resources>
```

As nice as Figure 8-9 is, the interaction is kind of boring given the capabilities of WPF. Let's see what we can do with style properties as the application is used.

Triggers

So far, we've seen styles as a collection of Setter elements. When a style is applied, the settings described in the Setter elements are applied unconditionally (unless overridden by per-instance settings). On the other hand, property triggers are a way to wrap one or more Setter elements in a condition. With a *property trigger*, if the condition is true, the corresponding Setter elements are executed to set one or more element properties. When the condition becomes false, the property values revert to their pre-trigger values.

---

* Moving groups of settings into styles also allows for easier skinning and theming, as described in Chapter 12.

Property triggers are not the only kinds of triggers that WPF supports, however. With an *event trigger*, the trigger is activated when an event is fired, which fires off another event to start or stop an animation.

Property Triggers

The simplest form of a trigger is a property trigger, which watches for a dependency property on the element to have a certain value. For example, we might want to set the tool tip over a button if neither player has yet chosen it for a move. We can do so by watching for the Content property to have a value of null,* as shown in Example 8-23.

Example 8-23. A simple property trigger

```
<Style TargetType="{x:Type Button}">
  ...
  <Style.Triggers>
    <Trigger Property="Content" Value="{x:Null}" >
      <Setter Property="ToolTip" Value="click to move here" />
    </Trigger>
  </Style.Triggers>
</Style>
```

Triggers are grouped together under the Style.Triggers element. In this case, we've added a Trigger element to the button style. When the Content property of our button is null, the ToolTip property of the button will be set to "click to move here," as shown in Figure 8-10.

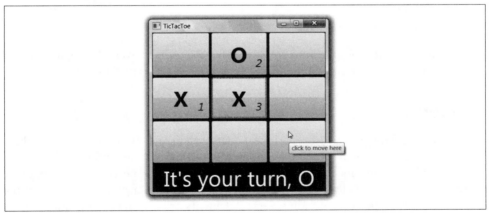

Figure 8-10. A property trigger in action (Color Plate 8)

---

* The null value is set via a XAML markup extension, which you can read more about in Appendix A.

There's no need to worry about setting a property back when the trigger is no longer true (e.g., watching for Content to be non-null). The WPF dependency property system watches for the property trigger to become inactive and reverts the property to the previous value.

You can set property triggers to watch any of the dependency properties on the control to which your style is targeted and to set any of the dependency properties on the control while the condition is true. In fact, you can use a single trigger to set multiple properties if you like.

Multiple Triggers

Although you can set as many properties as you like in a property trigger, there can be more than one trigger in a style. When grouped together under the Style.Triggers element, multiple triggers act independently of one another.

For example, we can update our example so that if the content is null on one of our buttons, it'll have one tool tip, but if the button has focus (the Tab and arrow keys move focus around), it'll have another tool tip, as shown in Example 8-24.

Example 8-24. Multiple property triggers

```
<Style TargetType="{x:Type Button}">
  ...
  <Style.Triggers>
    <Trigger Property="Content" Value="{x:Null}" >
      <Setter Property="ToolTip" Value="click to move here" />
    </Trigger>
    <Trigger Property="IsFocused" Value="True" >
      <Setter Property="ToolTip" Value="click or spacebar to move here" />
    </Trigger>
  </Style.Triggers>
</Style>
```

Figure 8-11 shows the result of one cell having both focus and the mouse hovering.

If multiple triggers set the same property, the last one wins. For example, in Figure 8-11, because the button has no content and focus, the tool tip will be the one associated with the keyboard focus because the trigger for the IsFocused trigger is last in the list.

Multicondition Property Triggers

One thing you may have noticed about Example 8-24 is that it checks only for keyboard focus. However, just checking for the focus isn't enough; we also need to check whether the button already has content. If you'd like to check more than one property before a trigger condition is activated, you can combine multiple conditions with a multiple condition property trigger, as shown in Example 8-25.

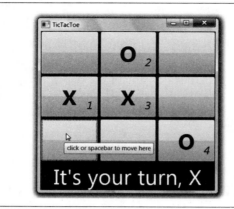

Figure 8-11. Multiple property triggers in action (Color Plate 9)

Example 8-25. A multiproperty trigger

```
<Style TargetType="{x:Type Button}">
  ...
  <Style.Triggers>
    <Trigger Property="Content" Value="{x:Null}" >
      <Setter Property="ToolTip" Value="click to move here" />
    </Trigger>
    <MultiTrigger>
      <MultiTrigger.Conditions>
        <Condition Property="IsFocused" Value="True" />
        <Condition Property="Content" Value="{x:Null}" />
      </MultiTrigger.Conditions>
      <Setter Property="ToolTip" Value="click or spacebar to move here" />
    </MultiTrigger>
  </Style.Triggers>
</Style>
```

Multicondition property triggers check all of the properties' values to be set as specified, not just one of them. Here, we're watching for both keyboard focus and the content to be null, reflecting the game logic that new moves can happen only in empty cells.

Property triggers are great for noticing when the user is interacting with an element displaying your program's state. However, we'd also like to be able to notice when the program's state itself changes—such as when a particular player makes a move—and update our style settings accordingly. For that, we have data triggers.

Data Triggers

Unlike property triggers, which check only WPF dependency properties, data triggers can check any old thing to which you can bind (e.g., a CLR object property, an XPath statement, etc.). Whereas property triggers are generally used to check WPF visual element properties, data triggers are normally used to check the properties of nonvisual objects used as content, like our PlayerMove objects (see Example 8-26).

Example 8-26. Two data triggers

```
<Window.Resources>
  <Style TargetType="{x:Type Button}">
    ...
  </Style>
  <Style x:Key="CellTextStyle" TargetType="{x:Type TextBlock}">
    ...
    <Style.Triggers>
      <DataTrigger Binding="{Binding Path=PlayerName}" Value="X">
        <Setter Property="Foreground" Value="Red" />
      </DataTrigger>
      <DataTrigger Binding="{Binding Path=PlayerName}" Value="O">
        <Setter Property="Foreground" Value="Green" />
      </DataTrigger>
    </Style.Triggers>
  </Style>
  <Style x:Key="MoveNumberStyle" TargetType="{x:Type TextBlock}">
    ...
  </Style>
  ...
  <DataTemplate DataType="{x:Type l:PlayerMove}">
    <Grid>
      <TextBlock
        TextContent="{Binding Path=PlayerName}"
        Style="{StaticResource CellTextStyle}" />
      <TextBlock
        TextContent="{Binding Path=MoveNumber}"
        Style="{StaticResource MoveNumberStyle}" />
    </Grid>
  </DataTemplate>
</Window.Resources>
```

DataTrigger elements go under the Style.Triggers element just like property triggers, and also just like property triggers, more than one of them can be active at any one time. Whereas a property trigger operates on the properties of the visual elements displaying the content, a data trigger operates on the content itself. In our case, the content of each cell is a PlayerMove object. In both of the data triggers, we're binding to the PlayerName property. If the value is "X," we're setting the foreground to red, and if it's "O," we're setting it to green.

We haven't had per-player colors since moving to data templates after setting styles programmatically in Figure 8-5, but data triggers bring that feature right back, along with all of the other features we've been building up, as shown in Figure 8-12.

Unlike property triggers, which rely on the change notification of dependency properties, data triggers can also use an implementation of the standard property change notification patterns built into .NET and discussed in Chapter 6 (e.g., INotifyPropertyChanged). Even our simple class needs to raise such notifications as the IsPartOfWin property changes (it's set when a win is detected). If you're using data triggers, chances are that you'll need to expose notifications from your data classes.

Figure 8-12. Data triggers in action (Color Plate 10)

One other especially handy feature of data triggers is that there's no need for an explicit check for null content. If the content is null, the trigger condition is automatically false, which is why the application isn't crashing trying to dereference a null PlayerMove to get to the PlayerName property.

Multicondition Data Triggers

Just as we can combine property triggers into "and" conditions using the MultiTrigger element, we can combine data triggers using the MultiDataTrigger element. For example, if we wanted to watch for winning moves and match the move number to the color of the player that won, we'd need two multicondition data triggers, one for each player, as shown in Example 8-27.

Example 8-27. A multidata trigger

```
<Style x:Key="MoveNumberStyle" TargetType="{x:Type TextBlock}">
  ...
  <Style.Triggers>
    <MultiDataTrigger>
      <MultiDataTrigger.Conditions>
        <Condition Binding="{Binding Path=PlayerName}" Value="X" />
        <Condition Binding="{Binding Path=IsPartOfWin}" Value="True" />
      </MultiDataTrigger.Conditions>
      <Setter Property="BitmapEffect">
        <Setter.Value>
          <OuterGlowBitmapEffect GlowColor="Red" GlowSize="10" />
        </Setter.Value>
      </Setter>
    </MultiDataTrigger>

    <MultiDataTrigger>
      <MultiDataTrigger.Conditions>
        <Condition Binding="{Binding Path=PlayerName}" Value="O" />
        <Condition Binding="{Binding Path=IsPartOfWin}" Value="True" />
```

Example 8-27. A multidata trigger (continued)

```
      </MultiDataTrigger.Conditions>
      <Setter Property="BitmapEffect">
        <Setter.Value>
          <OuterGlowBitmapEffect GlowColor="Green" GlowSize="10" />
        </Setter.Value>
      </Setter>
    </MultiDataTrigger>
  </Style.Triggers>
</Style>
```

Here we're setting a glow around the winning move numbers to make the crucial moves clear.* Figure 8-13 shows the results after a win.

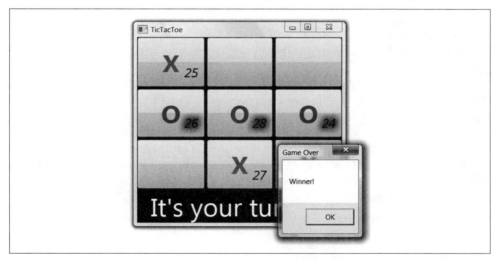

Figure 8-13. The winner aglow with pride (Color Plate 11)

The multicondition data trigger in Example 8-27 sets the move number to match the color of the winner to connote a cause for celebration, but you can use multicondition data triggers for celebrations of your own kinds. Also, I didn't show it in this example, but because data triggers support CLR property change notifications as well as dependency property change notifications, they are very handy inside the Triggers element of a data template.

Event Triggers

Whereas property triggers check for values on dependency properties and data triggers check for values on CLR properties, event triggers watch for events. When an event (like a Click event) happens, an event trigger responds by raising an animation-related event.

---

* For more information about bitmap effects, read Chapter 13.

Although animation is interesting enough to deserve its own chapter (Chapter 16), Example 8-28 shows a simple animation that will transition a button from transparent to opaque over two seconds when it's clicked.

Example 8-28. An event trigger

```
<Style TargetType="{x:Type Button}">
  ...
  <Style.Triggers>
    ...
    <EventTrigger RoutedEvent="Click">
      <BeginStoryboard>
        <Storyboard>
          <DoubleAnimation Storyboard.TargetProperty="Opacity"
                           From="0" To="1" Duration="0:0:2" />
        </Storyboard>
      </BeginStoryboard>
    </EventTrigger>
  </Style.Triggers>
</Style>
```

To add an animation to a style requires two things. The first is an event trigger with the name of the event that caused the trigger to fire (the Click event, in our case). The second is a *storyboard*, which is a grouping for animations. When the Click event happens, we begin the storyboard. Our storyboard happens to contain one animation, which animates the Opacity property on the button from fully transparent to fully opaque. Figure 8-14 shows the results of clicking the button in the upper left about halfway through the fade-in animation.

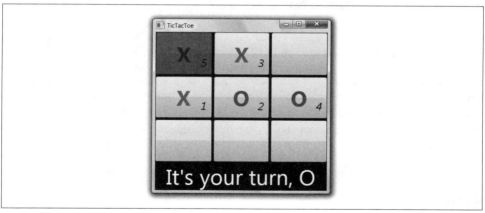

Figure 8-14. The event trigger and our fade-in animation (Color Plate 12)

Event triggers let you trigger animations when events happen. Property and data triggers let you set properties when properties change, but they also let you start or stop animations (discussed in Chapter 16). Both types of triggers let you add a degree of interactivity to your applications in a wonderfully declarative way with little or no code.

Where Are We?

Styles enable you to define a policy for setting the dependency properties of visual elements. You can apply sets of properties manually by name, programmatically by name, or automatically using element-typed styles. In addition to providing constant dependency property values, styles can contain condition-based property values based on other dependency properties, data properties, or events.

But that's not all there is to styles. For information about how animations work, you'll want to read Chapter 16, and for information about styles as related to resources, themes, and skins, you'll want to read Chapter 12. Finally, if setting style properties isn't enough to give your control the look you want, the very next chapter shows you how to replace the look of a control completely.

CHAPTER 9

Control Templates

Styles, as described in Chapter 8, are great if the changes you'd like to make to a control's look can be adjusted by the control's properties (according to your keen aesthetic sense), but what if the control author didn't leave you enough knobs to get the job done? Rather than diving in to build a custom control, as other presentation libraries would have you do, WPF provides the ability to replace the complete look of the built-in controls while maintaining the existing behavior.

Beyond Styles

Recall from Chapter 8 that we built a nice little tic-tac-toe game. However, if we take a closer look at it, we'll see that the Button isn't quite doing the job for us. What tic-tac-toe board has rounded inset corners (Figure 9-1)?

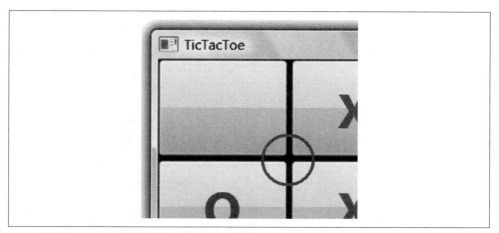

Figure 9-1. Tic-tac-toe boards don't have rounded insets!

What we really want here is to be able to keep the behavior (i.e., holding content and firing click events), but to take over the look of it. WPF allows this kind of thing because the intrinsic controls are built to be *lookless* (i.e., they provide behavior, but the control's user can swap out the look completely). The default look comes from the system-provided template, as described in Chapter 12.

Remember from Chapters 6 and 8 how we used data templates to provide the look of a nonvisual object? We can do the same to a control using a *control template*—a set of triggers, resources, and most important, elements that provide the look of a control.

To fix our buttons' looks, we'll build ourselves a control template resource. Let's start things off with a simple rectangle (see Example 9-1).

Example 9-1. A minimal control template

```
<!-- let's just try one button for now... -->
<Button Margin="0,0,2,2" Grid.Row="0" Grid.Column="0" Name="cell00">
  <Button.Template>
    <ControlTemplate>
      <Grid>
        <Rectangle />
      </Grid>
    </ControlTemplate>
  </Button.Template>
</Button>
```

Figure 9-2 shows the results of setting a single button's `Template` property.

Figure 9-2. Replacing the control template with something less visual than we'd like...

Notice that no vestiges of how the button used to look remain in Figure 9-2. Unfortunately, we can see no vestige of our rectangle, either. The problem is that without a fill explicitly set, the rectangle defaults to no fill, showing the grid's black background. Let's set it to our other favorite Halloween color instead:

```
<ControlTemplate>
  <Rectangle Fill="Orange" />
</ControlTemplate>
```

Now we're getting somewhere, as Figure 9-3 shows.

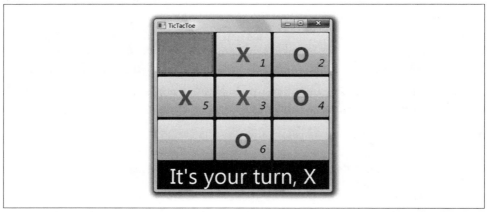

Figure 9-3. Replacing the button's control template with an orange rectangle (Color Plate 13)

Notice how square the corners are now? Also, if you click, you won't get the depression that normally happens with a button (and I don't mean "a sad feeling"). We have taken complete control over the look of the button or, to paraphrase some ancient pop culture, "all your button are belong to us..."

Control Templates and Styles

Now that we're making some progress on the control template, let's replicate it to the other buttons. We could do that by setting each button's Template property by hand, either to a copy of the control template or with a reference to a ControlTemplate element that's been created in a Resource element. However, it's often most convenient to bundle the control template with the button's style, as Example 9-2 illustrates.

Example 9-2. Putting a control template into a style

```
<Window.Resources>
  <Style TargetType="{x:Type Button}">
    ...
    <Setter Property="Template">
      <Setter.Value>
        <ControlTemplate>
          <Rectangle Fill="Orange" />
        </ControlTemplate>
      </Setter.Value>
    </Setter>
  </Style>
  ...
</Window.Resources>
...
```

Example 9-2. Putting a control template into a style (continued)

```
<!-- No need to set the Template property for each button -->
<Button ... Name="cell00" />
...
```

As Example 9-2 shows, the Template property is the same as any other and can be set with a style. Figure 9-4 shows the results.

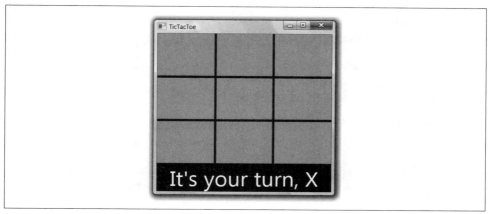

Figure 9-4. Spreading the orange (Color Plate 14)

Here we have the classic crosshatch we've been aiming for, but the orange is kind of jarring. What if the Button object's Background property was set to something more reasonable (maybe white?) and we're ignoring it, favoring colors from scary holidays not known for their design sense? We can solve this problem with template bindings.

Template Binding

If we wanted white buttons, we could hardcode the rectangle's fill to be white, but what happens when a style wants to change it (maybe somebody really wants an orange tic-tac-toe board)? Instead of hardcoding the fill of the rectangle, we can reach out of the template into the properties of the control by using template binding, as shown in Example 9-3.

Example 9-3. Template binding to the Background property

```
<Style TargetType="{x:Type Button}">
  <Setter Property="Background" Value="White" />
  ...
  <Setter Property="Template">
    <Setter.Value>
      <ControlTemplate>
        <Rectangle Fill="{TemplateBinding Property=Background}" />
      </ControlTemplate>
    </Setter.Value>
  </Setter>
</Style>
```

Template binding is like data binding, except that the properties to bind come from the control whose template you're replacing (called the *templated parent*). In our case, any dependency property on the Button class is fair game as a template binding source. And like data binding, template binds are smart enough to keep the properties of the items inside the template up-to-date with changing properties on the outside as set by styles, animations, and so on.

If you need the expanded options provided by a full binding, you use a Binding object inside a template with a RelativeSource of TemplatedParent to indicate how to resolve the Path (see Example 9-4).

Example 9-4. Binding inside a template using a RelativeSource of TemplatedParent

```
<Style TargetType="{x:Type Button}">
  <Setter Property="Background" Value="White" />
  ...
  <Setter Property="Template">
    <Setter.Value>
      <ControlTemplate>
        <Rectangle
          Fill="{Binding Path=Background,
                         RelativeSource={RelativeSource TemplatedParent}}" />
      </ControlTemplate>
    </Setter.Value>
</Style>
```

You should choose template binding over standard binding inside a template if it meets your needs, as template binding is optimized for just that use.

If you like, you can separate the control template from the style into a separate resource altogether:

```
<ControlTemplate x:Key="ButtonTemplate">
  <Grid>
    <Rectangle Fill="{TemplateBinding Property=Button.Background}" />
  </Grid>
</ControlTemplate>
<Style TargetType="{x:Type Button}">
  ...
  <Setter
    Property="Template"
    Value="{StaticResource ButtonTemplate}" />
</Style>
```

As with styles, we can avoid prefixing template binding property names with classes by setting the TargetType attribute on the ControlTemplate element:

```
<ControlTemplate x:Key="ButtonTemplate" TargetType="{x:Type Button}">
  <Grid>
    <Rectangle Fill="{TemplateBinding Property=Background}" />
  </Grid>
</ControlTemplate>
```

We're not quite through with our tic-tac-toe board yet, of course. If we're going to change the study in pumpkin that Figure 9-4 has become into a playable game, we have to show the moves. To do that, we'll need a content presenter.

Content Presenters

If you've ever driven by a billboard or a bus-stop bench that says "Your advertisement here!" that's all you need to know to understand content presenters. A *content presenter* is the WPF equivalent of "your content here" that allows content held by a ContentControl to be plugged in at runtime.

In our case, the content is the visualization of our PlayerMove object. Instead of reproducing all of that work inside the button's new control template, we'd just like to plug it in at the right spot. The job of the content presenter is to take the content provided by the templated parent and do all of the things necessary to get it to show up properly, including styles, triggers, and so on. You can drop the content presenter itself into your template wherever you'd like to see it. For this application, we'll compose a content presenter with the rectangle inside a grid, using techniques from Chapter 3:

```
<ControlTemplate TargetType="{x:Type Button}">
  <Grid>
    <Rectangle Fill="{TemplateBinding Property=Background}" />
    <ContentPresenter
      Content="{TemplateBinding Property=Content}" />
  </Grid>
</ControlTemplate>
```

Further, with the TargetType property in place, we can drop the explicit template binding on the Content property altogether, as it can be set automatically:

```
<ControlTemplate TargetType="{x:Type Button}">
  <Grid>
    <Rectangle Fill="{TemplateBinding Property=Background}" />
    <!-- with TargetType set, the template binding for the -->
    <!-- Content property is no longer required -->
    <ContentPresenter />
  </Grid>
</ControlTemplate>
```

I used the Grid here because it's an obvious way to compose the Rectangle and the ContentPresenter together into one cell that takes up the entire available space. However, I also used it to illustrate a possible performance issue.

When you're building control templates, you've got to keep in mind that they're likely to be used in multiple places—sometimes hundreds of places. Every element you include will be used each time your control template is expanded, so you want to make sure to use the minimum number of elements.

For example, in our simple control template, there's no reason to have a Rectangle to share the same cell in the Grid just to give the ContentPresenter a background color—instead, we can just use a Border, which has a background color and can contain our ContentPresenter. And because the Border is only one element, we don't need to use the Grid to arrange it. An optimized version of this template looks like this:

```
<ControlTemplate TargetType="{x:Type Button}">
  <Border Background="{TemplateBinding Property=Background}">
    <ContentPresenter />
  </Border>
</ControlTemplate>
```

For the purposes of our example, the control template is expanded only nine times, so there's no problem, but you should keep element count in mind when you're composing your content templates.

The content presenter is all we need to get our game back to being functional, as shown in Figure 9-5.

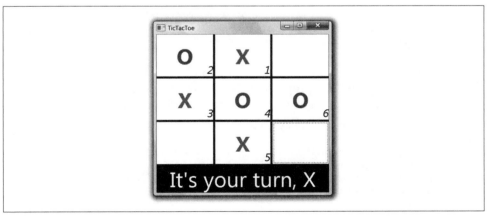

Figure 9-5. Adding a content presenter to our control template (Color Plate 15)

The last little bit of work in our sample is to get the padding to work. Because the content presenter doesn't have its own Padding property, we can't bind the Padding

---

property directly (it doesn't have a Background property, either, which is why we used the Rectangle and its Fill property). For properties that don't have a match on the content presenter, you have to find mappings or compose the elements that provide the functionality you're looking for. For example, Padding is an amount of space inside a control. Margin, on the other hand, is the amount of space around the outside of a control. Because they're both of the same type, System.Windows.Thickness, if we could map the Padding from the inside of our button to the outside of the content presenter,* our game would look very nice:

```
<ControlTemplate TargetType="{x:Type Button}">
  <Grid>
    <Rectangle Fill="{TemplateBinding Property=Background}" />
    <ContentPresenter Margin="{TemplateBinding Property=Padding}" />
  </Grid>
</ControlTemplate>
<Style TargetType="{x:Type Button}">
  <Setter Property="Background" Value="White" />
  <Setter Property="Padding" Value="8" />
  <Setter Property="Template" Value="{StaticResource ButtonTemplate}" />
  ...
</Style>
```

Figure 9-6 shows our completed tic-tac-toe variation.

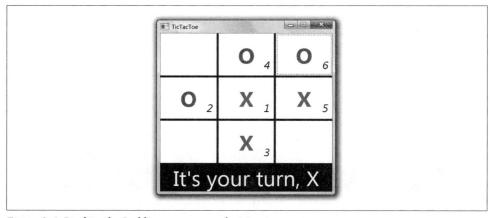

Figure 9-6. Binding the Padding property to the Margin property

Like the mapping between Padding and Margin, building up the elements that give you the look you want and binding the appropriate properties from the templated parent is going to be a lot of the work of creating your own control templates.

---

* You might be wondering whether we also need to bind our Margin property into the control template. It's a special case: WPF implements Margin for all elements as part of the layout process, so it's not something our template needs to worry about.

Template Triggers

Just like styles, control templates support triggers. These let us set up actions in the template itself, regardless of what other triggers the content of the control may or may not also have. For example, if we wanted to add a glow to our buttons as the user hovers, we can do so with a template trigger, as Example 9-5 illustrates.

Example 9-5. Control template triggers

```
<Style TargetType="{x:Type Button}">
  ...
  <Setter Property="Template">
    <Setter.Value>
      <ControlTemplate TargetType="{x:Type Button}">
        <Grid>
          <Rectangle Fill="{TemplateBinding Property=Background}"
                     Name="rect" />
          <ContentPresenter Margin="{TemplateBinding Property=Padding}" />
        </Grid>
        <ControlTemplate.Triggers>
          <Trigger Property="IsMouseOver" Value="True">
            <Setter TargetName="rect" Property="BitmapEffect">
              <Setter.Value>
                <OuterGlowBitmapEffect GlowColor="Yellow" GlowSize="10" />
              </Setter.Value>
            </Setter>
          </Trigger>
        </ControlTemplate.Triggers>
      </ControlTemplate>
    </Setter.Value>
  </Setter>
  ...
</Style>
```

In Example 9-5, we're setting a yellow glow whenever the mouse is hovered over the rectangle that fills the button. We're using a property trigger, so the value we're watching for is a property on the control itself (the IsMouseOver property, to be precise). However, we don't want to set a property on the button; instead, we want to set the BitmapEffect property on some inner part of the template (the rectangle, in our case). This is a very common thing to want to do, and because of that, a Setter object inside a control template allows an extra property to be set that can't be set in a style's Setter: the TargetName property. The TargetName is the name of some element in the template on which we'd like to set a property (e.g., the element named rect in our example).

Figure 9-7 shows the effect in all its glory.

Figure 9-7. A control template trigger in action (Color Plate 16)

Extending Templates

Take another look at the glow effect in which we swaddled our buttons:

```
<OuterGlowBitmapEffect GlowColor="Yellow" GlowSize="10" />
```

Do you notice a problem we've run into before? That's right—in the same way we were hardcoding the orange fill color a few pages ago, now we're hardcoding the glow color and size. "Oh," you think. "That's no problem. I'll just do what I did before and map the appropriate properties of the Button class to the GlowColor and GlowSize properties in the template." And I applaud you in the application of your recent learnin', but there ain't no properties on the Button that map to "glow." In fact, it is often the case in building control templates that there are more variables you'd like to expose than there are properties on the control being "templated."

Repurposing an existing property

One popular technique to let us default a custom property for use by the control template is to hijack an existing property for our purposes, as shown in Example 9-6.

Example 9-6. Extending a template by repurposing an existing property

```
<Style TargetType="{x:Type Button}">
  ...
  <Setter Property="Tag">
    <Setter.Value>
      <OuterGlowBitmapEffect GlowColor="Yellow" GlowSize="10" />
    </Setter.Value>
  </Setter>
  <Setter Property="Template">
    <Setter.Value>
```

Example 9-6. Extending a template by repurposing an existing property (continued)

```
      <ControlTemplate TargetType="{x:Type Button}">
        <Grid>
          ...
        </Grid>
        <ControlTemplate.Triggers>
          <Trigger Property="IsMouseOver" Value="True">
            <Setter TargetName="rect" Property="BitmapEffect"
                    Value="{Binding Path=Tag,
                        RelativeSource={RelativeSource TemplatedParent}}" />
          </Trigger>
        </ControlTemplate.Triggers>
      </ControlTemplate>
    </Setter.Value>
  </Setter>
...
<!-- use default bitmap effect set in the style -->
<Button Margin="2,0,2,2" Grid.Row="0" Grid.Column="1" Name="cell01" />
...
<!-- use custom bitmap effect, overriding the style's default -->
<Button Margin="2,2,2,2" Grid.Row="1" Grid.Column="1" Name="cell11">
  <Button.Tag>
    <BevelBitmapEffect BevelWidth="10" />
  </Button.Tag>
</Button>
...
```

In Example 9-6, our Button style uses the Tag property to pass in a bitmap effect object to use when the mouse is overhead. The control template's trigger uses the value of the Tag property when the IsMouseOver property is True. Notice that we're using normal binding (with the TemplatedParent RelativeSource) instead of template binding because the normal binding object has casting support at runtime, whereas template binding checks the types statically at compile time. The use of a normal binding enables us to pull a BitmapEffect out of the Tag property, which is of type Object.

When we create a button using this style, the Tag value acts as a default value, which we can override with any bitmap effect that tickles our fancy (as shown on the middle button in Example 9-6).

Defining a custom dependency property

The problem with repurposing any of the Button's properties is that somebody might actually use the one you pick for something (e.g., the Tag property is generally a place to store app-specific data). If this is a worry, the safest thing to do (short of defining your own custom control type) is to take a page from Chapter 18 and define your own custom dependency property:

```
namespace TicTacToe {
  public class MouseOverEffectProperties {
    public static DependencyProperty MouseOverEffectProperty;
    static MouseOverEffectProperties() {
```

```
    OuterGlowBitmapEffect defaultEffect = new OuterGlowBitmapEffect();
    defaultEffect.GlowColor = Colors.Yellow;
    defaultEffect.GlowSize = 10;

    MouseOverEffectProperty =
      DependencyProperty.RegisterAttached(
        "MouseOverEffect",
        typeof(BitmapEffect),
        typeof(MouseOverEffectProperties),
        new PropertyMetadata(defaultEffect));
  }
}
  public static BitmapEffect
    GetMouseOverEffect(DependencyObject target) {

    return (BitmapEffect)target.GetValue(MouseOverEffectProperty);
  }

  public static void
    SetMouseOverEffect(DependencyObject target, BitmapEffect value) {

    target.SetValue(MouseOverEffectProperty, value);
  }
}
```

Notice that this dependency property is registered as an attached property that can
be attached to any DependencyObject. Also notice that it has a built-in default, which
simplifies our style, as it needs to list a value for our new property only if it wants to
override the default. The static GetMouseOverEffect and SetMouseOverEffect methods
allow us to set the property value on any dependency object, including our buttons.
With this dependency property in place, we can write our control template trigger as
shown in Example 9-7.

Example 9-7. Using the custom attached dependency property to pass extra info

```
<Window ... xmlns:local="clr-namespace:TicTacToe">
  ...
  <ControlTemplate.Triggers>
    <Trigger Property="IsMouseOver" Value="True">
      <Setter ...
        Property="BitmapEffect"
        Value="{Binding
          Path=(local:MouseOverEffectProperties.MouseOverEffect),
          RelativeSource={RelativeSource TemplatedParent}}" />
    </Trigger>
  </ControlTemplate.Triggers>
  ...
  <Button ...
    Tag="howdy"
    local:MouseOverEffectProperties.MouseOverEffect="{x:Null}">
  ...
</window>
```

Notice that the Path expression in the Binding is surrounded by parentheses, which, as you'll recall from Chapter 6, means an explicit dependency property reference. Notice also that we've defined an XML namespace pointing to the CLR namespace where the class lives and that we use this to specify the path to the dependency property. However, instead of using the name of the dependency property field (which has a "Property" suffix), we use the name we registered with the RegisterAttached method (which doesn't have the "Property" suffix).

Also notice how Example 9-7 overrides the default value for the property by setting the attached property on an individual button (to null, in this example), while taking advantage of the newly available Tag property for a friendly Western U.S. greeting.

 Instead of creating a new attached dependency property, you can use one of the existing ones, even if it has nothing to do with your control. However, it can be difficult to find an attached property that a) will never be used for anything else on your control; b) is of the correct type; and c) has a name that suggests some kind of semantic relationship with the use of that property in your control template. It does save code, though, if you can use an existing property.

The simple usage of your custom template properties will always be a custom control that has those properties built in, of course. I recommend checking out Chapter 18 for more information about that.

The Control Template Contract

We haven't been explicit about this yet, but controls expect their templates to provide certain features. The exact set of features varies from one control to the next, but a contract is always in effect between the control and the template. The control's side of the contract is essentially the set of properties and commands it offers. The template's side of the contract is less obvious, and is sometimes implicit.

Remember that a control's job is to provide behavior. The control template provides the visuals. A control may provide a default set of visuals, but it should allow these to be replaced in order to offer the same flexibility as the built-in controls. If you need to provide both custom behavior and custom visuals, build two components: a control, and an element designed to be incorporated into the control's template. A control that conforms to this approach—where the visuals are separated from the control—is often described as *lookless*, because the control has no intrinsic appearance or "look." All of the controls built into WPF are lookless.

Of course, it is not possible for the control to be entirely independent of its visuals. Any control will impose some requirements that the template must satisfy if the control is to operate correctly. The extent of these requirements varies from one control to another. Button has fairly simple requirements: it needs nothing more than a placeholder in which to inject the content. The slider controls have much more extensive requirements: the visuals must supply two buttons (increase and decrease), the "thumb," and a track for the thumb to run in. Moreover, they need to be able to respond to clicks or drags on any of these elements, and to be able to position the thumb.

There is an implied contract between any control type and the style or template. The control allows its appearance to be customized by replacing the visual tree, but the tree must in turn provide certain features on behalf of the control. The nature of the contract will depend on the control—the built-in controls use several different techniques depending on how tightly they depend on the structure of their visuals. The following sections describe the various ways in which a control and its template can be related.

Property binding

The loosest form of contract between control and template is where the control simply defines public properties, and allows the template to decide which of these properties to make visible using the `TemplateBinding` markup extension. The control does not care what is in the template.

This is effectively a one-way contract: the control provides properties and demands nothing in return. Despite this, such a control can still respond to user input if necessary—event routing allows events to bubble up from the visuals to the control. The control can handle these events without needing to know anything about the nature of the visuals from which they originated.

Named parts

Sometimes it is necessary for a control to locate specific elements in the template. For example, if you write a template for a `ProgressBar`, the control will look for two parts: the element that it should resize to indicate progress, and a second so-called "track" element that represents the full extent of the control. The control modifies the progress indicator part to be a proportion of the size of the track, according to the current progress. When the bar's `Value` property is equal to the `Maximum` property, the indicator will be the same size as the track; when the `Value` is at `Minimum`, the indicator's size will be zero; and for values in between, the size is interpolated appropriately.

The `ProgressBar` locates these two template parts by name. It will expect the template to contain an element named `PART_Indicator`, and another element named `PART_Track`. Example 9-8 shows a very simple control template with these parts.

Example 9-8. Control template with named parts

```
<ProgressBar Width="100" Height="25" Value="4" Maximum="10">
  <ProgressBar.Template>
    <ControlTemplate TargetType="{x:Type ProgressBar}">
```

Example 9-8. Control template with named parts (continued)

```
    <Grid>
      <Rectangle Name="PART_Track" Fill="LightGray" Stroke="Black" />
      <Rectangle Name="PART_Indicator" HorizontalAlignment="Left"
                 Margin="2" RadiusX="5" RadiusY="5"
                 Fill="White" Stroke="Blue" />
    </Grid>
  </ControlTemplate>
  </ProgressBar.Template>
</ProgressBar>
```

Figure 9-8 shows the results. As you can see, the rectangle with the rounded corners and the white fill has been sized in proportion to the control's Value—it's filling about 40 percent of the space provided by the track.

Figure 9-8. ProgressBar with template

The intrinsic WPF controls mark their part usage with the TemplatePartAttribute, which makes it handy to figure out which controls have which parts (assuming you're handy with the metadata API in .NET). Table 9-1 shows the current set of template parts and their expected type for each WPF control.

Table 9-1. Controls with template parts

Control	Template part name	Expected type
ComboBox	PART_Popup	Popup
	PART_EditableTextBox	TextBox
DocumentViewer	PART_ContentHost	ScrollViewer
	PART_FindToolBarHost	ContentControl
FlowDocumentPageViewer	PART_FindToolBarHost	Decorator
FlowDocumentReader	PART_ContentHost	Decorator
	PART_FindToolBarHost	Decorator
FlowDocumentScrollViewer	PART_FindToolBarHost	Decorator
	PART_ToolBarHost	Decorator
	PART_ContentHost	ScrollViewer
Frame	PART_FrameCP	ContentPresenter
GridViewColumnHeader	PART_HeaderGripper	Thumb
	PART_FloatingHeaderCanvas	Canvas
MenuItem	PART_Popup	Popup
NavigationWindow	PART_NavWinCP	ContentPresenter
PasswordBox	PART_ContentHost	FrameworkElement

Table 9-1. Controls with template parts (continued)

Control	Template part name	Expected type
ProgressBar	PART_Track	FrameworkElement
	PART_Indicator	FrameworkElement
ScrollBar	PART_Track	Track
ScrollViewer	PART_HorizontalScrollBar	ScrollBar
	PART_VerticalScrollBar	ScrollBar
	PART_ScrollContentPresenter	ScrollContentPresenter
Slider	PART_Track	Track
	PART_SelectionRange	FrameworkElement
StickyNoteControl	PART_CopyMenuItem	MenuItem
	PART_CloseButton	Button
	PART_ResizeBottomRightThumb	Thumb
	PART_IconButton	Button
	PART_ContentControl	ContentControl
	PART_TitleThumb	Thumb
	PART_PasteMenuItem	MenuItem
	PART_InkMenuItem	MenuItem
	PART_SelectMenuItem	MenuItem
	PART_EraseMenuItem	MenuItem
TabControl	PART_SelectedContentHost	ContentPresenter
TextBoxBase	PART_ContentHost	FrameworkElement
ToolBar	PART_ToolBarPanel	ToolBarPanel
	PART_ToolBarOverflowPanel	ToolBarOverflowPanel
TreeViewItem	PART_Header	FrameworkElement

Content placeholders

Some controls expect to find a placeholder element of a certain type in the template. Controls that support the content model by deriving from ContentControl use the element type approach. They expect to find a ContentPresenter element in the template, as you've already seen.

> In practice, this is a loosely enforced contract. A ContentControl will not usually complain if there is no ContentPresenter in the template. The control doesn't absolutely depend on the content being presented in order to function.

In fact, some controls may require more than one placeholder. For example, controls derived from HeaderedContentControl require two—one for the body and one for the header. In this case, we can simply be explicit about which property the ContentPresenter presents, as Example 9-9 shows.

Example 9-9. ContentPresenter and HeaderedContentControl

```
<ControlTemplate TargetType="{x:Type local:MyContentControl}">
    <Grid>
        <Grid.RowDefinitions>
            <RowDefinition />
            <RowDefinition />
        </Grid.RowDefinitions>

        <ContentPresenter Grid.Row="0" Content="{TemplateBinding Content}" />
        <ContentPresenter Grid.Row="1" Content="{TemplateBinding Header}" />
    </Grid>
</ControlTemplate>
```

WPF defines two more placeholder types:

- `ScrollContentPresenter` indicates where the content hosted by a scroll viewer will go.

- You can use `ItemsPresenter` in an `ItemsControl` to indicate where generated items should be added.

In addition, if you don't want to replace the entire control template, `ItemsControl` lets you replace bits and pieces of itself, which it references in its default templates (and which you can reference in your own custom `ItemsControl` templates). In fact, there are two other options for templates on an `ItemsControl`. The first we've already seen in Chapter 7: you can supply a `DataTemplate` as the `ItemTemplate` property and this will customize the appearance of each individual item. The second alternative is that you can set the `ItemsPanel` property. This allows you to customize just the panel used to lay out the list contents. This uses another template class: `ItemsPanelTemplate`. Notice that neither the `ItemTemplate` property nor the `ItemsPanel` property is of the `ControlTemplate` type, but anyone customizing an `ItemsControl` will want to be familiar with all of the template types that WPF provides.

 At this point, we've rounded out the different kinds of templates available in WPF: data templates, hierarchical data templates, control templates, and items panel templates. Fundamentally, they're all about expanding a template as required (and they all derive from the `FrameworkTemplate` base class), but the specifics are different and you can't mix and match them.

The `ItemsPanelTemplate` lets you change the default panel that lays out items in the list:

```
<ListBox ItemsSource="{Binding}">
  <ListBox.ItemsPanel>
    <ItemsPanelTemplate>
      <StackPanel Orientation="Horizontal" />
    </ItemsPanelTemplate>
  </ListBox.ItemsPanel>
</ListBox>
```

```
<ComboBox ItemsSource="{Binding}">
  <ComboBox.ItemsPanel>
    <ItemsPanelTemplate>
      <UniformGrid />
    </ItemsPanelTemplate>
  </ComboBox.ItemsPanel>
</ComboBox>
```

In this code, we've replaced the vertical StackPanel provided by default in a ListBox with a horizontal one. This code also uses a UniformGrid to perform a grid layout of the list items in a combo box. These two changes produce the results you see in Figure 9-9.

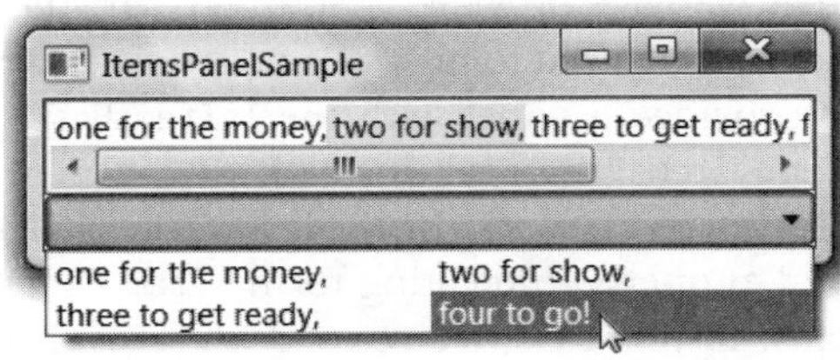

Figure 9-9. The items panel template in action

You can use any type derived from the Panel class as the panel template, including a custom panel if you've written such a thing to perform custom layout. The interesting thing about using a panel in this way is that although none of the panels supports data binding directly (e.g., none of them has an ItemsSource property like an ItemsControl), the ItemsControl knows how to manage items in a panel, so it effectively gives you data binding over the panel of your choice.

Placeholders indicated by properties

Some controls look for elements marked with a particular property. For example, controls derived from ItemsControl, such as ListBox and MenuItem, support templates containing an element with the Panel.IsItemsHost property set to true. This identifies the panel that will act as the host for the items in the control. ItemsControl uses an attached property instead of a placeholder to allow you to decide what type of panel to use to host the items. (ItemsControl also supports the use of the ItemsPresenter typed placeholder element. This is used when the template does not wish to impose a particular panel type, and wants to use whatever panel the ItemsPanelTemplate has specified in the ItemsPanel property.) Example 9-10 is a sample.

Example 9-10. Using IsItemsHost to indicate the items host

```
<ListBox ItemsSource="{StaticResource items}" Width="120" Height="67">
  <ListBox.Template>
    <ControlTemplate TargetType="{x:Type ListBox}">
      <Border BorderThickness="1" BorderBrush="Black" CornerRadius="10">
```

Example 9-10. Using IsItemsHost to indicate the items host (continued)

```
      <ScrollViewer>
        <ScrollViewer.Clip>
          <RectangleGeometry Rect="0, 0, 118, 65" />
        </ScrollViewer.Clip>
        <VirtualizingStackPanel IsItemsHost="True" />
      </ScrollViewer>
    </Border>
  </ControlTemplate>
  </ListBox.Template>
</ListBox>
```

Example 9-10 shows the use of a full control template replacing the entire set of visuals for a ListBox. Notice that we have provided a ScrollViewer; the default ListBox template supplies one of these, so we need to provide our own if we want scrolling to work. Notice also that we've provided a panel with the IsItemsHost property set to True. We could have used the ItemsPresenter instead, as we mentioned earlier, if we wanted the ItemsPanel property to work. Instead, this sample ignores the ItemsPanel and uses the IsItemsHost property, indicating to the ItemsControl to which panel it should add the list items. In this case, we've used a VirtualizingStackPanel, a special form of StackPanel optimized for a large number of items in the data source.* This is the same panel type that the default template for a ListBox uses. Figure 9-10 shows the results.

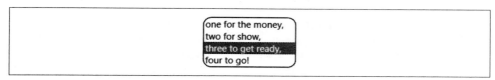

Figure 9-10. Setting the IsItemsHost property

If your goal is to re-create the default look and tweak it, you will want to use something like the template in Example 9-10. (Here we're just tweaking the template by supplying a Clip geometry in order to make the control an unusual shape.) However, if you want to radically change the appearance, the ScrollViewer is optional. The only hard requirement is that you supply a panel with the IsItemsHost property set to True or that you provide an ItemsPresenter.

The use of properties to indicate a content placeholder is effectively equivalent to the named parts approach described earlier. However, the named parts approach is far more common—few of the built-in controls use this property-based approach. We describe it here mainly for completeness.

---

* The VirtualizingStackPanel supports *item virtualization*, which is the ability to contain a large number of logical children, but instantiating UI elements only for the ones currently visible.

Special-Purpose Elements

Some controls define custom element types designed for use as a part of their template, which does more than merely marking the place where content is to be injected. For example, the Slider control requires the template to contain elements to represent the draggable thumb, and the clickable track in which the thumb runs. The control cannot function unless the template conforms to the required structure. To enforce this, Slider requires that the template contain elements of the special-purpose Thumb and Track types.

Neither of these control types is designed for use in isolation. To emphasize this, both Thumb and Track are defined in the System.Windows.Controls.Primitives namespace. The only places you would normally use Track are in the templates for a Slider or a ScrollBar. Thumb is slightly more general-purpose—you can use it anywhere you require something draggable. But it's still designed to be used as part of something else, and is not a control in its own right.

The Track control defines a fixed structure for part of a control template. It has three properties that contain nested controls. DecreaseRepeatButton and IncreaseRepeatButton must contain RepeatButton controls—these represent the clickable areas to either side of the thumb. The Thumb property contains the Thumb control itself. The Track manages the sizes and positions of all three controls, ensuring that they reflect the current properties of the control at all times.

Example 9-11 shows this technique in action. Notice that the slider uses the named part idiom as well as special-purpose element types.

Example 9-11. Slider template using special-purpose elements

```
<Slider Width="100" Height="20" Value="20" Maximum="100">
  <Slider.Template>
    <ControlTemplate TargetType="{x:Type Slider}">
      <Track x:Name="PART_Track">
        <Track.DecreaseRepeatButton>
          <RepeatButton Content="&lt;" />
        </Track.DecreaseRepeatButton>
        <Track.Thumb>
          <Thumb Width="10" />
        </Track.Thumb>
        <Track.IncreaseRepeatButton>
          <RepeatButton Content="&gt;" />
        </Track.IncreaseRepeatButton>
      </Track>
    </ControlTemplate>
  </Slider.Template>
</Slider>
```

Figure 9-11 shows the rather unadventurous results. In a real application, you would also provide templates for the two repeat buttons and the thumb.

Figure 9-11. Customized slider

The benefit of this approach is that it allows you to enforce relationships between different parts of the control template. Sliders and scroll bars use the Track element to keep the Thumb correctly positioned and sized in relation to the two clickable regions that form the track. In addition, this approach enforces the fact that the clickable regions are, in turn, represented by RepeatButtons. The downside is that it is more complex for the developers using the control because anyone wishing to define a template for the control must discover and understand the multiple element types involved.

Examining the Built-in Templates

A lot of the examples in this section talked about how one WPF template does one thing, while another WPF template does something else. If you're curious what the intrinsic WPF templates do, you can check out the ShowMeTheTemplate sample provided with this book, as seen in Figure 9-12.

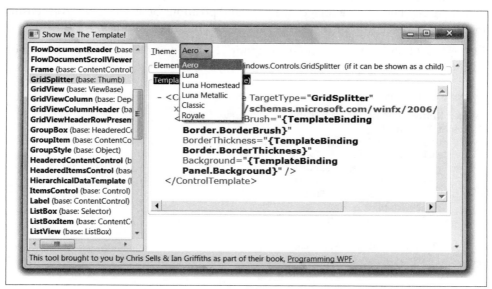

Figure 9-12. The ShowMeTheTemplate tool

On the lefthand side of the template tool are all of the framework elements that have template properties of any type. When one of them is selected, the template properties are shown on the right. For example, in Figure 9-12, we can see the Template property (of type `ControlTemplate`) of the `GridSplitter`. The templates shown on the right are produced by the XAML serializer, so you should be able to copy and paste them into your own code as a starting place if you'd prefer to tweak an existing template instead of starting over from scratch.

Logical and Visual Trees

The existence of templates leads to an API design dilemma that the WPF architects had to resolve. If a developer wishes to access the elements in the UI, should she see the fully expanded tree, containing all the instantiated templates? Although this would put the developer in full control, it might be rather cumbersome; often a developer only really cares that there is a `Button` present, not about the structure of its appearance. On the other hand, to present the simple pre-expansion view would be unnecessarily limiting.

To solve this problem, WPF lets you work with either the logical tree or the visual tree. The *visual tree* contains most* of the elements originally specified (either in markup or in code) plus all the extra elements added as a result of template instantiation. The *logical tree* is a subset of the visual tree that omits the elements added as a result of control template instantiation. WPF provides two helper classes for working with these two trees: `VisualTreeHelper` and `LogicalTreeHelper`.

For example, consider the following snippet of XAML:

```
<WrapPanel Name="rootPanel">
  <Button>_Click me</Button>
</WrapPanel>
```

Walking this logical tree at runtime using the `LogicalTreeHelper` looks like Example 9-12.

Example 9-12. Dumping the logical tree

```
public Window1( ) {
  InitializeComponent( );

  // Can dump the logical tree anytime after InitComp
  DumpLogicalTree(rootPanel, 0);
}

void DumpLogicalTree(object parent, int level) {
  string typeName = parent.GetType( ).Name;
  string name = null;
  DependencyObject doParent = parent as DependencyObject;
```

---

* As one example, no `FrameworkContentElement` objects, as described in Chapter 14, will show up in the visual tree even though they're in the logical tree.

Example 9-12. Dumping the logical tree (continued)

```
    // Not everything in the logical tree is a dependency object
    if( doParent != null ) {
      name = (string)(doParent.GetValue(FrameworkElement.NameProperty) ?? "");
    }
    else {
      name = parent.ToString( );
    }

    Debug.Write("                   ".Substring(0, level * 2));
    Debug.WriteLine(string.Format("{0}: {1}", typeName, name));
    if( doParent == null ) { return; }

    foreach( object child in LogicalTreeHelper.GetChildren(doParent) ) {
      DumpLogicalTree(child, level + 1);
    }
  }
}
```

Notice that we're watching for objects that aren't instances of the DependencyObject class (almost the lowest level in the WPF type hierarchy—only the DispatcherObject is lower). Not everything in the logical tree is part of the WPF type hierarchy (e.g., the string we pass in as the text content of the Button is going to stay a string when we examine it):

```
    WrapPanel: rootPanel
      Button:
        String: _Click me
```

The code to walk the instantiated objects with the VisualTreeHelper is simpler because everything it encounters is at least a DependencyObject (see Example 9-13).

Example 9-13. Dumping the visual tree

```
protected override void OnContentRendered(EventArgs e) {
  base.OnContentRendered(e);

  // Need to wait for layout before visual tree is ready
  Debug.WriteLine("Visual tree:");
  DumpVisualTree(rootPanel, 0);
}

void DumpVisualTree(DependencyObject parent, int level) {
  string typeName = parent.GetType( ).Name;
  string name = (string)(parent.GetValue(FrameworkElement.NameProperty) ?? "");
  Debug.Write("                   ".Substring(0, level * 2));
  Debug.WriteLine(string.Format("{0}: {1}", typeName, name));

  for( int i = 0; i != VisualTreeHelper.GetChildrenCount(parent); ++i ) {
    DependencyObject child = VisualTreeHelper.GetChild(parent, i);
    DumpVisualTree(child, level + 1);
  }
}
```

In Example 9-13, you'll notice that we're careful to only walk the visual tree in the OnContentRendered event, which guarantees that at least a portion of the visual tree has been rendered. This is important, because the visual tree isn't expanded until it needs to be. However, once it's instantiated, the visual tree is considerably more verbose than the logical tree:

```
WrapPanel: rootPanel
  Button:
    ButtonChrome: Chrome
      ContentPresenter:
        AccessText:
          TextBlock:
```

The difference, of course, is that the button control template was instantiated. If you'd like to explore the visual tree produced by a bit of XAML interactively, I suggest the XamlPad tool that comes with the Windows Platform SDK. XamlPad lets you type in XAML and shows you the results as soon as you've entered valid XAML. It also has a button that will show you the visual tree of the XAML you've typed in. Figure 9-13 shows the visual tree for our sample XAML in a slightly nicer way.

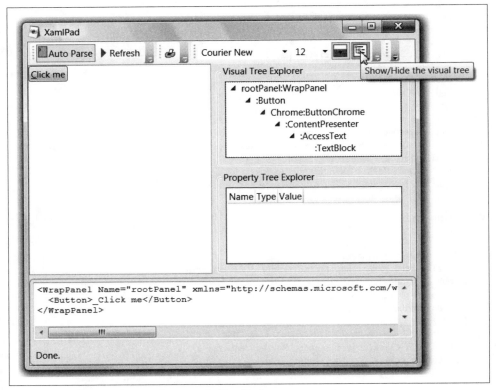

Figure 9-13. Showing the visual tree inside XamlPad

Data-Driven UI

Templates enable a certain kind of UI programming sometimes called *data-centric UI* and sometimes called *data-driven UI*. The idea is that the data is the most important thing in our application, and through the use of declarative UI techniques (as enabled by XAML) we shape the data into something suitable for presentation to the user. Ideally, we do this without changing the underlying data at all, but by instead transforming the data on its way to the user as appropriate.

For example, getting back to our tic-tac-toe program, we haven't been very data-driven at all, instead bundling up the manipulation of the data with the UI code (a.k.a. "putting your logic in the click handler"). A better way to start is to move our game logic into a class of its own that has nothing at all to do with the UI:[*]

```
class TicTacThree : INotifyPropertyChanged {
  public TicTacThree(int dimension) {...}
  public void NewGame() {...}
  public void Move(int cellNumber) {...}
  public IEnumerable<Cell> Cells { get {...} }
  public string CurrentPlayer { get {...} }
  public bool HasWinner { get {...} }
}

class Cell : INotifyPropertyChanged {
  public Cell(int cellNumber) {...}
  public int CellNumber { get {...} }
  public PlayerMove Move { get {...} set {...} }
}

class PlayerMove : INotifyPropertyChanged {
  public string PlayerName { get {...} set {...} }
  public int MoveNumber { get {...} set {...} }
  public bool IsPartOfWin { get {...} set {...} }
  public PlayerMove(string playerName, int moveNumber) {...}
}
```

With this change, the code to hook up our UI to the new game logic is reduced significantly:

```
class Window1 : Window {
  TicTacThree game = new TicTacThree(3); // 3x3 grid
  public Window1() {
    InitializeComponent();
    DataContext = game;
  }

  void cell_Click(object sender, RoutedEventArgs e) {
    Button cell = (Button)sender;
```

---

[*] In fact, this has nothing whatever to do with data-driven UI; as a good coding practice, you should separate your data and your logic from your UI.

```
    int cellNumber = int.Parse(cell.Tag.ToString( ));
    game.Move(cellNumber);
    if( game.HasWinner ) {
      MessageBox.Show("Winner!");
      game.NewGame( );
    }
  }
}
```

However, in addition to the styles and templates we've built up over the course of our discussion, our XAML is augmented with data binding to show the player moves and the current player:

```
<Window ...>
  ... <!-- styles and templates as before -->
  <Button ... Tag="0" Content="{Binding Cells[0].Move}" Click="cell_Click" />
  <Button ... Tag="1" Content="{Binding Cells[1].Move}" Click="cell_Click" />
  ...
    <TextBlock ...>
      It's your move, <TextBlock Text="{Binding CurrentPlayer}" />
    </TextBlock>
</Window>
```

At this point, we've moved further toward data-driven UI, as we've separated the data manipulation out of the UI code and are relying on our styles, templates, and data binding to translate the data appropriately for user interaction. However, we have hardcoded knowledge about how much data we are going to get: nine cells. That works great until we add an option to create a tic-tac-toe game of 4×4 or 5×5 cells, at which point it's clear we're not as data-driven as we'd like to be. Luckily, it's not hard to update our code-behind file:

```
class Window1 : Window {
  TicTacThree game = new TicTacThree(3); // 3x3 grid
  public Window1( ) {
    ...
    threeByThreeMenuItem.Click += gameDimensionMenuItem_Click;
    fourByFourMenuItem.Click += gameDimensionMenuItem_Click;
    fiveByFiveMenuItem.Click += gameDimensionMenuItem_Click;
  }

  void gameDimensionMenuItem_Click(object sender, RoutedEventArgs e) {
    if( sender == threeByThreeMenuItem ) { game = new TicTacThree(3); }
    if( sender == fourByFourMenuItem ) { game = new TicTacThree(4); }
    if( sender == fiveByFiveMenuItem ) { game = new TicTacThree(5); }
    DataContext = game;
  }

  ...
}
```

Updating the XAML is a bit trickier, however, as we need to handle a variable number of cells. In our case, the UniformGrid—which arranges things in even rows and columns—is exactly what we need, but the other panels will be useful for other kinds of data-driven layouts:

```
<Window ...>
  ...
  <Menu ...>
    <MenuItem Header="_Game">
      <MenuItem Header="_3x3 Game" Name="threeByThreeMenuItem" />
      <MenuItem Header="_4x4 Game" Name="fourByFourMenuItem" />
      <MenuItem Header="_5x5 Game" Name="fiveByFiveMenuItem" />
    </MenuItem>
  </Menu>
  ...
  <ItemsControl ... ItemsSource="{Binding Cells}">
    <ItemsControl.ItemsPanel>
      <ItemsPanelTemplate>
        <UniformGrid />
      </ItemsPanelTemplate>
    </ItemsControl.ItemsPanel>

    <ItemsControl.ItemTemplate>
      <DataTemplate>
        <Button Content="{Binding Move}" Tag="{Binding CellNumber}"
                Margin="2" Click="cell_Click" />
      </DataTemplate>
    </ItemsControl.ItemTemplate>
  </ItemsControl>
  ...
</Window>
```

Here, we've added the menu so that the user can control the dimensions of the game, and we've bound the cells in the game as the data source to drive our items control. (We're using an ItemsControl instead of a ListBox or a ListView because we don't want the selection behavior those controls provide.) For the panel, we're using a uniform grid, which will take however many items we provide and turn them into an even number of rows and columns. Likewise, for each item, we're expanding a data template into a button to show the current cell's move (or nothing, if no move has yet been made). We're also binding the Tag property of each Button to the CellNumber property of the cell so that we can use the same button Click event handler. However, as we saw in Chapter 7, we could just as easily use the DataContext of the sender, as it will point to the Cell that was used to instantiate the data template.

Figure 9-14 shows the results of our data-driven UI work.

The interesting thing to notice is that once we've structured our XAML to be free of the hardcoded amount of data to expect, the XAML itself doesn't get any more complicated, although it does have more functionality as the data changes, as Figure 9-14 shows.

If you decide you need even more control, you are of course free to take over the control templates as well:

```
<ItemsControl ... ItemsSource="{Binding Cells}">
  <ItemsControl.ItemsPanel>
    <ItemsPanelTemplate>
```

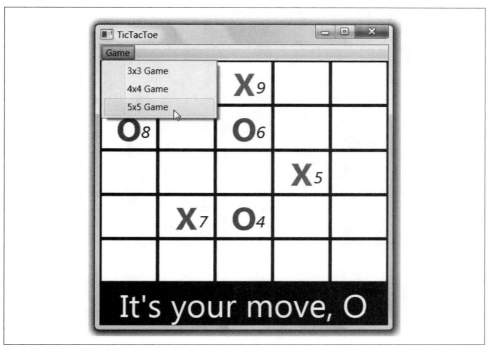

Figure 9-14. A data-driven game of tic-tac-toe

```xml
      <UniformGrid />
    </ItemsPanelTemplate>
  </ItemsControl.ItemsPanel>

  <ItemsControl.ItemTemplate>
    <DataTemplate>
      <Button Margin="2"
        Content="{Binding Move}"
              Tag="{Binding CellNumber}"
              Click="cell_Click" />
    </DataTemplate>
  </ItemsControl.ItemTemplate>

  <ItemsControl.Template>
    <ControlTemplate TargetType="{x:Type ItemsControl}">
      <Grid>
        <Rectangle Fill="Green" RadiusX="20" RadiusY="20" />
        <ItemsPresenter Margin="20" />
      </Grid>
    </ControlTemplate>
  </ItemsControl.Template>

</ItemsControl>
```

Here, we're replacing the control template with a border containing an ItemsPresenter, which, as you'll recall from earlier in this chapter, will display the items according to the templates set by the ItemsPanel and ItemsTemplate properties, as Figure 9-15 shows.

Figure 9-15. Replacing the control template in a data-driven application (Color Plate 17)

This use of the control template isn't particularly fancy (although it does give our game a nice felt-tabletop look), but it does illustrate just how much control we have over the UI using templates, even when our data is completely UI-agnostic.

Ultimately, driving your UI by the data means making a choice from a range of possibilities. We started by dropping data objects into buttons and using styles and templates to present those objects to the user. Moving to data binding and away from mingling the data manipulation code in with UI code moved us farther along the continuum, as did binding the cells to an items control hosting a uniform grid. However, there are always going to be trade-offs. For example, our menu supports only three dimension choices, no matter how many our game object might support. Further, we haven't supported the case where the game object might arrange the cells in nonuniform rows and columns. Like all software design choices, how "data-driven" you want your UI to be depends on the goals of your application.

However, whatever trade-offs you make, it is definitely the case that the various templates that WPF provides—data, control, and panel—all give us far more options than we've had in desktop presentation frameworks available before now. In fact, the reason I make a point of data-driven UI design is so that you don't approach WPF programming using the same techniques you used to program user interfaces of old.

As an example of where other UI frameworks don't quite provide the kind of data-driven capabilities we'd like, consider another UI framework that both authors are big fans of: Windows Forms. In Windows Forms, you absolutely have the ability to bind data to your controls. In fact, Windows Forms has more controls than WPF has, including the GridView, which has no equivalent in WPF v1.0.

However, although Windows Forms has more controls, each control has more limited support for what it can display. For example, although I can hand the Windows Forms ListBox a list of strings, I can't hand it a list of CheckBox objects or PlayerMove objects and have it do anything more than call each object's ToString method. If I want a container to meaningfully bind to a list of PlayerMove objects in Windows Forms, I have to build the custom PlayerMove container.

With WPF, on the other hand, I can plug custom data types and custom UI frameworks into *existing* containers by providing data and control templates. This turns out to be considerably less work for the same functionality. WPF is not your father's UI framework...

Where Are We?

If the control author didn't give you the right properties to tailor a control's look to your liking, you can replace the look completely with a control template (assuming the control author has allowed such a thing). To this end, all of the built-in controls are "lookless," picking up their default look from the system-wide theme, but leaving you to take it over completely, while keeping the existing behavior intact. If you want to plug into the existing behavior properly, however, some controls have more requirements, which we called the control template "contract."

If a custom template still doesn't give you enough control—perhaps you'd like customized behavior—you'll want to think about building a custom control, which is described in Chapter 18, along with how to support custom control templates on your own custom controls.

CHAPTER 10

Windows and Dialogs

The `Window` class, mentioned in Chapter 2, is the required class for the application's main window. To fit in with the rest of the Windows applications, the WPF `Window` class is flexible. It supports building top-level style main windows and dialogs, which we'll discuss in this chapter, as well as serving as the base class for the `NavigationWindow`, which we'll discuss in the next chapter.

Window

In Chapter 2, we looked at the lifetime and services of an application, often as related to the windows that constitute the UI of the application. However, we didn't talk much about the windows themselves. The `Window` class derives from the `ContentControl` (described in Chapter 5) and adds the chrome around the edges that contains the title; the minimize, maximize, and close buttons; and so on. The content can look however you want. The chrome itself has more limited options.

Window Look and Feel

The look and feel of the frame of a window is largely determined by the `Icon`, `Title`, and `WindowStyle` properties, the latter of which has four options (`None`, `SingleBorderWindow`, `ThreeDBorderWindow`, and `ToolWindow`), shown in Figure 10-1 (the default is `SingleBorderWindow`).

You'll notice that the icon and/or title are shown or not depending on the window style. You'll also notice that the `None` `WindowStyle` still contains a border. This is because, by default, a window can be resized, so it needs resizing edges. If you turn off resizing with the `ResizeMode` property, as discussed later in this chapter, the `None` `WindowStyle` will remove all window "crust," leaving only the "gooey center."

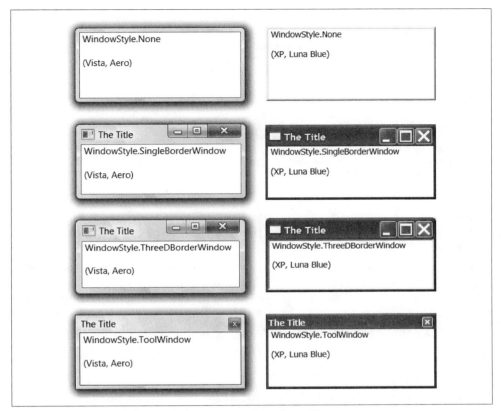

Figure 10-1. Window styles in Windows Vista and Windows XP

Window Lifetime

Before you can see a window, you need to create it and show it. Creating a window is as easy as calling new on the Window class or a class derived from Window. As you can see in Example 10-1, if you've defined a custom window in XAML—Visual Studio 2005 does this when you right-click on a project in the Solution Explorer and select Add → New Item and then choose Window (WPF)—the constructor will need to call the InitializeComponent method (as the Visual Studio 2005-generated Window classes already do).

Example 10-1. Calling InitializeComponent

```
<!-- Window1.xaml -->
<Window x:Class="WindowsApplication1.Window1" ...>
  ... <!-- XAML to initialize instance of custom Window class -->
</Window>

// Window1.xaml.cs
...
namespace WindowsApplication1 {
  public partial class Window1 : System.Windows.Window {
    public Window1() {
      // Use XAML to initialize object of custom Window class first
      InitializeComponent();
      ...
    }
    ...
  }
}
```

In the presence of the x:Class property, the WPF build task will generate a partial class with an InitializeComponent implementation. This will load the window's XAML and use it to initialize the properties that make up the window object and hook up the events. If you forget to call InitializeComponent or do something else before calling InitializeComponent, your window object will not be fully initialized.

After the window has been constructed, you can show it modally or modelessly (see Example 10-2).

Example 10-2. Showing a window modelessly and modally

```
Window1 window = new Window1();

// Show modelessly
window.Show();

// Show modally
if( window.ShowDialog() == true ) {
  // user clicked OK (or the equivalent)
}
```

When a window is shown modelessly using the Show method, the Show method returns immediately, not waiting for the newly shown window to close. This is the method to use to create a new top-level window in your application.

When a window is shown modally using the ShowDialog method, the ShowDialog method doesn't return until the newly shown window is closed, disabling the other windows in your application. The ShowDialog method is mostly used to show windows that act as dialogs, which we'll see in the "Dialogs" section, later in this chapter.

Once a window is created, it exposes a series of events to let you monitor and affect its lifetime, as shown in Figure 10-2.

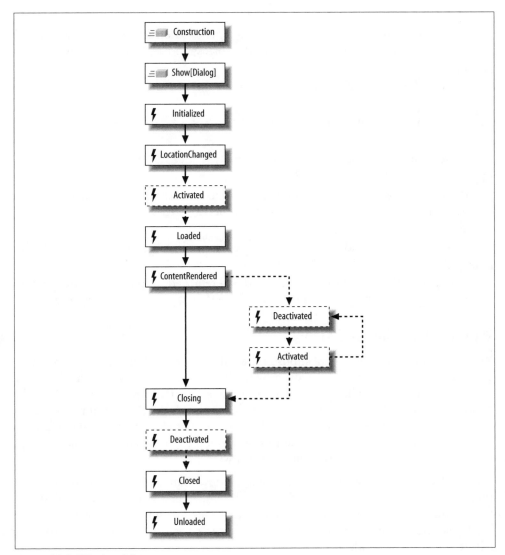

Figure 10-2. Window lifetime

The following is a description of these events:

Initialized

Raised when the FrameworkElement base of the Window is initialized (essentially when the InitializeComponent method is called).

LocationChanged

Fired when the window is moved.

Activated

Raised when the window is activated (e.g., clicked on). If the window is never activated, you won't get this event (or the corresponding Deactivated event).

Deactivated

Raised when some other window in the system is activated.

Loaded

Raised just before the window is shown.

ContentRendered

Raised when the window's content is visually rendered.

Closing

Raised when the window attempts to close itself. You can cancel this by setting the CancelEventArgs argument's Cancel property to true.

Closed

Raised when the window has been closed (cannot be canceled).

Unloaded

Raised after the window has been closed and removed from the visual tree. If closing the window causes the application to shut down, you won't see this event.

Window Location and Size

You can manage the *x* and *y* locations of a window with the Top and Left properties, whereas you can influence the Z order with the TopMost property. Across the entire desktop, all windows with the TopMost property set to true appear above all of the windows with the TopMost property set to false, although the Z order of the windows within their layer is determined by user interaction. For example, clicking on a non-topmost window will bring it to the top of the non-topmost layer of windows, but will not bring it in front of any topmost windows.

If you'd like to set the startup location of a window manually, you can do so by setting the Top and Left properties before showing the window. However, if you'd prefer to simply have the window centered on the screen or on the owner, you can set the WindowStartupLocation property to CenterScreen or CenterOwner as appropriate before showing the window:

```
Window1 window = new Window1();
window.WindowStartupLocation = WindowStartupLocation.CenterScreen;
window.Show(); // will be centered on the screen
```

If you don't change the WindowStartupLocation, Manual is the default. Manual lets you determine the initial position by setting Top and Left. If you don't care about the initial position, the Manual value lets the Windows shell determine where your window goes.

You can get the size of the window from the ActualWidth and ActualHeight properties of the Window class after (not during) the Initialized event (e.g., Loaded is a good place to get them). The actual size properties are expressed (like all Window-related sizes) in device-independent pixels measuring 1/96th of an inch.* However, the ActualWidth and ActualHeight properties are read-only, and therefore, you cannot use them to set the width and height. For that, you need the Width and Height properties.

The size properties (Width and Height) are separate from the "actual" size properties (ActualWidth and ActualHeight) because the actual size is calculated based on the size, the minimum size (MinWidth and MinHeight), and the maximum size (MaxWidth and MaxHeight). For example:

```
Window1 window = new Window1( );
window.Show( ); // render window so ActualWidth is calculated
window.MinWidth = 200;
window.MaxWidth = 400;
window.Width = 100;
Debug.Assert(window.Width == 100); // regardless of min/max settings
Debug.Assert(window.ActualWidth == 200); // bound by min/max settings
```

Here, we've set the width of the window outside the min/max bounds. The value of the Width property doesn't change based on the min/max bounds, but the value of the ActualWidth property does. This behavior lets you set a size outside of the min/max bounds, and that size will stick and potentially take effect if the min/max bounds change. This behavior also means that you should set the Width and Height properties to influence the size of your window, but you'll probably want to get the ActualWidth and ActualHeight properties to see what kind of influence you've had.

If, instead of sizing the window manually, you'd like the size of the window to be initially governed by the size of the content, you can change the SizeToContent property from the default SizeToContent enumeration value Manual to one of the other three enumeration values: Width, Height, or WidthAndHeight. If the content size falls outside the min/max bounds for one or both dimensions, the min/max bounds will still be honored. Likewise, if Width or Height is set manually, the SizeToContent setting will be ignored.

By default, all windows are resizable; however, you can change the behavior by setting the ResizeMode property with one of the values from the ResizeMode enumeration: NoResize, CanMinimize, CanResize, or CanResizeWithGrip, as shown in Figure 10-3.

You'll notice from Figure 10-3 that the NoResize resize mode causes the Minimize and Maximize buttons to go away. It also doesn't resize at the edges. Likewise, CanMinimize doesn't allow resizing at the edges, but it shows the Minimize and Maximize buttons (although only the Minimize button is functional). On the other hand, the CanResize mode makes the window fully resizable, whereas CanResizeWithGrip is just like CanResize except that it puts the grip in the lower-righthand corner. Because of the huge advances that WPF has provided in the area of layout functionality, there should be almost no reason to use a resize-disabling resize mode.

---

* For example, if you set the size of a WPF window to 400×400 in 120dpi mode, according to Spy++, the size of that window will be 500×500 as far as the operating system is concerned. However, at 96dpi, 400×400 is 400×400 for both WPF and the OS.

Figure 10-3. Window resize modes

Window Owners

We use the CenterOwner value of the WindowStartupLocation enumeration only if we also set the window's Owner property. The *owner* of a window dictates certain characteristics of the windows that are *owned* by it:

- An owned window always shows in front of its owner unless the owned window is minimized.
- When an owner window is minimized, all of the owned windows are minimized (and likewise for restoration).
- When the owner window is closed, so are all of the windows the owner owns.
- When an owner window is activated, all of the owned windows are brought to the foreground with it.

In practice, the chief visual use of an owned window is to create a floating tool window or modeless dialog (i.e., something that has minimizing and restoration behavior shared with the owner window).

However, you should get into the practice of setting the Owner property because it enables better accessibility support in WPF (which you can read about at *http://msdn2.microsoft.com/en-us/library/ms753388.aspx* or *http://tinysells.com/102*).

An owner window's set of owned windows is available from the OwnedWindows collection property.

Window Visibility and State

You can control the visibility of a window with the Visibility property, which has the following values from the Visibility enumeration: Visible, Hidden, and Collapsed. (The Window class treats Hidden and Collapsed as the same.) You can also use the Show and Hide methods. In addition to stopping the window from rendering, the Hide method takes it out of the taskbar (assuming the ShowInTaskbar property is set in the first place).

If you'd like to hide the window but leave it in the taskbar, you can set the WindowState property to the WindowState enumeration value Minimized. To restore it or make it take up the whole desktop (minus the taskbars and the sidebar), you can use Normal or Maximized.

Likewise, as the user interacts with the window, the WindowState will reflect the current state of the window. If, while the window is minimized or maximized, you'd like to know the location and size of what it will be upon restoration, you can use the RestoreBounds property. Unlike Left, Top, Width, Height, ActualWidth, and ActualHeight, all of which will reflect the current window state within the min/max bounds, RestoreBounds changes only if the window is moved or resized while it's in the Normal state. This makes RestoreBounds a handy property to keep in a user setting for window restoration,* as you can see in Example 10-3.

Example 10-3. Saving and restoring window state

```
public partial class MainWindow : System.Windows.Window {
  public MainWindow( ) {
    InitializeComponent( );

    try {
      // Restore state from user settings
      Rect restoreBounds = Properties.Settings.Default.MainRestoreBounds;
      WindowState = WindowState.Normal;
      Left = restoreBounds.Left;
      Top = restoreBounds.Top;
      Width = restoreBounds.Width;
      Height = restoreBounds.Height;

      WindowState = Properties.Settings.Default.MainWindowState;
    }
    catch { }

    // Watch for main window to close
    Closing += window_Closing;
  }
```

---

* Chapter 2 describes user settings.

Example 10-3. Saving and restoring window state (continued)

```
// Save state as window closes
void window_Closing(object sender, System.ComponentModel.CancelEventArgs e) {
    Properties.Settings.Default.MainRestoreBounds = RestoreBounds;
    Properties.Settings.Default.MainWindowState = WindowState;
    Properties.Settings.Default.Save();
}
...
}
```

This code assumes a couple of user settings variables named `MainRestoreBounds` and `MainWindowState` of type `Rect` and `WindowState`, respectively. With these in place, when the main window starts up, we set the window state temporarily to `Normal` so that we can set the left, top, width, and height from the restored bounds. After we do that, we can set the window state to whatever it was when we last ran the application, all of which happens before the window is shown, so there's no shake 'n' shimmy as the window goes between normal and another state. When the window is closing (but before it's closed), we tuck the data away for the next session and save the settings. Now, no matter what state the main window is in when we close it, we properly remember that state and the restored state.[*]

So far, we've talked about windows in the abstract, referring to some usages (e.g., top-level windows, toolbox windows, main windows, etc.). One other large use for windows in Windows applications is the humble dialog, which is the subject of the rest of this chapter.

Dialogs

Unlike the main window, where users can interact with any number of menu items, toolbar buttons, and data controls at will, a *dialog* is most often meant to be a short, focused conversation with the user to get some specific data before the rest of the application can continue. The File dialog is the classic example; when the application needs the name of a file, the File dialog provides a way for the user to specify it.

In Windows, dialogs were originally designed as *modal* (i.e., the application has entered a "mode" where the user must answer the questions posed by the dialog and click OK, or must abort the operation by clicking the Cancel button). However, it didn't take long for dialogs to need to continue running in concert with other accessible windows, leading to *modeless* operation, where the user can go back and forth between the dialog and other windows, using each at will. The Find dialog is the exemplar in this area. As users find something they've specified in the Find dialog, they're free to interact with that data without dismissing the Find dialog so that they can find the next thing that matches their query without starting over.

---

[*] For a multiple-monitor-safe version of this sample, check out the "Save Window Placement State Sample" in the SDK: *http://msdn2.microsoft.com/en-gb/library/aa972163.aspx* (*http://tinysells.com/103*).

In WPF, there is no special dialog class. Dialog interactions, both modal and modeless, are provided by either the `Window` or the `NavigationWindow` (discussed in the next chapter) as you choose. However, there is built-in support for dialog-like interactions with WPF application users, including modal operation, dialog styles, and data validation, as we'll explore in this chapter. And there are a few common dialog classes, which we'll explore now.

Common Dialogs

Since Windows 3.1, the operating system itself has provided common dialogs for use by applications to keep a consistent look and feel. WPF has three intrinsic dialogs that map to those provided by Windows—`OpenFileDialog`, `SaveFileDialog`, and `PrintDialog`—and they work the way you'd expect them to.[*] Example 10-4 shows the `OpenFileDialog` in action.

Example 10-4. Using the OpenFileDialog common dialog

```
using Microsoft.Win32; // home of OpenFileDialog and SaveFileDialog
using System.Windows.Controls; // home of PrintDialog
...
string filename;

void openFileDialogButton_Click(...) {
  OpenFileDialog dlg = new OpenFileDialog();
  dlg.FileName = filename;

  if (dlg.ShowDialog() == true) {
    filename = dlg.FileName;
    // open the file...
  }
}
```

If you'd like access to other common Windows Forms dialogs, like the folder browser dialog, you can bring in the `System.Windows.Forms` assembly[†] and use them without much trouble,[‡] as shown in Example 10-5.

Example 10-5. Showing the FolderBrowserDialog common Windows Forms dialog

```
string folder;

void folderBrowserDialogButton_Click(...) {
```

---

[*] Unlike the common dialogs provided by Windows Forms, the WPF `ShowDialog` returns a nullable Boolean value, not an enumerated value. We'll talk more about that later.

[†] Of course, now you're paying the cost of loading an additional assembly into your process, but that beats reimplementing the Windows Forms common dialogs in many scenarios.

[‡] If you'd like to take advantage of new Vista features in your common dialog usage, you can do so with samples provided in the SDK in the topic titled "Vista Bridge Samples," available at *http://msdn2.microsoft.com/en-us/library/ms756482.aspx* (*http://tinysells.com/95*).

Example 10-5. Showing the FolderBrowserDialog common Windows Forms dialog (continued)

```
System.Windows.Forms.FolderBrowserDialog dlg =
  new System.Windows.Forms.FolderBrowserDialog( );
dlg.SelectedPath = folder;

if( dlg.ShowDialog( ) == System.Windows.Forms.DialogResult.OK ) {
  folder = dlg.SelectedPath;
  // do something with the folder...
}
}
```

In Example 10-5, we're creating an instance of the `FolderBrowserDialog` class from the `System.Windows.Forms` namespace. The fully qualified type name is useful instead of the typical using statement at the top of the file so that we don't collide with any of the WPF types and thereby require those to be fully qualified, too.

After creation, the code in Example 10-5 calls the `ShowDialog` method, which shows the dialog modally until the dialog has closed. When that happens, `ShowDialog` returns with a result—generally, `OK` or `Cancel` (not `true` or `false`, like WPF dialogs). When it's `OK`, we can use the properties of the dialog set by the user.

Available common dialogs

Here's the list of common dialogs provided by a combination of WPF and Windows Forms (in case it isn't available in your personal short-term storage):

- `ColorDialog` (Windows Forms, but not good for use in WPF)
- `FolderBrowserDialog` (Windows Forms)
- `FontDialog` (Windows Forms, but not good for use in WPF)
- `OpenFileDialog` (WPF)
- `SaveFileDialog` (WPF)
- `PageSetupDialog` (Windows Forms)
- `PrintDialog` (WPF)
- `PrintPreviewDialog` (Windows Forms, but not good for use in WPF)

Most of them work exactly the way you'd expect them to because they deal in types that you can easily use in either Windows Forms or WPF (e.g., strings containing folder names or filenames work equally well in either). On the other hand, three of them (`ColorDialog`, `FontDialog`, and `PrintPreviewDialog`) don't work very well at all with WPF.

The problem with the `ColorDialog` is that it passes colors in and out using the GDI+ 4-byte representation of color from the `System.Drawing` namespace's `Color` class. WPF, on the other hand, has a much higher-fidelity `Color` class from the `System.Windows.Media` class that uses a four-float representation. Although it's possible to "dumb down" a

WPF color to work with the Windows Forms color dialog,* that's not your best option. Instead, if I were you, I'd check out the Color Picker Dialog sample that the WPF SDK team has put together and hosted on their blog.†

Things are similarly mismatched with the Windows Forms `FontDialog`, which relies on the GDI+ `Font` class from `System.Drawing`. WPF has many more font-rendering options than GDI+ and groups them differently, as individual properties instead of together into a single `Font` property (e.g., `FontFamily`, `FontSize`, `FontStretch`, `FontWeight`, etc.). It's possible to shoehorn some of the WPF font properties into the Windows Forms font dialog, and again, you'll want to check out a sample—this time bundled with the SDK itself.‡

 Although it's possible to use the Windows Forms color and font dialog from within your WPF programs (and in fact, the samples that come with this book show how to do it), I never did find a reasonable way to use the Windows Forms `PrintPreviewDialog` from WPF. The problem is that Windows Forms uses a completely different printing model than the one WPF uses, so you should check out Chapter 15 for the best way to render WYSIWYG documents to the screen in WPF.

Custom Dialogs

When the standard dialogs in WPF don't do the trick, you can, of course, implement your own custom dialogs. You can most easily define a custom dialog in WPF as a `Window`, like the `Settings` dialog for a mythical reporting application shown in Example 10-6.

Example 10-6. A simple custom settings dialog

```
<!-- SettingsDialog.xaml -->
<Window ...
  ResizeMode="CanResizeWithGrip"
  SizeToContent="WidthAndHeight"
  WindowStartupLocation="CenterOwner">
  <Window.Resources>
    <Style TargetType="Label">
      <Setter Property="VerticalAlignment" Value="Center" />
    </Style>
    <Style TargetType="TextBox">
      <Setter Property="VerticalAlignment" Value="Center" />
    </Style>
```

---

* The `FromArgb` method and the `A`, `R`, `G`, and `B` properties on both `Color` classes is the key to making the conversion between the GDI+ and WPF `Color` classes work.

† You can download it from *http://blogs.msdn.com/wpfsdk/archive/2006/10/26/Uncommon-Dialogs--Font-Chooser-and-Color-Picker-Dialogs.aspx* (*http://tinysells.com/89*).

‡ You can search for the "Font Dialog Box Demo" topic in your offline SDK or download it from *http:// msdn2.microsoft.com/en-gb/library/ms771765.aspx* (*http://tinysells.com/90*).

Example 10-6. A simple custom settings dialog (continued)

```xml
    <Style TargetType="Button">
      <Setter Property="Margin" Value="10" />
      <Setter Property="Padding" Value="5,2" />
    </Style>
  </Window.Resources>
  <Grid>
    <Grid.Resources>
      <SolidColorBrush x:Key="reportBrush" Color="{Binding ReportColor}" />
    </Grid.Resources>
    <Grid.RowDefinitions>
      <RowDefinition Height="Auto" />
      <RowDefinition Height="Auto" />
      <RowDefinition />
    </Grid.RowDefinitions>
    <Grid.ColumnDefinitions>
      <ColumnDefinition Width="Auto" />
      <ColumnDefinition MinWidth="200" />
      <ColumnDefinition Width="Auto" />
    </Grid.ColumnDefinitions>

    <!-- 1st row: report folder setting  -->
    <Label Grid.Row="0" Grid.Column="0"
      Target="{Binding ElementName=reportFolderTextBox}">Report _Folder</Label>
    <TextBox Grid.Row="0" Grid.Column="1" Name="reportFolderTextBox"
      Text="{Binding ReportFolder}" />
    <Button Grid.Row="0" Grid.Column="2" Name="folderBrowseButton">...</Button>

    <!-- 2nd row: report color setting -->
    <Button Grid.Row="1" Grid.Column="1" HorizontalAlignment="Left"
      Name="reportColorButton">
      <StackPanel Orientation="Horizontal">
        <Rectangle Width="15" Height="15" SnapsToDevicePixels="True"
                   Fill="{StaticResource reportBrush}" />
        <AccessText Text="Report _Color..." Margin="10,0,0,0" />
      </StackPanel>
    </Button>

    <!-- 3rd row: buttons -->
    <StackPanel Grid.Row="2" Grid.ColumnSpan="3" Orientation="Horizontal"
      HorizontalAlignment="Right" VerticalAlignment="Bottom">
      <Button Name="okButton" Width="72">OK</Button>
      <Button Name="cancelButton" Width="72">Cancel</Button>
    </StackPanel>
  </Grid>
</Window>
```

In Example 10-6, we haven't done anything that you wouldn't want to do in any window layout, as you've seen previously in this book. About the only thing we've done with a nod toward building a modal dialog box is to set the CenterOwner startup location and use a horizontal stack panel to keep the OK and Cancel buttons clustered together along the bottom right of the dialog. We're also using labels, access keys, and a resize grip, but those are just good practices and not dialog-specific. With the grid lines turned on, our settings dialog looks like Figure 10-4.

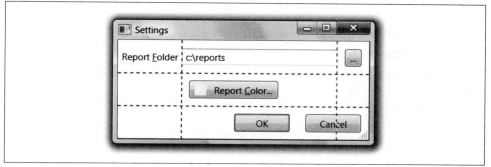

Figure 10-4. Using standard WPF techniques on a dialog

To take advantage of our custom dialog, we have but to create an instance and show it modally, as in Example 10-7.

Example 10-7. Showing a custom dialog

```
void settingsButton_Click(object sender, RoutedEventArgs e) {
  // Create dialog and show it modally, centered on the owner
  SettingsDialog dlg = new SettingsDialog();
  dlg.Owner = this;
  if (dlg.ShowDialog() == true) {
    // Do something with the dialog properties
    ...
  }
}
```

Although we've gotten a pretty good dialog using standard window techniques, dialogs need more to fit into a Windows world:

- The initial focus is set on the correct element.
- The dialog doesn't show in the taskbar.
- Data is passed in and out of the dialog.
- The OK button is shown as the default button (and is activated when the Enter key is pressed).
- Cancel is activated when the Esc key is pressed.
- Data is validated before "OK" is really "OK."

Dialog look and feel

Addressing issues on this list, we realize our dialog doesn't really feel like a dialog (e.g., the initial focus isn't set). Plus, like any window, the dialog shows as another window in the taskbar (which it shouldn't). We can fix both of these by setting two properties on the window, as shown in Example 10-8.

Example 10-8. Setting dialog-related Window properties

```
<!-- SettingsDialog.xaml -->
<Window ...
  ResizeMode="CanResizeWithGrip"
  WindowStartupLocation="CenterOwner"
  FocusManager.FocusedElement="{Binding ElementName=reportFolderTextBox}"
  ShowInTaskbar="False">
  ...
</Window>
```

In Example 10-8, the `FocusedElement` property allows us to bind to the element that we'd like to give the initial focus, and the `ShowInTaskBar` lets us keep the dialog out of the taskbar. Figure 10-5 shows the results.

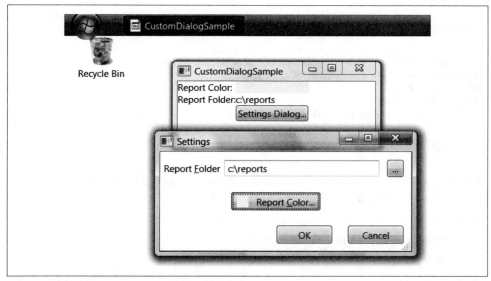

Figure 10-5. A good-looking dialog in WPF

The only traditional dialog feature that WPF doesn't support is the ? icon on the caption bar. However, as alternatives you can handle F1 (as described in Chapter 4), add a Help button, or use tool tips (as we'll see) as alternatives.

Dialog data exchange

Now that we've got our dialog looking like a dialog, we also want it to behave like one. A dialog's behavior is governed by its lifetime, which looks roughly like the following:

1. Create and initialize the dialog with initial values.
2. Show the dialog, letting the user choose new, validated values.
3. Harvest the values for use in your application.

Modal dialogs are generally provided to get data from a user so that some operation can be handled on his behalf. In the case of the sample settings dialog, I'm asking for a folder to store reports and specifying what color those reports should be. That information, like the information exposed from the standard dialogs, should be exposed as properties that I can set with initial values before showing the dialog and get after the user has changed them and clicked OK, as shown in Example 10-9.

Example 10-9. Exchanging data with a modal dialog

```
class Window1 : Window {
  ...
  Color reportColor;
  string reportFolder;

  void settingsButton_Click(object sender, RoutedEventArgs e) {
    // 1. Create and initialize the dialog with initial values
    SettingsDialog dlg = new SettingsDialog();
    dlg.Owner = this;
    dlg.ReportColor = reportColor;
    dlg.ReportFolder = reportFolder;

    // 2. Show the dialog, letting the user choose new, validated values
    if (dlg.ShowDialog() == true) {
      // 3. Harvest the values for use in your application
      reportColor = dlg.ReportColor;
      reportFolder = dlg.ReportFolder;
      // Do something with these values...
    }
  }
}
```

You'll notice that we're using a degree of good old-fashioned object-oriented encapsulation here, passing in and harvesting the values using .NET properties, but having no say about how the dialog shows those values to the user or how they're changed. All of this happens during the call to ShowDialog (which we'll get to directly). If the user clicks the OK button (or equivalent), we trust the dialog to let us know by returning a result of True so that we know to make use of the approved new values.

When you're implementing a custom dialog, how you implement the dialog properties is a matter of taste. Because I want to use data binding as part of the dialog implementation, I built a little class (Example 10-10) to hold the property data and fire change notifications.

Example 10-10. Managing custom dialog data

```
public partial class SettingsDialog : System.Windows.Window {

  // Data for the dialog that supports notification for data binding
  class DialogData : INotifyPropertyChanged {
    Color reportColor;
    public Color ReportColor {
      get { return reportColor; }
      set { reportColor = value; Notify("ReportColor"); }
    }

    string reportFolder;
    public string ReportFolder {
      get { return reportFolder; }
      set { reportFolder = value; Notify("ReportFolder"); }
    }

    // INotifyPropertyChanged Members
    public event PropertyChangedEventHandler PropertyChanged;
    void Notify(string prop) {
      if( PropertyChanged != null ) {
        PropertyChanged(this, new PropertyChangedEventArgs(prop));
      }
    }
  }

  DialogData data = new DialogData();

  public Color ReportColor {
    get { return data.ReportColor; }
    set { data.ReportColor = value; }
  }

  public string ReportFolder {
    get { return data.ReportFolder; }
    set { data.ReportFolder = value; }
  }

  public SettingsDialog() {
    InitializeComponent();

    // Allow binding to the data to keep UI bindings up-to-date
    DataContext = data;

    reportColorButton.Click += reportColorButton_Click;
    folderBrowseButton.Click += folderBrowseButton_Click;
    ...
  }
```

Example 10-10. Managing custom dialog data (continued)

```
  void reportColorButton_Click(object sender, RoutedEventArgs e) {
    // Set the ReportColor property, triggering a change notification
    // and updating the dialog UI
    ...
  }

  void folderBrowseButton_Click(object sender, RoutedEventArgs e) {
    // set the ReportFolder property, triggering a change notification
    // and updating the dialog UI
    ...
  }
  ...
}
```

Data Binding and Dialogs

You'll want to avoid binding directly to reference type objects passed into a dialog. The problem is that you could well be in a situation where the user makes changes to data and then clicks the Cancel button. In that case, WPF provides no facilities for rolling back changes made via data binding. That's why our example settings dialog keeps its own copies of the color and folder information.

The DialogData class in Example 10-10 is private to the dialog class and only serves as storage for the data that allows binding, which we enable by setting the DataContext to an instance of the class in the dialog's constructor. The dialog properties expose the data with properties that merely redirect to the instance of the DialogData class. When the data changes during the operation of the dialog (like when the user browses to a new folder or changes the color in a subdialog), setting the ReportColor and ReportFolder properties triggers a change notification, updating the dialog UI, which you'll recall is data bound as shown in Example 10-11.

Example 10-11. Binding property data in a custom dialog's GUI

```
<Window ...>
  ...
  <Grid>
    <Grid.Resources>
      <SolidColorBrush
        x:Key="reportBrush" Color="{Binding ReportColor}" />
    </Grid.Resources>
    ...
    <TextBox ... Text="{Binding ReportFolder}" />
    ...
    <Button ...
      Background="{StaticResource reportBrush}">Report _Color...</Button>
    ...
  </Grid>
</Window>
```

In Example 10-11, the report folder text box is binding to the ReportFolder property of the DialogData object. The button's background brush is binding to the brush (using the StaticResource markup extension described in Chapter 12) constructed via a binding to the ReportColor property (also of the DialogData object).

Figure 10-6 shows our settings dialog in various stages of data change.

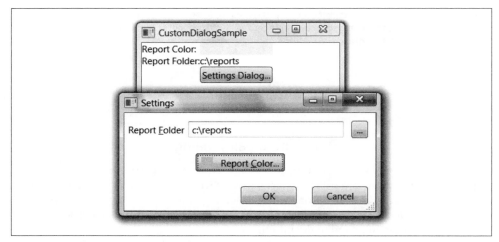

Figure 10-6. The custom settings dialog in action (Color Plate 18)

Handling OK and Cancel

Now that we know how to get the dialog running the way we want it to, we need to let the calling code know whether to process the data exposed after the dialog is closed. You can always close a dialog with the Window object's Close method, shown in Example 10-12.

Example 10-12. Closing a dialog manually

```
class SettingsDialog : Window {
  ...
  void cancelButton_Click(object sender, RoutedEventArgs e) {
    // The result from ShowDialog will be false
    Close();
  }
}
```

By default, when calling the Close method, or if the user clicks the Close button or presses Alt-F4, the result from ShowDialog will be false, indicating "cancel." If you'd like the return from ShowDialog to be true, to indicate "OK," you need to set the dialog's DialogResult property, as shown in Example 10-13.

Example 10-13. Changing the return value of ShowDialog

```
class SettingsDialog : Window {
  ...
  void okButton_Click(object sender, RoutedEventArgs e) {
    // The result from ShowDialog will be true
    DialogResult = true;
    Close();
  }
}
```

The DialogResult property is public, so it's available to users of your custom dialogs. The vast majority of the time, the dialog's DialogResult property will be the same as the return from ShowDialog. To understand the corner case, let's look at Example 10-14, which shows the definitions of ShowDialog and DialogResult.

Example 10-14. The nullable results of showing a dialog

```
namespace System.Windows {
  public class Window : ... {
  ...
    public bool? ShowDialog();
    public bool? DialogResult { get; set; }
  ...
}
```

If you're not familiar with the ? syntax, it designates the Boolean type of ShowDialog and DialogResult to be *nullable* (i.e., one of the legal values is null). However, even though both ShowDialog and DialogResult are of type bool?, ShowDialog will always return true or false.* Likewise, DialogResult will always be true or false after the dialog has been closed. Only after a dialog has been shown but before it's been closed is DialogResult null. This is useful when you're dealing with a modeless dialog while the dialog itself is still showing.

 You'll notice that ShowDialog doesn't return an enum with OK, Cancel, Yes, No, and so on, like Windows Forms does. ShowDialog indicates only whether the user OK'd the operation of the dialog in some way—what way that was is up to the implementer of the dialog to communicate.

Because DialogResult is null while the dialog is shown, WPF checks the DialogResult property after each Window event so that when it transitions to something non-null, the dialog will be closed (see Example 10-15).

---

* I wish the return type from ShowDialog was just a plain bool to indicate that it can return only true or false and never null.

Example 10-15. Closing a modal dialog automatically by changing DialogResult

```
void okButton_Click(object sender, RoutedEventArgs e) {
    // The return from ShowDialog will be true
    DialogResult = true;

    // No need to explicitly call the Close method
    // when DialogResult transitions to non-null
    //Close();
}
```

As a further shortcut, you can set the IsCancel property on the Cancel button to true, causing the Cancel button to automatically close the dialog without handling the Click event, as Example 10-16 illustrates.

Example 10-16. Cancel buttons transition DialogResult automatically

```
<!-- no need to handle the Click event to close dialog -->
<Button Name="cancelButton" IsCancel="True">Cancel</Button>
```

In addition to closing the dialog, setting IsCancel to true enables the Esc key as a shortcut to closing the dialog (and setting the DialogResult to false). However, whereas setting IsCancel is enough to cause the dialog to close when the Cancel button is clicked, the corresponding setting on the OK button, IsDefault, isn't enough to do the same. Transitioning the DialogResult to true, causing the dialog to close, must be handled manually, as shown in Example 10-17.

Example 10-17. Default buttons still need to transition DialogResult manually

```
...
<Button Name="okButton" IsDefault="True" ...>OK</Button>
...
void okButton_Click(object sender, RoutedEventArgs e) {
    // Need this to reflect "OK" back to dialog owner
    DialogResult = true;
}
```

Setting IsDefault provides a visual indication of the default button and enables the Enter key as a shortcut to the OK button (assuming the control with focus doesn't use the Enter key itself).

Data validation

Just because the user clicks the OK button doesn't mean that everything's OK: the data the user entered generally needs validation. You'll recall from Chapter 6 that WPF provides per-control validation as part of the binding engine. Dialogs, an example of which is shown in Example 10-18, are an excellent place to apply this technique.

Example 10-18. Data validation and dialogs

```
...
<!-- 1st row: report folder setting  -->
<Label ...>Report _Folder</Label>
<TextBox ...
  Name="reportFolderTextBox"
  ToolTip="
    {Binding
      RelativeSource={RelativeSource Self},
      Path=(Validation.Errors)[0].ErrorContent}">
  <TextBox.Text>
    <Binding Path="ReportFolder">
      <Binding.ValidationRules>
        <local:FolderMustExist />
      </Binding.ValidationRules>
    </Binding>
  </TextBox.Text>
</TextBox>
...
<!-- 3rd row: reporter setting -->
<Label ...>_Reporter</Label>
<TextBox ...
  Name="reporterTextBox"
  ToolTip="
    {Binding
      RelativeSource={RelativeSource Self},
      Path=(Validation.Errors)[0].ErrorContent}">
  <TextBox.Text>
    <Binding Path="Reporter">
      <Binding.ValidationRules>
        <local:NonZeroLength />
      </Binding.ValidationRules>
    </Binding>
  </TextBox.Text>
</TextBox>
...
```

In Example 10-18, I've added a validation rule to the report folder field that requires it to exist on disk. I've also added another field, this time to keep track of who's reporting the reports. The validation rule for this field is a class that makes sure something is entered in this field. The validation rule implementations, some of which are shown in Example 10-19, should not surprise you.

Example 10-19. Some example validation rules

```
public class FolderMustExist : ValidationRule {
  public override ValidationResult Validate(object value, ...) {
    if (!Directory.Exists((string)value)) {
      return new ValidationResult(false, "Folder doesn't exist");
    }
```

Example 10-19. Some example validation rules (continued)

```
    return new ValidationResult(true, null);
  }
}

public class NonZeroLength : ValidationRule {
  public override ValidationResult Validate(object value, ...) {
    if (string.IsNullOrEmpty((string)value)) {
      return new ValidationResult(false, "Please enter something");
    }

    return new ValidationResult(true, null);
  }
}
```

With these rules in place, as the user makes changes to the fields, the validation rules are fired and the controls are highlighted and tool-tipped with error indications, as shown in Figure 10-7.

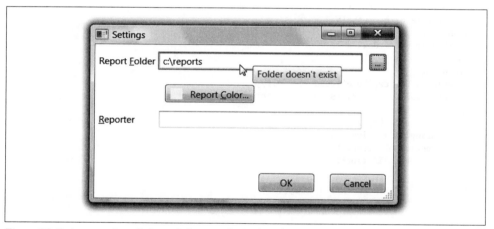

Figure 10-7. An error in a dialog validation rule (Color Plate 19)

However, if we don't make any changes or if we skip some fields before clicking the OK button, the user will have no way of knowing that some of the fields are invalid. Even worse, in the OK button handler, the Window class provides no facilities for manually checking all of the bindings to see whether there is any invalid data on the dialog. I assume a future version of WPF will provide this functionality, but in the meantime, I've built a little method called ValidateBindings that provides a first cut at this functionality, which you can use in your own custom dialogs in the OK button handler, as shown in Example 10-20.

Example 10-20. Validate all controls in the OK button

```
// This is here 'til future versions of WPF provide this functionality
public static bool ValidateBindings(DependencyObject parent) {
```

Example 10-20. Validate all controls in the OK button (continued)

```
    // Validate all the bindings on the parent
    bool valid = true;
    LocalValueEnumerator localValues = parent.GetLocalValueEnumerator( );
    while( localValues.MoveNext( ) ) {
      LocalValueEntry entry = localValues.Current;
      if( BindingOperations.IsDataBound(parent, entry.Property) ) {
        Binding binding = BindingOperations.GetBinding(parent, entry.Property);
        foreach( ValidationRule rule in binding.ValidationRules ) {
          ValidationResult result =
            rule.Validate(parent.GetValue(entry.Property), null);
          if( !result.IsValid ) {
            BindingExpression expression =
              BindingOperations.GetBindingExpression(parent, entry.Property);
            Validation.MarkInvalid(expression,
              new ValidationError(rule, expression, result.ErrorContent, null));
            valid = false;
          }
        }
      }
    }

    // Validate all the bindings on the children
    for( int i = 0; i != VisualTreeHelper.GetChildrenCount(parent); ++i ) {
      DependencyObject child = VisualTreeHelper.GetChild(parent, i);
      if( !ValidateBindings(child) ) { valid = false; }
    }

    return valid;
}

void okButton_Click(object sender, RoutedEventArgs e) {
  // Validate all controls
  if (ValidateBindings(this)) {
    DialogResult = true;
  }
}
```

With our validation helper method in place, when the user clicks the OK button, she gets a notification of all of the fields in error, not just the ones she's changed or the ones she's given focus to, as shown in Figure 10-8.

Modeless dialogs

We've been talking about modal dialogs so far, mostly because the similarities between a modal and a modeless dialog outweigh the differences. We still create an instance of a dialog class with style choices that make it look like a dialog. We still pass the data into and out of the dialog with properties. We still validate the data before notifying anyone that it's available. The only real differences between a modal and modeless dialog is that with a modeless dialog, we need some slightly different UI choices (generally "Apply" and "Close" instead of "OK" and "Cancel"), and we need to fire an event when the Apply button is clicked so that interested parties can pull out validated data.

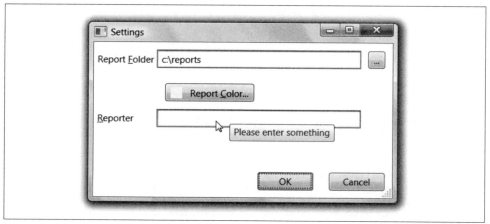

Figure 10-8. Validating all controls in the OK button handler (Color Plate 20)

Updating our settings dialog to operate modelessly starts with new buttons, as shown in Example 10-21.

Example 10-21. Apply and Close buttons for a modeless dialog

```
<StackPanel ...>
  <Button Name="applyButton" IsDefault="True" ...>Apply</Button>
  <Button Name="closeButton" IsCancel="True" ...>Close</Button>
</StackPanel>
```

Handling the button clicks is slightly different, too, as you can see in Example 10-22.

Example 10-22. Handling the Apply and Close buttons in a modeless dialog

```
public partial class SettingsDialog : System.Windows.Window {
  ...

  public SettingsDialog() {
    ...
    applyButton.Click += applyButton_Click;
    closeButton.Click += closeButton_Click;
  }

  // Fired when the Apply button is clicked
  public event EventHandler Apply;

  void applyButton_Click(object sender, RoutedEventArgs e) {
    // Validate all controls
    if (ValidateBindings(this)) {

      // Let modeless clients know
      if (Apply != null) { Apply(this, EventArgs.Empty); }
```

```
      // Don't close the dialog 'til Close is clicked
      // DialogResult = true;
    }
  }

  void closeButton_Click(object sender, RoutedEventArgs e) {
    // The IsCancel button doesn't close automatically
    // in the modeless case
    Close();
  }
}
```

In Example 10-22, we use the `ValidateBindings` helper method, and if everything is valid, we fire the `Apply` event to let the owner know, keeping the dialog open until the Close button is clicked. In the handler for the Close button, there's no more automatic closing of the dialog in the modeless case, so we close it ourselves.

The owner of the dialog changes a bit as well, as Example 10-23 illustrates.

Example 10-23. Handling the Apply event on a custom modeless dialog

```
public partial class Window1 : System.Windows.Window {
  ...
  Color reportColor;
  string reportFolder;
  string reporter;

  void settingsButton_Click(object sender, RoutedEventArgs e) {
    // Initialize the dialog
    SettingsDialog dlg = new SettingsDialog();
    dlg.Owner = this;
    dlg.ReportColor = reportColor;
    dlg.ReportFolder = reportFolder;
    dlg.Reporter = reporter;

    // Listen for the Apply button and show the dialog modelessly
    dlg.Apply += dlg_Apply;
    dlg.Show();
  }

  void dlg_Apply(object sender, EventArgs e) {
    // Pull the dialog out of the event args and apply the new settings
    SettingsDialog dlg = (SettingsDialog)sender;

    reportColor = dlg.ReportColor;
    reportFolder = dlg.ReportFolder;
    reporter = dlg.Reporter;

    // Do something with the dialog properties
  }
}
```

In Example 10-23, when the user asks to see the settings dialog, it's initialized as before, but because it's shown modelessly, we need to know when the user clicks Apply (and the data has been validated), so we subscribe to the Apply event. When that's fired, we pull the SettingsDialog object back out of the sender argument to the Apply event and pull out our settings as before. The only other thing you might want to do is to set a flag that a settings dialog is being shown so that you don't show more than one of them.

Where Are We?

The base class for top-level window functionality is Window, providing the features and flexibility you need to fit in with the rest of the applications on your desktop. In addition, the Window class provides for dialog-style user interactions, both modal and modeless. Finally, the NavigationWindow class, which derives from the Window class, forms the core of most standalone navigation-based applications, which we'll cover in the next chapter.

CHAPTER 11

Navigation

One of the mantras of the WPF team was "best of Windows, best of the Web," which drove much of the innovation in the platform. In the preceding chapter, we looked at windows in a very Windows-centric way, but there's one innovation that the Web has made popular that we haven't discussed: navigation between content one page at a time.

NavigationWindow

The idea of navigation in WPF is that instead of showing multiple windows in a cascading style—a popular Windows application style used in the preceding chapter—we show pages of content inside a single frame, using standard navigation metaphors, like the Back and Forward buttons, to go between pages. If you want to build an application that does this, you can derive from the NavigationWindow class instead of the Window class and navigate to any WPF content you like (see Example 11-1).

Example 11-1. Navigation basics

```
<!-- Window1.xaml -->
<NavigationWindow ...
  x:Class="NavigationBasics.Window1"
  Title="NavigationBasics" />

    // Window1.xaml.cs
    ...
    using System.Windows.Navigation; // home of the NavigationWindow

    public partial class Window1 : NavigationWindow {
      public Window1() {
        InitializeComponent();

        // Navigate to some content
        Navigate("Hello, World.");
      }
    }
```

In Example 11-1, we've defined a custom `NavigationWindow` that sets its initial content to a string using the `Navigate` method, which works as you'd expect (Figure 11-1).

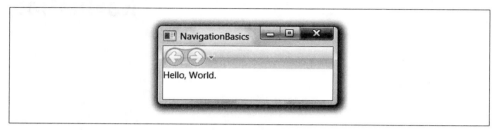

Figure 11-1. The simplest navigation application

Notice in Figure 11-1 the presence of the Back and Forward buttons, as well as the little triangle. These controls are provided and enabled/populated as appropriate based on the navigation history. In this case, we've navigated only once, so the navigation buttons are disabled (there's nowhere to go backward or forward to). The thing that navigates to our content, displays it, and shows the navigation controls is called a *navigation host*. The `NavigationWindow` is one of the three navigation hosts we'll discuss in this chapter.

Pages

If we want to get a little fancier than a string, we can create multiple "pages" of content, which is specifically what the `Page` class was invented for (see Example 11-2).

Example 11-2. Packaging content with a Page object

```xml
<!-- Page1.xaml -->
<Page ...
    x:Class="NavigationBasics.Page1"
    Title="Page 1"
    WindowTitle="Welcome to Page 1">
  <TextBlock VerticalAlignment="Bottom">
    <Hyperlink NavigateUri="Page2.xaml">Click to see page 2</Hyperlink>
  </TextBlock>
</Page>
```

```csharp
// Page1.xaml.cs
...
using System.Windows.Controls; // home of the Page

public partial class Page1 : Page {
  public Page1() {
    // Initialize page from XAML
    InitializeComponent();
  }
}
```

To get the basic skeleton of a new Page class, you can right-click on your project in the Visual Studio 2005 Solution Explorer, choosing Add → New Item, and select Page (WPF). Example 11-2 was started that way, adding the WindowTitle, the Title, and the content. The WindowTitle is what shows up in the caption of the navigation host. The Title property is what shows up in the history drop-down. If you don't set a page's Title property, it will be composed for you as *WindowTitle (foo.xaml)*, which isn't particularly friendly.

The content in Example 11-2 uses a Hyperlink, which is a nice little element that handles clicking for navigation applications.* We're setting the NavigateUri property to point to the page resource we'd like it to load for us. The NavigateUri supports the normal URI format (e.g., a URL to an HTTP file on the Web), as well as the pack URI format described in Chapter 12. Page two of our content is another custom Page class defined in XAML, as shown in Example 11-3.

Example 11-3. Using the navigation service

```
<!-- Page2.xaml -->
<Page ...
    x:Class="NavigationBasics.Page2"
    Title="Page 2"
    WindowTitle="Welcome to Page 2">
  <Button Name="backButton"
          VerticalAlignment="Center" HorizontalAlignment="Center">
    Click to go back to page 1
  </Button>
</Page>

    // Page2.xaml.cs
    ...
    public partial class Page2 : Page {
      public Page2() {
        InitializeComponent();

        // Handle the button Click event
        backButton.Click += backButton_Click;
      }

      void backButton_Click(object sender, RoutedEventArgs e) {
        // The Page class provides direct access to navigation services
        this.NavigationService.GoBack();
      }
    }
```

Example 11-3 looks pretty much like Example 11-2, except that in this case, we're assigning the hyperlink a name in the XAML so that we can handle the Click event and handle the "go back" navigation as though the user had clicked the Back button (which is enabled as soon as the user has navigated to another page).

---

* We describe the Hyperlink element and its role as part of the WPF text object model in Chapter 14.

To navigate programmatically, each navigation host provides a navigation service. The *navigation service* is responsible for fulfilling navigation requests, tracking history, providing events for handling navigation events (e.g., Navigating, Navigated, NavigationFailed, etc.), as well as methods of navigating history (e.g., GoBack, GoForward, Navigate, etc.).* To access the navigation service associated with a dependency object, you can use the static GetNavigationService method of the NavigationService class:

```
public Page2() {
  ...
  void backButton_Click(object sender, RoutedEventArgs e) {
    // get the page's navigation service
    NavigationService
      navService = NavigationService.GetNavigationService(this);
    navService.GoBack();
  }
}
```

As a shortcut, the Page class provides the NavigationService property. In addition, the Page class supports the set of navigation commands (as described in Chapter 4) on the NavigationCommands class (e.g., BrowseBack, BrowseForward, Refresh, etc.). You can use the commands to eliminate the need for any Click event handler code in our example Page 2, as shown in Example 11-4.

Example 11-4. Using navigation commands

```
<!-- Page2.xaml -->
<Page ...
    x:Class="NavigationBasics.Page2"
    Title="Page 2"
    WindowTitle="Welcome to Page 2">
  <Button Command="NavigationCommands.BrowseBack"
        VerticalAlignment="Center" HorizontalAlignment="Center">
    Click to go back to page 1
  </Button>
</Page>

    // Page2.xaml.cs
    ...
    public partial class Page2 : Page {
      public Page2() {
        InitializeComponent();
      }
    }
```

With our content hosted in pages, we can use the URI trick, shown in Example 11-5, to navigate to the first page from the navigation window.

---

* For a wonderful picture of the navigation events and when they happen, I recommend the SDK topic "Navigation Overview," available at *http://msdn2.microsoft.com/en-gb/library/ms750478.aspx#NavigationService* (*http://tinysells.com/92*).

Example 11-5. Navigating to the first page from the main window

```
// Window1.xaml.cs
...
public partial class Window1 : NavigationWindow {
  public Window1( ) {
    InitializeComponent( );

    // Show first page
    this.Navigate(new Uri("Page1.xaml", UriKind.Relative));
  }
}
```

In fact, the desire to define an entire application as a set of pages and to simply navigate to the first page without any muss or fuss is something that the Application object's StartupUri property supports directly, removing the need for a main window to host page content at all (see Example 11-6).

Example 11-6. Navigating to the first page using the StartupUri

```
<!-- App.xaml -->
<Application ... StartupUri="Page1.xaml">
  <!-- no need for a main window at all -->
</Application>
```

In the case of a standalone Windows application, the application will create a NavigationWindow for you and navigate to the page specified by the StartupUri property, as Figure 11-2 shows (after we've navigated to the second page).[*]

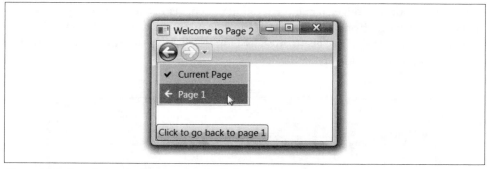

Figure 11-2. Populating the history with the Title property

Notice that setting the Title property on each Page has resulted in the name of the page instead of the WindowTitle property.

---

[*] In the case of an XBAP, the application will not create a NavigationWindow, as it doesn't have the permissions in partial trust to do so. Instead, it will create another navigation host that knows how to show your pages just like a page of HTML in Internet Explorer 6+, as you'll see later, in the "XBAPs" section.

Although setting the StartupUri property is a useful shortcut if your application's main window is going to be navigation-based, nothing is stopping you from using NavigationWindow-like dialogs to build wizards, even if your main window is not navigation-based. The WPF factoring of NavigationWindow allows it to be used like any other window.

Loose XAML

If you're willing to limit what you put in your XAML (e.g., removing all code-behind files, including the x:Class declaration), stick to only XAML filenames as navigation targets, and so on, you can double-click on XAML files in the shell and navigate between them. Example 11-7 is an updated *Page2.xaml* to start navigation directly from the shell.

Example 11-7. Limitations of loose XAML

```
<!-- Page2.xaml -->
<Page ...
    x:Class="NavigationBasics.Page2"
    Title="Page 2"
    WindowTitle="Welcome to Page 2">
  <TextBlock VerticalAlignment="Bottom">
    <Hyperlink NavigateUri="Page1.xaml">
      Click to go back to page 1</Hyperlink>
  </TextBlock>
</Page>
```

Notice that I am no longer using a Button here. This is because the navigation commands don't work from loose XAML and because I have no code-behind file in which to handle the Click event myself. Double-clicking on *Page1.xaml* and then clicking on the link yields Figure 11-3.

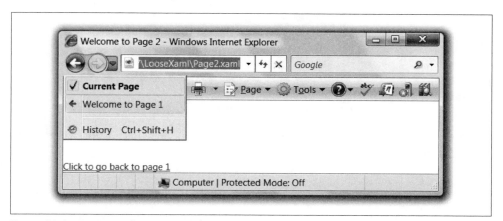

Figure 11-3. Navigating loose XAML pages in IE7

Due to these limitations, navigating between pages of loose XAML is largely a novelty. Instead, if you want to host your pages in the browser, you'll want to package them into an XBAP, discussed later in this chapter.

Fragment Navigation

If you're navigating to a page with a great deal of content (for example, a document such as one could construct using the techniques in Chapter 14), you might want to navigate not just to a page, but to a specific section of a page. You can do this with *fragment navigation*, which you can perform by composing the URI with a trailing fragment identifier, like so:

```
content.xaml#fragmentName
```

The fragment name maps to a named element on the target page. For instance, consider Example 11-8, which shows a piece of XAML that defines a longish chunk of text.

Example 11-8. A document with names suitable for fragment navigation

```
<Page x:Class="NavigationToFragments.Page2" ...>
  ...
  <ScrollViewer>
    <TextBlock TextWrapping="Wrap">
      <TextBlock Name="topic1">
        <TextBlock ...>Topic 1</TextBlock>
        <TextBlock>Lorem ipsum dolor sit amet, ...</TextBlock>
      </TextBlock>
      <TextBlock Name="topic2">...</TextBlock>
      ...
    </TextBlock>
  </ScrollViewer>
</Page.
```

Example 11-8 includes some named elements. We can refer to these names from a table of contents (see Example 11-9).

Example 11-9. A set of hyperlinks for fragment navigation

```
<Page x:Class="NavigationToFragments.Page1" ...>
  <TextBlock>
    <Hyperlink NavigateUri="Page2.xaml#topic1">Topic 1</Hyperlink>
    <Hyperlink NavigateUri="Page2.xaml#topic2">Topic 2</Hyperlink>
    ...
  </TextBlock>
</Page>
```

When navigation is performed against a fragment URI and the section is contained in a navigation target that supports scrolling, the section's content will be brought into view (or at least as much as will fit into the navigation host), as shown in Figure 11-4, after Topic 4 has been scrolled into view.

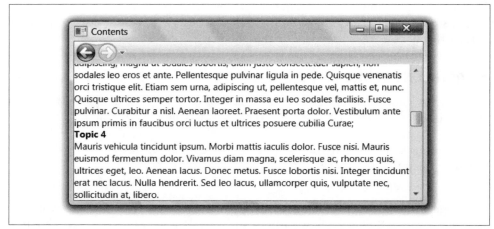

Figure 11-4. Fragment navigation

For those of you familiar with HTML name fragment navigation, note that the similarity of mechanism is not a coincidence. Because navigation in both WPF and HTML is based on URIs and the URI syntax supports fragments, we get the same syntax for both.[*]

Page Lifetime

As you begin to string several pages together, you may begin to wonder about the lifetime of a page. For example, consider a very simple guessing game that lets you guess a number, and if you don't get it in one guess, you lose. The idea is that you can have multiple guesses by backing up and trying again. The implementation of our first page isn't surprising, as you can see in Example 11-10.

Example 11-10. Exploring page state

```
<!-- Page1.xaml -->
<Page ...>
  <StackPanel Margin="10">
    <Label>Please guess a number between 0 and 2147483647:</Label>
    <TextBox Name="guessBox" />
    <TextBlock>
      (shh... the answer is <TextBlock Name="answerBox" />.)
    </TextBlock>
    <TextBlock HorizontalAlignment="Right">
      <Hyperlink NavigateUri="Page2.xaml">Guess</Hyperlink>
    </TextBlock>
  </StackPanel>
</Page>
// Page1.xaml.cs
```

---

[*] The URI syntax is defined by RFC 2396 and is available at *http://www.ietf.org/rfc/rfc2396.txt* (*http://tinysells.com/96*).

Example 11-10. Exploring page state (continued)

```
...
public partial class Page1 : Page {
  int answer = (new Random()).Next();

  public Page1() {
    InitializeComponent();
    answerBox.Text = answer.ToString();
  }
  ...
}
```

In the XAML, we're laying out the elements in a straightforward way, naming the guess and answer text boxes so that we can manipulate them. (Also, notice that we put the answer on the page so that we can see what's happening to the page's state as we navigate around.) In the code, when the page is created, we generate a random number, keep it in the page's state for subsequent guesses, and populate the text box. Figure 11-5 shows the results of showing the first page, navigating to the second page, and then navigating back.

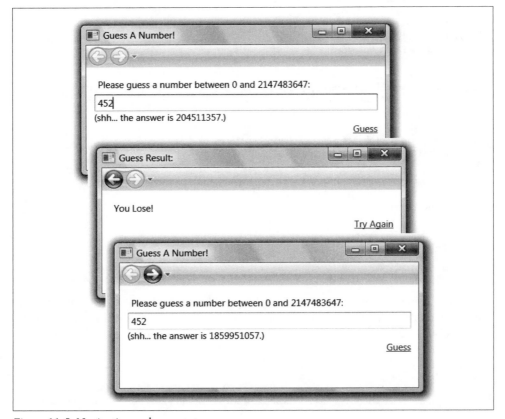

Figure 11-5. Navigating and page state

You'll notice that the answer the second time the first page is shown is different from the answer the first time. This is because, as a memory usage optimization, the navigation services of WPF do their best to keep the smallest amount of data associated with each page as they can get away with. In our case, because we're navigating between pages using a URI, the navigation services keeps the URI,[*] throwing away the page object itself (and all of the visuals associated with the page). What this means for us, of course, is that every time the user navigates to the first page, a new Page1 object is created, generating a new answer and making it even more difficult for the user to guess.

If you'd like to track the lifetime of a Page, you can do so with the Loaded and Unloaded events, shown in Example 11-11.

Example 11-11. Page lifetime

```
public partial class Page1 : Page {
  int answer = (new Random()).Next();

  public Page1() {
    Debug.WriteLine("Page1 constructed");
    InitializeComponent();
    answerBox.Text = answer.ToString();
    Loaded += Page1_Loaded;
    Unloaded += Page1_Unloaded;
  }

  void Page1_Loaded(object sender, RoutedEventArgs e) {
    Debug.WriteLine("Page1_Loaded");
  }

  void Page1_Unloaded(object sender, RoutedEventArgs e) {
    Debug.WriteLine("Page1_Unloaded");
  }
}
```

For example, the navigation sequence in Figure 11-5 looks like this:

```
Page1 constructed
Page1_Loaded
Page1_Unloaded
Page1 constructed
Page1_Loaded
```

One other thing that you'll notice about Figure 11-5 is that although the answer was regenerated along with the Page1 object, the answer text box state was properly restored the second time the first page is shown. This is because the WPF navigation

---

[*] The navigation service also keeps any data associated with navigation-aware controls using a mechanism we'll see in a moment.

services provide all kinds of different ways to keep state between page navigations while still maintaining the optimization of not actually keeping the page:[*]

- Adding to your page a custom dependency property marked with the FrameworkPropertyMetadataOptions.Journal flag. Several of the WPF controls, including TextBox, use this mechanism so that they can restore their state between navigations.

- Implementing the IProvideCustomContentState interface on your page, either with or without a corresponding CustomContentState object.

For large applications of navigation, you should absolutely take advantage of this navigation optimization (provided by default). Otherwise, the user could just keep navigating around in your application, adding pages to the history that he may never get back to, even though the visuals associated with those pages continue to take up memory.

However, for simpler applications, if you would like to turn off this optimization, you can with a flip of the KeepAlive switch (see Example 11-12).

Example 11-12. Setting KeepAlive to true

```
<!-- Page1.xaml -->
<Page ...
    KeepAlive="True"> <!-- keep the page between navigations -->
    ...
</Page>
```

The KeepAlive flag defaults to false, which means that the navigation history will attempt to destroy the page object (and all of the associated visuals) if it can, providing the hooks I listed to keep track of state between navigations. However, in certain cases, the navigation optimization can't be applied. For example, if we call the Navigate method with an object instead of a URI, the navigation service doesn't know how to re-create the object, so it caches it instead, which has the same effect as setting KeepAlive to true manually, as we did in Example 11-12.

Keeping data between navigations to a single page is only part of the story. If you're going to implement the second page that checks the answer, we'll need to pass it and the user's current guess from the first page.

Passing Data Between Pages

It's easy enough to define our Page2 class with a couple of properties to accept incoming data, as shown in Example 11-13.

---

[*] The various techniques for keeping state between page navigations are discussed in detail in the SDK topic "Navigation Overview," available at *http://msdn2.microsoft.com/en-gb/library/ms750478.aspx#NavigationService* (*http://tinysells.com/92*).

KeepAlive = False + Data Binding Considered Harmful

If you're planning to use data binding in your pages, you should set KeepAlive to True. Unfortunately, out of the box, the navigation optimization doesn't work with data binding and will not restore data binding options properly on instantiations. Because data binding is so darn useful (not only is it the foundation of keeping data in sync between your data objects and your UI, but it's also how the validation and data templates features are exposed, among others), it's likely you'll feel the tension between them, picking one or the other on any single page, but not both.

The good news is that, as of this writing, this is a high-priority issue scheduled to be fixed in the next version of the .NET Framework (code name "Orcas") as well as the next service pack for .NET 3.0.

Example 11-13. Accepting data into a page via properties

```xml
<!-- Page2.xaml -->
<Page ...> <!-- KeepAlive not set -->
  <StackPanel Margin="10">
    <TextBlock>
      You guessed: <TextBlock Name="guessBlock" />
    </TextBlock>
    <TextBlock FontSize="32" FontWeight="Bold" Name="resultBlock" />
    <TextBlock HorizontalAlignment="Right" VerticalAlignment="Bottom">
      <Hyperlink Name="tryAgainLink">Try Again</Hyperlink>
    </TextBlock>
  </StackPanel>
</Page>
```

```csharp
// Page2.xaml.cs
...
public partial class Page2 : Page {
  public Page2( ) {
    InitializeComponent( );
    Loaded += Page2_Loaded;
    backButton.Click += backButton_Click;
    playAgainLink.Click += playAgainLink_Click;
  }

  int answer;
  public int Answer {
    get { return answer; }
    set { answer = value; }
}

  int guess;
  public int Guess {
    get { return guess; }
    set { guess = value; }
  }
```

Example 11-13. Accepting data into a page via properties (continued)

```
void Page2_Loaded(object sender, RoutedEventArgs e) {
  guessBlock.Text = guess.ToString( );

  if( answer == guess ) { resultBlock.Text = "You win!"; }
  else if( answer < guess ) { resultBlock.Text = "Guess lower..."; }
  else { resultBlock.Text = "Guess higher..."; }
}

void backButton_Click(object sender, RoutedEventArgs e) {
  // Let them guess again
  NavigationService.GoBack( );
}

void playAgainLink_Click(object sender, RoutedEventArgs e) {
  // Start a new game
  NavigationService.Navigate(new Uri("Page1.xaml", UriKind.Relative));
}
}
```

In Example 11-13, we're defining two properties to be passed in from the first page—the answer we're looking for and the current guess.[*] When the page is loaded, we use those values to populate the UI.

You'll also notice that we're not setting KeepAlive to anything in *Page2.xaml*. By default, it's False, but that setting will be ignored because we're navigating to the page as an object and not as a URI (see Example 11-14).

Example 11-14. Passing data to a page

```
// Page1.xaml.cs
...
public partial class Page1 : Page {
  ...
  void guessLink_Click(object sender, RoutedEventArgs e) {
    Page2 page2 = new Page2( );
    page2.Answer = answer;
    page2.Guess = int.Parse(guessBox.Text);
    NavigationService.Navigate(page2);
  }
}
```

Figure 11-6 shows the state of an incorrect guess, and Figure 11-7 shows the history after a couple of successes.

The technique of passing in parameters directly to a new page object works fine, especially when you've got several instances of the same object to keep track of.

---

[*] Giving the Page2 class a constructor that takes arguments instead of passing them in via properties would work as well.

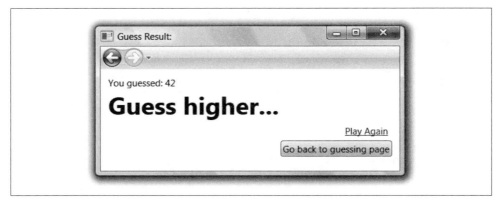

Figure 11-6. Guessing incorrectly

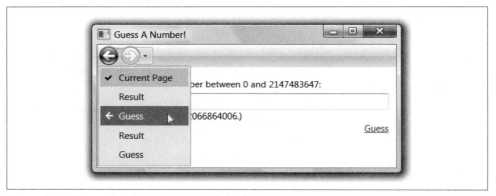

Figure 11-7. The results of guessing correctly in the history

However, sometimes you'd like to keep more "global" state (i.e., state that spans even multiple instances of a particular page type). For example, it would be inconvenient to have to pass the count of games played through every single page, not least because we'd have to stop navigating to the first page by URI, instead passing in a parameter. For these situations, WPF has provided the Properties dictionary on the Application, shown in Example 11-15.

Example 11-15. Keeping track of wins in the application's Properties collection

```
// Page2.xaml.cs
...
public partial class Page2 : Page {
  ...
  void Page2_Loaded(object sender, RoutedEventArgs e) {
    guessBlock.Text = guess.ToString();
```

Example 11-15. Keeping track of wins in the application's Properties collection (continued)

```
      if( answer == guess ) { resultBlock.Text = "You win!"; TrackWin( ); }
      else ...
  }

  // NOTE: uniqueness testing to make sure that every won game
  // is only tracked once is left as an exercise to the reader
  // (Send answers to csells@sellsbrothers.com...)
  void TrackWin( ) {
    IDictionary properties = Application.Current.Properties;
    if( !properties.Contains("GamesWon") ) { properties["GamesWon"] = 0; }
    properties["GamesWon"] = (int)properties["GamesWon"] + 1;
  }
}
```

In Example 11-15, we're tracking the number of games won by using a key of GamesWon and incrementing it on every win. The Properties dictionary is an object-to-object mapping, so you can keep whatever you want in there. By using a string, and a short one at that, we're risking the possibility of stepping on someone else's data, which is the problem with global data in general.

Page Functions

In the world of standard Windows applications, if you want to ask the user a quick question without disturbing the rest of your careful arrangement of visuals and windows, you simply pop up a modal dialog and ask 'im. However, in the world of navigation-based applications, external windows of any kind are considered rude at the very least (remember the pop-ad craze of the early 2000s?) and verboten in the worst case (XBAPs don't allow pop-up windows). So, the question is, how do we ask the user a quick question, returning him to whence he came, none the worse for wear? The answer is page functions.

A *page function* is a page that you call like a function, passing in input and getting output as desired. When the page function returns, the return value is provided to the calling page, where it can pick up where it left off. You can think of page functions as the modal dialog equivalent in navigation-based applications.

As a simple example, let's imagine that we wanted the user to say the magic word before she is allowed to play the guessing game. The UI for our page function looks like Figure 11-8.

Our page function to ask the user for the magic word looks like a page, but with a few minor differences, as shown in Example 11-16.

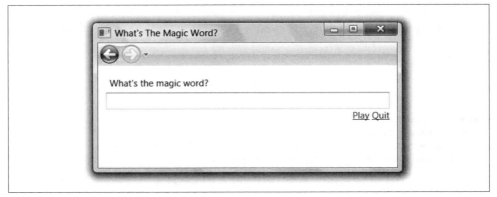

Figure 11-8. A page function UI

Example 11-16. Declaring a page function

```
<!-- MagicWordPageFunction.xaml -->
<PageFunction ... x:TypeArguments="sys:String">
  <StackPanel Margin="10">
    <Label>What's the magic word?</Label>
    <TextBox Name="wordBox" />
    <TextBlock HorizontalAlignment="Right">
      <Hyperlink Name="playLink">Play</Hyperlink>
      <Hyperlink Name="quitLink">Quit</Hyperlink>
    </TextBlock>
  </StackPanel>
</PageFunction>
```

The skeleton for Example 11-16 was generated in Visual Studio 2005 by right-clicking on the project, choosing Add → New Item, selecting PageFunction (WPF), entering a name, and clicking the OK button. Notice that Example 11-16 has a PageFunction element at the root to match the PageFunction<T> base class name. However, because the PageFunction<T> class is generic, we set the x:TypeArguments property to the type argument to use to construct the generic PageFunction<T> type.[*] The type passed will be the type of the result from our page "function call." The code needs to have a matching type argument, as shown in Example 11-17.

Example 11-17. Implementing a page function

```
// MagicWordPageFunction.xaml.cs
...
public partial class MagicWordPageFunction : PageFunction<string> {
  public MagicWordPageFunction() {
    InitializeComponent();
    playLink.Click += playLink_Click;
```

---

[*] The x:TypeArguments property is XAML's nod to generics and works only on elements at the root of a XAML document.

Example 11-17. Implementing a page function (continued)

```
    quitLink.Click += quitLink_Click;
    Loaded += MagicWordPageFunction_Loaded;
  }

  string magicWord;
  public string MagicWord {
    get { return magicWord; }
    set { magicWord = value; }
  }

  void playLink_Click(object sender, RoutedEventArgs e) {
    // Check to see if the magic word is the right one
    if( wordBox.Text == magicWord ) {
      OnReturn(new ReturnEventArgs<string>(wordBox.Text));
      Application.Current.Properties["MagicWordEntered"] = wordBox.Text;
    }
  }

  void quitLink_Click(object sender, RoutedEventArgs e) {
    OnReturn(null); // Cancel
  }

  void MagicWordPageFunction_Loaded(object sender, RoutedEventArgs e) {
    if( Application.Current.Properties.Contains("MagicWordEntered") &&
        (string)Application.Current.Properties["MagicWordEntered"] == magicWord ) {
      // No need to re-enter the magic word for subsequent games
      OnReturn(new ReturnEventArgs<string>(magicWord));
    }
  }
}
```

In addition to taking in the magic word to check for as a property (just like our page example earlier), we're checking the word the user enters when she clicks on the Play link. If the word is sufficiently magic, we return from the page function by calling the OnReturn method provided by the PageFunction<T> base class, passing the word the user entered so that the caller of the page function can inspect it. This is the page function equivalent of setting a modal dialog's DialogResult to true, and will trigger the page function to remove itself from the history and return to the caller.[*] In addition, we're storing the magic word the user entered into the application's Properties function so that she won't have to enter it again (as you'll see).

On the other hand, if the user clicked the Quit link, we call OnReturn, passing null to indicate the equivalent of the user clicking the Cancel button on a modal dialog, also returning to the caller.

---

[*] It often makes the most sense for a page function's page to be removed from the navigation history when it returns, just like a modal dialog removes itself from the screen. However, if you'd prefer to leave it in, you can set the page function's RemoveFromJournal property to false (it defaults to true).

Finally, so that the user doesn't have to enter the magic word more than once—no matter how many times the page function is navigated to in the application's lifetime—in the page function's Loaded event, we check for the presence of the magic word in the application's Properties collection, calling OnReturn right away if the user has already entered it.

Page Functions and KeepAlive

If you look at Example 11-16, you'll notice that we're not setting the KeepAlive property at all. Just like a Page, a PageFunction class will default the KeepAlive property to false. Further, even though we navigate to a page function by object instead of by URI, the WPF navigation service uses magic to figure out how to tear it down and rebuild it between navigations. This means that you'll have to keep in mind all of the KeepAlive issues mentioned earlier, but because page functions are meant to be short-lived, there is less chance of a memory usage problem if you want to set KeepAlive to true. (All of the page function's visuals will be torn down by default when you call OnReturn.)

Calling the page function from a "zeroth" page I'll show you presently looks like Example 11-18.

Example 11-18. Using a page function

```
// Page0.xaml.cs
...
public partial class Page0 : Page {
  ...
  void playLink_Click(object sender, RoutedEventArgs e) {
    MagicWordPageFunction fn = new MagicWordPageFunction();
    fn.MagicWord = "please";
    fn.Return += fn_Return;
    NavigationService.Navigate(fn);
  }

  void fn_Return(object sender, ReturnEventArgs<string> e) {
    // Get the navigation service from the sender
    // (the current page's hasn't yet been restored and
    // this.NavigationService is null
    NavigationService
      navService = ((PageFunctionBase)sender).NavigationService;

    // User canceled
    if( e == null ) {
      navService.Navigate(new Uri("QuitterPage.xaml", UriKind.Relative));
    }
    // Double-check the magic word
    else if( e.Result == "please" ) {
      navService.Navigate(new Uri("Page1.xaml", UriKind.Relative));
```

Example 11-18. Using a page function (continued)

```
        }
    }
}
```

At the click of a hyperlink, we create an instance of the page function, passing in the preferred magic word,* subscribing to the `Return` event (for the page equivalents of both "OK" and "Cancel"), and navigating to the page function just as though it were a normal page (and in fact, `Page` is in the inheritance hierarchy of the `PageFunction<T>` class).

In the `Return` event handler, the first thing we do is grab the current navigation service from the sender. Unfortunately, at this point in the action, the `NavigationService` property of the page function caller hasn't yet been set, so we have to rely on the one from the page function itself (the sender). Next, we check to see whether the `ReturnEventArgs<T>` (where `T` is `String` in our case) event argument is null. If it is, the page function called `OnReturn` passes null, and we should respond appropriately. On the other hand, if the return event argument isn't null, we can check the `Result` property for the data passed to `OnReturn`. In our example, we double-check that it was indeed the magic word we were looking for and navigate to the first page of our guessing game.

Figure 11-9 shows a nominal navigation session.

Clicking the Play link on the Welcome page causes the magic word page function to show and take its answer. When that returns, the Welcome page navigates to the first page of our guessing game. Notice that the history in Figure 11-9 doesn't show the magic word page function at all. Further, because the magic word page function keeps track of whether the magic word was already entered and short-circuits itself as appropriate, if we were to go back to the Welcome page and click the Play link again, the magic word UI would never show, the `Return` event handler would be fired immediately, and the user would go directly to the guessing page.

Frames

Thus far, we've spent a lot of time talking about the `NavigationWindow`, how it handles navigation, and how it integrates with pages and page functions. However, the navigation window is but one navigation host. A *navigation host* in WPF is anything that provides navigation support. Besides the navigation window, which provides top-level window navigation support, WPF also provides the `Frame`, for contained navigation support. For example, nothing is stopping us from hosting our guessing game in a frame, which is itself contained by something else, as shown in Example 11-19.

---

* You were perhaps expecting "abracadabra"?

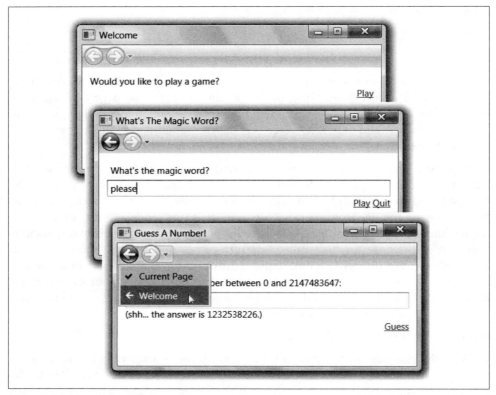

Figure 11-9. A page function in action

Example 11-19. Using a frame navigation host

```
<!-- Window1.xaml -->
<Window ...>
  <Border BorderBrush="Green" BorderThickness="10">
    <Frame Source="Page1.xaml" />
  </Border>
</Window>
```

In Example 11-19, we're hosting a Frame in a window, but you can host it equally well in a page. The main property you'll care about on the Frame class is the Source, which indicates where you'd like to start navigation. Figure 11-10 shows the results of making one guess on the history for the frame.

Frames are useful when you'd like to add navigation to part of your window (or to multiple parts), but you don't want the entire window dedicated to it. For example, your average web site is composed of a set of content that goes inside a navigation frame, including menus, graphics, and so on. The Frame element is one way to implement the content inside the outer navigation frame.

Figure 11-10. Using a frame navigation host

XBAPs

The final navigation host that WPF provides is an internal class called `RootBrowserWindow`. Like `NavigationWindow` and `Frame`, the `RootBrowserWindow` knows how to host content for navigation. However, `RootBrowserWindow` does it by integrating with versions 6 and later of Internet Explorer[*] in order to implement XAML Browser Applications (XBAPs). An *XBAP* is a WPF application with these characteristics:

- Hosted in IE6+ like loose XAML pages (although they're compiled), whether at the top level or inside an IFRAME. In fact, you're meant to be able to click back and forth between HTML and XBAPs without knowing that you're doing so (except that the XBAP pages are "better").

- No custom top-level windows. You must use the `RootBrowserWindow` provided and no other custom top-level windows (e.g., custom dialogs).

- Runs in partial trust that can't be elevated by users like normal ClickOnce applications.

- Can be deployed like ClickOnce "online-only" applications. The standard Click-Once "offline/online" deployment is available if your main window is a `NavigationWindow`, but it won't be hosted in Internet Explorer.

You can get a new XBAP application skeleton in Visual Studio 2005 by choosing the "XAML Browser Application (WPF)" project template. It will give you a standard navigation application without any window definition, just a page. The chief difference between an XBAP and a standard navigation-based application is the `HostInBrowser` property set in the project file:

```
<Project ...>
  <PropertyGroup>
    <HostInBrowser>true</HostInBrowser>
```

---

[*] Only IE7+ has an integrated navigation UI.

```
   ...
</PropertyGroup>
   ...
</Project>
```

In addition, an XBAP's ClickOnce manifests must be signed to build, which will be set up for you when you use Visual Studio 2005's project template. In fact, for the purposes of testing and debugging, you can execute an XBAP directly from Visual Studio 2005 (using Debug → Start Debugging or Debug → Start Without Debugging) to see it running inside the browser without first publishing, as shown in Figure 11-11.

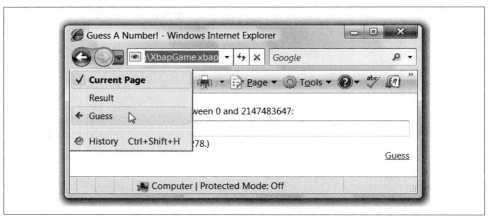

Figure 11-11. Hosting an XBAP in IE7

Notice that after a guess, the IE7 history looks pretty much like we'd expect from both the navigation window and the frame.

XBAP Publication and Deployment

The publication of an XBAP happens exactly like the publication of a WPF application via ClickOnce, as discussed in the Chapter 2. (I'll wait here while you refresh your memory.) Right-clicking on your XBAP project and choosing Publish brings up the Publish Wizard, which leads you through the publication process. Unlike the Publish Wizard for standalone ClickOnce applications, this time you won't get a *publish.htm*, but here's a template to get you started:

```
<html>
<head><title>Welcome to XBAP Fun!</title></head>
<body>
  <a href="http://localhost/XbapGame/XbapGame.xbap">XBAP Fun!</a>
</body>
</html>
```

Notice that the link to your XBAP ends in *.xbap*, unlike a standalone ClickOnce application, which ends in *.application*. Further, if you surf to this *publish.htm* file and click on the link, you'll get the download progress as you expect, but then nothing else (no security dialog) before the application shows itself. In fact, XBAPs are true "one-click" deployment, regardless of whether you've run the application before.* In addition, because we're surfing to it via URLs, the histories of both XBAP and HTML are merged, as shown in Figure 11-12.

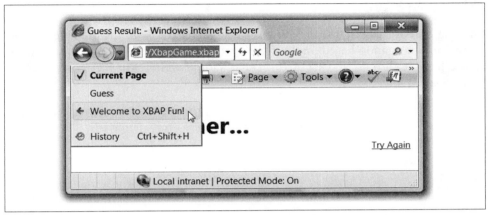

Figure 11-12. Mixing XAML and HTML in a single navigation history

XBAPs are your "best of the Web, best of Windows" WPF deployment mode of choice (assuming you can live with the limitations laid out earlier).

KeepAlive and XBAPs

Although the rules about KeepAlive and XBAPs still apply, there is one more wrinkle. If you navigate away from an XBAP and navigate back, the pages will have been flushed regardless of your KeepAlive settings.

Navigation to HTML

To further drive home the integration between WPF navigation and Internet Explorer, if you navigate to an HTML URL inside of a navigation host, the core OLE control that hosts HTML in IE will be used to show the content. For example:

```
<TextBlock>
  <Hyperlink
    NavigateUri="http://sellsbrothers.com">sellsbrothers.com</Hyperlink>
</TextBlock>
```

---

* Of course, that "one click" works only if your XBAP doesn't try to get more permissions than it's been awarded, in which case you can click all day long and it still ain't gonna run.

If you do this from within a standalone application using the navigation window or frame hosts, the HTML page will become part of the history along with everything else. If you do this within an XBAP, however, a new instance of IE will be spun up to handle the navigation (it's just too weird to host IE inside an XBAP hosted inside IE).

Where Are We?

Building on base Window functionality, the NavigationWindow forms the core of most standalone navigation-based applications, with Frame for navigating content while controlling the chrome, and RootBrowserWindow for providing XBAP Internet Explorer 6+ navigation integration.

CHAPTER 12

Resources

WPF offers us great flexibility in how we construct an application's user interface. But with great power comes great responsibility—we must avoid bewildering the user with a garish and inconsistent frontend. Styles and templates allow us to take control of our application's visuals, but these features depend on the resource system in WPF to make it easy to build visually consistent applications without sacrificing flexibility. If you want to build a graphically distinctive application, the resource system provides a straightforward way to *skin* your applications with customized yet consistent visuals. But by default, the resource mechanism simply ensures consistency with the system-wide OS theme chosen by the user.

In this chapter, we will look at how the resource system lets us plug in visual features where they are needed. Not only will we see how to ensure that the right look and feel is applied to our application at runtime, but we will also look at how the resource system lets you reuse objects or groups of objects such as drawings. Furthermore, we will look at how to manage binary resource streams and how to localize applications.

Creating and Using Resources

The term *resource* has a very broad meaning—in WPF, any object can be a resource. A brush or a color used in various parts of a user interface could be a resource. Snippets of graphics or text can be resources. An object does not have to do anything special to qualify as a resource. The resource handling infrastructure is entirely dedicated to making it possible to get hold of the resource you require, and it doesn't care what the resource is. It simply provides a mechanism for identifying and locating objects.

At the heart of resource management is the ResourceDictionary class. Outwardly, this is just a simple collection class. It behaves much like an ordinary Hashtable—it allows objects to be associated with keys, and it provides an indexer that lets you retrieve those objects using these keys. So, in theory, you could use the ResourceDictionary like a Hashtable, as Example 12-1 shows.

Example 12-1. Naïve ResourceDictionary programming

```
ResourceDictionary myDictionary = new ResourceDictionary();
myDictionary.Add("myBrush", Brushes.Green);
myDictionary.Add("HW", "Hello, world");

Console.WriteLine(myDictionary["myBrush"]);
Console.WriteLine(myDictionary["HW"]);
```

In practice, you will not often create your own `ResourceDictionary` in this way. Instead, you will normally use ones provided by WPF. For example, the `FrameworkElement` base class, from which most user interface elements derive, provides a resource dictionary in its Resources property. The calls to `Add` in Example 12-1 illustrate the usual way to add resources from code-behind files, but this dictionary can also be populated from markup, as Example 12-2 shows.

Example 12-2. Populating a ResourceDictionary from XAML

```
<Window x:Class="ResourcesExample.Window1" Title="Resources"
  xmlns="http://schemas.microsoft.com/winfx/2006/xaml/presentation"
  xmlns:x="http://schemas.microsoft.com/winfx/2006/xaml"
  xmlns:s="clr-namespace:System;assembly=mscorlib">

  <Window.Resources>
    <SolidColorBrush x:Key="myBrush" Color="Green" />
    <s:String x:Key="HW">Hello, world</s:String>
  </Window.Resources>

  <Grid x:Name="myGrid">
  </Grid>
</Window>
```

The `x:Key` attribute specifies the key that identifies the resource in the dictionary. It is equivalent to the first parameter of the calls to `Add` in Example 12-1. You can use any object as a key. Strings are the most common choice, although distinct object instances are often used to identify very broadly scoped resources, such as system resource.

 When you use compiled XAML to populate a resource dictionary, WPF defers creation of the resources. It leaves each resource in its serialized form (known as BAML), and expands this into real objects only on demand. This can significantly improve the startup time for a user interface in cases where not all of the objects are needed as soon as the UI appears. For the most part, this optimization will not have any direct effect on your code's behavior other than speeding it up. However, if there is something wrong with your markup, this deferred creation can cause the resulting errors to emerge later than you might have expected.

Example 12-3 shows code retrieving the resources defined in Example 12-2.

Example 12-3. Retrieving resources from an element's ResourceDictionary the wrong way

```
// NOT the best way to retrieve resources
Brush b = (Brush) this.Resources["myBrush"];
String s = (String) this.Resources["HW"];
```

This code accesses the ResourceDictionary using this.Resources. This is all very well for the code-behind file for the markup that defined the resources. However, it is not always this convenient to get hold of the right dictionary. What if we want to define resources accessible to all windows in the application? It would be both tedious and inefficient to copy the same resources into every window in the application. And what if we want a custom control to pick up resources specified by its parent window, rather than baking them into the control? To solve these problems, and to make it easy to achieve consistency across your user interface, FrameworkElement extends the basic ResourceDictionary facilities with a hierarchical resource scope.

Resource Scope

As well as providing a ResourceDictionary for every element, FrameworkElement also provides a FindResource method to retrieve resources. Example 12-4 shows the use of this to retrieve the same resources as Example 12-3.

Example 12-4. Using FindResource

```
Brush b = (Brush) this.FindResource("myBrush");
String s = (String) this.FindResource("HW");
```

This may seem pointless—why does this FindResource method exist when we could just use the dictionary's indexer as we did in Example 12-3? The reason is that FindResource doesn't give up if the resource is not in the specified element's resource dictionary. It will search elsewhere. Example 12-5 illustrates the difference between these two approaches.

Example 12-5. FrameworkElement.Resources versus FindResource

```
// Returns null
Brush b1 = (Brush) myGrid.Resources["myBrush"];

// Returns SolidColorBrush from Window.Resources
Brush b2 = (Brush) myGrid.FindResource("myBrush");
```

This code uses the myGrid element from Example 12-2 instead of this. The Grid doesn't have any resources, so the b1 variable will be set to null. However, because b2 is set using FindResources instead of the resource dictionary indexer, WPF considers all of the resources in scope, not just those directly set on the Grid. It starts at the Grid element, but then examines the parent, the parent's parent, and so on, all the way to the root element. (In this case, the parent happens to be the root element, so this is a short search. But in general, it searches as many elements as it needs to.) The result is that the b2 variable is set to the same Brush object as was retrieved in Examples 12-3 and 12-4.

It doesn't stop here. If FindResource gets all the way to the root of the UI without finding the specified resource, it will then look in the application. Not only do all framework elements have a Resources property, so does the Application object. Example 12-6 shows how to define application-scope resources in markup. (If you are using the normal Visual Studio WPF project template, you would put this in the *App.xaml* file.)

Example 12-6. Resources at application scope

```
<!-- App.xaml -->
<Application x:Class="MyResourcesExample.App"
  xmlns="http://schemas.microsoft.com/winfx/2006/xaml/presentation"
  xmlns:x="http://schemas.microsoft.com/winfx/2006/xaml"
  StartupUri="Window1.xaml"
  >
  <Application.Resources>
    <LinearGradientBrush x:Key="myBrush" StartPoint="0,0" EndPoint="1,1">
      <LinearGradientBrush.GradientStops>
        <GradientStop Offset="0" Color="Red"/>
        <GradientStop Offset="1" Color="Black"/>
      </LinearGradientBrush.GradientStops>
    </LinearGradientBrush>
  </Application.Resources>
</Application>
```

The application scope is helpful for objects that are used throughout your application. For example, if you use styles or control templates, you would typically put these in the application resources, to ensure that you get a consistent look across all the windows in your application.

Resource searching doesn't even stop at the application level. If a resource is not present in the UI tree or the application, FindResource will finally consult the system scope, which contains resources that represent system-wide settings, such as the configured color for selected items, the correct width for a scroll bar, and styles for built-in controls. The control styles WPF adds to the system scope will be based on the user's chosen "theme" (or "visual style").

Figure 12-1 shows a typical hierarchy of resource sources. Several applications are running, each application may have several windows, and each window has a tree consisting of multiple elements. If FindResource is called on the element labeled "1" in the figure, it will first look in that element's resource dictionary. If that fails, it will keep working its way up the hierarchy through the numbered items in order, until it reaches the system resources.

WPF uses the system scope to define brushes, fonts, and metrics that the user can configure at a system-wide level. The keys for these are provided as static properties of the SystemColors, SystemFonts, and SystemParameters classes, respectively. (These classes define more than 400 resources, so they are not listed here—consult the SDK documentation for each class to see the complete set.) Example 12-7 uses the system scope to retrieve a brush for the currently configured tool tip background color. (See Chapter 13 for more information on brushes.)

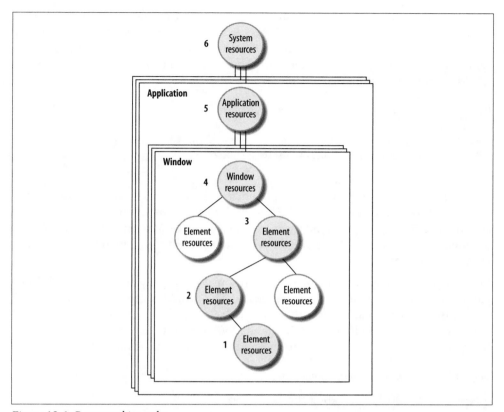

Figure 12-1. Resource hierarchy

Example 12-7. Retrieving a system scope resource

```
Brush toolTipBackground = (Brush) myGrid.FindResource(SystemColors.InfoBrushKey);
```

 These system resource classes use objects rather than strings as resource keys. This avoids the risk of naming collisions—system resources are always identified by a specific object, so there will never be any ambiguity between them and your own named resources.

Defining custom system-scope resources

All the built-in controls rely on the system scope to provide styles and templates suitable for the current OS theme. Without these resources, the controls would have no appearance by default. If you are writing a custom control, you will usually want to do the same thing. By providing a style for your control, you ensure that it has a default appearance. By putting that style into the system scope, you give developers the opportunity to customize the control by putting an alternative style in a narrower scope such as the application scope.

To add custom resources to the system scope, you must annotate your component with the ThemeInfo custom attribute. This indicates two things: whether your component has non-theme-specific system-scope resources, and whether it has theme-specific system-scope resources. As Example 12-8 shows, this is an assembly-level attribute. It would typically go in the *AssemblyInfo.cs* source file.

Example 12-8. Declaring custom system-scope resources

```
[assembly:ThemeInfo(
  ResourceDictionaryLocation.None,            // Theme-specific resources
  ResourceDictionaryLocation.SourceAssembly   // Generic resources
)]
```

This example declares that the component has generic resources, but no theme-specific resources. This instructs WPF to look in the component for an embedded ResourceDictionary called *themes\generic.xaml*, and to add any resources in that dictionary to the system scope. (We will show how to embed resource streams later in this chapter.)

You can also specify that theme-specific resources are present by setting the first parameter of the attribute to SourceAssembly. This would cause WPF to look for an embedded resource named after the currently selected theme. Table 12-1 shows the names of the embedded resources WPF will look for. If it cannot find a resource for the current theme, it will fall back to the generic resources instead.

Table 12-1. Themes and resource names

Theme	Embedded resource name
Aero (Windows Vista)	*themes\Aero.NormalColor.xaml*
Luna Blue (Windows XP)	*themes\Luna.NormalColor.xaml*
Luna Silver (Windows XP)	*themes\Luna.Metallic.xaml*
Luna Olive Green (Windows XP)	*themes\Luna.Homestead.xaml*
Royale (Windows Media Center)	*themes\Royale.NormalColor.xaml*
Classic (Any Windows version)	*themes\Classic.xaml*

The ResourceDictionaryLocation enumeration has one more value besides the two shown in Example 12-8: ExternalAssembly. This will cause WPF to look in a separate assembly for the resources. It will look for an assembly with a name formed by adding a period and then the current theme name to your assembly's name (which means you can specify this only for the theme-specific resources). It uses only the base theme name, without the color scheme appended. For example, if your component is called MyLibrary, and the user is running with the Windows Vista Aero theme, WPF will look for a MyLibrary.Aero component containing the *themes\Aero.NormalColor.xaml* resources.

For WPF to be able to find a custom system-scope resource, you must use a suitable key type: the key must incorporate information about which assembly contains the resource. For a custom control's style, you will normally use the control's Type object as a key. You typically do this by specifying a TargetType, as in Example 12-9. This automatically uses that type as the key, as well as the style's target type.

Example 12-9. Style using a Type object as key

```
<Style TargetType="{x:Type local:MyCustomControl}">
   ...
</Style>
```

When looking up a resource by type, WPF will locate the assembly referred to by the Type object's Assembly property. If the assembly has a ThemeInfo attribute indicating that system-scope resources are present, WPF will look for an embedded resource dictionary. In short, you simply add the ThemeInfo attribute, and put the resource streams in the same component as the custom control, and it all just works.

Sometimes it's useful to put resources other than styles into the system scope. You can do this, but you can't use a string to name the resource—a simple string won't tell WPF in which assembly it should be looking. WPF therefore provides the ComponentResourceKey type. This is a class designed to be used as a resource name. It incorporates both an identifier (which may be a string) and a Type object to indicate which assembly defines the type. WPF also defines a corresponding markup extension, offering a syntax for using these keys from XAML, which is shown in Example 12-10.

Example 12-10. Naming custom system-scope resources

```
<SolidColorBrush x:Key="{ComponentResourceKey {x:Type local:MyCustomType},
                         myBrush}" />
```

With a resource defined this way in your *themes\generic.xaml*, or in one of the theme-specific dictionaries, you can refer to the resource using the same syntax that Example 12-10 uses to name it. Because the ComponentResourceKey incorporates a type object, WPF will know which assembly defines the resource, and will be able to find it.

Using system-scope resources

The system resource classes also define static properties that let you retrieve the relevant object directly rather than having to go via the resource system. For example, SystemColors defines an InfoBrush property that returns the same value that FindResource returns when passed SystemColors.InfoBrushKey. So rather than writing the code in Example 12-7, we could have written the code in Example 12-11.

Example 12-11. Retrieving a system resource through its corresponding property

```
Brush toolTipBackground = SystemColors.InfoBrush;
```

When writing code, these properties are likely to be simpler to use than the resource system. However, using the resource key properties offers three advantages. First, if you want to let the user change your application's color scheme away from the system-wide default, you can override these system settings by putting resources into the application scope. Example 12-12 shows an application resource section that defines a new application-wide value for the InfoBrushKey resource.

Example 12-12. Application overriding system colors

```
// (Hypothetical function for retrieving settings)
Color col = GetColorFromUserSettings( );

Application.Current.Resources[SystemColors.InfoBrushKey] =
    new SolidColorBrush(Colors.Red);
```

This replacement value would be returned in Example 12-7, but not in Example 12-11. This is because in Example 12-11, SystemColors has no way of knowing what scope you would like to use, so it always goes straight to the system scope.

The second advantage offered by resource keys is that they provide a straightforward way of using system-defined resources from markup. Third, you can make your application respond automatically to changes in system resources. Both of these last two benefits come from using resource references.

Resource References

So far, we have seen how to retrieve the current value of a named resource in code. Because we usually use resource values to set element properties, we will now look at how to set an element's property to the value of a resource. This may seem like a ridiculously trivial step. You might expect it look like Example 12-13.

Example 12-13. How not to use a system resource value

```
this.Background = (Brush) this.FindResource(SystemColors.ControlBrushKey);
```

This is fine for some resource types, but here it will work only up to a point—it will successfully set the Background property to a brush that paints with whatever the currently selected color for control backgrounds is at the moment when this line of code runs. However, if the user changes the system color scheme, this Background property will not be updated automatically. The code in Example 12-13 effectively takes a snapshot of the resource value.

The code in Example 12-14 does not suffer from this problem. Instead of taking a snapshot, it associates the Background property with the resource.

Example 12-14. Self-updating system resource reference

```
this.SetResourceReference(Window.BackgroundProperty, SystemColors.ControlBrushKey);
```

Unlike Example 12-13, if the system resource value changes, the property will automatically receive the new value. The practical upshot of this is that if the user changes the color scheme using the Display Properties Control Panel applet, Example 12-14 will ensure that your user interface is updated automatically.

WPF defines markup extensions that are the XAML equivalent of the code in the previous two examples. (See Appendix A for more information on markup extensions.) These are the StaticResource and DynamicResource extensions. If you are using a system resource, or any other resource that might change at runtime, choose DynamicResource. If you know the resource will never change, use StaticResource, which takes a snapshot, avoiding the costs associated with tracking the resource for changes. (The cost is small, but you may as well avoid it for resources that never change.) Example 12-15 shows the use of both resource reference types.

Example 12-15. Using resources from markup

```
<Window x:Class="ResourcesExample.Window2" Title="Resources"
  xmlns="http://schemas.microsoft.com/winfx/2006/xaml/presentation"
  xmlns:x="http://schemas.microsoft.com/winfx/2006/xaml">

  <Window.Resources>
    <SolidColorBrush x:Key="myBrush" Color="LightGreen" />
  </Window.Resources>

  <Grid Background="{DynamicResource {x:Static SystemColors.ControlBrushKey}}">
    <TextBlock FontSize="36" Width="200" Height="200"
               Background="{StaticResource myBrush}">Hello!</TextBlock>
  </Grid>
</Window>
```

> A StaticResource reference must appear after the resource to which it refers. Forward references are not allowed.

The top-level Window defines a brush as a resource named myBrush. The TextBlock uses this for its Background property via a StaticResource reference. This has a similar effect to the code in Example 12-13. It takes a snapshot, and is appropriate for resources that will not change while the application runs.

The grid's Background has been set to the system "control" color. (This is typically battleship gray—the color often used as the background for dialogs.) Because this is a user-configurable color and could therefore change at runtime, we've used a DynamicResource, which has the same effect as the call to SetResourceReference in Example 12-14.

The DynamicSource syntax is a little more complex than for the StaticResource. This complexity is not because we are using DynamicResource. It is because the resource we wish to use is identified by an object, returned by the static SystemColors.ControlBrushKey property. We could have tried this:

```
<!-- This will not work as intended -->
<Grid Background="{DynamicResource SystemColors.ControlBrushKey}">
```

This is syntactically correct, but doesn't do what we want. It will be interpreted as a dynamic reference to a resource named by the *string* SystemColors.ControlBrushKey. There is no such resource, so the background will not be set. To use the real resource key (the object returned by the ControlBrushKey static property), we have to use the x:Static markup extension as Example 12-15 does—this tells the XAML compiler that the text should be treated as the name of a static property, not as a string.

Reusing Drawings

It is often useful to put drawings and shapes into resources. There are two main reasons for doing this. One is that drawings can be quite complex, and putting them inline as part of the main markup for a user interface can make the XAML hard to read. By putting drawings into the resources section, or even a separate file, the overall UI structure can be clearer. Another reason is to enable reuse; you may want to use the same graphic in multiple places. Performance can also be a factor—reusing drawing resources is much more efficient than duplicating them.

You can represent shapes and drawings in many different ways, as Chapter 13 shows, and all of them can be used as resources. Example 12-16 defines an Ellipse resource called "shape." It also shows how to use the resource.

Example 12-16. Using a FrameworkElement resource

```
<Window.Resources>
  <Ellipse x:Key="shape" Fill="Blue" Width="100" Height="80" />
</Window.Resources>

...

<StackPanel>
  <Button>Foo</Button>
  <StaticResource ResourceKey="shape" />
  <Button>Bar</Button>
</StackPanel>
```

The StaticResource element here will be replaced at runtime with the resource it names. The result will look like Figure 12-2.

There is a problem with this technique: if you use any element that derives from FrameworkElement as a resource, by default you can reference it only once. The reason for this restriction is that FrameworkElement is the basis of the user interface tree.

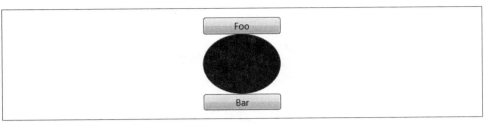

Figure 12-2. Reference to element resource

An element knows what its parent is and what children it has, so it is not possible for it to be in more than one place in the tree—its Parent property can point to only one element, after all. So if you were to add a second reference to the ellipse in Example 12-16, WPF would throw an exception complaining that the ellipse is already in use. However, there is a simple solution to this. By default, when you use a resource, you are not using a copy of the object, you are using the object itself, but you can change this behavior with the x:Shared attribute. Example 12-17 shows a modified version of Example 12-16. By enabling sharing of the ellipse resource, we can use the resource as many times as we like.

Example 12-17. Disabling sharing

```
<Window.Resources>
  <Ellipse x:Key="shape" Fill="Blue" Width="100" Height="80"
           x:Shared="False" />
</Window.Resources>

...

<StackPanel>
  <Button>Foo</Button>
  <StaticResource ResourceKey="shape" />
  <StaticResource ResourceKey="shape" />
  <Button>Bar</Button>
</StackPanel>
```

WPF will now build a new copy of the resource each time you use it.* As Figure 12-3 shows, this enables us to use the ellipse multiple times over. This is effective, but it is not the most efficient approach available, because it builds a new copy of the resource for each reference. For simple graphics this will not be a problem. However, if you are working with complex drawings containing many hundreds or even thousands of elements, the overhead of copying for each use can introduce performance problems.

---

* Copies are built using the deferred resource-loading mechanism described earlier—WPF goes back to the BAML each time it makes a new copy. Consequently, you can use this technique only in compiled XAML. It will not work in XamlPad because that parses the XAML at runtime.

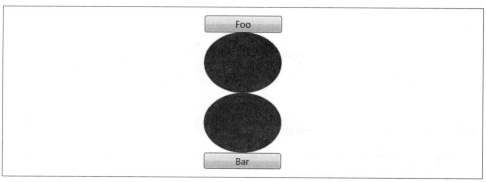

Figure 12-3. Multiple references to a single element resource

The Drawing classes, such as GeometryDrawing or DrawingGroup, are better candidates for storing drawings as resources. Because Drawing does not derive from FrameworkElement, you are free to use one instance in multiple places. DrawingGroup lets you put as many shapes and images into a single drawing as you like, and the various other types derived from Drawing provide access to all of WPF's graphics facilities. (See Chapter 13 for more details.)

Example 12-18 shows how to define and use a drawing resource. It uses a DrawingBrush to display the Drawing. Figure 12-4 shows the result.

Example 12-18. Using a Drawing resource

```
<Window.Resources>
  <GeometryDrawing x:Key="drawing" Brush="Green">
    <GeometryDrawing.Geometry>
      <EllipseGeometry RadiusX="200" RadiusY="10" />
    </GeometryDrawing.Geometry>
  </GeometryDrawing>
</Window.Resources>

...

<StackPanel Orientation="Vertical">
  <Rectangle Width="250" Height="50">
    <Rectangle.Fill>
      <DrawingBrush Drawing="{StaticResource drawing}" />
    </Rectangle.Fill>
  </Rectangle>
  <Rectangle Width="250" Height="50">
    <Rectangle.Fill>
      <DrawingBrush Drawing="{StaticResource drawing}" />
    </Rectangle.Fill>
  </Rectangle>
</StackPanel>
```

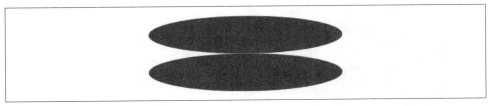

Figure 12-4. References to Drawing resource

You can also define the DrawingBrush as a resource. This moves some of the complexity into the Resources section, making the markup considerably simpler at the point at which you use the resource, as Example 12-19 shows. The results are the same as the preceding example, as shown in Figure 12-4, but the markup that uses the resource is just one line long instead of five.

Example 12-19. Using a DrawingBrush resource

```
<Window.Resources>
  <GeometryDrawing x:Key="drawing" Brush="Green">
    <GeometryDrawing.Geometry>
      <EllipseGeometry RadiusX="200" RadiusY="10" />
    </GeometryDrawing.Geometry>
  </GeometryDrawing>
  <DrawingBrush x:Key="dbrush" Drawing="{StaticResource drawing}" />
</Window.Resources>

...

<StackPanel Orientation="Vertical">
  <Rectangle Width="250" Height="50" Fill="{StaticResource dbrush}" />
  <Rectangle Width="250" Height="50" Fill="{StaticResource dbrush}" />
</StackPanel>
```

If you want the same shape to appear in multiple drawings, you might want to drop down a level and use individual geometry objects as resources. You can then refer to these from within drawings. Example 12-20 shows the use of a DrawingBrush with a GeometryDrawing that uses an EllipseGeometry resource. (Because this is yet another ellipse, we won't waste your time with another picture—it'll look much like Figure 12-4, only in cyan.)

Example 12-20. Using a Geometry resource

```
<Window.Resources>
  <EllipseGeometry x:Key="geom" RadiusX="200" RadiusY="30" />
</Window.Resources>

...
```

Example 12-20. Using a Geometry resource (continued)

```
<Rectangle Width="250" Height="50">
  <Rectangle.Fill>
    <DrawingBrush>
      <DrawingBrush.Drawing>
        <GeometryDrawing Brush="Cyan" Geometry="{StaticResource geom}" />
      </DrawingBrush.Drawing>
    </DrawingBrush>
  </Rectangle.Fill>
</Rectangle>
```

In this particular example, the use of resources may seem a little extreme—it would probably have required less effort just to create a new geometry from scratch. However, some geometries, such as PathGeometry, can become quite complex, in which case this kind of reuse makes more sense.

Although drawings and geometries are powerful, reusable, and lightweight, they have one disadvantage. They are not framework elements, so they cannot take advantage of WPF's layout system. You can scale them using the brush scaling features described in Chapter 13, but drawings cannot contain framework elements, so you cannot make them adapt their layout intelligently using the panels described in Chapter 3. If you need these framework-level features, use framework elements as Example 12-17 showed. But if you don't need to use FrameworkElement-based types in your drawing (maybe because you don't need the shapes laid out by a panel), the more lightweight DrawingBrush class is more efficient. And, if you are creating lots of drawings, all containing similar shapes, you can even go as far as sharing individual geometry objects as resources. Chapter 13 describes all of these drawing mechanisms in more detail.

Resources and Styles

WPF's styling mechanism depends on the resource system to locate styles. As you already saw in Chapter 8, styles are defined in the Resources section of an element and can be referred to by name, as Example 12-21 shows.

Example 12-21. Referencing a Style resource

```
<Window x:Class="ResourcesExample.Window1" Title="Resources"
  xmlns="http://schemas.microsoft.com/winfx/2006/xaml/presentation"
  xmlns:x="http://schemas.microsoft.com/winfx/2006/xaml">

  <Window.Resources>
    <Style x:Key="myStyle">
      <Setter Property="Button.FontSize" Value="36" />
    </Style>
  </Window.Resources>
```

Example 12-21. Referencing a Style resource (continued)

```
<Grid>
  <Button Style="{StaticResource myStyle}">Hello</Button>
</Grid>
</Window>
```

Further, it is also possible to define a style that is applied automatically to an element without the need for the explicit resource reference. This is useful if you want the style to be applied to all elements of a particular type without having to add resource references to every element. Example 12-22 shows a version of Example 12-21 modified to take advantage of this.

Example 12-22. Implicit use of a Style

```
<Window x:Class="ResourcesExample.StyleExplicitReference" Title="Resources"
  xmlns="http://schemas.microsoft.com/winfx/2006/xaml/presentation"
  xmlns:x="http://schemas.microsoft.com/winfx/2006/xaml">

  <Window.Resources>
    <Style TargetType="{x:Type Button}">
      <Setter Property="Button.FontSize" Value="36" />
    </Style>
  </Window.Resources>

  <Grid>
    <Button>Hello</Button>
  </Grid>
</Window>
```

Notice that the Button no longer has its Style property specified. However, the style will still be applied to the button because of its TargetType. If you were to add more buttons to the window, they would all pick up this style. Instead of defining a key, the style now has a TargetType set with the x:Type markup extension, which instructs XAML to provide the named class's System.Type object.

If a FrameworkElement does not have an explicitly specified Style, it will always look for a Style resource, using its own type as the key.

> When you create a Style with a TargetType and do not specify the x:Key, the x:Key is implicitly set to be the same as the TargetType. This key is used to locate the style. Data templates use a similar mechanism. In general, you should avoid setting the x:Key to a Type object unless the resource is a Style or DataTemplate that you want to be applied automatically.

Because elements look for their styles in resources, you can take advantage of the resource scoping system. You can define a style resource at a local scope if you wish to affect just a small number of elements, or at a broader scope such as in

`Window.Resources`, or at the application scope. If your application doesn't define a style for a particular element, its styles will be retrieved from the system scope. This relationship between styling and resources is the key to both theming and skinning.

Skins and Themes

Skinning and theming are both techniques for controlling the look and feel of a UI. A theme* is a system-wide look, such as the Classic Windows 2000 look, the Luna theme in Windows XP, and the Aero theme in Windows Vista. A skin is a look specific to a particular application, such as the distinctive styles available with media programs like WinAmp and Windows Media Player.

In WPF, skins and themes are both defined as sets of resources that apply the required styles to controls. By setting each resource key to the `Type` for the control to which the style applies, styles will apply themselves consistently and automatically. These styles will usually set the `Template` property in order to define the appearance of the control, and may also set other properties such as those for font handling. (Templates were discussed in Chapter 9.) The main difference between a skin and a theme is one of scope—a skin would typically be stored in the application's `Resources` property, whereas a theme lives at the system scope, and is not directly associated with any one application.

 There is currently no documented way of defining a new theme. All you can do is add features to the built-in themes. As we saw in the "Resource Scope" section, earlier in this chapter, you can provide sets of theme-specific resources that will be added to the system scope.

Because a skin's purpose is to control the appearance of a particular application, it may well provide more than just styles for standard controls. It might define various other named resources for use in specific parts of the application. For example, a music player application might present a `ListBox` whose purpose is to present a list of songs. A skin might well want to provide a particular look for this list without necessarily affecting all listboxes in the application. So the application would probably set that `ListBox` to use a specific named style, enabling the skin to define a style just for that `ListBox`.

A skin doesn't necessarily have to provide a comprehensive set of styles. If the application doesn't use every single WPF control type, the skin needs to supply styles only for the controls the application uses. Example 12-23 shows the XAML for an extremely simple skin.

---

* Strictly speaking, the proper name is *Visual Style*. According to official terminology, a *theme* can include other features, such as system sounds and mouse cursors, as well as the visual style. However, this distinction is rarely observed in practice, so we'll stick with the shorter name.

Example 12-23. BlueSkin.xaml—a very simple skin

```xml
<!-- BlueSkin.xaml -->
<ResourceDictionary
  xmlns="http://schemas.microsoft.com/winfx/2006/xaml/presentation"
  xmlns:x="http://schemas.microsoft.com/winfx/2006/xaml">

  <Style TargetType="{x:Type Button}">
    <Setter Property="Background" Value="Blue" />
    <Setter Property="Foreground" Value="White" />
  </Style>

  <SolidColorBrush x:Key="appBackground" Color="#EEF" />
</ResourceDictionary>
```

This sets the foreground and background for a Button. It also defines a brush—skins often define graphical resources such as brushes or drawings, as it sometimes takes more than just customizing controls to achieve a harmonious look for your application. A more complex skin would target more element types and set more properties. Most skins include some Template property setters in order to customize the appearance of controls. But even in this simple example, the underlying principles remain the same. Example 12-24 shows a UI, and Example 12-25 shows the corresponding code-behind file that allows skins to be switched. (This example assumes that two skins, BlueSkin and GreenSkin, have been defined* using the technique shown in Example 12-23.)

Example 12-24. Window1.xaml—switching skins

```xml
<Window x:Class="SimpleSkin.Window1" Title="SimpleSkin"
  xmlns="http://schemas.microsoft.com/winfx/2006/xaml/presentation"
  xmlns:x="http://schemas.microsoft.com/winfx/2006/xaml"
  Background="{DynamicResource appBackground}">

  <Grid Margin="1">
    <Grid.RowDefinitions>
      <RowDefinition Height="Auto" />
      <RowDefinition Height="Auto" />
      <RowDefinition Height="Auto" />
    </Grid.RowDefinitions>

    <RadioButton x:Name="chooseGreenSkin" Grid.Row="0" Content="Green" />
    <RadioButton x:Name="chooseBlueSkin" Grid.Row="1" Content="Blue" />

    <Button Grid.Row="2">Hello</Button>
  </Grid>
</Window>
```

---

* I haven't shown the *GreenSkin.xaml* file, as it's identical to *BlueSkin.xaml*, except the word *Green* replaces the word *Blue*.

Example 12-25. Window1.xaml.cs—code-behind file for switching skins

```csharp
using System;
using System.Collections.ObjectModel;
using System.Diagnostics;
using System.Windows;
using System.Windows.Controls;

namespace SimpleSkin {

    public partial class Window1 : Window {

        public Window1() {
            InitializeComponent();

            EnsureSkins();

            chooseGreenSkin.Click += SkinChanged;
            chooseBlueSkin.Click += SkinChanged;
        }

        static ResourceDictionary greenSkin;
        static ResourceDictionary blueSkin;

        void EnsureSkins() {
            // This method is called each time a new Window1 is constructed,
            // so make sure we only load the resources the first time
            if (greenSkin !- null) {
                greenSkin = new ResourceDictionary();
                greenSkin.Source = new Uri("GreenSkin.xaml", UriKind.Relative);
                blueSkin = new ResourceDictionary();
                blueSkin.Source = new Uri("BlueSkin.xaml", UriKind.Relative);
            }
        }

        void SkinChanged(object o, EventArgs e) {
            if (chooseGreenSkin.IsChecked.Value) {
                ApplySkin(greenSkin);
            } else {
                ApplySkin(blueSkin);
            }
        }

        void ApplySkin(ResourceDictionary newSkin) {
            Collection<ResourceDictionary> appMergedDictionaries =
                Application.Current.Resources.MergedDictionaries;

            // Remove the old skins (MergedDictionary.Clear won't do the trick)
            if (appMergedDictionaries.Count != 0) {
                appMergedDictionaries.Remove(appMergedDictionaries [0]);
            }
```

```
        // Add the new skin
        appMergedDictionaries.Add(newSkin);
    }
  }
}
```

This class contains some code to ensure that the skins get created just once. The code that changes skins over simply ensures that the application resource dictionary's `MergedDictionaries` collection contains the `ResourceDictionary` for the selected skin. The styling and resource systems react automatically to the change in resources, updating all of the affected controls and all `DynamicResource` references when you switch skins, so this is all the code that is required. Figure 12-5 shows the code in action.

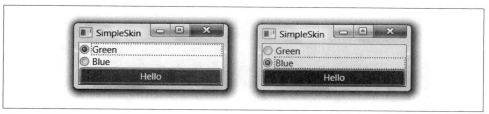

Figure 12-5. Changing skins (Color Plate 21)

Binary Resources

Although `ResourceDictionary` and the resource scope system are fine for data that can easily be contained in an object, not all resources fit comfortably into this model. Often we need to deal with binary streams. For example, images, audio, and video have efficient binary representations, but they are not particularly at home in markup, and in the world of objects they are usually represented by wrappers for the underlying data. Markup itself also presents a challenge: XAML pages must somehow get built into our applications. So a means of dealing with binary streams is needed.

WPF does not introduce any new technology for dealing with binary data. The .NET Framework has always provided mechanisms for dealing with embedded binary streams, and WPF simply uses these.

The lowest level of stream support lets you embed resource streams into any assembly. This is a simple matter of supplying the files you would like to embed to the compiler. In Visual Studio, you do this by setting a file's Build Action property to Embedded Resource. This copies the contents of the file into the assembly as an embedded stream. The stream can be retrieved at runtime using the `Assembly` class's `GetManifestResourceStream` method, as Example 12-26 shows.

Example 12-26. Retrieving assembly manifest resources

```
Assembly asm = Assembly.GetExecutingAssembly( );
Stream s = asm.GetManifestResourceStream("StreamName");
```

Streams embedded in this way are called *assembly manifest resources*. Although WPF ultimately depends on this embedded resource mechanism, it uses it indirectly through the ResourceManager class in the System.Resources namespace. The resource manager builds on the embedded resource system, adding two features: localization, and the ability to store multiple named streams in a single low-level stream. The ResourceManager API allows you to ask for resources by name, and it will attempt to locate the most appropriate resource based on the UI culture. The "Global Applications" section, later in this chapter, describes this in more detail.

By convention, a WPF application or component puts all of its resources into a single assembly manifest resource stream called *Appname*.g.resources, where *Appname* is the name of the component or executable without the file extension. We can learn how WPF uses this resource stream by examining it using a ResourceManager. (In a real application, you use a WPF-supplied wrapper for the ResourceManager that we'll look at shortly. We're just using ResourceManager to look under the hood.) Example 12-27 shows how to retrieve a list of resource names.

Example 12-27. Listing binary resources

```
static List<string> GetResourceNames(Assembly asm,
                        System.Globalization.CultureInfo culture) {

    string resourceName = asm.GetName( ).Name + ".g";
    ResourceManager rm = new ResourceManager(resourceName, asm);
    ResourceSet resourceSet = rm.GetResourceSet(culture, true, true);
    List<string> resources = new List<string>( );
    foreach (DictionaryEntry resource in resourceSet) {
        resources.Add((string) resource.Key);
    }
    rm.ReleaseAllResources( );
    return resources;
}
```

Let's use this to look at the resources found inside a typical application. Figure 12-6 shows the Visual Studio Solution Explorer view for a simple WPF project. It contains the usual *App.xaml* file defining the application, and a single *Window1.xaml* file defining the user interface. This application also has an *Images* directory, which contains two bitmap files. As you can see from the Properties panel in the bottom half of Figure 12-6, the Build Action of *Sunset.jpg* has been set to Resource.[*]

---

[*] This has a different effect than the Embedded Resource action we saw earlier. Embedded Resource embeds the file in its own distinct assembly manifest resource. Resource embeds the file inside the *Appname*.g.resources assembly manifest resource that is shared by all the files with a build action of Resource.

When you add a bitmap file to a project using Add → New Item or Add → Existing Item from the context menu in the Solution Explorer, its Build Action will be set to Resource automatically, because this is the simplest way to work with binary resources in WPF. *Wheel.jpg* has the same setting.

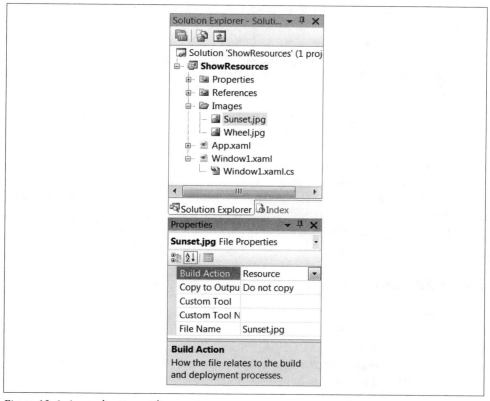

Figure 12-6. An application with resources

If we were to call the GetResourceNames function in Example 12-27, and print out each string it returns, we would see the following output:

```
window1.baml
images/wheel.jpg
images/sunset.jpg
```

As you can see, both of the bitmaps are present. You can use these embedded bitmaps from any element with a property of type ImageSource, as Example 12-28 shows.

Example 12-28. Using a bitmap resource

```
<Image Source="images/wheel.jpg" />
```

Using a relative URL such as this one indicates that the resource is local—relative URLs can be used either when the bitmap file is in the same directory, or when it is compiled in as a resource. Because the bitmap data is embedded inside the resource stream in the application binary, there is no need to ship a separate file containing bitmap data.

The resource list also shows a `window1.baml` resource. This corresponds to the `Window1.xaml` file.

 BAML is a binary representation of a XAML file—XAML is compiled into BAML during the compilation process. BAML is significantly more compact than XAML, so your executables are much smaller than they would be if XAML were built in.

In a WPF project, any file with a Build Action of Page is assumed to be XAML. It will be compiled into a BAML resource.

Although it's easy to load a resource with the `Image` element's `Source` property, or any property of type `ImageSource`, what if we want to use a resource from code? We shouldn't use the `ResourceManager` directly in a real application, because we would be depending on an implementation detail of WPF's resource handling. Instead, we should use the wrapper functionality provided by the `Application` class, because it's significantly simpler, as well as being the official documented mechanism.

Binary Resources and the Application Class

The `Application` class provides four helper functions for retrieving resources: `GetResourceStream`, `GetContentStream`, `GetRemoteResource`, and `LoadComponent`.

`GetResourceStream` is the proper way to retrieve resources compiled into the executable. This wraps the `ResourceManager` behavior described earlier. You simply need to pass in the URI of the resource, as shown in Example 12-29.

Example 12-29. Using GetResourceStream

```
Uri resourcePath = new Uri("Images/Sunset.jpg", UriKind.Relative);
StreamResourceInfo ri = Application.GetResourceStream(resourcePath);
Stream data = ri.Stream;
```

The method returns a `StreamResourceInfo`. This has two properties: `Stream` contains the resource stream, and `ContentType` is a string containing the MIME type of the stream.

`GetContentStream` is almost identical to `GetResourceStream`, as Example 12-30 shows. The only difference is that it retrieves streams stored in files in the same directory on disk as the executable.

Example 12-30. Using GetContentStream

```
Uri resourcePath = new Uri("Images/Sunset.jpg", UriKind.Relative);
StreamResourceInfo ri = Application.GetContentStream(resourcePath);
Stream data = ri.Stream;
```

GetContentStream won't open just any old stream that happens to be on the disk. The application is required to declare upfront which streams it expects to find. For each content stream you want to load, your executable must contain an assembly-level AssemblyAssociatedContentFile custom attribute specifying the filename. If you set a file's Build Action to Content, Visual Studio adds this attribute automatically when it builds the file.

GetRemoteResource looks just like the previous two methods. Again, the only difference is where it expects the resource to be. This method is intended for applications deployed to a web server (e.g., an XBAP; XBAPs are described in Chapter 11). The method can download files stored on the same web server from which the application itself came. You would use this method if your application has large resource files that would take a long time to download, not all of which are necessarily needed upfront. By separating the resources out into separate downloads, you can improve the initial startup time of your application.

The LoadComponent method is the odd one out here—this does more than simply retrieve a stream. It expects the stream to contain BAML—compiled XAML. It will parse the stream, and generate the tree of objects described by the XAML. The return value is the root of this tree. Example 12-31 uses this to load a resource dictionary.

Example 12-31. Application.LoadComponent

```
Uri resourcePath = new Uri("MyResources.xaml");
ResourceDictionary rd = (ResourceDictionary)
    Application.LoadComponent(resourcePath);
```

The LoadComponent method is aware of code behind. If the XAML you load has a corresponding code-behind class, it will create an instance of that. Otherwise, the object returned will be of the type specified by the root element of the XAML file.

LoadComponent has an overload that takes two parameters: an object and a URI. This loads and parses the XAML as before, but does not create the root object for you. Instead, you create the root object and pass this in to LoadComponent, which will then load all of the remaining content into the root you supply. This is how XAML normally gets loaded. The generated partial class that Visual Studio creates for a XAML file with code behind uses LoadComponent to populate your object with the objects described by the XAML, as this excerpt in Example 12-32 shows.

Example 12-32. Use of LoadComponent in generated code

```
System.Uri resourceLocater =
    new System.Uri("/BinaryResources;component/window1.xaml",
                   System.UriKind.Relative);
System.Windows.Application.LoadComponent(this, resourceLocater);
```

As we saw earlier, XAML gets compiled into binary files with a *.baml* extension. It's therefore slightly surprising to see a *.xaml* extension in these last two examples.

We use a *.xaml* extension because BAML is essentially an implementation detail. We always refer to resources by their original names, and we don't need to concern ourselves with the exact runtime representation. This is a good reason to use the methods provided by the `Application` class instead of going straight to `ResourceManager`.

The URI in Example 12-32 is a little more complex than the ones in the previous examples. WPF accepts several different forms of URI for resources. They are all variations around the pack URI scheme.

Pack URIs

Microsoft has defined a new URI scheme—the pack scheme. URIs that use this scheme are called *pack URIs*. This URI scheme is part of the Open Packaging Conventions, which are the basis of the Office 2007 file formats, and also the XPS file format. (The XPS file format is described in Chapter 15.) This URI scheme defines a convention for referring to resources embedded in files. We can use pack URIs to refer to resources in WPF. This is supported by the various resource methods defined by the `Application` class, and also within XAML files. For example, the `Image` element's `Source` property is set as a pack URI.

The most straightforward form of pack URI is a relative pack URI—all the examples we've looked at so far have been of this form. With a relative pack URI, we can specify just the name of the embedded resource. Example 12-31 used this form.

Example 12-32 illustrates a slightly more complex form of relative pack URI. It incorporates the name of the component that contains the resource. This makes it possible to refer to other components that are loaded by the application—you simply start the URI with */ComponentName*;component. The URI in Example 12-32 explicitly refers to a resource defined by a component named `BinaryResources`. Example 12-33 uses this same technique to refer to a system component (your code should appear on one line; here it's been split across two lines due to space constraints).

Example 12-33. Relative pack URI referring to external component

```
<StackPanel>
  <StackPanel.Resources>
    <ResourceDictionary
Source="/PresentationFramework.Luna;v3.0.0.0;31bf3856ad364e35;component/themes/
luna.normalcolor.xaml" />
  </StackPanel.Resources>

  <Button Content="Luna" />
  <CheckBox Content="Theme" />
</StackPanel>
```

This example grabs the resource dictionary containing the theme resources for the default Windows XP Luna color scheme. The controls inside this `StackPanel` will all have the Luna look regardless of which theme the user has selected.

Example 12-33 will work only in compiled XAML. If you are using runtime XAML parsing, such as XamlPad performs, you will need to use an absolute pack URI. The absolute form of a pack URI must begin with the text "pack://application:,,,/" in order to refer to a resource embedded in an assembly or a component used by the application. This verbose and slightly peculiar syntax is used because pack URIs support several different source types, not just embedded resources. The full capabilities of pack URIs are beyond the scope of this book.*

One of the main benefits WPF derives from using the ResourceManager mechanism to manage bitmaps, BAML files, and any other embedded binary resources is that it provides a way of making your application localizable. So, we will now look at how to take advantage of this.

Global Applications

If you plan to distribute your applications worldwide, you may need to prepare different versions of the user interface for different regions. At a minimum, this would involve translating text into the appropriate language. It may also involve other UI changes. You might need to adapt certain visuals to local cultural conventions. Or you might find that the original layout doesn't quite work after translation, because the words are of different lengths. (Although WPF's layout system makes it easy to build flexible layouts that can help to avoid that last problem.)

An extreme solution would be to build different versions of your software for different markets. However, a more common approach is to build a single version that can adapt to different locales, usually by selecting suitable resource files at runtime. The ResourceManager infrastructure that WPF uses makes this fairly straightforward.

 Microsoft draws a distinction between localization and globalization. *Localization* is the process of enabling an application to be used in a particular locale, by creating culture-specific resources such as translated text. *Globalization* is the process of ensuring that an application can be localized without needing to be recompiled. Using ResourceManager helps to globalize your application, because its runtime resource selection enables a single build of the application to be localized by supplying suitable resources. For more information on recommended globalization and localization practices in Windows, see Microsoft's internationalization site: *http://msdn2.microsoft.com/library/1021kkz0.aspx (http://tinysells.com/107).*

When a ResourceManager is asked to retrieve a named resource stream, the first thing it does is determine which culture it should use. A *culture* is the combination of a language and location, and it is typically represented as a short string.

---

* For full details on this URI scheme see *http://msdn2.microsoft.com/en-gb/library/aa970069.aspx*, or *http://tinysells.com/67*.

For example, en-US means the English language, as spoken in the United States. The en-GB culture represents English as spoken in Great Britain. The first two letters indicate the language and the last two, the region. Both language and location are specified because there are often variations in dialect and idiom where two cultures ostensibly share a language. For example, one of the authors of this book hails from en-GB, and therefore prefers *color* to be spelled *colour*.

The ResourceManager.GetStream method takes a CultureInfo object as a parameter. If you wish to use the end user's configured culture, you can simply pass null—this causes the ResourceManager to use the CultureInfo from the CurrentUICulture property of Thread.CurrentThread.

Although executables usually have resources compiled in, the ResourceManager will look for culture-specific resources before resorting to the built-in ones. It will look in the directory containing the application for a subdirectory named for the culture. So if you are running in a French Canadian culture it will look for an *fr-CA* subdirectory containing a file called *MyApp.resources.dll*, where *MyApp* is the name of your application or component. If that doesn't exist, it will then look for the same file in a directory called *fr*. This means that if your translation budget doesn't stretch to producing different versions for all of the various French-speaking regions of the world, you can instead provide a single set of French resources that will be used in any French-speaking region. If neither of these subdirectories exists, it will resort to using the built-in resources.

The resource DLLs that the ResourceManager looks for are called *satellite resource assemblies*, so called because they are small assemblies associated with a larger assembly nearby.

Note that if you supply a satellite assembly, you are not required to provide localized versions of all of the resources. It might be that some of the resources you embed in your main assembly work just fine for all cultures. For example, the application shown in Figure 12-6 had an embedded bitmap called *Sunset.jpg*. The sun sets in most parts of the world, so although you might need to do something special for Arctic and Antarctic editions, the basic *Sunset.jpg* probably works for most cultures. It would be a bit of a waste of space for every satellite resource assembly to contain a copy of the same image. Fortunately, they don't have to—if a particular named resource is not present in a satellite resource assembly, the ResourceManager will fall back to the built-in resources.

You can think of satellite resource assemblies as containing just the differences between the built-in resources and those required for the target culture. Any common resources will live in the main assembly alone. An assembly in a language-specific but location-generic subdirectory (e.g., in the *fr* subdirectory) contains resources that need to be different for the specified language. And then the fully culture-specific subdirectories (e.g., *fr-CA*, *fr-FR*, *fr-BE*, etc.) contain only those resources that need to be adjusted to take into account local idioms. (In this context, a *resource* is a single stream as retrieved by the ResourceManager, rather than an object retrieved from a ResourceDictionary.)

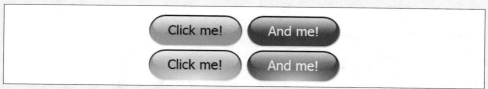

Color Plate 1 (Figures 1-18, 16-2). Buttons with animated glow

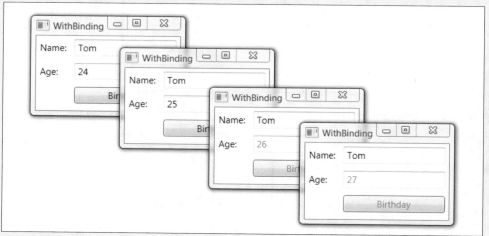

Color Plate 2 (Figures 1-21, 17-31). A 3D plot of data

Color Plate 3 (Figure 6-10). A value converter in action

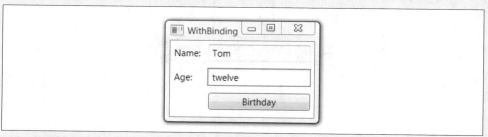

Color Plate 4 (Figure 6-12). A TextBox control highlighted as invalid

Color Plate 5 (Figure 7-3). Navigating between items in a list data source

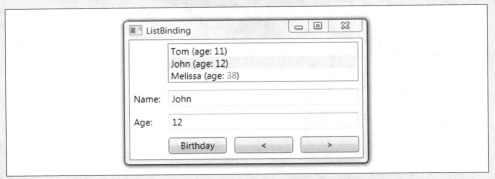

Color Plate 6 (Figure 7-7). Person objects being displayed in a ListBox with a data template

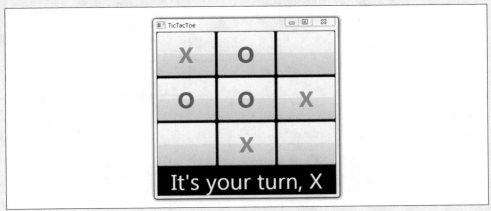

Color Plate 7 (Figure 8-5). Setting styles programmatically based on an object's content

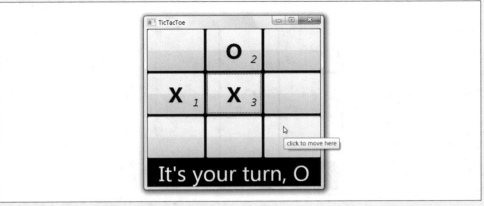

Color Plate 8 (Figure 8-10). A property trigger in action

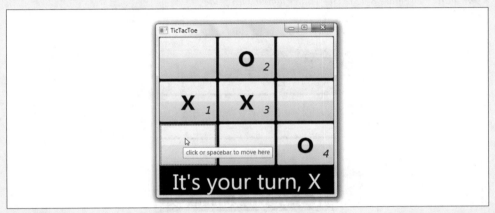

Color Plate 9 (Figure 8-11). Multiple property triggers in action

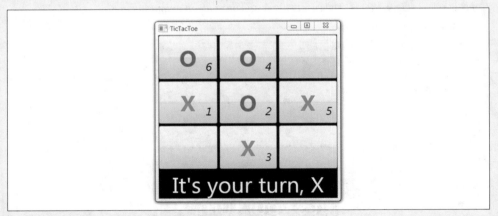

Color Plate 10 (Figure 8-12). Data triggers in action

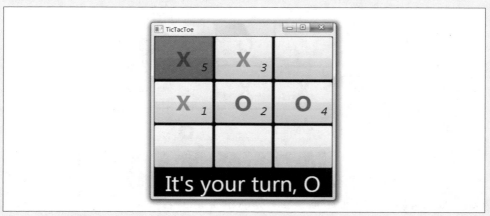

Color Plate 11 (Figure 8-13). The winner aglow with pride

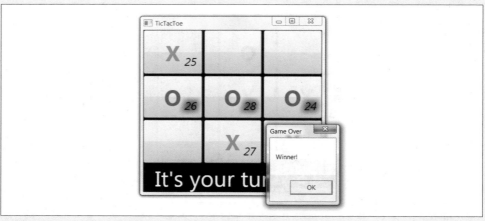

Color Plate 12 (Figure 8-14). The event trigger and our fade-in animation

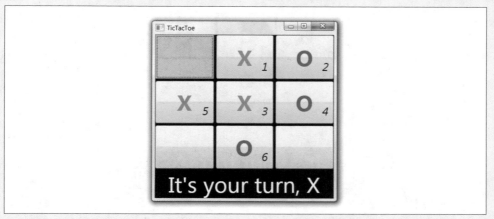

Color Plate 13 (Figure 9-3). Replacing the button's control template with an orange rectangle

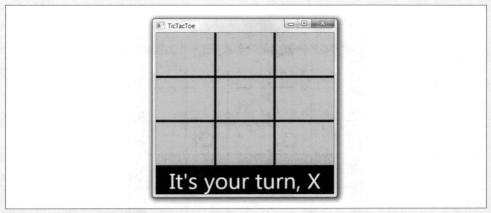

Color Plate 14 (Figure 9-4). Spreading the orange

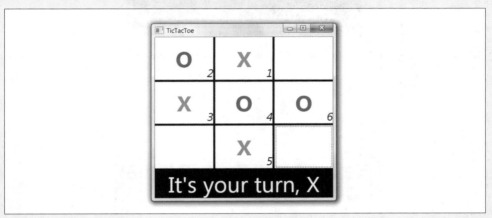

Color Plate 15 (Figure 9-5). Adding a content presenter to our control template

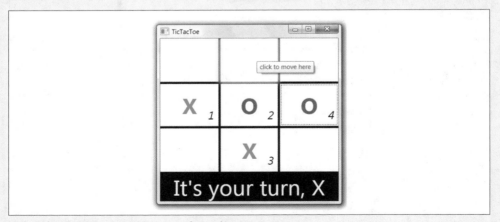

Color Plate 16 (Figure 9-7). A control template trigger in action

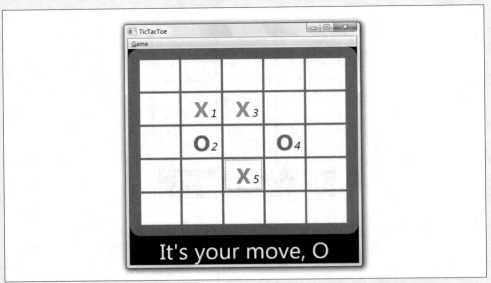

Color Plate 17 (Figure 9-15). Replacing the control template in a data-driven application

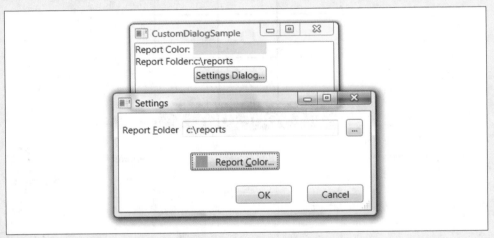

Color Plate 18 (Figure 10-6). The custom settings dialog in action

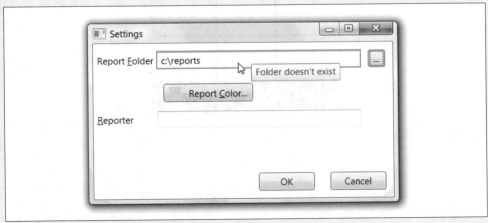

Color Plate 19 (Figure 10-7). An error in a dialog validation rule

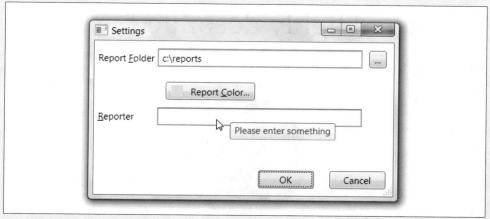

Color Plate 20 (Figure 10-8). Validating all controls in the OK button handler

Color Plate 21 (Figure 12-5). Changing skins

Color Plate 22 (Figure 13-40). Multiple gradient stops

Color Plate 23 (Figure 13-41). Simple lighting effects with linear fills

Color Plate 24 (Figure 13-42). Simple radial fill

Color Plate 25 (Figure 13-43). Radial fills

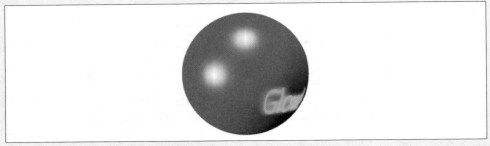

Color Plate 26 (Figure 14-4). Underline and strikethrough decorations

Color Plate 27 (Figure 17-15). MaterialGroup with EmissiveMaterial

Color Plate 28 (Figure A-1). Array of brushes provided by a ListBox

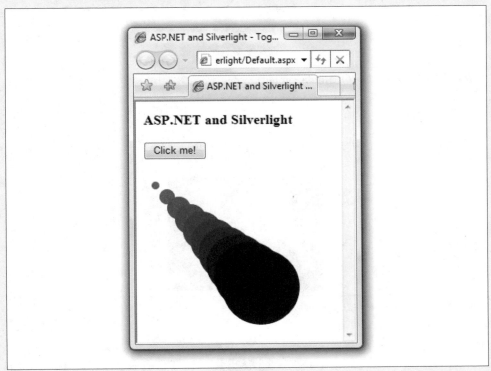

Color Plate 29 (Figure E-12). Default .aspx with dynamic XAML

Building Localizable Applications with XAML

Because XAML is compiled into BAML resources that are retrieved using a `ResourceManager`, localizability is an intrinsic feature of any WPF application built using XAML. If a satellite resource assembly for the current culture is present, and it contains a localized BAML resource, WPF will use that instead of the one in the main assembly. However, there is no built-in support for localizing WPF applications in Visual Studio 2005, so a few manual steps are involved.

 The localization process will no doubt be better streamlined and integrated in some future version of Visual Studio.

If you build a UI in XAML, localization effectively occurs one XAML file at a time—the `ResourceManager` cannot go more fine-grained than a single BAML resource, so each BAML resource is either localized or not. Because there is a close relationship between a XAML file and its code-behind file, however, it is important that the localized BAML resource has the same essential structure as the original. In principle, you could achieve this by writing a new XAML file for the localized version, and trying to keep its structure the same. However, there is a more robust way of guaranteeing consistency.

Instead of authoring a set of XAML files for every culture, you can write one master set of XAML files—one for each window or page in your application. Then, for each culture you wish to support, you can use a tool to generate culture-specific satellite resource assemblies containing localized resources. You supply the tool with configuration files indicating how the resources should be modified in order to create the localized versions. Figure 12-7 illustrates the overall process.

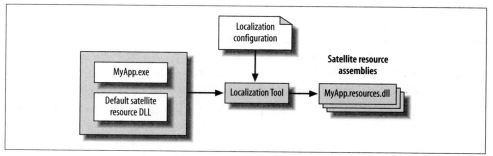

Figure 12-7. Localization process

First, you must make sure the project is set up to build a localizable application by specifying a default UI culture. Visual Studio provides no UI for doing this, so you must edit the *.csproj* file using a text editor. Add a `UICulture` element inside the `PropertyGroup` element. (It doesn't matter where it appears within this section.)

Set it to the default culture for your application—the culture in which you will create the main resources. This will cause Visual Studio to put all of the binary resources into a satellite resource assembly for this default culture (see Example 12-34).

Example 12-34. Specifying a UI culture for your project

```
<Project DefaultTargets="Build"
        xmlns="http://schemas.microsoft.com/developer/msbuild/2003">
  <PropertyGroup>
    ...
    <UICulture>en-US</UICulture>
  </PropertyGroup>
  ...
```

Next, you must add *Uids* to your XAML. A Uid (unique identifier) is a special attribute on a XAML element indicating content that may require localization. The localization configuration file containing localization instructions uses Uids to indicate which elements are being changed. Example 12-35 shows a TextBlock with a Uid.

Example 12-35. A Uid

```
<TextBlock x:Uid="TextBlock_1">Hello, world</TextBlock>
```

You can add these by hand if you want. Or, you can generate them automatically using msbuild. To add Uids to your XAML automatically, run this command:

```
msbuild /t:updateuid MyProject.csproj
```

If you have done this already, and have subsequently edited your XAML, you may want to check that you've not ended up with any duplicated Uids. You can do this with the following command:

```
msbuild /t:checkuid MyProject.csproj
```

Now you can build the project, either using Visual Studio or by running msbuild from the command line, passing just the project filename as a parameter. You should now find that as well as building an EXE or DLL, your project also adds a satellite resource assembly in a subdirectory. (The subdirectory will be the one you named when you added the UICulture element to the project file.)

The next step is to create the configuration file that will direct the localization process. This file will contain all localized items such as translated strings. You can create the skeleton of this file using the LocBaml command-line tool. This examines resource assemblies for BAML streams, and builds a file containing one line for each localizable piece of information in the file. You can then put your translated strings and whatever else is required into this file.

LocBaml is supplied in source code form only, so you will need to build it before you can run it. You can find the code in the SDK documentation's "Localize an Application" topic at *http://msdn2.microsoft.com/ library/ms746621.aspx* or *http://tinysells.com/106*. This provides the code for LocBaml. Once a version of Visual Studio with integrated WPF support ships, this "some assembly required" approach will hopefully no longer be necessary.

Example 12-36 shows how to run LocBaml to generate the skeleton configuration file. You should run this from the directory containing the built application (e.g., the *bin\ Debug* directory). You will need to copy the LocBaml executable into that directory in order for it to run without error.

Example 12-36. Generating a CSV file with LocBaml

```
LocBaml /parse en-US\MyApp.resources.dll /out:MyAppResources.csv
```

This will create a CSV file. Table 12-2 describes each column. To localize the resource, edit the "Value" column. (Note that the CSV file doesn't contain a heading line—it depends entirely on the column positions.)

Table 12-2. Columns generated by LocBaml

Column	Description
Baml Name	Identifies the BAML stream; the value will be of the form $AssemblyName:Stream\ Name$
Resource Key	Identifies the localizable resource; the value will be of the form $Uid:Element\ Type.\$Property$
Localization Category	An entry from the LocalizationCategory enumeration, indicating what kind of content this is
Readable	Indicates whether the resource is visible for translation
Modifiable	Indicates whether this value can be modified during translation
Comments	Localization comments
Value	The value of this resource (modify this field when localizing your WPF applications)

Example 12-37 shows a line from one of these configuration files. (It has been split across several lines here to make it fit on the page. In a real file, this would be on a single line.)

Example 12-37. Example configuration file

```
HelloApp.g.fr-FR.resources:window1.baml,
TextBlock_1:System.Windows.Controls.TextBlock.Text,
Text,True,True,,"Bonjour monde"
```

Once you have translated the Value column for each row, you can then run LocBaml again to generate the new resource DLL. You must pass in the path of the original resource DLL, the path of the CSV file containing translations, a target directory, and the target culture, as shown in Example 12-38. You must ensure that the target directory exists before running the tool—it will not create it for you. (Note that this example has been split across multiple lines to fit into the book. You should enter it as a single line in practice.)

Example 12-38. Generating a resource DLL with LocBaml

```
LocBaml /generate en-US\MyApp.resources.dll /trans:MyAppResource.csv
  /out:fr-FR /cul:fr-FR
```

This will generate a new satellite resource assembly in the specified directory, targeting the chosen culture. (If you want to build several resource assemblies, create one CSV file for each culture, and run LocBaml once for each file.) If you place the resulting resource assembly in a subdirectory of the application's directory named after the culture, it will automatically be picked up at runtime if the application is run with that particular culture selected.

Where Are We?

WPF provides resource facilities that let us plug bits of our user interface together dynamically but consistently. We can store any objects in resource dictionaries and then refer to these resources throughout our applications. WPF's styling mechanism relies on resource dictionaries to set properties and templates for our controls, based either on an application's skin or on the currently configured system theme. And, for binary resources—including the compiled BAML versions of our XAML files—WPF uses the localization-aware ResourceManager system, which chooses the most appropriate resources for the end user's chosen user interface culture.

CHAPTER 13

Graphics

WPF makes it easy to build visually stunning applications. It offers a rich array of drawing capabilities, and it is built to exploit the full power of modern graphics cards. This enables designers to create intricate designs and use animation to bring the UI to life much more easily than before.

WPF's graphics architecture is not just for designers. The key aspect of the graphics system is its deep integration with the rest of the programming model. It is easy to add graphical elements to any part of your application without the disconcerting change in programming techniques required by many user interface technologies.

Because WPF is a presentation technology, graphics are an important and substantial part of the framework. It would be possible to fill a whole book on WPF's graphical capabilities alone, so we can only really scratch the surface here. In this chapter, we will look at the fundamental concepts behind using graphics in WPF applications. In later chapters we will look at animation, media, and 3D support.

Graphics Fundamentals

WPF makes it easy to use graphics in your application, and to exploit the power of your graphics hardware. Many aspects of the graphics architecture contribute to this goal. The most important of these is *integration*.

Integration

Graphical elements can be integrated into any part of your user interface. Many GUI technologies split graphics into a separate world. This requires a "gearshift" when moving from a world of buttons, text boxes, and other controls into a world of shapes and images, because in many systems, these two worlds have different programming models.

For example, Windows Forms and Mac OS X's Cocoa both provide the ability to arrange controls within a window and build a program that interacts through those controls. They also both provide APIs offering advanced, fully scalable, two-dimensional drawing facilities (GDI+ in the case of Windows Forms, and Quartz 2D on OS X). But these drawing APIs are distinct from the control APIs. Drawing primitives are very different from controls in these systems—you cannot mix the two freely.

WPF, on the other hand, offers shape elements that can participate in the UI tree like any other. So we are free to mix them in with any other kind of element. Example 13-1 shows various examples of this.

Example 13-1. Mixing graphics with other elements

```
<DockPanel>
  <StackPanel DockPanel.Dock="Top" Orientation="Horizontal">
    <TextBlock Text="Mix text, " />
    <Ellipse Fill="Blue" Width="40" />
    <TextBlock Text=" and " />
    <Button>Controls</Button>
  </StackPanel>
  <Ellipse DockPanel.Dock="Left" Fill="Green" Width="100" />
  <Button DockPanel.Dock="Left">Foo</Button>
  <TextBlock FontSize="24" TextWrapping="Wrap">
    And of course you can put graphics into
    your text: <Ellipse Fill="Cyan" Width="50" Height="20" />
  </TextBlock>
</DockPanel>
```

As you can see, you can mix graphical elements seamlessly with other elements in the markup. Layout works with graphics exactly as it does for any other element. You can see the results in Figure 13-1.

> Although this example is in XAML, you can also use code to create elements. Most of the examples in this chapter use XAML because the structure of the markup directly reflects the structure of the objects being created. However, whether you use markup or code will depend on what you are doing. If you are creating drawings, you will most likely use a design program to create the XAML for these drawings. But if you are building up graphics from data, it might make more sense to do everything from code.
>
> You can use most of the techniques in this chapter in either code or markup. See Appendix A for more information on the relationship between XAML and code.

Figure 13-1. Mixed content

Not only can graphics and the other content live side by side in the markup, but they can even be intermingled. Notice how in Figure 13-1 the ellipse on the righthand side has been arranged within the flow of the containing TextBlock. If you want to achieve this sort of effect in Windows Forms, it is not possible with its Label control—you would have to write a whole new control from scratch that draws both the text and the ellipse. This mixing goes both ways—not only can you mix controls into your graphics, but you can also use graphical elements inside controls. For example, Figure 13-2 shows a button with mixed text and graphics as its caption.

Figure 13-2. Button with graphical content

Traditionally in Windows, you would get this effect by relying on the button's ability to display a bitmap. But bitmaps are just a block of fixed graphics—you can't easily make parts of a bitmap interactive, or animate selected pieces in response to user input. So, in WPF putting graphics in buttons works a little differently, as you can see in Example 13-2.

Example 13-2. Adding graphics to a Button

```
<Button>
  <StackPanel Orientation="Horizontal">
    <Canvas Width="20" Height="18" VerticalAlignment="Center">
      <Ellipse Canvas.Left="1" Canvas.Top="1" Width="16" Height="16"
               Fill="Yellow" Stroke="Black" />
      <Ellipse Canvas.Left="4.5" Canvas.Top="5" Width="2.5" Height="3"
               Fill="Black" />
      <Ellipse Canvas.Left="11" Canvas.Top="5" Width="2.5" Height="3"
               Fill="Black" />
      <Path Data="M 5,10 A 3,3 0 0 0 13,10" Stroke="Black" />
    </Canvas>
    <TextBlock VerticalAlignment="Center">Click!</TextBlock>
  </StackPanel>
</Button>
```

Of course, buttons with images are not a new idea. For example, the Windows Forms Button has an Image property, and in Cocoa, NSButton has a setImage method. But this is pretty inflexible—these controls allow a single caption and a single image to be set. Compare this to Example 13-2, which uses a StackPanel to lay out the interior of the button and just adds the content it requires. You can use any layout panel inside the Button, with any kind of content. Example 13-3 uses a Grid to arrange text and some ellipses within a Button. Figure 13-3 shows the results.

Example 13-3. Layout within a Button

```
<Button HorizontalAlignment="Center" VerticalAlignment="Center">
  <Grid>
    <Grid.ColumnDefinitions>
      <ColumnDefinition />
      <ColumnDefinition />
      <ColumnDefinition />
    </Grid.ColumnDefinitions>
    <Grid.RowDefinitions>
      <RowDefinition />
      <RowDefinition />
      <RowDefinition />
    </Grid.RowDefinitions>

    <Ellipse Grid.Column="0" Grid.Row="0" Fill="Blue" Width="10" Height="10" />
    <Ellipse Grid.Column="2" Grid.Row="0" Fill="Blue" Width="10" Height="10" />
    <Ellipse Grid.Column="0" Grid.Row="2" Fill="Blue" Width="10" Height="10" />
    <Ellipse Grid.Column="2" Grid.Row="2" Fill="Blue" Width="10" Height="10" />

    <Ellipse Grid.ColumnSpan="3" Grid.RowSpan="3" Stroke="LightGreen"
             StrokeThickness="3" />

    <TextBlock Grid.Column="1" Grid.Row="1" VerticalAlignment="Center"
               Text="Click!" />
  </Grid>
</Button>
```

Figure 13-3. Button with Grid content

In WPF, there is rarely any need for controls to provide properties, such as Text or Image. If it makes sense for a control to present nested content, it'll do just that by offering a content model—it will present whatever mixture of elements you choose to provide.

If you are familiar with two-dimensional drawing technologies such as Quartz 2D, GDI+, and GDI32, you may have been struck by another difference in the way drawing is done. We no longer need to write a function to respond to redraw requests—

WPF can keep the screen repainted for us. This is because WPF lets us represent drawings as objects.

Drawing Object Model

With many GUI technologies, applications that want customized visuals are required to be able to re-create their appearance from scratch. The usual technique for showing a custom appearance is to write code that performs a series of drawing operations in order to construct the display. This code runs when the relevant graphics first need to be displayed. In some systems, the OS does not retain a copy of what the application draws, so this method ends up running anytime an area needs repainting—for example, if a window was obscured and then uncovered.

Updating individual elements is often problematic in systems that use this on-demand rendering style. Even where the OS does retain a copy of the drawing, it is often retained as a bitmap. This means that if you want to change one part of the drawing, you often need to repaint everything in the area that has changed.

WPF offers a different approach: you can add objects representing graphical shapes to the tree of user interface elements. Shape elements are objects in the UI tree like any other, so your code can modify them at any time. If you change some property that has a visual impact—such as the size, location, or color—WPF will automatically update the display.

To illustrate this technique, Example 13-4 shows a simple window containing several ellipses. Each is represented by an `Ellipse` object, which we will use from the code-behind file to update the display.

Example 13-4. Changing graphical elements

```
<Window x:Class="ChangeItem.MainWindow"
    xmlns="http://schemas.microsoft.com/winfx/2006/xaml/presentation"
    xmlns:x="http://schemas.microsoft.com/winfx/2006/xaml"
    Title="Change Item">

  <Canvas x:Name="mainCanvas">
    <Ellipse Canvas.Left="10" Canvas.Top="30" Fill="Indigo"
            Width="40" Height="20" />
    <Ellipse Canvas.Left="20" Canvas.Top="40" Fill="Blue"
            Width="40" Height="20" />
    <Ellipse Canvas.Left="30" Canvas.Top="50" Fill="Cyan"
            Width="40" Height="20" />
    <Ellipse Canvas.Left="40" Canvas.Top="60" Fill="LightGreen"
            Width="40" Height="20" />
    <Ellipse Canvas.Left="50" Canvas.Top="70" Fill="Yellow"
            Width="40" Height="20" />
  </Canvas>
</Window>
```

Example 13-5 shows the code-behind file for this window. It attaches a handler to the main canvas's MouseLeftButtonDown event. Thanks to event bubbling, this OnClick handler method will be called whenever any of the ellipses is clicked. This method simply increases the Width property of whichever Ellipse raised the event. The result is that clicking on any ellipse will make it wider.

Example 13-5. Changing a shape at runtime

```
using System.Windows;
using System.Windows.Shapes;

namespace ChangeItem {
    public partial class MainWindow : Window {
        public MainWindow() : base() {
            InitializeComponent();
            mainCanvas.MouseLeftButtonDown += OnClick;
        }

        private void OnClick(object sender, RoutedEventArgs e) {
            Ellipse r = e.Source as Ellipse;
            if (r != null) {
                r.Width += 10;
            }
        }
    }
}
```

If we were using the old approach of drawing everything in a single rendering function, this code would not be sufficient to update the display. It would normally be necessary to tell the OS that the screen is no longer valid, causing it to raise a repaint request. But in WPF, this is not necessary—when you set a property on an Ellipse object, it ensures that the screen is updated appropriately. Moreover, WPF is aware that the items overlap, as shown in Figure 13-4, so it will also redraw the items beneath and above as necessary to get the right results. All you have to do is adjust the properties of the object.

Figure 13-4. Changing overlapping ellipses

Even though computer memory capacities have increased by orders of magnitude since GUIs first started to appear, in some situations this object model approach for drawing still might be too expensive. In particular, for applications dealing with vast data sets such as maps, having a complete set of objects in the UI tree mirroring the structure of the underlying data could use too much memory. Also, for certain kinds of graphics or data, it may be more convenient to use the old style of rendering code.

Because of this, WPF also supports some lighter weight modes of operation. The "Visual Layer Programming" section, later in this chapter, describes the on-demand rendering mechanisms. The "DrawingBrush" section, also later in this chapter, describes a third technique that is somewhere in between the two, trading off a little flexibility in exchange for better performance—it offers many of the benefits of a retained model, but without the overhead of a full WPF framework element.

You may have noticed that all of the drawing we've done so far has been with shapes and not bitmaps. WPF supports bitmaps, of course, but there is a good reason to use shapes—you can scale and rotate geometric shapes without losing image quality. This ability to perform high-quality transforms is an important feature of drawing in WPF.

Resolution Independence

Not only have graphics cards improved dramatically since the first GUIs appeared, but so have screens. For a long time, the only mainstream display technology was the CRT (cathode-ray tube). Color CRTs offer fairly low resolution—they struggle to display images with higher definition than about 100 pixels per inch. However, flat panel displays, which now outsell CRTs, can exceed this by a large margin.

One of the authors' laptops has a display with a resolution of 150 pixels per inch. Displays are available with more than 200 pixels per inch. It is technically possible to create even higher pixel densities. However, there is a potential problem with using these screens: either everything ends up being so small that it becomes unusable or, if the OS is able to scale things up, it may only be able to do so imperfectly, introducing blurring or other problems. This is because of a pixel-based development culture—the vast majority of applications measure their user interfaces in pixels.

This is not entirely the result of technical limitations. From the very first version of Windows NT, Win32 has made it possible to draw things in a resolution-independent way, because the drawing API—GDI32—allows you to apply transformations to all of your drawings. GDI+, introduced in 2001, offers the same facility. But just because a feature is available doesn't mean applications will use it—most applications don't fully exploit this scalability.

Unfortunately, the split between graphics and other UI elements in Win32 means that even if an application does exploit the scalability of the drawing APIs, the rest of the UI won't automatically follow. Figure 13-5 shows a Windows Forms application that uses GDI+ to draw text and graphics scaled to an arbitrary size.

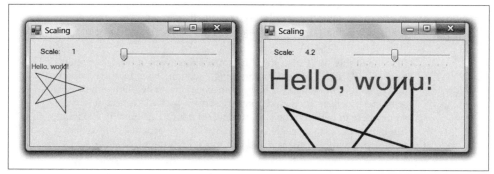

Figure 13-5. Incomplete UI scaling in Windows Forms

Notice in Figure 13-5 that although the star and the "Hello, world!" text have been scaled, the track bar and label controls have not. This is because drawing transformations affect only what you draw with GDI+—they do not affect the entire UI. And although Windows Forms offers some features to help with scaling the rest of the UI, it's not completely automatic; you have to take deliberate and nontrivial steps to build a resolution-independent UI in Windows Forms.

Scaling and rotation

WPF solves this problem by supporting transformations at a fundamental level. Instead of providing scalability just at the 2D drawing level, it is built into the underlying composition engine. The result is that everything in the UI can be transformed, not just the user-drawn graphics. Going back to our smiley face button in Figure 13-2, we can exploit this scalability with a simple addition just after the first line:

```
<Button>
  <Button.LayoutTransform>
    <ScaleTransform ScaleX="3" ScaleY="3" />
  </Button.LayoutTransform>
  ... as before ...
</Button>
```

The LayoutTransform property is available on all user interface elements in WPF, so you can scale the contents of an entire window just as easily as a single button. Many kinds of transformations are available, and we will discuss them in more detail later. For now, we are simply asking to enlarge the button by a factor of three in both *x* and *y* dimensions.

Figure 13-6 shows the enlarged button. When compared to the original Figure 13-2, it is larger, obviously. More significantly, the details have become crisper. The rounded edges of the button are easier to see than in the small version. The shapes of the letters are much better defined. And, our graphic is clearer. We get this clarity because WPF has rendered the button to look as good as it can at the specified size. Compare this with the examples in Figure 13-7.

Figure 13-6. Enlarged button with graphics

Figure 13-7. Enlarged bitmaps

Figure 13-7 shows what happens if you simply enlarge a bitmap of the original small button. There are several different ways of enlarging bitmaps. The example on the left uses the simplest algorithm, known as *nearest neighbor* or, sometimes, *pixel doubling*. To make the image larger, pixels have been repeated. This lends a very square feel to the image. The example on the right uses a more sophisticated interpolation algorithm. It has done a better job of keeping rounded edges looking round, and doesn't suffer from the chunky pixel effect, but it ends up looking very blurred. Clearly, neither of these comes close to Figure 13-6.

Resolution, coordinates, and "pixels"

This support for scaling graphics means that there is no fixed relationship between the coordinates your application uses and the pixels on-screen. This is true even if you do not use scaling transforms yourself—a transform may be applied automatically to your whole application if it is running on a high-DPI display.

What are the default units of measurement in a WPF application if not physical pixels? The answer is, somewhat confusingly, pixels! To be more precise, the real answer is *device-independent pixels*.

WPF defines a device-independent pixel as 1/96th of an inch. If you specify the width of a shape as 96 pixels, this means that it should be exactly 1 inch wide. WPF will use as many physical pixels as are required to fill 1 inch. For example, high-resolution laptop screens typically have a resolution of 150 pixels per inch. So, if you make a shape's width 96 "pixels," WPF will render it 150 physical pixels wide.

WPF discovers the physical pixel size from the system-wide display settings, so these need to be set accurately in order for elements to be displayed at the correct size. However, very few systems have this configured correctly, so the physical dimensions are often arbitrary in practice. But it's easy enough to configure your system correctly if you know the pixel density.

On Windows Vista, you can change this setting by right-clicking on the desktop, selecting Personalize, and then choosing "Adjust font size (DPI)" from the list of options that appears on the left. In the DPI scaling window that appears, click the Custom DPI button. Or in Windows XP, right-click on your desktop and select Properties to display the applet, and then go to the Settings tab. Click on the Advanced button, and in the dialog that opens, select the General tab. This lets you tell Windows your screen resolution. If you set the number to match the physical characteristics of your screen, WPF will render content at the correct physical size.

You might be wondering why WPF uses the somewhat curious choice of 1/96th of an inch, and why it calls this a "pixel." The reason is that 96 dpi is the default display DPI in Windows when it is running with Small Fonts, so this has long been considered the "normal" size for a pixel. This means that on screens with a normal pixel density, a device-independent pixel will correspond to a physical pixel. On screens with a high pixel density, if the system DPI is correctly configured, WPF will scale your drawings for you so that they remain at the correct physical size, so a device-independent pixel may not correspond to an exact number of physical pixels.

WPF's capability to optimize its rendering of graphical features for any scale means it is ideally placed to take advantage of increasing screen resolutions. For the first time, on-screen text and graphics will be able to compete with the crisp clarity we have come to expect from laser printers. Of course, for all of this to work in practice, we need a comprehensive suite of scalable drawing primitives.

Shapes, Brushes, and Pens

Most of the classes in WPF's drawing toolkit fall into one of three categories: shapes, brushes, and pens. There are many variations on these themes, and we will examine them in detail later. However, to get anywhere at all with graphics, we need a basic understanding.

Shapes are objects in the user interface tree that provide the basic building blocks for drawing. The Ellipse, Path, and Rectangle elements we have seen already are all examples of shape objects. There is also support for lines, both single- and multi-segment, using Line and Polyline, respectively. Polygon creates closed shapes whose edges are all straight. The Path class supports both open and closed shapes with any mixture of straight and curved edges. Figure 13-8 shows each of these shapes in action.

Figure 13-8. Rectangle, Ellipse, Line, Polyline, Polygon, and Path

Regardless of which shape you choose, you'll need to decide how it should be colored in. For this, you use a brush. Many brush types are available. The simplest is the single-color `SolidColorBrush`. You can achieve more interesting visual effects using the `LinearGradientBrush` or `RadialGradientBrush`. These allow the color to change over the surface of a shape, which can be a great way of providing an impression of depth. You can also create brushes based on images—the `ImageBrush` uses a bitmap, and the `DrawingBrush` uses a scalable drawing. Finally, the `VisualBrush` lets you take any visual tree—any chunk of user interface you like—and use that as a brush to paint some other shape. This makes it easy to achieve effects such as reflections of whole sections of your user interface, or wrapping a user interface around a 3D model.

Finally, pens are used to draw the outline of a shape. A pen is really just an augmented brush. When you create a `Pen` object, you give it a `Brush` to tell it how it should paint onto the screen. The `Pen` class just adds information like line thickness, dash patterns, and end cap details. Figure 13-9 shows a few of the effects available using brushes and pens.

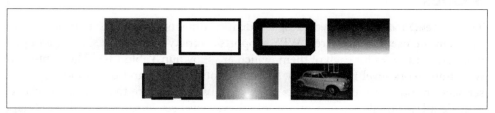

Figure 13-9. Brushes and pens

Composition

The final key feature of the graphics architecture is composition. In computer graphics, the term *composition* refers to the process of combining multiple shapes or images together to form the final output. WPF's composition model is very different from how Windows has traditionally worked, and it is crucial to enabling the creation of high-quality visuals.

In the classic Win32 model, each user interface element (each HWND) has exclusive ownership of some region of the application's window. Within each top-level window, any given pixel in that window is controlled completely by exactly one element. This prevents elements from being partially transparent. It also precludes the use of anti-aliasing around the edges of elements, a technique which is particularly important when combining nonrectangular elements. Although various hacks have been devised to provide the illusion of transparency in Win32, they all have limitations, and can be somewhat inconvenient to work with.

WPF's composition model supports elements of any shape, and allows them to overlap. It also allows elements to have any mixture of partially and completely transparent areas. This means that any given pixel on-screen may have multiple contributing visible elements. Moreover, WPF uses anti-aliasing around the edges of all shapes. This reduces the jagged appearance that simpler drawing techniques can produce on-screen, resulting in a smooth-looking image. Finally, the composition engine allows any element to have a transformation applied before composition.

WPF's composition engine makes use of the capabilities of modern graphics cards to accelerate the drawing process. Internally, it is implemented on top of Direct3D. This may seem odd because the majority of WPF's drawing functionality is two-dimensional, but most of the 3D-oriented functionality on a modern graphics card can also be used to draw 2D shapes. For example, WPF exploits the same ultra-fast polygon-drawing facilities used by 3D games to render primitive shapes.

Now that we've seen the core concepts underpinning the WPF graphics system, let's take a closer look at the details.

Shapes

The `System.Windows.Shapes` namespace defines drawing primitives that act as elements in the user interface tree. WPF supports a variety of different shapes, and provides element types for each of them, which are shown in Table 13-1. These integrate with framework-level functionality such as layout, styling, and data binding. These services are not without their costs, so it's useful to be aware that the shape classes provide a layer of abstraction on top of a lower-level set of services. See the "Shape Objects Versus Geometries" sidebar for details.

Table 13-1. Shapes

Shape Type	Usage
Ellipse	An ellipse
Line	A single straight line
Path	A shape using any mixture of straight lines and curves
Polygon	A closed shape made from straight lines
Polyline	An open shape made from straight lines
Rectangle	A rectangle, optionally with rounded corners

Base Shape Class

All of the elements described in this section derive from a common abstract base class, Shape. Shape defines a common set of features that you can use on all shapes. These common properties are mainly concerned with the way in which the interior and outline of the shape are painted.

The Fill property specifies the Brush that will be used to paint the interior. (The Line class doesn't have an interior, so it ignores this property. This was simpler than complicating the inheritance hierarchy by having separate Shape and FilledShape base classes.) The Stroke property specifies the Brush that will be used to paint the outline of the shape.

If you do not specify either a Fill or a Stroke for your shape, it will be invisible, because both of these properties are null by default.

It may seem peculiar that the Stroke property is of type Brush. As we saw earlier, WPF defines a Pen class for specifying a line's thickness, dash patterns, and the like, so it would make more sense if the Stroke property were of type Pen. WPF does in fact use a Pen internally to draw the outline of a shape. The Stroke property is of type Brush mainly for convenience—all of the Pen features are exposed through separate properties on Shape, as shown in Table 13-2. This simplifies the markup in scenarios where you're happy to use the default pen settings—you don't need to provide a full Pen definition just to set the outline color.

Table 13-2. Shape Stroke properties and Pen equivalents

Shape property	Equivalent Pen property
Stroke	Brush
StrokeThickness	Thickness
StrokeLineJoin	LineJoin
StrokeMiterLimit	MiterLimit
StrokeDashArray	DashArray
StrokeDashCap	DashCap
StrokeDashOffset	DashOffset
StrokeStartLineCap	StartLineCap
StrokeEndLineCap	EndLineCap

The "Brushes and Pens" section, later in this chapter, describes brushes and pens in detail.

The Shape class also defines a Stretch property, which determines how a shape will be adjusted if the available space doesn't match its preferred size. None means that the shape will simply be whatever size and shape you ask for. If you set this to Fill, the shape will be adjusted to fill the available space. Fill allows the shape to be distorted if necessary in order to fit exactly. Uniform and UniformToFill scale equally, in both directions. The former scales until the shape is large enough in at least one dimension to fill the available space, but will leave spare space on the other dimension if necessary so as to avoid cropping. You can see this on the lefthand side of Figure 13-10. The latter scales the shape until it's large enough to completely fill the space in both dimensions, even if this means cropping in one, as shown on the right of Figure 13-10.

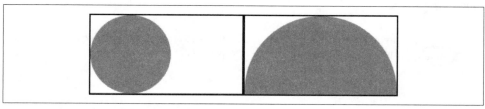

Figure 13-10. Uniform (left) and UniformToFill (right)

Rectangle and Ellipse default to a Stretch of Fill, whereas the other shapes all default to None.

The classes that derive from Shape all add properties specific to the kind of shape they represent. So, we will now look at each of these types, starting with Rectangle.

Rectangle

Rectangle does what its name suggests. As with any shape, it can be drawn either filled in, as an outline, or both filled in and outlined. As well as drawing a normal rectangle, it can also draw one with rounded corners.

Rectangle doesn't provide any properties for setting its location. It relies on the same layout mechanisms as any other UI element. The location is determined by the containing panel. The width and height can either be set automatically by the parent, or they can be set explicitly using the standard layout properties, Width and Height.

Example 13-6 shows a Rectangle on a Canvas panel. Here the Width and Height have been set explicitly, and the location has been specified using the attached Canvas.Left and Canvas.Top properties.

Example 13-6. Rectangle with explicit size and position

```
<Canvas>
    <Rectangle Fill="Yellow" Stroke="Black"
            Canvas.Left="30" Canvas.Top="10"
            Width="100" Height="20" />
</Canvas>
```

Example 13-7 shows the other approach; none of the rectangles has its location or size set explicitly. They are relying on the containing Grid to do this. Figure 13-11 shows the result.

Example 13-7. Rectangles with size and position controlled by parent

```
<Grid>
  <Grid.ColumnDefinitions>
    <ColumnDefinition />
    <ColumnDefinition />
  </Grid.ColumnDefinitions>

  <Grid.RowDefinitions>
    <RowDefinition />
    <RowDefinition />
  </Grid.RowDefinitions>

  <Rectangle Grid.Column="0" Grid.Row="0" Fill="LightGray" />
  <Rectangle Grid.Column="1" Grid.Row="0" Fill="Black" />
  <Rectangle Grid.Column="0" Grid.Row="1" Fill="DarkGray" />
  <Rectangle Grid.Column="1" Grid.Row="1" Fill="White" />
</Grid>
```

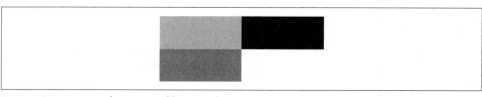

Figure 13-11. Rectangles arranged by a Grid

A Rectangle will usually be aligned with the coordinate system of its parent panel. This means that its edges will normally be horizontal and vertical, although if the parent panel has been rotated, Rectangle will of course be rotated along with it. If you want to rotate a Rectangle relative to its containing panel, you can use the RenderTransform property available on all user interface elements, as Example 13-8 shows.

Example 13-8. Rotating rectangles

```
<Canvas>
  <Rectangle Canvas.Left="50" Canvas.Top="50" Width="40" Height="10"
          Fill="Indigo" />
  <Rectangle Canvas.Left="50" Canvas.Top="50" Width="40" Height="10"
          Fill="Violet">
    <Rectangle.RenderTransform>
      <RotateTransform Angle="45" />
    </Rectangle.RenderTransform>
  </Rectangle>
  <Rectangle Canvas.Left="50" Canvas.Top="50" Width="40" Height="10"
          Fill="Blue">
    <Rectangle.RenderTransform>
      <RotateTransform Angle="90" />
    </Rectangle.RenderTransform>
  </Rectangle>
  <Rectangle Canvas.Left="50" Canvas.Top="50" Width="40" Height="10"
          Fill="Cyan">
    <Rectangle.RenderTransform>
      <RotateTransform Angle="135" />
    </Rectangle.RenderTransform>
  </Rectangle>
  <Rectangle Canvas.Left="50" Canvas.Top="50" Width="40" Height="10"
          Fill="Green">
    <Rectangle.RenderTransform>
      <RotateTransform Angle="180" />
    </Rectangle.RenderTransform>
  </Rectangle>
  <Rectangle Canvas.Left="50" Canvas.Top="50" Width="40" Height="10"
          Fill="Yellow">
    <Rectangle.RenderTransform>
      <RotateTransform Angle="225" />
    </Rectangle.RenderTransform>
  </Rectangle>
  <Rectangle Canvas.Left="50" Canvas.Top="50" Width="40" Height="10"
          Fill="Orange">
```

Example 13-8. Rotating rectangles (continued)

```
    <Rectangle.RenderTransform>
      <RotateTransform Angle="270" />
    </Rectangle.RenderTransform>
  </Rectangle>
  <Rectangle Canvas.Left="50" Canvas.Top="50" Width="40" Height="10"
          Fill="Red">
    <Rectangle.RenderTransform>
      <RotateTransform Angle="315" />
    </Rectangle.RenderTransform>
  </Rectangle>
</Canvas>
```

This uses `RenderTransform` to rotate a series of rectangles. Figure 13-12 shows the result.

Figure 13-12. Rotated rectangles

To draw a rectangle with rounded corners, use the `RadiusX` and `RadiusY` properties, as Example 13-9 illustrates.

Example 13-9. Rounded rectangle

```
<Rectangle Width="100" Height="50" Fill="Black" RadiusX="30" RadiusY="20" />
```

Figure 13-13 shows the result.

Figure 13-13. Rectangle with rounded corners

Ellipse

`Ellipse` is similar to `Rectangle`. Obviously it draws an ellipse rather than a rectangle, but the size, location, rotation, fill, and stroke of an `Ellipse` are controlled in exactly the same way as for a `Rectangle`, as Example 13-10 shows.

Example 13-10. Ellipse

```
<Ellipse Width="100" Height="50" Fill="Yellow" Stroke="Black" />
```

Figure 13-14 shows the result.

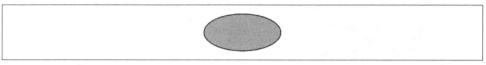

Figure 13-14. Ellipse

Line

The Line element draws a straight line from one point to another. It has four properties controlling the location: X1 and Y1 define the start point, and X2 and Y2 determine the end point. These coordinates are relative to wherever the parent panel chooses to locate the Line. Consider Example 13-11.

Example 13-11. Two Line elements in a StackPanel

```
<StackPanel Orientation="Vertical">
  <TextBlock Background="LightGray">Foo</TextBlock>
  <Line Stroke="Green" X1="20" Y1="10" X2="100" Y2="40" />
  <TextBlock Background="LightGray">Bar</TextBlock>
  <Line Stroke="Green" X1="0" Y1="10" X2="100" Y2="0" />
</StackPanel>
```

This uses a vertical StackPanel to arrange an alternating sequence of TextBlock and Line elements. The TextBlock elements have gray backgrounds to make it easier to see the vertical extent of each element (see Figure 13-15).

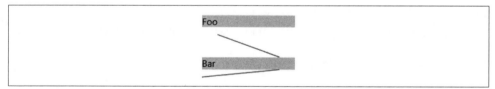

Figure 13-15. Two Line elements in a StackPanel

As you can see from Figure 13-15, the Line elements have been placed in the stack just like any other element. The StackPanel has allocated enough height to hold the line. The first of the lines is interesting in that there is some space between the TextBlock above it, and the start of the line. This is because the line's Y1 property has been set to 10, indicating that the line should start slightly below the top of the location allocated for the Line element. (In WPF, positive Y means down, unlike with a typical mathematical graph.) The second Line element goes all the way to the top because its Y2 property is set to 0, again illustrating that the coordinate system of the line end points is relative to the area allocated to the Line by the containing panel.

You can use the Stretch property to make the Line resize automatically with your layout. The Line in Example 13-12 has start and end points of 0,0 and 1,0. However, because its Stretch is set to Fill, the points will automatically be adjusted to fill the available width.

Example 13-12. Auto-sizing line

```
<Line Stroke="Black" X1="0" X2="1" Stretch="Fill" />
```

Polyline

A Polyline lets you draw a connected series of line segments. Instead of having properties for start and end points, Polyline has a Points property, containing a list of coordinate pairs, as Example 13-13 illustrates.

Example 13-13. Polyline

```
<Polyline Stroke="Blue"
    Points="0,30 10,30 15,0 18,60 23,30 35,30 40,0 43,60 48,30 160,30" />
```

WPF simply draws a line that goes through each point in turn, as shown in Figure 13-16.

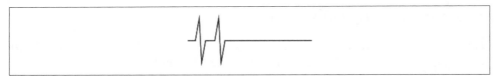

Figure 13-16. A Polyline

As with the Line class, the point coordinates in a Polyline are relative to wherever the containing panel chooses to locate the Polyline.

Polygon

Polygon is very similar to Polyline. It has a Points property that works in exactly the same way as Polyline's. The only difference is that whereas Polyline always draws an open shape, Polygon always draws a closed shape. To illustrate the difference, Example 13-14 contains a Polyline and a Polygon. They have all of the same properties set.

Example 13-14. A Polyline and a Polygon

```
<StackPanel Orientation="Horizontal">
  <Polyline Fill="Orange" Stroke="Blue" StrokeThickness="2"
          Points="40,10 70,50 10,50" />
  <Polygon  Fill="Orange" Stroke="Blue" StrokeThickness="2"
          Points="40,10 70,50 10,50"  />
</StackPanel>
```

As you can see in Figure 13-17, the Polyline has been left open. The Polygon, on the other hand, has closed the shape by drawing an extra line segment between the last and first points. Both shapes have painted interiors.

Figure 13-17. A Polyline (left) and a Polygon (right)

Because we are free to add points wherever we like to a Polygon, it is easy to end up with a self-intersecting shape (one whose edge crosses itself). With such shapes, what counts as the interior of the shape can be ambiguous. Figure 13-18 shows such a shape, and two possible ways of filling it.

Figure 13-18. Fill rules: EvenOdd (left) and Nonzero (right)

The Polygon class provides a FillRule property that tells WPF how to deal with ambiguous regions.* WPF supports two fill rules. Example 13-15 is the markup for Figure 13-18, and shows both fill rules in use.

Example 13-15. Fill rules

```
<StackPanel Orientation="Horizontal">
  <Polygon Fill="Orange" Stroke="Blue" StrokeThickness="2" FillRule="EvenOdd"
        Points="50,30 13,41 36,11 36,49 14,18" />
  <Polygon Fill="Orange" Stroke="Blue" StrokeThickness="2" FillRule="Nonzero"
        Points="50,30 13,41 36,11 36,49 14,18" />
</StackPanel>
```

The default rule is EvenOdd, and this is used on the left of Figure 13-18. This is the simplest rule to understand. To determine whether a particular enclosed region is inside or outside the shape, the EvenOdd rule counts the number of lines you have to cross to get from that point to one completely outside the shape. If this number is odd, the point was inside the shape. If it is even, the point is outside the shape. For example, if you start from inside the middle area of the star in Figure 13-18, you will need to cross over an even number of lines in order to get to the outside of the shape. This is why the central area of the star is unfilled when the EvenOdd rule is used.

The second fill rule, Nonzero, is subtler. From Figure 13-18, you might have thought that any enclosed area was deemed to be inside the shape, but it's not quite that simple. The Nonzero rule performs a similar process to EvenOdd, but rather than simply counting the number of lines, it takes into account the direction in which the line is running. It either increments or decrements the count for each line it crosses,

---

* In some graphics systems, this is described as the "winding" rule.

depending on the direction.* If the total at the end is nonzero, the point is considered to be inside the shape. The points making up the stars in Example 13-15 always proceed clockwise. This means that if you start from the center of the star, the two lines you must cross to get to the outside of the shape will always point in the same direction. This results in a count of 2 (or –2, depending on which direction you go), which is why the star on the right of Figure 13-18 has its central region filled.

In Figure 13-18, the Nonzero rule has resulted in all enclosed regions being part of the interior. However, if the outline of the shape follows a slightly more convoluted path, the results can be a little more mixed, as Example 13-16 shows.

Example 13-16. Nonzero fill rule with more complex shape

```
<Polygon Fill="Orange" Stroke="Blue" StrokeThickness="2" FillRule="Nonzero"
    Points="10,10 60,10 60,25 20,25 20,40 40,40 40,18 50,18 50,50 10,50" />
```

Figure 13-19 shows the results of Example 13-16. This illustrates that the nonzero rule is not quite as straightforward as it may at first seem.

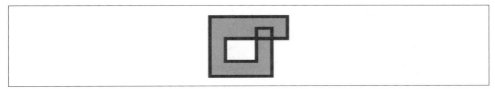

Figure 13-19. Nonzero rule in action

The nonzero rule is a bit of an oddity. It was popularized by PostScript, so most drawing systems support it, but it's not always easy to get useful results from a Polygon with this fill rule. It makes more sense in the context of the Path element, which supports multiple figures in a single shape.

Path

Path is by far the most powerful shape. All of the shapes we have looked at up to now have been supplied for convenience, because it is possible to draw all of them with a Path. Path also makes it possible to draw considerably more complex shapes than is possible with the previous shapes we have seen.

As mentioned earlier, the various classes derived from Shape are essentially high-level wrappers around underlying geometry objects. Path is explicit about this—its shape is defined by its Data property, which is of type Geometry. As we saw in the sidebar earlier, a Geometry object describes a particular shape. Table 13-3 shows the various concrete classes for representing different kinds of shapes.

---

* WPF doesn't document whether the positive direction is clockwise or counterclockwise. This is because it doesn't matter—as long as you are consistent, the final outcome is the same either way.

Table 13-3. Geometry types

Type	Usage
CombinedGeometry	Combines two geometry objects using set operations such as intersection or union
EllipseGeometry	An ellipse
GeometryGroup	Combines multiple geometries into one multifigure geometry
LineGeometry	A single straight line
PathGeometry	Defines shapes with any combination of straight lines, elliptical arcs, and Bézier curves
RectangleGeometry	A rectangle
StreamGeometry	More efficient alternative to PathGeometry—can define all the same shapes, but cannot modify the shapes after creation

Three geometry types—RectangleGeometry, EllipseGeometry, and LineGeometry—correspond to the Rectangle, Ellipse, and Line shape types shown earlier. So this Rectangle:

```
<Rectangle Fill="Blue" Width="40" Height="80" />
```

is effectively shorthand for this Path:

```
<Path Fill="Blue">
  <Path.Data>
    <RectangleGeometry Rect="0, 0, 40, 80" />
  </Path.Data>
</Path>
```

You might be wondering when you would ever use the RectangleGeometry, EllipseGeometry, or LineGeometry in a Path instead of the simpler Rectangle, Ellipse, and Line. One reason is that Path lets you use a special kind of geometry object called a GeometryGroup to create a shape with multiple geometries.

There is a significant difference between using multiple distinct shapes, and having a single shape with multiple geometries. Look at Example 13-17, for instance.

Example 13-17. Two Ellipse elements

```
<Canvas>
  <Ellipse Fill="Cyan" Stroke="Black" Width="40" Height="80" />
  <Ellipse Canvas.Left="10" Canvas.Top="10" Fill="Cyan" Stroke="Black"
        Width="20" Height="60" />
</Canvas>
```

This draws two ellipses, one on top of the other. They both have a black outline, so you can see the smaller one inside the larger one, as Figure 13-20 shows.

Because the Ellipse shape is just a simple way of creating an EllipseGeometry, the code in Example 13-17 is equivalent to the code in Example 13-18. (As you can see, using a Path is considerably more verbose. This is why the Ellipse and other simple shapes are provided.)

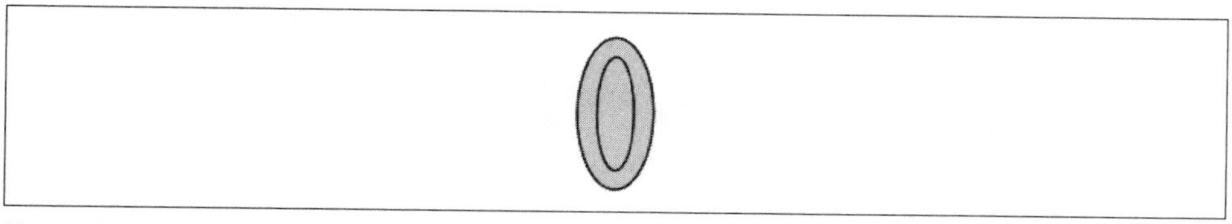

Figure 13-20. Two Ellipse elements

Example 13-18. Two Paths with EllipseGeometry elements

```
<Canvas>
  <Path Fill="Cyan" Stroke="Black">
    <Path.Data>
      <EllipseGeometry Center="20, 40" RadiusX="20" RadiusY="40" />
    </Path.Data>
  </Path>
  <Path Fill="Cyan" Stroke="Black">
    <Path.Data>
      <EllipseGeometry Center="20, 40" RadiusX="10" RadiusY="30" />
    </Path.Data>
  </Path>
</Canvas>
```

Because the code in Example 13-18 is equivalent to that in Example 13-17, it results in exactly the same output, as previously shown in Figure 13-20. So far, using geometries instead of shapes hasn't made a difference in the rendered results. This is because we are still using multiple shapes. So we will now show how you can put both ellipses into a single Path, and see how this affects the results. Example 13-19 shows the modified markup.

Example 13-19. One Path with two EllipseGeometry elements

```
<Canvas>
  <Path Fill="Cyan" Stroke="Black">
    <Path.Data>
      <GeometryGroup>
        <EllipseGeometry Center="20, 40" RadiusX="20" RadiusY="40" />
        <EllipseGeometry Center="20, 40" RadiusX="10" RadiusY="30" />
      </GeometryGroup>
    </Path.Data>
  </Path>
</Canvas>
```

This version has just a single path. Its Data property contains a GeometryGroup. This allows any number of geometry objects to be added to the same path. Here we have added the two EllipseGeometry elements that were previously in two separate paths. The result, shown in Figure 13-21, is clearly different from the one in Figure 13-20—there is now a hole in the middle of the shape. Because the default even-odd fill rule was in play, the smaller ellipse makes a hole in the larger one. (GeometryGroup has a FillRule property that lets you choose the nonzero rule instead if you need to.)

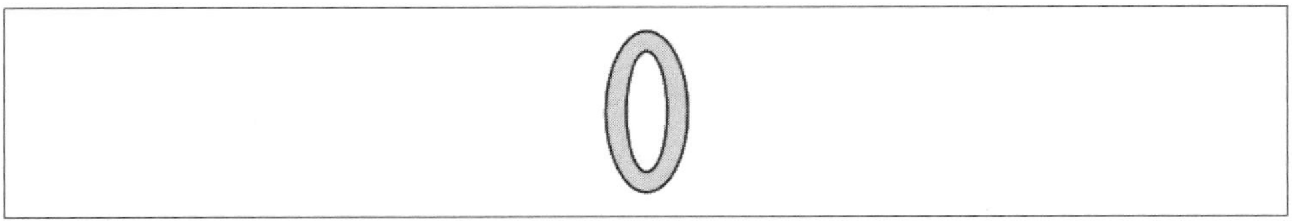

Figure 13-21. Path with two geometries

You can create shapes with holes only by combining multiple figures into a single shape. You could try to get a similar effect to that shown in Figure 13-21 by drawing the inner Ellipse with a Fill color of White, but that trick fails to work as soon as you draw the shape on top of something else, as Figure 13-22 shows.

Figure 13-22. Spot the fake hole

You might be wondering whether you could just draw the inner ellipse using the Transparent color, but that doesn't work either—if you tried this, you'd still see all of the larger ellipse, rather than what is behind it. Drawing something as totally transparent has the same effect as drawing nothing at all—that's what transparency means. Only by knocking a hole in the shape can we see through it.

To understand why, think about the drawing process. When it renders our elements to the screen, WPF draws the items one after the other. It starts with whatever's at the back—the text, in this case. Then it draws the shape on top of the text, which effectively obliterates the text that was underneath the shape. (It's still there in the element tree, of course, so WPF can always redraw it later if you change or remove the shape.) Because you just drew over the text, you can't draw another shape on top to "undraw" a hole into the first shape. So, if you want a hole in a shape, you'd better make sure that the hole is there before you draw it!

This is not to say you'd never use the Transparent color. It has a couple of uses. An animation might fade from a nontransparent color to Transparent in order to make an element disappear gradually. Also, objects that are Transparent are invisible to the eye, but not to the mouse—WPF's input system (which was described in Chapter 4) treats all brushes as equal, ignoring transparency. So the Transparent color provides a way of making invisible clickable targets.

We have not yet looked at the most flexible geometry: PathGeometry. This is the underlying geometry used by Polyline and Polygon, but it can draw many more shapes besides.

A PathGeometry contains one or more PathFigure objects, and each PathFigure represents a single open or closed shape in the path. To define the shape of each figure's outline, you use a sequence of PathSegment objects. Like GeometryGroup, PathGeometry also has a FillRule property to set the behavior for overlapping figures. Again, this defaults to the even-odd rule.

> PathGeometry's ability to contain multiple figures overlaps slightly with GeometryGroup's ability to contain multiple geometries. This is just for convenience—if you need to make a shape where every piece will be a PathGeometry object, it is more compact to have a single PathGeometry with multiple PathFigures. If you just want a group of simpler geometries like LineGeometry or RectangleGeometry, it is simpler to use a GeometryGroup and avoid PathGeometry altogether.

Example 13-20 shows a simple path. This contains just a single figure in the shape of a square.

Example 13-20. A square Path

```
<Path Fill="Cyan" Stroke="Black">
  <Path.Data>
    <PathGeometry>
      <PathGeometry.Figures>
        <PathFigure StartPoint="0,0" IsClosed="True">
          <PathFigure.Segments>
            <LineSegment Point="50,0" />
            <LineSegment Point="50,50" />
            <LineSegment Point="0,50" />
          </PathFigure.Segments>
        </PathFigure>
      </PathGeometry.Figures>
    </PathGeometry>
  </Path.Data>
</Path>
```

Figure 13-23 shows the result. This seems like a vast amount of effort for such a simple result—we've used 15 lines of markup to achieve what we could have achieved with a single Rectangle element. This is why WPF supplies classes for the simpler shapes and geometries. You don't strictly need any of them because you can use Path and PathGeometry instead, but the simpler shapes require much less effort. Normally you would use Path only for more complex shapes.

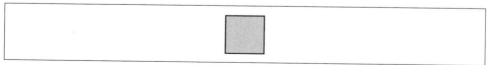

Figure 13-23. A square Path

Even though Example 13-20 produces a very simple result, it illustrates most of the important features of a Path with a PathGeometry. As with all the previous examples, the geometry is in the path's Data property. The PathGeometry is a collection of PathFigures, so all of the interesting data is inside its Figures property. This example contains just one PathFigure, but you can add as many as you like. The shape of the PathFigure is determined by the items in its Segments property.

The starting point of a PathFigure is determined by its StartPoint property. One or more segments describe the figure's shape. In Example 13-20, these are all LineSegments because the shape has only straight edges, but several types of curves are also on offer. This particular figure is a closed shape, which is determined by the IsClosed property.

 You might be wondering why LineSegments don't work like the Line shape or a LineGeometry. With those types, we specify start and end points, as in Example 13-11. This seems simpler than LineSegment, which needs us to specify a StartPoint in the PathFigure.

However, line segments in a PathFigure can't work like that because there cannot be any gaps in the outline of a figure. With the Line element, each Line is a distinct shape in its own right, but with a PathFigure, each segment is a part of the shape's outline. To define a figure fully and unambiguously, each segment must start off from where the previous one finished. This is why the LineSegment only specifies an end point for the line. All of the segment types work this way.

Example 13-20 isn't very exciting; it just uses straight line segments. We can create much more interesting shapes by using one of the curved segment types instead. Table 13-4 shows all of the segment types.

Table 13-4. Segment types

Segment type	Usage
LineSegment	Single straight line
PolyLineSegment	Sequence of straight lines
ArcSegment	Elliptical arc
BezierSegment	Cubic Bézier curve
QuadraticBezierSegment	Quadratic Bézier curve
PolyBezierSegment	Sequence of cubic Bézier curves
PolyQuadraticBezierSegment	Sequence of quadratic Bézier curves

ArcSegment lets you add elliptical curves to the edge of a shape. ArcSegment is a little more complex to use than a simple LineSegment. As well as specifying the end point of the segment, we must also specify two radii for the ellipse with the Size property.

The ellipse size and the line start and end points don't provide enough information to define the curve unambiguously, because there are several ways to draw an elliptical arc given these constraints. Consider a segment with a particular start and end point, and a given size and orientation of ellipse. For this segment, there will usually be two ways in which we can position the ellipse so that both the start and end points lie on the boundary of the ellipse, as Figure 13-24 shows. In other words, there will be two ways of "slicing" an ellipse with a particular line.

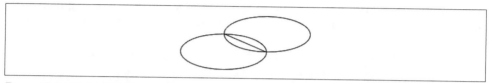

Figure 13-24. Potential ellipse positions

For each way of slicing the ellipse, there will be two resulting arc segments, a small one and a large one. This means that there are four ways in which the curve could be drawn between two points.

The ArcSegment provides two flags that enable you to select which of the curves you require. IsLargeArc determines whether you get the larger or smaller slice size. SweepDirection chooses on which side of the line the slice is drawn. Example 13-21 shows markup for all four combinations of these flags. It also shows the whole ellipse.

Example 13-21. ArcSegments

```
<Canvas>
  <Ellipse Fill="Cyan" Stroke="Black" Width="140" Height="60" />
  <Path Fill="Cyan" Stroke="Black" Canvas.Left="180">
    <Path.Data>
      <PathGeometry>
        <PathFigure StartPoint="0,11" IsClosed="True">
          <ArcSegment Point="50,61" Size="70,30"
                      SweepDirection="Counterclockwise" IsLargeArc="False" />
        </PathFigure>
        <PathFigure StartPoint="30,11" IsClosed="True">
          <ArcSegment Point="80,61" Size="70,30"
                      SweepDirection="Clockwise" IsLargeArc="True" />
        </PathFigure>
        <PathFigure StartPoint="240,1" IsClosed="True">
          <ArcSegment Point="290,51" Size="70,30"
                      SweepDirection="Counterclockwise" IsLargeArc="True" />
        </PathFigure>
        <PathFigure StartPoint="280,1" IsClosed="True">
          <ArcSegment Point="330,51" Size="70,30"
                      SweepDirection="Clockwise" IsLargeArc="False" />
        </PathFigure>
      </PathGeometry>
    </Path.Data>
  </Path>
</Canvas>
```

You may be wondering why the Ellipse has a width of 140 and a height of 60, which is double the Size of each ArcSegment. This is because the ArcSegment interprets the Size as the two radii of the ellipse, whereas the Width and Height properties on the Ellipse indicate the total size.

Figure 13-25 shows the results, and as you can see, each shape has one straight diagonal line and one elliptical curve. The straight line edge has the same length and orientation in all four cases. The curved edge is from different parts of the same ellipse.

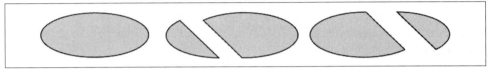

Figure 13-25. An ellipse and four arcs from that ellipse

In Figure 13-25, the ellipse's axes are horizontal and vertical. Sometimes you will want to use an ellipse where the axes are not aligned with your main drawing axes. ArcSegment provides a RotationAngle property, allowing you to specify the amount of rotation required in degrees.

Figure 13-26 shows four elliptical arcs. These use the same start and end points as Figure 13-25, and the same ellipse size. The only difference is that a RotationAngle of 45 degrees has been specified, rotating the ellipse before slicing it.

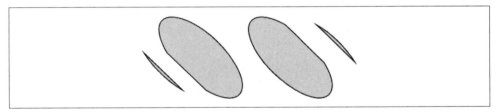

Figure 13-26. Four arcs from a rotated ellipse

There are two degenerate cases in which there will not be two ways of slicing the ellipse. The first is when the slice cuts the ellipse exactly in half. In this case, the IsLargeArc flag is irrelevant, because both slices are exactly the same size.

The other case is when the ellipse is too small—if the widest point at which the ellipse could be sliced is narrower than the segment is long, there is no way in which the segment can be drawn correctly. (If you do make the ellipse too small, WPF seems to scale the ellipse so that it is large enough, preserving the aspect ratio between the x- and y-axes.) You should avoid this.

The remaining curve types (BezierSegment, PolyBezierSegment, QuadraticBezierSegment, and PolyQuadraticBezierSegment) are variations on the same theme. They all draw Bézier curves.

Bézier curves

Bézier curves are curved line segments joining two points using a particular mathematical formula. It is not necessary to understand the details of the formula in order to use Bézier curves. What makes Bézier curves useful is that they offer a fair amount of flexibility in the shape of the curve. This has made them very popular—most vector drawing programs offer them.[*]

Figure 13-27 shows a variety of Bézier curve segments. Each of the five lines shown here is a single BezierSegment.

Figure 13-27. Bézier curve segments

As with all of the segment types, a BezierSegment starts from where the preceding segment left off, and defines a new end point. It also requires two "control points" to be defined, and it is these that determine the shape of the curve. Figure 13-28 shows the same curves again, but with the control points drawn on. It also shows lines connecting the control points to the segment end points, because this makes it easier to see how the control points affect the curve shapes.

Figure 13-28. Bézier curves with control points shown

The most obvious way in which the control points influence the shapes of these curves is that they determine the tangent. At the start and end of each segment, the direction in which the curve runs at that point is exactly the same as the direction of the line joining the start point to the corresponding control point.

There is a second, less obvious way in which control points work. The distance between the start or end point and its corresponding control point (i.e., the length of

---

[*] If you'd like to understand the formula for Bézier curves, *http://mathworld.wolfram.com/BezierCurve.html* (*http://tinysells.com/69*) and *http://en.wikipedia.org/wiki/B%C3%A9zier_curve* (*http://tinysells.com/70*) both provide good descriptions.

the straight lines added on Figure 13-28) also has an effect. This essentially determines how extreme the curvature is.

Figure 13-29 shows a set of Bézier curves similar to those in Figure 13-28. The tangents of both ends of the lines remain the same, but in each case, the distance between the start point and the first control point is reduced to one-quarter of what it was before, whereas the other is the same as before. As you can see, this reduces the influence of the first control point. In all four cases, the shape of the curve is dominated by the control point that is farther from its end point.

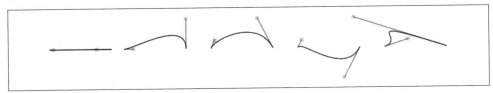

Figure 13-29. Bézier curves with less extreme control points

Example 13-22 shows the markup for the second curve segment in Figure 13-28. The Point1 property determines the location of the first control point—the one associated with the start point. Point2 positions the second control point. Point3 is the end point. (To keep things clear, the examples in this section just show the relevant PathFigure elements. If you want to see these shapes, you would of course need to put them inside a PathGeometry inside a Path, just as with the previous examples.)

Example 13-22. BezierSegment

```
<PathFigure StartPoint="0,50">
  <BezierSegment Point1="60,50" Point2="100,0" Point3="100,50" />
</PathFigure>
```

Flexible though Bézier curves are, you will rarely use just a single one. When defining shapes with curved edges, it is normal for a shape to have many Bézier curves defining its edge. WPF therefore supplies a PolyBezierSegment type, which allows multiple curves to be represented in a single segment. It defines a single Points property, which is an array of Point structures. Each Bézier curve requires three entries in this array: two control points and an end point. (As always, each segment starts from where the previous one left off.) Example 13-23 shows an example segment with two curves. Figure 13-30 shows the results.

Example 13-23. PolyBézierSegment

```
<PathFigure StartPoint="0,0">
  <PolyBezierSegment>
    <PolyBezierSegment.Points>
      <Point X="0" Y="10"/>
      <Point X="20" Y="10"/>
      <Point X="40" Y="10"/>
      <Point X="60" Y="10"/>
```

Example 13-23. PolyBézierSegment (continued)

```
        <Point X="120" Y="15"/>
        <Point X="100" Y="50"/>
      </PolyBezierSegment.Points>
    </PolyBezierSegment>
  </PathFigure>
```

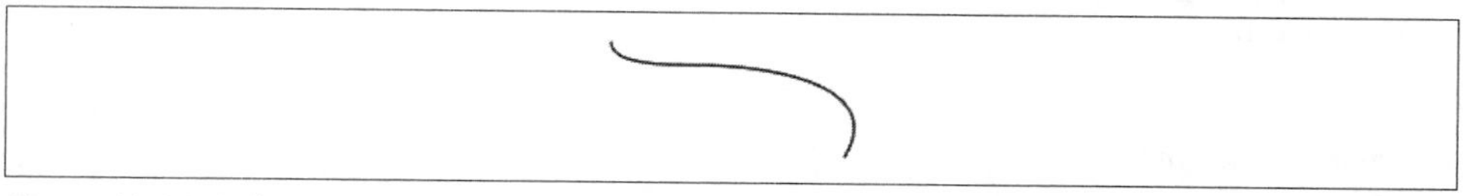

Figure 13-30. PolyBezierSegment

This markup is less convenient than simply using a sequence of `BezierSegment` elements, which rather defeats the point. Fortunately, you can provide all of the point data in string form. This is equivalent to Example 13-23:

```
<PathFigure StartPoint="0,0">
  <PolyBezierSegment Points="0,10 20,10 40,10 60,10 120,15 100,50" />
</PathFigure>
```

Also, if you are generating coordinates from code, dealing with a single `PolyBezierSegment` and passing it an array of `Point` data is often easier than working with lots of individual segments.

Cubic Bézier curves provide a lot of control over the shape of the line. However, you might not always need that level of flexibility. The `QuadraticBezierSegment` uses a simpler equation that uses just one control point to define the shape of the curve. This does not offer the same range of curve shapes as a cubic Bézier curve, but if all you want is a simple shape, this reduces the number of coordinate pairs you need to provide by one-third.

`QuadraticBezierSegment` is similar in use to the normal `BezierSegment`. The only difference is that it has no `Point3` property—just `Point1` and `Point2`. `Point1` is the single control point, and `Point2` is the end point. `PolyQuadraticBezierSegment` is the multi-curve equivalent. You use this in exactly the same way as `PolyBezierSegment`, except you need to provide only two points for each segment.

Combining shapes

Geometries can perform one more trick that we have not yet examined. We can combine geometries to form new geometries. This is different from adding two geometries to a `GeometryGroup`—it is possible to combine pairs of geometries in a way that forms a single geometry with a whole new shape.

Examples 13-24 and 13-25 define paths, both of which make use of the same `RectangleGeometry` and `EllipseGeometry`. The difference is that Example 13-24 puts both into a `GeometryGroup`, while Example 13-25 puts them into a `CombinedGeometry`.

Example 13-24. Multiple geometries

```
<Path Fill="Cyan" Stroke="Black">
  <Path.Data>
    <GeometryGroup>
      <RectangleGeometry Rect="0,0,50,50" />
      <EllipseGeometry Center="50,25" RadiusX="30" RadiusY="10" />
    </GeometryGroup>
  </Path.Data>
</Path>
```

Example 13-25. Combined geometries

```
<Path Fill="Cyan" Stroke="Black">
  <Path.Data>
    <CombinedGeometry GeometryCombineMode="Exclude">
      <CombinedGeometry.Geometry1>
        <RectangleGeometry Rect="0,0,50,50" />
      </CombinedGeometry.Geometry1>
      <CombinedGeometry.Geometry2>
        <EllipseGeometry Center="50,25" RadiusX="30" RadiusY="10" />
      </CombinedGeometry.Geometry2>
    </CombinedGeometry>
  </Path.Data>
</Path>
```

Figure 13-31 shows the results of Examples 13-24 and 13-25. Whereas the GeometryGroup has resulted in a shape with multiple figures (taking the default fill rule into account), the CombinedGeometry has produced a single figure. The ellipse geometry has taken a bite out of the rectangle geometry. This is just one of the ways in which geometries can be combined. The GeometryCombineMode property determines which is used, and Figure 13-32 shows all four available modes.

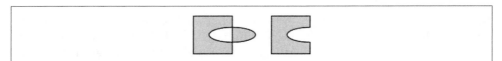

Figure 13-31. Grouping and combining geometries

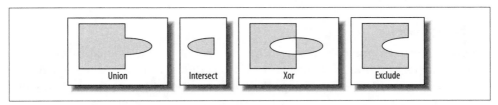

Figure 13-32. Combine modes: Union, Intersect, Xor, and Exclude

Union builds a shape in which any point that was inside either of the two original shapes will also be inside the new shape. Intersect creates a shape where only points that were inside both shapes will be in the new shape. Xor creates a shape where points that were in one shape or the other, but not both, will be in the new shape. Exclude creates a shape where points inside the first shape but not inside the second will be included.

Path geometry text format

We have now looked at all of the features that Path has to offer. As you have seen, we can end up with some pretty verbose markup. Fortunately, there is a shorthand mechanism that allows us to exploit most of the features we have seen without having to type quite so much.

So far, we have been setting the Data property using XAML's property element syntax. (See Appendix A for more details on this syntax.) However, we can supply a string instead. Example 13-26 shows both techniques. As you can see, the string form is some 12 lines shorter.

Example 13-26. Path.Data as text

```
<!-- Longhand -->

<Path Fill="Cyan" Stroke="Black">
  <Path.Data>
    <PathGeometry>
      <PathGeometry.Figures>
        <PathFigure StartPoint="0,0" IsClosed="True">
          <LineSegment Point="50,0" />
          <LineSegment Point="50,50" />
          <LineSegment Point="0,50" />
        </PathFigure>
      </PathGeometry.Figures>
    </PathGeometry>
  </Path.Data>
</Path>


<!-- Shorthand -->

<Path Fill="Cyan" Stroke="Black" Data="M 0,0 L 50,0 50,50 0,50 Z" />
```

The syntax for the text form of the Path.Data property is simple. The string must contain a sequence of commands. A command is a letter followed by some numeric parameters. The number of parameters required is determined by the chosen command. Lines require just a coordinate pair. Curves require more data.

If you omit the letter, the same command will be used as last time. For instance, Example 13-26 uses the L command—this is short for *Line,* and it represents a LineSegment. This requires only two numbers: the coordinates of the line end point. And yet, in our example, there are six numbers. This simply indicates that there are three lines in a row. Table 13-5 lists the commands, their equivalent segment types where applicable, and their usage.

Table 13-5. Path.Data commands

Command	Command name	Segment type	Parameters
M (or m)	Move		Coordinate pair: the StartPoint for a new PathFigure
L (or l)	Line	LineSegment	Coordinate pair: end point
H (or h)	Horizontal line	LineSegment	Single coordinate: end x coordinate (y coordinate will be the same as before)
V (or v)	Vertical line	LineSegment	Single coordinate: end y coordinate (x coordinate will be the same as before)
C (or c)	Cubic Bézier curve	BezierSegment	Three coordinate pairs: two control points and one end point
Q (or q)	Quadratic Bézier curve	QuadraticBezierSegment	Two coordinate pairs: control point and end point
S (or s)	Smooth Bézier curve	BezierSegment	Two coordinate pairs: second control point and end point (first control point generated automatically)
T (or t)	Smooth quadratic Bézier curve	QuadraticBezierSegment	One coordinate pair: end point (control point generated automatically)
A (or a)	Elliptical arc	ArcSegment	Seven numbers: x radius, y radius, RotationAngle, IsLargeArc, SweepDirection, and end point coordinate pair
Z (or z)	Close path		None
F0	Even-odd fill rule		None
F1	Nonzero fill rule		None

The commands M, Z, F0, and F1 do not correspond to segments. The M command causes a new PathFigure to be started, enabling multiple figures to be represented in this compact text format. Z sets the current figure's IsClosed property to true. F0 and F1 set the FillRule of the PathGeometry.

Notice that there are two ways to specify a BezierSegment. The C command lets you provide all of the control points. The S command generates the first control point for you—it looks at the preceding segment and makes the first control point a mirror image of the preceding one. This ensures that the segment's tangent aligns with the preceding segment's tangent, resulting in a smooth join between the lines.

Quadratic Bézier segments have a similar facility: the Q command lets you specify the control point, whereas the T command generates the control point for you in a way that guarantees a smooth line.

You can specify any of these commands in either uppercase or lowercase. In the uppercase form, coordinates are relative to the position of the Path element. If the command is lowercase, the coordinates are taken to be relative to the end point of the preceding segment in the path.

As well as being offered for the Path.Data property, this path syntax can also be used directly with a PathGeometry—its Figures property supports the same syntax. Another geometry type also supports this mini path language: StreamGeometry. This geometry type can represent all the same shapes as a PathGeometry, but you cannot modify it once it has been created. This is because it does not support the object model of path figures and segments—from markup, it only supports the path syntax. (If you are using code, you also can build a StreamGeometry with a StreamGeometryContext object, which lets you describe the shape with a series of method calls.)

Because a StreamGeometry is immutable and because it does not maintain a tree of objects representing the shape, it can use a more efficient internal representation than a PathGeometry. If you are working with very complex shapes, or a large number of shapes, this can significantly improve performance. If you are using XAML in such scenarios, you should prefer the path syntax over the object tree, because when you set Path.Data with the path syntax, WPF creates a StreamGeometry instead of a PathGeometry.

We have now examined all of the shapes on offer. However, not all visuals are best represented with scalable shapes—sometimes we need to work with bitmap images.

Bitmaps

WPF supports bitmaps in any of the following formats:[*] BMP, JPEG, PNG, TIFF, Windows Media Photo, GIF, and ICO (Windows icon files). You can use any image format to create a brush with which to paint any shape or text, as discussed later in the "ImageBrush" section of this chapter. The System.Windows.Media.Imaging namespace provides classes that let you work with the pixels and metadata of image files. However, the simplest way to use a bitmap is with the Image element.

---

[*] The imaging system is extensible, so it's possible to add support for custom formats. This requires unmanaged COM components to be written, and is beyond the scope of this book. See *http://msdn2.microsoft.com/en-us/library/ms737408.aspx* (*http://tinysells.com/111*) for information about the API for extending WPF imaging.

Image

Image simply displays an image. It derives from `FrameworkElement`, so you can place it anywhere in the visual tree, and it obeys the normal layout rules. You tell it what image to display by setting its `Source` property, as shown in Example 13-27.

Example 13-27. Image element

```
<Image Source="http://www.interact-sw.co.uk/images/M3/BackOfM3.jpeg" />
```

Setting the `Source` property to an absolute URL causes the image to be downloaded and displayed. Alternatively, if you embed an image file in your application as a resource, as described in Chapter 12, you can refer to it with a relative URL, as Example 13-28 illustrates.

Example 13-28. Using an image resource

```
<Image Source="/MyEmbeddedImage.jpeg" />
```

The Image element is able to resize the image. The exact behavior depends on your application's layout. If your layout permits the Image element to size to content, it will show the image at its natural size. (We discussed sizing to content in Chapter 3.) For example, the Canvas panel never imposes a particular size on its children, so the code in Example 13-29 will display the image at its native size.

Example 13-29. Showing an image at its natural size

```
<Canvas>
  <Image Source="/MyEmbeddedImage.jpeg" />
</Canvas>
```

However, if your layout provides the Image element with a specific amount of space, by default the bitmap will be scaled to fill that space. A window's content is constrained by the size of the window, so Example 13-30 will enlarge or reduce the image to fill the window.

Example 13-30. Scaling an image to fill the available space

```
<Window xmlns="http://schemas.microsoft.com/winfx/2006/xaml/presentation">
  <Image Source="http://www.interact-sw.co.uk/images/M3/BackOfM3.jpeg" />
</Window>
```

The default scaling behavior is to use the same scale factor horizontally and vertically. If the available space is the wrong shape for the image, it will be made as large as possible without being too large in either dimension. Figure 13-33 shows the result of Example 13-30, and even though the Image element fills the whole window, the window's white background is visible above and below when the window is too tall, or to the left and right where the window is too wide.

Figure 13-33. Uniform stretching

Images with a transparency channel are handled correctly—whatever is behind the image is visible through the transparent parts of the bitmap.

If you want the image to fill all of the space even when it is the wrong shape, you can set the element's Stretch property. This defaults to Uniform, but Fill or UniformToFill will cause the image to fill the full space. These values mean exactly the same as they do for the Shape types—Shape and Image use the same Stretch enumeration type. So, as Figure 13-34 shows, Fill will distort the image if necessary to make it fit, whereas UniformToFill scales uniformly and then crops if required.

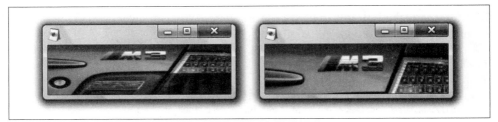

Figure 13-34. Fill (left) and UniformToFill (right)

The examples we've seen so far set the Image element's Source property with a URL. In fact, the Source property's type is ImageSource. XAML automatically uses the appropriate type converter to turn the URL into an ImageSource, but when working in code, you will use image source objects directly.

ImageSource

ImageSource is an abstract base class used throughout WPF to represent an image. Not only does the Image element's Source property use this type, but so do the ImageBrush class and the visual layer's DrawingContext.DrawImage method, both of which are described later.

Two classes derive from ImageSource: DrawingImage and BitmapSource. DrawingImage has nothing to do with bitmaps—it wraps a resolution-independent drawing object. (Drawings are described later.) This means that elements capable of using an image source can work with either resolution-independent drawings or bitmaps. But because we're looking at bitmaps right now, BitmapSource is the more interesting class. It too is abstract. Table 13-6 lists the derived concrete bitmap source types.

Table 13-6. BitmapSource types

Type	Usage
BitmapFrame	A single frame from a bitmap file (some file formats support multiple frames).
BitmapImage	Represents a bitmap at a specified URL; this is the type created when specifying a URL in XAML.
CachedBitmap	Wraps around any BitmapSource and caches it.
ColorConvertedBitmap	Wraps around any BitmapSource and converts it from one color space to another.
CroppedBitmap	Wraps around any BitmapSource and presents a cropped version.
FormatConvertedBitmap	Wraps around any BitmapSource and generates a copy with a different pixel format (e.g., grayscale).
RenderTargetBitmap	A bitmap whose contents are generated from a Visual.
TransformedBitmap	Wraps around any BitmapSource and presents a scaled and/or rotated copy.
WriteableBitmap	A bitmap whose contents can be modified at runtime.

BitmapImage is the simplest to use of these sources. You can give it a URL just as you would in XAML, as shown in Example 13-31.

Example 13-31. Using BitmapImage

```
Image imageElement = new Image();
imageElement.Source = new BitmapImage(new Uri(
  "http://www.nasa.gov/images/content/136054main_bm_072004.jpg"));
```

As you can see from Table 13-6, many of the bitmap source types are wrappers around other bitmap sources. You can chain sources together to perform operations such as rotation and cropping. This chaining model is used because you are often not able to modify the original image in any way—it might be compiled into your application as a resource, or it might live on an external web site. It might seem that the obvious way to handle this would be to load a bitmap and then modify it. However, this is at odds with how images are normally handled. In-memory copies are typically transient—WPF does not cache images unless you explicitly tell it to, either by using CachedBitmap or by setting the CacheOptions property of a BitmapImage.

That's not to say you can't use a load-then-modify approach; it's just that it's not necessary for cropping, transformation, color conversion, or pixel format conversion. Indeed, the chaining approach offers some advantages. For example, suppose you were writing an application that showed an image and allowed the user to crop it interactively. If you were cropping the image by modifying it, you'd need to keep a copy of the original around just in case the user decided he had cropped a little too much and wanted to go back. If you crop by chaining, say, a `BitmapImage` to a `CroppedBitmap`, you never modify the original image, so resetting the cropping is easy. (It's also more efficient—where possible, WPF avoids generating a copy, and just applies cropping or transformations as it renders.)

Sometimes building or modifying bitmaps at runtime is necessary. For example, maybe you want to do something to the image that you cannot achieve by chaining together the built-in image sources, or perhaps you need to build a brand-new image from scratch. `RenderTargetBitmap` and `WriteableBitmap` enable you to construct your own bitmaps either from scratch or by modifying a copy of an existing bitmap.

Creating Bitmaps

`RenderTargetBitmap` lets you create a new a bitmap from any visual. Example 13-32 renders a red ellipse into a bitmap.

Example 13-32. Using RenderTargetBitmap

```
RenderTargetBitmap bmp = new RenderTargetBitmap(
    300, 150,      // Dimensions in physical pixels
    300, 300,      // Pixel resolution (dpi)
    PixelFormats.Pbgra32);

Ellipse e = new Ellipse();
e.Fill = Brushes.Red;
e.Measure(new Size(96, 48));
e.Arrange(new Rect(0, 0, 96, 48));

bmp.Render(e);
```

You can choose any resolution you like for the output—in this case, we're creating a 300 dpi bitmap that's 1 inch wide and 0.5 inches high. Of course, WPF's coordinate system is resolution-independent—a device-independent pixel is always 1/96 of an inch regardless of the output resolution, so we make the ellipse's size 96×48 device-independent pixels in order to fill the bitmap.

 Although the `RenderTargetBitmap` constructor takes a parameter of type `PixelFormat`, it can create images in the `Pbgra32` format only. If you specify anything other than that or `PixelFormats.Default`, it will throw an exception. `Pbrga32` is a 32-bit-per-pixel format, with a pre-multiplied alpha channel.

Example 13-32 renders just one element, but because you can pass any visual, you are free to pass elements that have children, such as Grid and Canvas, enabling you to render multiple elements. However, there are two things to be aware of:

- If the visual is not already a visible part of a UI, it is your responsibility to call Measure and Arrange so that it knows how big it needs to be. The generated bitmap will be empty if you fail to do this.

- If you create a standalone visual with no parent, as Example 13-32 does, controls will not pick up their default styles and will be invisible. Consequently, only primitive elements such as Ellipse or TextBlock will appear. If you want to generate a bitmap of a UI, showing the UI in a real window before passing it to the Render method will fix this.

RenderTargetBitmap lets you build a bitmap out of any combination of WPF visuals. This provides a way to modify existing bitmaps. For example, if you want to overlay a text caption onto a bitmap, you could create a Grid containing an Image element displaying the original image, as well as a TextBlock containing the caption, and pass the Grid to the Render method, as shown in Example 13-33.

Example 13-33. Adding a caption to a bitmap

```
BitmapImage originalBmp = new BitmapImage( );
originalBmp.BeginInit( );
originalBmp.UriSource = new Uri(
    "http://www.interact-sw.co.uk/images/M3/BackOfM3.jpeg");
originalBmp.DownloadCompleted += delegate {
    Grid rootGrid = new Grid( );
    Image img = new Image();
    img.Source = originalBmp;
    rootGrid.Children.Add(img);
    TextBlock caption = new TextBlock();
    caption.Text = "Ian's car";
    caption.FontSize = 35;
    caption.Foreground = Brushes.White;
    caption.Background = new SolidColorBrush(Color.FromArgb(128, 0, 0, 0));
    caption.VerticalAlignment = VerticalAlignment.Bottom;
    caption.HorizontalAlignment = HorizontalAlignment.Center;
    caption.Margin = new Thickness(5);
    caption.Padding = new Thickness(5);
    caption.TextAlignment = TextAlignment.Center;
    caption.textWrapping = TextWrapping.Wrap;
    rootGrid.Children.Add(caption)

    RenderTargetBitmap bmp = newRenderTargetBitmap(
        originalBmp.PixelWidth, originalBmp.PixelHeight,
        originalBmp.DpiX, originalBmp.DpiY, PixelFormats.Pbgra32);
    rootGrid.Measure(new Size(originalBmp.Width, originalBmp.Height));
    rootGrid.Arrange(new Rect(0, 0, originalBmp.Width, originalBmp.Height));
    bmp.render(rootGrid);
```

Example 13-33. Adding a caption to a bitmap (continued)

```
    // bmp now ready for use
    ...
};
originalBmp.EndInit();
```

This brings to the surface something that was not previously evident: bitmaps are downloaded from the Web in the background. Normally this isn't a problem—if you connect a `BitmapImage` directly into an `Image` or `ImageBrush`, WPF automatically updates the display once the image is available. However, we're now trying to build a new image based on the original, so we must wait for the original image to arrive before we start. This is why most of the work is done in the `BitmapImage` object's `DownloadCompleted` event handler.

Example 13-33 does not modify the original bitmap file—in this case, it's up on a public web server, so there's no way the code could change it. Instead, the newly created `RenderTargetBitmap` contains the modified image. Figure 13-35 shows how it looks. (If you want to write the modified image out to disk, we'll see how to do that shortly.)

Figure 13-35. Bitmap modified with caption

`RenderTargetBitmap` is great if you want to build or modify a bitmap using WPF elements. However, if you want to work with raw pixel data, `WriteableBitmap` is a better choice. Example 13-34 uses this technique to invert all of the colors in a bitmap to form a negative image—something you could not do with a `RenderTargetBitmap`.

Example 13-34. Modifying pixels

```
BitmapImage originalBmp = new BitmapImage();
originalBmp.BeginInit();
originalBmp.UriSource = new Uri(
    "http://www.interact-sw.co.uk/images/M3/BackOfM3.jpeg");
originalBmp.DownloadCompleted += delegate {

    BitmapSource prgbaSource = new FormatConvertedBitmap(originalBmp,
                               PixelFormats.Pbgra32, null, 0);
    WriteableBitmap bmp = new WriteableBitmap(prgbaSource);
```

Example 13-34. Modifying pixels (continued)

```
    int w = bmp.PixelWidth;
    int h = bmp.PixelHeight;
    int[] pixelData = new int[w * h];
    int widthInBytes = 4 * w;

    bmp.CopyPixels(pixelData, widthInBytes, 0);
    for (int i = 0; i < pixelData.Length; ++i) {
        pixelData[i] ^= 0x00ffffff;
    }
    bmp.WritePixels(new Int32Rect(0, 0, w, h),
        pixelData, widthInBytes, 0);


    // bmp now ready for use
    ...
};

originalBmp.EndInit();
```

As before, the code waits until the image has been downloaded before proceeding. Once the image is available, the first thing the code does is ensure that the pixel data will be available in the format our code expects by wrapping the original in a FormatConvertedBitmap. If the original image uses a different pixel format, this will convert it for us.

Next, we load the results into a WriteableBitmap. We read out the pixel values using CopyPixels. CopyPixels is not unique to WriteableBitmap—you can read pixel values from any bitmap source—but only WriteableBitmap offers a WritePixels method to change the image. After we've flipped the bits of the red, green, and blue channels of the pixel, we use WritePixels to put these modified pixels back into the bitmap. Finally, we can use the WriteableBitmap as an image source—for example, we could set it as an Image element's Source property. Figure 13-36 shows the resulting negative image.

Figure 13-36. Bitmap with inverted colors

If you are generating bitmaps with either WriteableBitmap or RenderTargetBitmap, you may not want to put the results on-screen—you might want to write them out to disk. You can do this with a bitmap encoder.

Bitmap Encoders and Decoders

A *bitmap encoder* is a class that knows how to generate a bitmap stream in a particular format. WPF provides encoders for all the image formats listed earlier. Encoders are named after their format (e.g., `PngBitmapEncoder`, `JpegBitmapEncoder`, etc.).

Example 13-35 shows how to write a bitmap out to disk as a JPEG file. This function works with any `BitmapSource`.

Example 13-35. Creating a JPEG file

```
static void WriteJpeg(string fileName, int quality, BitmapSource bmp) {

    JpegBitmapEncoder encoder = new JpegBitmapEncoder( );
    BitmapFrame outputFrame = BitmapFrame.Create(bmp);
    encoder.Frames.Add(outputFrame);
    encoder.QualityLevel = quality;

    using (FileStream file = File.OpenWrite(fileName)) {
        encoder.Save(file);
    }
}
```

Decoders work in the opposite direction—they know how to read bitmap streams of a particular format. Decoders are used implicitly whenever you load a bitmap stream into a `BitmapImage`, but you can also use them explicitly. This is necessary if you wish to access bitmap metadata or retrieve all the frames in a multiframe image file.

Example 13-36 shows how to load a JPEG image with a decoder to discover the type of camera used to take the image.

Example 13-36. Reading bitmap metadata

```
static string GetCamera(string myJpegPath) {
    JpegBitmapDecoder decoder = new JpegBitmapDecoder(new Uri(myJpegPath),
        BitmapCreateOptions.None, BitmapCacheOption.None);
    BitmapMetadata bmpData = (BitmapMetadata) decoder.Frames[0].Metadata;
    return bmpData.CameraModel;
}
```

Notice that both the encoder and the decoder have a property called `Frames` to represent the frames of the image. For single-frame formats, this cannot contain more than one frame, but an animated GIF would contain multiple frames.

 Metadata is returned only at the level of individual frames. The decoder classes all offer a `Metadata` property, but it is always null for all of the decoders that ship as part of the first release of WPF. Use the `Metadata` property of the frame instead.

There is one last bitmap feature we will examine. It is a little different from the rest, because it allows bitmap processing to be applied to any part of the UI, not just bitmaps.

Bitmap Effects

All user interface elements have a `BitmapEffects` property. You can use it to apply a visual effect to the element and all of its children. All of these effects use bitmap processing algorithms, hence the name. Example 13-37 applies a `BlurBitmapEffect` to one of its `StackPanel` elements.

Example 13-37. Bitmap effect

```
<StackPanel Orientation="Horizontal">
  <StackPanel Orientation="Vertical">
    <TextBlock Text="Abcdef" TextAlignment="Center" FontWeight="Bold" />
    <RadioButton Content="Better in position 1?" GroupName="r" />
  </StackPanel>
  <StackPanel Orientation="Vertical" Margin="10,0">
    <StackPanel.BitmapEffect>
      <BlurBitmapEffect Radius="1" />
    </StackPanel.BitmapEffect>
    <TextBlock Text="Abcdef" TextAlignment="Center" FontWeight="Bold" />
    <RadioButton Content="Or position 2?" GroupName="r" />
  </StackPanel>
</StackPanel>
```

As you can see in Figure 13-37, the righthand side is out of focus, thanks to the blur effect. Despite this, it's still live—as you can see, the radio button on the righthand side has been selected. Even if you made the panel completely illegible by cranking up the blur's `Radius` property to 10, the controls would continue to function because WPF's input handling completely ignores bitmap effects.

Figure 13-37. BlurBitmapEffect

Table 13-7 lists all of the built-in effects. It is possible to write custom effects, but this requires an unmanaged COM component to be written, and is beyond the scope of this book.*

---

* See *http://msdn2.microsoft.com/en-us/library/ms735322.aspx* (*http://tinysells.com/108*) for information on the API for building custom WPF bitmap effects.

Table 13-7. BitmapEffects

Type	Usage
BevelBitmapEffect	Creates a pseudo-3D relief effect at the edges of the content
BitmapEffectGroup	Allows multiple effects to be used on a single element
BlurBitmapEffect	Makes the image look out of focus
DropShadowBitmapEffect	Draws a soft shadow around the outline of the content
EmbossBitmapEffect	Performs a bump mapping algorithm to apply a pseudo-3D relief across the whole of the content
OuterGlowBitmapEffect	Adds a soft halo around the outline of the content

Bitmap effects are expensive. Use them sparingly.

To apply a bitmap effect, WPF must first render the content to which the effect will be applied, and then run the bitmap effect algorithm over the rendered content in order to generate the final results. This has two significant performance implications. First, it involves the creation of an *intermediate render target*—a block of memory in which to build the rendered content prior to processing. This increases memory usage. Second, many bitmap effects run in software. This in turn means that the content to which the effect is applied will be rendered in software.

Tempting though it may be, applying a bitmap effect to a large region (e.g., the whole window) is a very bad idea. It disables hardware rendering for the whole region, which is likely to reduce performance drastically.

So far, we've seen how to use bitmaps and define simple shapes, but we have been rather unadventurous in our choice of fills and outlines for our shapes. We have used nothing but standard named colors and simple outline styles. And although we've seen how to render bitmaps as standalone rectangles of content, we've not yet seen how we can combine bitmaps with shapes. So, it's time to look at how WPF's brush and pen classes enable more interesting drawing styles.

Brushes and Pens

To draw a shape on the screen, WPF needs to know how you would like that shape to be colored in and how its outline should be drawn. WPF provides several Brush types supporting a variety of painting styles. The Pen class extends this to provide information about stroke thickness, dash patterns, and the like.

In this section, we will look at all of the available brush types and the Pen class. However, because all brushes and pens are ultimately about deciding what colors to use where and how they are combined, we must first look at how colors are represented.

Color

WPF uses the Color structure in the System.Windows.Media namespace to represent a color. If you have worked with Windows Forms, ASP.NET, or GDI+ in the past, note that this is not the same structure as those technologies use. They use the Color structure in the System.Drawing namespace. WPF introduces this new Color structure because it can work with floating-point color values, enabling much higher color precision and greater flexibility.

The Color structure uses four numbers or "channels" to represent a color. These channels are red, green, blue, and alpha. Red, green, and blue channels are the traditional way of representing color in computer graphics. (This is because color screens work by adding these three primary colors together.) A value of 0 indicates that the color component is not present at all; 0 on all three channels corresponds to black. The alpha channel represents the level of opacity—a Color can be opaque, completely transparent, or anywhere in between these two extremes. WPF's composition engine allows anything to be drawn with any level of transparency. A value of 0 is used to represent complete transparency, and 1 means completely opaque.

Windows has traditionally used 24 bits of color information (8 bits per channel) to represent "true" or "full" color, and 32 bits for full color with transparency. This is just about sufficient for the average computer screen. The color and brightness range of most computer displays means that 24 bits of color has always been adequate (albeit barely) for most purposes, although a sufficiently good screen can reveal the limitations. However, for many imaging applications, this is not sufficient. For example, film can accommodate a much wider range of brightness than a computer screen, so 24-bit color is simply not good enough for graphics work with film as its output medium. The same is true for many medical imaging applications. And, even for computer or video images, 24-bit color can cause problems—if images are going through many stages of processing, these can amplify the limitations of 24-bit source material.

WPF therefore supports a much higher level of detail in its representation of color. Each color channel uses 16 bits instead of 8. The Color structure still supports the use of 8-bit channels where required, because a lot of imaging software depends on such a representation. Color exposes the 8-bit channels through the A, R, G, and B properties, which accept values in the range of 0–255.[*] The higher definition representations are available through the ScA, ScR, ScG, and ScB properties, which present the channels as single-precision floating-point values ranging from 0–1.

---

[*] The old GDI+ Color structure exposed 8-bit properties of the same names, which may be useful if you need to port code.

The "Sc" in the ScA, ScR, ScG, and ScB properties refers to the fact that these support the standard "Extended RGB colour space—scRGB" color space defined in the IEC 61966-2-2 specification. (This is an international specification, hence the *u* in *colour*.) Strangely, the *sc* is not officially short for anything. During its development, the scRGB spec went through various names. As is often the way with standards committees, various parties had objections to the names that made any sense, so they settled on something unobjectionable but meaningless.

Various post hoc theories as to what *sc* might stand for have been developed. One is that it is an abbreviation of *specular*, suggesting the high-headroom support offered by the out-of-gamut capability. Another theory is that it could be short for *standard compositing*, to indicate that the color space is designed for compositing rather than for physical devices. This same thinking informed the theory that it is short for *scene referred* (although one member of the standards committee maintains that this last theory is absolutely wrong).

The Color class also allows color values to go out of range. This can lead to counterintuitive color values where a particular color channel may be negative, or more than 100 percent. Even though this may seem to make no sense, it can be useful to accommodate excursions outside of the 0–1 range if you are performing several image processing steps. For example, suppose you want to increase the brightness but decrease the contrast of an image—the first step might take the brightness over 100 percent, but the second step could bring it back into range. As long as your final output values are within the 0–1 range, it doesn't necessarily matter where they went during image processing. However, if a color system is unable to accommodate out-of-range values, it must clip all colors to be within the valid range at every single stage. This range limiting can result in a degradation of image quality.

There is also a Colors class. This provides a set of standard named colors, with all the old favorites such as PapayaWhip, BurlyWood, LightGoldenrodYellow, and Brown.

You cannot use a Color directly for drawing. To draw, you need either a Brush or a Pen.

SolidColorBrush

SolidColorBrush is the simplest brush. It uses one color across the whole area being painted. It has just one property, Color. Note that this color is allowed to use transparency, despite what the word *Solid* suggests.

We have already been using the SolidColorBrush extensively even though we have not yet referred to it by name. This is because WPF creates this kind of brush if you specify the name of a color in markup—if you work mostly with XAML, you very rarely need to specify that you require a SolidColorBrush, because you'll get one by default. (The only reason you would normally specify it in full is if you want to use data binding with the brush's properties.) Consider this example:

```
<Rectangle Fill="Yellow" Width="100" Height="20" />
```

The XAML compiler will recognize *Yellow* as one of the standard named colors from the Colors class, and will supply a suitable SolidColorBrush. (See Appendix A for more information on how XAML maps from strings to property values.) It does not need to create the brush, because there is a Brushes class, providing a set of brushes for each of the named colors in Colors.

You will also be provided with a SolidColorBrush if your markup uses a numeric color value. Example 13-38 shows various examples of numeric colors. All but the last two begin with a # symbol and contain hexadecimal digits. A three-digit number is taken to be one digit each of red, green, and blue. A four-digit number is interpreted as alpha, red, green, and blue. These are compact formats providing just 4 bits per channel. Six- or eight-digit numbers allow 8 bits per channel for RGB or ARGB, respectively. To exploit the full accuracy of scRGB, you provide a string that starts with "sc#" followed by a space, and then four comma-separated decimal numbers representing the A, R, G, and B values. Finally, if the string starts with ContextColor, you can define a color that refers to a specific International Color Consortium (ICC) or Image Color Manager (ICM) color profile file.

Example 13-38. Numeric color values

```
<Rectangle Fill="#8f8"       Width="100" Height="20" />
<Rectangle Fill="#1168ff"    Width="50" Height="40" />
<Rectangle Fill="#8ff0"      Width="130" Height="10" />
<Rectangle Fill="#72ff8890" Width="70" Height="30" />
<Rectangle Fill="sc# 0.8,0.1442,0.429,0.94" Width="10" Height="20" />
<Rectangle Fill="ContextColor
file://C:/Windows/System32/spool/drivers/color/sRGB%20Color%20Space%20Profile.icm
 1.0,0.0,1.0,0.0" Width="10" Height="20" />
```

The SolidColorBrush is lightweight and straightforward. However, it makes for fairly flat-looking visuals. WPF offers some more interesting brushes if you want to make your user interface look a little more appealing.

LinearGradientBrush

With a LinearGradientBrush, the painted area transitions from one color to another, or even through a sequence of colors. Figure 13-38 shows a simple example.

Figure 13-38. LinearGradientBrush

This brush fades from black to white, starting at the top-left corner and finishing at the bottom-right corner. The fade always runs in a straight line—this brush cannot do curved transitions, hence the name "linear." Example 13-39 shows the markup for Figure 13-38.

Example 13-39. Using a LinearGradientBrush

```
<Rectangle Width="80" Height="60">
  <Rectangle.Fill>
    <LinearGradientBrush StartPoint="0,0" EndPoint="1,1">
      <GradientStop Color="Black" Offset="0" />
      <GradientStop Color="White" Offset="1" />
    </LinearGradientBrush>
  </Rectangle.Fill>
</Rectangle>
```

The StartPoint and EndPoint properties indicate where the color transition begins and ends. These coordinates are relative to the area being filled, so 0,0 is the top left and 1,1 is the bottom right, as shown in Figure 13-39. (Note that if the brush is painting an area that is narrow or wide, the coordinate system is squashed accordingly.) You are allowed to put the StartPoint and EndPoint outside of the rectangle. For example, you could change the StartPoint of Figure 13-39 to –1,0. This would mean that only half of the fill's color range would be used. This might seem pointless—setting the first gradient stop's color to a shade of gray would have the same effect. However, sometimes it's easier to tweak the look of a fill by adjusting the end points rather than by adjusting the colors.

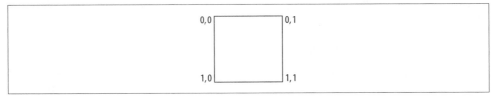

Figure 13-39. Fill coordinate system

Each GradientStop has an Offset property as well as a Color. This enables the fill to pass through multiple colors. Example 13-40 shows a LinearGradientBrush with multiple colors.

Example 13-40. Multiple gradient stops

```
<Rectangle Width="80" Height="60">
  <Rectangle.Fill>
    <LinearGradientBrush StartPoint="0,0" EndPoint="1,1">
      <GradientStop Color="Black" Offset="0" />
      <GradientStop Color="Orange" Offset="0.2" />
      <GradientStop Color="Red" Offset="0.4" />
      <GradientStop Color="Black" Offset="0.6" />
      <GradientStop Color="Blue" Offset="0.8" />
      <GradientStop Color="White" Offset="1" />
    </LinearGradientBrush>
  </Rectangle.Fill>
</Rectangle>
```

Figure 13-40 shows the result.

Figure 13-40. Multiple gradient stops (Color Plate 22)

LinearGradientBrush is often used to provide a feeling of depth to a user interface. Example 13-41 shows a typical example. It uses just two shapes—a pair of rounded Rectangle elements. (The Grid doesn't contribute directly to the appearance. It is there to make it easy to resize the graphic—changing the grid's Width and Height will cause both rectangles to resize appropriately.) The second rectangle's gradient fill fades from a partially transparent shade of white to a completely transparent color, which provides an interesting visual effect.

Example 13-41. Simulating lighting effects with linear fills

```
<Grid Width="80" Height="26">
  <Grid.RowDefinitions>
    <RowDefinition Height="2*" />
    <RowDefinition Height="*" />
  </Grid.RowDefinitions>

  <Rectangle Grid.RowSpan="2" RadiusX="13" RadiusY="13">
    <Rectangle.Fill>
      <LinearGradientBrush StartPoint="0,0" EndPoint="0,1">
        <GradientStop Color="Green" Offset="0" />
        <GradientStop Color="DarkGreen" Offset="1" />
      </LinearGradientBrush>
    </Rectangle.Fill>
    <Rectangle.Stroke>
      <LinearGradientBrush StartPoint="0,0" EndPoint="0,1">
        <GradientStop Color="Black" Offset="0" />
        <GradientStop Color="LightGray" Offset="1" />
      </LinearGradientBrush>
    </Rectangle.Stroke>
  </Rectangle>

  <Rectangle Margin="3,2" RadiusX="8" RadiusY="12">
    <Rectangle.Fill>
      <LinearGradientBrush StartPoint="0,0" EndPoint="0,1">
        <GradientStop Color="#dfff" Offset="0" />
        <GradientStop Color="#0fff" Offset="1" />
      </LinearGradientBrush>
    </Rectangle.Fill>
  </Rectangle>
</Grid>
```

Figure 13-41 shows the result. This is an extremely simple graphic, containing just two shapes. The use of gradient fills has added an impression of depth that these shapes would otherwise not have conveyed.

Figure 13-41. Simple lighting effects with linear fills (Color Plate 23)

RadialGradientBrush

RadialGradientBrush is very similar to LinearGradientBrush. Both transition through a series of colors. But whereas LinearGradientBrush paints these transitions in a straight line, the RadialGradientBrush fades from a starting point out to an elliptical boundary. This opens more opportunities for making your user interface appear less flat. Example 13-42 shows an example.

Example 13-42. Using a RadialGradientBrush

```
<Rectangle Width="200" Height="150">
  <Rectangle.Fill>
    <RadialGradientBrush Center="0.45,0.5" RadiusX="0.3" RadiusY="0.5"
                         GradientOrigin="0.25,0.4">
      <GradientStop Color="White" Offset="0" />
      <GradientStop Color="DarkBlue" Offset="1" />
    </RadialGradientBrush>
  </Rectangle.Fill>
</Rectangle>
```

The RadialGradientBrush takes a list of GradientStop objects to determine the colors that the fill runs through, just like LinearGradientBrush. This example uses the RadiusX and RadiusY properties to determine the size of the elliptical boundary, and the Center property to set the position of the ellipse. The values chosen here make the fill boundary fit entirely into the shape, as Figure 13-42 shows. The area of the shape that falls outside of this boundary is filled with the color of the final GradientStop. Notice that the focal point of the fill is to the left. This is because the GradientOrigin has been set. (By default, the focal point is in the center of the ellipse.)

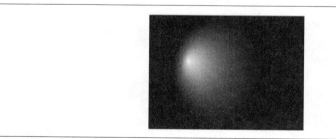

Figure 13-42. Simple radial fill (Color Plate 24)

Example 13-42 makes it easy to see the effects of the properties of the RadialGradientBrush, but it's not a very exciting example. Example 13-43 shows something a little more adventurous. It is similar to Example 13-41—both use a small number of shapes with gradient fills to convey a feeling of depth and reflection—but this example uses radial fills as well as a linear fill.

Example 13-43. Radial gradient fills

```
<Grid Width="16" Height="16" Margin="0,0,5,0" >
  <Grid.ColumnDefinitions>
    <ColumnDefinition Width="*" />
    <ColumnDefinition Width="10*" />
    <ColumnDefinition Width="*" />
  </Grid.ColumnDefinitions>

  <Grid.RowDefinitions>
    <RowDefinition Height="*" />
    <RowDefinition Height="20*" />
    <RowDefinition Height="6*" />
  </Grid.RowDefinitions>


  <Ellipse Grid.RowSpan="3" Grid.ColumnSpan="3" Margin="0.5">
    <Ellipse.Fill>
      <RadialGradientBrush Center="0.5,0.9" GradientOrigin="0.5,0.9"
                           RadiusX="0.7" RadiusY="0.5">
        <GradientStop Color="PaleGreen" Offset="0" />
        <GradientStop Color="Green" Offset="1" />
      </RadialGradientBrush>
    </Ellipse.Fill>
  </Ellipse>
  <Ellipse Grid.Row="1" Grid.Column="1">
    <Ellipse.Fill>
      <RadialGradientBrush Center="0.5,0.1" GradientOrigin="0.5,0.1"
                           RadiusX="0.7" RadiusY="0.5">
        <GradientStop Color="#efff" Offset="0" />
        <GradientStop Color="Transparent" Offset="1" />
      </RadialGradientBrush>
    </Ellipse.Fill>
  </Ellipse>
  <Ellipse Grid.RowSpan="3" Grid.ColumnSpan="3">
    <Ellipse.Stroke>
      <LinearGradientBrush StartPoint="0,0" EndPoint="0,1">
        <GradientStop Color="Gray" Offset="0" />
        <GradientStop Color="LightGray" Offset="1" />
      </LinearGradientBrush>
    </Ellipse.Stroke>
  </Ellipse>
</Grid>
```

This time, three ellipses have been used. Two have `RadialGradientBrush` fills, and one has a `LinearGradientBrush` stroke. The fill in the first ellipse creates the glow at the bottom of the drawing. The second adds the reflective highlight at the top. The third draws a bezel around the outside. Figure 13-43 shows the result. The radial fills suggest a curved surface and give the graphic a slightly translucent look.

Figure 13-43. Radial fills (Color Plate 25)

ImageBrush, DrawingBrush, and VisualBrush

The ability to fill shapes with a pattern or image of some kind is often useful. WPF provides three brushes that allow us to paint shapes with whatever graphics we choose. The ImageBrush lets us paint with a bitmap. With DrawingBrush, we use a scalable drawing. VisualBrush allows us to use any UI element as the brush image—we can in effect use one piece of our user interface to paint another.

All of these brushes have a certain amount in common, so they all derive from the same base class, TileBrush.

TileBrush

ImageBrush, DrawingBrush, and VisualBrush all paint using some form of source picture. Their base class, TileBrush, decides how to stretch the source image to fill the available space, whether to repeat (tile) the image, and how to position the image within the shape. TileBrush is an abstract base class, so you cannot use it directly. It exists to define the features common to the ImageBrush, DrawingBrush, and VisualBrush.

Figure 13-44 shows the default TileBrush behavior. This figure shows three rectangles so that you can see what happens when the brush is made narrow or wide, as well as how it looks when the brush shape matches the target area shape. All three are rectangles painted with an ImageBrush specifying just the image.

Figure 13-44. Default stretching and placement (Stretch.Fill)

The stretching behavior would be exactly the same for any of the tile brushes—we are using ImageBrush just as an example. Indeed, all the features discussed in this section apply to any TileBrush. Example 13-44 shows the markup used for each rectangle in Figure 13-44.

Example 13-44. Using an ImageBrush

```
<Rectangle>
  <Rectangle.Fill>
    <ImageBrush ImageSource="Images\Moggie.jpg" />
  </Rectangle.Fill>
</Rectangle>
```

Because this specifies nothing more than which image to display, it gets the default TileBrush behavior: the brush has stretched the source image to fill the available space. We can change this behavior by modifying the brush's Stretch property. It defaults to Fill, but we can show the image at its native size by specifying None, as Example 13-45 shows.

Example 13-45. Specifying a Stretch of None

```
<Rectangle>
  <Rectangle.Fill>
    <ImageBrush ImageSource="Images\Moggie.jpg" Stretch="None" />
  </Rectangle.Fill>
</Rectangle>
```

The None stretch mode preserves the aspect ratio, but if the image is too large, it will simply be cropped to fit the space available, as Figure 13-45 shows.

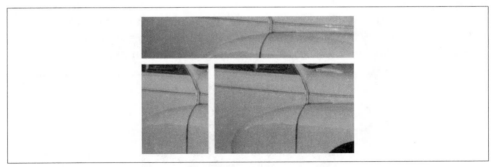

Figure 13-45. Stretch.None

For displaying images, you may want to stretch the image to match the available space without distorting the aspect ratio. TileBrush supports this with the Uniform stretch mode, shown in Figure 13-46. This scales the source image so that it fits entirely within the space available.

Figure 13-46. Stretch.Uniform

The `Uniform` stretch mode typically results in the image being made smaller than the area being filled, leaving the remainder of the space transparent. Alternatively, you can scale the image so that it completely fills the space available while preserving the aspect ratio, cropping in one dimension if necessary. The `UniformToFill` stretch mode does this, and it is shown in Figure 13-47.

Figure 13-47. Stretch.UniformToFill

`UniformToFill` is most appropriate if you are filling an area with some nonrepeating textured pattern, because it guarantees to paint the whole area. It is probably less appropriate if your goal is simply to display a picture—as Figure 13-47 shows, this stretch mode will crop images where necessary. If you want to show the whole picture, `Uniform` is the best choice.

All of the stretch modes except for `Fill` present an extra question: how should the image be positioned? With `None` and `UniformToFill`, cropping occurs, so WPF needs to decide which part of the image to show. With `Uniform`, the image may be smaller than the space being filled, so WPF needs to decide where to put it.

Images are centered by default. In the examples where the image has been cropped (Figures 13-45 and 13-47) the most central parts are shown. In the case of `Uniform`, where the image is smaller than the area being painted, it has been placed in the middle of that area (Figure 13-46). You can change this with the `AlignmentX` and

AlignmentY properties. You can set these to Left, Middle, or Right, and Top, Middle, or Bottom, respectively. Example 13-46 shows the UniformToFill stretch mode again, but this time with alignments of Left and Bottom. Figure 13-48 shows the results.

Example 13-46. Specifying a Stretch and alignment

```
<Rectangle>
  <Rectangle.Fill>
    <ImageBrush ImageSource="Images\Moggie.jpg" Stretch="UniformToFill"
                AlignmentX="Left" AlignmentY="Bottom" />
  </Rectangle.Fill>
</Rectangle>
```

Figure 13-48. Stretch.UniformToFill, bottom-left-aligned

The stretch and alignment properties are convenient to use, but they do not allow you to focus on any arbitrary part of the image, or choose specific scale factors. TileBrush supports these features through the Viewbox, Viewport, ViewboxUnits, and ViewportUnits properties.

The Viewbox property chooses the portion of the image to be displayed. By default, this property is set to encompass the whole image, but you can change it to focus on a particular part. Figure 13-49 shows the UniformToFill stretch mode, but with a Viewbox set to zoom in on the front of the car.

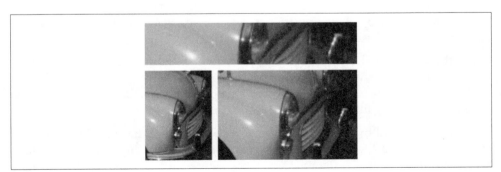

Figure 13-49. Stretch.UniformToFill with Viewbox

As Example 13-47 shows, the Viewbox is specified as four numbers. The first two are the coordinates of the upper-lefthand corner of the Viewbox; the second two are the width and height of the box. By default, coordinates of 1,1 represent the entire source image.

Example 13-47. Specifying a Viewbox

```
<ImageBrush Stretch="UniformToFill" Viewbox="0.75,0.42,0.25,0.34"
        ImageSource="Images\Moggie.jpg" />
```

Sometimes it can be more convenient to work in the coordinates of the source image itself. As Example 13-48 shows, you can do this by setting the ViewboxUnits property to Absolute. (It defaults to RelativeToBoundingBox.)

Example 13-48. Viewbox with absolute units

```
<ImageBrush Stretch="UniformToFill"
        ViewboxUnits="Absolute" Viewbox="593,250,200,200"
        ImageSource="Images\Moggie.jpg" />
```

In this case, because an ImageBrush is being used, these are coordinates in the source bitmap. In the case of a DrawingBrush or VisualBrush, the Viewbox would use the coordinate system of the source drawing.

Although the last two examples chose which portion of the source image to focus on by specifying a Viewbox, they still relied on the Stretch property to choose how to size and position the output. If you want more precise control, you can use Viewport to choose exactly where the image should end up in the brush.

Figure 13-50 illustrates the relationship between Viewbox and Viewport. On the left is the source image—a bitmap, in this case, but it could also be a drawing or visual tree. The Viewbox specifies an area of this source image. On the right is the brush. The Viewport specifies an area within this brush. WPF will scale and position the source image so that the area specified in Viewbox ends up being painted into the area specified by Viewport.

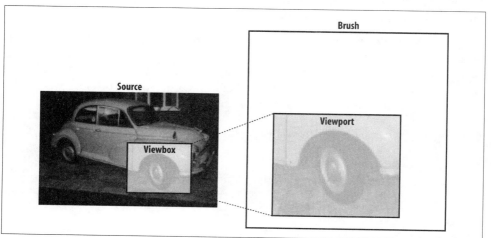

Figure 13-50. Viewbox and Viewport

As well as indicating where the contents of the Viewbox end up, the Viewport specifies the extent of the brush; it will be clipped to the size of the Viewport. Example 13-49 shows Viewport and Viewbox settings that correspond to the areas highlighted in Figure 13-50.

Example 13-49. Using Viewbox and Viewport

```
<ImageBrush ViewboxUnits="Absolute" Viewbox="380,285,308,243"
            Viewport="0.1,0.321,0.7, 0.557"
            ImageSource="Images\Moggie.jpg" />
```

Like the Viewbox, by default the Viewport coordinates range from 0–1. The position 0,0 is the top left of the brush, and 1,1 is the bottom right. This means that the part of the image shown by the brush will always be the same, regardless of the brush size or shape. This results in a distorting behavior similar to the default StretchMode of Fill, as shown in Figure 13-51. (In fact, the Fill stretch mode is equivalent to setting the Viewbox and Viewport to be 0,0,1,1.)

Figure 13-51. Viewbox and Viewport

As with the Viewbox, you can specify different units for the Viewport. The ViewportUnits property defaults to RelativeToBoundingBox, but if you change it to Absolute, the Viewport is measured using output coordinates. Note that setting the Viewport in absolute units means the image will no longer scale as the brush resizes.

In several of the preceding examples, the source image has not completely filled the area of the brush. By default, the brush is transparent in the remaining space. However, if you have specified a Viewport, you can choose other behaviors for the spare space with the TileMode property. The default is None, but if you specify Tile, as Example 13-50 does, the image will be repeated to fill the space available.

Example 13-50. Specifying a Stretch and a TileMode

```
<Rectangle>
  <Rectangle.Fill>
    <ImageBrush ImageSource="Images\Moggie.jpg"
                Viewport="0,0,100,100" ViewportUnits="Absolute"
                TileMode="Tile" />
  </Rectangle.Fill>
</Rectangle>
```

Figure 13-52 shows the effect of the Tile tile mode. There is one potential problem with tiling. It can often be very obvious where each repeated tile starts. If your goal is simply to fill in an area with a texture, these discontinuities can jar somewhat. To alleviate this, TileBrush supports three other modes of tiling: FlipX, FlipY, and FlipXY. These mirror alternate images as shown in Figure 13-53. Although mirroring can reduce the discontinuity between tiles, for some source images it can change the look of the brush quite substantially. Flipping is typically better suited to more uniform texture-like images than pictures.

Figure 13-52. Tiling

Figure 13-53. FlipXY tiling

Remember that all of this scaling and positioning functionality is common to all of the brushes derived from TileBrush. However, some features are specific to the individual brush types, so we will now look at each in turn.

ImageBrush

ImageBrush paints areas of the screen using a bitmap. The ImageBrush was used to create all of the pictures in the preceding section. This brush is straightforward—you simply need to tell it what bitmap to use with the ImageSource property, as Example 13-51 shows.

Example 13-51. Using an ImageBrush

```
<Rectangle>
  <Rectangle.Fill>
    <ImageBrush ImageSource="Images\Moggie.jpg" />
  </Rectangle.Fill>
</Rectangle>
```

To make a bitmap file available to the ImageBrush, you can add one to your project in Visual Studio. The file in Example 13-51 was in a subdirectory of the project called Images, and was built into the project as a resource. To do this, select the bitmap file in Visual Studio's Solution Explorer and then, in the Properties panel, make sure the Build Action property is set to Resource. This embeds the bitmap into the executable, enabling the ImageBrush to find it at runtime. (See Chapter 12 for more information on how binary resources are managed.) Alternatively, you can specify an absolute URL for this property—you could, for example, display an image from a web site.[*]

 ImageBrush is quite happy to deal with images with a transparency channel (also known as an alpha channel). Not all image formats support partial transparency, but some—such as the PNG, WMP, and BMP formats—can. (And, to a lesser extent, GIF. It supports only fully transparent or fully opaque pixels. This is effectively a 1-bit alpha channel.) Where an alpha channel is present, the ImageBrush will honor it.

DrawingBrush

The ImageBrush is convenient if you have a bitmap you need to paint with. However, bitmaps do not fit in well with resolution independence. The ImageBrush will scale bitmaps correctly for your screen's resolution, but bitmaps tend to become blurred when scaled. DrawingBrush does not suffer from this problem, because you usually provide a scalable vector image as its source. This enables a DrawingBrush to remain clear and sharp at any size and resolution.

The vector image is represented by a Drawing object. This is an abstract base class. You can draw shapes with a GeometryDrawing—this allows you to construct drawings using all of the same geometry elements supported by Path. You can also use bitmaps and video with ImageDrawing and VideoDrawing. Text is supported with GlyphRunDrawing. Finally, you can combine these using the DrawingGroup.

Even if you use nothing but shapes, you will still probably want to group the shapes with a DrawingGroup. Each GeometryDrawing is effectively equivalent to a single Path, so if you want to draw using different pens and brushes, or if you want your shapes to overlap rather than combine, you will need to use multiple GeometryDrawing elements.

---

[*] If you don't use an absolute URL, a property of type ImageSource will be treated as a relative *pack URI*. So, the image in Example 13-51 is handled as a relative pack URI, which resolves to a resource compiled into the component. Pack URIs and resources were described in Chapter 12.

Example 13-52 shows a Rectangle that uses a DrawingBrush for its Fill. This brush paints the same visuals seen earlier in Figure 13-41. Because each rectangular element that makes up the drawing uses different linear gradient fills, they both get their own GeometryDrawing, nested inside a DrawingGroup.

Example 13-52. Using DrawingBrush

```
<Rectangle Width="80" Height="30">
  <Rectangle.Fill>
    <DrawingBrush>
      <DrawingBrush.Drawing>
        <DrawingGroup>
          <DrawingGroup.Children>
            <GeometryDrawing>
              <GeometryDrawing.Brush>
                <LinearGradientBrush StartPoint="0,0" EndPoint="0,1">
                  <GradientStop Color="Green" Offset="0" />
                  <GradientStop Color="DarkGreen" Offset="1" />
                </LinearGradientBrush>
              </GeometryDrawing.Brush>

              <GeometryDrawing.Pen>
                <Pen Thickness="0.02">
                  <Pen.Brush>
                    <LinearGradientBrush StartPoint="0,0" EndPoint="0,1">
                      <GradientStop Color="Black" Offset="0" />
                      <GradientStop Color="LightGray" Offset="1" />
                    </LinearGradientBrush>
                  </Pen.Brush>
                </Pen>
              </GeometryDrawing.Pen>
              <GeometryDrawing.Geometry>
                <RectangleGeometry RadiusX="0.2" RadiusY="0.5"
                                Rect="0.02,0.02,0.96,0.96" />
              </GeometryDrawing.Geometry>
            </GeometryDrawing>

            <GeometryDrawing>
              <GeometryDrawing.Brush>
                <LinearGradientBrush StartPoint="0,0" EndPoint="0,1">
                  <GradientStop Color="#dfff" Offset="0" />
                  <GradientStop Color="#0fff" Offset="1" />
                </LinearGradientBrush>
              </GeometryDrawing.Brush>
              <GeometryDrawing.Geometry>
                <RectangleGeometry RadiusX="0.1" RadiusY="0.5"
                                Rect="0.1,0.07,0.8,0.5" />
              </GeometryDrawing.Geometry>
            </GeometryDrawing>
          </DrawingGroup.Children>
        </DrawingGroup>
      </DrawingBrush.Drawing>
    </DrawingBrush>
  </Rectangle.Fill>
</Rectangle>
```

With a `DrawingBrush`, the `Viewbox` defaults to 0,0,1,1. All of the coordinates and sizes in Example 13-52 are relative to this coordinate system. If you would prefer to work with coordinates over a wider range, you can simply set the `Viewbox` to the range you require, and the `ViewboxUnits` to `Absolute`. We already saw how to use the `Viewbox` in Example 13-47. The only difference with `DrawingBrush` is that you're using it to indicate an area of the drawing, rather than a bitmap.

Note that we can use the `Viewbox` to focus on some subsection of the picture, just as we did earlier with the `ImageBrush`. We can modify the `DrawingBrush` in Example 13-52 to use a smaller `Viewbox`, as shown in Example 13-53.

Example 13-53. Viewbox and DrawingBrush

```
<DrawingBrush Viewbox="0.5,0,0.5,0.25">
```

The result of this is that most of the drawing is now outside of the `Viewbox`, so the brush shows only a part of the whole drawing, as Figure 13-54 shows.

Figure 13-54. DrawingBrush with small Viewbox

`DrawingBrush` is very powerful, as it lets you use more or less any graphics you like as a brush, and because it is vector-based, the results remain crisp at any scale. It does have one drawback if you are using it from markup, though: it is somewhat cumbersome to use from XAML. Consider that Example 13-52 produces the same appearance as Example 13-41, but these examples are 48 lines long and 30 lines long, respectively.

The `DrawingBrush` is much more verbose because it requires us to work with geometry objects rather than higher-level constructs such as the `Grid` or `Rectangle` used in Example 13-41. (Note that this problem is less acute when using this brush from code, where the higher-level objects are not much more convenient to use than geometries. The verbosity is really only a XAML issue.) Moreover, higher-level features such as the ability to exploit layout or controls are not available in a `DrawingBrush`. Fortunately, `VisualBrush` allows us to paint with these higher-level elements.

VisualBrush

The `VisualBrush` can paint with the contents of any element derived from `Visual`. Because `Visual` is the base class of all WPF user interface elements, this means that in practice, you can plug any markup you like into a `VisualBrush`. The brush is "live" in that if the brush's source visual changes, anything painted with the brush will automatically update.

Example 13-54 shows a `Rectangle` filled using a `VisualBrush`. The brush's visuals have been copied directly from Example 13-41, resulting in a much simpler brush than the equivalent `DrawingBrush`. (The results look exactly the same as Figure 13-41—the whole point of the `VisualBrush` is that it paints areas to look just like the visuals it wraps.)

Example 13-54. Using a VisualBrush

```
<Rectangle Width="80" Height="30">
  <Rectangle.Fill>
    <VisualBrush>
      <VisualBrush.Visual>
        <Grid Width="80" Height="26">
          <Grid.RowDefinitions>
            <RowDefinition Height="2*" />
            <RowDefinition Height="*" />
          </Grid.RowDefinitions>
          <Rectangle Grid.RowSpan="2" RadiusX="13" RadiusY="13">
            <Rectangle.Fill>
              <LinearGradientBrush StartPoint="0,0" EndPoint="0,1">
                <GradientStop Color="Green" Offset="0" />
                <GradientStop Color="DarkGreen" Offset="1" />
              </LinearGradientBrush>
            </Rectangle.Fill>
            <Rectangle.Stroke>
              <LinearGradientBrush StartPoint="0,0" EndPoint="0,1">
                <GradientStop Color="Black" Offset="0" />
                <GradientStop Color="LightGray" Offset="1" />
              </LinearGradientBrush>
            </Rectangle.Stroke>
          </Rectangle>

          <Rectangle Margin="3,2" RadiusX="8" RadiusY="12">
            <Rectangle.Fill>
              <LinearGradientBrush StartPoint="0,0" EndPoint="0,1">
                <GradientStop Color="#dfff" Offset="0" />
                <GradientStop Color="#0fff" Offset="1" />
              </LinearGradientBrush>
            </Rectangle.Fill>
          </Rectangle>

        </Grid>
      </VisualBrush.Visual>
    </VisualBrush>
  </Rectangle.Fill>
</Rectangle>
```

You might be wondering why on earth you would ever use a DrawingBrush when VisualBrush is so much more flexible—VisualBrush can support any element, whereas DrawingBrush supports only the low-level Drawing and Geometry classes. However, DrawingBrush is more efficient. A drawing doesn't carry the overhead of a full FrameworkElement for every drawing primitive. Although it takes more effort to create a DrawingBrush, it consumes fewer resources at runtime. If you want your user interface to have particularly intricate visuals, the DrawingBrush will enable you to do this with lower overhead. If you plan to use animation, this low overhead may translate to smoother-looking animations.

VisualBrush makes it very easy to create a brush that looks exactly like some part of your user interface. You could use this to create effects such as reflections, as Figure 13-55 shows, or to project the user interface onto a 3D surface. (We show this latter technique in Chapter 17.)

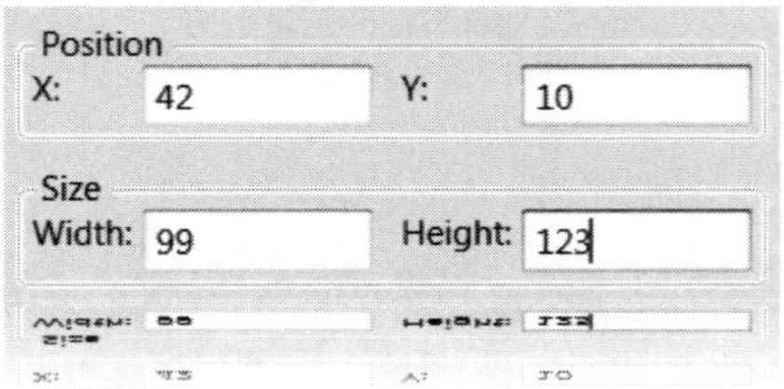

Figure 13-55. Reflection effect with VisualBrush

Example 13-55 shows how to create a reflection effect with a VisualBrush. The user interface to be reflected has been omitted for clarity—you would place this inside the Grid named mainUI. The important part is the Rectangle, which has been painted with a VisualBrush based on mainUI. This example also uses a ScaleTransform to flip the image upside down.

Example 13-55. Simulating a reflection with VisualBrush

```
<Grid>
  <Grid.RowDefinitions>
    <RowDefinition />
    <RowDefinition Height="40"/>
  </Grid.RowDefinitions>

  <Grid x:Name="mainUI">

    ...User interface to be reflected goes here...

  </Grid>
```

Example 13-55. Simulating a reflection with VisualBrush (continued)

```
  <Rectangle Grid.Row="1">
    <Rectangle.LayoutTransform>
     <ScaleTransform ScaleY="-1" />
    </Rectangle.LayoutTransform>

    <Rectangle.Fill>
      <VisualBrush Visual="{Binding ElementName=mainUI}" />
    </Rectangle.Fill>

    <Rectangle.OpacityMask>
      <LinearGradientBrush StartPoint="0,0" EndPoint="0,1">
        <GradientStop Offset="0" Color="Transparent" />
        <GradientStop Offset="1" Color="White" />
      </LinearGradientBrush>
    </Rectangle.OpacityMask>
  </Rectangle>

</Grid>
```

 The reflection is live in only one direction: if the main UI updates, the reflection will update to match, but you cannot interact with it.

As you can see from Figure 13-55, the image fades out toward the bottom. We achieved this by applying an OpacityMask. All user interface elements support this OpacityMask property. Its type is Brush. Only the transparency channel of the brush is used; the opacity of the element to which the mask is applied is determined by the opacity of the brush. In this case, we've used a LinearGradientBrush that fades to transparent, and this is what causes the Rectangle to fade to transparency.

Remember that VisualBrush derives from TileBrush. This means that you are not obliged to paint the target element with the whole of the source visual—you can use Viewport and Viewbox to be more selective. For example, you could use this to implement a magnifying glass feature.*

Pen

Brushes are used to fill the interior of a shape. To draw the outline of a shape, WPF needs a little more information—not only does it need a brush in order to color in the line, but it also needs to know how thick you would like the line to be drawn, and whether you want a dash pattern and/or end caps. The Pen class provides this information.

---

* For an example of this technique, see *http://www.interact-sw.co.uk/iangblog/2007/03/28/wpfmagnifyupdate*, or *http://tinysells.com/100*.

A Pen is always based on a brush, meaning that we can use all of the drawing effects we've seen so far when drawing outlines. You set the brush using the Brush property of the Pen class.

 Remember that if you are working with any of the high-level shape elements, you will not work with a Pen directly. A Pen is used under the covers; you set all of the properties indirectly. Table 13-2 showed how Shape properties correspond to Pen properties.

You will typically deal directly with a Pen only if you work at a lower level, such as with the GeometryDrawing in a DrawingBrush.

You set the line width with the Thickness property. For simple outlines, this and Brush may be the only properties you set. However, Pen has more to offer. For example, you can set a dash pattern with the DashArray property. This is simply an array of numbers. Each number corresponds to the length of a particular segment in the dash pattern. Example 13-56 illustrates the simplest possible pattern.

Example 13-56. DashArray

```
<Rectangle Stroke="Black" StrokeThickness="5" StrokeDashArray="1" />
```

This indicates that the first segment in the dash pattern is of length 1. The dash pattern repeats, and because only one segment has been specified, every segment will be of length 1. Figure 13-56 shows the result.

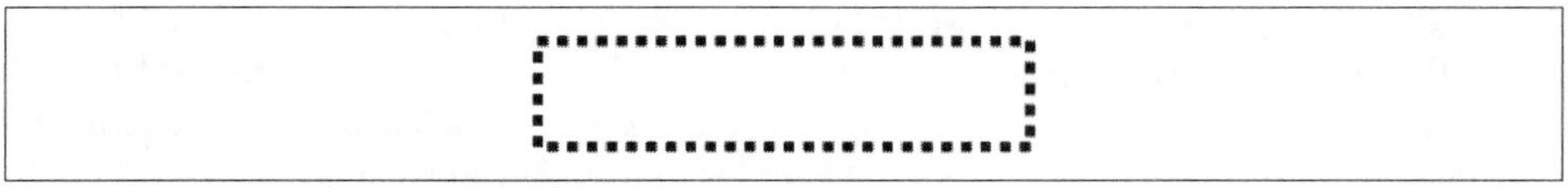

Figure 13-56. Simple dash pattern

Example 13-57 shows two slightly more interesting pattern sequences. Note that the second case supplies an odd number of segments. This means that the first time around, the solid segments will be of size 6 and the gap will be of size 1, but when the sequence repeats, the solid segment will be of length 1 and the gaps of size 6. So the effective length of the dash pattern is doubled. Figure 13-57 shows the results of both patterns.

Example 13-57. Dash patterns

```
<Rectangle Stroke="Black" StrokeThickness="5" StrokeDashArray="10 1 3 1" />
<Rectangle Stroke="Black" StrokeThickness="5" StrokeDashArray="6 1 6" />
```

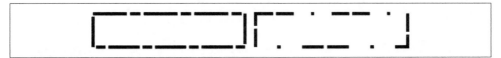

Figure 13-57. Longer dash patterns

WPF can draw corners in three different ways. You can set the LineJoin property to Miter, Bevel, or Round. These are shown in Figure 13-58.

Figure 13-58. LineJoin types: Miter, Bevel, and Round

For open shapes such as Line and PolyLine, you can specify the shape of the starts and ends of lines with the StartLineCap and EndLineCap properties. The DashCap property specifies the shape with which dashes start and end. These properties support four styles of caps: Round, Triangle, Flat, and Square. These are shown in Figure 13-59. Flat and Square both square off the ends of lines. The distinction is that with Flat, the flat end intersects the end point of the line, but with Square, it extends beyond it. The amount by which it overshoots the line is equal to half the line thickness.

Figure 13-59. Line cap styles: Round, Triangle, Flat, and Square

Transformations

Support for high-resolution displays is an important feature of WPF. This is enabled in part by the emphasis on the use of scalable vector graphics rather than bitmaps. But as experience with GDI+ and GDI32 has shown, if scalability is not integrated completely into the graphics architecture, resolution independence is very hard to achieve consistently in practice.

WPF's support for scaling is built in at a fundamental level. Any element in the user interface can have a transformation applied, making it easy to scale or rotate anything in the user interface.

As we saw in Chapter 3, all user interface elements have RenderTransform and LayoutTransform properties. These are of type Transform, which is an abstract base class. There are derived classes implementing various affine transformations,[*] listed in Table 13-8.

---

[*] An *affine transformation* is one in which features arranged in a straight line before the transform remain in a straight line after the transform. Note that 3D perspective transformations do not preserve straight lines.

Table 13-8. Transform types

Transform class	Usage
MatrixTransform	General-purpose transform based on 3 × 3 matrix
RotateTransform	Rotates around a point
ScaleTransform	Scales in x and/or y
SkewTransform	Shears (e.g., converts a square into a rhombus)
TransformGroup	Combines several transforms into one
TranslateTransform	Moves items by a specified vector

Most of these are just convenience classes—you can represent all supported transformations by the MatrixTransform class. This contains a 3×3 matrix, allowing any affine transformation to be used. However, the other transform types are often easier to work with than the set of numbers in a matrix.

Example 13-58 shows the use of a TransformGroup to apply a ScaleTransform and a RotateTransform to the RenderTransform property of a TextBlock.

Example 13-58. Using RenderTransform

```
<StackPanel Orientation="Horizontal">
  <TextBlock>
    <TextBlock.RenderTransform>
      <TransformGroup>
        <ScaleTransform ScaleX="2" ScaleY="2" />
        <RotateTransform Angle="10" />
      </TransformGroup>
    </TextBlock.RenderTransform>
    Hello,
  </TextBlock>
  <TextBlock>world</TextBlock>
</StackPanel>
```

Notice that we have used a TransformGroup here to combine the effects of two transforms. (Note that the rotation angle is specified in degrees in a RotateTransform, rather than radians, which are slightly more common in computational geometry. Likewise, positive numbers are clockwise, contrary to the usual mathematical convention.) Figure 13-60 shows the results.

Figure 13-60. RenderTransform

The order in which you apply transforms is usually significant, because each transform in a TransformGroup builds on the ones before it. For example, if you add a TranslateTransform to Example 13-58 to move the *Hello* text right by 30 device-independent pixels, the effect is different depending on whether it appears before or after the other transforms. The lefthand side of Figure 13-61 shows the result when the translation occurs first, and the righthand side shows the result when it occurs last. In the first case, the text has moved twice as far to the left; this is because the ScaleTransform was applied after the translation, doubling its effects.

world Hello, world Hello,

Figure 13-61. Adding a TranslateTransform before (left) and after (right)

Visual Layer Programming

The shape elements can provide a convenient way to work with graphics. However, in some situations, creating all the shape elements required to represent a drawing, and adding them to the UI tree, may be more trouble than it's worth. Data binding can often provide a solution—the shape classes all derive from FrameworkElement, so they can participate in data binding like any other user interface element. However, sometimes your data may be structured in such a way that it's easier or more efficient to write code that performs a series of drawing operations based on the data. For this reason, WPF provides a "visual layer" API as a lower-level alternative to shape elements. (In fact, the shape elements are all implemented on top of this visual layer.) This API lets us write code that renders content on demand.

 A *visual* is a visible object. A WPF application's appearance is formed by composing all of its visuals onto the screen. Because WPF builds on top of the visual layer, every element is a visual—the FrameworkElement base class derives indirectly from Visual. Programming at the visual layer simply involves creating a visual and writing code that tells WPF what we'd like to appear in that visual.

Even at this low level, WPF behaves very differently from Win32. The way in which graphics acceleration is managed means that your on-demand rendering code is called much less often than it would be in a classic Windows application.

Rendering On Demand

The key to custom on-demand rendering is the OnRender method. WPF calls this method when it needs your component to generate its appearance. (This is how the built-in shape classes render themselves.)

 The virtual OnRender method is defined by the UIElement class. Most elements derive from this indirectly via FrameworkElement, which adds core features such as layout and data binding.

Example 13-59 shows a custom element that overrides `OnRender`.

Example 13-59. A custom OnRender implementation

```
class MyFramedTextRenderer : FrameworkElement {
    protected override void OnRender(DrawingContext drawingContext) {
        Debug.WriteLine("OnRender");

        drawingContext.DrawRectangle(Brushes.Red, null, new Rect(0, 0, 100, 50));

        FormattedText text = new FormattedText("Hello, world",
            CultureInfo.CurrentUICulture, FlowDirection.LeftToRight,
            new Typeface("Verdana"), 24, Brushes.Black);
        drawingContext.DrawText(text, new Point(3, 3));
    }
}
```

The `OnRender` method is passed a single parameter of type `DrawingContext`. This is the low-level drawing API in WPF. It provides a set of primitive drawing operations, which are listed in Table 13-9. Example 13-59 uses the `DrawRectangle` and `DrawText` methods.

Note that the `DrawingContext` uses the `Brush` and `Pen` classes to indicate how shapes should be filled and outlined. We can also pass in the same `Geometry` and `Drawing` objects we saw earlier in the chapter.

Table 13-9. DrawingContext drawing operations

Operation	Usage
DrawDrawing	Draws a Drawing object.
DrawEllipse	Draws an ellipse.
DrawGeometry	Draws any Geometry object.
DrawGlyphRun	Draws a series of glyphs (i.e., text elements) offering detailed control over typography.
DrawImage	Draws a bitmap image.
DrawLine	Draws a line (a single segment).
DrawRectangle	Draws a rectangle.
DrawRoundedRectangle	Draws a rectangle with rounded corners.
DrawText	Draws text.
DrawVideo	Draws a rectangular region that can display video.
PushTransform	Sets a transform that will be applied to all subsequent drawing operations until Pop is called; if a transform is already in place, the net effect will be the combination of all the transforms currently pushed.
PushClip	Sets a clip region that will be applied to all subsequent drawing operations until Pop is called; as with PushTransform, multiple active clip regions will combine with one another.
PushEffect	Applies a BitmapEffect to all subsequent drawing operations until Pop is called; as with transforms and clips, multiple calls to this method will combine effects.

Table 13-9. DrawingContext drawing operations (continued)

Operation	Usage
PushOpacity	Sets a level of opacity that will be applied to all subsequent drawing operations until Pop is called; as with transforms and clips, multiple opacities are combined.
Pop	Removes the transform, clip region, or opacity added most recently by PushTransform, PushClip, or PushOpacity. If those methods have been called multiple times, calls to Pop remove their effects in reverse order. (The transforms, clip regions, and opacities behave like a stack.)

Because our custom element derives from FrameworkElement, it integrates naturally into any WPF application. Example 13-60 shows markup for a window that uses this custom element—we can use it just like we'd use any custom element. Figure 13-62 shows this window.

Example 13-60. Loading a custom visual into a window

```
<Window x:Class="VisualRender.Window1"
  xmlns="http://schemas.microsoft.com/winfx/2006/xaml/presentation"
  xmlns:x="http://schemas.microsoft.com/winfx/2006/xaml"
  xmlns:local="clr-namespace:VisualRender"
  Title="Visual Layer Rendering">
  <Canvas>
    <local:MyFramedTextRenderer Canvas.Top="10" Canvas.Left="10"
        x:Name="customRender" />
  </Canvas>
</Window>
```

Figure 13-62. Visual layer rendering in action

Notice that the OnRender function in Example 13-59 calls Debug.WriteLine. If the program is run inside a debugger, this will print a message to the debugger output window each time OnRender is called. This enables us to see how often WPF asks our custom visual to render itself. If you are accustomed to how the standard on-demand painting in Win32 and Windows Forms works, you might expect to see this called regularly whenever the window is resized, or partially obscured and uncovered. In fact, it is called just once!

It turns out that on-demand rendering is not as similar to old-style Win32 rendering as you might think. WPF will call your OnRender function when it needs to know what content your visual displays, but the way graphics acceleration works in WPF means that this happens far less often than the equivalent repaints in Win32. WPF caches the rendering instructions. (This rendering style is sometimes referred to as *retained mode*, whereas the Win32 style is *immediate mode*.) The extent and form of this caching are not documented, but caching clearly occurs. Moreover, it is subtler than simple bitmap-based caching. We can add this code to the host window in Example 13-60 (this would go in the code-behind file):

```
protected override void OnMouseLeftButtonDown(MouseButtonEventArgs e) {
    customRender.RenderTransform = new ScaleTransform(6, 6);
}
```

This applies a transform to our element, scaling it up by a factor of 6. When clicking on the user interface, the custom visual expands as you would expect, and yet OnRender is not called. Moreover, the enlarged visual does not show any of the pixelation or blurring artifacts you would see with a simple bitmap scale—it continues to be sharp, as you can see in Figure 13-63.

Figure 13-63. Scaled custom rendering

This outcome indicates that WPF is retaining scalable information about the contents of the visual. It is able to redraw our visual's on-screen appearance without bothering our OnRender method, even when the transformation has changed. This is in part due to the acceleration architecture, but also because transformation support is built into WPF at the most fundamental levels. WPF's ability to redraw without calling OnRender allows the user interface to remain intact on-screen even if our application is busy.

If the state of our object should change in a way that needs the appearance to be updated, we can call the InvalidateVisual method. This will cause WPF to call our OnRender method, allowing us to rebuild the appearance.

Note that when you override OnRender, you would typically also override the MeasureOverride and ArrangeOverride methods. Otherwise, WPF's layout system will have no idea how large your element is. The only reason we got away without doing this here is that we used the element on a Canvas, which doesn't care how large its children are. To work in other panels, it is essential to let the layout system know your size. Example 13-61 shows custom rendering of text along with layout logic.

Example 13-61. Custom rendering with layout logic

```
class CustomTextRenderer : FrameworkElement {
    FormattedText text = new FormattedText("Hello, world",
        CultureInfo.CurrentUICulture, FlowDirection.LeftToRight,
        new Typeface("Verdana"), 24, Brushes.Black);

    protected override void OnRender(DrawingContext drawingContext) {
        drawingContext.DrawText(text, new Point(0, 0));
    }

    protected override Size MeasureOverride(Size availableSize) {
        text.MaxTextWidth = availableSize.Width;
        text.MaxTextHeight = availableSize.Height;
        return new Size(text.Width, text.Height);
    }

    protected override Size ArrangeOverride(Size finalSize) {
        text.MaxTextWidth = finalSize.Width;
        text.MaxTextHeight = finalSize.Height;
        return finalSize;
    }
}
```

Chapter 3 described the MeasureOverride and ArrangeOverride methods in more detail. Example 13-61 defers to the FormattedText class to work out how much space is required. We describe FormattedText in the next chapter.

Where Are We?

WPF provides a range of high-quality rendering and composition services. A set of shape elements supports various drawing primitives. Several brush types are available for determining how shapes are painted, and pens augment brushes to define how outlines are drawn. Transformability is supported at all levels, making it easy to scale a user interface to any resolution or size. And, a low-level API is available for working at the "visual" layer when necessary.

CHAPTER 14

Text and Flow Documents

Text in WPF applications need never be plain. Any place a user interface displays text, all of WPF's text rendering features are available. Basic text formatting is offered, including word wrapping, text alignment, and any mixture of fonts and text styles. Nontextual UI elements such as controls or graphics may be intermingled with text. ClearType text rendering is used on flat-panel screens, significantly enhancing the clarity, shape, and readability of characters. The various typography features available in OpenType fonts can be exploited. And, as you would expect, there is full support for international applications.

As well as enabling fine control over textual details, WPF also defines types that represent documents. It offers two kinds: fixed documents and flow documents. Fixed documents have a fixed layout and size, and are often created in order to be printed. These are described in Chapter 15. Flow documents are more flexible—instead of prescribing a particular layout, they are formatted dynamically to fit the space available. This makes them ideal for presenting text on-screen, because most applications cannot know in advance the exact dimensions of the end user's screen, or whether the user will resize her window.

In this chapter, we will explore the options for presenting text, and we will examine the object model used by flow documents.

Fonts and Text Styles

You can work with text at several levels in WPF, but regardless of which level you choose, there are some common types and properties that control features—such as typeface, font weight, underlines, and so on—that you should know about. Because these types and properties crop up throughout the API, we will look at them first.

Common Text Properties

WPF defines a class called TextElement. This is part of the text object model used to define the structure and appearance of text, which we describe later in this chapter, but TextElement also defines a set of attached properties for formatting text. Many of these are inherited properties, meaning that if you apply them to some containing element, such as the Button in Example 14-1, the setting applies to any text inside that element. For example, if you were to apply these properties to a Window element, they would affect all text inside the window.

Example 14-1. Using common TextElement attached properties

```
<Button TextElement.FontFamily="Parchment" TextElement.FontSize="80">
  Cancel
</Button>
```

As Figure 14-1 shows, the font settings applied to the button have had an impact on the text element inside the button that provides the caption.[*]

Although an inherited property applies to all of the children of the element to which it is applied, it can be overruled. Obviously, giving the property a different value on a child element overrules the inherited value. More subtly, a property setter in a style will overrule an inherited property value, even if the style is picked up implicitly.

A few controls have default styles that set common TextElement properties, which results in inconsistencies if you set these properties on a Window. One example is Menu, which ignores the inherited font family and font size properties because its style sets the font to the system's configured font menu. It does this because users are allowed to change this font with the Windows Control Panel. StatusBar and ToolTip also set the font in their styles for the same reason. Consequently, these elements will ignore window-level font settings.

Figure 14-1. TextElement properties applied to descendents of a button

Table 14-1 lists the inherited attached properties defined by TextElement.

---

[*] Recall that the default template for a Button includes a ContentPresenter to host the content. If the content is plain text, a ContentPresenter will generate a TextBlock to display that text. This TextBlock inherits the two TextElement properties set on the Button.

Table 14-1. TextElement inherited properties

Property	Usage
FontFamily	Typeface family (e.g., Palatino Linotype, or Arial).
FontSize	Font size in device-independent pixels. (XAML can specify alternative units with a suffix: in, cm, px, and pt indicate inches, centimeters, pixels, and points, respectively. These are all converted at compile-time to a numeric value in pixel units.)
FontStretch	A value from FontStretches, such as Condensed, Normal or Expanded.
FontStyle	A value from FontStyles, such as Italic or Normal.
FontWeight	A value from FontWeights, such as Normal, Bold, or Light.
Foreground	Brush with which text is painted.

Because the need to control text properties crops up so often, several elements provide aliases for these properties. For instance, we can rewrite Example 14-1 as shown in Example 14-2.

Example 14-2. Using text format property aliases

```
<Button FontFamily="Parchment" FontSize="80">
  Cancel
</Button>
```

The two examples are exactly equivalent—we are setting the FontFamily and FontSize properties defined by TextElement in both cases. The Control. FontFamilyProperty field refers to the very same DependencyProperty object as the field of the same name in TextElement. The Control, AccessText, and TextBlock classes all provide aliases for the properties in Table 14-1. Page provides aliases for FontFamily, FontSize, and Foreground.

The following sections describe these properties and the associated types.

Fonts and Font Families

The common FontFamily property's type is FontFamily. This is one of the three classes WPF offers for working with fonts, which are listed in Table 14-2.

Table 14-2. WPF font classes

Class	Usage
FontFamily	Represents a named family of fonts such as Arial, Times New Roman, or Palatino Linotype.
GlyphTypeface	Wraps a specific font file on disk, such as *C:\Windows\Fonts\timesbi.ttf*. This will contain a particular weight and style of a font family, such as the bold, italic version of Times New Roman.
Typeface	Encapsulates a FontFamily, weight (e.g., bold), style (e.g., italic), and stretch (e.g., condensed). This is just a description, and unlike GlyphTypeface, you can create a Typeface representing a font that is not present on your system (e.g., one used by a document created on some other machine that has the font).

FontFamily just identifies a named family of fonts, rather than any particular weight or style. Example 14-1 used this to select the Parchment font family. In order to render text, WPF needs more than this—most font families have variants such as bold and italic. For elements using the common text properties in Table 14-1, these facets are managed by separate properties. This is useful because it lets you control features such as weight and italics independently—if you just choose a font weight of bold without specifying a font family, the element will inherit the family from its parent.

Property inheritance does not apply automatically to the low-level text handling APIs. These offer very fine control, but they require the font to be specified comprehensively and explicitly. This is why WPF offers the other two types, Typeface and GlyphTypeface. We will illustrate their use later when we look at the visual-level text APIs.

You should not count on all variants of a font being available for any particular font family. For example, some fonts do not have bold versions, or may be available only in bold. You can discover which variants are available by retrieving the list of Typeface objects from a FontFamily object's GetTypefaces method.

FontSize

The FontSize property is of type Double. It specifies the font's size in pixels. If you're working in XAML, you can specify other units by adding a suffix, as Example 14-3 shows.

Example 14-3. FontSize units

```
<StackPanel>
  <TextBlock Text="10 pixels"     FontSize="10" />
  <TextBlock Text="10 points"     FontSize="10pt" />
  <TextBlock Text="1 centimetre"  FontSize="1cm" />
  <TextBlock Text="0.2 inches"    FontSize="0.2in" />
</StackPanel>
```

Stretch

The FontStretch property lets you choose a condensed or expanded variant of the typeface. It accepts any of the values provided by the FontStretches class. These are: UltraCondensed, ExtraCondensed, Condensed, SemiCondensed, Normal, Medium, SemiExpanded, Expanded, ExtraExpanded, and UltraExpanded.

Stretched variants of fonts are not created simply by scaling. Doubling or halving the width of a character would distort it, changing the width of horizontal features without changing vertical aspects to match. Each stretch type requires a separate font file. A font family will not normally offer all of the stretch types listed previously. Most fonts offer either exactly one (usually Normal), or a handful. For example, the Gill Sans MT font that ships with various versions of Microsoft Office comes in Normal, Condensed, and `ExtraCondensed`, but the latter is available only in bold.[*] If the font family does not offer the stretch you request, WPF will choose the nearest matching stretch.

Style

The `FontStyle` property indicates whether a font should be upright or slanted. This can be any of the three values from the `FontStyles` class: `Normal`, `Italic`, or `Oblique`. The distinction between italic and oblique is that an italic font is a distinct font, where the character shapes are typically different from (but harmonious with) the normal version, and are defined in a separate file. An oblique style is formed by skewing a normal font—it does not require a separate font file, as it just transforms the shapes of an existing font. Figure 14-2 shows the Palatino Linotype font family in all three styles.

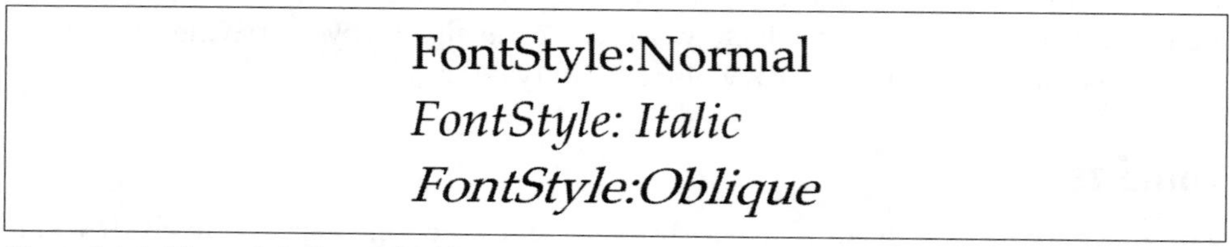

FontStyle:Normal

FontStyle: Italic

FontStyle:Oblique

Figure 14-2. Normal, Italic, and Oblique

As you can see, the italic font has letters that are of a significantly different shape from the equivalent characters in the normal style. This is partly because italic fonts typically have a slightly more decorative style, but also because simply skewing the character shapes—which is what an oblique font does—produces rather low-quality results, distorting the letter shapes. You would normally use an oblique font only as a fallback when an italic font is missing for some reason.

Weight

The `FontWeight` property determines how dark the text appears. You specify one of the values from the `FontWeights` class. Where two values are listed in the same table entry, it means they are different names for the same weight—for historical reason-scertain weights go by more than one name. The available `FontWeights` are `Thin`, `ExtraLight`/`UltraLight`, `Light`, `Normal`/`Regular`, `Medium`, `DemiBold`/`SemiBold`, `Bold`, `ExtraBold`/`UltraBold`, `Black`/`Heavy`, and `ExtraBlack`/`UltraHeavy`.

As with `FontStretch`, most font families do not offer variants for every weight. WPF will choose the nearest match. It has no facility for adjusting character shapes to

---

[*] Just to confuse matters, Office also provides a font called Gill Sans, which is a different family—note the missing "MT." This offers only `Normal` and `Condensed`, and only in ultra-bold.

"lighten" or "embolden" text—each font weight requires a font file defining the character shapes for that weight.

The properties discussed so far in this section are all defined by the `TextElement` class. There are a few properties that are widely used by WPF's text facilities, but which are defined by other more specialized types because they apply only to certain types of textual element—text alignment makes sense for paragraphs or blocks of text, but not for an individual word, for example. The following sections examine these properties.

Decorations

A *decoration* is a line drawn through a piece of text, such as an underline or strikethrough. The `Inline` class, which is part of the text object model described later in this chapter, defines an attached `TextDecorations` property, which is aliased by both `AccessText` and `TextBlock`. This property supports the four decoration styles shown in Example 14-4.

Example 14-4. Text decorations

```
<TextBlock TextWrapping="Wrap" TextAlignment="Center">
  <Span TextDecorations="Underline">Underline</Span>,
  <Span TextDecorations="Baseline">Baseline</Span>,
  <Span TextDecorations="Strikethrough">Strikethrough</Span>,
  <Span TextDecorations="Overline">Overline</Span>,
  <Span TextDecorations="Underline,Overline,Baseline,Strikethrough">
    Full house
  </Span>
</TextBlock>
```

Figure 14-3 shows the results. As you can see from the final item, it is possible to use multiple decorations. This is because the `TextDecorations` property is of type `TextDecorationCollection`.

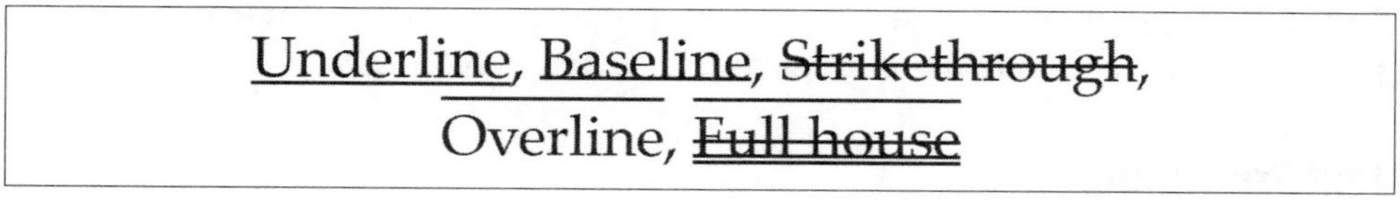

Figure 14-3. Text decorations

The syntax shown in Example 14-4 is easy to use but slightly limited. If you create the `TextDecoration` elements explicitly, you can control the pen used to paint the decoration, and its exact vertical position. Example 14-5 sets two decorations on an element: a blue underline and a thicker green strikethrough.

Example 14-5. Setting text decorations

```
<Span>
  <Span.TextDecorations>
    <TextDecoration Location="Underline" PenOffset="4">
      <TextDecoration.Pen>
        <Pen Brush="Blue" Thickness="1" />
      </TextDecoration.Pen>
    </TextDecoration>
    <TextDecoration Location="StrikeThrough">
      <TextDecoration.Pen>
        <Pen Brush="LightGreen" Thickness="2" />
      </TextDecoration.Pen>
    </TextDecoration>
  </Span.TextDecorations>
  Highly decorated
</Span>
```

Figure 14-4 shows the results.

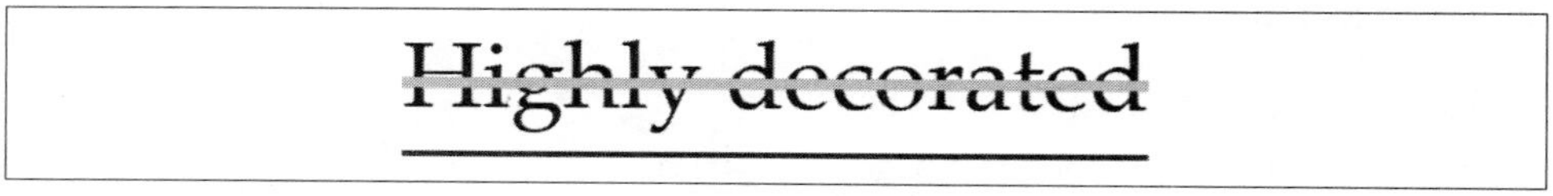

Figure 14-4. Underline and strikethrough decorations (Color Plate 26)

The shorter syntax shown in Example 14-4 is available only in XAML—it's provided by a type converter class. However, WPF makes it just as easy to set simple decorations from code. It provides the TextDecorations class, which offers static properties containing text decoration collections holding exactly one decoration, such as an underline or a strikethrough. Example 14-6 uses this to apply a simple underline decoration.

Example 14-6. Simple underline decoration

```
text.TextDecorations = TextDecorations.Underline;
```

As this example shows, the static properties offered by TextDecorations make it as simple to set a single decoration from code as it is from XAML.

Text Trimming

If you try to display more text than fits in the space available, something has to give. Some of the text viewing elements described later in this chapter deal with this by scrolling or paging through the text. However, the TextBlock and AccessText elements both simply crop the text. They each offer a TextTrimming property, shown in Example 14-7, which takes a value from the TextTrimming enumeration, allowing the cropping behavior to be modified.

Example 14-7. TextTrimming

```
<TextBlock TextTrimming="None" Text="Too much text." />
```

The effect of the None setting (which is the default) is shown in Figure 14-5—the text has been cut off mid-character. A black border has been added to the edges of the figures in this section to illustrate where cropping occurs relative to the available space, and with this setting, the whole space is used.

Figure 14-5. TextTrimming.None

Figure 14-6 shows one of the other two options: CharacterEllipsis. This crops to an exact number of characters. It also adds an ellipsis to indicate that cropping has occurred, which has the side effect of reducing the number of visible characters. It also means that the space available is not filled completely—with this setting, WPF cannot show a partial character in order to fill the space, as it did in Figure 14-5.

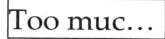

Figure 14-6. TextTrimming.CharacterEllipsis

The final option is WordEllipsis, which crops at a word boundary. As Figure 14-7 shows, this can reduce the amount of text that is shown further still, particularly when only a handful of words will fit. WPF has had to cut the text off after the first word because where wasn't room to fit both *much* and an ellipsis, resulting in a lot of unused space. However, even though this is the least space-efficient option, it can sometimes lead to less confusing results—cropping text at a word boundary reduces the chances of changing the apparent meaning of the text.

Figure 14-7. TextTrimming.WordEllipsis

Text Wrapping and Hyphenation

Often, a UI layout will have insufficient horizontal width to show some text, but spare vertical space. Not all text elements will exploit this space by default. Figure 14-8 shows a traditional English tongue twister displayed by a TextBlock, and as you can see, it has failed to use the available vertical space.

I'm not a pheasant plucker, I'm

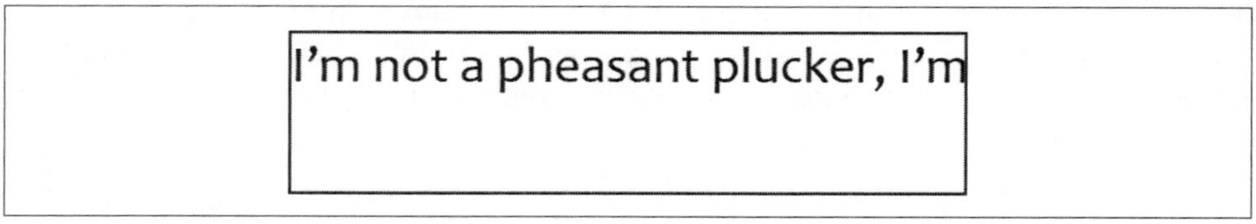

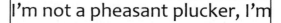

Figure 14-8. Vertical space not used by default

To use the vertical space, we must enable text wrapping. Both `TextBlock` and `AccessText` offer a `TextWrapping` property, which takes a value from the `TextWrapping` enumeration. This defaults to `NoWrap`, but Figure 14-9 shows the effect of setting it to `Wrap`.

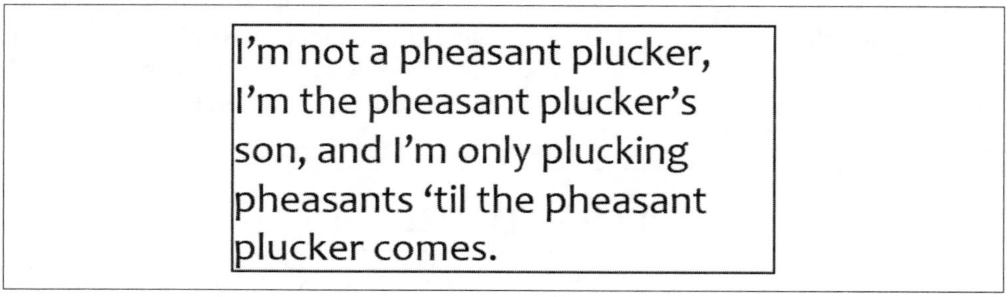

I'm not a pheasant plucker,
I'm the pheasant plucker's
son, and I'm only plucking
pheasants 'til the pheasant
plucker comes.

Figure 14-9. Word wrapping

The `TextWrapping` enumeration offers a third value: `WrapWithOverflow`. The distinction between the two wrapping styles is in the way they deal with individual words that are longer than the available space. Figure 14-10 shows a piece of text with this problem.

A
cumbersom
e word.
A
cumbersom
word.

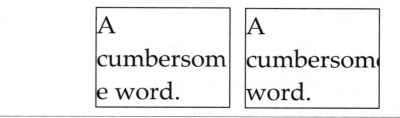

Figure 14-10. Wrap (left) and WrapWithOverflow (right)

The left of Figure 14-10 shows how `Wrap` deals with this—it simply breaks the word across multiple lines. On the right, we see the `WrapWithOverflow` behavior: over-long words are cropped.

A more elegant solution to this problem is commonly used in print: hyphenation. Splitting words with hyphens can enable word wrapping to work better in confined spaces. The `Block` class, which is part of the text object model described later in this chapter, defines an attached IsHyphenationEnabled property, and TextBlock provides an alias for this, as Example 14-8 shows.

Example 14-8. Enabling hyphenation

```
<TextBlock TextWrapping="Wrap" IsHyphenationEnabled="True">
  A cumbersome word.
</TextBlock>
```

As Figure 14-11 shows, hyphenation enables the text to fit on fewer lines than in Figure 14-10, and with less compromise. Because hyphenation seems to be better in every respect, it may seem strange that it is disabled by default. However, the hyphenation algorithm is complex, and there are nontrivial costs to enabling it. Because hyphenation is appropriate only for certain scenarios—presenting bodies of text in relatively narrow spaces—it makes sense for it to be off by default.

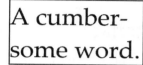

Figure 14-11. Hyphenation

 Hyphenation is a language-specific process. WPF takes the element tree's language into account for both hyphenation and spellchecking. In XAML, you can set the language using the standard xml:lang attribute—you can set this to any culture string, such as en-GB or fr-CA, which represent British English and French Canadian, respectively. From code, you can set the Language property of any FrameworkElement or FrameworkContentElement object. Text editing controls with the SpellCheck.IsEnabled attached property set to True also honor the language setting.

Hyphenation and spelling dictionaries are shipped as part of the .NET 3.0 language packs provided by Microsoft. At the time of this writing, dictionaries are provided for English, German, French, and Spanish.

Text Alignment

TextAlignment is an attached property defined by the Block class. The property accepts any value from the TextAlignment enumeration type. This offers four values, all of which will be familiar to you if you've ever used a word processor: Left, Right, Center, and Justify.

Figure 14-12 shows the effect of the Justify setting. As you can see, the righthand edge is now flush with the available space, as opposed to the ragged-right edge shown in Figure 14-9.

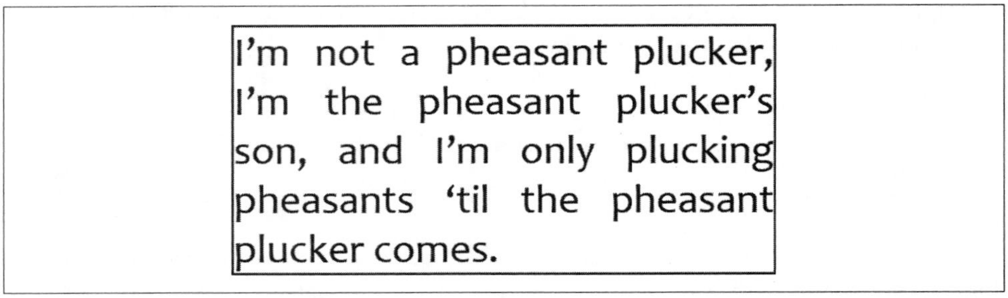

> I'm not a pheasant plucker,
> I'm the pheasant plucker's
> son, and I'm only plucking
> pheasants 'til the pheasant
> plucker comes.

Figure 14-12. Justified text

We've looked at the mechanisms available for describing how text should be formatted. However, a description of formatted text isn't much use unless we can somehow display that text, so it is time to look at the elements available to us for presenting text in a user interface.

Text and the User Interface

As we saw in the Introduction and Chapter 13, a WPF application's appearance is defined by its visual tree—a tree of objects derived from the Visual base class. Text must fit into this model, but we have several different options for adding text into the visual tree depending on the balance we require between control and ease of use.

The lowest level at which we can work with text is to use the visual layer drawing techniques introduced in Chapter 13. The next level up is to use the Glyphs class, which offers a similar level of control as visual layer programming, but packaged into a framework element. This enables it to be used from markup and to provide the usual framework-level features, such as event support and participation in layout. The GlyphRunDrawing class offers similar features, but you can incorporate it into a drawing. Finally, you can use the text object model in conjunction with one of the elements that knows how to render this form of text, such as TextBlock or FlowDocumentReader. TextBlock is the most widely used, as it offers a good balance between simplicity and flexibility.

TextBlock

The TextBlock element is usually the best choice for presenting simple text. It can handle both plain text and formatted text, and can cope easily with anything from a single character to a few paragraphs. Example 14-9 shows TextBlock at its simplest.

Example 14-9. Simple TextBlock

```
<TextBlock Text="Some text" />
```

Because TextBlock derives from FrameworkElement, its position and size will be determined by WPF's normal layout mechanisms (which we described in Chapter 3).

A TextBlock can span multiple lines. A straightforward though inflexible way to do this is to put either a carriage return or a linefeed (character values 13 and 10) or both* into the Text property. Example 14-10 shows this technique. Note that because all three of the popular representations for a new line are treated equivalently, there's no need to use .NET's Environment.NewLine property in WPF.

Example 14-10. Multiline Text value

```
<TextBlock Text="Some&#x0a;text" />
```

Although this hardcoded line break works fine, a better solution might be to switch on word wrapping, enabling the TextBlock to choose where to put line breaks. This is controlled with the TextWrapping property, one of the common text properties, described earlier in this chapter, in the "Fonts and Text Styles" section. TextBlock defines aliases for all of these common properties.

As an alternative to setting the Text property of a TextBlock, you can supply content inside the element. Example 14-11 uses this technique to create the same result as Example 14-9.

Example 14-11. Text as content

```
<TextBlock>Some text</TextBlock>
```

Moving the text inside the element doesn't add anything very useful for this particular example. However, by representing the text as content, we can go beyond plain strings, as Example 14-12 shows.

Example 14-12. Text with mixed content

```
<TextBlock><Bold>Some</Bold> text</TextBlock>
```

As Figure 14-13 shows, this renders the word "Some" in bold, and the word "text" with the normal font weight.

Some text

Figure 14-13. Mixed bold and ordinary text

---

* A carriage return followed directly by a line feed is treated as a single new line. This is the most common convention for representing line ends in Windows. It originates from the days when computer terminals had a keyboard and printer but no screen. The printer used separate control characters to feed a new line of paper (10), and to return the print head to the start of the line (13). This character sequence is completely redundant today, but it is still the norm in Windows thanks to backward compatibility and developer inertia.

When you add content to a `TextBlock` in this way, you are adding items to its `Inlines` property. This is a collection of objects, all derived from `Inline`. This class and its derivatives (such as `Bold` and `Italic`) are described in detail in the "Text Object Model" section, later in this chapter. For now, it is enough to think of an `Inline` as some formatted text contained within a single paragraph. This means that a good way to think of `TextBlock` is as a framework element that renders a sequence of `Inline` text elements.

Label and AccessText

WPF defines a `Label` control, which is also able to display text. If you have used Windows Forms, `Label` might look like the obvious choice for displaying text, because Windows Forms also defined a `Label` control, which was used for displaying simple text. However, the purpose of WPF's `Label` control is different.

As mentioned in Chapter 5, WPF's `Label` control's purpose is to place the focus into another control such as a `TextBox` when an access key is pressed. Using a `Label` control simply as a plain-text label is wasteful—it creates a `TextBlock` internally to render plain text for you, so you might as well just create the `TextBlock` yourself.

`Label` has one other trick: you can use it to add underlines for access keys when the user presses the Alt key. As Example 14-13 shows, you denote the access key with an underscore.

Example 14-13. Access key underline with Label

```
<Label Content="S_hortcut" />
```

When the user presses the Alt key (or if he has configured Windows to show access key underlines at all times), the relevant letter will be underlined, as shown in Figure 14-14.

Sh̲ortcut

Figure 14-14. Access key underline

However, if the only reason you're using `Label` is to show an access key underline, there's a better alternative. When you provide `Label` (or any control that supports the content model) with a string containing an underscore, it generates an `AccessText` element to present that string instead of a `TextBlock`. So, it would be more efficient to use this directly, as Example 14-14 does.

Example 14-14. Access key underline with AccessText

```
<AccessText Text="S_hortcut" />
```

The rule is simple: use the Label control if you need its focus management. If all you need to do is present text, use a text presentation element: AccessText if you need the underline and TextBlock otherwise.

The TextBlock is designed for fairly small volumes of text. It is possible to put multiple paragraphs into a TextBlock either by embedding suitable line break characters in its Text property, or by using the LineBreak inline element. However, WPF provides other elements that are better suited to presenting large quantities of text.

Flow Documents and Viewer Controls

The full text object model of WPF supports more than just the inline elements supported by TextBlock. It contains types that represent paragraphs, lists, and tables; collectively these are known as *block* types, and we will describe them in detail in the "Text Object Model" section. These elements can only appear inside a FlowDocument. WPF provides three controls for displaying flow documents.

FlowDocumentScrollViewer is the simplest of the flow document controls. Its behavior is very similar to the HTML control: it formats the document to fill the available width, and provides a vertical scroll bar if the document is taller than the available height. This is a very simple element to use, as Example 14-15 shows.

Example 14-15. Using a FlowDocumentScrollViewer

```
<Window ...>
  <FlowDocumentScrollViewer x:Name="viewer" />
</Window>
```

All you need to do is set the viewer's Document property to a FlowDocument. We will show how to write a FlowDocument in the "Text Object Model" section, but for now assume that your application contains a XAML file called *MyFlowDocument.xaml*[*] containing a FlowDocument in XAML form. You could load it in the code-behind file for the file that contains the viewer in Example 14-15 with the code in Example 14-16.

Example 14-16. Loading a FlowDocument into a viewer

```
partial class Window1 : Window {
    public Window1( ) {
        InitializeComponent( );
        viewer.Document = (FlowDocument) Application.LoadComponent(
            new Uri("MyFlowDocument.xaml", UriKind.Relative));
    }
}
```

---

[*] This example flow document is provided in the examples for this book, which you can download from *http://sellsbrothers.com/writing/wpfbook*.

Figure 14-15 shows how the FlowDocumentScrollViewer presents a document.

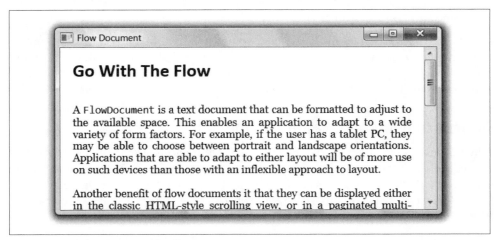

Figure 14-15. FlowDocumentScrollViewer

A problem with this control is that it doesn't make very effective use of wide spaces. As the available width increases, it simply makes the lines of text wider to match. This can be unhelpful because wide lines are hard to read—when we reach the end of one line and our eyes track back to the start of the next line, the likelihood of missing a line gets higher with longer lines. Ideally you don't want more than 15 words per line.

The traditional solution to this problem in the world of printed media is to split the text into multiple columns. This keeps the line length readable, while exploiting the available width. On paper, a column's height is fixed, being dictated by the page size and layout. On screen, we need to be a little more flexible—columns need to be as tall as the available space, which can change as the user resizes the application. The worst thing we could do is create columns that are too tall, requiring the user to scroll up and down to read across the columns. If you've ever had to read a column-formatted PDF file on a computer, you'll know what a horrible reading experience that is. Even with suitably sized columns, there may be too much text to fit, in which case we'll need some mechanism for moving from page to page.

WPF provides the FlowDocumentPageViewer to solve these problems. It splits text into columns of the appropriate height, reformatting the text should the layout change for any reason (such as the user resizing the window). And, it provides paging controls to navigate through the document. In markup and code, it is used in exactly the same way as the FlowDocumentScrollViewer, as you can see from Example 14-17. Figure 14-16 shows how it looks.

Example 14-17. FlowDocumentPageViewer

```
<FlowDocumentPageViewer x:Name="viewer" />
```

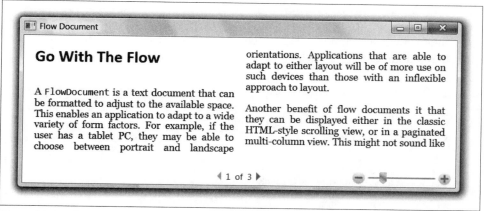

Figure 14-16. *FlowDocumentPageViewer*

Figure 14-16 shows two columns because that was how many happened to fit for that window size. As Figure 14-17 shows, the control will add more columns if space permits. Notice that the viewer also provides a set of controls at the bottom. In the center are the paging controls, indicating the current page, the total number of pages, and buttons for moving backward and forward. To the right is a zoom control, allowing the user to adjust the magnification.

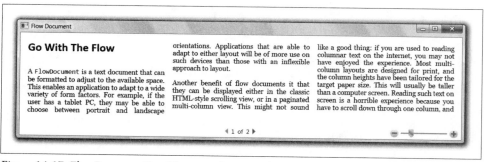

Figure 14-17. *FlowDocumentPageViewer with more columns*

If you want to let the user choose whether to have a scrolling view or a column-based paginated view, you can use the `FlowDocumentReader` control. This provides buttons that let the user choose between scrolling and pagination. As Figure 14-18 shows, these appear to the left of the zoom control.

Figure 14-18. *FlowDocumentReader controls*

`FlowDocumentReader` provides three modes. The leftmost button selects paginated viewing, and the rightmost selects scrolling. The middle button selects the double-page view shown in Figure 14-19, which is reminiscent of reading a double-sided printed and bound material such as a book or a magazine.

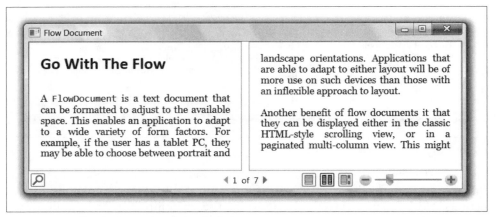

Figure 14-19. FlowDocumentReader in dual-page view

 WPF provides a fourth document viewer: the `DocumentViewer` control. This displays a `FixedDocument` instead of a `FlowDocument`. It is described in Chapter 15.

Whether you are using simple formatted text in a `TextBlock` or a full flow document in one of the viewer controls, you will be making use of WPF's text object model in order to manage the structure and formatting of the text. We describe this in detail in the "Text Object Model" section. However, before we look at that, there are some lower-level options for rendering text. These offer finer control than the text object model, but are considerably harder to use.

Visual Layer Text

The visual layer is the lowest level at which you can work with text. In practice, you will probably not use this approach very often—it is most useful when you are already writing visual layer graphics code and need to present some text. However, the visual layer underpins all forms of text rendering in WPF, so it is useful to understand how it works.

Even at the visual layer, two levels of abstraction are available. At the very lowest level, we work with *glyph runs*, which are sequences of characters sharing a single font and style. A glyph run offers very precise control over how text is rendered, but it is a lot of work to use. Alternatively, you can work with the higher-level `FormattedText` class, which provides simple formatting for small blocks of text.

Glyph runs

Glyph runs are the lowest-level representation of text in WPF. They provide extremely precise control, but they are very inconvenient to use as a result, as Example 14-18 shows.

Example 14-18. "Hello, world" with GlyphRuns

```
public class MyGlyphsElement : FrameworkElement {
    protected override void OnRender(DrawingContext drawingContext) {
        GlyphRun run = BuildGlyphRun("Hello, world!");
        if (run != null) {
            drawingContext.DrawGlyphRun(Brushes.Black, run);
        }
    }

    public static GlyphRun BuildGlyphRun(string text) {
        double fontSize = 50;
        GlyphRun glyphs = null;

        Typeface font = new Typeface("Calibri");
        GlyphTypeface glyphFace;
        if (font.TryGetGlyphTypeface(out glyphFace)) {
            glyphs = new GlyphRun();
            ISupportInitialize isi = glyphs;
            isi.BeginInit();
            glyphs.GlyphTypeface = glyphFace;
            glyphs.FontRenderingEmSize = fontSize;

            char[] textChars = text.ToCharArray();
            glyphs.Characters = textChars;
            ushort[] glyphIndices = new ushort[textChars.Length];
            double[] advanceWidths = new double[textChars.Length];

            for (int i = 0; i < textChars.Length; ++i) {
                int codepoint = textChars[i];
                ushort glyphIndex = glyphFace.CharacterToGlyphMap[codepoint];
                double glyphWidth = glyphFace.AdvanceWidths[glyphIndex];

                glyphIndices[i] = glyphIndex;
                advanceWidths[i] = glyphWidth * fontSize;
            }
            glyphs.GlyphIndices = glyphIndices;
            glyphs.AdvanceWidths = advanceWidths;

            glyphs.BaselineOrigin = new Point(0, glyphFace.Baseline * fontSize);
            isi.EndInit();
        }
        return glyphs;
    }
}
```

This example overrides `OnRender` in order to work with the visual layer API. As we saw in Chapter 13, WPF passes this method a `DrawingContext`, with which we define the appearance of our element. Here, we call the `DrawGlyphRun` method to render text. Figure 14-20 shows the result.

Figure 14-20. Rendered GlyphRun

The bulk of the work is done in the `BuildGlyphRun` method, which creates the `GlyphRun` object. A `GlyphRun` needs to know which font to use, specified by a `GlyphTypeface` object. As mentioned earlier, in the "Fonts and Font Families" section, WPF offers three classes for working with fonts. `GlyphTypeface` is the lowest-level one, representing a specific font file.

If you know the exact location of the font file on disk, you can build a `GlyphTypeface` from scratch. However, Example 14-18 does not presume the location of the font. Instead, it creates a `Typeface` object that describes the font, and then uses its `TryGetGlyphFace` method to do the work of locating the relevant font file and creating a `GlyphTypeface` object.

We have to provide the `GlyphRun` with detailed information about the characters we would like it to draw. Not only must we provide an array containing the characters themselves, but we also need to tell it where to find each character in the font file—this is the purpose of the `glyphIndices` array in Example 14-18. We obtain the glyph index by looking it up in the `GlyphTypeface` object. Note that glyph indices are not standardized—a particular character's glyph index will change from one font file to another.

`GlyphRun` also requires us to be explicit about horizontal character positioning: the `advanceWidths` array contains the nominal width of each character. The visible width of a character is always determined by its shape, and the *advance widths* do not change this—characters are not squashed or stretched to fit. These so-called widths simply determine where each character is positioned. If you imagine a typewriter, the advance width for a character would indicate how far the paper should be advanced horizontally after that character is typed. `GlyphRun` gives us control over this to allow nonstandard spacing where necessary. We could use this to perform *tracking* (i.e., reducing or increasing the spacing uniformly for every letter). We might also use this to perform *kerning*, where the spacing between a particular pair of characters is adjusted. We could also place multiple characters on top of one another by using a zero advance width. Example 14-18 does none of these things—it simply asks the GlyphTypeface for each character's default width.

Finally, we set the BaselineOrigin property to indicate where we would like the text to be rendered. Because we just want to render text in a straightforward fashion, we use the GlyphTypeface object to look up the baseline offset, just as we did for the glyph indices and advance widths.

Example 14-18 passes the GlyphRun object to the DrawGlyphRun method of the DrawingContext. You can also use a GlyphRun with a GlyphRunDrawing, in order to incorporate text into a drawing. Example 14-19 calls the BuildGlyphRun method defined in Example 14-18 and wraps it as a drawing, which it then presents in a window. (We described drawing objects in Chapter 13.) Because this uses the same text as the previous example, the results will look much the same as Figure 14-20.

Example 14-19. GlyphRunDrawing

```
public class FontDrawingWindow : Window {
    public FontDrawingWindow( ) {

        GlyphRunDrawing drawing = new GlyphRunDrawing(
                Brushes.Blue, MyGlyphsElement.BuildGlyphRun("Hello, world!"));

        // Host drawing in an Image so we can see it.
        Image imageElement = new Image( );
        imageElement.Stretch = Stretch.None;
        imageElement.Source = new DrawingImage(drawing);
        this.Content = imageElement;
    }
}
```

Although GlyphRun gives you very fine control over text rendering, it involves a lot of work. You will probably not want to write code like that in Example 14-18 every time you want to put some text on the screen. So even down at the visual layer, we have a higher-level alternative: FormattedText.

FormattedText

The most convenient way to work with text at the visual layer is to use the FormattedText class. As Example 14-20 shows, we can build a FormattedText object representing the text we would like to render, and then pass it to the DrawingContext. This is considerably simpler than building a GlyphRun.

Example 14-20. Visual layer text rendering

```
public class MyTextElement : FrameworkElement {
    protected override void OnRender(DrawingContext drawingContext) {
        FormattedText text = new FormattedText(
            "Hello, world!",
            Thread.CurrentThread.CurrentUICulture,
```

Example 14-20. Visual layer text rendering (continued)

```
        FlowDirection.LeftToRight,
        new Typeface("Candara"),
        60,     // Font size in pixels
        Brushes.Black);

    drawingContext.DrawText(text, new Point(0, 0));
  }
}
```

As you can see, the `FormattedText` object contains the text to be displayed, but it also contains some other settings. We provide culture and text direction information—WPF's text rendering takes the culture into account, as certain text features may need to be handled differently in different cultures. (For example, a particular Unicode character can have different shapes in different regions.) The `FormattedText` object also needs to know the font, font size, and brush to be used. Figure 14-21 shows the results.

Figure 14-21. FormattedText results

`FormattedText` is able to perform word wrapping. This is off by default—text will simply be cropped if it doesn't fit. The result is the same as the default `TextBlock` behavior shown earlier in Figure 14-8. To use wrapping, we must tell WPF how much space is available. All we need to do is add one line of code, shown in Example 14-21, before passing the `FormattedText` object to `DrawText`.

Example 14-21. Specifying the text width

```
text.MaxTextWidth = this.ActualWidth;
```

Specifying a width has the effect of turning on word wrapping, so the results will look the same as those shown earlier in Figure 14-9.

This example may have you wondering whether `FormattedText` also has a `MaxTextHeight` property. Indeed it does. Figure 14-22 shows the result of specifying a maximum width and height, and then making the window slightly too small to hold the text.

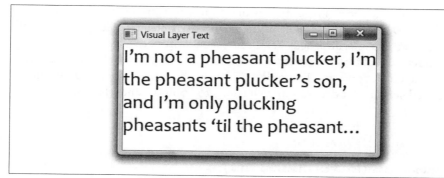

Figure 14-22. Cropped text

WPF will render only as much text as fits completely. The cropping behavior is determined by setting the FormattedText object's Trimming property to a value from the TextTrimming enumeration. We described the available enumeration values earlier, in the "Text Trimming" section of this chapter.

FormattedText also offers a TextAlignment property that supports the four alignment styles defined by the TextAlignment enumeration, as described earlier in the "Text Alignment" section of the chapter.

Example 14-20 specified only the typeface name. The Typeface object passed to the FormattedText constructor can contain more information. Example 14-22 shows a more detailed typeface description.

Example 14-22. Typeface

```
FontFamily preferredFont = new FontFamily("Candara");
FontFamily fallbackFont = new FontFamily("Verdana");

Typeface tf = new Typeface(
    preferredFont,
    FontStyles.Italic,
    FontWeights.Bold,
    FontStretches.Normal,
    fallbackFont);
```

This creates a Typeface object that incorporates two font families: the first (Candara) will be used if available, but the second one (Verdana) indicates the family to use if the first is unavailable. The constructor used here also takes FontStyle, FontWeight, and FontStretch values, all of which work in the same way as the font style, weight, and stretch properties described earlier in the chapter, in the "Fonts and Text Styles" section. In this case, we have asked for an italic, bold, unstretched version of the font.

> If you need a mixture of fonts or styles, you will need to create a FormattedText object for each distinct style, and make multiple calls to DrawText.

FormattedText also supports lines, such as underlines and strikethroughs. As we saw earlier, in the "Decorations" section of the chapter, UI elements support this with the TextElement class's attached TextDecorations property, which is of type TextDecorationCollection. FormattedText offers a SetTextDecoration method that uses this same collection type. Example 14-23 uses this in conjunction with one of the predefined simple text decoration collections to apply an underline.

Example 14-23. Simple underline decoration

```
FormattedText text = ...; // As before
```

text.SetTextDecorations(TextDecorations.Underline);

The FormattedText class offers a useful service that is not directly related to text rendering, but which is well worth knowing about: it can convert text into a Geometry. As we saw in Chapter 13, geometries define shapes, and you can use them at the visual layer or in conjunction with a Path object, as well as to specify clip regions for any UI element. The FormattedText class's BuildGeometry method does the work, as Example 14-24 shows.

Example 14-24. Converting text to geometry

```
FormattedText text = new FormattedText(
    "CLIP!",
    Thread.CurrentThread.CurrentUICulture,
    FlowDirection.LeftToRight,
    new Typeface("Gill Sans Ultra Bold"),
    20,
    Brushes.Black);
```

Geometry textGeometry = text.BuildGeometry(new Point(0,0));
```
button1.Clip = textGeometry;
```

This example builds a geometry from some text and then applies it as the Clip property of a button element. Figure 14-23 shows the results.

Figure 14-23. Text as a clip geometry

The visual layer API offers powerful text rendering services—all of WPF's text rendering builds on either GlyphRun or FormattedText. However, you will not want to write code every time you need to get text to appear. In many cases, TextBlock or the various flow document viewers will be ideal, but sometimes it is useful to exploit the full control offered by glyph runs from markup. This is the purpose of the Glyphs element.

Glyphs

The Glyphs class allows a glyph run to be incorporated into an application's UI tree. It is very similar in nature to the Path class we saw in Chapter 13. Both types derive from Shape (which in turn derives from FrameworkElement). Whereas Path lets you add any geometry object to the visual tree, Glyphs lets you add any glyph run.

You don't build the GlyphRun object yourself—Glyphs constructs it for you. Glyphs can use exactly the same information as we used when building a GlyphRun earlier in this chapter. However, it is quite happy to generate default glyph indices, advance widths, and cluster maps for us. This makes it simpler to use—as Example 14-25 shows, we need to provide only a font, the font size, the text, the fill brush, and the position.

Example 14-25. Glyphs

```
<Glyphs FontUri="C:\Windows\Fonts\Calibri.ttf" FontRenderingEmSize="40"
        UnicodeString="Hello, world" Fill="Black" OriginY="30" />
```

Note that as with GlyphRuns, Glyphs needs to know the location of the font file. In Example 14-18, we were able to get Typeface to find the file for us by calling its TryGetGlyphTypeface method. In code, you could do the same thing with a Glyphs object. But if you are using Glyphs from markup, there is no straightforward way to look up the font location, which is why Example 14-25 hardcodes the path. In practice, you should avoid doing this unless the path is a relative URI referring to a font embedded in your application as a resource. (You can package a font into your application just as you would any other binary resource.* See Chapter 12 for information on embedding binary resources.) If you need to use a system font in a Glyphs element, you will unfortunately need to write some code to look up the URI. Example 14-26 shows one general-purpose solution to this problem.

Example 14-26. Font URI markup extension

```
using System;
using System.Windows.Markup;
using System.Windows.Media;

namespace GlyphsUriLookup {
    public class FontUriExtension : MarkupExtension {
        string fontFamilyName;

        public FontUriExtension(string fontFamilyName) {
            this.fontFamilyName = fontFamilyName;
        }
```

---

* You should of course check whether the license for your font permits you to do this.

Example 14-26. Font URI markup extension (continued)

```
        public override object ProvideValue(IServiceProvider serviceProvider) {
            Typeface tf = new Typeface(this.fontFamilyName);
            GlyphTypeface gtf = null;
            if (!tf.TryGetGlyphTypeface(out gtf)) {
                throw new ArgumentException("Font family not found");
            }
            return gtf.FontUri;
        }
    }
}
```

This is a markup extension—a class that contains code used to determine the value of a property. (See Appendix A for more information about XAML and markup extensions.) It contains the code necessary to map from a font name to a font URI. You can use this to set the FontUri property of a Glyphs element, as Example 14-27 shows.

Example 14-27. Setting FontUri with a custom markup extension

```
<Canvas xmlns:loc="clr-namespace:GlyphsUriLookup">
  <Glyphs FontUri="{loc:FontUri Calibri}" FontRenderingEmSize="40"
          UnicodeString="Hello, world" Fill="Black" OriginY="30" />
</Canvas>
```

Although Glyphs will generate sensible default values for glyph indices and advance widths, you can specify nonstandard values manually if necessary, as you would for a GlyphRun. However, the way you specify these values looks a little different. GlyphRun takes separate arrays for indices and widths, but with Glyphs, these are encoded into a single text property, Indices, shown in Example 14-28.

Example 14-28. Using Indices

```
<Glyphs FontUri="C:\Windows\Fonts\Calibri.ttf"
        FontRenderingEmSize="40"
        Indices="44,60;286,60;367,60;367,60;381,60;853,60;3,60;
                 449,60;381,60;396,60;367,60;282,60;842,60"
        UnicodeString="Hello, world!"
        Fill="Black"
        OriginY="30" />
```

The Indices property consists of semicolon-separated sets of numbers. Each set corresponds to one character in the text. The first number is the glyph index.

 Remember that glyph indices are specific to a particular font file. If you change the FontUri without updating the Indices, you are likely to see complete garbage as a result.

The number after the glyph index is the advance width (i.e., the nominal width of the character). Example 14-28 sets this to 60 for every single character. Figure 14-24

---

shows the results. It looks pretty horrible because this particular font is designed for proportional spacing, and not the monospaced layout shown here.

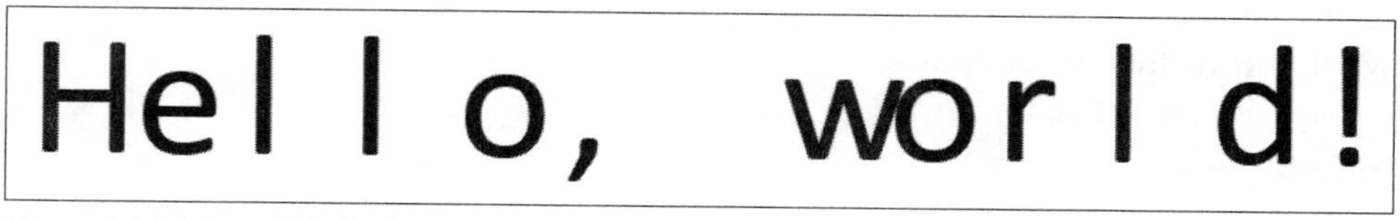

Figure 14-24. Nondefault character spacing

You can optionally supply two more numbers for each entry in Indices to control the position of combining characters. Some characters, such as accents, are designed to be added to other characters. Their default position is usually appropriate, but occasionally it's useful to adjust them. You would do this by providing an *x* and *y* offset after the advance width.

Now that we've seen all of the elements available for rendering text, it's time to look at this text object model in more detail.

Text Object Model

Text has distinctive layout requirements. With most user interface elements, the goal of layout is typically to define the basic UI structure (e.g., menu and toolbars at the top, status bar at the bottom, tree view on the left, scrollable work area on the right) and have the layout system make simple adjustments to the size and position of each element in order to fit the available space. But with text, we typically have a continuous stream of content where sequencing is more important than exact position. For example, we often don't care whether a particular figure appears at the top, bottom, or middle of a page as long as it is adjacent to the paragraph that refers to the figure.

There is some overlap between the requirements of text layout and UI layout. For example, the WrapPanel arranges elements in a similar manner to word-wrapped text layout. Although it would have been technically possible to use a single layout system for both textual content and user interface structure, this would have involved compromises on both sides. WPF's object model for representing formatted text is therefore separate from the layout panels and controls we've seen in previous chapters.

The element types that make up the text model all derive from a common abstract base class: TextElement. As you saw in Table 14-1, this defines a set of properties for controlling aspects of the text's appearance, such as its font and color. The TextElement type does not derive from FrameworkElement. Instead, it derives from FrameworkContentElement, meaning that all text objects are not intrinsically visible—they rely on some hosting element derived from Visual, such as TextBlock or FlowDocumentPageViewer, in order to render them. But although text elements do not form part of the visual tree, they are still a part of the logical tree—if you walk the tree using the LogicalTreeHelper class, it will report all textual content. We described the distinction between the logical and visual trees in Chapter 9.

Text elements fall into two main categories: inline elements and block elements. We'll start by looking at inlines.

Inline

Inline text elements represent a stretch of text contained within a paragraph. They derive from the Inline base class, which in turn derives from TextElement. Some inlines simply apply formatting to their content, and some do a little more than that.

Because Inline derives from TextElement, it supports all the standard properties shown in Table 14-1. It also defines a few more, listed in Table 14-3.

Table 14-3. Inline text formatting properties

Property	Usage
BaselineAlignment	Determines vertical alignment relative to the current line of text
FlowDirection	LeftToRight or RightToLeft
TextDecorations	Controls lines such as underlining and strikethrough

We covered the TextDecorations property earlier because decorations are also used in the low-level text rendering APIs. FlowDirection is straightforward enough—in some languages text runs from left to right, whereas in others it runs from right to left—but it may seem surprising for this to be applied to an inline rather than, say, a paragraph. The reason is that a paragraph might contain a mixture of languages, so each inline can have a different flow direction if necessary. BaselineAlignment supports these values: Baseline, Bottom, Center, Subscript, Superscript, TextBottom, TextTop, and Top.

Example 14-29 illustrates the use of BaselineAlignment.

Example 14-29. BaselineAlignment

```
<TextBlock Background="LightGreen">
  Alignment:
  <Span FontSize="20" BaselineAlignment="Baseline">Baseline</Span>
  <Span BaselineAlignment="Center">Center</Span>
  <Span BaselineAlignment="Top">Top</Span>
  <Span BaselineAlignment="Superscript">Superscript</Span>
  <Span BaselineAlignment="Bottom">Bottom</Span>
  <Span BaselineAlignment="Subscript">Subscript</Span>
</TextBlock>
```

We made one piece of text in this example larger than the rest in order to highlight the difference between Center and Baseline. If every item in a line is the same height, these two values have the same effect. Figure 14-25 shows the results.

Example 14-29 does not show the TextTop and TextBottom settings, because in this particular example, they behave in the same way as Top and Bottom. The distinction

Alignment: **Baseline** Center Top Superscript Bottom Subscript

Figure 14-25. BaselineAlignment

matters only if you take the fairly unusual step of forcing the effective line height to be different from the natural height of the text. You can do this by setting the LineStackingStrategy property to BlockLineHeight, and setting the BlockLineHeight property, as shown in Example 14-30.

Example 14-30. Top and Bottom versus TextTop and TextBottom

```
<TextBlock Background="LightGreen"
          LineStackingStrategy="BlockLineHeight" LineHeight="40">
  Alignment:
  <Span FontSize="20" BaselineAlignment="Baseline">Baseline</Span>
  <Span BaselineAlignment="TextTop">TextTop</Span>
  <Span BaselineAlignment="Top">Top</Span>
  <Span BaselineAlignment="TextBottom">TextBottom</Span>
  <Span BaselineAlignment="Bottom">Bottom</Span>
</TextBlock>
```

As Figure 14-26 shows, Top and Bottom appear at the top and bottom of the TextBlock. TextTop and TextBottom appear at the top and bottom of the text's natural vertical extent.

Alignment: **Baseline** TextTop Top TextBottom Bottom

Figure 14-26. Top and Bottom versus TextTop and TextBottom

The following sections describe each concrete type derived from Inline.

Run

Run is the most widely used text element type, because it's the only one capable of containing actual text. This can come as a surprise, as you rarely see the type used explicitly in XAML. However, Run elements are generated automatically. For example, this:

```
<TextBlock>
  Simple text
</TextBlock>
```

is equivalent to this:

```
<TextBlock>
  <Run Text="Simple text" />
</TextBlock>
```

The XAML compiler knows to generate the Run element automatically thanks to custom attributes applied to the relevant classes. As Example 14-31 shows, the TextBlock element is annotated with a ContentProperty attribute indicating that child content should be added to its Inlines property. That property is of type InlineCollection, and as you can see, that is annotated with two ContentWrapper attributes. We describe the process by which XAML is converted into objects in Appendix A; the net result of these attributes is that plain text inside any InlineCollection will automatically be wrapped in Run elements, whereas user interface elements will automatically be wrapped in InlineUIContainer elements.

Example 14-31. Attributes responsible for Run element generation

```
[ContentProperty("Inlines"), ...]
public class TextBlock : FrameworkElement, ...

[ContentWrapper(typeof(Run)), ContentWrapper(typeof(InlineUIContainer)),
    WhitespaceSignificantCollection]
public class InlineCollection : TextElementCollection<Inline>, ...
```

Because Run elements are generated automatically, you don't often use them in XAML. However, they offer one advantage over bare text: XML parsers often ignore whitespace in element content, but will never ignore it inside an attribute. Consider Example 14-32.

Example 14-32. Whitespace as content and as attribute

```
<TextBlock>
   A     B
   <Run Text="A       B" />
</TextBlock>
```

This TextBlock looks like it should contain the same text twice. The plain-text content will automatically be wrapped with a Run element, which is then followed by another Run with the same text. However, as Figure 14-27 shows, the text has been handled differently. The spaces in the first block of text have collapsed into a single space. Only in the second case, where the text was wrapped explicitly in a Run, is the whitespace preserved.

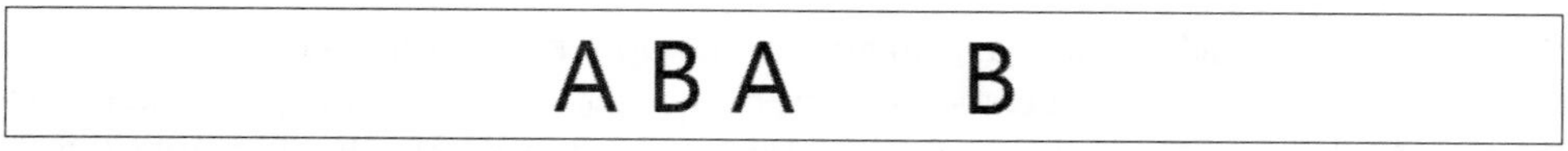

A B A   B

Figure 14-27. Whitespace handling

This reduction of whitespace is often useful. It enables us to indent text and add new lines without affecting the final outcome. Indeed, although we can disable this behavior, doing so illustrates why we often don't want to. Example 14-33 uses a standard XML attribute to force whitespace to be preserved.

Example 14-33. Preserving whitespace in mixed content

```
<TextBlock xml:space="preserve" Background="LightBlue">
  A       B
  <Run Text="A        B" />
</TextBlock>
```

Figure 14-28 shows the results. A background color has been specified to make it clear what is happening. Although both blocks of text now correctly preserve the amount of space between the two letters, the example also preserves some things we may not have wanted. There is now some space to the left of both *As*—this is because we indented the contents of the TextBlock. If we want the content to be flush to the left of the TextBlock, we would have to avoid indenting it wherever xml:space="preserve" is used. This can be inconvenient because a lot of XML editors will automatically indent both elements and their content based on the depth of nesting.

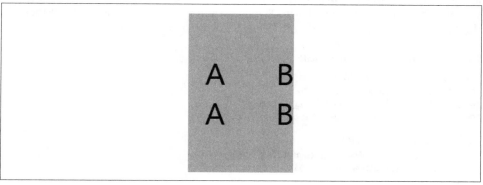

Figure 14-28. Preserved whitespace

The example also now spans multiple lines. As you can see from the empty areas painted with the background color, we have blank lines at the top and the bottom. This is because the content is defined on separate lines from the opening and closing TextBlock tags—there are line end characters in our XAML after the opening TextBlock, before the Run, and before the closing TextBlock, and these have all been faithfully preserved. If you use the xml:space="preserve" attribute, the only way to get just one line of output is to make sure that the TextBlock is all on one line in your XAML source. In practice, it's often more convenient to use explicit Run elements instead when you need to control whitespace.

The XAML compiler automatically generates Run wrapper elements for text content. If you are working with the text object model from code, you will need to deal with Run elements regardless of whether you need precise control over whitespace.

Because Run derives from TextElement, it can use all of the TextElement formatting properties shown in Table 14-1. Run elements are always the leaves of a tree of text elements—they cannot have children. This can make them a little cumbersome for mixing styles together. It may be easier to use Span or one of its derivatives.

Span

Span allows you to apply text formatting properties to a range of text. Unlike Run, a Span can contain child elements. This allows you to combine styles, as shown in Example 14-34.

Example 14-34. Nested Span elements

```
<TextBlock>
  <Span FontFamily="Cambria">
    This uses <Span FontWeight="Bold">a
    <Span FontStyle="Italic">mixture</Span> of</Span> styles.
  </Span>
</TextBlock>
```

The Span class has an Inlines property. Just as with TextBlock, child content will be added to this property, which is of type InlineCollection. This means that plain text will automatically be wrapped with Run elements, just as it is inside a TextBlock. So the XAML in Example 14-34 is equivalent to the code in Example 14-35.

Example 14-35. Nested Span elements in code

```
TextBlock txt = new TextBlock();
Span rootSpan = new Span();
rootSpan.FontFamily = new FontFamily("Cambria");
rootSpan.Inlines.Add(new Run("This uses "));

Span boldSpan = new Span();
boldSpan.FontWeight = FontWeights.Bold;
boldSpan.Inlines.Add(new Run("a "));

Span italicSpan = new Span();
italicSpan.Inlines.Add(new Run("mixture"));

boldSpan.Inlines.Add(italicSpan);
boldSpan.Inlines.Add(new Run(" of"));

rootSpan.Inlines.Add(boldSpan);
rootSpan.Inlines.Add(new Run(" styles"));
```

Figure 14-29 shows the results.

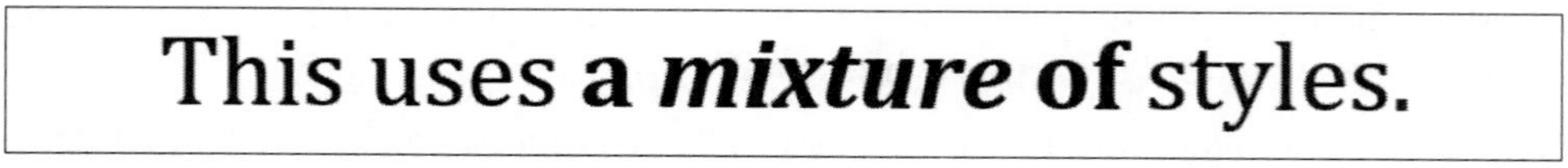

This uses **a *mixture* of** styles.

Figure 14-29. Nested Span elements

For convenience, WPF defines four types derived from Span that apply common formatting to their contents: Bold, Hyperlink, Italic, and Underline.

These allow the content in Example 14-34 to be expressed more compactly. Example 14-36 will produce the same result as that shown in Figure 14-29.

Example 14-36. Using the derived span types

```
<TextBlock>
  <Span FontFamily="Cambria">
    This uses <Bold>a <Italic>mixture</Italic> of</Bold> styles.
  </Span>
</TextBlock>
```

Unlike Bold and Italic, the Hyperlink class does more than define a standard look. It also offers a NavigateUri property. If you set this on a Hyperlink in a navigation application, the application will navigate to the specified URI if the element is clicked. It also offers a Click event and a Command property, both of which behave in exactly the same way as the equivalently named members of the Button class, which we described in Chapter 5.

LineBreak

The LineBreak element is a bit of an oddball. It derives from Inline, meaning that it is for use within a paragraph, but it appears to introduce a new paragraph. Strictly speaking, from the point of view of the text object model, it introduces a new line in the middle of a paragraph. Example 14-37 shows LineBreak in use.

Example 14-37. LineBreak

```
<TextBlock TextWrapping="Wrap">
  This is the first sentence in a paragraph.
  <LineBreak />
  This is technically the second sentence of the same paragraph.
</TextBlock>
```

Figure 14-30 shows the results. As you can see, it certainly looks like two paragraphs. But as far as the text object model is concerned, it is treated as a single paragraph.

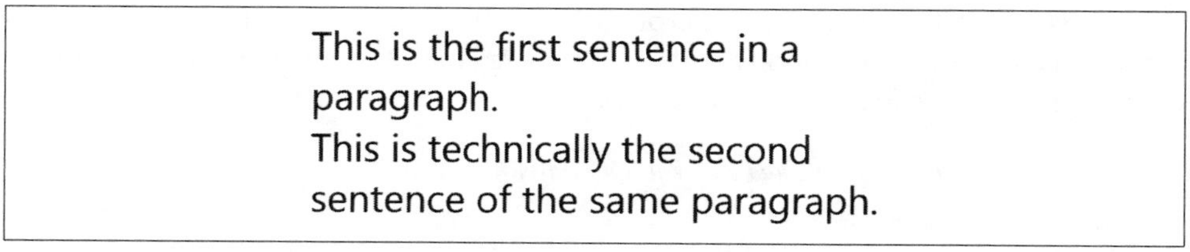

This is the first sentence in a paragraph.
This is technically the second sentence of the same paragraph.

Figure 14-30. LineBreak

Although this may seem to be a rather pedantic distinction, it is a useful one. A TextBlock is not capable of dealing with WPF's Paragraph element, but it can deal with LineBreak because that's an Inline. By using LineBreak, you can show what appear to be multiple paragraphs of text without having to use a full FlowDocument in a reader control. In performance-sensitive scenarios, this can be important, because TextBlock uses fewer resources than any of the FlowDocument viewers.

InlineUIContainer

Although types derived from `TextElement` use a different layout strategy from those derived from `FrameworkElement`, it is possible to mix both element types. Just as elements such as `TextBlock` or `FlowDocumentReader` can host text in a visual tree, there are also text elements that can host UI elements in a text tree. The `InlineUIContainer` type wraps any object derived from `UIElement`. Because `InlineUIContainer` derives from `Inline`, you can place it in any element that contains inlines, such as a `TextBlock` or a `Span`. Example 14-38 uses this to host a `Button`.

Example 14-38. InlineUIContainer

```
<TextBlock>
  Text with a
  <InlineUIContainer>
    <Button Content="Control" />
  </InlineUIContainer>
  in the middle.
</TextBlock>
```

Figure 14-31 shows the result. Elements hosted by an `InlineUIContainer` will size to content unless the containing element has its `LineHeight` property set. In that case, the hosted element will size to content horizontally, but would be vertically constrained to the line height.

Figure 14-31. InlineUIContainer

As you can see in Figure 14-31, the default alignment for a hosted element is that its bottom is aligned with the baseline of the text. Because `InlineUIContainer` derives from `Inline`, you can modify this by setting the `BaselineAlignment` property described earlier, as Example 14-39 shows.

Example 14-39. Positioning a hosted element with BaselineAlignment

```
<TextBlock TextWrapping="Wrap">
  Text with a
  <InlineUIContainer BaselineAlignment="Center">
    <Button Content="Control" />
  </InlineUIContainer>
  in the middle.
</TextBlock>
```

Figure 14-32 shows the results.

Text with a Control in the middle.

Figure 14-32. InlineUIContainer aligned centrally

InlineUIContainer offers all the same properties as any other inline element. If you do not need to set any of these, you can omit it from your XAML because, as we saw in Example 14-31, the InlineCollection class is annotated with a ContentWrapper attribute. This instructs the XAML compiler to wrap UI elements in InlineUIContainer elements automatically. So, instead of the markup in Example 14-38, we can use the shorter equivalent in Example 14-40.

Example 14-40. Automatic InlineUIContainer generation

```
<TextBlock>
  Text with a
  <Button Content="Control" />
  in the middle.
</TextBlock>
```

InlineUIContainer is not limited to controls. It enables you to integrate any content type into your text—you can host video, bitmaps, and 2D and 3D graphics in an InlineUIContainer.

We've now looked at all of the text element types that we can use within a single paragraph. However, for any reasonable quantity of text, you will want to break the text into multiple paragraphs, and maybe add features such as lists and tables. This is where the Block type comes in.

Block

Block is an abstract base class that derives from TextElement. It represents blocks of text such as paragraphs, tables, and lists. You can't use a Block inside a TextBlock—that can contain only inline elements. Blocks belong inside a FlowDocument, and must therefore be presented by one of the flow document viewer controls described earlier in this chapter.

The Block base class defines a set of common properties. This includes all of those from TextElement, of course, which are listed in Table 14-1. Block adds many more properties common to all elements derived from Block. Two of these, TextAlignment and IsHyphenationEnabled, are aliased by TextBlock and were described earlier. Table 14-4 shows the complete set.

Table 14-4. Common block properties

Property	Usage
BorderBrush	Brush with which to paint a border around the block; null if no border required.
BorderThickness	Thickness of border.
BreakColumnBefore	True if this block should start in a new column.
BreakPageBefore	True if this block should start on a new page.
ClearFloaters	Controls how floaters for this block are positioned—see the "Figures and Floaters" section, later in this chapter, for details on floaters.
FlowDirection	Sets text flow direction for block—either LeftToRight or RightToLeft.
IsHyphenated	If True, enables words to be hyphenated when word wrapping.
LineHeight	Line height in device-independent pixels. (XAML can specify other units with a suffix: in, cm, and pt indicate inches, centimeters, and points, respectively.) A value of NaN (Auto in XAML) means the default height for the font.
LineStackingStrategy	Determines whether the actual line height is determined by LineHeight, or the height of the tallest element on the line.
Margin	Space to be left between this block and its neighbors.
Padding	Space to be left between the block's border and its content.
TextAlignment	One of the TextAlignment enumeration values: Left, Right, Center, or Justify.

We describe the block element types in the following sections.

Paragraph

The Paragraph element groups a collection of Inline elements into a paragraph. Example 14-41 shows a FlowDocument containing two paragraphs.

Example 14-41. Paragraph elements

```
<FlowDocument>
  <Paragraph>
    This is a paragraph.
  </Paragraph>
  <Paragraph>
    <Italic>This</Italic> is <Bold>another</Bold> paragraph. It
    contains more text than the first, and with more
    <Span FontFamily="Old English Text MT">styles</Span>.
  </Paragraph>
</FlowDocument>
```

Figure 14-33 shows the results. As you can see, each paragraph starts on a new line.

There is also space between the paragraphs—by default, a paragraph has a vertical margin that is the same as the line height. You can override this by setting an explicit Margin property value. Figure 14-34 shows the effect of changing the Margin to 0 on both paragraphs.

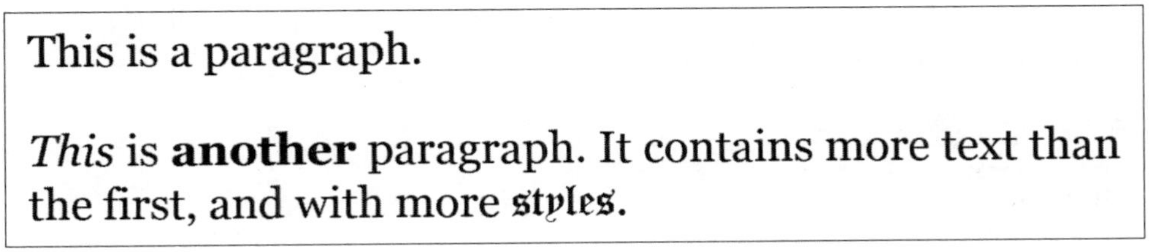

> This is a paragraph.
>
> *This* is **another** paragraph. It contains more text than the first, and with more 𝔰𝔱𝔶𝔩𝔢𝔰.

Figure 14-33. FlowDocument with two paragraphs

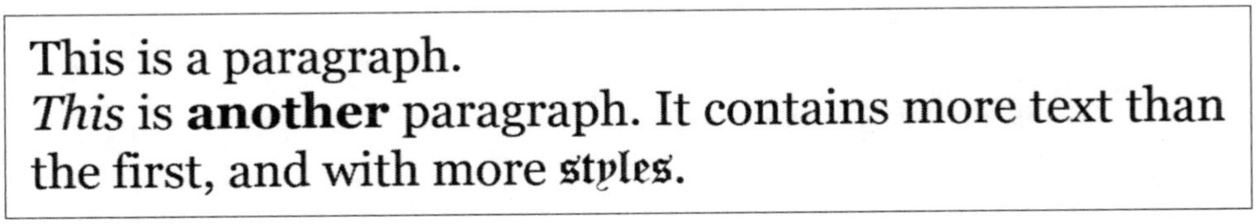

> This is a paragraph.
> *This* is **another** paragraph. It contains more text than the first, and with more 𝔰𝔱𝔶𝔩𝔢𝔰.

Figure 14-34. Paragraphs with margin of 0

The contents of a Paragraph are contained in its Inlines property. Just as with TextBlock and Span, this is of type InlineCollection, so again, Run and InlineUIContainer elements will be generated automatically for nested text and FrameworkElements when the XAML is processed.

List

The List block defines a numbered or bulleted list. The list's contents are held in the ListItems property—a collection of ListItem elements. The ListItemCollection type is not annotated with a ContentWrapper attribute, so you are required to define the ListItem elements explicitly, as Example 14-42 shows.

Example 14-42. List with ListItems

```
<List>
  <ListItem>
    <Paragraph>
      This is an item.
    </Paragraph>
  </ListItem>
  <ListItem>
    <Paragraph>
      This item contains two paragraphs. This is the first.
    </Paragraph>
    <Paragraph>
      This is the second.
    </Paragraph>
  </ListItem>
</List>
```

ListItem derives directly from TextElement, because the only place in which it occurs is inside a List—it is neither an Inline nor a Block. Its content is held in the Blocks property, which is a collection of Block elements. In Example 14-42, the two items contain a paragraph and a pair of paragraphs, respectively, but any block type will do. You can even nest lists, as Example 14-43 shows.

Example 14-43. Nested lists

```
<List MarkerStyle="Square">
  <ListItem>
    <Paragraph>
      This item contains a paragraph followed by a nested list.
    </Paragraph>
    <List MarkerStyle="Decimal">
      <ListItem>
        <Paragraph>
          This is a nested list item.
        </Paragraph>
      </ListItem>
      <ListItem>
        <Paragraph>
          This is a second nested list item.
        </Paragraph>
      </ListItem>
    </List>
  </ListItem>
  <ListItem>
    <Paragraph>
      Is the second item in the first list.
    </Paragraph>
    <List MarkerStyle="Decimal" StartIndex="3">
      <ListItem>
        <Paragraph>
          This nested list carries on from the previous list numbering.
        </Paragraph>
      </ListItem>
      <ListItem>
        <Paragraph>
          This is the second item in the second nested list.
        </Paragraph>
      </ListItem>
    </List>
  </ListItem>
</List>
```

This example also illustrates the use of the MarkerStyle property, as Figure 14-35 shows. The top-level list uses a hollow square, but more interestingly, the nested lists are numbered. There is no way to get one list to automatically pick up the numbering from where another left off, but this example gets the required result by manually specifying the StartIndex for the second nested list.

MarkerStyle supports a variety of styles, which are shown in Figure 14-36.

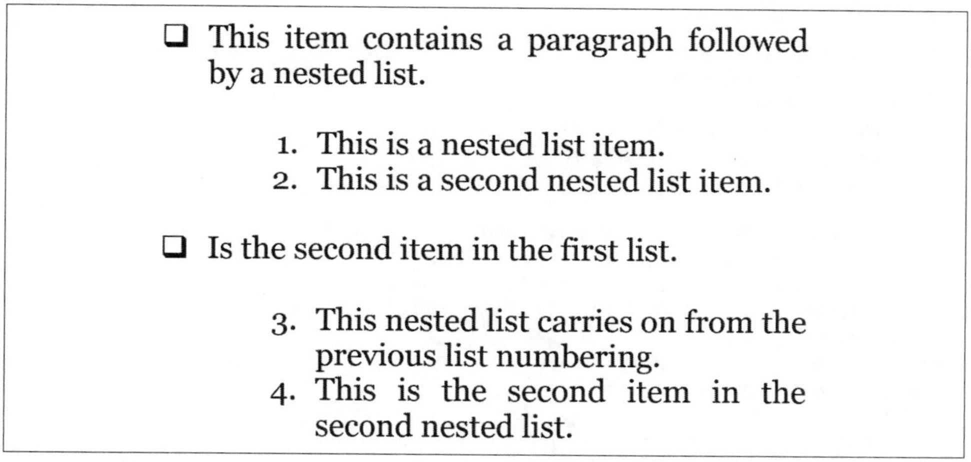

> ❑ This item contains a paragraph followed by a nested list.
>
> 1. This is a nested list item.
> 2. This is a second nested list item.
>
> ❑ Is the second item in the first list.
>
> 3. This nested list carries on from the previous list numbering.
> 4. This is the second item in the second nested list.

Figure 14-35. Nested and numbered lists

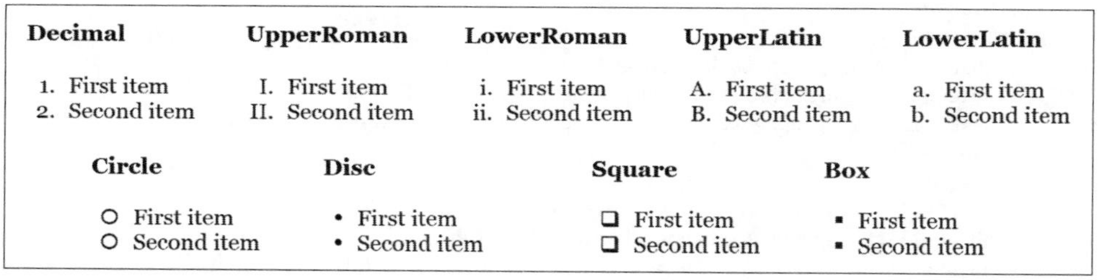

Decimal	UpperRoman	LowerRoman	UpperLatin	LowerLatin
1. First item	I. First item	i. First item	A. First item	a. First item
2. Second item	II. Second item	ii. Second item	B. Second item	b. Second item

Circle	Disc	Square	Box
○ First item	• First item	❑ First item	▪ First item
○ Second item	• Second item	❑ Second item	▪ Second item

Figure 14-36. Marker styles

There is no direct support for customizing the marker—MarkerStyle accepts values only from the TextMarkerStyle enumeration, so the set of values is closed, and there is no "custom" style. However, you could easily create your own list by defining a two-column Table, with the list items in the second column and the custom markers in the first.

Table

The Table element presents information in tabular form. Its capabilities overlap somewhat with the Grid. Think of it as the TextElement equivalent of the Grid—you would only use a Table inside a FlowDocument, whereas a UI would use a Grid. However, not only are these elements designed for use in different contexts, but also the style of use is slightly different. Whereas the position of an element within a Grid is set by attached Grid.Column and Grid.Row properties, table elements' positions are based on the order in which they are added—Example 14-44 contains no explicit positioning information.

Example 14-44. Table

```
<Table CellSpacing="6">
  <TableRowGroup FontWeight="Bold">
    <TableRow FontSize="24">
      <TableCell ColumnSpan="3" TextAlignment="Center" >
        <Paragraph>Ice Cream</Paragraph>
      </TableCell>
    </TableRow>
    <TableRow FontSize="18" Background="LightGray">
      <TableCell><Paragraph>Type</Paragraph></TableCell>
      <TableCell><Paragraph>Description</Paragraph></TableCell>
      <TableCell><Paragraph>Availability</Paragraph></TableCell>
    </TableRow>
  </TableRowGroup>
  <TableRowGroup>
    <TableRow>
      <TableCell><Paragraph>Chocolate</Paragraph></TableCell>
      <TableCell><Paragraph>Yummy</Paragraph></TableCell>
      <TableCell><Paragraph>Widespread</Paragraph></TableCell>
    </TableRow>
    <TableRow>
      <TableCell><Paragraph>Cookie Dough</Paragraph></TableCell>
      <TableCell><Paragraph>Extra yummy</Paragraph></TableCell>
      <TableCell><Paragraph>Scarce - Ian ate it all</Paragraph></TableCell>
    </TableRow>
    <TableRow>
      <TableCell><Paragraph>Artichoke</Paragraph></TableCell>
      <TableCell><Paragraph>Gruesome</Paragraph></TableCell>
      <TableCell><Paragraph>Rarely available</Paragraph></TableCell>
    </TableRow>
  </TableRowGroup>
</Table>
```

Figure 14-37 shows the results. Each item in the table is defined in a TableCell element, which is contained by a TableRow. The first cell in a row will be in the first column, the second cell in the second column, and so on. You can make a single item span multiple cells using the ColumnSpan or RowSpan property—the title on the first row has a ColumnSpan of 3 in order to fill the whole width. But unlike the Grid, a single Table cell cannot contain multiple overlapping items.

Ice Cream		
Type	**Description**	**Availability**
Chocolate	Yummy	Widespread
Cookie Dough	Extra yummy	Scarce - Ian ate it all
Artichoke	Gruesome	Rarely available

Figure 14-37. Table

The rows in a table are always contained by a TableRowGroup. This provides a single place to apply formatting to multiple rows. Example 14-44 uses a TableRowGroup to set the FontWeight of the first two rows to Bold. The remaining rows use the default font weight because they are in a separate TableRowGroup that does not specify any formatting.

 A Table must always contain at least one TableRowGroup even if you do not need to apply formatting to groups of rows. The object model requires this—the Table class's content is held in its RowGroups property.

The number of columns in a table is determined automatically unless you choose to specify columns explicitly. Example 14-45 defines the columns explicitly in order to fix the first column's width. The TableColumn.Width property is of type GridLength, meaning it supports the same sizing mechanisms as Grid: fixed size, star sizing, and automatic sizing. We described these in Chapter 3.

Example 14-45. Explicit table columns

```
<Table BorderThickness="1" BorderBrush="Black">
  <Table.Columns>
    <TableColumn Width="25" />
    <TableColumn />
  </Table.Columns>
  <TableRowGroup>
    <TableRow>
      <TableCell><Paragraph>&#x2665;</Paragraph></TableCell>
      <TableCell><Paragraph>Raspberry</Paragraph></TableCell>
    </TableRow>
    <TableRow>
      <TableCell><Paragraph>&#x2665;</Paragraph></TableCell>
      <TableCell><Paragraph>Vanilla</Paragraph></TableCell>
    </TableRow>
  </TableRowGroup>
</Table>
```

Figure 14-38 shows the results. Example 14-45 sets a border on the table so that you can see its bounds. This makes the effect of the fixed-width column clear; by default, the two columns would have been the same width.

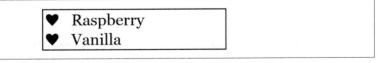

Figure 14-38. Table with fixed-width column

The only other property offered by TableColumn is Background, enabling you to set a background brush for the column.

In Examples 14-44 and 14-45, each cell contains a Paragraph. A TableCell can contain any sequence of block elements, so you can also nest lists, or even other tables, inside a table cell.

Section

The Section block type contains a sequence of other blocks. A Section has no default intrinsic behavior: wrapping some blocks in a Section will not change their appearance unless you set some formatting properties on the Section. The purpose of Section is to allow you to apply a set of formatting properties to several blocks at once. Example 14-46 uses a Section to apply an italic font style to two paragraphs.

Example 14-46. Section

```
<Section FontStyle="Italic">
  <Paragraph>
    This paragraph is in italics because the containing section's
    FontStyle property is set to Italic.
  </Paragraph>
  <Paragraph FontWeight="Bold">
    This paragraph is in bold italics because its FontWeight is set
    to Bold, and it inherits the Italic FontStyle from its containing
    section.
  </Paragraph>
</Section>
```

As you can see from Figure 14-39, both paragraphs pick up the italic style from their parent section. The second paragraph combines this inherited italic style with a locally specified bold font weight.

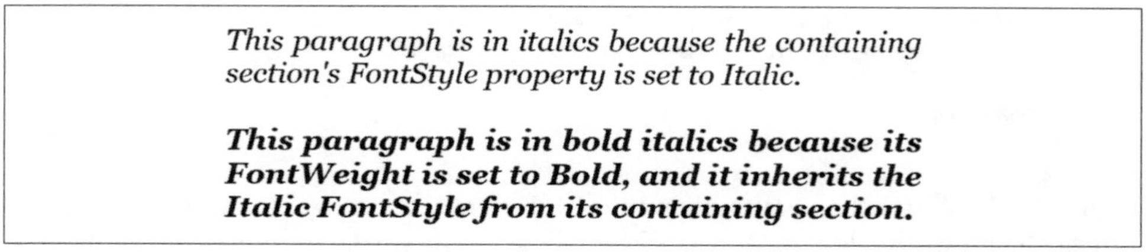

> *This paragraph is in italics because the containing section's FontStyle property is set to Italic.*
>
> ***This paragraph is in bold italics because its FontWeight is set to Bold, and it inherits the Italic FontStyle from its containing section.***

Figure 14-39. Section

BlockUIContainer

Earlier, we saw the InlineUIContainer, which allows any UIElement to be hosted inside a paragraph. This allowed controls, video, bitmap, 2D graphics, or 3D graphics to be integrated into a document. BlockUIContainer is similar: it can host any UIElement, but it wraps it as a Block instead of an Inline. Example 14-47 uses this to put a Button between two paragraphs.

Example 14-47. BlockUIContainer

```
<Paragraph>
  This is a paragraph.
</Paragraph>
<BlockUIContainer>
  <Button Content="Button" />
</BlockUIContainer>
<Paragraph>
  This is another paragraph.
</Paragraph>
```

Figure 14-40 shows the result. As you can see, the button has turned out rather wide. This is because a `BlockUIContainer` will offer the entire column width to the element it contains. The contained element will size to content vertically, but not horizontally.

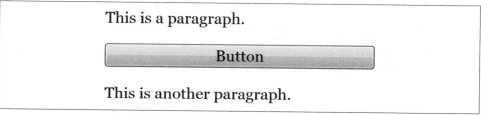

Figure 14-40. BlockUIContainer

If you don't want the contained element to fill the whole width, you must use `FrameworkElement` layout settings. For example, setting the `HorizontalAlignment` property of the `Button` to `Left` will cause the button to left-align within the container, as Figure 14-41 shows. Setting the `TextAlignment` property of the `BlockUIContainer` to `Left` will not work—this block type always fills the full width of the column, so the horizontal alignment options mean nothing on the `BlockUIContainer` itself.

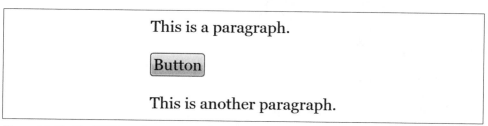

Figure 14-41. BlockUIContainer content alignment

We have now looked at all of the block types. However, there are two remaining text element types we've not yet looked at: `Figure` and `Floater`. These are not blocks, but they are normally used from within blocks.

Figures and Floaters

The Figure and Floater types are used to host blocks of content around which other content flows. They are typically used for hosting figures, sidebars, or tables. Both types derive from the AnchoredBlock abstract base class. This derives from Inline, so these are technically inline elements. However, their content is a collection of Block elements, so you cannot use them in a TextBlock—figures and floaters must appear inside a flow document. Example 14-48 shows a Floater.

Example 14-48. Floater

```
<FlowDocument>
  <Paragraph>
    This paragraph contains a 'floater'. It is the table you can see to
    the right.
    <Floater HorizontalAlignment="Right" Width="150">
      <Table BorderThickness="1" BorderBrush="Black">
        <Table.Columns>
          <TableColumn Width="25" />
          <TableColumn />
        </Table.Columns>
        <TableRowGroup>
          <TableRow>
            <TableCell><Paragraph>&#x2665;</Paragraph></TableCell>
            <TableCell><Paragraph>Raspberry</Paragraph></TableCell>
          </TableRow>
          <TableRow>
            <TableCell><Paragraph>&#x2665;</Paragraph></TableCell>
            <TableCell><Paragraph>Vanilla</Paragraph></TableCell>
          </TableRow>
          <TableRow>
            <TableCell ColumnSpan="2">
              <Paragraph TextAlignment="Center" FontStyle="Italic"
                         Margin="0,5,0,0">
                Example ice cream flavors
              </Paragraph>
            </TableCell>
          </TableRow>
        </TableRowGroup>
      </Table>
    </Floater>

    This table is anchored to this paragraph because the Floater element
    appears inside of this paragraph.
  </Paragraph>
  <Paragraph>
    This second paragraph also flows around the Floater because the table
    is tall enough to span two paragraphs.
  </Paragraph>
</FlowDocument>
```

Notice that the Floater element appears inside the first Paragraph. The position at which the Floater or Figure appears determines the anchor point, which will have an impact on where the hosted block appears—WPF will try to position it as close to the anchor point as possible. In Figure 14-42, the table appears on the line immediately after the one containing the anchor point.

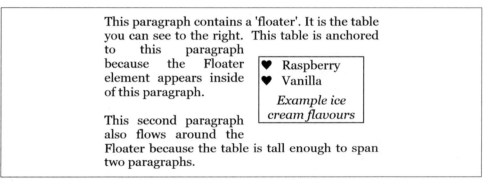

Figure 14-42. Floater

Whereas a Floater is positioned vertically as close as possible to its anchor point, its horizontal position is determined by the HorizontalAlignment property. In Example 14-48, this is set to Right. Figure 14-43 shows the effect of setting this to Center. The other options are Left and Stretch. The latter causes the block to fill the whole column width, preventing text from flowing around either side.

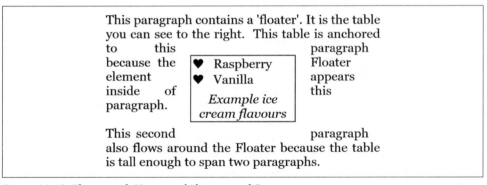

Figure 14-43. Floater with HorizontalAlignment of Center

Figure is very similar to Floater, the main difference being that it offers more flexibility in specifying the position relative to the anchor point. The horizontal position is set with the HorizontalAnchor property. This can be any of the values in the FigureHorizontalAnchor enumeration, which are shown in Table 14-5.

Table 14-5. FigureHorizontalAnchor enumeration

Value	Figure position
ColumnCenter	The center of the current column
ColumnLeft	The left of the current column
ColumnRight	The right of the current column
ContentCenter	The center of the content-holding area of the page
ContentLeft	The left of the content-holding area of the page
ContentRight	The right of the content-holding area of the page
PageCenter	The center of the page
PageLeft	The left of the page
PageRight	The right of the page

You can control the vertical position using the VerticalAnchor property. Table 14-6 shows the available values.

Table 14-6. FigureVerticalAnchor enumeration

Value	Figure position
ContentBottom	The bottom of the content-holding area of the page
ContentCenter	The center of the content-holding area of the page
ContentTop	The top of the content-holding area of the page
PageBottom	The bottom of the page
PageCenter	The center of the page
PageTop	The top of the page
ParagraphTop	The top of the current paragraph

Notice that almost all of the available anchor values are concerned with columns or pages. This means that some of the higher level of control offered by a Figure over a Floater is significant only if you are using a column-based paginated view. If you are using the FlowDocumentScrollViewer, there is no distinction between ColumnLeft and ContentLeft, because there is just one big scrolling column. Both of these do the same thing as a Floater with a HorizontalAlignment of Left. Likewise, the FigureVerticalAnchor settings are meaningful only in a paginated view. So, you would normally use Figure only on a document likely to be viewed in pages (e.g., a document you intend to print or one that will be viewed in a FlowDocumentPageViewer).

The horizontal column-based positions in Table 14-5 are self-explanatory. The difference between the page-based position and the positions relative to the "content" area is less obvious. This distinction exists because a FlowDocument does not necessarily fill the entire page. If you set its PagePadding property, WPF will leave space between the edge of the page and the document. Choosing a page-relative alignment such as PageLeft will position a figure relative to the page, ignoring the space added due to `PagePadding`. Figure 14-44 shows a document with 50 pixels of page padding, and a figure horizontally aligned with `PageLeft`. As you can see, this causes the figure to appear outside of the horizontal bounds of the column. Had we specified `ContentLeft`, the figure would have remained within the column's bounds.

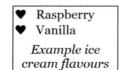

This paragraph contains a 'floater'. It is the table you can see to the right. This table is anchored to this paragraph because the Floater element appears inside of this paragraph.

This second paragraph also flows around the Floater because the table is tall enough to span two paragraphs.

Figure 14-44. PageLeft horizontal anchor

`Figure` offers extra flexibility for specifying the `Width` and `Height` of a figure. Whereas with a `Floater` these properties are of type `Double`—representing the absolute size in pixels—on a `Figure` they are of type `FigureLength`. This value type has a `FigureUnitType` property, indicating the units in which the size is specified. You can set this to `Pixel` in order to specify absolute dimensions. But you can also set it to `Column`, `Content`, or `Page` to specify the size relative to the column, content, or page size. For example, a width of 0.25 and unit of `Page` mean the figure should be one-quarter the width of the page. When using `Page` or `Content`, the size must be less than or equal to one. But you can specify multiple columns. Example 14-49 shows the XAML syntax for specifying a figure width in columns.

Example 14-49. Specifying figure widths in "columns" units

```
<Figure HorizontalAnchor="ContentLeft" VerticalAnchor="ContentTop"
    Width="2 columns">
    ...figure content...
</Figure>
```

This example would place a figure at the top left of the page content area, and it would span two columns. Figure 14-45 shows how this would look when the document is displayed in a paginated viewer wide enough to show three columns.

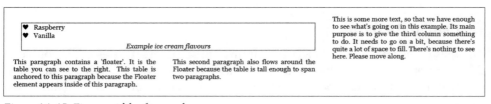

Figure 14-45. Figure width of two columns

We've now seen all of the types in the text object model, and yet we've not yet seen how to add an image to a document. It turns out that we can embed images easily using features we've already seen.

Images

The text object model doesn't have any direct support for hosting images. Although this is hardly surprising for a *text* object model, hosting images is a reasonably common requirement. There is no explicit support for images because you can use either of the UI container elements to add an Image element to the document.

By default, the images will try to fill the entire width available. If this is not what you require, you should specify the width or height as Example 14-50 does. Figure 14-46 shows the results.

Example 14-50. FlowDocument with images

```
<FlowDocument>
  <Paragraph>
    This paragraph is followed by an image in a block container:
  </Paragraph>

  <BlockUIContainer>
    <Image Source="Picture.jpg" Width="200" />
  </BlockUIContainer>

  <Paragraph>
    This paragraph uses an inline UI container to host an image:
    <InlineUIContainer BaselineAlignment="Center">
      <Image Source="Picture2.jpg" Height="40" />
    </InlineUIContainer>
  </Paragraph>
</FlowDocument>
```

All of the text object model examples we've seen so far have shown hardcoded content. Because text is represented with objects, you are of course free to generate content from code. As you saw in Chapters 6 and 7, data binding can offer a powerful way to generate content dynamically from data with a minimal amount of code. However, although data binding is supported in the text object model, it is somewhat limited.

Text and Data Binding

All types in the text object model derive from FrameworkContentElement. This provides data binding support, including a DataContext property, just like its counterpart, FrameworkElement. Data binding relies on the dependency property system: a data

This paragraph is followed by an image in a block container:

This paragraph uses an inline UI container to host an image:

Figure 14-46. Images in a flow document

binding target must be a dependency property. Unfortunately, the Text property of the Run class, which is where all the text in any tree of text objects is ultimately defined, is an ordinary CLR property and not a dependency property. This means it cannot be the target of a data binding expression. Indeed, the dependency properties available in the text object model are mainly concerned with formatting rather than textual content.

The only elements that offer dependency properties that you can use to display text are not text elements at all—they derive from FrameworkElement. You can use TextBlock—its Text property can be the target for a binding expression. Alternatively, you can use any type derived from ContentControl—if you bind text to its Content property, it will host that text in a TextBlock for you. Example 14-51 shows data binding with TextBlock elements.

Example 14-51. Text and data binding

```
<TextBlock>
  Name:
  <TextBlock Text="{Binding FirstName}" />
  <TextBlock Text="{Binding LastName}" />
</TextBlock>
```

This example contains two binding expressions, bound to a hypothetical data source offering two properties, FirstName and LastName. In order to provide a binding target for each property, we've used two TextBlock elements. These are nested inside a third TextBlock, allowing us to mix data-bound content with fixed content. As we saw earlier, the content of a TextBlock is a collection of inline elements, so this is really shorthand for the markup in Example 14-52.

Example 14-52. Text and data binding in full

```
<TextBlock>
  <Run Text="Name: " />
  <InlineUIContainer>
    <TextBlock Text="{Binding FirstName}" />
  </InlineUIContainer>
  <Run Text=" " />
  <InlineUIContainer>
    <TextBlock Text="{Binding LastName}" />
  </InlineUIContainer>
</TextBlock>
```

You don't need to specify the InlineUIContainer elements explicitly—as we saw earlier, they are generated automatically for you thanks to the ContentWrapper attributes on the InlineCollection class. So, Examples 14-51 and 14-52 are functionally equivalent. There is one problem with this: each nested TextBlock element will be treated by the top-level TextBlock as a single indivisible element for word-wrapping purposes. To see why this is a problem, consider the following two examples. Example 14-53 uses a nested TextBlock to display the title of a book. (It's not data-bound, but you could easily imagine wanting to retrieve a book title with data binding.)

Example 14-53. Nested TextBlock

```
<TextBlock Margin="5" Background="PaleGreen" TextWrapping="Wrap">
  This book is called
  '<TextBlock FontWeight="Bold" Text="Programming WPF" />'
</TextBlock>
```

Example 14-54 displays the same text, but without using a nested TextBlock. Instead, it uses a Bold span to make the book title bold.

Example 14-54. Simple content

```
<TextBlock Margin="5" Background="PaleGreen" TextWrapping="Wrap">
  This book is called
  '<Bold>Programming WPF</Bold>'
</TextBlock>
```

Figure 14-47 shows the results. The nested TextBlock version is shown on the left, and as you can see, some things have gone wrong. It has wrapped the entire "Programming WPF" string into a new line, even though there was space to fit the word "Programming" on the first line. WPF was unable to break the line in between "Programming" and "WPF" because the text was inside an InlineUIContainer. It has failed to keep the opening apostrophe adjacent to the word "Programming" for exactly the same reason. As far as the text layout engine is concerned, the "Programming WPF" content is part of a completely different body of text than the rest of the sentence. By contrast, the example on the right has just the one text tree, so it has been able to break the text in the right place. (And, if we were to force it to break the line earlier by narrowing the space, it would keep each apostrophe on the same line as the word to which it belongs.)

| This book is called '
Programming WPF' | This book is called '**Programming
WPF**' |

Figure 14-47. Nested TextBlock

Unfortunately, there is no straightforward solution to this problem. None of the element types in the text object model provides a way to bind data into a text tree, so if you want to inject code into the middle of a body of text without disrupting the formatting, you will need to write some code to do it instead of relying on data binding.[*]

In the `FrameworkElement` world, `ItemsControl` provides powerful support for binding to list-like data sources, and generating multiple UI items from those sources. Unfortunately, there is no equivalent of this in the text object model world: you cannot generate either a `Table` or a `List` from a list-like data source with data binding. If you want to build data-driven textual lists, you will need to write code.

Coding with the Text Object Model

Generating a flow document from code is straightforward. It is slightly more long-winded than using XAML, because you need to create the `Run` elements that hold the text explicitly. Example 14-55 shows how to build a `FlowDocument` containing a `List` in code.

Example 14-55. Building a List in code

```
FlowDocument doc = new FlowDocument();
List myList = new List();
for (int item = 1; item <= 5; ++item) {
    string itemText = "Item " + item;
    Run itemRun = new Run(itemText);
    Paragraph itemBlock = new Paragraph(itemRun);
    ListItem listItem = new ListItem(itemBlock);
    myList.ListItems.Add(listItem);
}
doc.Blocks.Add(myList);
```

This creates a list of numbered items, as Figure 14-48 shows.

Creating text object models from scratch in code is very similar to creating text in markup. However, manipulating existing text gets special handling. You can just add and remove items from the collections of blocks and inlines, but the text object model also provides features for navigating and modifying trees of text, using the `TextPointer` type.

---

[*] You can find an example of how to do this at *http://fortes.com/2007/03/20/bindablerun* (*http://tinysells.com/109*).

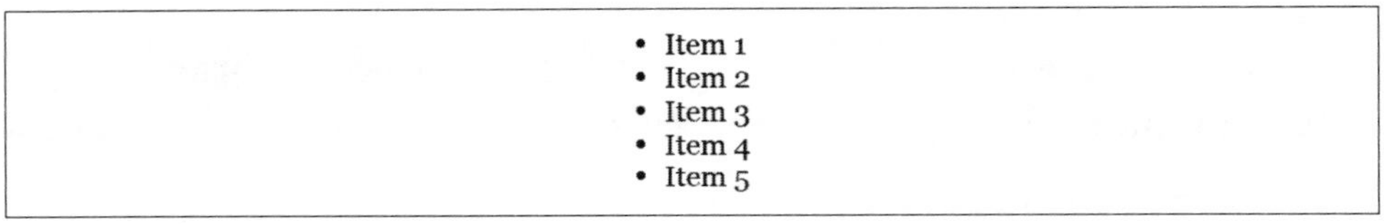

```
• Item 1
• Item 2
• Item 3
• Item 4
• Item 5
```

Figure 14-48. Generated List

TextPointer

A TextPointer object represents a particular position within either a FlowDocument or a TextBlock. You can retrieve a TextPointer from any TextElement—the ContentStart and ContentEnd properties return pointers to the start and end of the content represented by the element. Or, you can ask a TextBlock to return a pointer for a particular location (e.g., the current mouse pointer position) using its GetPositionFromPoint method. TextPointer is also used anywhere an API needs to indicate a position within a body of text, such as the start and end of the current selection in a RichTextBox.[*]

TextPointer provides methods for navigating through the text structure. Example 14-56 iterates through a range of text represented by a start and end pair of text pointers by calling GetNextContextPosition. It builds a string by appending the text from all of the runs it finds, and it uses GetPointerContext to discover which of the elements it encounters are Run elements.

Example 14-56. Extracting text content

```
static string GetText(TextPointer textStart, TextPointer textEnd) {
    StringBuilder output = new StringBuilder( );

    TextPointer tp = textStart;

    while (tp != null && tp.CompareTo(textEnd) < 0) {
        if (tp.GetPointerContext(LogicalDirection.Forward) ==
                TextPointerContext.Text) {
            output.Append(tp.GetTextInRun(LogicalDirection.Forward));
        }
        tp = tp.GetNextContextPosition(LogicalDirection.Forward);
    }
    return output.ToString( );
}
```

As well as being able to examine the text, a TextPointer allows you to insert text. Not all points in a text tree can accept new content, so TextPointer offers a GetInsertionPosition method that returns the nearest place where new text may be added. Example 14-57 uses this to insert text at the beginning of the current selection in a RichTextBox. (If there is no selected text, the Selection property returns the location of the caret.)

---

[*] RichTextBox uses a FlowDocument to represent the text being edited.

Example 14-57. Inserting text with a TextPointer

```
TextPointer insertionPoint =
  richTextBox.Selection.Start.GetInsertionPosition(LogicalDirection.Forward);
insertionPoint.InsertTextInRun("Text added from code");
```

The RichTextBox type's Selection property is of type TextRange. TextRange encapsulates a pair of TextPointer objects to denote a range of text that is available through the Start and End properties. It also offers a helper Text property that extracts all of the text in the range as a string (so in practice, you wouldn't need to write the code in Example 14-56—you can use a TextRange to do the work for you).

Sometimes it is useful to get from a TextPointer to an element in the tree of text objects. TextPointer therefore offers a GetAdjacentElement method, enabling you to retrieve the object containing the location to which the pointer refers. Alternatively, you can use the TextPointer object's Paragraph property. If the TextPointer points to a Paragraph, or an element contained by a Paragraph, this property gives you access to that Paragraph.

Whether you're using the full text object model as supported by flow documents, or just the inline subset available with a TextBlock, you can take advantage of WPF's typography support.

Typography

WPF supports both TrueType and OpenType fonts. OpenType fonts often contain many alternates to the basic set of character shapes in order to support advanced typographical functionality. If you are using a low-level text-handling feature such as GlyphRun, you can use these alternates directly, referring to them by glyph index. But if you are using the higher-level elements, such as TextBlock or the FlowDocument viewers, these can locate and use the appropriate glyphs for you. You can control which character shapes are used with the attached properties defined by the Typography class.

Because WPF supports all of OpenType's typography features, we will not provide a complete list here.[*] We'll show just one example: ligatures.

Most fonts offer ligatures: single shapes representing a group of letters. Historically, ligatures were invented out of necessity. In the past, typesetting involved an individual block of metal or wood for each letter. Certain combinations were problematic. For example, the top of a lowercase letter *f* extends to the right of the main stem of the letter. If you put two of them next to each other, with some typefaces this results in too much space between the stems—you couldn't get the letters close enough together to look right. To solve this, printers used a single block of metal with two *f*s on it.

---

[*] The MSDN documentation already does a fine job of that. For details, see *http://msdn2.microsoft.com/en-us/system.windows.documents.typography.aspx* or *http://tinysells.com/74*.

This single block is called a ligature. Figure 14-49 shows an example from the Palatino Linotype typeface: the two lowercase *f*s are displayed as a single shape here because the font offers them as a standard ligature, and WPF will use a font's standard ligatures by default.

Effusive

Figure 14-49. Ligature

Digital printing technology renders ligatures unnecessary. However, they are still widely used, mainly because we have become accustomed to seeing them. When reading at full speed, we recognize words as much by their overall shape as by the shapes of the individual letters in the words, and getting rid of ligatures can have a negative impact on reading speed. Moreover, most fonts are designed with the use of ligatures in mind, so they tend to look better with ligatures than without. Palatino Linotype is a case in point—as you can see from Figure 14-49, its lowercase *f* is relatively narrow at the top, so a ligature is not strictly necessary, but the font has still been designed to use a ligature for this case.

OpenType fonts can designate ligatures for various purposes. Some are *standard*, meaning they should be used by default. This set will typically include "ff," "fi," and "ffi." Some are marked as *discretionary*, meaning their use is optional. Palatino Linotype defines a discretionary ligature for the "Th" pair. Figure 14-50 shows the default appearance for this pair, as well as the discretionary ligature.

Th Th

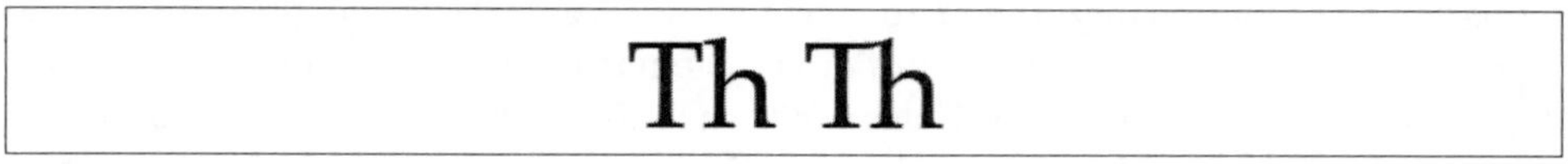

Figure 14-50. Default "Th" and discretionary "Th" ligature

The Typography class defines various attached properties for controlling the use of ligatures, which are listed in Table 14-7. Each is a Boolean property. StandardLigatures defaults to True, and you can enable the rest in the way shown in Example 14-58.

Table 14-7. Typography class ligature attached properties

Attached property	Usage
ContextualLigatures	Ligatures to be used only in specific contexts (e.g., only after certain letters)
DiscretionaryLigatures	Decorative ligatures, not necessarily appropriate in ordinary text
HistoricalLigatures	Decorative ligatures using old-fashioned styles
StandardLigatures	Ligatures suitable for use in ordinary text

Example 14-58. Enabling discretionary ligatures

```
<Span Typography.DiscretionaryLigatures="True">Th</Span>
```

All of the typography features are controlled in a similar way: the Typography class defines attached properties that you can set on any TextElement. All of these are inherited properties, so you can set them on the root FlowDocument or TextBlock element in order to apply a consistent typography style to all of the text.

Where Are We?

WPF supports any mixture of typefaces and formatting styles anywhere text is used. If you need fine control, you can work at a very low level with glyphs, using either GlyphRun at the visual layer, or Glyphs at the FrameworkElement level. It is typically easier to work at a higher level. TextBlock provides a simple but powerful way to incorporate small volumes of formatted text into an application, and it is the workhorse of basic text presentation for most WPF applications. But if you need to represent a multiparagraph document, FlowDocument is the way to go, as it supports the full WPF text object model. The document viewer controls offer either a simple single-column scrolling view, or a column-based paginating viewer. Whichever representation you use, WPF provides access to all the typographical features of your fonts.

CHAPTER 15

Printing and XPS

WPF provides powerful printing support, allowing you to use the majority of its graphical features in print as well as on-screen. Dynamic features such as animation and event handling don't translate to static paper output, of course, but you can use any stationary graphics. You can also use framework services such as data binding and layout to construct output for printing.

For many years, Windows has used a print spool system based on the Win32 Enhanced Meta File (EMF) format. This does not support the full WPF rendering feature set, so a new format has been introduced: XPS, the XML Paper Specification. This enables WPF-based graphics to be sent for printing without any loss of fidelity.

XPS is a fixed-layout page description format, and not only is it the basis for WPF print spooling, but also you can use it as a standalone file format. For example, you might build an XPS file so that you can email it to someone as a preview of what the printed output will look like.

Whether your WPF application is sending output directly to the printer or creating an XPS file containing the output, you will use the XPS APIs. So, in order to look at printing in WPF, we must begin by looking at XPS.

XPS

XPS is an open specification[*] for a file format designed to hold printable output from a WPF application. As the name suggests, an XPS file describes exactly how the document should look on paper.

The XPS format has been designed to be easy to create and consume. It builds on two very widely supported standards: the ZIP file format and XML. There are a few binary elements of an XPS file, such as embedded fonts and bitmaps, but these also

---

[*] You can download the specification from *http://www.microsoft.com/whdc/xps/default.mspx* (*http://tinysells.com/72*).

use common standards—OpenType and TrueType for fonts, and TIFF, PNG, JPEG, and WMP for bitmaps.

The way XPS uses ZIP and XML is very similar to the XML-based file formats introduced in Office 2007. This is no coincidence. All of these files share a common system, described by the Open Packaging Conventions.

Open Packaging Conventions

The Open Packaging Conventions (OPC) specification is part of the Office Open XML suite of standards. These standards are owned by ECMA.* OPC describes a consistent scheme for packaging multiple streams into a single ZIP file, and a standard mechanism by which one stream can refer to the contents of another stream. For example, in XPS, each page is represented by a stream of XML. If the page uses a bitmap, the bitmap would be stored in a separate stream, and the page XML would point to that stream with a relative URL. As well as defining the means by which one stream refers to another, the packaging conventions also define mechanisms for incorporating common file properties (title, creator, etc.), thumbnail images, and digital signatures.

OPC makes it very easy to inspect the contents of a file manually. If you change the extension of an XPS file to *.zip*, you can then extract its contents as you would any normal ZIP file. Although this offers a very useful way to learn about an OPC-based format by inspecting example files, it's important not to presume too much about the exact structure of the file. Even though you might observe common patterns, you often cannot count on these. For example, XPS files often contain a *FixedDocSeq. fdseq* stream in the root of the package, which typically defines the overall structure of the document. Similarly, Word files typically contain a *document.xml* stream in the *word* subdirectory in which you will find the document contents. However, you should not rely on these parts always having these names, as the names are of no significance. Parts are always located by relationships or references embedded within other parts. Only one well-known part will always be present: a stream called *_rels/. rel*. Applications start by opening this, and work out where to go next from there. Example 15-1 shows the contents of this stream from an XPS file. (A couple of lines have been split because they are too long to fit across the page.)

Example 15-1. Package relationships

```
<?xml version="1.0" encoding="UTF-8" standalone="yes"?>
<Relationships
    xmlns="http://schemas.openxmlformats.org/package/2006/relationships">
  <Relationship Id="rId3"
    Type="http://schemas.openxmlformats.org/package/2006/relationships/metadata/
```

---

* You can find the specifications at *http://www.ecma-international.org/memento/TC45.htm* (*http://tinysells.com/ 110*).

Example 15-1. Package relationships (continued)

```
core-properties"
    Target="docProps/core.xml"/>
  <Relationship Id="rId2"
    Type="http://schemas.openxmlformats.org/package/2006/relationships/metadata/
thumbnail"
    Target="docProps/thumbnail.jpeg"/>
  <Relationship Id="rId1"
    Type="http://schemas.microsoft.com/xps/2005/06/fixedrepresentation"
    Target="FixedDocSeq.fdseq"/>
</Relationships>
```

This shows where to locate three parts of the document. Each is identified with a fixed URI. To find the thumbnail image for this file, for example, an application would open this well-known *_rels/.rel* stream, locate the Relationship element with the relevant Type URI, and then open the stream to which it refers with its Target property.

So, although you can learn a lot about the structure of an OPC-based file by looking inside it, you should never rely on the parts having particular names or locations. You should always use relationships to locate the parts. Moreover, if you're using XPS, this issue will typically be dealt with for you, because WPF will use relationships and locate parts on your behalf if you use the XPS-specific classes it provides.

XPS Document Classes

The classes for working with XPS documents are spread across several namespaces, because there are several different levels at which you may wish to work. Table 15-1 shows the various namespaces that contain XPS functionality, and the scenarios for which they are intended.

Table 15-1. Namespaces for working with XPS

Namespace	Purpose of classes
System.Windows.Documents	Contains classes that represent the logical internal structure of XPS documents, and which also add extra runtime functionality for constructing documents
System.Windows.Xps	Abstract API for creating XPS documents, for either printing or writing to disk
System.Windows.Xps.Serialization	Provides fine-grained control of how the XPS file's contents are generated
System.Windows.Xps.Packaging	Provides access to package-level aspects of XPS, such as loading and saving XPS documents, or adding thumbnail images
System.IO.Packaging	Allows reading and writing of any OPC file (not limited to XPS)

XPS file structure is most directly represented by the classes in the System.Windows. Xps.Packaging namespace. If you want to work directly with the streams of data that make up an XPS file, these classes will give you the most control. However, they are not all that convenient to use because of their low-level nature. There is an even lower level beneath the XPS packaging classes: the System.IO.Packaging namespace implements OPC. This is the foundation on which the XPS packaging classes are built. Although you could use the lowest-level classes to open an XPS file or any other OPC file, they don't give you any more control—they merely take more work. In practice, the XPS-specific packaging classes are as low-level as you need. We mention System.IO.Packaging here because the System.Windows.Xps.Packaging classes use it—some types from the lower-level packaging API crop up in the XPS packaging API.

The classes in System.Windows.Documents also reflect the physical structure of the file, but add higher-level WPF services such as data binding and layout. So, we will start by looking at these higher-level classes.

The basic structure of an XPS file is very simple: a single XPS file contains one or more documents, and each document consists of one or more pages. (In printing terms, you could think of an XPS file as analogous to a print job containing one or more documents.) The System.Windows.Documents namespace represents this structure with three classes. FixedDocumentSequence represents the set of documents in the file. This contains a collection of FixedDocument objects, one for each document. These in turn contain a collection of FixedPage objects, one for each page.

 All of the XPS document structure classes begin with Fixed to make it clear that the formatting of any XPS document is frozen. This distinguishes these classes from the flow document classes, which are also in the System.Windows.Documents namespace.

If you unzip an XPS file, its physical structure will typically embody this logical structure. For example, Figure 15-1 shows the parts in an XPS file that correspond to the classes just discussed. (The file we dissected here happens to be the XPS 1.0 specification itself—it is distributed as an XPS file.) In the root is a file corresponding to the FixedDocumentSequence: *FixedDocSeq.fdseq*, in this case. (Remember, this root file may not always have this name. The reliable way to find it is to follow the link in the *_rels/.rel* file.) The root also contains a *Documents* folder, with a subdirectory for each document in the sequence.

This particular file contains just one document, so there is a single subdirectory, *1*. This contains a *FixedDoc.fdoc* file, which would be represented by a corresponding FixedDocument object if you loaded the XPS file into memory. The directory also has a *Pages* subfolder. This contains a series of *.fpage* files, each corresponding to a FixedPage object. Each page file contains graphical elements describing the exact appearance of the page.

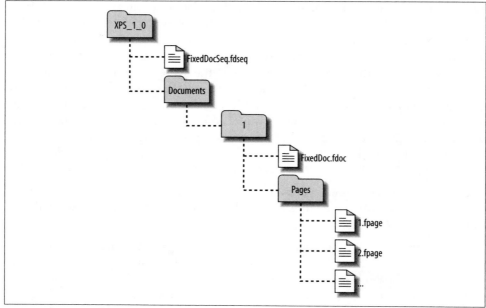

Figure 15-1. Example XPS file contents

All three levels—fixed document sequence, fixed document, and fixed page—are stored as XAML. We will now look at the classes WPF supplies for working with each of these structural levels, and the corresponding XAML in the XPS file.

FixedDocumentSequence

Logically, a `FixedDocumentSequence` is a collection of `FixedDocument` objects. Very often, it will contain just one `FixedDocument`, but the structure supports any number. Although this logical structure is simple, the details are slightly more involved. Example 15-2 shows the steps required to create a `FixedDocumentSequence` and add a single `FixedDocument` to it.

Example 15-2. Creating a FixedDocumentSequence containing a FixedDocument

```
FixedDocumentSequence fds = new FixedDocumentSequence( );
FixedDocument doc = new FixedDocument( );

DocumentReference docReference = new DocumentReference( );
docReference.SetDocument(doc);

fds.References.Add(docReference);
```

The slightly surprising part of this example is that we are required to wrap the `FixedDocument` in a `DocumentReference` object. Surely it would be simpler if documents could be added directly to a collection in some property of the document sequence.

However, the XAML in Example 15-3 offers a clue to why this would not be a good idea. This is the `FixedDocSeq.fdseq` stream from an XPS file—the serialized version of a `FixedDocumentSequence`.

Example 15-3. FixedDocumentSequence XAML

```
<FixedDocumentSequence xmlns="http://schemas.microsoft.com/xps/2005/06">
  <DocumentReference Source="/Documents/1/FixedDoc.fdoc"/>
</FixedDocumentSequence>
```

If the documents were held directly inside a property of the fixed document sequence, they would need to appear inline in this XAML. If this approach were used consistently throughout the file, the fixed pages would appear inline, too—the entire structure of the document would be stored in one huge XAML stream. This would be unwieldy for large documents, particularly for a viewer that wants to start displaying a document before the file is completely downloaded. To avoid having one huge XAML stream for the whole document, each `FixedPage` and each `FixedDocument` gets its own stream. (Separation of documents is typically less critical than separation of pages because it's more common to have a high page count than a large number of documents in a single file, but it's more consistent to have distinct streams at all levels.)

The purpose of the `DocumentReference` is to provide an extra level of indirection that enables this separation. The exact location of the relevant XAML stream in the file is determined by a relative URL—the `Source` property of the `DocumentReference`, in this case. The physical structure is not required to mirror the logical structure, even though it often does in practice.

Example 15-2 showed how to create from scratch a `FixedDocumentSequence` containing a `FixedDocument`. You can also use these classes to inspect an existing XPS file—Example 15-4 shows how to load a file from disk into these objects.

Example 15-4. Extracting FixedDocument objects from an XPS file

```
FixedDocumentSequence fds;
using (XpsDocument xpsDocumentFile = new XpsDocument("MyXpsDoc.xps",
                                                     FileAccess.Read)) {
    fds = xpsDocumentFile.GetFixedDocumentSequence();
}

foreach (DocumentReference docRef in fds.References) {
    FixedDocument document = docRef.GetDocument(false);

    ...use document...
}
```

The `XpsDocument` class reads the file and is able to return a `FixedDocumentSequence` object representing the top level of the file structure. We can then iterate through the `DocumentReference` objects in the `References` property. We call `GetDocument`, passing `false` to tell WPF that we don't require it to reload the document from disk—WPF caches parts of the file in memory, and if you expect the file to have changed, you can pass true here instead. We don't expect the file to have changed in between constructing the XpsDocument and calling GetDocument—you would normally pass true here only if you kept the document open for long enough that changes might have occurred. GetDocument returns the FixedDocument object representing the document to which the reference points.

FixedDocument

The FixedDocument class represents a single document. Logically, it consists of a sequence of pages, but as with the FixedDocumentSequence, an extra level of indirection enables its children to be defined in separate streams in the package.

Adding pages to a document is very similar to adding documents to a document sequence. Just as each document must be wrapped in a DocumentReference, each page must be wrapped in a PageContent object, although as Example 15-5 shows, the way you provide a PageContent with its FixedPage is slightly different. You need to call the IAddChild.AddChild method.

Example 15-5. Adding FixedPages to a FixedDocument

```
FixedDocument doc = new FixedDocument( );

FixedPage page1 = new FixedPage( );
PageContent page1Content = new PageContent( );
((IAddChild)page1Content).AddChild(page1);
doc.Pages.Add(page1Content);

FixedPage page2 = new FixedPage( );
PageContent page2Content = new PageContent( );
((IAddChild) page2Content).AddChild(page2);
doc.Pages.Add(page2Content);
```

Example 15-6 shows how the FixedDocument created in Example 15-5 looks in XAML.

Example 15-6. FixedDocument in XAML

```
<FixedDocument xmlns="http://schemas.microsoft.com/xps/2005/06">
  <PageContent Source="Pages/1.fpage" />
  <PageContent Source="Pages/2.fpage" />
</FixedDocument>
```

Although we now have enough code to create a complete document, it's not very interesting because all the pages are empty. For a document to be worth printing or viewing, the pages will need some content. This means working with the FixedPage class.

FixedPage

The XPS specification places very strict limitations on what is allowed inside a FixedPage. Page content must be built from just three element types: Canvas, Glyphs, and Path. Of course, Canvas has no intrinsic appearance—it is a layout panel. In XPS, it is used simply to group items, enabling a single transform to be applied to a collection of objects. So, we are left with just two elements for describing the page content: Glyphs, the lowest-level mechanism in WPF for presenting text, and Path, the general-purpose shape element.

At first glance, the FixedPage class seems not to enforce these restrictions. Example 15-7 populates a FixedPage with a Canvas containing a TextBlock. This appears to contravene the XPS specification, which requires us to represent text with Glyphs, not TextBlock.

Example 15-7. Adding content to a FixedPage

```
FixedPage page1 = new FixedPage( );

Canvas content1 = new Canvas( );
page1.Children.Add(content1);
TextBlock text1 = new TextBlock( );
text1.Text = "Hello, world!";
text1.FontFamily = new FontFamily("Palatino Linotype");
text1.FontSize = 50;
Canvas.SetLeft(text1, 100);
Canvas.SetTop(text1, 200);
content1.Children.Add(text1);
```

In fact, the FixedPage class fully supports the XPS specification. But instead of imposing restrictions on the FixedPage object's contents, WPF meets the XPS requirements by converting page content into the lower-level types when necessary. This conversion occurs when you print, or when you write a FixedDocument into an XPS file. Example 15-8 shows the results of the conversion.

Example 15-8. Text content converted into Glyphs in XPS file

```
<FixedPage xmlns="http://schemas.microsoft.com/xps/2005/06"
  xmlns:x="http://schemas.microsoft.com/xps/2005/06/resourcedictionary-key"
  xml:lang="en-us" Width="816" Height="1056">
  <Glyphs OriginX="100" OriginY="252.49" FontRenderingEmSize="50"
      FontUri="/Resources/53698881-83d0-479f-a8a4-5e5a58691f15.ODTTF"
      UnicodeString="Hello, world!" Fill="#FF000000" />
</FixedPage>
```

The TextBlock has been replaced by a Glyphs element. And, because WPF has determined that the Canvas we added was serving no purpose beyond positioning the text, it has omitted that entirely.

This illustrates that the conversion to XPS is a one-way trip. WPF preserves just the information required to create the right appearance and discards everything else. You cannot reconstruct the original UI from the XPS file—there is no way to tell from Example 15-8 that it started life as a TextBlock. The output would have looked exactly the same if we had used a Label or a Glyphs element in Example 15-7 to create the text. So, if you load a generated XPS file back in, its structure will usually not be the same as the original—only the appearance will be preserved.

Note that although the OriginX property matches the position we specified with a call to Canvas.SetLeft, the OriginY property is slightly different from the position we set. This is because the attached Canvas.Top property indicates where the *top* of an element's bounding box should be, whereas the OriginY property indicates the position of the text baseline for the Glyphs.

The FixedPage itself has a Width and Height of 816×1056. As always in WPF, these are in units of device-independent pixels, which are 1/96th of an inch in size. So these dimensions correspond to 8.5×11 inches. This is the default size for a FixedPage, even if you live in a country where, say, A4 is more popular. You are free to set any size you like, although if you are generating XPS for the purposes of printing, you would normally set the size to match the target media, which is the topic of the next section.

Page sizing

FixedPage allows you to specify three sizes for your page. The Width and Height properties are obvious enough—these specify the size of the paper for which the output is intended. The other two sizes are necessary to deal with the technical limitations of printing.

Most printers cannot print right to the edge of the paper. Control over the paper position is somewhat approximate, so printers always leave a blank area near the edge of the paper to ensure that they don't attempt to deposit ink or toner onto the rollers that feed the paper. A FixedPage can designate the area of the page in which it is intending to print by setting the ContentBox property. As Figure 15-2 shows, the ContentBox typically identifies an area smaller than the physical page.

By default, this is just information—setting ContentBox does not imply any particular behavior. However, a helpful XPS viewer application could use this to check that a document's content fits into the printable area of the target printer, and scale the output to fit if necessary or at least alert users of a potential problem.

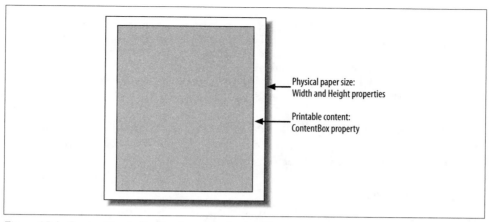

Figure 15-2. ContentBox indicating location of printable content

The final page size measure relates to the standard workaround for printing to the edge of the page. If you really need ink all the way to the edge of a page, you simply print onto a larger sheet of paper and then trim it down. As long as the printable area of the printer is bigger than the size to which you will be trimming, you will be able to print across the entire area of your final output. However, it's not quite as simple as printing something the exact size of the final, trimmed page—if you did that, even the slightest paper misalignment during the trimming process would result in an annoying white gap at the edge of the page. The standard solution to this is to print a slightly larger image than is required. This is referred to as *bleed*—the content bleeds out of the page area and into the area destined to be trimmed. Often, the bleed area also contains marks used in the print production process, such as crop lines and registration marks. The BleedBox indicates how large this area is, as Figure 15-3 shows.

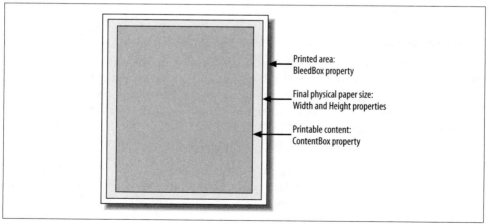

Figure 15-3. BleedBox indicates printing outside of target page size

If the bleed area is being used only to hold production features such as printing marks, the content box may still be smaller than the physical page size, as shown in Figure 15-3. However, if the bleed box is being used in order to allow ink all the way to the edge of the page, this implies that the page is completely full, so the content box will fill the whole page.

Again, the BleedBox is usually just for information. But it could be important information for a print bureau producing the finished output—it could use this to verify that everything is set up correctly before committing to a print run.

Page content limitations

It is convenient to be able to add any WPF content to a FixedPage and have it automatically converted to the element types supported in XPS. However, this conversion process has its limitations. WPF offers a couple of features that cannot be represented directly with the limited repertoire available in an XPS file's FixedPage: 3D and bitmap effects.

You can use these features in a FixedPage, but if you print the page or save it to an XPS file, then all 3D content, and all elements that use the BitmapEffect property, will be converted into bitmaps. They will be represented in the FixedPage as a Path object with a rectangular shape and a bitmap fill. This does not guarantee perfect fidelity—the image quality for such features is only as good as the resolution of the generated bitmap.

If you want to print content that uses effects such as drop shadows, you might be better off trying to approximate the effects you require using opacity masks and gradient brushes. Although these are not as convenient as the bitmap effects, they can be represented in an XPS file without any loss of fidelity.

Fonts, bitmaps, and other resources

The Glyphs element in Example 15-8 indicates the font through its FontUri property. This does not name the font—instead it refers to a font file embedded in the XPS file. Fonts, bitmaps, thumbnails, color profiles, and any other necessary resources are embedded as separate streams in the package. These are then referred to by path. For example, the FontUri in Example 15-8 is:

```
/Resources/53698881-83d0-479f-a8a4-5e5a58691f15.ODTTF
```

This indicates that the XPS package contains a Resources folder, and that this contains an embedded font file with the specified name. In general, you do not need to worry about creating these resources, unless you choose to work with the lower-level System.Windows.Xps.Packaging API. If you print or save a fixed document using the higher-level API, WPF adds the necessary resources for you.

It is important to be aware that WPF can automatically embed font files, or subsets of a font file. It does this to guarantee that a document can be displayed or printed correctly. However, it is your responsibility to ensure that you do not generate XPS files that contravene font licensing terms.

We have now seen all the high-level classes that represent the structure of an XPS document. We saw in Example 15-4 how to read an existing XPS file off the disk and into a tree of objects representing its structure. But what about the creation process, where we build an XPS document structure, and want to either print it or save it to disk? For this, we must use the XpsDocumentWriter class.

Generating XPS Output

Whether you are printing, or writing your output to an XPS file, you can use the same API: the XpsDocumentWriter class. If you wish to print, you can obtain one of these from the printing API, as Example 15-9 shows.

Example 15-9. Obtaining an XpsDocumentWriter for printing

```
PrintDocumentImageableArea imageArea = null;
XpsDocumentWriter xpdw = PrintQueue.CreateXpsDocumentWriter(ref imageArea);
if (xpdw != null) {
    ...provide XpsDocumentWriter with output here...
}
```

This will cause the standard print dialog to be shown, allowing the user to select a printer. If the user cancels the dialog, CreateXpsDocumentWriter returns null, but otherwise it returns an XpsDocumentWriter, along with an object that describes the size of the target's paper and the margins of the printable area. If you wish to exercise more control over the print dialog and printer selection, there are several variations on this theme, described later in this chapter.

If you wish to send your output to an XPS file instead of a printer, you can obtain the document writer using the code shown in Example 15-10.

Example 15-10. Obtaining an XpsDocumentWriter for file output

```
using (XpsDocument xpsFile = new XpsDocument(xpsOutputPath, FileAccess.Write)) {
    XpsDocumentWriter xpdw = XpsDocument.CreateXpsDocumentWriter(xpsFile);

    ...provide XpsDocumentWriter with output here...

}
```

Once you have obtained an XPS document writer, you can use the same code whether you are writing to an XPS file or to a printer. For clarity, we will use the term *printing* to refer to both kinds of output; unless otherwise specified, any discussion of printing in the following sections also applies to generating XPS files.

You can provide an XpsDocumentWriter with content in many forms. For most of the supported content types, you call a suitable overload of the Write method. This is a one-shot process: once you've called Write, it will print the document straight away, and any further calls to Write will throw an exception. The following sections describe the various types of content accepted by a document writer.

Printing Fixed Documents

XpsDocumentWriter offers overloads of its Write method that accept a FixedPage, a FixedDocument, or a FixedDocumentSequence. These allow you to submit a single page, a whole document, or a job containing several documents for printing, respectively. If you want to print more than one fixed page you *must* pass either a FixedDocument or a FixedDocumentSequence, because you get to call the Write method only once. Example 15-11 creates and prints a FixedDocument.

Example 15-11. Creating and printing a FixedDocument

```
FixedDocument doc = new FixedDocument( );

// Add first page to document
FixedPage page1 = new FixedPage( );
PageContent page1Content = new PageContent( );
((IAddChild)page1Content).AddChild(page1);
doc.Pages.Add(page1Content);


// Add content to first page
Canvas content1 = new Canvas( );
page1.Children.Add(content1);
TextBlock text1 = new TextBlock( );
text1.Text = "Hello";
text1.FontSize = 50;
Canvas.SetLeft(text1, 100);
Canvas.SetTop(text1, 200);
content1.Children.Add(text1);


// Add second page to document
FixedPage page2 = new FixedPage( );
PageContent page2Content = new PageContent( );
((IAddChild) page2Content).AddChild(page2);
doc.Pages.Add(page2Content);


// Add content to second page
Canvas content2 = new Canvas( );
page2.Children.Add(content2);
TextBlock text2 = new TextBlock( );
text2.Text = "World";
text2.FontSize = 50;
```

Example 15-11. Creating and printing a FixedDocument (continued)

```
Canvas.SetLeft(text2, 100);
Canvas.SetTop(text2, 200);
content2.Children.Add(text2);


// Print document
PrintDocumentImageableArea imageArea = null;
XpsDocumentWriter xpsdw = PrintQueue.CreateXpsDocumentWriter(ref imageArea);
if (xpsdw != null) {
    xpsdw.Write(doc);
}
```

This builds a `FixedDocument` with two `FixedPages`. The first contains the text "Hello," and the second contains the text "World". The user will be shown the print dialog at the point at which the code asks `PrintQueue` for the document writer. The print job will be submitted to the print queue when it calls `Write`—when that method returns, print spooling will already be complete, and the job will be in the Windows print queue for the target printer.

If your `FixedPage` objects use any WPF element types other than `Canvas`, `Glyphs`, or `Path`, the conversion to these simple element types occurs when you call the `XpsDocumentWriter.Write` method.

Printing Visuals

You do not need to create `FixedDocument` or `FixedPage` objects explicitly. WPF is able to generate a fixed page automatically from any object that derives from `Visual`. Because `Visual` is the base class of all WPF user interface elements, this means you can print any element. It will even accept elements that are already part of a visual tree, enabling you to print a screenshot of a user interface.

Unlike the ordinary bitmap-based screenshots you get by pressing PrtScn or Alt-PrtScn in Windows, these screenshots will be resolution-independent. Also, they aren't screenshots in the sense of being a direct copy of what's visible on-screen—they will contain your application's visuals and nothing else, even if your application is currently obscured by other programs.

To print a `Visual`, just pass it to the relevant overload of the `Write` method. Example 15-12 shows how to print a `TextBlock` element.

Example 15-12. Printing a single Visual

```
PrintDocumentImageableArea area = null;
XpsDocumentWriter xpsdw = PrintQueue.CreateXpsDocumentWriter(ref area);
if (xpsdw != null) {
    TextBlock myVisual = new TextBlock();
```

Example 15-12. Printing a single Visual (continued)

```
    double leftMargin = area.OriginWidth;
    double topMargin = area.OriginHeight;
    double rightMargin = area.MediaSizeWidth - area.ExtentWidth - leftMargin;
    double bottomMargin = area.MediaSizeHeight - area.ExtentHeight - topMargin;
    myVisual.Margin = new Thickness(leftMargin, topMargin,
                                    rightMargin, bottomMargin);

    myVisual.Text = "Hello, world";

    Size outputSize = new Size(area.MediaSizeWidth, area.MediaSizeHeight);
    myVisual.Measure(outputSize);
    myVisual.Arrange(new Rect(outputSize));
    myVisual.UpdateLayout( );

    xpsdw.Write(myVisual);
}
```

This example performs layout on the TextBlock explicitly. WPF does this automatically for elements in a user interface, but because this TextBlock is not hosted in a window, it is our responsibility to perform the layout. Otherwise, it would not have a valid width and height, so it would be invisible when we try to print it. If we were trying to print an element that was already in the visual tree of a window, this layout step would not be necessary.

Note that the margin and size of the TextBlock have been based on the page size information in the PrintDocumentImageableArea returned by PrintQueue, ensuring that the TextBlock doesn't fall into the unprintable area around the edge of the paper. PrintDocumentImageableArea reports the total page size with its MediaSizeWidth and MediaSizeHeight properties. The top-left position of the printable area within the page is indicated by the OriginWidth and OriginHeight properties. The ExtentWidth and ExtentHeight properties describe the size of the printable area.

Although basing the print margins on the physical capabilities of the printer guarantees to make full use of the available space, it means that output will vary from one printer to another. In practice, it's common to choose fixed margins with sufficiently conservative values that the content is likely to fit with any printer's printable region. Example 15-13 shows modifications to Example 15-12 that hardcode the margins. For some applications it may be appropriate to provide the user with a way to modify the margins; WPF doesn't have a built-in page setup dialog,* so it's up to you how to present such settings.

---

* You could always use the PageSetupDialog class provided by Windows Forms. However, be aware that you will pay the usual working set overhead for using Windows Forms features on top of the costs of using WPF. If you are already using Windows Forms in your application (e.g., you are hosting Windows Forms controls via interop, as described in Appendix B), incremental cost of using this dialog will be low. But if it's the only Windows Forms feature you use, you might want to consider whether it's worth the impact.

Example 15-13. Setting fixed print margins

```
. . .

TextBlock myVisual = new TextBlock( );

double leftMargin = 96;      // 1 inch
double topMargin = 144;      // 1.5 inches
double rightMargin = 96;     // 1 inch
double bottomMargin = 144;   // 1.5 inches

// Making sure that we're inside the physical
// limitations of the printer

Debug.Assert(leftMargin >= area.OriginWidth);
Debug.Assert(topMargin >= area.OriginHeight);
Debug.Assert(rightMargin <= area.OriginWidth + area.ExtentWidth);
Debug.Assert(topMargin <= area.OriginHeight + area.ExtentHeight);

myVisual.Margin = new Thickness(leftMargin, topMargin,
                                rightMargin, bottomMargin);

. . .
```

The use of Debug.Assert in Example 15-13 is for illustration only. In practice, there is no one correct way to respond if the configured margins fail to place the content entirely within the printable area. An application might show the user a warning dialog the first time the problem occurs for a particular document. Alternatively, it might choose to adjust the content to fit.

Because the overload of the Write method used in Example 15-12 accepts any object that has Visual as a base class, we are free to pass in whole trees of objects. For example, Grid derives from Visual, so you can pass any Grid, and it will print the grid and all its contents.

However, if you need to print multiple pages, you need to take a slightly different approach. As with the previous examples, you are allowed to call this overload of the Write method only once, meaning you can print only a single page. If you want to print multiple pages as visuals, you need to use a different method of the XpsDocumentWriter class: CreateVisualsCollator.

CreateVisualsCollator returns a SerializerWriterCollator object. This offers a Write method that accepts a visual, just like XpsDocumentWrite.Write. The difference is that you can call it several times in a row, once for each page. Example 15-14 uses this technique to print 10 pages, with a TextBlock showing each page's number.

Example 15-14. Printing multiple Visuals

```
PrintDocumentImageableArea area = null;
XpsDocumentWriter xpsdw = PrintQueue.CreateXpsDocumentWriter(ref area);
if (xpsdw != null) {
    SerializerWriterCollator c = xpsdw.CreateVisualsCollator( );
    c.BeginBatchWrite( );
    for (int i = 1; i <= 10; ++i) {
        TextBlock tb = new TextBlock( );
        tb.Text = i.ToString( );
        tb.TextAlignment = TextAlignment.Center;
        tb.VerticalAlignment = VerticalAlignment.Center;
        tb.FontSize = 500;
        tb.FontFamily = new FontFamily("Verdana");

        tb.Margin = new Thickness(area.OriginWidth, area.OriginHeight, 0, 0);
        Size outputSize = new Size(area.ExtentWidth, area.ExtentHeight);
        tb.Measure(outputSize);
        tb.Arrange(new Rect(outputSize));
        tb.UpdateLayout( );

        c.Write(tb);
    }
    c.EndBatchWrite( );
}
```

We must indicate the start and end of the range of pages by calling BeginBatchWrite and EndBatchWrite so that WPF knows when to start and complete the print spooling process. Once you have called EndBatchWrite, you cannot perform any more output with either the collator or the document writer.

Printing with Document Paginators

Some WPF classes have an intrinsic ability to split their content into pages. The FlowDocument, FixedDocument, and FixedDocumentSequence classes all advertise this capability by implementing the IDocumentPaginatorSource interface. XpsDocumentWriter can work with self-paginating objects directly, which can make multipage printing much simpler than the previous example. Example 15-15 shows a function that you can use to print an instance of any type that implements IDocumentPaginatorSource.

Example 15-15. Printing with DocumentPaginator

```
public static void PrintPaginatedDocument(IDocumentPaginatorSource dps) {
    PrintDocumentImageableArea area = null;
    XpsDocumentWriter xpsdw = PrintQueue.CreateXpsDocumentWriter(ref area);
    if (xpsdw != null) {
        xpsdw.Write(dps.DocumentPaginator);
    }
}
```

If the document paginator source is a fixed document or a fixed document sequence, Example 15-15 will generate an output page for each fixed page in the source.

This is not usefully different from just passing the fixed document or fixed document sequence directly to the `Write` overload that accepts those types, so in practice, you will not usually print fixed documents this way. However, if the source document is a `FlowDocument` (which was described in Chapter 14), it will not have a fixed idea of how many pages it contains. In this case, the paginator is more useful, because you can use it to split the document into pages that fit the target media.

You might expect the `FlowDocument` pagination to be based automatically on the target page size. In fact, this is not the case: the paginator it returns defaults to a page size of 816×1056 pixels (i.e., 8.5×11 inches regardless of the real paper size). You can inspect or change the paginator's page size using its `PageSize` property. If you are writing to an XPS file instead of printing, the generated XPS file will have pages of this size. If you are printing, the flow document will be split into pages of this size regardless of whether they fit onto the target paper. If you want to be sure that the flow document's output will fit the available space offered by the target printer, you should use the information returned in the `PrintDocumentImageableArea` to adjust the `PageSize` property, as shown in Example 15-16.

Example 15-16. Setting a DocumentPaginator's PageSize

```
PrintDocumentImageableArea area = null;
XpsDocumentWriter xpsdw = PrintQueue.CreateXpsDocumentWriter(ref area);
if (xpsdw != null) {
    DocumentPaginator paginator = dps.DocumentPaginator;
    paginator.PageSize = new Size(area.ExtentWidth, area.ExtentHeight);
    xpsdw.Write(paginator);
}
```

This will ensure that the flow document is broken into pages that fit into the available space, whatever the paper size may be.

There is a limitation with printing a `FlowDocument` in this way: you cannot add other features to the page, such as page numbers, without doing a little more work. You have two options: either you can implement your own `DocumentPaginator` as a wrapper around the one provided by the `FlowDocument`, or you can call into the provided paginator directly to retrieve the pages, and incorporate this into the content you require to represent the whole page.

Example 15-17 shows some code that uses the second technique to print a `FlowDocument` with page numbers.

Example 15-17. Printing a FlowDocument with page numbers

```
public static void PrintFlowDocWithPageNumbers(FlowDocument myFlowDoc) {
    PrintDocumentImageableArea area = null;
    XpsDocumentWriter xpsdw = PrintQueue.CreateXpsDocumentWriter(ref area);
    if (xpsdw != null) {
        IDocumentPaginatorSource dps = myFlowDoc;
        DocumentPaginator sourceFlowDocPaginator = dps.DocumentPaginator;
```

Example 15-17. Printing a FlowDocument with page numbers (continued)

```
        const int HeaderFooterHeight = 30;
        sourceFlowDocPaginator.PageSize = new Size(area.ExtentWidth,
            area.ExtentHeight - 2 * HeaderFooterHeight);

        if (!sourceFlowDocPaginator.IsPageCountValid) {
            sourceFlowDocPaginator.ComputePageCount();
        }

        FixedDocument outputFixedDoc = BuildFixedDocument(myFlowDoc, area,
            sourceFlowDocPaginator, HeaderFooterHeight);

        xpsdw.Write(outputFixedDoc);
    }
}
```

This obtains an `XpsDocumentWriter` in the usual way. It then retrieves the document paginator for the flow document we wish to print. Next, it sets the `PageSize` on the paginator, specifying the full width of the printable page area, but reducing the height in order to allow space for a header and footer to be added. This ensures that the content, header, and footer fit within the printable area of the page.

Next, we make sure the paginator has an up-to-date page count—we changed the page size, which is likely to have changed the number of pages required for the document. If `IsPageCountValid` indicates that the page count is no longer up-to-date, we call `ComputePageCount`.

Finally, Example 15-17 builds a `FixedDocument` to hold the paginated output, combined with the header and footer, and prints it by calling the `Write` method of the `XpsDocumentWriter`. The document is created by the `BuildFixedDocument` helper method, which is shown in Example 15-18.

Example 15-18. Building a FixedDocument from a FlowDocument

```
static FixedDocument BuildFixedDocument(FlowDocument myFlowDoc,
        PrintDocumentImageableArea area, DocumentPaginator sourceFlowDocPaginator,
        int headerFooterHeight) {

    FixedDocument outputFixedDoc = new FixedDocument();

    for (int pageNo = 0; pageNo < sourceFlowDocPaginator.PageCount; ++pageNo) {
        Canvas pageCanvas = new Canvas();
        pageCanvas.Margin = new Thickness(192);

        AddHeaderAndFooter(myFlowDoc, area, sourceFlowDocPaginator,
                            headerFooterHeight, pageNo, pageCanvas);
        AddPageBody(sourceFlowDocPaginator,
                    headerFooterHeight, pageNo, pageCanvas);

        AddPageToDocument(area, outputFixedDoc, pageCanvas);

    }
```

Example 15-18. Building a FixedDocument from a FlowDocument (continued)

```
    return outputFixedDoc;
}
```

This iterates through the pages provided by the paginator, creating a Canvas for each page. The Canvas will hold the page content, and the header and footer. We set the Margin on this canvas to ensure that it appears within the printable area of the page. The fixed margin of 2 inches (192 device-independent pixels) all around should be enough for any normal printer.

Next, we add the header and footer to the canvas, making sure they appear horizontally centered, and at the appropriate vertical position on the page. We add these with the AddHeaderAndFooter helper function, which is shown in Example 15-19.

Example 15-19. Adding the header and footer

```
static void AddHeaderAndFooter(FlowDocument myFlowDoc,
        PrintDocumentImageableArea area,
        DocumentPaginator sourceFlowDocPaginator,
        int headerFooterHeight, int pageNo, Canvas pageCanvas) {

    TextBlock header = new TextBlock( );
    header.Text = "My Document";
    header.FontSize = 20;
    header.FontWeight = FontWeights.Bold;
    header.TextAlignment = TextAlignment.Center;
    header.Width = sourceFlowDocPaginator.PageSize.Width;
    pageCanvas.Children.Add(header);

    TextBlock footer = new TextBlock( );
    footer.Text += "Page " + (pageNo + 1);
    footer.TextAlignment = TextAlignment.Center;
    footer.FontFamily = myFlowDoc.FontFamily;
    footer.Width = sourceFlowDocPaginator.PageSize.Width;
    Canvas.SetTop(footer, area.ExtentHeight - headerFooterHeight);
    pageCanvas.Children.Add(footer);
}
```

Finally, we need to incorporate the page content from the flow document. WPF offers a special element type, DocumentPageView, for hosting content from a particular page of a paginated document, which is used by the AddPageBody helper function shown in Example 15-20.

Example 15-20. Adding the page body

```
static void AddPageBody(DocumentPaginator sourceFlowDocPaginator,
        int headerFooterHeight, int pageNo, Canvas pageCanvas) {

    DocumentPageView dpv = new DocumentPageView( );
    dpv.DocumentPaginator = sourceFlowDocPaginator;
    dpv.PageNumber = pageNo;
```

Example 15-20. Adding the page body (continued)

```
    Canvas.SetTop(dpv, headerFooterHeight);
    pageCanvas.Children.Add(dpv);
}
```

The Canvas defining the appearance of our page is now complete. The last thing the loop in Example 15-18 does is to create a FixedPage to host the Canvas, wrap it in a PageContent, and add that to the FixedDocument that will be returned to Example 15-17. This is accomplished by the AddPageToDocument helper shown in Example 15-21.

Example 15-21. Adding pages to the FixedDocument

```
static void AddPageToDocument(PrintDocumentImageableArea area,
        FixedDocument outputFixedDoc, Canvas pageCanvas) {

    FixedPage fp = new FixedPage();
    fp.Width = area.MediaSizeWidth;
    fp.Height = area.MediaSizeHeight;
    fp.Children.Add(pageCanvas);

    PageContent pc = new PageContent();
     ((IAddChild) pc).AddChild(fp);
    outputFixedDoc.Pages.Add(pc);
}
```

You can use the code in Example 15-17, along with its various helper functions, to print any flow document. It will add a header to each page with the text "My Document," and a footer showing the page number.

Asynchronous Printing

Printing a large document can be a slow process. The Write methods shown in the previous sections are synchronous (i.e., they do not return until the document has been completely spooled out to the print queue). This can be bad news for the user—if you print from the main thread, the application will become unresponsive until printing finishes. Fortunately, WPF offers asynchronous versions of all of these Write methods. Each overload of Write has a corresponding WriteAsync method.

The WriteAsync methods return immediately. Printing will then progress during idle time. However, because WPF will be using the objects you passed in, you should make sure you don't attempt to change them until printing is complete. The simplest way to ensure that is to create objects especially for printing. For example, build a FixedDocument that will be passed to an XPS document writer's WriteAsync method, and which will never be used for anything else. (This rule also applies to each FixedPage object and all the objects that make up the page content.)

The XpsDocumentWriter will periodically raise the WritingProgressChanged event to tell you how far along it is. It will raise its WritingCompleted event once printing has completed spooling. The document may still be in the print queue at this point, so this event doesn't necessarily mean the document is sitting on the printer awaiting collection; it just means that the application has finished generating the printer output—the application could exit without losing the output. Example 15-22 shows a version of Example 15-17 modified to use asynchronous printing.

Example 15-22. Asynchronous printing

```
void PrintPaginatedDocument(IDocumentPaginatorSource dps) {
    PrintDocumentImageableArea area = null;
    XpsDocumentWriter xpsdw = PrintQueue.CreateXpsDocumentWriter(ref area);
    xpsdw.WritingCompleted += OnPrinted;
    if (xpsdw != null) {
        xpsdw.WriteAsync(dps.DocumentPaginator);
    }
}

void OnPrinted(object sender, WritingCompletedEventArgs e) {
    MessageBox.Show("Printing completed!");
}
```

Sometimes users need to cancel print jobs. They can, of course, do this via the printing user interface in Windows. Alternatively, your application could call the CancelAsync method on the XpsDocumentWriter anytime before it signals completion. If the document is cancelled, the WritingCancelled event will be raised instead of the WritingCompleted event.

Everything in the preceding sections applies equally to generating XPS files and sending output to a printer. However, some tasks are specific to XPS file generation, and some apply only in printing scenarios. The next section describes parts of the .NET 3.0 API that are concerned solely with XPS file generation.

XPS File Generation Features

As we've seen, you can use the same code path to generate both printed output and XPS files by using the XpsDocumentWriter class. However, you can build some extra features into an XPS file that would not be useful for print output, but which can enhance its usefulness as a standalone file. Indeed, unless you plan to exploit some of these features, there's probably not much point in adding a "save as XPS" feature to your application—Windows automatically offers basic XPS generation to any application that can print.

Any machine with either .NET 3.0 or the Microsoft XPS Essentials Pack* installed will have a "Microsoft XPS Document Writer" printer. Windows Vista has .NET 3.0 built in. You can install .NET 3.0 on Windows XP or Windows Server 2003. You can install the XPS Essentials Pack on these systems, and on Windows 2000 machines.

When an application "prints" to this printer, an XPS file is created. At the start of the print process, a dialog opens asking the user where he'd like to save the XPS file, and once printing is complete, the XPS viewer application will run, displaying the results.

This is very useful because it means that any print-enabled application can generate an XPS file. However, it is possible for applications to build a richer, more useful XPS file than this pseudoprinter can. An application knows things about its documents that the print system cannot, and can use this to enhance the XPS file. For example, XPS files can contain hyperlinks to allow easy navigation within documents. An application may also wish to control aspects of the file creation process, such as whether the compression strategy favors speed of decoding, or minimizing the file size.

Package-Level XPS API

The XpsDocumentWriter class is convenient in that it lets us use functionality not directly supported by the XPS file format itself. As we've seen, if we use non-XPS elements in a FixedPage, or we choose to work with Visual objects directly, the document writer will convert these objects to glyphs and paths for us. However, there is a price to pay: XpsDocumentWriter does not give you complete control over all XPS file features.

WPF provides a lower-level API that lets you work directly with the streams of an XPS file, giving you full control over all of the features, while still providing XPS-specific features that you don't get from the low-level System.IO.Packaging classes, such as an intrinsic understanding of the parts and relationships required in an XPS file. Of course, the downside is that you have to do more work to build up a complete document from scratch. Fortunately, in a lot of cases, you can use both techniques: you can build the basic document using the higher-level API, and then use the lower-level API on the same file to add the XPS features you require.

The package-level API is defined in the System.Windows.Xps.Packaging namespace. Table 15-2 shows the types it provides for dealing with the core XPS structural elements, and the nearest equivalents in the high-level API.

---

* See *http://www.microsoft.com/whdc/xps/viewxps.mspx* (*http://tinysells.com/71*).

Table 15-2. Package-level XPS API

Document structures	Type	System.Windows.Documents equivalent
XPS file	XpsDocument	None
Document sequence	IXpsFixedDocumentSequenceReader, IXpsFixedDocumentSequenceWriter	FixedDocumentSequence
Document	IXpsFixedDocumentReader, IXpsFixedDocumentWriter	FixedDocument
Page	IXpsFixedPageReader, IXpsFixedPageWriter	FixedPage

Working with the package-level API requires a procedural style. Instead of building up a data structure in memory representing the documents and their pages, you issue a series of instructions in strict order, describing which things to write out. Example 15-23 shows how to create a document from scratch at this level.

Example 15-23. Generating an XPS file from scratch

```
using (XpsDocument xpsDoc = new XpsDocument("Out.xps", FileAccess.Write)) {
    IXpsFixedDocumentSequenceWriter sequenceWriter =
        xpsDoc.AddFixedDocumentSequence();
    IXpsFixedDocumentWriter docWriter = sequenceWriter.AddFixedDocument();
    IXpsFixedPageWriter pageWriter = docWriter.AddFixedPage();

    XmlWriter pageXml = pageWriter.XmlWriter;
    pageXml.WriteStartElement("FixedPage");
        pageXml.WriteAttributeString("xmlns",
                "http://schemas.microsoft.com/xps/2005/06");
        pageXml.WriteAttributeString("Width", "793.7");
        pageXml.WriteAttributeString("Height", "1122.5");
        pageXml.WriteAttributeString("xml:lang", "en-GB");

        pageXml.WriteStartElement("Path");
            pageXml.WriteAttributeString("Data",
                "M 10,550 L 396,164 782,550 396,936 z");
            pageXml.WriteAttributeString("Fill", "#ffff0000");

        pageXml.WriteEndElement();

    pageXml.WriteEndElement();

    pageWriter.Commit();
    docWriter.Commit();
    sequenceWriter.Commit();
}
```

Figure 15-4 shows how this generated page looks in the XPS viewer.

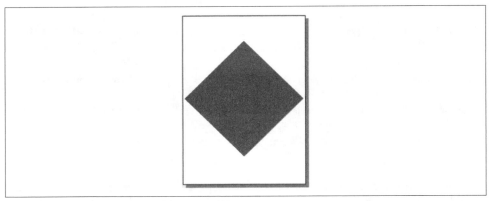

Figure 15-4. XPS file generated from scratch

As you can see, you need to generate the raw XML for the fixed page content by hand if you are working at this level, and it is your responsibility to ensure that it conforms to the requirements laid out in the XPS specification. You cannot use the FixedPage class or any WPF elements with these APIs. Life gets even more complex if you wish to use text, as you need to generate embedded font resources. This is why it's often preferable to use a hybrid approach. Example 15-24 shows how to generate the basic output with XpsDocumentWriter, and then use the package-level API to set a file property.

Example 15-24. Using both XPS API styles

```
using (Package xpsPackage = Package.Open("Out.xps", FileMode.Create,
                                    FileAccess.ReadWrite))
using (XpsDocument doc = new XpsDocument(xpsPackage)) {
    FixedPage page = new FixedPage( );
    Path p = new Path( );
    p.Data = StreamGeometry.Parse("M 10,550 L 396,164 782,550 396,936 z");
    p.Fill = Brushes.Red;
    page.Children.Add(p);

    TextBlock text = new TextBlock( );
    text.Text = "XPS Output";
    text.FontSize = 150;
    page.Children.Add(text);

    XpsDocumentWriter dw = XpsDocument.CreateXpsDocumentWriter(doc);
    dw.Write(page);

    doc.CoreDocumentProperties.Description = "Some text and a red square";
}
```

There are some limitations to this technique, because you are leaving certain parts of the XPS file generation to the XpsDocumentWriter. For example, if you want fine control over the generated XML, you will have to stick to the lower-level technique.

However, most of the techniques described in the following sections can use this hybrid approach, where the bulk of the XPS file is generated with XpsDocumentWriter, and then a few details are edited with the System.Windows.Xps.Packaging API.

Core Document Properties

OPC defines a representation for a set of document properties. These enable documents to supply common properties such as title, description, and keywords in a standard way. These properties are embedded in an XML stream in the package, with one element per property.

Several of the supported properties are defined by the Dublin Core Metadata Initiative,[*] a standard that defines how to represent certain common types of metadata in markup. There are also a number of properties not found in the Dublin Core, but which are common to all OPC-based file formats, including XPS and all of the Office Open XML file formats. Table 15-3 shows all the properties, indicating which are shared with the Dublin Core.

Table 15-3. Core document properties shared with Dublin Core

Property	Usage	In Dublin Core
Category	Categorization of document	No
ContentStatus	Status of document (e.g., "Draft")	No
ContentType	Type of content, such as "Whitepaper" (note: this is *not* a MIME content type)	No
Created	Creation date	Yes
Creator	Entity primarily responsible for creating document	Yes
Description	Short description of the content	Yes
Identifier	An unambiguous reference to the document within a given context	Yes
Keywords	Set of keywords to facilitate searching	No
Language	Language in which document is written	Yes
LastModifiedBy	User who last modified the document	No
LastPrinted	Date on which the document was last printed	No
Modified	Date of last change	Yes
Revision	Revision number	No
Subject	Topic of document	Yes
Title	Name of document	Yes
Version	Version number	No

You're not obliged to set any of these properties—set just those that make sense for your application. You do so using the XpsDocument class's CoreDocumentProperties

---

[*] *http://dublincore.org.*

property. This contains an instance of the `PackageProperties` type that defines CLR properties corresponding to each available core document property. Example 15-25 shows how to use this.

Example 15-25. Setting core document properties

```
PackageProperties props = xpsOutput.CoreDocumentProperties;

props.Creator = "Ian Griffiths";
props.Title = "XPS Output";
props.Subject = "Example XPS output document";
props.Description = "XPS document generated by example from " +
    "the book 'Programming WPF' published by O'Reilly";
props.Category = "Demo output";
props.ContentStatus = "Final";
props.Keywords = "XPS; Demo; WPF";
```

Once you have set these properties, Windows Explorer is able to extract them, because it knows how to retrieve core properties from XPS files. Figure 15-5 shows how this looks. The labels Windows uses do not always correspond to the underlying property names. This is because Windows has some long-standing conventions for property names that predate the adoption of the Dublin Core properties by the OPC.

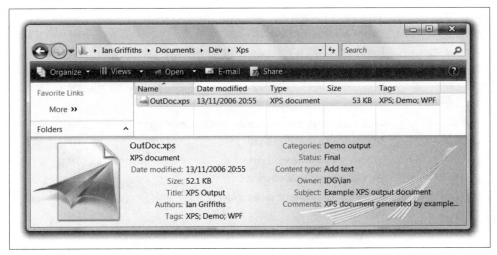

Figure 15-5. XPS core properties shown by Windows Explorer

Windows Explorer allows the user to edit metadata on certain file formats. (Applications can register handlers to enable this editing. There is a built-in handler for XPS files.) You can see this in Figure 15-5: look at the "Content type" entry. Our code did not set this property, so the shell has shown an "Add text" prompt. If the user moves the mouse over this or any of the other editable properties, the value will take on a text-box-like appearance to let the user know she can edit the value. If she edits or adds values, a Save button appears, allowing her to commit the changes to disk. So be aware that the properties you write into an XPS file at creation time are not necessarily the properties that it will have for its lifetime.

Thumbnails

OPC defines a way to embed thumbnail bitmap images. A *thumbnail* is a small bitmap containing a preview of the document. Windows Vista can use this as the document's icon in Explorer. Thumbnails enable a rough image of a document to be presented quickly, because they require very little processing—loading and rendering a small bitmap is likely to be faster than loading and rendering a FixedPage for all but the most trivial of documents.

The most common style of thumbnail is a small view of the first page of the document (or if the XPS file contains multiple fixed documents, the first page of the first document). XPS allows thumbnails to be provided for each page, but the default viewer does not use these, and neither the XPS Print Driver nor Microsoft Office's XPS export feature generates them. In practice, a single thumbnail for the file should suffice.

To set the file's thumbnail, you just call the XpsDocument object's AddThumbnail method, passing an XpsImageType value to specify the image type. Although the XpsImageType enumeration lists four bitmap types, the specification requires thumbnails to be in either JPEG or PNG format, so you should not use the other types here—the enumeration includes the TIFF and WDP types because those are supported in other parts of an XPS document. AddThumbnail returns an object of type XpsThumbnail, which provides a method called GetStream. We then write the bitmap into that stream. It is our job to provide the raw JPEG or PNG byte stream. Example 15-26 shows how to generate a suitable bitmap and add it as a thumbnail.

Example 15-26. Adding a thumbnail to an XPS document

```
void AddThumbnailToXpsDocument(XpsDocument xpsOutput) {
    Size thumbnailSize = new Size(256, 256);
    Visual thumbnailVisual = CreateThumbnailVisual(thumbnailSize);

    XpsThumbnail docThumbnail = xpsOutput.AddThumbnail(XpsImageType.JpegImageType);
    WriteVisualAsThumbnail(thumbnailSize, thumbnailVisual, docThumbnail);

}

Visual CreateThumbnailVisual(Size thumbnailSize) {
    Grid myThumbnail = new Grid();
    myThumbnail.Background = new LinearGradientBrush(
        Colors.LightBlue, Colors.White, 90);
```

Example 15-26. Adding a thumbnail to an XPS document (continued)

```
    TextBlock thumbText = new TextBlock( );
    thumbText.FontSize = 50;
    thumbText.Text = "My XPS Document";
    thumbText.TextAlignment = TextAlignment.Center;
    thumbText.VerticalAlignment = VerticalAlignment.Center;
    thumbText.TextWrapping = TextWrapping.Wrap;
    myThumbnail.Children.Add(thumbText);

    myThumbnail.Measure(thumbnailSize);
    myThumbnail.Arrange(new Rect(new Point( ), thumbnailSize));

    return myThumbnail;
}

void WriteVisualAsThumbnail(Size thumbnailSize, Visual thumbnailVisual,
                            XpsThumbnail thumbnail) {

    RenderTargetBitmap bmp = new RenderTargetBitmap(
        (int) thumbnailSize.Width, (int) thumbnailSize.Height,
        96, 96, PixelFormats.Default);
    bmp.Render(thumbnailVisual);

    JpegBitmapEncoder encoder = new JpegBitmapEncoder( );
    encoder.Frames.Add(BitmapFrame.Create(bmp));

    encoder.Save(**thumbnail.GetStream( )**);
}
```

Most of the code in this example is there to generate a JPEG bitmap. Only two lines of code are XPS-specific: the call to XpsDocument.AddThumbnail near the top, and the call to GetStream near the bottom.

This example generates a 256×256-pixel bitmap. The XPS specification doesn't mandate any particular size, beyond saying that it should be "small." However, Explorer in Windows Vista expects high-resolution icons to be 256×256, and because it is able to extract the thumbnail from an XPS and show it, 256×256 seems like a sensible default for an XPS thumbnail. Figure 15-6 shows how Windows Explorer displays the thumbnail created by Example 15-26 in its Large Icons view.

Figure 15-6. XPS document thumbnail shown by Explorer in Windows Vista

Hyperlinks

XPS documents can contain hyperlinks. These may be either internal links within the document or links to external sites. If you are building an XPS document using XpsDocumentWriter, the simplest way to generate hyperlinks is to use the WPF Hyperlink element.

In practice, navigation with XPS is slightly more complicated than what we saw in Chapter 11 because the XPS file format itself does not support the Hyperlink element directly. Instead, it requires you to set the FixedPage.NavigateUri attached property on the Canvas, Glyph, or Path elements that you would like to act as links. However, the XpsDocumentWriter can convert a Hyperlink into suitably annotated elements. It generates three elements for each hyperlink: the link text, a Path representing the underline, and a rectangular Path element with a transparent fill. This covers the whole area of the Hyperlink to ensure that it functions correctly as a click target even if the Hyperlink itself has a transparent background. Without this, the link would be much harder to click—clicking in, say, the space in the middle of a letter *o* or anywhere outside of the letter shapes would fail to activate the link.*

Adding a hyperlink to an external resource, such as a web site, is simple: just set the link's NavigateUri to an absolute URL. But if you want a link on one page to be able to refer to another page, you must use a fragment URI (i.e., one beginning with a # character). The text following the # refers to a named element somewhere in the document.

For an element to be a valid target for a link, you must do two things. First, you must set the element's Name property to match the fragment URI in the link. (For example, if the link's NavigateUri is "#Heading_1" its target is an element named "Heading_1".) Second, you must advertise the existence of the target with a LinkTarget object associated with the containing page's PageContent object.

This second requirement exists to make sure XPS document viewers don't need to parse every single page in order to find the link target. As we saw earlier, the FixedDocument part of an XPS file contains a sequence of PageContent elements describing the pages that make up the document, such as the one shown in Example 15-6. If you are using hyperlinks, this part must declare which pages contain which link targets. Example 15-27 shows such a document.

Example 15-27. FixedDocument with LinkTargets

```
<FixedDocument xmlns="http://schemas.microsoft.com/xps/2005/06">
  <PageContent Source="Pages/1.fpage" />
  <PageContent Source="Pages/2.fpage">
```

---

* If you choose to generate an XPS document with the package-level APIs, you will need to do something similar when creating hyperlinks in order to make them usable.

Example 15-27. FixedDocument with LinkTargets (continued)

```
    <PageContent.LinkTargets>
      <LinkTarget Name="FirstItem" />
    </PageContent.LinkTargets>
  </PageContent>
  <PageContent Source="Pages/3.fpage">
    <PageContent.LinkTargets>
      <LinkTarget Name="SecondTarget" />
      <LinkTarget Name="Third" />
    </PageContent.LinkTargets>
  </PageContent>
</FixedDocument>
```

By declaring link targets in the FixedDocument part, it becomes possible for an XPS reader to follow internal links quickly. When the user clicks on a link, an XPS document viewer needs to scan only the FixedDocument to find the named link, and then open the containing page. Without this structure, it would need to scan every single page looking for the named element. This is not an optional performance enhancement—you are required to advertise link targets. Failure to do this will cause the links not to work.

> This linking mechanism requires you to ensure that your fragment names are unique across the scope of the whole document. Indeed, the XPS specification recommends (but does not absolutely require) that if a single XPS file contains multiple documents, the fragment names should be unique across the scope of the whole file.

The code in Examples 15-28 through 15-30 creates a document with a table of contents as its first page, containing a set of links to 10 more pages that make up the remainder of the document. Figure 15-7 shows how this first page will look. Clicking on any of these links in an XPS document viewer will jump directly to the relevant page.

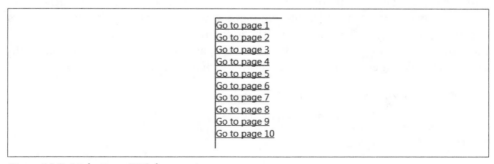

Figure 15-7. Links in an XPS document

Example 15-28 builds this FixedDocument. It begins by adding a page to contain the table of contents. This first page contains a TextBlock, which is initially empty.

The for loop builds 10 more pages and creates hyperlinks to these pages, adding those links to the TextBlock on the first page, and building up the list of links as shown in Figure 15-7.

Example 15-28. Using hyperlinks: creating the document

```
public static FixedDocument MakeDocWithToc( ) {
    FixedDocument doc = new FixedDocument( );

    FixedPage tocPage = new FixedPage( );
    TextBlock tableOfContents = new TextBlock( );
    tocPage.Children.Add(tableOfContents);

    PageContent pc = new PageContent( );
     ((IAddChild) pc).AddChild(tocPage);
    doc.Pages.Add(pc);

    for (int pageNumber = 1; pageNumber <= 10; ++pageNumber) {
        pc = MakePage(pageNumber);
        doc.Pages.Add(pc);

        Hyperlink link = MakeLink(pageNumber);
        tableOfContents.Inlines.Add(link);
        tableOfContents.Inlines.Add(new LineBreak( ));
    }
    return doc;
}
```

This code relies on a helper function, MakePage, to generate each page. Although a single page can contain any number of targets, Example 15-29 keeps things simple by creating a page for each target. It adds a TextBlock to act as the target itself. The fragment IDs[*] take the form Page1, Page2, and so on.

Example 15-29. Using hyperlinks: creating pages with targets

```
static PageContent MakePage(int pageNumber) {
    PageContent pc;
    string fragmentId = "Page" + pageNumber;

    TextBlock tb = new TextBlock( );
    tb.Text = "This is page " + pageNumber;
    tb.Name = fragmentId;

    FixedPage page = new FixedPage( );
    page.Children.Add(tb);
    pc = new PageContent( );
    ((IAddChild) pc).AddChild(page);
```

---

[*] Fragment IDs are the part of the URL following a # symbol. These are a standard URL feature. WPF uses these for much the same purpose as web pages: to identify a particular target location within a page.

Example 15-29. Using hyperlinks: creating pages with targets (continued)

```
    LinkTarget lt = new LinkTarget( );
    lt.Name = tb.Name;
    pc.LinkTargets.Add(lt);
    return pc;
}
```

We must also advertise the existence of the targets in the PageContent so that an XPS reader can find the targets without opening all of the FixedPage parts. This is why Example 15-29 creates a LinkTarget for each page.

After calling MakePage, Example 15-28 creates a Hyperlink for each page, using the MakeLink helper function shown in Example 15-30. This sets the NavigateUri property to a fragment URI matching the Name of the target.

Example 15-30. Using hyperlinks: creating the Hyperlink

```
static Hyperlink MakeLink(int pageNumber) {
    string fragmentId = "Page" + pageNumber;
    Run linkText = new Run("Go to page " + pageNumber);
    Uri linkTarget = new Uri("#" + fragmentId, UriKind.Relative);

    Hyperlink link = new Hyperlink(linkText);
    link.NavigateUri = linkTarget;

    return link;
}
```

If the FixedDocument created by Examples 15-28 through 15-30 is written to an XPS file using an XpsDocumentWriter, the table of contents pages will contain the hyperlink, converted into Glyphs and Path elements as the XPS specification requires. If the user opens the file in the XPS viewer provided with .NET 3.0 and clicks on a link, it will take him straight to the target. Example 15-31 shows an excerpt from the first fixed page in the XPS file that the preceding example generates.

Example 15-31. Generated FixedPage with hyperlink

```
<FixedPage xmlns="http://schemas.microsoft.com/xps/2005/06"
  xmlns:x="http://schemas.microsoft.com/xps/2005/06/resourcedictionary-key"
  xml:lang="en-us" Width="816" Height="1056">
  <Glyphs OriginX="0" OriginY="12.95" FontRenderingEmSize="12"
        FontUri="/Resources/19775d40-e839-41d3-a9fe-ca4670f35840.0DTTF"
        UnicodeString="Go to page 1" Fill="#FF0000FF" />
  <Path Fill="#FF0000FF" Data="M0,13.65L69.19,13.65 69.19,14.34 0,14.34Z" />
...
  <Path FixedPage.NavigateUri="../FixedDocument.fdoc#Page1" Fill="#00000000"
        Data="F1M0,0L69.19,0 69.19,15.96 0,15.96Z" />
...
</FixedPage>
```

This shows only the elements for the first link. The Glyphs element presents the text of the link: "Go to page 1." The first Path renders the underline—hyperlinks are displayed in the usual "blue with underline" style by default. The second Path defines a rectangle that covers the area occupied by the hyperlink, ensuring that the whole area is clickable. (It has a transparent fill, ensuring that it is invisible, but still presents a click target.) As you can see, this final Path element has the FixedPage.NavigateUri attached property. The XpsDocumentWriter has replaced our fragment URI with a relative URI pointing to the LinkTarget as declared in the fixed document part—this is the URI form that XPS readers will expect to see in the final output to represent a hyperlink. The result is that when the user clicks on a link in the contents page, he is taken to the corresponding target page.

Compression

When you create an XpsDocument, you have the option to specify the type of compression you would like to use. If you do not pass a CompressionOption, it will default to maximum compression. However, if you would like to favor speed over file size, you can pass in either Fast (as in Example 15-32) or SuperFast.

Example 15-32. Choosing fast compression

```
XpsDocument doc = new XpsDocument("out.xps", FileAccess.Write,
                                  CompressionOption.Fast);
```

In this section, we saw that many XPS features are of interest only when the output is destined for a file. The .NET 3.0 Framework also provides a number of features that are concerned solely with printing.

System.Printing

The System.Printing namespace defines types that provide printing services including managing settings of print jobs, discovering and selecting print queues, and configuring printers and print servers. We will explore the most commonly used types from this namespace.

PrintQueue

PrintQueue represents an output destination for printing—anytime you print something, you are sending it to a PrintQueue. The standard print dialog presents a list of available printers, and each printer in this list corresponds to a PrintQueue.

You have already seen several examples using PrintQueue—it offers a static CreateXpsDocumentWriter method that can return an XpsDocumentWriter. Although this method does not explicitly return a PrintQueue object, the writer it returns is implicitly bound to the PrintQueue of the printer the user selected in the print dialog.

The examples shown earlier in this chapter call an overload of CreateXpsDocumentWriter that does not specify a target PrintQueue, causing a print dialog to be shown automatically. However, if you have a PrintQueue object, you can call one of the overloads that accepts a PrintQueue, in which case no dialog will be shown, and the document writer will target the specified queue. Example 15-33 shows one way to do this.

Example 15-33. Creating a document writer with a specific PrintQueue

```
LocalPrintServer local = new LocalPrintServer( );
PrintQueue pq = local.DefaultPrintQueue;

XpsDocumentWriter xpsdw = PrintQueue.CreateXpsDocumentWriter(pq);
```

This example uses the default queue on the local machine. You can also obtain a PrintQueue from the PrintServer or the PrintDialog class. PrintQueue provides numerous properties (more than 60). Some of these provide static information about the queue, such as its name (FullName) and print speed (AveragePagesPerMinute). Others provide dynamic status information, such as IsPaperJammed and IsTonerLow.

PrintServer

PrintServer represents a machine offering one or more print queues. It provides a GetPrintQueues method that can return a collection of all the PrintQueue objects associated with the machine.

You can create a PrintServer by passing the machine name to the constructor. An alternative is a special derived class we saw in Example 15-33, called LocalPrintServer, which provides access to the local machine. This derived class adds a DefaultPrintQueue property, which returns the PrintQueue currently configured as the default print target.

GetPrintQueues offers overloads that enable you to filter the list of print queues. You can pass in an array of EnumeratedPrintQueueTypes values, specifying the kinds of printers you would like to see (e.g., print queues representing faxes, or print queues published in directory services).

If you already know exactly which print queue you want, you can call GetPrintQueue, passing in the queue name.

PrintServer even enables suitably privileged users to add and remove print queues. InstallPrintQueue allows you to specify the queue name, driver name, port names, processor name, and optionally the share name, comment, and location description. DeletePrintQueue removes a print queue.

PrintSystemJobInfo

The `PrintQueue` class defines a `GetPrintJobInfoCollection` method. This returns a collection of `PrintSystemJobInfo` objects. This collection provides roughly the same information you can see by opening the window showing active print jobs for the printer in Windows.

Some of the information in `PrintSystemJobInfo` is static for the job lifetime, such as `JobName` and `NumberOfPages`. Some properties provide status information; for example, `IsPrinting`, `TimeSinceStartedPrinting`, and `IsPaperOut`. `PrintSystemJobInfo` also offers a `Cancel` method to cancel the print job, and `Pause` and `Resume` methods to allow a job to be suspended and then resumed.

PrintTicket and PrintCapabilities

When you print from a Windows application, the print dialog provides access to various printing options. These include generic features such as the number of copies to be printed and collation settings. There may also be features common to many printers but not universally supported, such as double-sided printing. In some cases, you may wish to configure features specific to your particular printer type. A `PrintTicket` object encapsulates all such print settings.

The `PrintCapabilities` class is related to `PrintTicket`. Given a `PrintQueue`, you can call its `GetPrintCapabilities` method to discover the supported set of features you can add to a `PrintTicket` for that queue (see Example 15-34). If you call the overload of `GetPrintCapabilities` that takes no parameters, it will return a `PrintCapabilities` object with properties indicating which common features are available.

Example 15-34. Examining print capabilities

```
PrintCapabilities caps = pq.GetPrintCapabilities();
foreach (Duplexing duplexType in caps.DuplexingCapability) {
    Console.WriteLine(duplexType);
}
```

The `PrintCapabilities` class is convenient. However, it does not provide a complete list of the features the printer has to offer. It defines only the properties for common features. To get the complete set, you need to call the `GetPrintCapabilitiesAsXml` method. This returns an XML document containing all of the features, including those specific to the model of printer attached to the queue. This document will contain XML elements named `Feature` for each available feature. Example 15-35 shows one such element.

Example 15-35. Feature from a PrintCapabilities XML document

```
<psf:Feature name="ns0000:JobEnhancedPCL5Enable">
  <psf:Property name="psf:SelectionType">
    <psf:Value xsi:type="xsd:QName">psk:PickOne</psf:Value>
  </psf:Property>
  <psf:Property name="psk:DisplayName">
    <psf:Value xsi:type="xsd:string">EnhancedPCL5Enable</psf:Value>
  </psf:Property>
  <psf:Option name="ns0000:False" constrained="psk:None">
    <psf:Property name="psk:DisplayName">
      <psf:Value xsi:type="xsd:string">False</psf:Value>
    </psf:Property>
  </psf:Option>
  <psf:Option name="ns0000:True" constrained="psk:None">
    <psf:Property name="psk:DisplayName">
      <psf:Value xsi:type="xsd:string">True</psf:Value>
    </psf:Property>
  </psf:Option>
</psf:Feature>
```

Example 15-36 uses XPath to extract all of the Feature elements, and to print their DisplayName properties in order to show the names of the features. It then retrieves the Option elements inside each Feature to display the available settings.

Example 15-36. Working with print capabilities in XML form

```
Stream capsStream = pq.GetPrintCapabilitiesAsXml();
XmlDocument capsDoc = new XmlDocument();
capsDoc.Load(capsStream);

XmlNamespaceManager nsm = new XmlNamespaceManager(capsDoc.NameTable);
nsm.AddNamespace("psf",
  "http://schemas.microsoft.com/windows/2003/08/printing/printschemaframework");

XmlNodeList features = capsDoc.SelectNodes("//psf:Feature", nsm);
foreach (XmlElement feature in features) {
    XmlNode featureName = feature.SelectSingleNode(
        "psf:Property[@name='psk:DisplayName']/psf:Value/text()", nsm);
    Console.WriteLine("Feature: " + featureName.Value);

    XmlNodeList options = feature.SelectNodes("psf:Option", nsm);
    foreach (XmlElement option in options) {
        XmlNode optionName = option.SelectSingleNode(
            "psf:Property[@name='psk:DisplayName']/psf:Value/text()", nsm);
        if (optionName != null) {
            Console.WriteLine(" option: " + optionName.Value);
        }
    }
}
```

Running this against a real printer generates a lot of output—about 40 features, each with a few options. Because that wouldn't make very interesting reading, Example 15-37 shows just a short excerpt that corresponds to the XML in Example 15-35. It shows a printer-specific feature from one of the authors' printers, along with the possible settings for that feature.

Example 15-37. Printer-specific feature

```
Feature: EnhancedPCL5Enable
  option: False
  option: True
```

If you are interested in only certain features (e.g., you wish to know whether the printer at the end of the `PrintQueue` supports color and duplex printing), you can build a `PrintTicket` containing the features you are interested in and pass that to either of the methods for retrieving capabilities. This filters the results, listing only features that are both supported by the target printer and that were in your `PrintTicket`.

It is sometimes appropriate to specify print settings on a more fine-grained level than an entire print job. For example, if you are printing to a color printer, you might require color only on certain pages, and could indicate to the printer that black-and-white printing should be used on the rest. To exploit this, you would associate a `PrintTicket` for each `FixedPage` and `FixedDocument`, as well as providing one for the whole job. You would set the ticket's `OutputColor` property to `OutputColor.Color` for the color pages, and `OutputColor.Grayscale` for the other tickets. (For the job-level ticket, either you can let the user provide the settings via a print dialog, or you can pass one in to `PrintQueue.CreateXpsDocumentWriter`.)

Although print tickets are used to control print settings, it may be appropriate to provide them when writing an XPS file. For example, your application may generate XPS file output that is ultimately destined for a print bureau. In this case, either you can set the ticket on the `FixedPage`, `FixedDocument`, and `FixedDocumentSequence` classes (just as you would for printing) or you can use the package-level API. The writer interfaces for fixed pages, documents, and document sequences offer a settable `PrintTicket` property.

PrintDialog

As we've already seen, if you ask the `PrintQueue` class to create an `XpsDocumentWriter` without passing in a specific `PrintQueue`, it automatically shows the standard print dialog. However, sometimes you will need to exercise more control. For example, you may wish to enable the page range selection functionality, allowing the user to print a specific range of pages from the document. You may also wish to select an initial print queue and print ticket—rather than accepting the current defaults, you might wish to show the same settings the user chose the last time a particular document was printed, for example. Alternatively, although you may be happy with the default print dialog behavior, you might want to examine the PrintQueue or PrintTicket chosen by the user. In these cases, you will need to write code to display the PrintDialog.

Example 15-38 shows how to enable user page range selection in the PrintDialog. This also sets an initial selected range of pages.

Example 15-38. Using PrintDialog

```
PrintDialog pd = new PrintDialog( );
pd.MinPage = 1;
pd.MaxPage = 20;
pd.UserPageRangeEnabled = true;
pd.PageRangeSelection = PageRangeSelection.UserPages;
pd.PageRange = new PageRange(4, 8);

if (pd.ShowDialog( ) == true) {
    PrintQueue pq = pd.PrintQueue;
    PrintTicket pt = pd.PrintTicket;
    ...
}
```

If the user clicks the Print button, ShowDialog will return true. (The return type is a nullable bool, hence explicit comparison with true in the if statement.) The code goes on to retrieve the print queue and ticket reflecting the user's chosen print settings. These could then be passed to PrintQueue.CreateXpsDocumentWriter, in order to start printing to the chosen queue with the configured settings.

Media Description

Several classes are available in the System.Printing namespace for working with the size and resolution of the output media. These are described in Table 15-4. The reason for having several different classes to represent "paper size" is that different scenarios require different amounts of information.

Table 15-4. Media description types

Class	Usage
PageMediaSize	Describes the paper size
PageImageableArea	Describes the area of the paper in which printing is possible
PrintDocumentImageableArea	Combines a description of the paper size and the printable area
PageResolution	Describes the horizontal and vertical resolution of the target, and contains a "qualitative" resolution such as Draft or High

Displaying Fixed Documents

The easiest way to display an XPS file is to use the XPS viewer application supplied with the .NET 3.0 Framework. This viewer runs when you double-click on an XPS file. As mentioned earlier, Microsoft also supplies a free viewer for displaying documents on machines without the framework installed. However, it is sometimes useful to be able to display an XPS file within an application. WPF supplies the DocumentViewer control for this. Simply set its Document property to refer to either a FixedDocument or a FixedDocumentSequence, and it will render the document, providing navigation and zoom controls. Example 15-39 shows a simple window containing a DocumentViewer.

Example 15-39. Window with DocumentViewer

```
<Window x:Class="ShowFixedDocument.Window1"
    xmlns="http://schemas.microsoft.com/winfx/2006/xaml/presentation"
    xmlns:x="http://schemas.microsoft.com/winfx/2006/xaml"
    Title="Show FixedDocument" Height="300" Width="300">

  <DocumentViewer x:Name="viewer" />

</Window>
```

Given this XAML, the code-behind file can load an XPS document as shown in Example 15-40.

Example 15-40. Loading an XPS document into a DocumentViewer

```
string docPath = Environment.GetCommandLineArgs()[1];
XpsDocument doc = new XpsDocument(docPath, FileAccess.Read);
viewer.Document = doc.GetFixedDocumentSequence();
```

This reads the XPS file specified by the first command-line parameter. You could also use a FixedDocument or FixedDocumentSequence built from scratch. Figure 15-8 shows the XPS specification itself loaded into this UI.

Where Are We?

The XML Paper Specification is at the heart of printing in WPF. It also acts as a file format for accurately capturing an application's printable output. WPF lets us work with XPS files at various levels. There are the high-level FixedDocumentSequence, FixedDocument, and FixedPage classes, which mirror the basic structure of an XPS file but allow us to use WPF elements such as layout primitives that are not directly supported in XPS. The XpsDocumentWriter maps between this framework element world and the lower-level world of the XPS file.

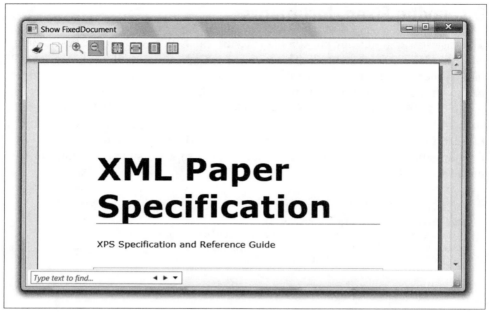

Figure 15-8. DocumentViewer control

We can either build an XPS file on disk or send it directly to the print system. If we provide a "save as XPS" feature, we may choose to add extra structure to enhance the resulting XPS files, typically working directly at the XPS package level with the System.Windows.Xps.Packaging namespace. Or, if we wish, we can go lower still, using the System.IO.Packaging namespace to work directly at the OPC level.

The System.Printing namespace provides us with various types to control the printing process, such as choosing output servers and queues, and configuring the print settings.

CHAPTER 16

Animation and Media

Imagine an application with a completely static appearance, which offers no visible reaction to mouse clicks or other input—it would sometimes be hard to tell whether that application was functioning or had frozen. We depend on visual feedback to assure us that applications are responding to input. Adding movement to your user interface can bring it to life, enhancing the interactive feel of the application. Animation can improve the realism of visual transitions intended to suggest physical movement, such as buttons that become visibly pushed in when clicked.

Animation is also useful for dealing with transitions from one view to another. In the real world, we are not used to seeing items materialize instantaneously out of nowhere, but computer programs often use abrupt transitions. In the very early days of cinema, editing shots to make objects or people appear suddenly was an effective way of scaring the audience, because it was such an unnatural thing to see. These days we are accustomed to unreal imagery and are not so easily shocked, but sudden transitions can still jar. Careful and subtle use of animation can make it much easier for a user to follow visual transitions, such as a move from one page to another or the appearance and disappearance of UI features.

For many years, Windows has been able to play video clips, but only as isolated islands of moving content. Animating features of ordinary controls has typically been much harder. WPF makes it easy to add animation to your application, by providing comprehensive support for animating almost any visible aspect of any user interface element. It can, of course, play video and audio clips as well, and it can even synchronize media playback with animations.

Animation Fundamentals

Animation involves changing some visible characteristic of part of a user interface, such as its size, position, or color, over some period of time. You could do this the hard way, by creating a timer and modifying the user interface's appearance on each timer tick. Indeed, this is how animation is typically done in Win32 and Windows Forms.

Fortunately, WPF takes care of these low-level details. Animation, like many features of WPF, simply requires us to declare what we would like to happen. The system takes care of doing it for us.

All of WPF's animation support boils down to changing one or more properties over time. This means that there are some limitations on what WPF's animation system can do for you. For example, the structure of the visual tree remains the same throughout. An animation will not add and remove elements for you (although it is possible for animation to set properties that will change elements' visibility). You cannot provide "before" and "after" scenes, and have WPF interpolate between the two. This means there is no automatic way to animate a transition from one layout to another so that all of the elements slide from their start positions to their end positions—you would need to write a special-purpose custom panel to make that happen.*

The key to knowing what WPF animation can or cannot do is to understand its property-focused nature—it changes only those properties you tell it to change. When deciding how to animate a UI, ask yourself what you would expect to see halfway through the animation, and work out how the properties would need to be set in order to capture that intermediate point. If you apply this thought process for animating from a horizontal to a vertical StackPanel, it's obvious that there's a problem. You can't set a property on a StackPanel to make it display something halfway between horizontal and vertical—and if you can't, neither can the animation system.

Before we look at any of the parts of the animation framework in detail, let's examine a simple example. Example 16-1 shows the markup for a single red ellipse that will act as the target for an animation.

Example 16-1. A target to be animated

```
<Ellipse Name="myEllipse" Fill="Red" Height="100" Width="10" />
```

Example 16-2 creates an animation object and applies it to the ellipse's Width property in order to make the ellipse grow wider over five seconds.

Example 16-2. A simple animation

```
DoubleAnimation animate = new DoubleAnimation( );
animate.To = 300;
animate.Duration = new Duration(TimeSpan.FromSeconds(5));
animate.RepeatBehavior = RepeatBehavior.Forever;
myEllipse.BeginAnimation(Ellipse.WidthProperty, animate);
```

The animation in this example is of type DoubleAnimation, which is defined in the System.Windows.Media.Animation namespace. The significance of the Double is that the property being animated is of type Double, as opposed to Int32, Point, Size, or

---

* You can find an example of an animating panel in Kevin Moore's WPF Bag-O-Tricks at *http://wpf.netfx3.com/ files/folders/controls/entry8196.aspx* or *http://tinysells.com/112.*

some other type. Not all types are animated in the same way. For example, Point is a two-dimensional value, meaning we may want control over aspects of its animation that wouldn't make sense for a one-dimensional type such as Double.

The DoubleAnimation describes how the animated property should change over time. Example 16-2 sets the To property to 300, and it sets a Duration of five seconds. As you might guess, this means the width will start from the initial value of 10 specified in Example 16-1, and will gradually change to 300 over the course of five seconds. The RepeatBehavior property has been set to Forever, indicating that once the animation reaches the end, it should go back to the start and repeat indefinitely.

The animation created by Example 16-2 will start to run the moment it calls the BeginAnimation method. Note that BeginAnimation requires us to pass an object identifying the property to be animated—this must be a DependencyProperty object; types that define dependency properties usually make the corresponding DependencyProperty object available in a static read-only field, such as the WidthProperty field used in Example 16-2. Figure 16-1 shows how the ellipse appears at various stages during the animation.

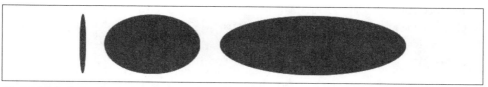

Figure 16-1. Animation at start, after two and a half seconds, and after five seconds

As we will see, there are several ways to choose exactly how the properties change. For example, we can use curved motion and changes in speed. But these are just ways of getting WPF to set properties to the right value at the right time.

You can animate the majority of properties that have an impact on an element's appearance. There are just three requirements to be able to animate a property: the property must be a dependency property, a suitable animation type must be available, and the target type that defines the property must implement IAnimatable.

The animation system relies on the dependency property system to be able to update property values automatically. The main reason for this is that animations are always transient—they never change the underlying value of the property, they just temporarily change the effective value. This means that if your code decides to change the underlying property value halfway through an animation, the property will correctly revert to this new underlying value when the animation completes, rather than reverting to the old value and thereby losing your change. Dependency properties have special support to allow the animation system to temporarily change the effective property value without modifying the underlying value. Chapter 18 describes dependency properties in detail. The majority of properties of WPF elements are dependency properties, so in practice this first requirement is rarely a problem.

The second requirement, that the property's type must have a corresponding animation type, refers to types such as DoubleAnimation and PointAnimation. (We'll look at the third requirement, IAnimatable, after we've looked at the animation types.)

Animation Types

An animation type defines how a property should change over time. WPF provides many animation types, each one designed to animate properties of a particular type. For example, you can animate properties of type Double using a DoubleAnimation, whereas for a Color property, you can use ColorAnimation. All of these types follow the same naming convention of *Type*Animation, as you can see from the list in Table 16-1. All animation types conform to the same design, so although there are many examples, you need to learn only the one basic pattern.

Table 16-1. Animation types

ByteAnimation	Int64Animation	SingleAnimation
ColorAnimation	Point3DAnimation	SizeAnimation
DecimalAnimation	PointAnimation	ThicknessAnimation
DoubleAnimation	QuaternionAnimation	Vector3DAnimation
Int16Animation	RectAnimation	VectorAnimation
Int32Animation	Rotation3DAnimation	

Although this list covers most of the common types needed to influence the appearance of a WPF UI, it does not include any enumeration types. For example, the Orientation type used by StackPanel has no corresponding animation type. This makes sense when you consider that this enumeration supports just two values: Horizontal and Vertical. There is no way to represent some intermediate value between these choices.

If you really need to change such properties during the course of an animation, you can do so using DiscreteObjectKeyFrame, which allows you to set properties of any type. You can only use this inside a keyframe animation, as described later in the "Keyframe Animations" section. However, the fundamental limitation that enumerations support only discrete values still applies—all you can do is perform abrupt changes from one value to another at the moment of your choosing.

 You can write your own animation types. This can be useful if you write a custom element that has properties of some custom type that you would like to animate. Your animation type would derive from AnimationTimeline, the base class of the built-in animation types, and would implement the features described in this section. For more information about custom animations, see *http://msdn2.microsoft.com/library/aa970564.aspx* (*http://tinysells.com/113*).

All of the built-in animation types provide To and From properties to set the start and end values. Example 16-2 used the To property; if you use this without setting From, the animation takes the current property value as its starting point. As an alternative, they also offer a By property, which lets you modify the property without needing to know its current value. Example 16-3 makes the target ellipse 100 logical pixels wider than its initial Width, whatever that might be.

Example 16-3. Animating "by" with By

```
DoubleAnimation animate = new DoubleAnimation( );
animate.By = 100;
animate.Duration = new Duration(TimeSpan.FromSeconds(5));
myEllipse.BeginAnimation(Ellipse.WidthProperty, animate);
```

 The target property must have a valid value for a By animation to work. Some properties have no value at all by default, so you may get an error if you apply such an animation if the target property has not previously been set. The same is true of animations that specify only To or only From. Animations that specify both To and From can safely be applied to an unset property.

The types of these To, From, and By properties match the target type—on a ColorAnimation, these properties are of type Color, whereas on a DoubleAnimation they are of type Double. The essential behavior is the same in all cases. The animation simply interpolates from the initial value to the final value over the animation's duration.

By default, this interpolation is linear—the value changes with constant speed over the duration of the whole animation. However, you can change this with the AccelerationRatio and DecelerationRatio properties. Example 16-4 uses these to provide a "soft" start and finish to the animation.

Example 16-4. Acceleration and deceleration

```
animate.AccelerationRatio = 0.2;
animate.DecelerationRatio = 0.1;
```

Both properties are of type double. The AccelerationRatio of 0.2 causes the animation's rate of change to start at zero, and then gradually accelerate up to full speed over the first one-fifth of the animation's duration. Likewise, the DecelerationRatio of 0.1 means progress will slow to a halt over the last one-tenth of the animation.

 AccelerationRatio and DecelerationRatio do not change the effective duration of the animation. An animation will run for the time specified in its Duration property regardless of acceleration or deceleration.

There is one last requirement for animation support. The target element for animation must implement the IAnimatable interface.

IAnimatable

IAnimatable provides an API for controlling animation. Example 16-5 shows the interface definition. The methods for starting animations include the BeginAnimation method used in Example 16-2. Recall that AnimationTimeline is the base class of all animation types, so you can pass any animation object into the overloaded BeginAnimation method. There are other methods to allow the use of clocks and hand-off, techniques we will look at later. GetAnimationBaseValue allows you to retrieve the value an animated property would have had if it were not being animated.

Example 16-5. IAnimatable interface

```
public interface IAnimatable {
    void ApplyAnimationClock(DependencyProperty dp, AnimationClock clock);
    void ApplyAnimationClock(DependencyProperty dp, AnimationClock clock,
                             HandoffBehavior handoffBehavior);
    void BeginAnimation(DependencyProperty dp, AnimationTimeline animation);
    void BeginAnimation(DependencyProperty dp, AnimationTimeline animation,
                        HandoffBehavior handoffBehavior);
    object GetAnimationBaseValue(DependencyProperty dp);
    bool HasAnimatedProperties { get; }
}
```

A wide range of WPF classes implement IAnimatable. The UIElement and ContentElement base classes both provide implementations, enabling you to apply animations to the majority of user interface elements. IAnimatable is also implemented by Animatable, which is the base class of many graphical elements such as Drawing, Geometry, Brush, and classes used to build 3D models. (See Appendix D for more information about these core base types.) In practice, you can animate almost any UI feature in WPF.

 If you want a custom type to support animation, you should derive from one of WPF's existing implementations. IAnimatable defines a consistent API for controlling animations, but it is not intended as an interface that your own types would ever implement from scratch. If you try to build your own implementation, it won't work, because WPF will animate only the implementations it knows about.

The examples we've seen so far used code to launch the animation. Although this is often an appropriate technique, it can sometimes be easier to let WPF launch the animation automatically. We can tell WPF when we would like an animation to run by defining a *trigger*.

Triggers

WPF can start animations automatically when events are raised. Example 16-6 defines an animation identical to the one created in Example 16-2, but arranges for WPF to start it anytime the ellipse raises the MouseEnter event. Triggers enable us to use just XAML—the techniques shown previously involve calling a method, which required code.

Example 16-6. Starting an animation with a trigger

```
<Ellipse Name="myEllipse" Fill="Red" Height="100" Width="10">
  <Ellipse.Triggers>
    <EventTrigger RoutedEvent="Ellipse.MouseEnter">
      <BeginStoryboard>
        <Storyboard>
          <DoubleAnimation Storyboard.TargetProperty="(Ellipse.Width)"
                           To="300" Duration="0:0:5" />
        </Storyboard>
      </BeginStoryboard>
    </EventTrigger>
  </Ellipse.Triggers>
</Ellipse>
```

 When defining an animation in markup, any duration value should be specified as at least three parts: hours, minutes, and seconds. The value "0:0:5" in Example 16-6 means five seconds. You may optionally specify the number of days (e.g., the value "1.10:0:15" means one day, 10 hours, and 15 seconds). If you specify just a single number, WPF treats that as the number of days, so if we had just written "5," it would mean five days!

This markup adds an EventTrigger to the ellipse. An EventTrigger can be associated with any routed event. (We described routed events in Chapter 4.) In this case, we've chosen Ellipse.MouseEnter, meaning that this trigger will fire when the mouse pointer enters the ellipse.

An event trigger contains a collection of actions that define what happens when the trigger is activated. These must be of a type derived from the TriggerAction base class. Table 16-2 lists the available action types and their usage.

Table 16-2. Trigger action types and usage

Type	Usage
BeginStoryboard	Starts an animation storyboard
PauseStoryboard	Pauses a running storyboard
RemoveStoryboard	Removes a storyboard and the resources it consumes
ResumeStoryboard	Allows a paused storyboard to continue

Table 16-2. Trigger action types and usage (continued)

Type	Usage
SeekStoryboard	Moves a storyboard to a particular moment in time
SetStoryboardSpeedRatio	Changes the speed at which a storyboard plays
SkipStoryboardToFill	Advances a storyboard to the end
SoundPlayerAction	Plays a sound
StopStoryboard	Stops a running storyboard, allowing any animated properties to revert to their original values

Example 16-6 uses a `BeginStoryboard` as the trigger's only action. This action runs a storyboard, which is a collection of animations. The purpose of storyboards is to let you orchestrate several animations, enabling a single trigger to launch anything from the simplest possible transition to a feature-length extravaganza. The `Storyboard` in Example 16-6 contains just one animation, but it could contain as many as you like. For example, you could add a second `DoubleAnimation` to animate the ellipse's height at the same time as its width, or you could add more animations to change these properties further after the first animations are complete.

Although the animation in Example 16-6 has the same effect as that in Example 16-2, we use a different technique to indicate the target property. In code, we just pass the `DependencyProperty` object for the target property as a parameter to `BeginAnimation`. But in markup, we must set the `Storyboard.TargetProperty` attached property. Notice that this attached property requires us to specify both the property to be animated and the class that defines the property (i.e., `"(Ellipse.Width)"` instead of just `"Width"`). This is because properties do not always have to be defined by the class to which they are applied—you might want to animate attached properties such as `Canvas.Left`. For consistency, you are required to always specify both class and property, even when the property is a member of the target object, as it is in this case.

Although `BeginStoryboard` lets you start an animation, most of the other trigger action types let you control a storyboard after it has been started. To use these, you must give the `BeginStoryboard` action a name so that the other actions can indicate which storyboard they are controlling. Example 16-7 uses this technique—as before, it starts animating the width when the mouse enters the ellipse, but it also pauses and resumes the animation when the left mouse button is pressed and released, respectively.

Example 16-7. Pausing and resuming a storyboard with triggers

```
<Ellipse Name="myEllipse" Fill="Red" Height="100" Width="10">
  <Ellipse.Triggers>
    <EventTrigger RoutedEvent="Ellipse.MouseEnter">
      <BeginStoryboard Name="changeWidth">
```

Example 16-7. Pausing and resuming a storyboard with triggers (continued)

```
      <Storyboard>
        <DoubleAnimation Storyboard.TargetProperty="(Ellipse.Width)"
                         To="300" Duration="0:0:5" />
      </Storyboard>
    </BeginStoryboard>
  </EventTrigger>

  <EventTrigger RoutedEvent="Ellipse.MouseLeftButtonDown">
    <PauseStoryboard BeginStoryboardName="changeWidth" />
  </EventTrigger>

  <EventTrigger RoutedEvent="Ellipse.MouseLeftButtonUp">
    <ResumeStoryboard BeginStoryboardName="changeWidth" />
  </EventTrigger>
  </Ellipse.Triggers>
</Ellipse>
```

Although most of the storyboard trigger types are straightforward, the distinction between `StopStoryboard` and `RemoveStoryboard` is not so obvious. The difference is that you can use a seek action with a stopped storyboard to rewind to an earlier position, allowing it to run again. You cannot do this (or anything else) to a storyboard once it has been removed, because the storyboard effectively no longer exists. `RemoveStoryboard` is slightly more efficient, because it allows WPF to free up all resources associated with the storyboard. For simple animations, the resource costs are not high, but there is one case where it is important to ensure that storyboards are removed. You should do so when using the "compose" style of handoff behavior (which we will describe later in this chapter).

One of the trigger action types is not concerned with storyboards. `SoundPlayerAction` just plays a sound. Example 16-8 plays the system "ding" sound whenever the mouse enters a rectangle.

Example 16-8. Playing a sound with a trigger

```
<Rectangle Fill="Green">
  <Rectangle.Triggers>
    <EventTrigger RoutedEvent="Rectangle.MouseEnter">
      <SoundPlayerAction Source="c:\windows\media\ding.wav" />
    </EventTrigger>
  </Rectangle.Triggers>
</Rectangle>
```

You can add triggers to any `FrameworkElement`, `DataTemplate`, `ControlTemplate`, or `Style`. Other trigger types besides `EventTrigger` can control animations. In Chapter 8, you saw data and property triggers being added to the `Triggers` collection of templates and styles. We used these to set properties of elements, but you also can use them to control animations.

Using animation is slightly different with DataTrigger and Trigger. This is because of a fundamental difference between these trigger types and EventTrigger. An EventTrigger is not active for any length of time—it simply fires at the moment its corresponding event is raised, invoking its actions at that instant. But the other trigger types are not instantaneous—they are active for as long as their conditions are met.* Despite this, the other trigger types can still run animations. They have two sets of actions associated with them: one to be used when the trigger moves from being inactive to active, and a second set to be used when it returns to the inactive state. These are called the *enter actions* and the *exit actions*, respectively. Example 16-9 shows these in use in a style.

Example 16-9. Enter and exit actions

```
...
<Style x:Key="widthOnFocus">
  <Style.Triggers>
    <Trigger Property="FrameworkElement.IsFocused" Value="True">
      <Trigger.EnterActions>
        <BeginStoryboard Name="changeWidth">
          <Storyboard>
            <DoubleAnimation Storyboard.TargetProperty="(FrameworkElement.Width)"
                             To="300" Duration="0:0:5" />
          </Storyboard>
        </BeginStoryboard>
      </Trigger.EnterActions>
      <Trigger.ExitActions>
        <RemoveStoryboard BeginStoryboardName="changeWidth" />
      </Trigger.ExitActions>
    </Trigger>
  </Style.Triggers>
</Style>
...
```

This style causes an element's width to be animated when it acquires the focus. The animation is removed when it loses the focus.

 The Triggers property of a FrameworkElement can contain only EventTriggers. You can use enter and exit actions only with styles and templates.

When using triggers, you may find yourself in a situation where one storyboard starts before the preceding one has finished. This is not a problem, but it does raise a question regarding what happens when both storyboards contain animations that target the same property. The behavior depends on the nature of the second animation. If it specifies a From value, the preceding animation is stopped and has no further effect.

---

* If you are familiar with electronics terminology, you could think of EventTrigger as being edge-driven, and all the other triggers as level-driven.

However, it might have no From value, specifying either By, To, or none of these (the final case indicating that the animation returns the value to its original unanimated state). In these cases, a process called *handoff* occurs.

There are two forms of handoff. If you are starting animations from code, there are overloads of the members of the IAnimatable interface, which was shown in Example 16-5, that take a HandoffBehavior enumeration value. Alternatively, you can set the HandoffBehavior property of a BeginStoryboard object. The default handoff behavior is SnapshotAndReplace, which means that the preceding animation stops, but its current value is used as the starting point for the new animation. The alternative is Compose. When new storyboards or animations are started with this behavior, existing animations targeting the same properties are not stopped. Instead, the animations run simultaneously, and their results are combined. The second storyboard in Example 16-10 uses this technique.

Example 16-10. HandoffBehavior.Compose

```
<Ellipse Fill="Green" Width="20" Height="100">
  <Ellipse.Triggers>
    <EventTrigger RoutedEvent="Ellipse.MouseEnter">
      <BeginStoryboard Name="enterAnim">
        <Storyboard>
          <DoubleAnimation By="400" Duration="0:0:4"
              Storyboard.TargetProperty="Width" />
        </Storyboard>
      </BeginStoryboard>
    </EventTrigger>
    <EventTrigger RoutedEvent="Ellipse.MouseLeave">
      <BeginStoryboard HandoffBehavior="Compose" Name="leaveAnim">
        <Storyboard>
          <DoubleAnimation By="-400" Duration="0:0:4"
              Storyboard.TargetProperty="Width" />
        </Storyboard>
      </BeginStoryboard>
    </EventTrigger>
    <EventTrigger RoutedEvent="Ellipse.Unloaded">
      <RemoveStoryboard BeginStoryboardName="enterAnim" />
      <RemoveStoryboard BeginStoryboardName="leaveAnim" />
    </EventTrigger>
  </Ellipse.Triggers>
</Ellipse>
```

The first storyboard is run normally, launched by a trigger when the mouse moves into the ellipse. The second runs when the mouse leaves. Both target the ellipse's Width property, but they animate it in opposite directions—the first animates by 400, and the second animates by −400. If you move the mouse into the ellipse and then wait for the first animation to complete before removing the mouse, the animations do not overlap. However, if you remove the mouse before the first animation completes, handoff will occur because we have two animations targeting the same property.

Because we are using the Compose handoff behavior, the effect of the two animations will be combined. Because they are working in equal and opposite ways, the effect will be that the ellipse's width will stop changing while both animations are active, and will start to shrink only when the first animation completes.

 As mentioned earlier, it is recommended that you remove storyboards that use this Compose behavior as early as you can. WPF cannot shut down the original animation when the new one starts, because its effect must be taken into account. It would be worse if both storyboards in Example 16-10 had used this behavior, because a new set of animations would have to be created every time the mouse enters and leaves the ellipse! Because (as will become clear later) most animations have an infinite effective duration by default, continuing to apply their final value on completion, this would mean that the animations would never go away. Example 16-10 explicitly removes the animations when the ellipse unloads. But if you are making heavy use of multiple composing animations, you may need to remove storyboards a little earlier.

Animations in a single storyboard can target properties of multiple elements. By default, the target is determined by the storyboard's location—if the containing trigger belongs to an element, that element will be the target; if the trigger belongs to a style or a template, the style or template's target will be the animation's target. However, it is often useful to target some other element.

For example, if you define a template for a control, it might contain features that do not correspond directly to properties on the element, but that you may want to animate nonetheless. For example, Figure 16-2 shows two pairs of buttons. On the top row, the buttons are shown with custom visuals with a rounded reflective look. The bottom row is similar, but a radial fill has been added to suggest an inner glow to the button. We might want to animate that glow to make the button pulsate gradually.

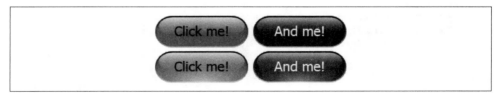

Figure 16-2. Buttons with animated glow (Color Plate 1)

The Button type does not provide a property we can use to represent the glow color, so in order to animate the glow, the animation needs to target that specific element within the control template. If we set the x:Name attribute on the relevant element in the template, we can then refer to this in the animation using the Storyboard.TargetName attached property. Example 16-11 shows the markup for Figure 16-2.

Example 16-11. Templates and animation targets

```
<StackPanel Orientation="Horizontal">
  <StackPanel.Resources>
    <Style TargetType="{x:Type Button}">
      <Setter Property="Background" Value="CornflowerBlue" />
      <Setter Property="Height" Value="26" />
      <Setter Property="Template">
        <Setter.Value>

          <ControlTemplate TargetType="{x:Type Button}">
            <Grid Height="{TemplateBinding Height}">
              <Grid.RowDefinitions>
                <RowDefinition Height="1.8*" />
                <RowDefinition Height="*" />
              </Grid.RowDefinitions>

              <Rectangle Grid.RowSpan="2" RadiusX="13" RadiusY="13"
                                    Fill="{TemplateBinding Background}">
                <Rectangle.Stroke>
                  <LinearGradientBrush StartPoint="0,0" EndPoint="0,1">
                      <GradientStop Offset="0" Color="Black" />
                      <GradientStop Offset="1" Color="LightGray" />
                  </LinearGradientBrush>
                </Rectangle.Stroke>
              </Rectangle>


              <!-- Glow -->

              <Rectangle Grid.RowSpan="2" RadiusX="13" RadiusY="13">
                <Rectangle.Fill>
                  <RadialGradientBrush Center="0.5, 1" GradientOrigin="0.5,1"
                                        RadiusX="0.7" RadiusY="0.8">
                    <RadialGradientBrush.GradientStops>
                      <GradientStop x:Name="glowStop" Offset="0" Color="White" />
                      <GradientStop Offset="1" Color="Transparent" />
                    </RadialGradientBrush.GradientStops>
                  </RadialGradientBrush>
                </Rectangle.Fill>
              </Rectangle>

              <Rectangle Margin="3,1.1" RadiusX="11" RadiusY="12">
                <Rectangle.Fill>
                  <LinearGradientBrush StartPoint="0,0" EndPoint="0,1">
                      <GradientStop Offset="0" Color="#dfff" />
                      <GradientStop Offset="1" Color="#0fff" />
                  </LinearGradientBrush>
                </Rectangle.Fill>
              </Rectangle>
```

Example 16-11. Templates and animation targets (continued)

```
                <ContentPresenter Grid.RowSpan="3" Margin="13,2,13,4"
                                              HorizontalAlignment="Center"
                                              VerticalAlignment="Center" />

            </Grid>

            <ControlTemplate.Triggers>
              <EventTrigger RoutedEvent="Button.Loaded">
                <BeginStoryboard>
                  <Storyboard>

                    <ColorAnimation From="#1fff" To="#cfff"
                          Storyboard.TargetName="glowStop"
                          Storyboard.TargetProperty="(GradientStop.Color)"
                          Duration="0:0:1"
                          AutoReverse="True" RepeatBehavior="Forever"
                          AccelerationRatio="0.4" DecelerationRatio="0.6"/>
                  </Storyboard>
                </BeginStoryboard>
              </EventTrigger>
            </ControlTemplate.Triggers>
          </ControlTemplate>
        </Setter.Value>
      </Setter>
    </Style>
  </StackPanel.Resources>

  <Button Margin="4,0">Click me!</Button>
  <Button Background="DarkRed" Foreground="White">And me!</Button>
</StackPanel>
```

Most of the template is static, but the glow is animated. Note the x:Name attribute
with a value of glowStop on the relevant gradient stop. The animation targets this
item. This technique is not limited to templates. You can use it from storyboards in
an element's Triggers property. Example 16-12 shows a storyboard defined in a grid
that applies animations to a couple of named ellipses.

Example 16-12. Targeting named elements

```
<Grid>
  <Grid.Triggers>
    <EventTrigger RoutedEvent="Grid.Loaded">
      <BeginStoryboard>
        <Storyboard>
          <DoubleAnimation To="300" Duration="0:0:1"
              Storyboard.TargetName="left"
              Storyboard.TargetProperty="Width" />

          <DoubleAnimation To="300" Duration="0:0:1"
              Storyboard.TargetName="right"
              Storyboard.TargetProperty="Height" />
```

Example 16-12. Targeting named elements (continued)

```
        </Storyboard>
      </BeginStoryboard>
    </EventTrigger>
  </Grid.Triggers>
  <Grid.ColumnDefinitions>
    <ColumnDefinition />
    <ColumnDefinition />
  </Grid.ColumnDefinitions>

  <Ellipse Name="left"  Grid.Column="0" Fill="Red" Width="100" Height="10" />
  <Ellipse Name="right" Grid.Column="1" Fill="Green" Width="100" Height="10" />

</Grid>
```

Sometimes it can be convenient to animate nested properties of properties. For example, the ellipse in Example 16-1 is red, and we might want to animate this color. This is not quite as straightforward as it may seem, because the Fill property's type is Brush. So, we cannot target it directly with a ColorAnimation, and there is no BrushAnimation type. One way to deal with this is to make the Brush the animation target, just as we made a GradientStop the target in Example 16-11. All we would need to do is give the brush a name, as shown in Example 16-13.

Example 16-13. Ellipse with explicit SolidColorBrush

```
<Ellipse Name="myEllipse" Height="100">
  <Ellipse.Fill>
    <SolidColorBrush x:Name="myBrush" Color="Red" />
  </Ellipse.Fill>
</Ellipse>
```

Here we've expanded the Fill property. This is effectively the same as the original in Example 16-1—the XAML compiler interprets the value of Red as shorthand for a SolidColorBrush property. (We discuss how XAML converts strings to objects in Appendix A.)

We could now make this named brush the target of an animation using the technique already shown in Example 16-12. However, there is a more succinct option. An animation can target nested properties—Storyboard.TargetProperty can drill into subobjects inside a property. We can use that to animate properties of brushes, and other types, without having to expand them out and name them. Example 16-14 uses this technique to animate the color of an ellipse.

Example 16-14. Animating nested properties

```
<Ellipse Fill="Red" Height="100" Width="200">
  <Ellipse.Triggers>
    <EventTrigger RoutedEvent="Ellipse.Loaded">
      <BeginStoryboard>
        <Storyboard>
```

Example 16-14. Animating nested properties (continued)

```
        <ColorAnimation
          Storyboard.TargetProperty="(Ellipse.Fill).(SolidColorBrush.Color)"
          Duration="0:0:7" From="Red" To="Purple"
          RepeatBehavior="Forever" AutoReverse="True" />
      </Storyboard>
    </BeginStoryboard>
  </EventTrigger>
 </Ellipse.Triggers>
</Ellipse>
```

The `StoryBoard.TargetProperty` property first identifies the `Ellipse.Fill` property, then indicates that it wants to drill into that property, which is a `SolidColorBrush`, and set its nested `Color` property. The `ColorAnimation` then specifies that the color should fade between red and purple every seven seconds.

 All `Brush` properties set to `Red` in XAML will share the same `SolidColorBrush` instance: the one returned by `Brushes.Red`. So, you could be forgiven for worrying that Example 16-14 would change the color of everything using this brush, and not just our ellipse. In fact, this doesn't happen. The brush returned by `Brushes.Red` is "frozen," meaning that it cannot be changed. When you ask the animation system to animate properties that contain frozen objects, it replaces them with unfrozen copies. (The `Freezable` base class defines a `Clone` method to enable this.) Example 16-14 therefore ends up animating a local copy of the brush, and not the original one returned by `Brushes.Red`.

`Storyboard.TargetProperty` can drill down to any depth. It can also index into collections. Example 16-15 shows this technique—this is how a `ColorAnimation` for a `LinearGradientBrush` might look.

Example 16-15. Animation path with index

```
<ColorAnimation Storyboard.TargetName="gradientBrush"
    Storyboard.TargetProperty="
        (LinearGradientBrush.GradientStops)[2].(GradientStop.Color)"
    To="Green" Duration="0:0:4" />
```

The [*index*] syntax indicates an item at a particular zero-based offset inside a collection. This example uses it to animate the color of the brush's third gradient stop.

We've now looked at the core features of WPF's animation system: the property-centric approach, launching of animations either from code or via triggers, the animation types that describe the animations to be performed, and how we can use storyboards to group animations. Animation types and storyboards share a certain amount in common. They are both *timelines*. Timelines are a critical concept for managing complex animations in WPF.

Timelines

A timeline represents a stretch of time. It usually also describes one or more things that happen during that time. All timeline types derive from the Timeline base class, which defines various common properties. For example, the animation types described in the preceding section are timelines. Consider this DoubleAnimation:

```
<DoubleAnimation From="10" To="300" BeginTime="0:0:2" Duration="0:0:5" />
```

Timelines of all kinds have a start time and a duration identifying the particular stretch of time they describe. The Duration property indicates that this DoubleAnimation represents a five-second stint. As the BeginTime property indicates, it starts at an offset of two seconds. BeginTime is relative to the timeline's container. For example, if an animation is defined inside a storyboard, the start time is relative to when the storyboard begins. If the start time is not specified, it defaults to 0:0:0. BeginTime and Duration are just two of the standard properties available on every timeline. Table 16-3 shows the properties common to all timelines.

Table 16-3. Timeline properties

Property	Usage
AccelerationRatio	Causes the timeline to ramp up to speed at the start
AutoReverse	Makes the timeline run in reverse once it reaches the end
BeginTime	Start time, relative to parent
DecelerationRatio	Causes the timeline to slow down toward the end
Duration	The length of the timeline
FillBehavior	How the timeline behaves when it reaches its natural end
Name	An optional name
RepeatBehavior	Indicates whether the timeline repeats
SpeedRatio	The speed at which this timeline runs relative to its parent's speed

All of the animation types described earlier are timelines, but these are not the only kinds. Later, when we look at playback of media such as audio and video, we will use the MediaTimeline type. There are also timelines used for grouping. These enable you to orchestrate complex animations by combining multiple simpler ones into a hierarchy of timelines.

Hierarchy

Timelines are often arranged in a hierarchy. We've already seen the Storyboard as a parent of a DoubleAnimation, but it is common to have deeper nesting than this to manage more complex animations. For example, if you want the first part of an animation to repeat a few times before the second phase begins, it would be best to define this first part as a single group and make that group repeat, rather than duplicating the relevant animations. We do this using `ParallelTimeline`, a type of timeline intended for grouping other timelines.

 Storyboard derives from `ParallelTimeline`. It's a special case of a `ParallelTimeline`, found only at the root of an animation hierarchy.

The storyboard in Example 16-16 uses two `ParallelTimeline` elements to group several animations together.

Example 16-16. A hierarchy of timelines

```
<StackPanel Orientation="Horizontal" VerticalAlignment="Center">
  <StackPanel.Triggers>
    <EventTrigger RoutedEvent="StackPanel.Loaded">
      <BeginStoryboard>
        <Storyboard>
          <ParallelTimeline RepeatBehavior="Forever">

            <DoubleAnimation BeginTime="0:0:0" Duration="0:0:0.2"
                Storyboard.TargetName="button1"
                Storyboard.TargetProperty="(Button.Height)"
                By="30" AutoReverse="True" />

            <DoubleAnimation BeginTime="0:0:1" Duration="0:0:0.2"
                Storyboard.TargetName="button2"
                Storyboard.TargetProperty="(Button.Height)"
                By="30" AutoReverse="True" />

            <ParallelTimeline BeginTime="0:0:2">

              <DoubleAnimation BeginTime="0:0:0" Duration="0:0:0.2"
                  Storyboard.TargetName="button3"
                  Storyboard.TargetProperty="(Button.Height)"
                  By="30" AutoReverse="True" />

              <DoubleAnimation BeginTime="0:0:1" Duration="0:0:0.2"
                  Storyboard.TargetName="button4"
                  Storyboard.TargetProperty="(Button.Height)"
                  By="30" AutoReverse="True" />

            </ParallelTimeline>

          </ParallelTimeline>
        </Storyboard>
      </BeginStoryboard>
    </EventTrigger>
  </StackPanel.Triggers>
```

Example 16-16. A hierarchy of timelines (continued)

```
    <Button Name="button1" Height="25">One</Button>
    <Button Name="button2" Height="25">Two</Button>
    <Button Name="button3" Height="25">Three</Button>
    <Button Name="button4" Height="25">Four</Button>
</StackPanel>
```

The animation modifies each button's height in sequence, enlarging the button and then shrinking it back to its initial size. Figure 16-3 shows the animation partway through the sequence.

 This illustrates that using a "parallel" timeline doesn't necessarily prevent you from making your animations run sequentially. The default behavior for a ParallelTimeline is to run all its child animations simultaneously, but we've chosen to stagger them here by giving each one a different BeginTime.

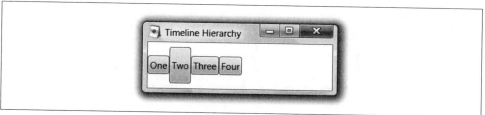

Figure 16-3. Hierarchical animation in action

The storyboard's structure is not as straightforward as this simple sequence suggests—it has a somewhat contrived structure in order to show the effects of a timeline hierarchy. Each button has a DoubleAnimation animating its height. The first two of these are simple enough—they are both children of the first ParallelTimeline, and their BeginTime properties are set to 0:0:0 and 0:0:1, respectively. This means that the second button expands and contracts one second after the first button. However, the third and fourth buttons are slightly surprising—they also have their BeginTime properties set to 0:0:0 and 0:0:1. Despite this, they do not expand and contract at the same time as the first two buttons—if they did, Figure 16-3 would show the fourth button at the same size as the second one.

The buttons animate one after the other from left to right. This works even though the third and fourth buttons have the same BeginTime as the first and second because they are nested inside another ParallelTimeline, which is in turn nested inside the top-level ParallelTimeline. The third and fourth animations' BeginTime properties are relative to this nested ParallelTimeline, rather than the top-level ParallelTimeline. This nested ParallelTimeline has a BeginTime of 0:0:2, meaning that it will not start to run until two seconds into the top-level timeline, after the first two buttons have been animated. The BeginTime properties of the nested animations for the third and fourth buttons will be relative to this second ParallelTimeline.

Figure 16-4 illustrates the structure of the storyboard in Example 16-16. Each timeline (including the DoubleAnimation timelines) is represented as a horizontal line, with a dot at the start and end. Its horizontal position indicates when the timeline runs—as the scale along the top shows, the further to the right a timeline appears, the later it runs. This scale is relative to when the storyboard started (i.e., when the StackPanel raises its Loaded event).

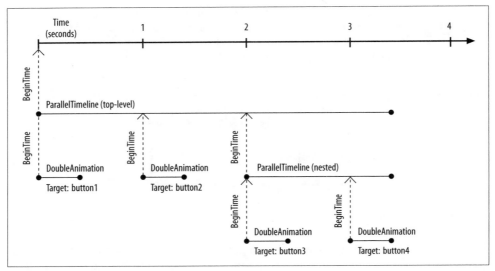

Figure 16-4. Animation hierarchy structure

This hierarchical structure makes it easy to change when an animation sequence starts, without having to edit any of the details of that sequence. Because each BeginTime property refers to its parent, we can move sequences around by adjusting a single BeginTime. For example, we can change when the third and fourth buttons are animated by changing only the BeginTime of their parents. One way to picture this is to imagine picking up part of the structure in Figure 16-4 by one of the vertical arrows labeled BeginTime—if you move the line from side to side, everything beneath the line moves with it.

Notice in Figure 16-4 that to the righthand side of the diagram, all three active timelines come to an end at exactly the same moment. This is not mere coincidence. It's not even the result of careful coding. In Example 16-16, you'll see that the only timelines with a specified duration are the DoubleAnimation elements. All of the other timelines' durations are determined automatically.

Duration

If you do not provide a Duration property, a parallel timeline will attempt to work out what its duration should be. It will base this on the duration of its children, setting its own duration to be just long enough to contain whichever child timeline finishes last. Consider Example 16-17.

Example 16-17. Implicit duration of parent timeline

```
<ParallelTimeline>

  <DoubleAnimation BeginTime="0:0:0" Duration="0:0:0.2"
      Storyboard.TargetName="button1"
      Storyboard.TargetProperty="(Button.Height)"
      By="30" />

  <DoubleAnimation BeginTime="0:0:1" Duration="0:0:0.2"
      Storyboard.TargetName="button2"
      Storyboard.TargetProperty="(Button.Height)"
      By="30" />

</ParallelTimeline>
```

Each DoubleAnimation has an explicit Duration, but the parent ParallelTimeline does not. Its duration will be determined by its children. It contains two DoubleAnimation elements, both with durations of 0.2 seconds. The second of the two DoubleAnimation objects has a BeginTime of 0:0:1 (i.e., one second after its parent ParallelTimeline begins). Because this child's duration is 0.2 seconds, it will not finish until 1.2 seconds after its parent begins, meaning its parent has an implicit duration of 1.2.

> All timelines offer an AutoReverse property. If this is set to true, the timeline will run in reverse when it reaches the end. This doubles its duration. This can be slightly confusing when used in conjunction with an explicit Duration. An element with an explicit Duration of 0:0:0.2 and an AutoReverse set to true has an effective duration of 0.4 seconds. This is why the timelines in Figure 16-4 are slightly longer than you might have expected.

In general, the implicit duration mechanism works well, and it can save you a lot of effort. However, in some situations it can cause surprises. Indeed, it causes a slight glitch in one of the earlier examples. If you try out Example 16-16, you will notice that there is a gap of just over half a second between each button expanding and contracting, except for when the sequence repeats. There is no gap between when the fourth button finishes contracting and the first button starts to expand. This glitch is visible in Figure 16-4—you can see that each DoubleAnimation starts a whole number of seconds into the sequence. The first button animates immediately, the next after one second, the third after two, and the fourth after three. But the animation has a total length of 3.4 seconds. This causes a slightly lopsided feel when it repeats—it would be better if it repeated after four seconds.

There are two easy ways to fix this. We could just set the duration of the top-level ParallelTimeline to be four seconds. More subtly, we could set the duration of the nested ParallelTimeline to be two seconds long. Because this starts two seconds in, this would make the top-level ParallelTimeline four seconds long. Although this second approach looks less straightforward, it avoids hardcoding the duration of the top-level timeline, meaning that if you were to add more child animations later, you wouldn't need to go back and adjust the top-level duration.

Repetition

By default, a timeline starts at the offset specified by its BeginTime, and then stops when it reaches the end of its Duration. However, all timelines have a RepeatBehavior property, enabling them to repeat one or more times.

We have seen this already in Example 16-16, where the top-level ParallelTimeline had a RepeatBehavior of Forever. This has a straightforward enough meaning for top-level elements: they will repeat for as long as the UI is running. For nested timelines, it is not quite this simple. When a nested timeline with a RepeatBehavior of Forever reaches the end of its duration, it goes back to the start and continues to repeat until the end of time, but only for small values of "the end of time."

Remember that any nested timeline's BeginTime is relative to its parent. In fact, its whole view of time is determined by its parent. So for a nested timeline, "the end of time" means the end of its parent's duration. Example 16-18 shows how a RepeatBehavior of Forever can be cut off after only a short time.

Example 16-18. When "forever" isn't

```
<Button Background="Red" VerticalAlignment="Center"
        HorizontalAlignment="Center" Content="I feel fine">
  <Button.Triggers>
    <EventTrigger RoutedEvent="Button.Loaded">
      <BeginStoryboard>
        <Storyboard>
          <ParallelTimeline Duration="0:0:5">

              <ColorAnimation BeginTime="0:0:2" Duration="0:0:1"
                          Storyboard.TargetProperty="
                              (Button.Background).(SolidColorBrush.Color)"
                          From="Red" To="Yellow" AutoReverse="True"
                          RepeatBehavior="Forever" />

          </ParallelTimeline>
        </Storyboard>
      </BeginStoryboard>
```

Example 16-18. When "forever" isn't (continued)

```
      </EventTrigger>
    </Button.Triggers>
</Button>
```

In this example, a button's background is animated to fade between red and yellow. It uses a `ColorAnimation` with a `RepeatBehavior` of `Forever`. Running this shows a button that is red for two seconds, fades to yellow and back once, fades to yellow one more time, and then stays that way indefinitely. The two-second delay is caused by the `BeginTime` of 0:0:2. The animation stops after only one and a half cycles (three seconds) because the top-level `ParallelTimeline` has an explicit duration of 0:0:5. Once this is reached, the timeline and all of its descendants are finished, so the animation stops.

Figure 16-5 shows the structure of the timeline in Example 16-18. As you can see, the `ColorAnimation` starts after two seconds because its `BeginTime` is 0:0:2. Its `Duration` property is set to 0:0:1, but this is not the effective duration. First, the `AutoReverse` property is set to `True`, doubling the effective length. Moreover, because its `RepeatBehavior` is `Forever`, it will run for as long as it is allowed to, so its effective duration is constrained only by its context: the explicit five-second duration of the parent `ParallelTimeline`.

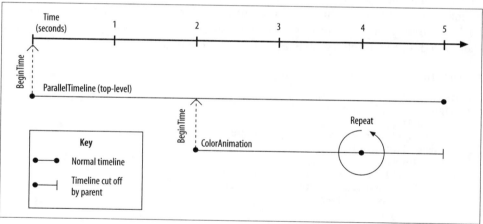

Figure 16-5. Cutting off RepeatBehavior.Forever

 If you use a `RepeatBehavior` of `Forever` and do not cut it off with an explicit duration in the parent, the implicit duration of the parent element will be indefinite. Removing the `Duration` property from the `ParallelTimeline` in Example 16-18 allows the color animation to run indefinitely.

The RepeatBehavior property also supports finite repetition. You can instruct a time-line to repeat either for a particular length of time or for a fixed number of iterations. Example 16-19 shows examples of both techniques.

Example 16-19. Repetition count and duration

```
<ColorAnimation From="Red" To="Yellow" Duration="0:0:1"
                Storyboard.TargetProperty="(Ellipse.Fill).(SolidColorBrush.Color)"
                RepeatBehavior="3x" />
...
<DoubleAnimation By="20" Duration="0:0:0.25"
                Storyboard.TargetProperty="(Ellipse.Width)"
                RepeatBehavior="0:0:2" />
```

The ColorAnimation in Example 16-19 has a RepeatBehavior of 3x. This indicates that the animation should repeat three times and then stop. The effective duration of the animation ends up being three seconds—three times longer than it would be with-out repetition. The DoubleAnimation has a RepeatBehavior of 0:0:2. This means the animation will repeat until two seconds have elapsed.

Filling

Many animations have finite duration. This raises a question: what happens to the animated property when the animation finishes? Many of the examples presented so far have either repeated forever or put the property back to its original value before they ended, but Example 16-20 uses neither of these tricks.

Example 16-20. A simple, finite animation

```
<Canvas>
  <Ellipse Name="myEllipse" Height="100" Fill="Red">
    <Ellipse.Triggers>
      <EventTrigger RoutedEvent="Ellipse.Loaded">
        <BeginStoryboard>
          <Storyboard>
            <DoubleAnimation BeginTime="0:0:2" Duration="0:0:5"
                Storyboard.TargetProperty="(Ellipse.Width)"
                From="10" To="300" />
          </Storyboard>
        </BeginStoryboard>
      </EventTrigger>
    </Ellipse.Triggers>
  </Ellipse>
</Canvas>
```

When you run this program, the ellipse will initially be invisible because no Width property is set. After two seconds, it appears, and then gradually it expands as before. At the end of the five-second animation, the ellipse stays at its final size. We can add some code to look at this in a little more detail, such as that shown in Example 16-21.

Example 16-21. Code-behind file for Example 16-20

```
using System;
using System.Windows;
using System.Windows.Threading;
using System.Diagnostics;

namespace Holding {
    public partial class Window1 : Window {
        public Window1() {
            InitializeComponent();

            t = new DispatcherTimer();
            t.Tick += new EventHandler(OnTimerTick);
            t.Interval = TimeSpan.FromSeconds(0.5);
            t.Start();
            start = DateTime.Now;
        }

        DispatcherTimer t;
        DateTime start;

        void OnTimerTick(object sender, EventArgs e) {
            TimeSpan elapsedTime = DateTime.Now - start;
            Debug.WriteLine(elapsedTime.ToString() + ": " +
                myEllipse.Width);
        }
    }
}
```

This sets up a timer to call our OnTimerTick function twice per second. The DispatcherTimer is a special WPF timer guaranteed to call our timer function in a context where it is safe to do UI work. This means we don't need to worry about whether we're on the right thread. See Appendix C for more information on threading in WPF.

On each timer tick, the ellipse's width is printed with the Debug class. Running the program in Visual Studio 2005 lets us see these messages in the Output panel. Here's the output I get:

```
00:00:00.4911795: NaN
00:00:00.9931005: NaN
00:00:01.4891625: NaN
00:00:02.0369790: NaN
00:00:02.5408530: 28.1700834
00:00:03.0417975: 59.1043138
00:00:03.5407890: 87.1383412
00:00:04.0358745: 116.139565
00:00:04.5358425: 145.1403364
00:00:05.0397165: 174.1407308
00:00:05.5426140: 204.1083274
00:00:06.0396525: 232.1420242
00:00:06.5347380: 261.1428652
00:00:07.0366590: 290.1434162
00:00:07.5366270: 300
00:00:08.0375715: 300
```

This illustrates two potentially surprising points. First, don't rely on a `DispatcherTimer` to be especially precise about when it calls you back, particularly if you're running in the debugger. Second, before the animation runs, the actual width reported by the ellipse is "NaN." This is short for *Not a Number*, and it indicates that the `Width` property doesn't have a value.

> NaN is one of a few special values supported by the `Double` floating-point type. This is not particular to WPF—the IEEE standard for floating point defines special values for positive and negative infinities, and this "not a number" value. NaN usually arises from questionable operations such as attempting to divide zero by zero, or subtracting infinity from infinity.
>
> Although NaN is a standard value, WPF's use of it here is slightly unusual. It is acting as a kind of sentinel value, indicating that the `Width` property is not set.

We shouldn't be surprised that the ellipse initially has no width, because we haven't set the ellipse's `Width` property directly in the markup. We set it indirectly using the animation, so the `Width` property has a meaningful value only once that animation starts. We can fix this by setting the ellipse's `Width`:

```
<Ellipse Name="myEllipse" Height="100" Fill="Red" Width="42" />
```

Having made this change, the ellipse is visible before the animation starts—it is initially 42 pixels wide. (As it was before, it is 300 pixels wide once the animation has finished.) The debug output reflects this, showing the value 42 for the width at the start of the animation, instead of NaN:

```
00:00:00.4921560: 42
00:00:00.9911475: 42
00:00:01.4920920: 42
00:00:01.9910835: 42
00:00:02.5320645: 31.7818768
00:00:03.0212910: 60.7827294
00:00:03.5437185: 90.7498562
00:00:04.0534515: 119.7509988
00:00:04.5534195: 148.7517702
00:00:05.0533875: 177.7524082
00:00:05.5562850: 206.7534232
00:00:06.0533235: 235.7539336
00:00:06.5542680: 264.7546876
00:00:07.0532595: 293.7556968
00:00:07.5532275: 300
00:00:08.0541720: 300
```

This is the default behavior of animations—when they reach their end, their final value continues to apply for as long as their parent timeline continues to be active. This may not always be the behavior you require—in some circumstances, you might want to be sure that the property returns to its original value. Even when the default behavior is what you require, it's not quite as straightforward as it may seem.

When an animation reaches the end of its duration, it isn't quite finished yet. We see the animation's final value applied in the earlier example because the animation is still active, even though it has reached the end of its duration. This twilight zone between the end of the animation's duration and its final deactivation is called the *fill period*.

All timelines have a `FillBehavior` property that specifies what happens after the timeline reaches the end of its effective duration. The default value is `HoldEnd`, meaning the animation will continue to apply its final value until the UI closes, unless something causes it to be deactivated. The alternative `FillBehavior`, shown in Example 16-22, is `Stop`. This deactivates the animation as soon as it reaches the end of its duration, meaning the relevant property will revert to the value it had before the animation began.

Example 16-22. Stop in fill period

```
<DoubleAnimation BeginTime="0:0:2" Duration="0:0:5"
    Storyboard.TargetProperty="(Ellipse.Width)"
    From="10" To="300" FillBehavior="Stop" />
```

As the following output shows, the property now reverts to 42 at the end of the animation:

```
00:00:00.4980150: 42
00:00:00.9999360: 42
00:00:01.4950215: 42
00:00:01.9949895: 42
00:00:02.5232760: 31.3482572
00:00:03.0427740: 61.3153898
00:00:03.5495775: 90.3162598
00:00:04.0475925: 119.3171878
00:00:04.5426780: 148.3175996
00:00:05.0455755: 177.3179012
00:00:05.5484730: 206.3190264
00:00:06.0425820: 235.3201864
00:00:06.5435265: 263.3539528
00:00:07.1050140: 296.2216596
00:00:07.6088880: 42
00:00:08.1049500: 42
```

Note that unlike `RepeatBehavior`, the `FillBehavior` property has no impact on the effective duration of a timeline. A fill behavior of `HoldEnd` means something only if the parent timeline runs for longer than the duration of the child timeline. Example 16-23 shows such a scenario—the parent `ParallelTimeline` has a duration of 10 seconds, whereas the child has a duration of five seconds, leaving it a fill period of five seconds. The child's `FillBehavior` has not been set, so it will default to `HoldEnd`.

Example 16-23. A child with a fill period

```
<ParallelTimeline Duration="0:0:10" FillBehavior="Stop">
  <DoubleAnimation From="10" To="300" Duration="0:0:5"
                   Storyboard.TargetProperty="(Ellipse.Width)" />
</ParallelTimeline>
```

Figure 16-6 illustrates this pair of timelines. Because the parent timeline's FillBehavior is Stop, it deactivates at the end of its natural duration. When a parent deactivates, all its children are deactivated, so this causes the child's fill period to come to an end, meaning that all the corresponding properties will revert to the values they had before the animation started.

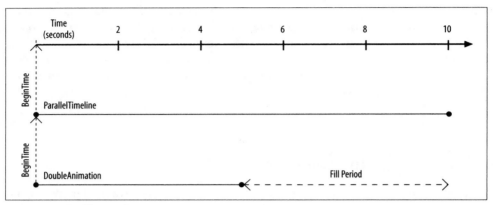

Figure 16-6. A fill period

If a parent timeline has the default FillBehavior of HoldEnd, its fill period will be indefinite. This in turn means its children's fill periods will also be indefinite. Example 16-24 shows such a timeline hierarchy.

Example 16-24. Parent and child timelines with default HoldEnd FillBehavior

```
<ParallelTimeline BeginTime="0:0:2">
  <DoubleAnimation From="10" To="300" Duration="0:0:5"
                   Storyboard.TargetProperty="(Ellipse.Width)" />
</ParallelTimeline>
```

Here, neither the DoubleAnimation nor the ParallelTimeline has an explicit FillBehavior, so they default to HoldEnd. This means that both animations have an indefinite fill period—they will run until the UI closes or a containing timeline stops. This is indicated by the double-headed arrows in Figure 16-7. The upshot is that with the storyboard in Example 16-24, the ellipse's width grows from 10 to 300, and then stays at 300.

The default fill behavior means animations typically end up with an indefinite fill period. This results in what is usually the desired behavior: an animation's final value is the value that remains in place once the animation's duration is over.

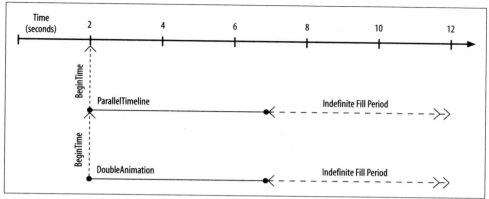

Figure 16-7. An indefinite fill period

Speed

You may sometimes find that you want to change the speed at which some part of an animation runs. For a simple animation consisting of a single element, you can just change the duration. For a more complex animation consisting of many timelines, it would become tedious to adjust each duration by hand. A simpler solution is to warp time, using the `SpeedRatio` property available on any timeline.

`SpeedRatio` allows you to change the rate at which a timeline is played back. Its default value is 1, meaning that all timelines advance by one second for each second of real time that elapses. However, if you modify one of your timelines to have a `SpeedRatio` of 2, that timeline and all its children will be advanced by two seconds for each second of real time that elapses.

Strictly speaking, `SpeedRatio` is relative to the rate at which the parent timeline progresses, rather than absolute elapsed time. This becomes important if you modify speed in multiple places in a timeline hierarchy. Example 16-25 shows a modified version of the animations from Example 16-16, with a `SpeedRatio` attribute added to some of the timelines.

Example 16-25. Using SpeedRatio in a hierarchy

```
<ParallelTimeline RepeatBehavior="Forever">

  <DoubleAnimation BeginTime="0:0:0" Duration="0:0:0.2"
              Storyboard.TargetName="button1"
              Storyboard.TargetProperty="(Button.Height)"
              By="30" AutoReverse="True" />
```

Example 16-25. Using SpeedRatio in a hierarchy (continued)

```
<DoubleAnimation SpeedRatio="2" BeginTime="0:0:1" Duration="0:0:0.2"
                 Storyboard.TargetName="button2"
                 Storyboard.TargetProperty="(Button.Height)"
                 By="30" AutoReverse="True" />

<ParallelTimeline BeginTime="0:0:2" SpeedRatio="4">

  <DoubleAnimation SpeedRatio="0.25" BeginTime="0:0:0" Duration="0:0:0.2"
                   Storyboard.TargetName="button3"
                   Storyboard.TargetProperty="(Button.Height)"
                   By="30" AutoReverse="True" />

  <DoubleAnimation SpeedRatio="0.125" BeginTime="0:0:1" Duration="0:0:0.2"
                   Storyboard.TargetName="button4"
                   Storyboard.TargetProperty="(Button.Height)"
                   By="30" AutoReverse="True" />

</ParallelTimeline>

</ParallelTimeline>
```

Figure 16-8 shows the effect of these changes. The top-level timeline's speed is not specified, so it will default to 1 and will progress at a normal rate. So will its first `DoubleAnimation` child. The second `DoubleAnimation` has a `SpeedRatio` of 2. This does not affect the time at which this timeline starts—its `BeginTime` is relative to its parent and therefore depends on its parent's speed. But the `DoubleAnimation` itself will run twice as fast as normal, so it will be as though this animation's duration is set to 0.1 rather than 0.2 seconds. The result is that the second button expands and contracts in half the time that the first one expands and contracts.

The third and final child of the top-level timeline is a `ParallelTimeline` element with a `SpeedRatio` of 4. This quadruples the rate at which it runs its child timelines. However, its first child is a `DoubleAnimation` with a `SpeedRatio` of 0.25. Consequently, the animation will run at normal speed. The next nested `DoubleAnimation`, which controls the fourth button, has a `BeginTime` of 0:0:1, but because its parent's `SpeedRatio` is 4, it will start only one-quarter of a second into that timeline, causing it to overlap slightly with the preceding animation, as Figure 16-8 shows. Its speed is 0.125, but that is relative to its parent's speed of 4, meaning that this timeline runs at half speed and its effective duration is therefore 0.4. And, because its `AutoReverse` property is set to true, it will run in reverse after completing, so its total duration will in fact be 0.8 seconds.

SpeedRatio is compatible with `AccelerationRatio` and `DecelerationRatio`. These properties are similar, in that each allows you to adjust the rate at which an animation runs. The difference is that `SpeedRatio` applies uniformly to the whole animation, whereas the other two cause the speed to vary as the animation progresses. If you modify the `SpeedRatio` of an animation that uses acceleration or deceleration, the animation will still accelerate or decelerate; it will just do everything faster or slower.

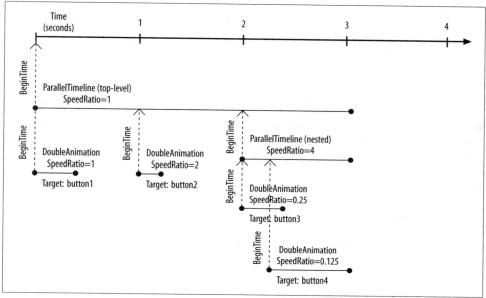

Figure 16-8. Speed in a timeline hierarchy

You can use the animation types and other timelines we've looked at so far to build fairly complex animations. However, for animations that need to make a series of changes to the same property, a set of animation types is available that enables us to be more succinct: keyframe animations.

Keyframe Animations

So far, we have looked at only simple point-to-point animations. Whether we use the To and From properties, or the By property, animations run from some start value to an end value. This is fine for simple animations, and although we could create more complex animations by building sequences of simple animations, this would be very cumbersome. Fortunately, there is a better way. WPF provides animation objects that allow us to specify a series of times and values.

In traditional animation in television and cinema, it is common to start by drawing the most important steps of the animation. These *keyframes* define the basic flow of the scene, capturing its most important points. Only once these keyframes are satisfactory are the remaining frames drawn. The drawings in between the keyframes do not require much creative input—they are simply meant to interpolate from one keyframe to the next. WPF uses the same concept. You could consider the simple From and To approach to be equivalent to providing just two keyframes: a "before" frame and an "after" frame where WPF interpolates between the two for you. Keyframe animations simply extend this concept to multiple frames.

As with the simpler animation types, keyframe animations still target one property at a time. So, they are not quite the same as keyframes in traditional animation where each frame would consist of a whole drawing. You cannot provide two drawings and tell WPF to morph from one to the other.

Keyframe animation types use the naming convention of *Type*AnimationUsingKeyFrames. Example 16-26 shows a simple animation of a bouncing rectangle. The horizontal position is controlled by an ordinary DoubleAnimation, but the vertical position is set by a DoubleAnimationUsingKeyFrames.

Example 16-26. Keyframe animation

```
<Canvas>
  <Rectangle Fill="Red" Width="20" Height="20">
    <Rectangle.Triggers>
      <EventTrigger RoutedEvent="Rectangle.Loaded">
        <BeginStoryboard>
          <Storyboard>

            <DoubleAnimation From="0" To="800" Duration="0:0:10"
                Storyboard.TargetProperty="(Canvas.Left)"
                RepeatBehavior="Forever" AutoReverse="True" />


            <DoubleAnimationUsingKeyFrames Duration="0:0:2"
                Storyboard.TargetProperty="(Canvas.Top)"
                                        RepeatBehavior="Forever">
              <DoubleAnimationUsingKeyFrames.KeyFrames>
                <LinearDoubleKeyFrame Value="0" KeyTime="0:0:0" />
                <LinearDoubleKeyFrame Value="50" KeyTime="0:0:0.5" />
                <LinearDoubleKeyFrame Value="200" KeyTime="0:0:1" />
                <LinearDoubleKeyFrame Value="50" KeyTime="0:0:1.5" />
                <LinearDoubleKeyFrame Value="0" KeyTime="0:0:2" />
              </DoubleAnimationUsingKeyFrames.KeyFrames>
            </DoubleAnimationUsingKeyFrames>
          </Storyboard>
        </BeginStoryboard>
      </EventTrigger>
    </Rectangle.Triggers>
  </Rectangle>
</Canvas>
```

The DoubleAnimationUsingKeyFrames controlling the vertical position contains five keyframes, specifying the required vertical position of the rectangle at half-second intervals. As Figure 16-9 shows, the keyframes show the rectangle at the top and bottom of its bounce, with the midway point being slightly higher than halfway up to indicate the gradual change in speed over time. WPF interpolates between these positions for us.

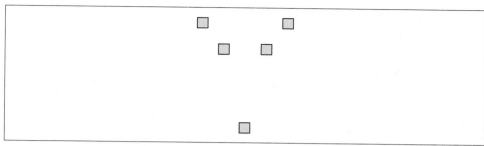

Figure 16-9. Keyframes

Each keyframe value in Example 16-26 is specified with a LinearDoubleKeyFrame. This indicates that linear interpolation should be used—the rate of change will be constant between any two frames. This results in motion that is not especially smooth. The rectangle speeds up as it falls, but the changes in speed take place in visible "steps" moving from one stage of the animation to the next. We could reduce this effect by adding more keyframes, but there is an easier way. Rather than the simple linear interpolation shown on the left of Figure 16-10, it is possible to get a curved interpolation like that shown on the right, improving the smoothness without needing to add more keyframes.

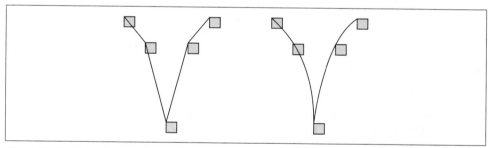

Figure 16-10. Smoothness of interpolation

To get the smoother changes in animation speed we want, we can use SplineDoubleKeyFrame. With a spline keyframe, a Bézier curve specifies how the animation value should change. However, the way in which the curve is used is not completely straightforward. As we saw in Chapter 13, you can use Bézier curves to define curved shapes. However, the animation does not simply follow the path defined by the Bézier curve in this example. It's possible to do that by using path animations, which we describe later, but that's not what happens with a spline keyframe.

Instead of defining the path of a point, the Bézier curve in a spline keyframe defines the shape of a mathematical function. This function takes as its input the proportion of the keyframe's time that has elapsed. As its output, it provides a number indicating the proportion in which the previous and current values should be mixed.

The curve always moves from 0,0 to 1,1, but you position the two control points that determine its shape in between these extremes. You can set these using the KeySpline property of the keyframe.

Figure 16-11 shows three example animation splines, with the control points marked as small squares. Remember that these curves simply determine the rate at which the animation progresses. The first "curve" is a straight line, meaning that the animation progresses at a constant rate. This is equivalent to a LinearDoubleKeyFrame. The second indicates that the animation should start slowly and then speed up. The third shows that the animation should start quickly and then gradually slow to a halt.

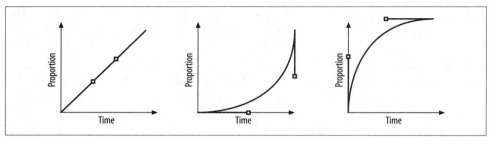

Figure 16-11. Spline animation curves

Example 16-27 is a modified version of the keyframe animation in Example 16-26. The animation passes through the same keyframe values, but uses splines to indicate that the rate of animation should gradually change. This makes the animation feel much smoother without needing to add more keyframes.

Example 16-27. Keyframe spline animation

```
<DoubleAnimationUsingKeyFrames Duration="0:0:2" RepeatBehavior="Forever"
        Storyboard.TargetProperty="(Canvas.Top)">
  <DoubleAnimationUsingKeyFrames.KeyFrames>
    <LinearDoubleKeyFrame Value="0" KeyTime="0:0:0" />
    <SplineDoubleKeyFrame Value="50" KeyTime="0:0:0.5"
                          KeySpline="0.4,0 0.7,0.7" />
    <SplineDoubleKeyFrame Value="200" KeyTime="0:0:1"
                          KeySpline="0.2,0.2 0.7,0.4" />
    <SplineDoubleKeyFrame Value="50" KeyTime="0:0:1.5"
                          KeySpline="0,0.3 0.75,0.75" />
    <SplineDoubleKeyFrame Value="0" KeyTime="0:0:2"
                          KeySpline="0.25,0.25 0.6,1" />
  </DoubleAnimationUsingKeyFrames.KeyFrames>
</DoubleAnimationUsingKeyFrames>
```

The first frame still uses a LinearDoubleKeyFrame, because there is no "before" frame from which to interpolate. The two "downward" keyframes use curve shapes similar to the one in the middle of Figure 16-11. This causes the animation to start slowly and then speed up, as you would expect in an animation of a falling object.

The two "upward" keyframes use curve shapes similar to the one on the right of Figure 16-11, causing the animation to slow gradually as the object rises to the top. This provides a more convincing visual approximation of how a real object would move.

There is one more keyframe style available: discrete. If you use a discrete keyframe, WPF doesn't interpolate at all—it jumps instantaneously to the specified value. This makes it easy to introduce discontinuities into your animation if necessary.

Note that WPF provides keyframe versions of most of the animation types it supports, not just Double. Table 16-4 lists these types.

Table 16-4. Keyframe animation types

BooleanAnimationUsingKeyFrames	Point3DAnimationUsingKeyFrames
ByteAnimationUsingKeyFrames	PointAnimationUsingKeyFrames
CharAnimationUsingKeyFrames	QuaternionAnimationUsingKeyFrames
ColorAnimationUsingKeyFrames	RectAnimationUsingKeyFrames
DecimalAnimationUsingKeyFrames	Rotation3DAnimationUsingKeyFrames
DoubleAnimationUsingKeyFrames	SingleAnimationUsingKeyFrames
Int16AnimationUsingKeyFrames	SizeAnimationUsingKeyFrames
Int32AnimationUsingKeyFrames	StringAnimationUsingKeyFrames
Int64AnimationUsingKeyFrames	ThicknessAnimationUsingKeyFrames
MatrixAnimationUsingKeyFrames	Vector3DAnimationUsingKeyFrames
ObjectAnimationUsingKeyFrames	VectorAnimationUsingKeyFrames

Notice that four of these keyframe animation types do not have a corresponding simple animation type. This is because the target types in question—Char, Matrix, Object, and String—cannot be usefully interpolated. You can use them only with discrete keyframes. Example 16-28 shows one way of using discrete object keyframe animations.

Example 16-28. Setting enumeration values with discrete animations

```
<ObjectAnimationUsingKeyFrames Storyboard.TargetProperty="(Button.Visibility)">
  <DiscreteObjectKeyFrame KeyTime="0:0:1.5">
    <DiscreteObjectKeyFrame.Value>
      <Visibility>Hidden</Visibility>
    </DiscreteObjectKeyFrame.Value>
  </DiscreteObjectKeyFrame>
</ObjectAnimationUsingKeyFrames>
```

This sets the value of a button's Visibility property. This property's type, Visibility, is an enumeration type. As mentioned earlier, you cannot set such properties with ordinary animation types, because enumeration values cannot meaningfully be interpolated. But here, we are using a discrete keyframe, avoiding the need for interpolation.

You can mix different keyframe types freely within a single keyframe animation. You can also mix keyframe animations and simple animations within a storyboard or parallel timeline. Use whichever is most convenient for the task at hand.

Although keyframe animations are good at defining animations through a series of snapshot values, there's an alternative way of defining animations that move items around. Path animations can sometimes make this task much simpler.

Path Animations

A path animation lets you animate an object so that its position follows a path defined by a PathGeometry. This is often a more convenient way of defining the motion of an object than using keyframe animations.

DoubleAnimationUsingPath, MatrixAnimationUsingPath, and PointAnimationUsingPath are the three path animation types. As their names suggest, they can target properties of type Double, Matrix, and Point, respectively.

PointAnimationUsingPath is the most straightforward type. It targets a property of type Point, and it will move the location of that point along the path described by the animation's PathGeometry property. Example 16-29 shows this technique being used to animate one end of a LineGeometry.

Example 16-29. Point path animation

```
<Path Stroke="Black" StrokeThickness="4">
  <Path.Data>
    <LineGeometry StartPoint="50,50" EndPoint="0,0" />
  </Path.Data>
  <Path.Triggers>
    <EventTrigger RoutedEvent="Path.Loaded">
      <BeginStoryboard>
        <Storyboard>
          <PointAnimationUsingPath AutoReverse="True"
                RepeatBehavior="Forever" Duration="0:0:2"
                Storyboard.TargetProperty="(Path.Data).(LineGeometry.EndPoint)">
            <PointAnimationUsingPath.PathGeometry>
              <PathGeometry Figures="M 14.64,14.64 A 50,50 90, 0 1 85.36,14.64" />
            </PointAnimationUsingPath.PathGeometry>
          </PointAnimationUsingPath>
        </Storyboard>
      </BeginStoryboard>
    </EventTrigger>
  </Path.Triggers>
</Path>
```

The PathGeometry describing the animation path contains a single elliptical arc segment. This sweeps out a 90 degree angle, and its center coincides with the fixed StartPoint of the LineGeometry. The result is that the line swings from side to side like a metronome. Figure 16-12 shows three snapshots from the animated line's progress.

Figure 16-12. Point animation with path

Not all of the properties you might wish to animate in this way will be of type Point. For example, you might want to use a path animation to modify an object's position on a Canvas. This requires you to set two properties: Canvas.Left and Canvas.Top. Both are of type Double. Example 16-30 shows how to animate these using DoubleAnimationUsingPath.

Example 16-30. Double animation with path

```
<Canvas>
  <Canvas.Resources>
    <PathGeometry x:Key="animPath"
                  Figures="M 0,30 A 30,30 180 0 1 60,30   30,30 180 0 1 0,30" />
  </Canvas.Resources>

  <Path Stroke="Blue" StrokeThickness="2" Data="{StaticResource animPath}" />

  <Path Stroke="Black" StrokeThickness="2" Data="M0,0 H20 M15,-5 L20,0 15,5">
    <Path.Triggers>
      <EventTrigger RoutedEvent="Line.Loaded">
        <BeginStoryboard>
          <Storyboard>

              <DoubleAnimationUsingPath Source="X"
                  RepeatBehavior="Forever" Duration="0:0:5"
                  Storyboard.TargetProperty="(Canvas.Left)"
                  PathGeometry="{StaticResource animPath}" />

              <DoubleAnimationUsingPath Source="Y"
                  RepeatBehavior="Forever" Duration="0:0:5"
                  Storyboard.TargetProperty="(Canvas.Top)"
                  PathGeometry="{StaticResource animPath}" />

          </Storyboard>
        </BeginStoryboard>
      </EventTrigger>
    </Path.Triggers>
  </Path>
</Canvas>
```

The storyboard in this example contains two animations, one for each property. The Source property indicates whether the DoubleAnimationUsingPath is to provide the *x* or *y* position for the current location. Because both animations need to share the same PathGeometry, it is defined as a resource. The first Path in the example displays this same path so that we can see its shape. The second Path is in the shape of an arrow, and its position is animated around this PathGeometry. Figure 16-13 shows three snapshots from this animation.

Figure 16-13. Point animation with path

Figure 16-13 highlights an extra feature we might want from a path animation. In all three snapshots in the figure, the arrow points in the same direction. But what if we would like to have it pointing in the direction of travel? In general, when animating an object along a path, it might make sense for it to face in the direction it's moving. To enable this, DoubleAnimationUsingPath supports a third option for its Source property: Angle. We could add a RotateTransform to the animation target, and animate its Angle property with such a DoubleAnimationUsingPath. However, in this case there's an easier way.

A MatrixAnimationUsingPath can animate a single object's position and orientation in one step. It builds a transformation matrix that includes the necessary translation, and if you set its DoesRotateWithTangent property to true, the matrix also incorporates rotation. Example 16-31 shows a version of the arrow-shaped second Path from Example 16-30 modified to use this technique.

Example 16-31. Matrix animation with path

```
...
<Path Stroke="Black" StrokeThickness="2" Data="M0,0 H20 M15,-5 L20,0 15,5">
  <Path.RenderTransform>
    <MatrixTransform />
  </Path.RenderTransform>
  <Path.Triggers>
    <EventTrigger RoutedEvent="Line.Loaded">
      <BeginStoryboard>
        <Storyboard>

          <MatrixAnimationUsingPath DoesRotateWithTangent="True"
              RepeatBehavior="Forever" Duration="0:0:5"
              Storyboard.TargetProperty="
                  (Path.RenderTransform).(MatrixTransform.Matrix)"
              PathGeometry="{StaticResource animPath}" />
```

Example 16-31. Matrix animation with path (continued)

```
        </Storyboard>
      </BeginStoryboard>
    </EventTrigger>
  </Path.Triggers>
</Path>
...
```

The path's `RenderTransform` property contains a `MatrixTransform`. By default, this will apply the identity matrix—it will have no effect. However, it is present because the animation modifies this transform's `Matrix` property to set the position and rotation of the element. Figure 16-14 shows the result.

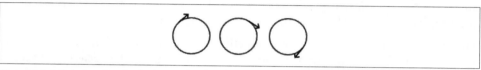

Figure 16-14. Animating both position and tangent rotation

You can use any segment type in the `PathGeometry` for a path animation—see Chapter 13 for more information on the available path segment types. However, there is one thing to watch out for if you are using Bézier curves: if you animate the tangent, it's tricky to keep this smooth when transitioning from one Bézier segment to the next. It's not sufficient to keep the control point tangents of adjacent segments aligned—this produces a smooth-looking join, but it can result in a visible jolt in the rate at which the rotation changes. Tangent alignment guarantees only first order continuity, or *C1 continuity* as it's sometimes called. For smooth tangent animation, you require second order, or C2, continuity. The mathematics for guaranteeing C2 continuity is beyond the scope of this book. However, if you have a drawing tool that is able to draw B-splines and can export them to XAML as Bézier curves, that will provide the continuity required for smooth tangent animation.

Now that we've seen all of the ways in which timelines can describe animations, it's time to look at how we can control the execution of timelines from code.

Clocks and Control

When launching an animation from code, we've had only a limited amount of control over the progress of the animation. We may have defined the sequence and structure of events we require in great detail, but then we just kicked them off by calling `BeginAnimation`, leaving the animation system to deal with them. To gain more control, we have two options. Either we can use the control features offered by storyboards, or we can work with a timeline's clock.

Controlling Animations with Storyboards

We've already seen how to exercise a little control by using event triggers. These offer actions to pause, stop, or resume an animation, or even to seek to a particular location within an animation. Example 16-7 showed how to use these. One limitation with triggers is that they always run the same storyboard. Sometimes it can be useful to write code that decides which storyboard to use at runtime. This means controlling the storyboards from code.

Trigger actions rely on control features offered by storyboards, so if you wish to control animations from code rather than with triggers, you can use these same services. The `Storyboard` class provides a set of methods for controlling the execution of the animations it contains: `Begin`, `Pause`, `Remove`, `Resume`, `Seek`, `SeekAlignedToLastTick`, `SetSpeedRatio`, `SkipToFill`, and `Stop`.

The majority of these correspond directly to the trigger action types listed in Table 16-2, with two exceptions. There is no counterpart to the `SoundPlayerAction`, because that trigger type does not correspond to a `Storyboard`—it plays sounds rather than animations. Also, `Storyboard` offers a variation on the `Seek` method, called `SeekAlignedToLastTick`, for which there is no corresponding trigger action.

These two seek methods do more or less the same thing. The only distinction is the instant at which they will take effect. `Seek` sets the storyboard's position for the *next* time the animation system updates all of the animated properties. `SeekAlignedToLastTick` updates the animation system's state so that everything looks as though the storyboard had been moved to the specified position on the *most recent* tick to have occurred. This means that if you call `SeekAlignedToLastTick`, its effect will immediately be visible to your code if you should read the current value of any animated property. But if you call `Seek`, any affected properties will not change until the next animation update. In general, you should prefer `Seek` unless you really need to see the effects straight away, because `SeekAlignedToLastTick` requires the animation system to do more work. The distinction between these two methods typically matters only from code, which is why trigger actions offer only one kind of seek.

To use these control methods, you must create a storyboard outside a trigger. You could do this from code, but a common approach is to define the storyboard as a resource, as shown in Example 16-32.

Example 16-32. Storyboard resources

```
<Window.Resources>
  <Storyboard x:Key="sunrise">
    <DoubleAnimation Storyboard.TargetProperty="(Canvas.Top)"
                     From="100" To="0" Duration="0:0:3" />
    <ColorAnimation Storyboard.TargetProperty="
                    (Ellipse.Fill).(SolidColorBrush.Color)"
                    From="Red" To="Yellow" Duration="0:0:3" />
  </Storyboard>
```

Example 16-32. Storyboard resources (continued)

```
<Storyboard x:Key="sunset">
  <DoubleAnimation Storyboard.TargetProperty="(Canvas.Top)"
              From="0" To="100" Duration="0:0:3" />
  <ColorAnimation Storyboard.TargetProperty="
              (Ellipse.Fill).(SolidColorBrush.Color)"
              From="Yellow" To="Red" Duration="0:0:3" />
</Storyboard>
</Window.Resources>
```

Having defined the storyboards, you can then retrieve them from code and launch them with the Begin method. You must pass a parameter to Begin indicating the animation target of the storyboard, as Example 16-33 shows.

Example 16-33. Selecting a storyboard at runtime

```
bool isMorning = DateTime.Now.Hour < 12;
string storyboardKey = isMorning ? "sunrise" : "sunset";
Storyboard sb = (Storyboard) FindResource(storyboardKey);

sb.Begin(myEllipse);
```

This example chooses which storyboard to run based on the time of day, something an event trigger cannot do.

As well as controlling a Storyboard, you can also monitor its progress. Table 16-5 lists the methods for doing this. Because you can apply a Storyboard to multiple different targets, you must pass in the target for which you wish to examine the state. Note that these facilities are available only if you make the storyboard *controllable*. You do this by using an overload of the Begin method that accepts a Boolean as well as a target element, and pass in True for this final parameter. Storyboards are not controllable by default.

Table 16-5. Methods for monitoring storyboard progress

Method	Usage
GetCurrentGlobalSpeed	Returns the rate of progress of this storyboard relative to real time. Returns null if the animation has stopped.
GetCurrentIteration	1-based iteration count. (Useful only if the storyboard repeats.) Returns null if the animation has stopped.
GetCurrentProgress	Returns a number from 0 to 1 indicating how far the storyboard is through its current iteration. If the storyboard has an indefinite duration, this will always be 0. Returns null if the animation has stopped.
GetCurrentState	Indicates whether the animation is in the Active, Filling, or Stopped state.
GetCurrentTime	Indicates the current time relative to the start of the storyboard. Returns null if the animation has stopped.
GetIsPaused	Returns true if the storyboard is paused.

Storyboard provides the members listed previously for convenience. All of the same services are available on any timeline if you obtain the timeline's *clock*. In fact, Storyboard defers to its own clock to provide each of these methods.

Controlling Animations with Clocks

Sometimes it is useful to have control over an individual animation's progress without having to wrap it in a Storyboard. You can do this by working with the animation's clock.

A clock is an object created at runtime that keeps track of the current position in a timeline and executes whatever actions the timeline defines. If you refer back to one of the timeline diagrams, such as Figure 16-8, the clock is the thing that knows where we are on the time scale at the top of the diagram. All running timelines have clocks associated with them.

 The relationship between timelines and clocks is similar to the relationship between code and threads. Executable code defines what operations are to be performed, but a thread is required to execute the code. Likewise, a timeline describes what happens over a particular length of time, but a clock is required to run the timeline.

If you use BeginAnimation or a Storyboard, WPF will create the clock for you, but if you want the same kind of control over an individual animation object as you can have with the storyboard control methods, you must create the clock yourself. Example 16-34 creates an animation identical to the one in Example 16-2, but it creates a clock explicitly and starts the animation using ApplyAnimationClock.

Example 16-34. Controlling animations with a clock

```
AnimationClock clock;

void StartAnimation() {
    DoubleAnimation animate = new DoubleAnimation();
    animate.To = 300;
    animate.Duration = new Duration(TimeSpan.FromSeconds(5));
    animate.RepeatBehavior = RepeatBehavior.Forever;

    clock = animate.CreateClock();
    myEllipse.ApplyAnimationClock(Ellipse.WidthProperty, clock);
}

void PauseAnimation() {
    clock.Controller.Pause();
}

void ResumeAnimation() {
    clock.Controller.Resume();
}
```

This example contains methods that can pause and resume the animation, using the clock's Controller property. The operations offered by the clock controller are identical to the control methods offered by Storyboard; it also has a set of properties that correspond closely to the methods shown in Table 16-5. These properties are shown in Table 16-6, which also shows how they correspond to the Storyboard methods.

Table 16-6. Properties for monitoring clock progress

Property	Storyboard equivalent
CurrentGlobalSpeed	GetCurrentGlobalSpeed
CurrentIteration	GetCurrentIteration
CurrentProgress	GetCurrentProgress
CurrentState	GetCurrentState
CurrentTime	GetCurrentTime
IsPaused	GetIsPaused

One kind of animation you would normally control from code is a *transition animation*—an animation from one part of a UI to another.

Transition Animations

Sometimes it can be useful to use animations to ease the transition between one part of the user interface and another. Many user interfaces present multiple different contexts and allow the user to navigate between them. For example, a modal dialog presents a different context from the main user interface. In navigation-style applications, each page is its own context. Most applications switch between these contexts more or less instantaneously. However, we can provide a smoother experience for the user if we animate the transition from one part of the UI to another (e.g., fade).

Unfortunately, the current version of WPF does not provide any automatic support for transition animations. For example, you can't simply supply a NavigationWindow or Frame with an animation to use when moving from one page to another. You need to do a little more work.

To provide transition animations in a navigation application, we need to handle both the Navigating and the Navigated events. In the Navigating event handler, we can capture a copy of the current page's appearance in the form of a VisualBrush. In the Navigated event, we can use this to provide a transition animation.

 We can't handle it all in a single event. In the Navigated event handler, it's too late to get hold of the old page. And, in the Navigating handler, it's too early to start the animation: we don't yet know whether navigation will definitely occur, because it may be cancelled.

Example 16-35 shows the markup for an application that will perform navigation transition animation. It contains a Frame, which will host the application's pages. It also contains a Canvas element placed on top of the Frame. This will hold the copied page as it is animated out of view. The IsHitTestVisible property has been used to make the element invisible to the mouse—we want this Canvas to be a cosmetic element whose presence has no effect on the application's behavior. This example also contains the Storyboard that will be used to perform the transition animation.

Example 16-35. Markup for navigation transition animations

```
<Window ...>

  <Window.Resources>
    <Storyboard x:Key="transitionAnimation"
                TargetName="transitionPlaceholder">
      <DoubleAnimation Storyboard.TargetProperty="Opacity"
                       From="1" To="0" DecelerationRatio="1"
                       Duration="0:0:0.4" />
    </Storyboard>
  </Window.Resources>

  <Grid>
    <Frame Name="mainFrame" Source="Page1.xaml" />
    <Canvas Name="transitionPlaceholder" IsHitTestVisible="False" />
  </Grid>

</Window>
```

In the code-behind file, the Navigating event handler makes a copy of the outgoing page's appearance in the form of a VisualBrush, as Example 16-36 shows.

Example 16-36. Copying the outgoing page to a VisualBrush

```
VisualBrush lastPageBrush;
void mainFrame_Navigating(object sender, NavigatingCancelEventArgs e) {
    Page lastPage = mainFrame.Content as Page;
    if (lastPage != null) {
        lastPageBrush = new VisualBrush(lastPage);
        lastPageBrush.Viewbox = new Rect(0, 0, lastPage.ActualWidth,
                                               lastPage.ActualHeight);
        lastPageBrush.ViewboxUnits = BrushMappingMode.Absolute;
        lastPageBrush.Stretch = Stretch.None;


        // Page won't be at origin, thanks to navigation bar.
        // Discover the offset.
        Point pageOffset =
            lastPage.TransformToVisual(this).Transform(new Point( ));
        transitionPlaceholder.Margin = new Thickness(pageOffset.X, pageOffset.Y,
                                                      0, 0);
```

Example 16-36. Copying the outgoing page to a VisualBrush (continued)

```
    }
    else {
        lastPageBrush = null;
    }
}
```

This code also discovers the position of the page relative to the window by calling TransformToVisual. We need to do this because the navigation bar provided by the Frame will push the page down, and we want to make sure that the copy of the page we use for animation is in the same location. Our navigation placeholder Canvas is a child of the main Grid—we can't make it a child of the Frame because the Frame contains just one child: the Page. So, we need to adjust the placeholder's position to match that of the Page. We do this by adjusting the placeholder's Margin.

In the Navigated event handler, we display the copy of the previous page in the placeholder and run the transition animation, as shown in Example 16-37.

Example 16-37. Running the transition animation

```
void mainFrame_Navigated(object sender, NavigationEventArgs e) {
    if (lastPageBrush != null) {
        transitionPlaceholder.Background = lastPageBrush;
        lastPageBrush = null;

        Storyboard sb = (Storyboard) FindResource("transitionAnimation");
        sb.Begin(this);
    }
}
```

Now, when the user navigates from one page to another, the preceding page will fade away instead of vanishing immediately. Figure 16-15 shows a snapshot of a transition. This fading is fairly unambitious, but with this code in place, we could create more exciting transitions by changing the storyboard in Example 16-35.

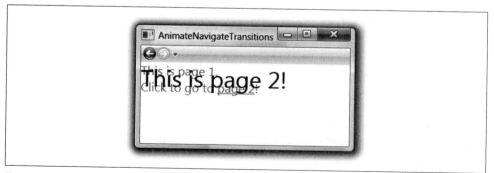

Figure 16-15. Transition animation

All of the animation examples we've looked at so far have involved properties of ordinary elements. However, the animation's timing system can also integrate with that of media playback.

Audio and Video

WPF can incorporate video and audio into a user interface. The relationship between video and animation goes deeper than the superficial fact that they are both ways of showing moving images. The timeline and clock mechanisms you use in animation you can also use to control video and audio playback.

The fact that video or audio can connect with the animation timing system is useful if you want to synchronize animation with media. For example, suppose you wanted to present a recording in an application with a series of clickable bookmarks to jump directly to key points in the recording. You might want to arrange for these bookmarks to change appearance as the playback reaches the relevant point, allowing the user to see at a glance where the playback has reached. One way to do this is to create a timeline that changes each bookmark item at the appropriate time. By connecting this timeline with the media playback, you could guarantee that the visual changes to the bookmarks were always properly synchronized with the video or audio playback.

It's not always necessary to synchronize media and animations. WPF also lets you play media in a simpler "independent" mode. We'll look at this simple usage before seeing how to synchronize playback with animations.

Simple Media Playback

The easiest way to play video or audio media in WPF is to use the MediaElement, pointing its Source property at the media file you wish to play. Example 16-38 shows a MediaElement that will play one of the sample videos that ship with Windows Vista.

Example 16-38. Simple MediaElement

```
<MediaElement Source="C:\Users\Public\Videos\Sample Videos\Butterfly.wmv" />
```

Used this way, the MediaElement will play the material as soon as it loads, and you will have no control over its progress. You can change this by setting the LoadedBehavior property. This defaults to Play, but if you set it to Manual, you can control the media element from the code-behind file, using the Play, Pause, and Stop methods, and you can jump to a particular position in the media by setting the Position property.

 You can use these control methods only if LoadedBehavior is set to Manual. They will throw exceptions otherwise. LoadedBehavior has a default value of Play.

By default, the MediaElement will resize video content to match the space available. Its Stretch property supports the same stretch styles we saw in Chapter 13—None, Fill, Uniform, and UniformToFill. The default is Uniform, meaning it will enlarge the content as far as possible without clipping it, but will preserve the aspect ratio.

The MediaElement will have a width and height of 0 until it has loaded the video. It does not take on a size until it knows the size of the video stream. It raises the MediaOpened event once it has successfully opened the stream and determined the size. You can discover the size of the source material by reading the element's NaturalVideoWidth and NaturalVideoHeight properties after the MediaOpened event has been raised.

If a MediaElement is playing audio content, its size will be zero even once the stream starts to play.

When you use a MediaElement in this fashion, it is said to be running in *independent mode*—it plays the media at its own rate, independent of the animation timing system. Although the MediaElement provides basic control methods when used in independent mode, you will need to use it in *clock mode* if you want to synchronize animation events with media playback.

Using MediaElement in Clock Mode

To use a media element in clock mode, you must create a MediaTimeline with the media element as its target. The MediaTimeline is responsible for specifying the source media. Example 16-39 shows a MediaTimeline in a storyboard that contains several other animations. (Note that this example presumes that a *VoiceRecording.wma* file containing an audio recording exists.)

Example 16-39. Media element in clock mode

```
<StackPanel>
  <TextBlock Name="ten" Text="10 seconds" Background="White" />
  <TextBlock Name="fifteen" Text="15 seconds" Background="White" />
  <TextBlock Name="twentyfive" Text="25 seconds" Background="White" />

  <MediaElement Name="media" />

  <StackPanel.Triggers>
    <EventTrigger RoutedEvent="StackPanel.Loaded">
      <BeginStoryboard>
        <Storyboard SlipBehavior="Slip">

          <MediaTimeline Source="VoiceRecording.wma"
            Storyboard.TargetName="media" />

          <ColorAnimation BeginTime="0:0:10" Duration="0:0:0.2"
            Storyboard.TargetName="ten" To="PaleGreen"
```

Example 16-39. Media element in clock mode (continued)

```
        Storyboard.TargetProperty=
            "(TextBlock.Background).(SolidColorBrush.Color)" />

    <ColorAnimation BeginTime="0:0:15" Duration="0:0:0.2"
        Storyboard.TargetName="fifteen" To="PaleGreen"
        Storyboard.TargetProperty=
            "(TextBlock.Background).(SolidColorBrush.Color)" />

    <ColorAnimation BeginTime="0:0:25" Duration="0:0:0.2"
        Storyboard.TargetName="twentyfive" To="PaleGreen"
        Storyboard.TargetProperty=
            "(TextBlock.Background).(SolidColorBrush.Color)" />

        </Storyboard>
      </BeginStoryboard>
    </EventTrigger>
  </StackPanel.Triggers>
</StackPanel>
```

This example contains three TextBlock elements. The storyboard contains animations that change these elements' background colors at various points during the timeline. Figure 16-16 shows three snapshots from this UI, illustrating how the background is filled in as time progresses.

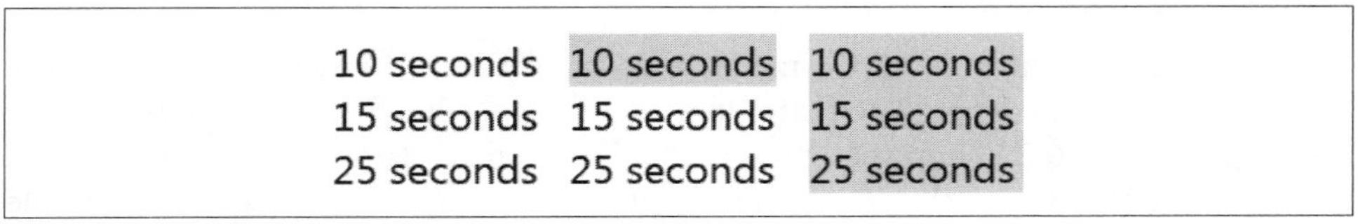

10 seconds	10 seconds	10 seconds
15 seconds	15 seconds	15 seconds
25 seconds	25 seconds	25 seconds

Figure 16-16. Highlights indicating media progress

Because these animations are part of the same storyboard as the MediaTimeline, they will be synchronized—the first animation has a BeginTime of 0:0:10, so it will run exactly 10 seconds into the animation, and therefore also 10 seconds into the media playback. If you were to pause the storyboard, both the media playback and the animations would be paused. They would remain in sync when you resumed the storyboard.

Slipping

One problem with media playback is that it is sometimes not possible to play the source material in real time. If the material is being downloaded, network problems may prevent the data from arriving in time to be played. In this case, the system has no option but to suspend playback for a while. There may be delays even when the material is local—there is often a short delay from when you ask to play material to when playback begins. The net result is that a MediaTimeline may occupy more real time than the theoretical natural duration of the source material. This is referred to as *slipping*.

Slipping causes a problem when playing media in clock mode: it can compromise the relationship between the media playback and any synchronized animations. WPF can deal with slipping in two ways, chosen by the SlipBehavior property of the storyboard.

The default SlipBehavior is Grow. In this mode, timelines that slip are treated as though they have simply grown in length. So, if media playback starts one second late due to startup delays, it will be one second behind throughout and will finish one second late—the MediaTimeline has effectively grown one second longer. This means that all the other animations will be unaffected by the slippage, which can minimize visual disruption. However, this has the unfortunate effect that any synchronized animations will appear to run early. In fact, they're running exactly on time and it's the media that's late, but if the user attention is focused on the media, it will look like the animations are coming in ahead of cue.

To avoid this timing mismatch, Example 16-39 sets the SlipBehavior to Slip. With this setting, when the MediaTimeline slips, the Storyboard forces all of its other timelines to slip with it—any animations that were in progress when slippage began will be suspended until the MediaTimeline is able to progress. This increases the disruption when slippage occurs—the whole storyboard grinds to a halt instead of just the media playback. But it keeps the animations in sync, and because synchronization of animations and media playback is the normal reason for using a media element in clock mode, the Slip mode will normally make more sense.

 If you want some of the animations to slip in order to remain synchronized, but other animations to progress as normal, you can use two separate storyboards.

Where Are We?

Animation can enhance an application's interactive feel. It can make for smoother transitions when items appear and disappear. Of course, you should use animation with taste and restraint—if you animate everything in your application, it will be a bewildering mess. You should also take care not to frustrate your users by forcing them to wait for animations to finish before proceeding. Fortunately, WPF keeps all user interface elements active while animations are in progress.

All animations are described by timelines, which are objects that describe what happens over some particular stretch of time. Timelines form a hierarchy, allowing the relationships between different parts of an animation to be expressed. The execution of animations is controlled by "clocks," which provide us with a means of starting and stopping animations. You can add animations to the triggers section of any element, and to styles and templates. The animation's timing system can synchronize with media playback, enabling animations to coincide with events in audio or video sources.

CHAPTER 17

3D Graphics

WPF applications can incorporate three-dimensional content. A data visualization application might use this to produce a 3D plot of a field of values. A shopping application could offer a 3D model of a product in order to give potential customers a better idea of what the item looks like. WPF provides a simple mechanism for integrating such 3D content into your application.

Note that if you wish to fully exploit your graphics card's 3D capabilities, WPF is unlikely to be the best choice of technology. The main benefits WPF offers in 3D are ease of use and the ability to integrate 3D content anywhere in a WPF application. The performance cannot compete with lower-level APIs such as DirectX and OpenGL, and you should continue to use these if your application has very demanding 3D requirements. But if you wish to incorporate fairly simple models into an otherwise two-dimensional application, WPF's 3D features make this easy.

This chapter is not an introduction to 3D graphics in general, or the mathematics behind it. We will focus just on how WPF does 3D graphics.[*]

3D Content in a 2D World

WPF is essentially a two-dimensional technology. The panel-based layout system knows how to arrange 2D elements onto a 2D screen. Likewise, the flow document system knows how to flow text onto a two-dimensional page. So how does 3D content fit into this world?

The Viewport3D element bridges the gap between 2D and 3D. As far as the WPF layout system is concerned, Viewport3D is just a rectangular element. It is similar in nature to the MediaElement type: both are rectangular elements that can display moving images. Whereas MediaElement displays a recorded video stream, a Viewport3D works more like a live video feed from a camera—a virtual camera in a 3D model.

---

[*] You can find a thorough tutorial on the mathematics and geometry of 3D graphics at *http://chortle.ccsu.edu/ VectorLessons/index.html* (*http://tinysells.com/81*).

Viewport3D fits into the WPF layout model like any other element. You can give it an explicit width and height, or you can let it pick up its height from a containing panel such as a Grid. You can host it inside a panel or a content control just like any other element. And, of course, all the normal layout properties, such as Margin and HorizontalLayout, are available.

Viewport3D requires us to supply three things: a camera description, one or more light sources, and a 3D model. Without a model, there is nothing to display. Without a light source, there is no way to see the model. And, the Viewport3D needs a camera description so that it knows the point of view from which it should render the scene.

Cameras

You must set the Viewport3D's Camera property to one of the three available camera types: PerspectiveCamera, OrthographicCamera, or MatrixCamera. The type of camera determines how the 3D model will be turned into a 2D image on-screen.

The PerspectiveCamera is often the most natural choice. With this camera, the farther away objects are, the smaller they appear. Because that's how things look in real life, this produces a reasonably natural-looking image.

The OrthographicCamera uses a more simplistic approach. A 3D object of a particular size will always be rendered at exactly the same size, regardless of how far away it is. This tends to produce rather unnatural-looking images, but it can occasionally be useful—sometimes consistency is more important than a natural appearance. If you are rendering 3D models representing the design of something physical, such as a planned piece of woodwork or the layout of a room, you might want objects of the same size in the model to appear the same size on-screen. Likewise, if you are producing a 3D graph, consistency of size might be more important than realism. An OrthographicCamera can guarantee this, whereas a PerspectiveCamera can, by design, show equal-size objects as different sizes on-screen. Figure 17-1 shows an example— on the left is a series of identical columns rendered with a PerspectiveCamera, and on the right is the same model as shown by an OrthographicCamera.

Figure 17-1. PerspectiveCamera and OrthographicCamera

If you are using either the PerspectiveCamera or the OrthographicCamera, you need to provide information about the camera's position and orientation. You set its location relative to the coordinate space of the Viewport3D's model with the Position property. The LookDirection property indicates which direction the camera is pointing. This isn't quite enough to establish the camera's orientation—a camera in a particular location pointed in a particular direction can still be rotated around the axis in which it is pointing. For example, when taking a photograph with a real camera, you can rotate it to choose between a portrait or landscape shot. So, you must also specify an UpDirection.

This pins down the location and orientation of the camera, but you still need to indicate how wide a shot you require. (In real camera terms, this is equivalent to adjusting the focal length of a zoom lens.) With the PerspectiveCamera, you do this with the FieldOfView property, specifying an angle in degrees. Narrowing the angle has the effect of zooming in, and increasing the angle zooms out.

Example 17-1 shows a PerspectiveCamera. This is positioned and oriented such that the model's x- and y-axes will appear horizontal and vertical in the Viewport3D, respectively. The camera is looking directly at the origin, and it is positioned on the z-axis itself, four units away from the origin in the positive z direction. The position we've chosen for this camera means that lower values of z are farther away from the camera.

Example 17-1. PerspectiveCamera

```
<PerspectiveCamera Position="0,0,4" LookDirection="0,0,-1"
                   UpDirection="0,1,0" FieldOfView="45" />
```

To demonstrate the impact of the various camera settings, we'll look at how making small changes to each property affects what the camera sees. The model in all cases will be the same. It will consist of five cylinders, similar to those shown in Figure 17-1, but with a couple of the cylinders colored black to make it easier to see which way around things are—with a 3D view it is possible to look at a scene from any angle, so it's useful to have something to help keep your bearings. Figure 17-3 shows a plan view of the model viewed from above.

The cylinders are positioned in a line near the center. Figure 17-3 also shows a symbol that appears three times toward the bottom—a circle with a cross through it. These indicate camera locations, and the arrow indicates the direction in which the camera is pointing (i.e., the LookDirection). The middle one corresponds to the camera in Example 17-1, and the ones on either side correspond to similar cameras, but with the Position property modified to –1,0,4 and 1,0,4. This is equivalent to moving the camera one unit to the left or one unit to the right. Figure 17-2 shows the three camera positions. The leftmost image shows the leftmost camera position, which results in the leftmost column appearing in the center of the frame, because that column appears directly in front of the camera. Likewise, the rightmost image has the rightmost column dead center, as it is directly in front of the camera. The middle image may look surprising, as it appears slightly lopsided. However, this is just the effect of perspective. The central column is in the center of the frame, and the columns on the right appear nearer to the center than those on the left simply because they are farther away.

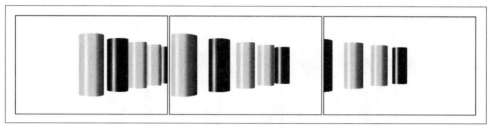

Figure 17-2. Position: −1,0,4; 0,0,4; and 1,0,4

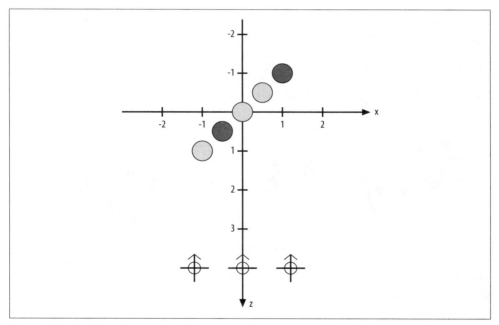

Figure 17-3. Model and camera positions

By changing just the Position, we adjust the camera location without changing the direction in which it is pointing. In cinematic terminology, this is equivalent to a *tracking shot*, in which the camera is typically on rails so that it can move around. With a real camera, an alternative to moving around is to use a *panning shot*, where the camera remains stationary, but the direction in which it points changes. We can achieve this effect in WPF by changing the camera's LookDirection. In Figure 17-4, the Position is the same for all three shots—it is back at 0,0,4.

Instead, the LookDirection has been adjusted to point the camera at the leftmost column, the central column, and the rightmost column. The difference between this and Figure 17-2 is subtle, but clear—the effect of perspective is different. In Figure 17-2, the columns in the lefthand shot are bunched together fairly closely, and the spacing increases as the camera moves to the right. This effect is sometimes called *parallax*, and it occurs with any tracking shot. But in Figure 17-4 this effect does not occur, because the camera has not moved; again, with a real camera, parallax effects do not occur with panning shots.

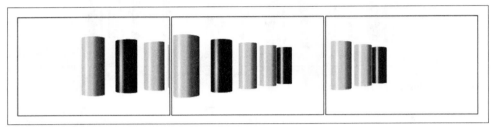

Figure 17-4. LookDirection: –0.33,0,–1; 0,0,–1; and 0.33,0,–1

The third property in Example 17-1 is UpDirection. On a real camera, this would correspond to tilting the camera while keeping it pointed in the same direction. Figure 17-5 shows the effect of changing this property.

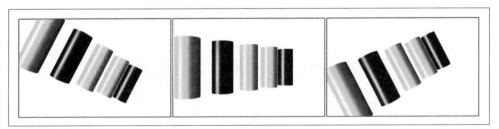

Figure 17-5. UpDirection: –0.5,1,0; 0,1,0; and 0.5,1,0

The final property in Example 17-1 is FieldOfView. This has the same effect as changing the focal length of the lens on a real camera, either by adjusting the zoom or by changing lenses. Figure 17-6 shows three shots where all the parameters are the same as in Example 17-1, except for the FieldOfView.

A zoom facility may seem redundant in a virtual 3D model, because it's very easy to move the camera around. However, moving a camera close to an item has a different effect than zooming in. The closer a camera gets to its subject, the more distortion is caused by perspective effects. Fitting a very wide angle lens, such as a so-called "fisheye" lens, to a real camera will take this to extremes, producing strangely distorted-looking images. Moving a PerspectiveCamera farther away from a subject and then zooming back in by narrowing the FieldOfView will reduce the effects of perspective.

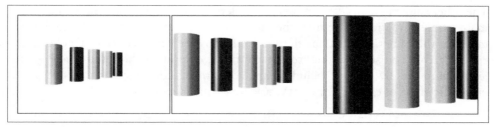

Figure 17-6. FieldOfView: 65; 45; and 25

Figure 17-7 shows three shots where the `Position` has been adjusted to move the camera away from or toward the scene, but the `FieldOfView` has been adjusted so that the whole model remains in shot and at about the same size, in all three cases. As you can see, the farther away from the model the camera is, the less effect perspective has.

Figure 17-7. Position/FieldOfView: 0,0,2/108; 0,0,4/45; and 0,0,8/20

Although most of the camera settings described apply to the `OrthographicCamera`, the `OrthographicCamera` doesn't adjust objects' sizes for perspective, so a field-of-view angle would make no sense for this camera. Instead, it has a `Width` property, which serves a similar purpose—it determines how wide a view the camera takes—but rather than taking an angle, it takes a size, measured in the coordinate space of the 3D model. Figure 17-8 shows the same scene as the previous examples, with the same `Position`, `LookDirection`, and `UpDirection`, but shown by an `OrthographicCamera` with various `Width` settings.

Figure 17-8. Width: "5"; "4"; and "3"

The other camera type is `MatrixCamera`. This lets you define the camera with a pair of matrix transformations. The first, the `ViewMatrix`, determines the position and orientation of the camera (i.e., it has the same effect as the `Position`, `LookDirection`, and `UpDirection`). The second, the `ProjectionMatrix`, determines how the image is projected onto the 2D output, including any adjustments for perspective.[*] You can re-create the effect of either a `PerspectiveCamera` or an `OrthographicCamera`.

The `MatrixCamera` is harder to set up than the other two camera types—4×4 matrix values are rather cryptic compared to position and direction properties. The main reason the `MatrixCamera` exists is that this matrix representation is fairly common in 3D graphics packages. If you already have code that knows how to set up a camera this way, you can plug the matrices it generates directly into a `MatrixCamera`.

In 2D, WPF's coordinate system is arranged so that increasing the x position moves to the right and increasing the y position moves down. In 3D, the orientation of x and y depends entirely on the camera's position and orientation.

For example, you can place the camera so that increasing x values are to the right, and increasing y values are down, making these axes consistent with 2D. This will mean that increasing z values will move away from the camera, because WPF uses a so-called *right-handed* coordinate system. If you orient your thumb, index finger, and middle finger of your right hand at right angles to each other and label them x, y, and z, respectively, they are arranged in the same way as the 3D axes in WPF. This is inconsistent with WPF's convention for Z order in 2D. As discussed in Chapter 3, even in 2D there is some notion of a third dimension in the form of Z order. The Z order uses the convention that a higher Z index is nearer to the viewer. And because positive x means right and positive y means down, this tells us that 2D effectively uses a *left-handed* system.

A camera is not much use without something to look at. So, we must add a model to the `Viewport3D`.

Models

We describe three-dimensional objects in WPF by building a tree of `Model3D` objects. `Model3D` is an abstract class, and we use the derived `GeometryModel3D` type to define a particular 3D shape. Another derived type, `Model3DGroup`, allows us to combine several `Model3D` objects into one composite `Model3D`. There are also various light source types derived from `Model3D`, which we describe later in the "Lights" section.

---

[*] This may seem rather surprising, because perspective transformations are nonaffine and are therefore something you can't do with matrix multiplication. The trick is that all of these matrices work with four-dimensional coordinates, where the fourth dimension is used for perspective. After the matrix multiplication has been done, these 4D coordinates are then turned back into 3D coordinates by dividing each of the first three dimensions by the value in the fourth dimension. It's this division operation that enables perspective.

Example 17-2 shows the basic structure of a very simple model.

Example 17-2. A simple 3D model

```
<Model3DGroup>

  <DirectionalLight Direction="0,0,-1" />

  <GeometryModel3D>
    ...
  </GeometryModel3D>

</Model3DGroup>
```

This uses a Model3DGroup to build a model containing a light source (a DirectionalLight, in this case) and a GeometryModel3D. The example is not complete, as we need to provide the GeometryModel3D with two pieces of information. It needs to know what the surface of the shape should look like—what color it should be, and whether its finish should be matte or reflective. It also needs a description of the shape, which a Geometry3D provides.

Geometry3D

As you saw in Chapter 13, WPF defines 2D shapes with the various types derived from Geometry. It should therefore come as no surprise that 3D shapes are defined by classes derived from Geometry3D. However, whereas the 2D world offers various different kinds of geometries, such as EllipseGeometry, RectangleGeometry, and PathGeometry, WPF currently offers only one concrete Geometry3D: MeshGeometry3D.

A MeshGeometry3D defines the shape of a surface as a collection of triangles. A so-called "mesh" of triangles is a very common way to represent shapes in 3D, because modern graphics cards are designed to render triangles very quickly, and it's possible to build all sorts of complex shapes by stitching enough triangles together. Any modern 3D modeling software will be able to generate triangle-based representations of the 3D models you design. In WPF, you create a mesh by specifying a collection of 3D points and then describing how those points are joined up as triangles. We also provide surface normals for each point—vectors indicating the direction in which the surface is facing at that particular point. Example 17-3 shows the simplest possible MeshGeometry3D.

Example 17-3. MeshGeometry3D

```
<MeshGeometry3D Positions="0,1,0  1,-1,0  -1,-1,0"
                Normals="0,0,1  0,0,1  0,0,1"
                TriangleIndices="0,2,1" />
```

This defines a single triangle. The Positions property contains three sets of three numbers. Each group of three numbers in the XAML is turned into a Point3D value.

The Normals property is a collection of Vector3D values that indicate the direction in which the surface is facing at each point. WPF needs to know this in order to perform lighting calculations—the angle between a surface and a light source can have an impact on how the surface should be rendered. In this example, all three vectors are pointing in the same direction, because this is a flat surface.

The TriangleIndices property is a collection of integers, indexing into the Positions collection. This serves two purposes. The first is that it indicates how the points are joined into triangles. (In this case, it's trivial: there are only three points, so there's only one possible triangle. But for meshes containing hundreds of points, WPF needs to know how you want them joined together.)

More subtly, the TriangleIndices property also indicates which way each triangle is facing. Surfaces have a front and a back, which may be painted in different ways. (For a completely enclosed shape, you wouldn't bother painting the back at all, because all the triangle backs are on the inside of the shape.) The ordering of the points determines which side is which: if the points appear in counterclockwise order, you're looking at the front.

Figure 17-9 shows the triangle described by Example 17-3, drawn so that x and y are horizontal and vertical, viewed from the positive z direction. The TriangleIndices in Example 17-3 list the points in the order 0,2,1—a counterclockwise order. This means that the triangle's front is the one facing us in Figure 17-9 (i.e., the one facing in the positive z direction). If TriangleIndices had been set to 0,1,2, the triangle would be facing away from us, and Figure 17-9 would be showing its back.

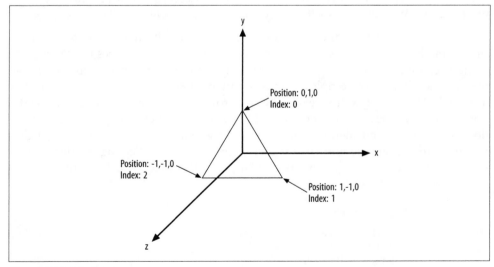

Figure 17-9. Mesh points

Now that we have defined a shape, albeit a very simple one, we can plug this MeshGeometry3D into the unfinished GeometryModel3D in Example 17-2. Example 17-4 shows this fleshed-out version.

Example 17-4. GeometryModel3D with MeshGeometry3D

```
<GeometryModel3D>
    <GeometryModel3D.Geometry>
        <MeshGeometry3D Positions="0,1,0  1,-1,0  -1,-1,0"
                        Normals="0,0,1  0,0,1  0,0,1"
                        TriangleIndices="0,2,1" />
    </GeometryModel3D.Geometry>

    ...
</GeometryModel3D>
```

We're not done yet, though. A GeometryModel3D requires two pieces of information: the shape and a description of how to paint the surface. For this second part, we need to supply a Material object.

Materials

A Material is the 3D equivalent of a Brush. Just as a Brush describes how to paint a 2D shape, a Material describes how to paint a 3D shape. In fact, a Material incorporates at least one 2D Brush to define the surface's coloring, but it also provides information such as whether it is shiny or matte.

Material is an abstract class. WPF provides four concrete subclasses. DiffuseMaterial defines a surface with a matte finish. SpecularMaterial defines a somewhat shiny finish—one that will have reflective highlights. An EmissiveMaterial is one that lights up of its own accord—it does not need a light source in order to be visible. Finally, MaterialGroup allows multiple material types to be combined into a single material.

DiffuseMaterial

DiffuseMaterial describes a surface with a matte finish. This means the brightness for any particular part of the surface is determined only by how the various light sources strike it. The position of the camera does not have any impact.

You set the surface color or texture by setting the Brush property. This will accept any WPF brush, so you can use a solid color, a gradient, a bitmap, a drawing, or even a Visual to paint the 3D surface. Example 17-5 shows a DiffuseMaterial based on a SolidColorBrush.

Example 17-5. DiffuseMaterial

```
<DiffuseMaterial Brush="#00FFFF" />
```

Figure 17-10 shows this material applied to a model of a sphere. (The sphere model itself is not shown because it contains several thousand triangles, and is therefore rather large.)

Figure 17-10. Sphere with DiffuseMaterial

SpecularMaterial

SpecularMaterial models a shiny surface. A SpecularMaterial shows highlights where it reflects the light source, and as with a real object, these highlights will shift as the point of view moves around. Example 17-6 shows a SpecularMaterial.

Example 17-6. SpecularMaterial

```
<SpecularMaterial SpecularPower="30" Brush="White" />
```

Figure 17-11 shows this material applied to the same sphere as in Figure 17-10. (Two highlights have appeared because this particular example scene contains two light sources.) This has been rendered onto a black background because the material would be invisible on a white background.

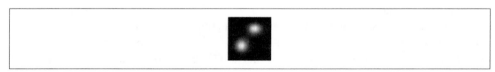

Figure 17-11. Sphere with SpecularMaterial

Figure 17-11 looks a little odd. This is because you would not normally use a SpecularMaterial in isolation. The material is designed to be used in a MaterialGroup in combination with other material types such as a DiffuseMaterial. The highlights provided by a SpecularMaterial are added onto whatever is underneath.

The way a SpecularMaterial combines with what is underneath is different from ordinary transparency. Normal transparent rendering in 2D graphics in WPF generates weighted averages of colors. But a SpecularMaterial is additive. For example, suppose a specular material's brush is bright green—a color of #00FF00. Imagine it appears on top of something bright red (i.e., #FF0000); for example, it is part of a material group, on top of a red diffuse material. The resultant highlight will be the color you get when adding red to green: #FFFF00, which is yellow. This is a different result from the averaging used by ordinary semitransparent alpha blending.

If you had a rectangle of color #FF0000 and then painted one on top of it with the color #00FF00 and an Opacity of 0.5, the outcome for this combination would be the average of the R, G, and B channels for those colors, #808000, which is a rather dull shade of brown.

If adding in the highlight takes any of the red, green, or blue color channels past 100 percent, they will simply be clipped at 100 percent. This causes the highlight to bleach out, a bit like an overexposed area of a photograph. This is why Figure 17-11 has been rendered on a black background—a white background is already at maximum brightness, and attempting to add highlights won't make it any whiter.

As with the DiffuseMaterial, you can provide any 2D Brush object to determine the color or texture of the material. In addition, you can specify a SpecularPower. This determines how much the highlights are spread out. A low number results in a wide spread, and a high number results in a more tightly focused highlight.

Figure 17-12 shows the same sphere as Figure 17-11 twice, with different SpecularPower values. On the left, the low value of 5 has caused the two highlights to spread out so far that they have merged into one. On the right, the high value of 100 has caused the two highlights to become very small.

Figure 17-12. SpecularPower of 5 (left) and 100 (right)

 Lighting calculations are performed on a per-point basis. If you choose a high specular power, meaning that the highlights should look small and focused, you will need a fairly detailed model for the highlights to look correct. The triangles that make up the surface need to be significantly smaller than the size of the specular highlights in order to avoid strange artifacts. The example on the righthand side of Figure 17-12 is pushing it a little—the highlights look a little uneven, even though the sphere model contains 4,000 facets and fills more than 400 KB of XAML.

EmissiveMaterial

Both DiffuseMaterial and SpecularMaterial require external light sources to be visible. If all your light is coming from one direction, these materials will look completely black on the shadow side. But an EmissiveMaterial is its own light source.

An emissive material contributes to the output in the same way as a specular material: it adds to whatever was behind it. However, whereas a specular material's contribution is based on viewing angles and light positions, an emissive material is unaffected by the light sources in a scene—it always contributes evenly across the whole surface.

Although an `EmissiveMaterial` illuminates itself, it does not act as a light source to other objects in the same 3D model. Shaped light sources are computationally complex to render and are beyond the 3D capabilities offered by WPF. However, if you want to create a 3D object that looks like a light source, you can fake it by placing a light source in the scene at the same location.

Example 17-7 shows a simple `EmissiveMaterial`. In practice, you would not normally use as simple a brush as this. As Figure 17-13 shows, when this is applied to the same sphere as the earlier examples, it produces a rather dull result.

Example 17-7. EmissiveMaterial

```
<EmissiveMaterial x:Key="emissiveBlueMaterial" Brush="#00FFFF" />
```

As with the `SpecularMaterial` example, this figure has been rendered onto a black background—additive rendering onto white only ever results in white.

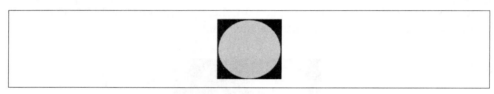

Figure 17-13. Sphere with EmissiveMaterial

In practice, an `EmissiveMaterial` would usually be used only with a more varied brush, such as an `ImageBrush`. Also, like a `SpecularMaterial`, it would typically be used as part of a `MaterialGroup`.

MaterialGroup

`MaterialGroup` allows multiple materials to be combined into a single material. For example, you might want to use a `DiffuseMaterial` to define the basic solid appearance, but provide a less dull finish by adding a `SpecularMaterial`. Example 17-8 shows such a material.

Example 17-8. Diffuse and specular materials in a MaterialGroup

```
<MaterialGroup>
  <DiffuseMaterial Brush="#00FFFF" />
  <SpecularMaterial SpecularPower="30" Brush="White" />
</MaterialGroup>
```

Figure 17-14 shows the results. Note that the diffuse material provides a complete solid basic finish for the shape to which the specular material can add highlights. We no longer need a black background to be able to see the highlights. This is the normal way to use a specular material.

Figure 17-14. Sphere with MaterialGroup

By combining with other materials in a `MaterialGroup`, `EmissiveMaterial` can play a more convincing role than the rather dull example in Figure 17-13. Figure 17-15 shows a sphere with a similar material group to that in Figure 17-14, but with an added `EmissiveMaterial`.

Figure 17-15. MaterialGroup with EmissiveMaterial (Color Plate 27)

Notice how the text "glow" is visible and bright even though it runs into the part of the sphere that is in shadow. This is because it is rendered as an `EmissiveMaterial` and is therefore unaffected by the scene's lighting. This illustrates `EmissiveMaterial`'s main purpose: to make areas of a shape "light up." Example 17-9 shows the material for Figure 17-15.

Example 17-9. MaterialGroup with EmissiveMaterial

```
<MaterialGroup>
  <DiffuseMaterial Brush="#0000FF" />
  <SpecularMaterial SpecularPower="30" Brush="White" />
  <EmissiveMaterial>
    <EmissiveMaterial.Brush>
      <VisualBrush ViewboxUnits="Absolute" Viewbox="0,0,150,50">
        <VisualBrush.Transform>
          <TransformGroup>
            <TranslateTransform X="0.35" Y="0.5" />
          </TransformGroup>
        </VisualBrush.Transform>
        <VisualBrush.Visual>
          <Grid Width="150" Height="50">
            <TextBlock FontSize="8" Text="Glow!" Foreground="#ff80a0"
                      HorizontalAlignment="Center">
              <TextBlock.BitmapEffect>
```

Example 17-9. MaterialGroup with EmissiveMaterial (continued)

```
                <OuterGlowBitmapEffect GlowColor="#ff8000" GlowSize="1" />
            </TextBlock.BitmapEffect>
          </TextBlock>
        </Grid>
      </VisualBrush.Visual>
    </VisualBrush>
  </EmissiveMaterial.Brush>
  </EmissiveMaterial>
</MaterialGroup>
```

Now that we have seen how to define materials, we can finally complete the GeometryModel3D we started building earlier. Example 17-10 shows the full model item, with both a geometry and a material.

Example 17-10. Complete GeometryModel3D

```
<GeometryModel3D>
  <GeometryModel3D.Geometry>
    <MeshGeometry3D Positions="0,1,0  1,-1,0  -1,-1,0"
                    Normals="0,0,1  0,0,1  0,0,1"
                    TriangleIndices="0,2,1" />
  </GeometryModel3D.Geometry>

  <GeometryModel3D.Material>
    <DiffuseMaterial Brush="Red" />
  </GeometryModel3D.Material>

  <GeometryModel3D.BackMaterial>
    <DiffuseMaterial Brush="Green" />
  </GeometryModel3D.BackMaterial>
</GeometryModel3D>
```

Notice that we've added two materials, one for the front and one for the back. This is because our shape is open, so the surface can be seen from either side. Some shapes, such as a sphere, are closed, so only one side of the mesh will ever be visible (assuming you don't move the camera into and out of the shape). For such shapes, you would supply just a single material.

Now that have a complete model, we need to connect this into the Viewport3D. However, we can't connect it in directly—there's one more step.

ModelVisual3D

The various classes derived from Model3D that make up our model are just a description of the scene. They are in many ways analogous to the elements that make up a Drawing in the 2D world: both are descriptions of visual content; both are shareable objects that derive from Freezable;* and neither can render something on-screen of its own accord.

---

* We describe the Freezable base class in Appendix C.

A Drawing needs to be connected to some kind of Visual object to be rendered and to enable input handling. Likewise, a Model3D needs to be connected to a ModelVisual3D in order to be rendered and to support hit testing.

 ModelVisual3D does not derive from Visual. It derives from Visual3D instead. However, it does form part of the visual tree. If you use the VisualTreeHelper class to navigate the tree, it reports both kinds of elements. We described VisualTreeHelper in Chapter 9.

Example 17-11 brings together the various other pieces we've looked at so far to form a complete, if rather simple, example. This adds the completed GeometryModel3D from Example 17-10 to the Model3DGroup in Example 17-2. This Model3DGroup provides the Content of a ModelVisual3D. This in turn is the child of a Viewport3D, which lets us host this 3D content in a 2D WPF user interface. Finally, in order to describe the point of view from which we would like to render the scene, we have added the PerspectiveCamera from Example 17-1.

Example 17-11. Complete 3D example

```
<Viewport3D>
  <Viewport3D.Camera>
    <PerspectiveCamera Position="0,0,10" LookDirection="0,0,-1"
                       UpDirection="0,1,0" FieldOfView="45" />
  </Viewport3D.Camera>

  <ModelVisual3D>
    <ModelVisual3D.Content>
      <Model3DGroup>

        <DirectionalLight Direction="0,0,-1" />

        <GeometryModel3D>
          <GeometryModel3D.Geometry>
            <MeshGeometry3D Positions="0,1,0  1,-1,0  -1,-1,0"
                            Normals="0,0,1  0,0,1  0,0,1"
                            TriangleIndices="0,2,1" />
          </GeometryModel3D.Geometry>

          <GeometryModel3D.Material>
            <DiffuseMaterial Brush="Red" />
          </GeometryModel3D.Material>

          <GeometryModel3D.BackMaterial>
            <DiffuseMaterial Brush="Green" />
          </GeometryModel3D.BackMaterial>
        </GeometryModel3D>

      </Model3DGroup>
    </ModelVisual3D.Content>
  </ModelVisual3D>
</Viewport3D>
```

For all our efforts, we might have expected something slightly more impressive than the result shown in Figure 17-16. But remember, we did set out to create the simplest possible MeshGeometry3D, so we cannot be too surprised at the modest results.

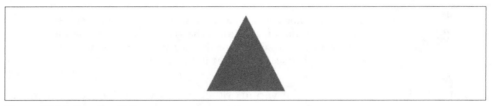

Figure 17-16. Rendered 3D content

Creating 3D shapes by typing in mesh data is a slow and awkward process. In practice, most 3D models will be designed in interactive modeling applications or generated by code. However, Figure 17-16 is so flat that before moving on, we should at least tweak the model so that it looks like it's three-dimensional. Example 17-12 shows modified versions of the camera and mesh.

Example 17-12. Tweaking the model

```
<PerspectiveCamera Position="-4,1,10" LookDirection="4,-1,-10"
                UpDirection="0,1,0" FieldOfView="45" />
...
<MeshGeometry3D Positions="0,1,0  1,-1,1  -1,-1,1  1,-1,-1  -1,-1,-1"
             Normals="0,1,0  -1,0,1  1,0,1  -1,0,-1  1,0,-1"
             TriangleIndices="0,2,1  0,3,1  0,3,4  0,2,4" />
```

Figure 17-17 shows the resulting tetrahedron. To make the faces more visually distinctive, alternate faces in the model have been turned backward by reversing the index order in TriangleIndices. So, the front face in this example is red, but the face visible on the side is green—the color of the back material. (Although this is a convenient hack for making the faces stand out, it has the unfortunate side effect of inverting the lighting calculations for those faces, so the shading looks inconsistent. In practice, if you want different faces of your model to have different materials, using multiple Geometry3D objects would be a better technique.)

Figure 17-17. Visibly three-dimensional content

We have now examined the core types at the heart of WPF's 3D API. As you've seen, many of these are analogous to WPF's 2D types. Table 17-1 summarizes the similarities between these types. (For completeness, the table also contains a type we have not covered yet: Transform3D, which we will describe later.)

Table 17-1. Analogous 3D and 2D types

3D type	2D equivalent	Purpose
Visual3D	Visual	Abstract base class for elements in the visual tree
ModelVisual3D	Canvas	A visual element that can contain a group of visual elements
Model3D	Drawing	Abstract base class for model or drawing parts
GeometryModel3D	GeometryDrawing	A shape plus a material or brush (part of a model or drawing)
Model3DGroup	DrawingGroup	A collection of model or drawing parts
Geometry3D	Geometry	Abstract base class for shapes
MeshGeometry3D	PathGeometry	A shape
Material	Brush	Abstract base of classes describing how to paint a shape
Transform3D	Transform	Abstract base class of transformations such as scaling or rotation

Now that we've looked at the basics, it's time to look at a few of the ways we can enhance the appearance of our 3D visuals. We'll start by looking at the various kinds of light sources.

Lights

A 3D model can incorporate any number of light sources. It should include at least one so that you are able to see the objects in the model. In practice, you might want to add a few—a single light source can produce a somewhat stark appearance. WPF offers four different kinds of light.

Although lights form part of the model—the base Light class derives from Model3D—they are not visible. They affect only the way in which other elements in the 3D scene are rendered. If you want a bright-looking object to be visible, representing the light, you would need to add one or more 3D shapes to provide that appearance.

AmbientLight

The simplest light source is AmbientLight. This provides an even illumination of all objects in the scene regardless of their location or orientation. Example 17-13 shows an AmbientLight.

Example 17-13. AmbientLight

```
<AmbientLight Color="White" />
```

The only property to set on an ambient light is Color. This property is present on all lights, and it indicates the color of the light emitted by the source. Note that the Color property determines not just the color of illumination, but also the intensity— White is the brightest color; a darker color such as Gray will provide less illumination. Figure 17-18 shows the results. This makes it clear that you would not normally use an AmbientLight as your only source of illumination. The sphere rendered in this example is the same one shown in Figure 17-14, but in that earlier figure, we could see reflected highlights and shadows thanks to the SpecularMaterial and DiffuseMaterial in the object's material group. The same material is in use here, but because AmbientLight illuminates the scene in a completely uniform way, the sphere looks flat.

Figure 17-18. Ambient lighting

You would not normally use an AmbientLight in isolation like this unless your goal was to create an exaggeratedly artificial look. AmbientLight is designed to be used in conjunction with some directional or positional light sources. The other sources would provide most of the light, with a dim AmbientLight ensuring that any parts of the model in shadow are not plunged into complete darkness.

DirectionalLight

DirectionalLight provides a slightly more natural form of illumination. It models a bright distant light source such as the sun. So, you do not specify a position for DirectionalLight, you merely configure the direction from which it illuminates, as Example 17-14 shows. The light in this example arrives from behind and slightly above the viewer. (This assumes that the camera is positioned so that a positive y direction means up, and positive z means toward the viewer.)

Example 17-14. DirectionalLight

```
<DirectionalLight Color="White" Direction="0,-1,-0.5" />
```

Figure 17-19 shows the same sphere as Figure 17-18, but illuminated with this directional light. As you can see, the materials are now able to do their job. The upper half is brighter than the lower half thanks to the diffuse material, and there is a reflective highlight from the specular material. These effects reveal the curvature of the surface.

Figure 17-19. Directional lighting

 Although the sphere clearly has a side that is in shadow, this is simply a result of how the DiffuseMaterial works: parts of the shape that face away from any light source will be painted dark, giving the appearance of a shadow. However, objects cannot cast shadows onto each other. For example, if we added a flat surface representing the ground to the model in Figure 17-19, it would not show a shadow of the sphere. This is because WPF uses a simple lighting model—each object's illumination is calculated in isolation, so one object cannot cast a shadow on another.

PointLight

PointLight is useful for simulating a local light source, such as a lamp in a room. The relative position of a PointLight and an object has an impact on how the one illuminates the other. The simplest use of a PointLight involves setting its color and position, as shown in Example 17-15.

Example 17-15. PointLight

```
<PointLight Color="White" Position="0,1,1.5" />
```

Figure 17-20 shows the effect of this on a scene containing two spheres. The spheres are centered on the x-axis, at x positions of –0.6 and 0.6. This means the PointLight is slightly above and in front of the spheres, but horizontally centered between them. This positioning is evident in the shadows and highlights on the spheres—the highlights point toward the position of the PointLight.

Figure 17-20. Point lighting

If you were to animate the position of the light, the highlights would follow the light around. Figure 17-21 shows the same scene with the Position of the PointLight changed to 4, –2, 1.5.

Figure 17-21. Moving a point light

Real light sources provide more illumination when they are nearby than when they are distant. By default, a PointLight does not behave this way—a very distant PointLight illuminates just as brightly as a nearby one. However, you can configure it to attenuate the brightness over distance in order to model a real light source more realistically.

Attenuation of a PointLight is calculated as a quadratic function of distance (i.e., a function with three terms: the square of the distance, the distance itself, and a constant). This is designed to correspond to how light sources attenuate naturally. Two factors contribute to how real light sources diminish with distance.

The first factor is that light spreads out. For example, put a light in a small room with dimensions of $10 \times 10 \times 10$ feet. The area of each wall is 100 square feet, so including the floor and ceiling as well as the walls, the light has to illuminate a total surface area of 600 square feet. Now put the same light in a larger room with dimensions of $30 \times 30 \times 30$ feet. Each wall is now 900 square feet, a total area of 5,400 square feet to illuminate. We increased the dimensions by a factor of 3, but the total area to be illuminated by our lamp went up by a factor of 9—the square of the change. Because it's the same lamp, it'll be giving out just as much light as before, but as this light is spread over an area nine times larger, the walls would appear nine times darker.

You can model this by setting the QuadraticAttenuation property—this sets the multiplier for the square term of the attenuation equation. Figure 17-22 shows the effect of this. The two spheres' centers are 1.6 units apart, and the light source is just to the right of the rightmost sphere. The QuadraticAttenuation has been set to 0.2, and as you can see, this causes the left sphere to be darker than the right sphere.

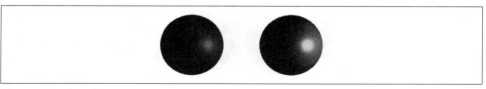

Figure 17-22. Attenuation

The second cause of natural attenuation is dust and other small airborne obstacles. These gradually diminish the intensity of light over distance. The effect of this is proportional to the distance the light has traveled—the farther it has to go, the more stuff gets in its way. You can model this by setting the LinearAttenuation property.

There is a third term for the attenuation equation, set by the `ConstantAttenuation` property. By default, this is set to 1, and the other two attenuation properties default to 0. This ensures that the level of attenuation is constant by default. (A sum total attenuation of 1 means no attenuation—only values higher than 1 will cause attenuation to occur.)

> `PointLight` is more expensive than either `AmbientLight` or `DirectionalLight`, because it requires more complex lighting calculations. If you have more than a handful of such lights and you encounter performance problems with 3D content, try reducing the number of point lights. The same applies to the `SpotLight` described in the next section.

SpotLight

`SpotLight` is very similar to `PointLight`—it supports all the same properties. However, whereas a `PointLight` casts light in all directions, a `SpotLight` casts a cone of light in a specific direction. You specify the direction with the `Direction` property. You set the width of the cone with `InnerConeAngle` and `OuterConeAngle` properties. Everything inside `InnerConeAngle` is fully illuminated, and then the degree of illumination fades to nothing by the time the `OuterConeAngle` is reached. Example 17-16 shows a `SpotLight`.

Example 17-16. SpotLight

```
<SpotLight Color="White" Position="-2,2,6" Direction="2,-2,-6"
           InnerConeAngle="8" OuterConeAngle="12" />
```

Figure 17-23 shows the result. As you can see, only a circular region to the upper left of the sphere has been illuminated. The rest falls outside of the `OuterConeAngle`, so it is in darkness.

Figure 17-23. SpotLight

Remember that WPF performs illumination calculations on a per-point basis. So if you take a surface that contains very few points, and you shine a spotlight onto the surface expecting to see a spot appear, you will be disappointed. Figure 17-24 illustrates this. Both of the images are of a simple flat square surface. Both surfaces have the same material and have been lit with the same spotlight from the same angle. The two models are identical in every respect except one: the surface on the left has been subdivided into a 64×64 grid of evenly spaced points, whereas the surface on the right is defined by just the four corner points. Figure 17-25 gives an impression of the difference between the two models—it shows the outlines of the triangles that make up the two squares. (In fact, the model on the left of Figure 17-25 is only a 16×16 grid—Figure 17-24 has been subdivided into pieces one-quarter the height and width. However, those would have been too small to see what's going on.)

Figure 17-24. Impact of point density on illumination

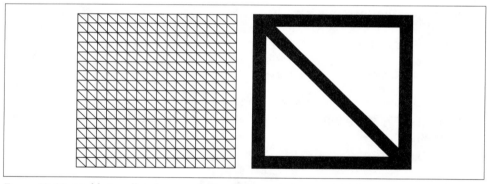

Figure 17-25. Highly tessellated square (left) and four-point square (right)

Geometrically speaking, the two surfaces have exactly the same shape: the grid of points making up the first surface lies in the same plane and within the same bounds. But as you can see, the two look very different. The surface on the left has sufficiently densely packed points that you can easily make out the shape of the spot cast by the SpotLight. With the shape on the right, however, only four lighting calculations have been performed—one for each corner—and the results have been interpolated across the shape, so the result is just a gradual color fade to one corner. (If we point the spotlight directly in the middle of the surface on the right, it remains completely black, because none of the four points falls inside the spotlight's cone.)

Although you need a fairly dense mesh for detailed lighting effects to work, you might be able to achieve a similar effect using materials instead. Rather than using a spotlight to project a spot onto a surface, you could use an EmissiveMaterial in conjunction with a suitable brush texture. Texture mapping does not require a high point density to work correctly, as you're about to see.

Textures

Because DiffuseMaterial, SpecularMaterial, and EmissiveMaterial are based on brushes, we need not be limited to plain colors for our surfaces. We are free to paint 3D objects with gradient brushes, bitmaps, or drawings. We can even use any part of a user interface as a brush with which to paint a 3D object. An image or pattern used to paint a 3D surface is often referred to as a *texture*.

To use a textured material, we must tell WPF exactly how the brush should be positioned on the surface. With a solid color, this is a nonissue—the entire surface is of uniform color. But with a bitmap, we need to specify exactly where the image is projected onto the surface.

MeshGeometry3D provides the TextureCoordinates property for exactly this purpose. For each 3D point in the Positions, you can specify a 2D texture coordinate. Example 17-17 defines a simple square surface with four points, joined together with two triangles.

Example 17-17. MeshGeometry3D with TextureCoordinates

```
<MeshGeometry3D Positions="-1,1,0  1,1,0  -1,-1,0,  1,-1,0"
                Normals="0,0,1  0,0,1  0,0,1  0,0,1"
                TextureCoordinates="0,0  1,0  0,1  1,1"
                TriangleIndices="0,2,3  0,3,1" />
```

Figure 17-26 shows the texture coordinates specified for each corner of the square, and how the TriangleIndices collection joins these together with triangles. Texture coordinates are specified in the coordinate space of the brush's Viewport. As we saw in Chapter 13, by default tile brushes use a mapping mode of RelativeToBoundingBox, which means that their viewport ranges from 0,0 to 1,1. So, the texture coordinates in Example 17-17 tell the brush to fill the surface area completely.

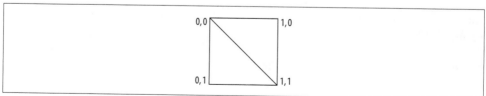

Figure 17-26. Texture coordinate positions

With the texture coordinates specified, we can now use any tile brush to form the material for this shape. Example 17-18 uses an ImageBrush to paint the surface with a bitmap.

Example 17-18. Painting a 3D surface with a bitmap

```
<GeometryModel3D>
  <GeometryModel3D.Geometry>
    <MeshGeometry3D Positions="-1,1,0  1,1,0  -1,-1,0, 1,-1,0"
                    Normals="0,0,1  0,0,1  0,0,1 0,0,1"
                    TextureCoordinates="0,0 1,0 0,1 1,1"
                    TriangleIndices="0,2,3 0,3,1" />
  </GeometryModel3D.Geometry>

  <GeometryModel3D.Material>
    <DiffuseMaterial>
      <DiffuseMaterial.Brush>
        <ImageBrush ImageSource="MyImage.jpg" />
      </DiffuseMaterial.Brush>
    </DiffuseMaterial>
  </GeometryModel3D.Material>
</GeometryModel3D>
```

Figure 17-27 shows the results.

 A common practice in 3D applications is to use a mixture of textures and bump mapping to enhance the realism of a surface. (*Bump maps* allow the basic shape defined by a mesh to be modulated in order to give a richer impression of texture.) However, although WPF supports textures, it does not currently support bump maps.

Figure 17-27. Material with ImageBrush

Alternatively, you could paint the surface with a video by using the Material in Example 17-19.

Example 17-19. Painting a surface with video

```
<DiffuseMaterial>
  <DiffuseMaterial.Brush>
    <VisualBrush>
      <VisualBrush.Visual>
        <MediaElement Source="MyVideo.wmv" />
```

Example 17-19. Painting a surface with video (continued)

```
      </VisualBrush.Visual>
    </VisualBrush>
  </DiffuseMaterial.Brush>
</DiffuseMaterial>
```

This example uses a `VisualBrush` to create a material based on a `MediaElement`. We can use the same brush type with any UI element. For example, we could map a whole 2D UI onto a 3D surface. Figure 17-28 shows an ordinary data entry UI mapped onto our simple square surface and viewed from an angle.

Figure 17-28. 2D UI mapped onto a 3D surface

Although this technique makes for nifty-looking demos, it has a fundamental limitation: you cannot click on any of the controls on the 3D surface. `VisualBrush` lets us paint 2D or 3D elements with the contents of a visual, but it only lets us create an image. It does not provide a built-in way to route mouse input aimed at the surface back to the original visual. The user interface in this example is strictly a "look but don't touch" affair.

 Although WPF does not provide any built-in means of routing user input back to the original visual, it is possible to make this happen with a little extra work. Microsoft has released a library of WPF 3D tools that include the necessary code. This library also contains other useful utilities such as a "trackball" that allow the user to rotate 3D models with a mouse. You can download the library (including source code) from *http://www.codeplex.com/3DTools* (*http://tinysells.com/76*).

Transforms

Just as you can apply a transform to any 2D element in WPF, you can also transform any `ModelVisual3D`, or any of the types derived from `Model3D`. The set of transforms is much the same—you can rotate, scale, shear, or translate any part of the 3D model. However, to effect these operations in three dimensions requires slightly more information than it does in two dimensions, so we cannot simply use the 2D transform classes in 3D. WPF therefore defines a set of 3D transform types, all of which derive from the abstract `Transform3D` class.

TranslateTransform3D

TranslateTransform3D changes the position of an object. It has three properties: OffsetX, OffsetY, and OffsetZ, indicating the distance to move in each direction.

Translation can provide a convenient means of reusing the same 3D shape many times over. Example 17-20 shows an example of this—it defines the scene that was shown in Figure 17-1, consisting of five identical cylinders in a row.

Example 17-20. Positioning models with TranslateTransform3D

```
<ModelVisual3D Content="{StaticResource cylinderModel}">
  <ModelVisual3D.Transform>
    <TranslateTransform3D OffsetX="-1" OffsetZ="0" />
  </ModelVisual3D.Transform>
</ModelVisual3D>
<ModelVisual3D Content="{StaticResource cylinderModel}">
  <ModelVisual3D.Transform>
    <TranslateTransform3D OffsetX="-0.5" OffsetZ="-0.5" />
  </ModelVisual3D.Transform>
</ModelVisual3D>
<ModelVisual3D Content="{StaticResource cylinderModel}">
  <ModelVisual3D.Transform>
    <TranslateTransform3D OffsetX="0" OffsetZ="-1" />
  </ModelVisual3D.Transform>
</ModelVisual3D>
<ModelVisual3D Content="{StaticResource cylinderModel}">
  <ModelVisual3D.Transform>
    <TranslateTransform3D OffsetX="0.5" OffsetZ="-1.5" />
  </ModelVisual3D.Transform>
</ModelVisual3D>
<ModelVisual3D Content="{StaticResource cylinderModel}">
  <ModelVisual3D.Transform>
    <TranslateTransform3D OffsetX="1" OffsetZ="-2" />
  </ModelVisual3D.Transform>
</ModelVisual3D>
```

In this example, the cylinder model has been defined just once as a resource. The resource is not shown here, because the mesh defining the shape is about 100 KB of XAML. (The model is this big because it uses a large number of small triangles to approximate the cylinder's curved surface.) With a model this large, it's obviously preferable to use one copy five times over than to create separate models for each of the five positions. By using a TranslateTransform3D, we can place multiple instances of the same model into the scene in different locations.

ScaleTransform3D

A ScaleTransform3D enlarges or reduces an object. The scale factors are specified independently for each dimension with the ScaleX, ScaleY, and ScaleZ properties.

There are also three properties to specify the center of scaling: CenterX, CenterY, and CenterZ. (The center of scaling is the point that remains in the same place before and after the scale operation.)

Example 17-21 uses a ScaleTransform3D to display a model stretched to double its normal width and depth, and one-quarter its normal height. This will use the default scale center of 0,0,0.

Example 17-21. ScaleTransform3D

```
<ModelVisual3D Content="{StaticResource cylinderModel}">
  <ModelVisual3D.Transform>
    <ScaleTransform3D ScaleX="2" ScaleY="0.25" ScaleZ="2" />
  </ModelVisual3D.Transform>
</ModelVisual3D>
```

Figure 17-29 shows the results. This is the same cylinder model as used for Figure 17-1, but the scaling has made it look shorter and squatter.

Figure 17-29. ScaleTransform3D

RotateTransform3D

RotateTransform3D allows objects to be rotated. Two pieces of information are required: the angle of rotation and the axis around which to rotate. Example 17-22 rotates a model by 45 degrees around the x-axis. WPF follows the usual mathematical convention that a positive angle indicates a counterclockwise rotation.

Example 17-22. Rotation around the x-axis

```
<ModelVisual3D Content="{StaticResource cylinderModel}">
  <ModelVisual3D.Transform>
    <RotateTransform3D>
      <RotateTransform3D.Rotation>
        <AxisAngleRotation3D Axis="1,0,0" Angle="45" />
      </RotateTransform3D.Rotation>
    </RotateTransform3D>
  </ModelVisual3D.Transform>
</ModelVisual3D>
```

Figure 17-30 shows the original unrotated model on the left. In the center is the model as rotated by Example 17-22. The righthand side shows how the model would look if rotated around the z-axis (i.e., if the Axis property had been set to 0,0,1). Rotation around the y-axis is not shown, because this particular model has rotational symmetry about that axis, so there would be no visible difference. (If the object had a bitmap texture material instead of a plain color, such a rotation would have a visible effect.)

Figure 17-30. 2D Rotation

Many 3D graphics systems use *quaternions* to represent rotations. A quaternion is a number with four components, and there are some standard rules for how to perform mathematical operations on quaternions. There is also a widely adopted system for encoding a 3D rotation into a quaternion.[*] Example 17-23 shows how to apply a rotation expressed as a quaternion. This particular quaternion happens to correspond to a rotation of 120 degrees around the axis –1,1,1.

Example 17-23. QuaternionRotation

```
<RotateTransform3D>
  <RotateTransform3D.Rotation>
    <QuaternionRotation3D Quaternion="-0.5,0.5,0.5,0.5" />
  </RotateTransform3D.Rotation>
</RotateTransform3D>
```

The relationship between the numbers in a quaternion and the resultant rotation is somewhat opaque compared to the AxisAngleRotation3D representation. However, there are two useful characteristics of quaternions that explain their ubiquity in 3D graphics systems. First, it is easy to concatenate multiple rotations—you can simply multiply two quaternions together, and the result is a quaternion that represents the combined rotations. Second, there is a fairly straightforward way of interpolating between two quaternions that guarantees to offer the shortest transition between any two rotations. Without quaternions, this is not always straightforward if the two rotations are around different axes.

RotateTransform3D therefore accepts for the Rotation property either an AxisAngleRotation3D or a QuaternianRotation3D. WPF defines a Quaternion structure to represent a quaternion. This supports interpolation between two quaternions with its Slerp method. (*Slerp* is short for Spherical Linear intERPolation.) The QuaternionAnimation class also uses this interpolation method to animate between two rotations.

---

[*] The details are beyond the scope of this chapter, but there is an excellent explanation of quaternions and how they are used in 3D graphics at *http://www.sjbrown.co.uk/?article=quaternions* (*http://tinysells.com/77*).

Transform3DGroup

It is sometimes useful to combine a sequence of transformations. For example, you might wish to translate and rotate a model. The Transform3DGroup makes this simple—it can combine any number of individual transforms. Example 17-24 concatenates a scale transform and a translation.

Example 17-24. Transform3DGroup

```
<Transform3DGroup>
  <ScaleTransform3D ScaleX="2" ScaleY="2" />
  <TranslateTransform3D OffsetX="1" OffsetZ="-2" />
</Transform3DGroup>
```

The order in which you specify transforms is significant. If we moved the TranslateTransform3D before the ScaleTransform3D, the scale would then have the effect of scaling up the translation as well as enlarging the objects in the scene. In general, if you need to combine all three of the previous transform types into a group, the easiest order is scale, rotate, translate—this produces the results most people intuitively expect.

MatrixTransform3D

All of the transforms discussed so far are provided mainly for convenience. There is a single type of transform capable of representing any of these transforms, including transform groups: the MatrixTransform3D. This uses a Matrix3D to encode the transformation.

A Matrix3D is a set of 16 numbers, arranged into four columns. The mathematics behind matrices is beyond the scope of this book, but it is sufficient to know that each basic transform type can be represented in such a matrix, and that transforms can be combined into a single matrix by multiplying together the matrices for the individual transforms. To apply the transformation to a point, you simply multiply the point by the matrix. Matrices are very widely used in graphical systems.

Example 17-25 shows a MatrixTransform3D that reverses an object in the x direction. This is equivalent to a ScaleTransform3D with ScaleX set to −1, and with ScaleY and ScaleZ set to 1.

Example 17-25. MatrixTransform3D

```
<MatrixTransform3D Matrix="-1,0,0,0
                    0,1,0,0
                    0,0,1,0
                    0,0,0,1" />
```

Strange though it may seem to have a 4×4 matrix to represent three-dimensional operations, this is normal practice in 3D graphics. The fourth dimension is a kind of hack, and it is used for two purposes. The first three columns of the fourth row encode offsets; this is how translations are performed—you cannot perform 3D translations with a 3×3 matrix. The fourth column would normally be left as three zeros and a 1 because this column is reserved for perspective operations. The one place you'd normally put other numbers in here is in the ProjectionMatrix of a MatrixCamera. However, if you want to play eye-bending tricks with perspective, you can put other numbers in there for any MatrixTransform3D.

3D Data Visualization

You can represent some kinds of data as a three-dimensional graph. For example, certain mathematical functions can be visualized this way. So can some sets of physical measurements (e.g., height information from map data). Figure 17-31 shows an example.

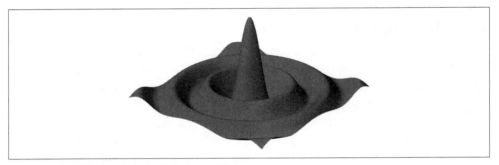

Figure 17-31. 3D plot of data (Color Plate 2)

To display data in this form, you need to write code that will generate a mesh from the data. Let's look at an example that creates the MeshGeometry3D shown in Figure 17-31 from a two-dimensional array of floating-point numbers. To be able to display a 3D model, we will of course need a Viewport3D. Example 17-26 shows the XAML for a window containing a Viewport3D with a camera and some light sources.

Example 17-26. XAML to host 3D model

```
<Window x:Class="Generate3DMesh.Window1"
    xmlns="http://schemas.microsoft.com/winfx/2006/xaml/presentation"
    xmlns:x="http://schemas.microsoft.com/winfx/2006/xaml"
    Title="Generate3DMesh" Height="400" Width="400">

    <Grid x:Name="mainGrid">
      <Viewport3D x:Name="vp">
        <Viewport3D.Camera>
```

Example 17-26. XAML to host 3D model (continued)

```xaml
          <PerspectiveCamera Position="5,4,6" LookDirection="-5,-3.75,-6"
                             UpDirection="0,1,0" FieldOfView="10" />
        </Viewport3D.Camera>

        <ModelVisual3D>
          <ModelVisual3D.Content>
            <Model3DGroup>
              <AmbientLight Color="#222" />
              <DirectionalLight Color="#aaa" Direction="-1,-1,-1" />
              <DirectionalLight Color="#aaa" Direction="1,-1,-1" />
            </Model3DGroup>
          </ModelVisual3D.Content>

          <ModelVisual3D x:Name="modelHost" />

        </ModelVisual3D>
      </Viewport3D>
    </Grid>
</Window>
```

Notice that this example contains an empty `ModelVisual3D` element named `modelHost`.
This is where we will add the 3D model that we build to represent the graph.
Example 17-27 shows how the code-behind file initializes the window: it builds the
data for the graph, builds a 3D model from the data, and then adds that model to
the `modelHost` placeholder.

Example 17-27. Adding a generated model to the view

```csharp
public partial class Window1 : Window {

    public Window1() {
        InitializeComponent();

        double[,] points = GraphDataBuilder.BuildSincFunction(100, 100, 2.5, 5);
        ModelVisual3D vis3D = BuildModelVisual3DFromPoints(points);
        modelHost.Children.Add(vis3D);
    }
    ...
}
```

Example 17-28 shows the function that generates the data. It contains no 3D-specific
code—it just builds a suitable two-dimensional array, using the mathematical *sinc*
function, a popular function in signal processing applications that also happens to
look good in 3D graphs. (.NET doesn't provide a built-in implementation of *sinc*, so
this code provides its own. The *sinc* function is defined to be $sin(x)/x$, except for when
x is 0, where it is defined to be 1.)

Example 17-28. Generating data for the graph

```
class GraphDataBuilder {
    public static double[,] BuildSincFunction(int xPoints, int yPoints,
                                              double cycles, double height) {
        double[,] points = new double[xPoints, yPoints];
        for (int yIndex = 0; yIndex < yPoints; ++yIndex) {
            double y = yIndex; y /= ((yPoints - 1) / 2.0); y -= 1;
            for (int xIndex = 0; xIndex < xPoints; ++xIndex) {
                double x = xIndex; x /= ((xPoints - 1) / 2.0); x -= 1;

                double d = Math.Sqrt(x * x + y * y) * 2 * Math.PI * cycles;
                points[xIndex, yIndex] = (d == 0 ? 1 : Math.Sin(d) / d) * height;
            }
        }
        return points;
    }
}
```

After calling this `BuildSincFunction` method to generate the data, Example 17-27 calls the `BuildModelVisual3DFromPoints` method shown in Example 17-29 to convert this into a `ModelVisual3D`.

Example 17-29. Creating the ModelVisual3D

```
public partial class Window1 : Window {
    ...
    static ModelVisual3D BuildModelVisual3DFromPoints(double[,] points) {
        MeshGeometry3D mesh = MeshBuilder.BuildMeshFromPoints(points, 1, 1);
        GeometryModel3D model = BuildModel3DFromMesh(mesh);
        ModelVisual3D vis3D = new ModelVisual3D();
        vis3D.Content = model;
        return vis3D;
    }
```

The structure of this method reflects the structure of elements we need to create in order to build a complete 3D model. We need a mesh to represent the shape of the surface. This must be connected to a `GeometryModel3D` in order to define the materials for the surface. This model is then wrapped in a `ModelVisual3D`, allowing the `InitializeComponent` method in Example 17-27 to add it to the 3D visual tree.

Example 17-29 calls a helper method to build the mesh: `BuildMeshFromPoints`. This is shown in Example 17-30.

Example 17-30. Creating a mesh: Initialization

```
class MeshBuilder {
    public static MeshGeometry3D BuildMeshFromPoints(double[,] data,
                    double textureWidth, double textureHeight) {
        Point3DCollection points;
        PointCollection textureCoordinates;
        Int32Collection triangleIndices;
        BuildMeshData(data, textureWidth, textureHeight,
                out points, out textureCoordinates, out triangleIndices);
```

Example 17-30. Creating a mesh: Initialization (continued)

```
            points.Freeze( );
            textureCoordinates.Freeze( );
            triangleIndices.Freeze( );

            MeshGeometry3D mesh = new MeshGeometry3D( );
            mesh.Positions = points;
            mesh.TextureCoordinates = textureCoordinates;
            mesh.TriangleIndices = triangleIndices;

            return mesh;
        }
        ...
}
```

This assembles the constituent parts of a `MeshGeometry3D`—the points and triangle indices defining the surface shape, and the texture coordinates that define how a texture is mapped onto the surface. Notice that this code freezes the collections containing the data. Calling `Freeze` tells WPF that we will not be changing any of these collections again. This enables it to handle the data more efficiently—it doesn't need to do any of the housekeeping that would be necessary to be able to respond to changes to the data.

`BuildMeshData`, another helper function, shown in Example 17-31, performs all of the work of generating the mesh data.

Example 17-31. Building the mesh data

```
class MeshBuilder {
    ...

    static void BuildMeshData(double[,] data,
                       double textureWidth, double textureHeight,
                       out Point3DCollection points,
                       out PointCollection textureCoordinates,
                       out Int32Collection triangleIndices) {

        // 1: initialization
        int width = data.GetLength(0);
        int height = data.GetLength(1);

        int pointCount = width * height;
        points = new Point3DCollection(pointCount);
        textureCoordinates = new PointCollection(pointCount);

        int triangleCount = 2 * (width - 1) * (height - 1);
        triangleIndices = new Int32Collection(3 * triangleCount);

        // 2: iteration
        for (int yDataIndex = 0; yDataIndex < height; ++yDataIndex) {
            double yProportion = yDataIndex; yProportion /= (height - 1);
```

Example 17-31. Building the mesh data (continued)

```
                // Adding points from top to bottom.
                // In 3D up means increasing Y, but in
                // 2D 0 is at the top.
                double outY = 0.5 - yProportion;
                double textureY = textureHeight * yProportion;

                for (int xDataIndex = 0; xDataIndex < width; ++xDataIndex) {
                    double xProportion = xDataIndex; xProportion /= (width - 1);
                    double outX = xProportion - 0.5;
                    double textureX = textureWidth * xProportion;


                    // 3: adding points
                    points.Add(new Point3D(outX, outY, data[xDataIndex, yDataIndex]));
                    textureCoordinates.Add(new Point(textureX, textureY));


                    // Add triangles for everything but the last row and column.
                    if (xDataIndex < (width - 1) && yDataIndex < (height - 1)) {
                        int topLeftIndex = xDataIndex + yDataIndex * width;
                        int bottomLeftIndex = topLeftIndex + width;

                        triangleIndices.Add(bottomLeftIndex);
                        triangleIndices.Add(bottomLeftIndex + 1);
                        triangleIndices.Add(topLeftIndex);

                        triangleIndices.Add(bottomLeftIndex + 1);
                        triangleIndices.Add(topLeftIndex + 1);
                        triangleIndices.Add(topLeftIndex);
                    }
                }
            }
        }
    }
}
```

The function begins by working out how many points and triangles will be required in the mesh to present all the data in the array. It also allocates the various collections to hold the mesh data.

The code tells each collection how many items will be created through the constructor parameter. This enables the collection to allocate exactly enough space upfront. We don't have to do this—the collections can automatically allocate space on demand. But without preallocation, the collections will initially allocate a fairly small amount of space, and will then reallocate as we populate the collections, possibly causing several reallocations. That would make unnecessary work, both for the collection class and for the garbage collector. And because 3D work can involve large quantities of data, efficiency is often particularly important. So, you should usually tell the collections in advance how many items you intend to provide.

Next, we start the nested loops that will iterate over the point data in the two-dimensional input array—we do this with the two `for` loops in the part of Example 17-31 labeled "2: iteration."

The xProportion and yProportion variables track how far we are through the data, expressed as a number from 0 to 1. We then calculate two coordinates. The outX and outY coordinates are in 3D space, and will range over a unit square centered on the origin. The textureX and textureY coordinates will be used to generate the TextureCoordinates entries, and will range over the texture size passed into the function. Note that these coordinate systems use different conventions. The 3D coordinates use the common convention that increasing values of y mean "up," but the texture coordinates use the TileBrush convention that increasing y values mean "down."

Finally, the inner part of the loop adds the points—this is the part of Example 17-31 labeled "3: add points." It creates both a 3D point for the mesh's Positions collection, and the corresponding 2D point for the TextureCoordinates collection. The latter enables us to use a textured material to paint the mesh, should we wish to.

The inner loop also generates the triangles that join the points to form the surface by adding entries to the triangleIndices collection. (We skip this for the final row and column of points, because those will already have been joined to triangles from the previous line and column.)

 We have not defined any surface normals. This is OK, because WPF will build them for us based on the shape of the surface described by the positions.

Our work is nearly done. The mesh data returned by BuildMeshData will be wrapped in a MeshGeometry3D by BuildMeshFromPoints. As we saw in Example 17-29, our BuildModelVisual3DFromPoints helper will then wrap this in a GeometryModel3D by calling another helper, BuildModel3DFromMesh, shown in Example 17-32.

Example 17-32. Creating a GeometryModel3D

```
public partial class Window1 : Window {
    ...
    private static GeometryModel3D BuildModel3DFromMesh(MeshGeometry3D mesh) {
        Material front = new DiffuseMaterial(Brushes.Red);
        GeometryModel3D model = new GeometryModel3D(mesh, front);
        model.BackMaterial = new DiffuseMaterial(Brushes.Green);
        return model;
    }
}
```

This adds red and green materials for the front and back of the surface. As we saw in Example 17-29, this will then be wrapped in a ModelVisual3D by the BuildModelVisual3DFromPoints helper function. And, as Example 17-27 showed, this is added to the modelHost placeholder defined in the XAML shown in Example 17-26, enabling our generated model to be displayed by the Viewport3D.

Hit Testing

The normal WPF mouse events and properties work when the mouse is over a Viewport3D just like they do for any other UI element. The shapes of the elements in the model will be taken into account—if your scene has areas with nothing in it, the Viewport3D will effectively be transparent in those areas, and if you move the mouse over those, it will be considered to be over whatever is behind the Viewport3D rather than over the Viewport3D itself. But as long as the mouse is over some 3D object, all the usual mouse events will be reported.

 You can disable hit testing by setting IsHitTestVisible to false on the Viewport3D. This is recommended for very complex 3D models if hit testing is not required, as 3D hit testing can be expensive.

Sometimes it is useful to know exactly which part of your 3D model the mouse is over. For example, in an application that displays the graph shown in Figure 17-31, you might want to display the exact coordinates and value for the point currently under the mouse. You can call the VisualTreeHelper.HitTest method to retrieve all the necessary information. You can pass in a 2D position relative to the Viewport3D (e.g., the current mouse location), as Example 17-33 shows.

Example 17-33. Hit testing with a 2D starting point

```
public partial class Window1 : Window {
    ...
    void myViewport_MouseMove(object sender, MouseEventArgs e) {
        Point mousePos = e.GetPosition(vp);
        PointHitTestParameters hitParams = new PointHitTestParameters(mousePos);
        VisualTreeHelper.HitTest(vp, null, delegate (HitTestResult hr) {
            RayMeshGeometry3DHitTestResult rayHit = hr as
                    RayMeshGeometry3DHitTestResult;
            if (rayHit != null) {
                Debug.WriteLine(rayHit.PointHit);
            }
            return HitTestResultBehavior.Continue;
        }, hitParams);
    }
}
```

This shows an event handler for the MouseMove event of a Viewport3D. It uses the VisualTreeHelper class's HitTest method in exactly the same way as you would for 2D hit testing. HitTest calls a callback method (the anonymous method in this example) for each item it finds at the specified position, and if one of the items is part of a 3D model, it will pass a RayMeshGeometry3DHitTestResult object as the parameter. This provides information about the item that was hit.

This particular example just prints the 3D location to the debugger by printing out the PointHit property. The result object also contains information about which Visual3D contained the model, and which Model3D and mesh were hit. It even tells you which triangle in the mesh was hit, and the position within that triangle. In the graph example, you can use this information to calculate the corresponding coordinates in the original graph data. Example 17-34 illustrates how to modify Example 17-33 to use this technique.

Example 17-34. Extracting hit test details

```
void myViewport_MouseMove(object sender, MouseEventArgs e) {
    Point mousePos = e.GetPosition(vp);
    PointHitTestParameters hitParams = new PointHitTestParameters(mousePos);
    VisualTreeHelper.HitTest(vp, null, delegate (HitTestResult hr) {
        RayMeshGeometry3DHitTestResult rayHit = hr as
                RayMeshGeometry3DHitTestResult;
        if (rayHit != null) {
            MeshGeometry3D mesh = rayHit.MeshHit as MeshGeometry3D;
            if (mesh != null) {
                int pointsWidth = points.GetLength(0);
                int y = rayHit.VertexIndex1 / pointsWidth;
                int x = rayHit.VertexIndex1 - (y * pointsWidth);

                Debug.WriteLine(string.Format("Point: {0},{1} value = {2}",
                    x, y, points[x, y]));
            }
        }
        return HitTestResultBehavior.Continue;
    }, hitParams);
}
```

This uses the RayMeshGeometry3DHitTestResult object's VertexIndex1 property to discover which point in the mesh has been hit. It then works out which of the entries in the points array created in Example 17-31 this corresponds to.

The mouse will rarely be exactly over a vertex—it will usually be somewhere within the area of one of the mesh's triangles. In this example, we don't care about this because we're just trying to correlate the mouse position back to one of the original data points, so we don't need to know the exact location within the triangle. However, sometimes extra precision is necessary.

To enable you to work out the exact 3D position of the mouse, RayMeshGeometry3DHitTestResult provides a property for each corner of the triangle the mouse was over: VertexIndex1, VertexIndex2, and VertexIndex3. The relative position of the mouse within the triangle is indicated by the VertexWeight1, VertexWeight2, and VertexWeight3 properties. To calculate the exact position, you would calculate the sum of the three vertex positions, multiplied by the three weight properties, as shown in Example 17-35.

Example 17-35. Calculating the exact hit position

```
Point3D pointInMesh1 = mesh.Positions[rayHit.VertexIndex1];
Point3D pointInMesh2 = mesh.Positions[rayHit.VertexIndex2];
Point3D pointInMesh3 = mesh.Positions[rayHit.VertexIndex3];
double x = pointInMesh1.X * rayHit.VertexWeight1 +
           pointInMesh2.X * rayHit.VertexWeight2 +
           pointInMesh3.X * rayHit.VertexWeight3;
double y = pointInMesh1.Y * rayHit.VertexWeight1 +
           pointInMesh2.Y * rayHit.VertexWeight2 +
           pointInMesh3.Y * rayHit.VertexWeight3;
double z = pointInMesh1.Z * rayHit.VertexWeight1 +
           pointInMesh2.Z * rayHit.VertexWeight2 +
           pointInMesh3.Z * rayHit.VertexWeight3;

Point3D exactLocation = new Point3D(x, y, z);
```

Where Are We?

The Viewport3D class allows you to add simple 3D models your user interface. The scene is built up with shapes defined by mesh geometries. These might be imported from a 3D modeling program, or generated at runtime from data. The appearance of the shapes is described by materials—combinations of 2D brushes and various lighting models. Because you can use any 2D brush, you can paint 3D surfaces with bitmaps, drawings, videos, or even a visual copy of a user interface. Finally, hit testing services enable you to find out with which part of a 3D model the user is interacting.

CHAPTER 18

Custom Controls

One of the benefits of WPF is that you don't need to write custom controls as often as you would have to in many user interface frameworks. If you need to customize the appearance of an existing control or adjust its superficial interactive behavior, WPF provides various tools that can let you do this. In earlier chapters, we saw features such as composability, content models, styling, templates, animation, and integrated graphics support. These let you customize existing controls extensively without having to write a new control type.

Custom controls still have a place, of course. As we saw in Chapter 5, the role of a control is to define essential behavior. For example, although you can customize and animate the visuals of a button to your heart's content, it still retains its essence—it is just something clickable. If the behavior you require is not provided by any existing controls, and you cannot create it by bolting a few controls together, you will need to write a custom control.

If you want your control to be reusable, you will want it to have the same kind of flexibility that the built-in controls offer, such as support for rich content, styling, and templates. In this chapter, we will see how to make your custom controls take advantage of the same powerful flexibility as the built-in controls.

Custom Control Basics

Before you write a custom control, the first question you should ask is:

Do I really need a custom control?

One of the main reasons for writing custom controls in older user interface technologies is to modify the appearance of a control, but as we've seen in earlier chapters, content models and templates mean this is often unnecessary. WPF offers a progressive scale of customization techniques that you should bear in mind when considering writing a custom control:

1. Use properties to modify the appearance or behavior of an existing control.

2. Compose existing controls.

3. Nest content in an existing control.

4. Replace the template of an existing control.

5. Create a custom control or other custom element.

This sequence offers increasing levels of power in exchange for slightly more effort at each step. Only if 1–4 don't meet your needs is writing some kind of custom element such as a custom control likely to be the answer.

An important indicator of whether you need to write a new control (or some other custom visual element type) is whether you plan to add new API features. Even in this case, you should consider carefully what type of custom element to write—controls are not the only kind of element. You might get more flexibility by writing a lower-level element that you can integrate into the visuals of an existing control. For example, a lot of the elements that make WPF so flexible, such as layout classes and shapes, derive from FrameworkElement, but are not in fact controls (i.e., they do not derive from the Control base class).

If you are certain that a custom element is the best way to proceed, you will need to work through a number of design steps. First, you must pick the base class—will it derive from FrameworkElement, Control, or one of the other base types provided by WPF? Then you must define the API, deciding what properties, events, and commands your class will provide. Finally, if your new element is to provide the same flexibility that built-in classes offer, you will need to pay careful attention to the interface between the element and its template.

Choosing a Base Class

WPF provides many classes from which you can derive when creating custom elements. Figure 18-1 shows a set of classes that are most likely to be suitable base classes, and illustrates the inheritance relationship between them. Note that this is by no means a complete inheritance diagram—it simply shows the classes you should consider as possible base classes.

Whichever base class you choose, your element will derive directly or indirectly from FrameworkElement. This offers event routing, advanced property handling, animation, data binding, layout support, styling, and logical tree integration.

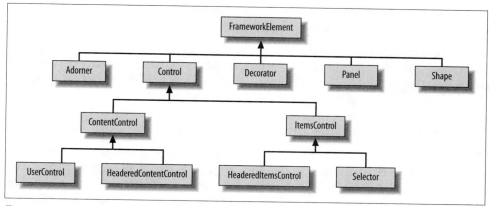

Figure 18-1. Partial class hierarchy, showing candidate base classes for custom elements

It is not an absolute requirement to derive from FrameworkElement. Chapter 13 discussed the low-level *visual layer* graphics API, and although the example in that chapter derived from FrameworkElement, you can derive directly from UIElement when using the low-level drawing API. However, you would lose all of the services FrameworkElement offers. The main reason UIElement exists is that Microsoft wanted to make it possible to use WPF's low-level rendering services without being obliged to use the whole WPF framework. In practice, you would not normally do this.

Deriving directly from FrameworkElement might be appropriate for an element designed to be composed into other elements. For example, consider an element that binds to a data source and renders the data as a graph. You might be tempted to make this derive from Control. However, the raw graph drawing element would usually be used in conjunction with other elements such as TextBlock to provide labels for the graph and its axes. It might therefore make more sense to separate the graph drawing into a low-level element, which could then be incorporated into the visuals of any number of different controls.

It is possible to use controls inside the template of other controls. But if you find yourself writing a custom control purely to be used in the template of another custom control, you probably need to review your choice of base class.

If you are writing an element that performs custom layout logic, you should derive from Panel to be consistent with the built-in layout elements.

If you are writing an element that wraps around another element, augmenting it in some way, consider deriving from Decorator. Many built-in elements derive from Decorator. For example, there is Border, which adds a border around an element. There is also ViewBox, which automatically scales the element that it wraps to fill the available space. If you wish to provide some kind of wrapper that adds functionality around other content, consider deriving from Decorator.

The Adorner base class is designed for elements such as selection outlines and drag handles. WPF renders adorners so that they appear on top of all other elements. For example, if a selected shape in a drawing program were mostly obscured by other shapes on top of it, its selection outline would still be visible if rendered as an adorner. The "Adorners" section, later in this chapter, describes how to write an adorner.

Shape is the base class of elements such as Rectangle and Path. If your application makes heavy use of some shape that can be represented with a PathGeometry, you can derive your own shape class instead of having to use the Path type every time. For example, if you wanted lots of stars in your application, you could derive a Star class from Shape. When writing your own shape, you generate the appearance by overriding the DefiningGeometry property. The base Shape class's OnRender will render the Geometry you provide, and will automatically handle the Stretch property for you by applying a transform. If you want to handle how your object changes shape when stretched—the default behavior might distort the shape in an unacceptable way—you can take complete control by overriding the OnRender method, as shown in Chapter 13.

If your element provides behavior, or supports user interactions not available from built-in components, it is appropriate to derive from Control, either directly or indirectly. For example, if you want to make an interactive graphing component, where the user can click on items in the graph to inspect them, or zoom around, you would typically write this as a control (and its template might use the lower-level graph rendering element you wrote earlier).

Control offers several derived classes, augmenting the basic control functionality. If you are writing a control that provides a space in which the user can place some content (e.g., a caption), you should derive from ContentControl—this provides your control with support for the content model. If your control supports content in both a header caption and the main area (like a tab page), consider deriving from HeaderedContentControl.

If you need to present multiple child items, first consider whether the combination of ListBox, data binding, templates, and styles will meet your requirements. Data binding and styling enable WPF's list controls such as ListBox and TreeView to handle a wide range of scenarios for which their Win32 and Windows Forms forebears are unsuited.

If you need extra functionality not provided by the built-in list controls, you should consider deriving your custom element type from either Selector or its base class, ItemsControl. ItemsControl provides the basic support for controls containing lists of items, including optional data binding functionality. Selector augments this with the ability to track a currently selected item or set of items.

Custom Functionality

Once you have picked a base class, you will need to devise an API for your control. WPF elements usually expose the majority of their functionality through properties, events, and commands, because these get extensive support from the framework and are easily used from XAML. WPF can provide automatic support for routing of events and commands, and its *dependency property* system provides support for many framework features such as data binding, styling, triggers, and animation. You can, of course, write methods as well, and for certain kinds of functionality, methods are the best approach. (For example, the ListBox has a ScrollIntoView method that ensures that a particular item is visible. This is a useful thing to be able to do from code.) But, you should prefer properties, events, and commands where they are a reasonable fit.

Properties

The .NET type system provides a standard way of defining properties for an object. It prescribes a convention for supplying get and set accessor methods, but the implementation of these, and the way in which the property value is stored, is left up to the developer.[*] In WPF, elements normally use the *dependency property* system. .NET-style property accessors are typically provided, but these are just wrappers around dependency properties (DPs), added for convenience.

The get and set accessors required to wrap the DP system are trivial—just a single method call for each, as you'll see shortly. In exchange for this minimal amount of code, the DP system adds a number of features that standard .NET properties do not normally offer. For example, a DP can *inherit* its value from a parent element. Confusingly, this is different from the classic OO meaning of inheritance, where a derived class inherits features from its base class (although DPs also support inheritance in that sense). Property value inheritance is a more dynamic feature, allowing a property to be set on a single element and automatically propagate to all of its children. For example, all elements have a Cursor property to control the mouse cursor. This property uses value inheritance, meaning that if you set the Cursor on an element, all of the child elements will automatically get the same Cursor property value.

---

[*] Some languages, including VB.NET and C++/CLI, provide a default implementation of properties. This consists simply of a field wrapped by get and set accessors.

(You will be familiar with this idea if you've used Windows Forms, in which *ambient properties* offer the same feature.)

Besides supporting inheritance, DPs can also pick up their values automatically from elsewhere, such as data binding expressions, triggers, or styles. The animation system also relies on DPs—it uses the DP infrastructure to adjust property values over time. They also provide a mechanism for defining a default value. That's a lot of functionality in exchange for a tiny amount of code.

By implementing your element's properties as DPs, not only do you get all of these features automatically, but also the DP system manages the storage of the value for you—you do not need to define any instance fields to hold property values.

Storage management may seem like a small thing—after all, how hard is it to add a field to a class? However, this feature can offer surprisingly significant memory savings.

Simply by inheriting from Control, your element will support more than 80 properties (plus any attached properties) of varying complexity, most of which are likely to be left at their default values on most objects. If each element had its own set of fields to hold these values, this would take hundreds of bytes per element. A complex user interface may have hundreds or even thousands of elements. (Even if the logical tree is not that complex, the visual tree can multiply the number of elements greatly.)

If most of the properties on these many elements are either inheriting values from their parents or are set to their default values, using per-element fields to hold these values could waste hundreds of kilobytes of memory. DPs use a more sophisticated storage approach that exploits the fact that most properties are left unset. And although memory is cheap, moving data into and out of the CPU is expensive. The CPU can execute code far faster than it can fetch data from main memory. Only cache memory is fast enough to keep up with the processor, and most modern processors typically have only a few hundred kilobytes of cache. Even high-end systems have only a few megabytes of cache. Saving a few hundred kilobytes can therefore sometimes improve performance dramatically.

By deferring to the DP system, we can let it handle the information more efficiently by storing just the property values that have been set explicitly.

Finally, the DP system tracks changes to values. This means that if any interested party wants to know when a property value changes, it can register for notifications with the DP system. (Data binding relies on this.) We do not need to write any special code to make this happen—the DP system manages storage of our property values, so it knows whenever a property changes.

Any custom WPF element you create will automatically have everything it requires to support DPs, because FrameworkElement derives indirectly from the DependencyObject base class. To define a new property on our custom element, we must create a new DependencyProperty object in the element's static constructor. This object acts as an identifier for the property—all the DPs of built-in controls have a corresponding DependencyProperty object. By convention, this property object is stored in a public static field of our class, and the field's name is formed by adding *Property* to the end of the property's name (see Example 18-1).

Example 18-1. Defining a dependency property

```
public class MyCustomControl : ContentControl {

    public static readonly DependencyProperty StripeBrushProperty;

    static MyCustomControl( ) {
        PropertyMetadata stripeBrushMetadata =
            new PropertyMetadata(Brushes.Green); // default value
        StripeBrushProperty = DependencyProperty.Register("StripeBrush",
            typeof(Brush), typeof(MyCustomControl), stripeBrushMetadata);
    }

    public Brush StripeBrush {
        get { return (Brush) GetValue(StripeBrushProperty); }
        set { SetValue(StripeBrushProperty, value); }
    }
}
```

This custom control defines a single DP called StripeBrush, of type Brush with a default color of green. The control's template could use this to determine the color of a stripe drawn as part of its appearance, using a TemplateBinding as described in Chapter 9. It is common to define properties whose only purpose is to provide TemplateBinding sources. Many common properties of built-in controls, such as Foreground and Background, have no intrinsic behavior of their own—they just provide a place for users of the control to set information that will be relayed to the control's template. For such properties, it is common for the control class itself to do nothing with the property other than defining it. So, although Example 18-1 is a pretty minimal implementation, it is entirely sufficient for its purpose.

It is often useful to define a default value for a property. The control in Example 18-1 specifies a default value of Brushes.Green by passing in a PropertyMetadata object when registering the StripeBrush property.

 You might wonder why WPF invents these new DependencyProperty and PropertyMetadata types to represent properties and associated metadata when the Reflection API already provides the PropertyInfo class, and an extension mechanism in the form of custom attributes. Unfortunately, the Reflection API was unable to provide the combination of flexibility and performance WPF requires, which is why there is some overlap between the DP metadata system and reflection.

Example 18-1 also defines normal .NET get and set property accessors. These are not strictly necessary—you could access the properties using the public GetValue and SetValue methods inherited from DependencyObject like so:

```
myControl.SetValue(MyCustomControl.StripeBrushProperty, Brushes.Red);
```

However, in most .NET languages it is easier to use a normal CLR property, and more important, the XAML compiler will complain if you use a DP that has no corresponding CLR property, so you would normally provide a property wrapper as Example 18-1 does. As you can see, the accessors simply defer to the GetValue and SetValue methods inherited from the DependencyObject base class.

 The Visual Studio Extensions for .NET 3.0 define a code snippet to help write dependency properties. Put the caret inside the class to which you would like to add a DP. Type **propdp** and then press the Tab key. (If the IntelliSense pop up is open, you'll need to press Tab twice—once to get rid of the pop up and once to expand the snippet.) This will insert code very similar to Example 18-1.

Example 18-2 shows how to use this custom property from XAML. (This assumes that the namespace containing this control has been associated with the XML namespace prefix local. See Appendix A for more information on the relationship between .NET namespaces and XML namespaces.)

Example 18-2. Using properties from XAML

```
<local:MyCustomControl StripeBrush="Blue" />
```

Because our property's type is Brush, we can use the same text format for representing brushes as we saw in Chapter 13. Example 18-2 exploits this to create a brush based on a named color, but you could also use one of the numerical formats, such as #0000FF.

Attached properties

If you wish to define an *attached property*—one that you can apply to elements other than the defining element—you register it with a different call: RegisterAttached. As Example 18-3 shows, this is called in much the same way as the normal Register method.

Example 18-3. Registering attached properties

```
public class ElementWithAttachedProp : Panel {

    public static readonly DependencyProperty IsSkewedProperty;

    static ElementWithAttachedProp () {
        PropertyMetadata isSkewedMetadata = new PropertyMetadata(false);
        IsSkewedProperty = DependencyProperty.RegisterAttached("IsSkewed",
            typeof(bool), typeof(ElementWithAttachedProp), isSkewedMetadata);
    }
}
```

Example 18-3. Registering attached properties (continued)

```
    public static bool GetIsSkewed(DependencyObject target) {
        return (bool) target.GetValue(IsSkewedProperty);
    }

    public static void SetIsSkewed(DependencyObject target, bool value) {
        target.SetValue(IsSkewedProperty, value);
    }
    ...
}
```

Note that the accessors look different. .NET does not specify a standard way for properties defined by one type to be applied to another. XAML and WPF recognize the idiom used in Example 18-3, where we define a pair of static methods called Get*PropName* and Set*PropName*. Both of the set methods are passed the target object to which the property is to be attached.

The class in Example 18-3 derives from Panel, indicating that it offers some kind of custom layout service, as described in Chapter 3. Although any custom element can define attached properties, it is particularly common for custom panels to do so, to enable child elements to tell the panel how they would like to be arranged. Example 18-3 is just a hypothetical example, so the layout implementation is not shown, but the name suggests that when the panel encounters a child with the IsSkewed attached property set to true, it will arrange it askew. Example 18-4 shows how to apply this custom attached property to a Button element in XAML.

Example 18-4. Using an attached property from XAML

```
<Button local:ElementWithAttachedProp.IsSkewed="True" />
```

XAML also offers the property element syntax, which is useful for when the property value is too complex to express as an attribute. This works in the same way for attached properties as it does for ordinary properties: use an element name of the form `<ClassName.PropertyName>` to set a property. Example 18-5 uses this syntax to set three properties: the unattached Background property, the built-in Grid.Row attached property, and the custom IsSkewed attached property.

Example 18-5. Property element syntax

```
<Button>
  <Button.Background>
    <SolidColorBrush Color="Blue" />
  </Button.Background>
  <Grid.Row>1</Grid.Row>
  <local:ElementWithAttachedProp.IsSkewed>
    True
  </local:ElementWithAttachedProp.IsSkewed>
</Button>
```

Value change notification

Your properties will not always be set using the accessor methods. For example, data binding and animation use the DP system to modify property values directly. If you need to know when a property value is changed, you *must not* depend on your accessors being called, because they often won't be—this is true for both instance properties and attached properties. Instead, you should register for change notifications. You do this by passing a callback to the PropertyMetadata during property registration.

 You can register a change handler for both normal and attached properties. The same technique is used in either case.

Example 18-6 shows the modifications you would make to Example 18-3 in order to be notified when the property value changes.

Example 18-6. Handling property changes

```
...
static ElementWithAttachedProp () {
    PropertyChangedCallback isSkewedChanged =
        new PropertyChangedCallback(OnIsSkewedChanged);
    PropertyMetadata isSkewedMetadata =
        new PropertyMetadata(false, isSkewedChanged);
    IsSkewedProperty = DependencyProperty.RegisterAttached("IsSkewed",
        typeof(bool), typeof(ElementWithAttachedProp), isSkewedMetadata);
}
...
static void OnIsSkewedChanged(DependencyObject target,
                             DependencyPropertyChangedEventArgs e) {
    Debug.WriteLine("IsSkewed just changed: " + e.NewValue);
}
...
```

The change handler function will be called whenever the property is changed, whether it is altered by a call to the static SetIsSkewed method shown in Example 18-3, or by code that uses the DP system to change the value directly, such as a trigger in a style. Your change handler is passed two parameters. The first indicates the target object to which the property has been attached. If your property's behavior requires you to do something to target objects, you would do it in the property change handler. For example, when you set the built-in SpellCheck.IsEnabled attached property to a text editing control, this hooks up dynamic spellchecking functionality. Because you are given a reference to the target, your property change handler can do whatever it deems fit.

The second parameter is a simple struct containing self-explanatory OldValue and NewValue properties. The NewValue property is just for convenience—Example 18-6 could also have retrieved the new value by calling the GetIsSkewed accessor.

Whether you need a property change handler depends on the nature of the attached property. Some attached properties are passive. For example, panel layout properties have no intrinsic behavior of their own and have no direct effect on the elements to which they are applied—instead, they tell the containing panel what to do with the elements. Moreover, layout properties mean anything only when they are applied to children of the panel that defined them. For this kind of panel, you don't need a property change handler. However, for a more proactive property, such as SpellCheck.IsEnabled, you would need to supply a change handler in order to discover to which elements your property has been applied.

Change notifications for property consumers

The change handling technique shown in the preceding section is perfect for custom properties. But what if you want to be notified of changes to dependency properties you didn't create? For example, if you've written a custom control, you might want to know when the Background property changes. (There is no BackgroundChanged event, because most controls rely on templates to render their background, and template bindings handle property changes for you.) There are two options, depending on whether you wish to receive notifications for properties on an object of a custom type written by you, or properties on an object of a type you do not control.

A custom type can have two types of properties not written by you: attached properties, and properties defined by the base class. You can handle changes for both kinds of properties by overriding the OnPropertyChanged method. This virtual method is defined by DependencyObject, and it will be called anytime any of the object's properties change. Example 18-7 uses this to change the background color anytime the IsMouseOver property changes. (This is just to illustrate the OnPropertyChanged method. In practice, you would normally use a Style with a Trigger if you want one property's value to be changed by another, as described in Chapter 8.)

Example 18-7. Handling change notifications in a custom type

```
partial class MyWindow : Window {
    ...
    protected override void OnPropertyChanged(
            DependencyPropertyChangedEventArgs e) {

        base.OnPropertyChanged(e);
        if (e.Property == UIElement.IsMouseOverProperty) {
            this.Background = this.IsMouseOver ? Brushes.Red : Brushes.Blue;
        }
    }
}
```

You can override the OnPropertyChanged method only if you are writing a custom type. What if you want to be notified of property changes on an object of a type you do not control, such as Button? In this case, we must rely on the PropertyDescriptor class.

You can retrieve a property descriptor for any CLR property using the TypeDescriptor class's static GetProperties method. You pass it either a type or an object, and it returns a complete list of descriptors, one for each property. By default, the .NET Framework generates property descriptors automatically, using reflection to discover the available properties. However, one of the most important features of the property descriptor system is that objects are allowed to provide their own descriptors if they want to.* DependencyObject offers custom property descriptors for all dependency properties. This enables us to retrieve them in the same way we would for any object.

Example 18-8 shows how we can provide the property descriptor with a change handler. The OnButtonIsPressedChanged method in this example will be called whenever the myButton object's IsPressed property changes.

Example 18-8. Obtaining a PropertyDescriptor from TypeDescriptor

```
partial class Window1 : Window {

    public Window1() {
        InitializeComponent();

        // myButton refers to a <Button> in the XAML (not shown)
        PropertyDescriptor buttonIsPressedProp =
            TypeDescriptor.GetProperties(myButton)["IsPressed"];

        buttonIsPressedProp.AddValueChanged(myButton, OnButtonIsPressedChanged);
    }

    void OnButtonIsPressedChanged(object sender, EventArgs e) {
        this.Background = myButton.IsPressed ? Brushes.Red : Brushes.Blue;
    }
}
```

Although the normal mechanism for retrieving a property descriptor used by Example 18-8 works fine, WPF provides a more direct mechanism, as Example 18-9 shows.

Example 18-9. Obtaining a PropertyDescriptor from a DependencyProperty

```
PropertyDescriptor buttonIsPressedProp =
    DependencyPropertyDescriptor.FromProperty(Button.IsPressedProperty,
                                              typeof(Button));
```

This is a little more verbose than Example 18-8, but it offers a useful advantage. Instead of passing in a property name, we pass in the DependencyProperty object for the property we require. This removes the potential for a runtime error. If we mistype the property name, we will get a compiler error, whereas if we use the technique in Example 18-8, the mistake will not be detected until runtime.

---

* The DataRow class in ADO.NET uses this to advertise what columns it has, for example.

You would use the techniques shown in Examples 18-8 and 18-9 only when you are not deriving from the class that defines the DP. The previous techniques are preferable when you are able to use them, for two reasons. First, your handler will be notified if you use XAML to set the property's initial value—the PropertyDescriptor technique won't do that because you can attach the handler only after initialization is complete. Second, using the earlier techniques you will be passed both the old and the new values, whereas with the PropertyDescriptor, you will be able to see only the new value.

Property metadata options

Certain common property behaviors crop up time and time again. For example, if you are writing a custom element that overrides OnRender in order to work at the visual layer, it is likely to have properties that affect its appearance. Suppose you had written a custom element called Star that renders a star shape, with a Points property defining how many points the star should have. The obvious thing to do would be to register a change handler, and to call InvalidateVisual in this handler in order to trigger another call to OnRender. In fact, you don't have to do this. Example 18-10 shows how to get WPF to do this work for you.

Example 18-10. Automatic visual invalidation

```
public class Star : FrameworkElement {
    public static readonly DependencyProperty PointsProperty;

    public int Points {
        get { return (int) GetValue(PointsProperty); }
        set { SetValue(PointsProperty, value); }
    }

    static Star() {
        FrameworkPropertyMetadata pointsMetadata =
            new FrameworkPropertyMetadata(5, // default value
                FrameworkPropertyMetadataOptions.AffectsRender);

        PointsProperty = DependencyProperty.Register("Points",
            typeof(int), typeof(Star), pointsMetadata);
    }
    ...
}
```

Instead of using the basic PropertyMetadata class, we've used the derived FrameworkPropertyMetadata type. This is designed for properties defined by a FrameworkElement, and it adds various features not available to dependency properties defined on types that derive directly from lower-level base classes such as UIElement. You can pass in any of the flags defined by the FrameworkPropertyMetadataOptions enumeration, which are described in Table 18-1.

Table 18-1. FrameworkPropertyMetadataOptions

Flag	Meaning
AffectsArrange	The arrange layout phase will be redone when the property changes.
AffectsMeasure	The layout will be completely redone when the property changes.
AffectsParentArrange	The arrange layout phase of the parent will be redone when the property changes.
AffectsParentMeasure	The parent's layout will be completely redone when the property changes.
AffectsRender	The element's visuals will be invalidated when the property changes, causing OnRender to be called if the element is visible.
BindsTwoWayByDefault	Data binding expressions will use a Mode of TwoWay by default. (The default is usually OneWay.)
Inherits	The property's value will be inherited by child elements.
Journal	The property value will be stored in the navigation journal when navigating away, and restored when returning.
NotDataBindable	Data binding expressions will not be allowed to target this property.
OverridesInheritanceBehavior	The property is inherited by descendants even when a child element disables inheritance with the InheritanceBehavior property.
SubPropertiesDoNotAffectRender	Used in conjunction with AffectsRender. Changes to nested properties defined by this property's value do not affect rendering—OnRender should be called only if the property value itself changes (i.e., the property value is replaced with a new object).

By enabling metadata options, you can often avoid the need to write a property change handler.

> You should not use the AffectsRender flag unless your element overrides OnRender. You do not need to set this for all properties that have an impact on appearance. If the property affects a control's appearance via a TemplateBinding in the template—which is how the property defined in Example 18-1 is intended to be used—the template binding will automatically detect property changes without you needing to set AffectsRender.

FrameworkPropertyMetadata also defines a couple of properties that can affect property behavior. DefaultUpdateSourceTrigger lets you specify when two-way data bindings to this property will normally update the source. The usual default is LostFocus, but by setting this to PropertyChanged, you can force the source to be updated every time the property changes. Alternatively, you can set it to Explicit, indicating that the source will be updated only if the code calls the binding's UpdateSource method.

Finally, you can disable the use of animation with the property by setting the IsAnimationProhibited property to true. This might be appropriate if changing the property would be a calamitously expensive thing to try to do tens of times per second.

Events

We looked at the handling of routed events in Chapter 4. If you wish to define custom events for your control, it makes sense to implement them as routed events. Not only will this make your element consistent with other WPF elements, but also you can take advantage of the same bubbling and tunneling routing strategies where appropriate.

Creating custom routed events is similar to creating custom properties. You simply create them in your class's static constructor. For convenience, you would normally also add a .NET style event to wrap the underlying routed event handling.

Example 18-11 shows the definition of a pair of events: a tunneling `PreviewAlarm` event and a bubbling `Alarm` event. It provides .NET event accessors for convenience—these just defer to the `AddHandler` and `RemoveHandler` methods built into the base class.

This example also provides an `OnAlarm` method to raise the event. This raises the preview event, and if that isn't marked as handled, it goes on to raise the main `Alarm` event. The `RaiseEvent` method provided by the base `UIElement` class does the work of event routing and calling any registered handlers. Note that just as with normal CLR events, routed events are raised synchronously—`RaiseEvent` will call the event handlers sequentially, and will not return until all of them have run.

Example 18-11. Defining a custom RoutedEvent

```
public class ClockControl : ContentControl {

    public static RoutedEvent AlarmEvent;
    public static RoutedEvent PreviewAlarmEvent;

    static ClockControl() {
        AlarmEvent = EventManager.RegisterRoutedEvent(
            "Alarm", RoutingStrategy.Bubble,
            typeof(RoutedEventHandler), typeof(ClockControl));
        PreviewAlarmEvent = EventManager.RegisterRoutedEvent(
            "PreviewAlarm", RoutingStrategy.Tunnel,
            typeof(RoutedEventHandler), typeof(ClockControl));
    }

    public event RoutedEventHandler Alarm {
        add { AddHandler(AlarmEvent, value); }
        remove { RemoveHandler(AlarmEvent, value); }
    }
    public event RoutedEventHandler PreviewAlarm {
        add { AddHandler(PreviewAlarmEvent, value); }
        remove { RemoveHandler(PreviewAlarmEvent, value); }
    }

    protected virtual void OnAlarm() {
        RoutedEventArgs args = new RoutedEventArgs(PreviewAlarmEvent);
```

Example 18-11. Defining a custom RoutedEvent (continued)

```
        RaiseEvent(args);
        if (!args.Handled) {
            args = new RoutedEventArgs(AlarmEvent);
            RaiseEvent(args);
        }
    }
    ...
}
```

 Example 18-11 used the built-in RoutedEventArgs class. If you want to pass extra information about the event, as with normal .NET events you are free to define your own custom event argument type. It should derive from RoutedEventArgs, because this incorporates some routing functionality required by WPF to route events correctly.

Attached events

Just as some properties can be attached to types other than their defining types, so can events. Unlike dependency properties, routed events do not need to be registered in a different way in order to work as attached events. For example, you could attach a handler for the ClockControl.Alarm event defined in Example 18-11 to a Button using the code shown in Example 18-12.

Example 18-12. Attached event handler

```
RoutedEventHandler handler = MyAlarmHandlerMethod;
myButton.AddHandler(ClockControl.AlarmEvent, handler);
```

The MyAlarmHandlerMethod referred to in this example is the event handler method that will get called when the Alarm event is raised on this button. Of course, the button knows nothing about the Alarm event, so we would need to write the code to raise the event. This is shown in Example 18-13.

Example 18-13. Raising an attached event

```
RoutedEventArgs re = new RoutedEventArgs(ClockControl.AlarmEvent);
myButton.RaiseEvent(re);
```

Attached events enable you to introduce your own events into the UI tree even though the source element may have no intrinsic understanding of the event.

Commands

We saw in Chapter 4 that WPF's RoutedUICommand class represents a particular user action, which may be invoked through any number of different inputs. There are two ways in which a custom control might want to interact with the command system. It might define new command types. Or, it could handle commands defined elsewhere.

Example 18-14 shows how to register a custom command. Note that we provide two strings to name the command. The first is a display name. Because this may appear in the UI (e.g., if the command is associated with a menu item), you would not hardcode the string like this if the application were localizable. Instead, you would typically read the value from a ResourceManager, as with any localizable string. The second name is not localized—this is the real name of the command, and should always be the same regardless of locale.

Example 18-14. Registering a custom command

```
public class ClockControl : Control {
    public static RoutedUICommand SnoozeCommand;

    static ClockControl( ) {
        InputGestureCollection boomInputs = new InputGestureCollection( );
        boomInputs.Add(new KeyGesture(Key.F,
                            ModifierKeys.Control|ModifierKeys.Shift));
        SnoozeCommand = new RoutedUICommand("Snooze", "Snooze",
                            typeof(ClockControl), boomInputs);
    }
    ...
}
```

Example 18-15 shows XAML that configures a Button to invoke this custom command when it is clicked.

Example 18-15. Invoke a command from XAML

```
<Button Command="local:ClockControl.SnoozeCommand">Click me</Button>
```

You will often want to make your control handle any custom commands it defines. You might also want it to handle other commands. For example, you might wish to respond to some of the standard commands provided by classes such as ApplicationCommands. In Chapter 4, we saw how to achieve this by adding a CommandBinding to our custom control's CommandBindings collection. However, although this technique will work, it is usually not an appropriate technique for a custom control. You will normally want all instances of your control to respond to the command in the same way, so instead of setting up command bindings for every instance, it would be better to register a *class handler*. This lets you set up a command handling association just once in your static constructor, and it will work for all instances of your custom element. Example 18-16 shows how.

Example 18-16. Adding a class-level command handler

```
public class MyCustomControl : ContentControl {

    static MyCustomControl( ) {
        CommandBinding copyCommandBinding = new CommandBinding(
            ApplicationCommands.Copy,
            HandleCopyCommand);
```

Example 18-16. Adding a class-level command handler (continued)

```
        CommandManager.RegisterClassCommandBinding(typeof(MyCustomControl),
            copyCommandBinding);
    }

    static void HandleCopyCommand(object target,
                                             ExecutedRoutedEventArgs e) {
        MyCustomControl myControl = (MyCustomControl) target;
        ...
    }
}
```

Note that the handler must be a static method—when your static constructor runs, there will not yet be any instances of your custom element. Besides, this handler will be registered once on behalf of all instances, so it would not make sense for it to be an instance method. When the command is invoked, the handler will be passed a reference to the target element as its first parameter.

Supporting Templates in Custom Controls

The final design consideration for any custom element is how it will connect with its visuals. If the element derives directly from FrameworkElement, it might be appropriate for it to generate its own visuals. (Chapter 13 described how to create a graphical appearance.) In particular, if you are creating an element whose purpose is to provide a particular form of visualization—such as an element that renders a three-dimensional graph—the element should take complete control of how this is managed. However, if you are writing a control, you would not normally hard-wire the graphics into the control.

Remember that a control's job is to provide behavior. The visuals are provided by the control template. A control may provide a default set of visuals, but it should allow these to be replaced in order to offer the same flexibility as the built-in controls. (Chapter 9 described how to replace a control's visuals with a template.) A control that conforms to this approach, where the visuals are separated from the control, is often described as *lookless*, because the control has no intrinsic appearance or "look." All of the controls built into WPF are lookless.

Of course, it is not possible for the control to be entirely independent of its visuals. As we saw in Chapter 9, there is an implied contract between a control and its template. The control allows its appearance to be customized by replacing the template, but the template should in turn provide certain features on behalf of the control. Chapter 9 described the various styles of contract; some controls use a mixture of these styles. The following sections describe how to support these contract types in a custom control.

Property Binding

Property binding is where the control template projects properties from the control onto properties of elements in the control template. It does this with the `TemplateBinding` markup extension.

To support this model, all you need to do is implement properties using the dependency property mechanism described earlier in this chapter. Example 18-1 showed a custom control that defined a single dependency property called `StripeBrush`, of type `Brush`. This enables users of this control to refer to it in a template, as Example 18-17 shows.

Example 18-17. Using property binding

```
<ControlTemplate TargetType="{x:Type local:MyCustomControl}">
  <Grid>
    <Line Stroke="{TemplateBinding StripeBrush}" StrokeThickness="1"
          X1="0" Y1="0" X2="100" Y2="100" />
  </Grid>
</ControlTemplate>
```

All dependency properties automatically support property binding. The "contract" in this case is implied by the set of dependency properties your control offers.

Named Parts

The named parts style is where the control locates required template parts by name. Example 18-18 shows a very simple control template with two named parts.

Example 18-18. Control template with named parts

```
<ControlTemplate TargetType="{x:Type loc:ControlWithNamedParts}">
  <Grid Width="80" Height="100">
    <Ellipse Fill="Black" Stroke="Gray" StrokeThickness="3" Margin="0,20,0,0" />
    <ContentControl x:Name="PART_Body"
                    Foreground="White" HorizontalAlignment="Center"
                    VerticalAlignment="Center" Margin="0,15,0,0" />
    <Line x:Name="PART_Fuse"
          Stroke="Blue" StrokeThickness="3" X1="55" Y1="40" X2="75" Y2="5" />
  </Grid>
</ControlTemplate>
```

Writing a control that uses this style of template is straightforward. First, you should declare which parts your control expects by annotating the class with the `TemplatePartAttribute` custom attribute, which is defined in the `System.Windows` namespace. This indicates the names and types of elements you expect to see. Design tools can use this information to ensure that a template is correct. To hook your control to these named parts, you should override the `OnApplyTemplate` method (see Example 18-19).

Example 18-19. Connecting with named parts

```
[TemplatePart(Name="PART_Body", Type=typeof(ContentControl))]
[TemplatePart(Name="PART_Fuse", Type=typeof(FrameworkElement))]
public class ControlWithNamedParts : Control {
    ContentControl body;
    FrameworkElement fuse;

    public override void OnApplyTemplate() {
        base.OnApplyTemplate();

        body = Template.FindName("PART_Body", this) as ContentControl;
        fuse = Template.FindName("PART_Fuse", this) as FrameworkElement;
    }
    ...
}
```

This retrieves the `ControlTemplate` from the `Template` property, and calls its `FindName` method to locate named elements within the template. Notice that we have to pass in the `this` reference—this is because one `ControlTemplate` object is typically shared by many controls, so it needs to know which particular instance of the template we'd like to connect with. The method returns null if it cannot find the element.

In general, you should try to make your control robust in the face of missing elements. The built-in controls do not raise errors when parts are missing; they simply stop providing the functionality that depended on the part in question (even if that means becoming completely nonfunctional). For example, the `Button` control requires its template to contain a `ContentPresenter` in order for the `Content` property to work. If the template does not contain a `ContentPresenter`, the `Content` property stops doing anything, but otherwise the control continues to function as normal. Users of your control may not be interested in exploiting all the available features, and so may give you an incomplete template. Even if they intend to provide a full template, it is likely that at the start of the design process, the template will be incomplete.

Your template may be replaced during the lifetime of your control. If you do things to the template parts, such as hooking up event handlers, you must be prepared to undo this work in the event that your template is replaced. Example 18-20 shows how to do this.

Example 18-20. Handling a change of template

```
[TemplatePart(Name="PART_Target", Type=typeof(FrameworkElement))]
public class MyControl : Control {
    private FrameworkElement targetPart;

    public override void OnApplyTemplate() {
        base.OnApplyTemplate();

        FrameworkElement oldTargetPart = targetPart;
        targetPart = Template.FindName("PART_Target", this) as FrameworkElement;
```

Example 18-20. Handling a change of template (continued)

```
        if (!object.ReferenceEquals(oldTargetPart, targetPart)) {
            if (oldTargetPart != null) {
                oldTargetPart.MouseEnter -=
                    new MouseEventHandler(targetPart_MouseEnter);
                oldTargetPart.MouseLeave -=
                    new MouseEventHandler(targetPart_MouseLeave);
            }

            if (targetPart != null) {
                targetPart.MouseEnter +=
                    new MouseEventHandler(targetPart_MouseEnter);
                targetPart.MouseLeave +=
                    new MouseEventHandler(targetPart_MouseLeave);
            }
        }
    }

    void targetPart_MouseLeave(object sender, MouseEventArgs e) {
        ...
    }
    void targetPart_MouseEnter(object sender, MouseEventArgs e) {
        ...
    }
    ...
}
```

Content Placeholders

Some controls expect the template to provide a placeholder for content, typically using a ContentPresenter element. You do not need to do anything special to enable the use of a ContentPresenter—if you derive from ContentControl, it will just work. Users of your control will be able to write templates such as that shown in Example 18-21.

Example 18-21. Using a ContentPresenter

```
<ControlTemplate TargetType="{x:Type local:MyContentControl}">
  <Grid>
    <Rectangle Fill="White" />
    <ContentPresenter />
  </Grid>
</ControlTemplate>
```

Your control may require more than one placeholder. For example, controls derived from HeaderedContentControl require two—one for the body and one for the header. In this case, we can simply be explicit about which property the ContentPresenter presents, as Example 18-22 shows.

Example 18-22. ContentPresenter and HeaderedContentControl

```
<ControlTemplate TargetType="{x:Type local:MyHeaderedContentControl}">
  <Grid>
    <Grid.RowDefinitions>
      <RowDefinition />
      <RowDefinition />
    </Grid.RowDefinitions>

    <ContentPresenter Grid.Row="0" Content="{TemplateBinding Content}" />
    <ContentPresenter Grid.Row="1" Content="{TemplateBinding Header}" />
  </Grid>
</ControlTemplate>
```

ContentPresenter does not require the template control to derive from ContentControl. You can use this technique in the template of any custom control, although you get to omit the Content property template binding as in Example 18-21 only if your control derives from ContentControl—all other control types will require the template to contain explicit bindings as in Example 18-22.

WPF defines two more placeholder types. You can use ItemsPresenter in an ItemsControl in order to show where generated items should be added. And, ScrollContentPresenter is designed for use in the scroll viewer control, indicating where the scrollable content will go. If you were defining a new kind of control that hosts content in some way (e.g., a paginating viewer), it might be appropriate to define a custom placeholder type. However, you should do this only if the built-in ones do not meet your needs.

Placeholders Indicated by Properties

There is an alternative to the named parts approach described earlier: you can define attached properties whose job is to mark certain elements as special. For example, Panel.IsItemsHost is an attached property used in an ItemsControl template to indicate the panel that will hold generated items. The advantage of this property-based technique is that it is more amenable to compile-time checking: if you misspell the name of a named part, the failure is typically not detected until runtime. A misspelled property name is detected at compile time. The TemplatePartAttribute provides a mechanism by which a template could be verified for the correct named parts, but the current WPF build tools do not make use of this. However, the named part approach is far more common and simpler to implement. The marker property approach is described here mainly for completeness.

To implement a control that denotes a placeholder with a marker property, you will need to define a custom attached dependency property. This should be a Boolean property. Example 18-23 registers such an attached property and defines the usual accessor functions.

Example 18-23. Registering the attached placeholder property

```
public class ControlWithPlaceholder : Control {
    public static readonly DependencyProperty IsMyPlaceholderProperty;

    static ControlWithPlaceholder() {

        PropertyMetadata isMyPlaceholderMetadata = new PropertyMetadata(false,
            new PropertyChangedCallback(OnIsMyPlaceholderChanged));

        IsMyPlaceholderProperty = DependencyProperty.RegisterAttached(
            "IsMyPlaceholder", typeof(bool),
            typeof(ControlWithPlaceholder), isMyPlaceholderMetadata);
    }

    public static bool GetIsMyPlaceholder(DependencyObject target) {
        return (bool) target.GetValue(IsMyPlaceholderProperty);
    }
    public static void SetIsMyPlaceholder(DependencyObject target, bool value) {
        target.SetValue(IsMyPlaceholderProperty, value);
    }
...
```

Notice that in Example 18-23, a `PropertyChangedCallback` is supplied to the `PropertyMetadata`. This denotes a method that is to be called anytime this attached property is set or modified on any element. It is in this method that our control will discover which element was set as the placeholder. Example 18-24 shows the method.

Example 18-24. Discovering when the placeholder property is applied

```
    ...
    static void OnIsMyPlaceholderChanged(DependencyObject target,
                                DependencyPropertyChangedEventArgs e) {

        FrameworkElement targetElement = target as FrameworkElement;
        if (targetElement != null && GetIsMyPlaceholder(targetElement)) {
            ControlWithPlaceholder containingControl =
                targetElement.TemplatedParent as ControlWithPlaceholder;
            if (containingControl != null) {
                containingControl.placeholder = targetElement;
            }
        }
    }

    FrameworkElement placeholder;

    ...
}
```

This example starts by checking that the property was applied to an object derived from `FrameworkElement`. Remember that we're expecting this to be applied to a particular element inside the control template, so if it is applied to something other than a `FrameworkElement`, there's nothing useful we can do with it.

Next, we check the value of the property by calling the `GetIsMyPlaceholder` accessor method we defined for the attached property in Example 18-23. It would be slightly odd if someone explicitly set this property to false, but if he does, we definitely shouldn't treat the element as the placeholder.

If the property was set to true, we go on to retrieve the target element's `TemplatedParent` property. For elements that are part of a control's template, this returns the control that owns the template. (It returns null if the element is not a member of a control. Because our property only has any meaning for elements inside a template, we just do nothing when there is no templated parent.) We also check that the parent is an instance of our control type, and ignore the property if it is applied to an element in the template of some other kind of control.

If the target element was a member of a template for an instance of this custom control type, we know we've found the placeholder. This example stores a reference to the placeholder in a private field of the control so that the control can then go on to do whatever it needs to do with the placeholder, such as add child elements or set its size.

Example 18-25 shows how you would use this property in a control template to indicate which element is the placeholder.

Example 18-25. Specifying a placeholder with a property

```
<ControlTemplate TargetType="{x:Type local:ControlWithPlaceholder}">
  <Grid local:ControlWithPlaceholder.IsMyPlaceholder="True" />
</ControlTemplate>
```

Default Styles

Although the ability to provide a custom look for a control is useful, developers should be able to use a control without having to supply custom visuals. The control should just work when used in its most straightforward way, which means that it should supply a default set of visuals. This is normally done by providing a style that sets default property values, including a default control template.

Logically speaking, these default styles live in the system resource scope. As we saw in Chapter 12, this scope contains system-defined resources such as system colors, and default styles for built-in controls. If you write a custom control, you can add your own resources to this scope by adding a *themes\generic.xaml* file to your project. See Chapter 12 for more information on custom system-scope resources.

For each custom control, you should define a system-scope style with a TargetType specifying your control. This style must set the Template property with a ControlTemplate defining the default visuals for your control, such as the one shown in Example 18-26. See Chapters 8 and 9 for more information on how to define a style that supplies a template.

Example 18-26. Default visuals

```
<!-- themes/generic.xaml -->
<ResourceDictionary
    xmlns="http://schemas.microsoft.com/winfx/2006/xaml/presentation"
    xmlns:x="http://schemas.microsoft.com/winfx/2006/xaml"
    xmlns:local="clr-namespace:CustomControlLib">
  <Style TargetType="{x:Type local:MyCustomControl}">
    <Setter Property="Template">
      <Setter.Value>
        <ControlTemplate TargetType="{x:Type local:MyCustomControl}">
          <Border Background="{TemplateBinding Background}"
                  BorderBrush="{TemplateBinding BorderBrush}"
                  BorderThickness="{TemplateBinding BorderThickness}">
            <ContentPresenter />
          </Border>
        </ControlTemplate>
      </Setter.Value>
    </Setter>
  </Style>
</ResourceDictionary>
```

To make sure your control picks up this default theme, you need to let the dependency property system know that the style is there. If you don't, the control will just pick up the default style for its base class. Example 18-27 shows how to ensure that the correct style is used.

Example 18-27. Ensuring that your default style is used

```
public class MyCustomControl : ContentControl {
    static MyCustomControl() {
        ...
        DefaultStyleKeyProperty.OverrideMetadata(typeof(MyCustomControl),
            new FrameworkPropertyMetadata(typeof(MyCustomControl)));
    }
    ...
}
```

Note that the Visual Studio extensions for .NET 3.0 generate this code for you when you add a new custom control to a WPF project.

UserControl

User controls offer a way of building custom controls that works rather differently than everything we've looked at so far. These are intended to offer a similar model to user controls in other UI frameworks such as Windows Forms and ASP.NET. In those technologies, user controls are built with the visual designer in the same way as a window or page would be created, using the same event handling and code-behind mechanisms.

UserControl is a very simple class that derives from ContentControl and adds very little. It defines no new public members, and merely makes minor changes to some default behaviors: it prevents the control from acting as a target for focus and tab navigation (we typically want the elements inside the user control to act as focus targets, not the containing user control itself). The main purpose of UserControl is to signal intent: by deriving from UserControl, you are indicating to the development environment how you would like to build and edit the control. It also offers a clue to developers using your control that it is unlikely to be lookless—user controls use the same tightly coupled relationship between markup and code behind as a window or page, so they do not usually support customization through templates.

 Strictly speaking, user controls have templates—all controls do. However, the default template contains just a single ContentPresenter, which hosts the UI defined in your markup. So in practice, a user control supplies its own visuals.

Example 18-28 shows the XAML and code behind for a very simple user control.

Example 18-28. Markup and code behind for UserControl

```
<!-- CustomElement.xaml -->
<UserControl x:Class="CustomElement"
    xmlns="http://schemas.microsoft.com/winfx/2006/xaml/presentation"
    xmlns:x="http://schemas.microsoft.com/winfx/2006/xaml">
  <Grid>
    <Button Click="OnButtonClick" Content="_Click me" />
  </Grid>
</UserControl>

// CustomElement.xaml.cs
public partial class CustomElement : UserControl {
    public CustomElement(){
        InitializeComponent();
    }

    void OnButtonClick(object sender, RoutedEventArgs e) {
        MessageBox.Show("Clicked");
    }
}
```

Having written a user control, you use it in the same way as any other custom element. Example 18-29 shows how you might use the control defined in Example 18-28.

Example 18-29. Using a user control

```
<Window ...
    xmlns:local="clr-namespace:MyNamespace">
  <Grid>
    <local:CustomElement />
  </Grid>
</Window>
```

One of the reasons UserControl is so simple is that we don't technically need it—features intrinsic to user controls in other UI frameworks are supported throughout all of WPF, so you can build custom elements using markup with code behind without deriving from UserControl. XAML is quite happy to use any root element type, so you can derive from any base class you like. Example 18-30 shows a pair of markup and code-behind files for a custom element that derives directly from Grid. This behaves in much the same way as the user control defined in Example 18-28.

Example 18-30. Markup and code behind without UserControl

```
<!-- CustomElement.xaml -->
<Grid x:Class="CustomElement"
    xmlns="http://schemas.microsoft.com/winfx/2006/xaml/presentation"
    xmlns:x="http://schemas.microsoft.com/winfx/2006/xaml">

  <Button Click="OnButtonClick" Content="_Click me" />

</Grid>

// CustomElement.xaml.cs
public partial class CustomElement : Grid {
    public CustomElement(){
        InitializeComponent();
    }

    void OnButtonClick(object sender, RoutedEventArgs e) {
        MessageBox.Show("Clicked");
    }
}
```

As you can see, we add elements and attach event handlers to this code in the same way as with a user control. The current preview .NET 3.0 extensions for Visual Studio 2005 will even let you edit the design of such an element interactively—it doesn't care that it's not a user control.

Today, there is very little difference between these two ways of creating custom elements. This illustrates that the UserControl class doesn't offer any unique functionality.

It exists mainly to signal explicitly that you are using the markup and code-behind idiom. And this is A Good Thing—the minimal functionality doesn't mean that class is useless. If another developer is using your element, she might be misled if it derives directly from Grid—she could reasonably think that it is intended as a custom layout element. But if it derives from UserControl, that provides a clear indication of its nature.

Adorners

An *adorner* is a special-purpose custom element whose purpose is to add visual features to a UI element. An adorner appears at the same position as the element it adorns, but it will be at top of the Z order—it appears above all nonadorner elements in the window. Adorners are typically used in interactive editing scenarios to display selection outlines or handles. Figure 18-2 shows a typical example from Microsoft Expression Blend.

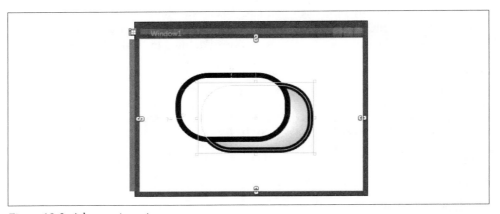

Figure 18-2. Adorners in action

Figure 18-2 shows two rounded rectangles. The one with the white fill is on top of the gray one, partially obscuring it. The gray one underneath has been selected, causing various handles, shapes, and labels to light up. For example, there's a rectangle showing the bounding box, with small, square resize handles at each corner, and there's an outline version of the shape itself. Notice that the white rectangle has obscured none of these features. Even though the gray rectangle is beneath the white rectangle, all of the handles appear on top, making it easy to edit the shape even though it is mostly obscured. These handles and other features appear on top because they use WPF's adorner system.

Adorners are able to appear on top because WPF creates a special AdornerLayer element at the top of the Z order. There is nothing magic about this—you could achieve the same effect without using the adorner infrastructure simply by creating a suitably placed panel to host your adorners. However, it would require a considerable amount of work to ensure that the elements on this panel appeared in the correct position. This is what makes the adorner system attractive—it ensures that the objects in the adorner layer are always in the same position as the elements they adorn, despite being in completely different parts of the UI tree.

The AdornerLayer can contain multiple elements, so you might expect it to be a panel. However, it derives directly from FrameworkElement, not Panel, for a couple of reasons. First, it can only contain elements that derive from Adorner, whereas panels can contain any UI elements. Second, AdornerLayer has no layout logic of its own— adorners are positioned on the adorner layer according to the location of the elements they adorn. This means that adorners do not participate in layout in the normal way.

No public classes are derived from the Adorner abstract base class, so you are obliged to derive your own. And, because the Adorner class does not provide a way to define the appearance through properties, you can't simply use XAML. A common approach for writing adorners is to use visual layer programming, which we described in Chapter 13. Example 18-31 shows an example of this approach.

Example 18-31. Adorner using visual layer

```
class BoxingAdorner : Adorner {
    public BoxingAdorner(UIElement adornedElement)
        : base(adornedElement) { }

    protected override void OnRender(DrawingContext drawingContext) {
        drawingContext.DrawRectangle(null, new Pen(Brushes.Blue, 2),
            new Rect(0, 0, 100, 40));
    }
}
```

This adorner will render a blue box 100 device-independent pixels wide and 40 high. Notice that the constructor takes as its parameter the element to be adorned. All adorners must do this because the Adorner base class has no default constructors— you must provide it with a reference to the element being adorned. Example 18-32 shows the XAML and code behind for a window that uses this adorner.

Example 18-32. Using an adorner

```
<Window ... >
  <Grid>
    <TextBlock x:Name="targetElement" Margin="40,40,0,0" Text="Test" />
  </Grid>
</Window>

// Code behind
partial class Window1 : Window {

    public Window1() {
        InitializeComponent();
```

Example 18-32. Using an adorner (continued)

```
        this.Loaded += new RoutedEventHandler(Window1_Loaded);
    }

    void Window1_Loaded(object sender, RoutedEventArgs e) {
        AdornerLayer al = AdornerLayer.GetAdornerLayer(targetElement);
        BoxingAdorner myAdorner = new BoxingAdorner(targetElement);
        al.Add(myAdorner);
    }
}
```

The work is done in the Loaded event handler, because the adorner layer is not available until then. In the event handler, we ask WPF for the AdornerLayer to use for the target element, we create an instance of our adorner class, and then we add that to the adorner layer. Figure 18-3 shows the results: a box around the text block.

Figure 18-3. TextBlock with adorner

Note that the adorner is significantly larger than the content of the TextBlock. Adorners are often larger than the element they adorn. The resize box in Figure 18-2 is a typical example. You can draw your adorner outside the adorned element's area by passing in suitable coordinates when drawing—modifying Example 18-31 to pass negative x and y values would move the top left of the adorner above and to the left of the text block. Alternatively, you can override the GetDesiredTransform method, returning the transform you would like to have applied to your adorner. (We discussed transforms in Chapter 13.) Either way, the adorner can fill the whole adorner layer if it wants.

Example 18-32 had to do its work in the Loaded event handler because the adorner layer wasn't ready sooner. This raises the question: where does the adorner layer come from? The answer is the AdornerDecorator class.

AdornerDecorator

The adorner layer's location in the visual tree of an application is always determined by an AdornerDecorator element. Window provides an AdornerDecorator by default, which is why we didn't need to supply one earlier. It's part of the window's default template, which is why we needed to wait until the Loaded event before trying to use it—any earlier, and the template would not yet have been instantiated.

AdornerDecorator is a potentially confusing name—you could be forgiven for thinking that it might be used to decorate an element with an adorner, or that it might decorate an adorner. The reason for the name is that it derives from the Decorator class, which we describe in Appendix D. Decorators provide their content with a service. AdornerDecorator is a decorator that provides its content with an adorner layer, hence the name.

Sometimes it can be useful to provide your own adorner decorator. For example, you might want to crop the adorner layer so that it doesn't fill the whole window. A drawing program would typically want to do this to make sure that its selection handles did not encroach into the tool palettes. Example 18-33 shows how to use AdornerDecorator to supply your own adorner layer.

Example 18-33. Using AdornerDecorator

```
<Window ... >
  <Grid>
    <Grid.ColumnDefinitions>
      <ColumnDefinition />
      <ColumnDefinition />
    </Grid.ColumnDefinitions>

    <AdornerDecorator Grid.Column="1">
      <TextBlock x:Name="targetElement" Margin="40,40,0,0" Text="Test" />
    </AdornerDecorator>
  </Grid>
</Window>
```

If an adorner is applied to the targetElement, as before, WPF will now use the AdornerDecorator supplied here, instead of the one that the Window provided. When asked for an adorner layer, WPF walks the tree starting from the adorned element and uses the first adorner decorator it finds. It generates an AdornerLayer as a child of the decorator in the visual tree. You are free to have multiple adorner layers. WPF uses the first one it finds for each adorner you create. Because the decorator in Example 18-33 is in the second column of the grid, the adorners will be cropped if necessary to ensure that they only appear inside that grid column, whereas by default, they would have been able to appear anywhere in the window.

Where Are We?

You should write a custom element only if the underlying behavior you require is not offered by any of the built-in types, and you cannot build it by composing existing elements. Even if you do write a custom type, it will not necessarily be a control. When you write a custom element of any kind, you will use the dependency property system to provide properties that support data binding and animation. You will use the routed event infrastructure to expose events. If your element defines a particular interactive behavior, it should be a control. If you want to write a "lookless" control that allows its visuals to be replaced just like the built-in controls, you must consider how your control and template will interact with one another. You will also most likely want to supply a default style with a template that provides a default set of visuals.

XAML

XAML—the eXtensible Application Markup Language—is an XML-based language for creating trees of .NET objects. XAML provides a convenient way of constructing WPF user interfaces. This appendix explores the syntax of XAML and its relationship to .NET code.

Although XAML is seen as being strongly associated with WPF, the two are, strictly speaking, separate. You do not have to use XAML in order to write a WPF application, and it is possible to use XAML for technologies other than WPF. For example, the Windows Workflow Foundation can use XAML to represent workflows. WPF is designed to be convenient to use from XAML, but to understand XAML fully, it's important to realize that it has no special connection with the WPF framework. As we said, XAML is essentially just a language for constructing trees of .NET objects.

XAML Essentials

To examine the relationship between XAML and .NET, we will work through a simple XAML example (see Example A-1).

Example A-1. Simple XAML file

```
<Window
    xmlns="http://schemas.microsoft.com/winfx/2006/xaml/presentation"
    xmlns:x="http://schemas.microsoft.com/winfx/2006/xaml"
    x:Class="XamlProj.Window1"
    Title="Main Window">

  <Grid>
    <Ellipse Fill="LightBlue" />
    <TextBlock>
      Name: <TextBlock Text="{Binding Name}" />
    </TextBlock>
  </Grid>
</Window>
```

Example A-1 is a simple but typical XAML file. Let's look at it in detail to understand what the XAML compiler will do with it.

Namespaces

The first thing to examine is the file's use of XML namespaces. There are two here:

```
<Window
    xmlns="http://schemas.microsoft.com/winfx/2006/xaml/presentation"
    xmlns:x="http://schemas.microsoft.com/winfx/2006/xaml"
    x:Class="XamlProj.Window1"
    Title="Main Window">
```

XAML relies on XML namespaces to determine the meaning of elements. For example, the root element of this file is a Window, but WPF needs to know to what .NET type this corresponds. Many class names are ambiguous. For example, there are three different classes called Control in the .NET 3.0 class library. The .NET Framework has a namespace system that is used for disambiguation. Standard XML also has a namespace system that is used for the same purpose. XAML uses XML namespaces to represent .NET namespaces.

There is not a one-to-one correspondence between XML namespaces in XAML and .NET namespaces. One XML namespace can encompass several .NET namespaces. This makes XAML less verbose—WPF's types are spread across a number of namespaces, so a one-to-one mapping would require XAML to contain a lot more XML namespace boilerplate. This one-to-many mapping is workable because no naming collisions result from merging these particular .NET namespaces into a single XML namespace.

To define the relationship between an XML namespace and one or more .NET namespaces, you apply the XmlnsDefinitionAttribute to the assembly that contains the types you would like to make accessible in XAML. As Example A-2 shows, you can apply the attribute several times in order to add multiple .NET namespaces to a single XML namespace, or to define multiple XML namespaces.

Example A-2. XmlnsDefinitionAttribute

```
[assembly:XmlnsDefinition("http://example.com/mywpftypes",
                          "MyNamespace")]
[assembly:XmlnsDefinition("http://example.com/mywpftypes",
                          "MyNamespace.NestedNamespace")]
[assembly:XmlnsDefinition("http://example.com/otherwpftypes",
                          "MyOtherNamespace ")]
```

When you build a WPF project, the XAML compiler will look for these XML namespace definition attributes on all of the libraries your project uses, including any system libraries. WPF's WindowsBase, PresentationCore, and PresentationFramework assemblies use this attribute to define certain XML namespaces, including the two in Example A-1. The first indicates types that are part of the WPF framework.

(This particular XML namespace encompasses several .NET namespaces, including System.Windows and many of its children.) Because this is declared as the default XML namespace in our XAML file (there is no colon after the xmlns), this indicates that unless specified otherwise, all elements in this file are WPF elements.

The second namespace used by Example A-1, associated here with the x prefix, represents various XAML utility features not specific to WPF, such as the ability to represent type objects, or a null reference. This is a special namespace, in that not everything in it corresponds to a type—some features in this namespace are used to control the XAML compiler's behavior.

 There is no particular significance to XML namespace prefixes—you are free to associate any prefix with any namespace. Prefixes are local to the XML within the element that declares the prefix, and there is no requirement that you use the same prefixes from one file to the next. However, the usual convention in XAML is to associate x with the XAML namespace. Nothing depends on this convention,* but it makes it easier for others to understand your XAML.

XAML also supports a way to refer to types in namespaces for which the XmlnsDefinitionAttribute has not been used. This lets you refer to types in existing assemblies that may not have been designed with XAML in mind; you might want to do this when defining a DataTemplate keyed off a particular type—the target data type might be from a component that knows nothing about the UI. Also, WPF projects in Visual Studio 2005 cannot use namespaces introduced by XmlnsDefinitionAttribute from XAML that lives in the same assembly. If you want to refer to locally defined types, you must use the alternative mechanism, which is shown in Example A-3.

Example A-3. Namespace mapping URI syntax

```
<Grid  xmlns:local="clr-namespace:MyProject"
       xmlns:mylib="clr-namespace:MyLibraryNamespace;assembly=MyLibrary">

  <!-- MyProject.MyLocalType in local assembly -->
  <local:MyLocalType />

  <!-- MyLibraryNamespace.MyLibraryType in MyLibrary assembly -->
  <mylib:MyLibraryType />
</Grid>
```

The XAML compiler recognizes a special URI scheme. If an XML namespace URI begins with clr-namespace: it will not be treated as a simple opaque identifier, as namespace URIs normally are—the XAML compiler will parse the URI to extract the .NET namespace, and optionally an assembly name.

---

* At least, nothing in WPF depends on it. Given the ubiquity of the convention, it wouldn't be wholly surprising to come across tools elsewhere that do in fact depend on this, so it would be wise to follow the convention in your own XAML.

If the URI contains no semicolon, the text following the `clr-namespace:` is interpreted as a .NET namespace. The XML namespace is deemed to contain all types in that namespace that are defined in the same assembly as the XAML file. So, in Example A-3, the namespace prefix `local` provides access to any types in the local assembly in the `MyProject` namespace. The first child element of the `Grid` is of type `MyProject.MyLocalType`, as defined in the same assembly as the XAML file.

If the URI string contains a semicolon, the text up to the semicolon is treated as a .NET namespace, and the text that follows is expected to begin with `assembly=` and be followed by the assembly name. The second namespace declaration in Example A-3 is of this form. So, the second child of the `Grid` is an instance of a type called `MyLibraryNamespace.MyLibraryType`, which is defined in an assembly called `MyLibrary`. The assembly name can be fully qualified (i.e., containing the version culture and public key token as shown in Example A-4), but this is not necessary for assemblies to which the project has a reference.

Example A-4. Fully qualified namespace mapping URI

```
<!-- Split onto multiple lines in order to fit in book. Must appear
     on one line in practice. -->
<DataTemplate
    xmlns:dat="clr-namespace:System.Data;assembly=System.Data,
        Version=2.0.0.0,Culture=Neutral,PublicKeyToken=b77a5c561934e089"
    DataType="{x:Type dat:DataRow}">

  <TextBlock Text="{Binding Path=ItemArray[0]}" />
</DataTemplate>
```

Again, the XML namespace prefix has no particular significance. We could change every instance of the text "local" in Example A-3 to "foo" without changing the XAML's meaning. However, it is a fairly common convention to use either "local" or "loc" to signify local types.

 You must not include any whitespace in a `clr-namespace` URI.

Because the root `Window` element in Example A-1 is qualified by the WPF XML namespace, the XAML compiler knows that this refers to the `System.Windows.Window` class. The XAML compiler imposes no restrictions on the type of the top-level element, although in WPF applications, the most common choices are `Window`, `Page`, `FlowDocument`, `UserControl`, and `Application`.

Generating Classes

Example A-1 has an x:Class attribute on the root element, shown again here:

```
<Window
    xmlns="http://schemas.microsoft.com/winfx/2006/xaml/presentation"
    xmlns:x="http://schemas.microsoft.com/winfx/2006/xaml"
    x:Class="XamlProj.Window1"
    Title="Main Window">
```

The x: prefix is standard XML shorthand to indicate that this particular attribute is in the namespace specified by the xmlns:x attribute. As explained earlier, this is the XAML namespace. The x:Class attribute is a signal to the XAML compiler that it should generate a class definition based on this XAML file. The x:Class attribute determines the name of the generated class, and it will derive from the type of the root element.

You do not have to specify an x:Class attribute. If we were to omit the attribute from this example, the root object's type would be Window, rather than the generated Window1 class.

 It is possible to parse XAML at runtime. This technique, which is shown later, has certain limitations compared to build-time XAML compilation. You can use code generation features only at build time. If you use the x:Class attribute with runtime parsing, you will cause an error. You will see this if you try to use the x:Class attribute in the XamlPad utility that comes with the Windows SDK.

When you opt to generate a class, this provides an easy way to build the tree of objects represented by the XAML. Each Window1 instance we generated will contain a set of objects as specified by the XAML, so we can just use normal object construction syntax:

```
Window1 myWindow = new Window1();
```

If you do not provide an x:Class attribute, creating the object tree is a little more involved. There are several ways to do this, and we discuss them later in the "Loading Compiled XAML (BAML)" section.

Properties

Next, consider the Title attribute on the Window element:

```
<Window
    xmlns="http://schemas.microsoft.com/winfx/2006/xaml/presentation"
    xmlns:x="http://schemas.microsoft.com/winfx/2006/xaml"
    x:Class="XamlProj.Window1"
    Title="Main Window">
```

This attribute has no namespace qualifier. In XAML, unqualified attributes usually correspond to properties on the .NET object to which the element refers. (They can also refer to events, as we'll see later.) The Title attribute indicates that when an instance of this generated XamlProj.Window1 class is constructed, it should set its own Title property to "Main Window". This is equivalent to the following code:

```
myWindow.Title = "Main Window";
```

Children

Next, consider the contents of the Window element in Example A-1:

```
<Grid>
  <Ellipse />
  <TextBlock>
    Name: <TextBlock Text="{Binding Name}" />
  </TextBlock>
</Grid>
```

The default XML namespace specified by the xmlns attribute in the Window element is in scope for all of the XML file, so these elements are also in the WPF XML namespace. The Grid element therefore corresponds to the System.Windows.Controls.Grid class. But what does it mean for this to be "inside" the window? There isn't any single model for nesting one object inside another in .NET, so there are potentially many different interpretations. XAML does not impose a model—instead it lets the parent object decide how to deal with child elements.

Whenever you attempt to provide nested content, the XAML compiler will require the parent type (Window, in this case) or its base class to be annotated with the ContentPropertyAttribute. In this particular case, Window does not have this attribute, but its base type, ContentControl, does, as Example A-5 shows.

Example A-5. Handling child content

```
[ContentProperty("Content"), ...]
public class ContentControl : Control {
    ...
    public Object Content { get { ... } set { ... } }
}
```

This attribute tells the XAML compiler the name of the property that will contain the child content. So, in this example, the compiler will arrange for a Grid object to be created and assigned to the Content property. Example A-6 shows the code equivalent.

Example A-6. Window content

```
Grid g = new Grid();
myWindow.Content = g;
```

The Content property is of type Object, which means that the Window element supports only a single child. Elements that can contain multiple children, such as panels, simply designate a property with a collection type as the content property, as Example A-7 shows.

Example A-7. Handling multiple children

```
[ContentProperty("Children"), ...]
public class Panel : FrameworkElement {
    ...
    public UIElementCollection Children { get { ... } }
}
```

Panel is the base class of Grid, so this tells us how the XAML compiler will add the children inside the Grid in our example. It will be equivalent to Example A-8.

Example A-8. Adding content to the Grid

```
Grid g = new Grid();
myWindow.Content = g;
Ellipse e = new Ellipse();
TextBlock t = new TextBlock();
...
g.Children.Add(e);
g.Children.Add(t);
```

The TextBlock in Example A-1 has further nested content—some text and a second TextBlock. This particular example turns out to be a little more complex, because in this case, the XAML compiler will generate automatic wrapper objects for the children. As Chapter 14 shows, if you add plain text inside a text element, such as a TextBlock or a Paragraph, it will automatically be wrapped in a Run object. Likewise, FrameworkElement children will automatically be wrapped in InlineUIContainer elements. The TextBlock from our example here, shown again in Example A-9, exploits both of these features.

Example A-9. Implicit Run and InlineUIContainer

```
<TextBlock>
  Name: <TextBlock Text="{Binding Name}" />
</TextBlock>
```

This is shorthand for the markup in Example A-10.

Example A-10. Explicit Run and InlineUIContainer

```
<TextBlock>
  <Run Text="Name: " />
  <InlineUIContainer>
    <TextBlock Text="{Binding Name}" />
  </InlineUIContainer>
</TextBlock
```

This works because of a couple of custom attributes. TextBlock is annotated with ContentPropertyAttribute, indicating that its child content should go into its Inlines property. That property's type is InlineCollection, which is annotated with a couple of ContentWrapperAttribute custom attributes, as Example A-11 shows.

Example A-11. ContentWrapperAttribute

```
[ContentWrapper(typeof(Run)), ContentWrapper(typeof(InlineUIContainer)),
    WhitespaceSignificantCollection]
public class InlineCollection : TextElementCollection<Inline>, ...
```

This tells us that Example A-9 is equivalent to the code shown in Example A-12.

Example A-12. TextBlock equivalent code

```
TextBlock t = new TextBlock( );
t.Inlines.Add(new Run("Name: "));
TextBlock t2 = new TextBlock( );
t.Inlines.Add(new InlineUIContainer(t2));
t2.SetBinding(new Binding("Name"));
```

This example illustrates one last feature of XAML: markup extensions. The nested TextBlock in Example A-9 sets the Text property with a data binding expression, and Example A-12 shows the equivalent code. We described binding expressions in Chapters 6 and 7, but they are an example of a more general XAML construct: a markup extension. Markup extensions allow you to customize the way in which a property is set—in this case, the markup extension sets the property by calling SetBinding on the target TextBlock. Each markup extension's behavior is different, and we describe all the built-in ones in detail later in this appendix.

The steps we've just seen illustrate more or less all of what XAML does. The XAML file causes a type to be defined, and the contents cause objects to be created and properties to be set. Everything else is just a refinement of these basics. Now let's look at each feature in more depth.

Properties

In Example A-1, we set the Window element's Title property. This property's type was String. Pure text properties are a natural fit with XML, because XML is a text-based format. But what about other property types? Example A-13 uses a slightly wider range of types.

Example A-13. Nonstring properties

```
<Rectangle Width="100"
           Height="20"
           Stroke="Black"
           Fill="#80FF40EE" />
```

None of the properties set here is a string. Both Width and Height are of type Double, whereas both Stroke and Fill require a Brush. In order to support diverse property types, XAML relies on .NET's TypeConverter system. This has been around since v1.0 of .NET, and it is used in design-time scenarios. A TypeConverter maps between different representations of a value, most commonly between String and a property's native type.[*]

The Width and Height properties are converted using the LengthConverter type. (WPF knows to use this type because the FrameworkElement class's Width and Height properties are marked with a TypeConverterAttribute indicating which converter to use.) The BrushConverter class is used for the other two properties, because although they do not have a TypeConverterAttribute, they are of type Brush, and the Brush type has a TypeConverterAttribute indicating that BrushConverter should be used. Example A-14 illustrates how the attribute was applied in each case.

Example A-14. Specifying a TypeConverter

```
public class FrameworkElement : UIElement, ... {
    ...
    [TypeConverter(typeof(LengthConverter)) ...]
    public double Width { ... }
    [TypeConverter(typeof(LengthConverter)) ...]
    public double Height { ...  }
    ...
}

[TypeConverter(typeof(BrushConverter)) ...]
public abstract class Brush : Animatable, ...
```

The Stroke is set to a standard named color, so this will cause the relevant SolidColorBrush to be fetched from the Brushes class. The Fill in this example uses one of the numerical color formats described in Chapter 13. This causes a new SolidColorBrush of the specified color to be created. Example A-15 shows the equivalent code for the whole of Example A-13.

Example A-15. Nonstring properties, equivalent code

```
Rectangle r = new Rectangle( );
r.Width = 100.0;
r.Height = 20.0;
r.Stroke = Brushes.Black;
r.Fill = new SolidColorBrush(Color.FromArgb(0x80, 0xff, 0x40, 0xEE));
```

Custom components can provide their own type converters if they wish to allow properties with nonstandard types to be set easily from XAML.

---

[*] You should not confuse type converters with value converters, which are strictly for data binding scenarios.

Property Element Syntax

Although the type converter system often makes it possible to specify property values using attributes in your XAML, it sometimes falls short; either a suitable type converter is not available, or you need to do something too complex to fit into a string. For example, the BrushConverter does not provide a way of specifying a gradient fill. For these situations, XAML supports the *property element* syntax.

With the property element syntax, you set the property using a nested element instead of an attribute. The nested element's name is of the form *Parent.PropertyName*, where *Parent* is the name of the element whose property is being set, and *PropertyName* is the name of the property, as Example A-16 shows. This dotted syntax marks the element as being a property value rather than child content.

Example A-16. Property element syntax

```
<Button>
  <Button.Background>
    <SolidColorBrush Color="#FF4444FF" />
  </Button.Background>
  Click me
</Button>
```

Example A-16 uses the property element syntax to set a Button element's Background property. It is equivalent to this code:

```
Button btn = new Button();
SolidColorBrush brush = new SolidColorBrush();
brush.Color = Color.FromArgb(0xFF, 0x44, 0x44, 0xFF);
btn.Background = brush;
btn.Content = "Click me";
```

This particular example has the same effect as a simple Background="#FF4444FF" attribute would—if you specify a numeric color value as a brush, the BrushConverter converts it into a SolidColorBrush. Although this property element version is a lot more verbose, it is also more explicit—we can see exactly what kind of a brush will be created here.

Although this more verbose syntax can help demystify some of the magic that type converters do behind the scenes, this is not the normal reason for using the property element syntax. It is typically necessary because we need to nest more complex definitions inside the property. Example A-17 uses property element syntax for a Button element's Background in order to use a relatively complex brush. The brush itself also uses property element syntax for a list of GradientStops.

Example A-17. Nested property elements

```
<Button VerticalAlignment="Center" HorizontalAlignment="Center">
  <Button.Background>
    <LinearGradientBrush StartPoint="0,0" EndPoint="0,1">
      <LinearGradientBrush.GradientStops>
```

```
        <GradientStop Offset="0"    Color="#800" />
        <GradientStop Offset="0.35" Color="Red" />
        <GradientStop Offset="1"    Color="#500" />
      </LinearGradientBrush.GradientStops>
    </LinearGradientBrush>
  </Button.Background>
  Click me
</Button>
```

Example A-18 shows the equivalent code.

Example A-18. Code equivalent of property elements

```
Button b = new Button( );
b.VerticalAlignment = VerticalAlignment.Center;
b.HorizontalAlignment = HorizontalAlignment.Center;
LinearGradientBrush brush = new LinearGradientBrush( );
brush.StartPoint = new Point(0,0);
brush.EndPoint = new Point(0,1);
GradientStop gs = new GradientStop( );
gs.Offset = 0;
gs.Color = Color.FromRgb(0x80, 0, 0);
brush.GradientStops.Add(gs);
gs = new GradientStop( );
gs.Offset = 0.35;
gs.Color = Colors.Red;
brush.GradientStops.Add(gs);
gs = new GradientStop( );
gs.Offset = 0.35;
gs.Color = Color.FromRgb(0x50, 0, 0);
brush.GradientStops.Add(gs);
b.Background = brush;
b.Content = "Click me";
```

Note that in Example A-17, we could have left out the lines that open and close the LinearGradientBrush.GradientStops element. This is because the LinearGradientBrush has the ContentPropertyAttribute applied, meaning you can just add the GradientStop elements directly as children of the brush. We used the more verbose approach here simply to illustrate that the nested property elements syntax works for collection-like properties as well as singular properties. Normally, you would use the more compact syntax here.

Attached Properties

As well as allowing normal .NET properties to be set, XAML also supports *attached properties*. An attached property is one where the property is defined by a different type than the element to which the property is applied. Most of WPF's layout elements exploit this to allow attributes specific to the layout type to be applied to child elements, as Example A-19 shows.

Example A-19. Attached properties

```
<Button Grid.Row="1" Name="myButton" />
```

The syntax for attached properties is straightforward—they are always of the form *DefiningType.PropertyName*, where *DefiningType* is the name of the type that defines the property, and *PropertyName* is the name of the property. XAML interprets this as a call to the static *DefiningType.SetPropertyName* method, passing in the target object and value. Example A-20 shows the code for setting the same attached property set in markup in Example A-19.

Example A-20. Setting an attached property in code

```
Grid.SetRow(myButton, 1);
```

Attached properties are not a standard .NET feature—they are a useful idiom recognized by XAML. Attached properties are used extensively in WPF and make an important contribution to its flexibility.

For example, the use of attached properties helps keep the layout system open to extension. Properties specific to a particular layout style are always attached properties. Otherwise, properties such as `Grid.Row`, `DockPanel.Dock`, and `Canvas.Left` would have to be built into the base `FrameworkElement` class, making it difficult to add new layout algorithms. With attached properties, you can define your own new layout systems with a corresponding set of attachable properties. All you need to do is provide a pair of static *SetPropertyName* and *GetPropertyName* methods on the defining class for each attached property.

Example A-21 defines an attached property called `Foo.Bar`, of type `Brush`. (The XAML compiler doesn't care how you implement these accessors, so the details have not been shown.)

Example A-21. Defining a custom attached property

```
namespace MyNamespace {
  public class Foo {
    public void SetBar(DependencyObject target, Brush b) { ... }
    public Brush GetBar(DependencyObject target) { ... }
  }
}
```

To use this property from XAML you would need a suitable XML namespace declaration to get access to the type, just as you would to use a custom element. Example A-22 shows this syntax.

Example A-22. Using a custom attached property

```
<Window
    xmlns="http://schemas.microsoft.com/winfx/2006/xaml/presentation"
    xmlns:x="http://schemas.microsoft.com/winfx/2006/xaml"
```

Example A-22. Using a custom attached property (continued)

```
    xmlns:my="clr-namespace:MyNamespace">

  <Button my:Foo.Bar="Blue" />

</Window>
```

This example shows the syntax required to use a custom attached property. As with any attached property, it follows the *TypeName.PropertyName* pattern. But because the defining type is not in the default namespace, the *TypeName* must be qualified by a namespace prefix. So, the syntax is, in effect, *xmlNamespacePrefix:TypeName.PropertyName*.

Attached properties and the property element syntax

The property element syntax shown earlier works for attached properties as well as normal ones. For example, we could write Example A-19 as shown in Example A-23.

Example A-23. Attached property as property element

```
<Button Name="myButton">
  <Grid.Row>1</Grid.Row>
</Button>
```

You can also use property element syntax with custom attached properties. You simply include the relevant XML namespace, just as you do for the normal attached property syntax. Example A-24 shows how to use the custom property defined in Example A-21 with the property element syntax.

Example A-24. Custom attached property element

```
<Window
    xmlns="http://schemas.microsoft.com/winfx/2006/xaml/presentation"
    xmlns:x="http://schemas.microsoft.com/winfx/2006/xaml"
    xmlns:my="clr-namespace:MyNamespace">

  <Button>
    <my:Foo.Bar>
      <LinearGradientBrush StartPoint="0,0" EndPoint="0,1">
        <LinearGradientBrush.GradientStops>
          <GradientStop Offset="0"    Color="#800" />
          <GradientStop Offset="0.35" Color="Red" />
          <GradientStop Offset="1"    Color="#500" />
        </LinearGradientBrush.GradientStops>
      </LinearGradientBrush>
    </my:Foo.Bar>
  </Button>
</Window>
```

Markup Extensions

Type converters and property elements let us initialize most properties to constant values or fixed structures. However, in certain situations we need a little more flexibility. For example, we might want to set a property to be equal to the value of some particular static property, but we don't know at compile time what that value will be, like the properties representing user-configured colors. XAML provides a powerful solution in the form of *markup extensions*. A markup extension is a class that decides at runtime how to set a property's value.

Markup extension classes derive from MarkupExtension, the nonprivate members of which are shown in Example A-25. This class is defined in the System.Windows.Markup namespace.

Example A-25. MarkupExtension class

```
public abstract class MarkupExtension {
    protected MarkupExtension () { }

    public abstract object ProvideValue(IServiceProvider serviceProvider);
}
```

Example A-26 shows an example of a markup extension in use.

Example A-26. Using a markup extension

```
...
<Style TargetType="{x:Type Button}">
...
```

The TargetType property of the Style has a value enclosed in curly braces. This indicates to the XAML compiler that a markup extension is being used. The first string inside the curly braces is the name of the markup extension class, and the remaining contents are passed to the markup extension during initialization.

We are using x:Type in Example A-26. There is no class called Type in any of the .NET namespaces represented by the XAML namespace, but when the XAML compiler fails to find the markup extension class, it appends Extension to the name and tries again. There is a TypeExtension class, so the XAML compiler will use that, passing the string "Button" to its constructor. Then it will call the extension's ProvideValue method, to obtain the real value to be used for the property. The TypeExtension will return the Type object for the Button class.

As you can see from Example A-25, ProvideValue takes a single parameter of type IServiceProvider. This is a standard .NET interface that allows a set of services to be made available, where each service is an implementation of some interface. In this case, the provider will typically offer two services: IProvideValueTarget and IXamlTypeResolver. The former allows the extension to discover for which object and which property it is providing a value (the `Style` object's `TargetType` property, in this scenario). The latter converts type names to types, taking into account the set of XML namespaces in scope where the markup extension was used. The `TypeExtension` uses this to convert its parameter to a `Type` object.

The XAML compiler singles out certain markup extension classes for special treatment, evaluating them at compile time, because the compiler writers know those extensions will always return the same value for a particular input. (Most extensions are evaluated at runtime, including any custom extensions you write.) `TypeExtension` is one of these special cases. So, at compile time, the compiler will do the equivalent of the code in Example A-27. (The service provider passed to `ProvideValue` is an implementation detail of the XAML compiler, and is not shown here.)

Example A-27. Compile-time effect of TypeExtension

```
TypeExtension te = new TypeExtension("Button");
object val = te.ProvideValue(serviceProviderImpl);
```

The runtime effect of using the `TypeExtension` in Example A-26 is equivalent to the code in Example A-28. The main reason for this special handling is efficiency—`TypeExtension` is widely used, so looking up type names at runtime would slow things down.

Example A-28. Runtime effect of TypeExtension

```
Style s = new Style();
s.TargetType = typeof(Button);
```

XAML can pass data into a markup extension in two ways. One is to provide constructor parameters as Example A-26 shows—`TypeExtension` offers a constructor that takes a string, and this example passes the string `"Button"` to that constructor. (You can pass multiple parameters, separating each one with a comma.) The other is to set properties, which you can do by putting *PropertyName=Value* pairs into the list, as Example A-29 shows.

Example A-29. Using Name=Value pairs with a markup extension

```
<TextBlock Text="{Binding Path=SimpleProperty, Mode=OneTime}"/>
```

Properties passed to a type extension are parsed using type converters, just like all other properties. Example A-29 is equivalent to the code in Example A-30.

Example A-30. Setting properties on a Binding

```
Binding b = new Binding();
b.Path = new PropertyPath("SimpleProperty");
b.Mode = BindingMode.OneTime;
```

You can nest markup extensions, enabling you to set an extension's property with another extension, as shown in Example A-31.

Example A-31. Nested markup extensions

```
<TextBlock Text="{Binding Path=MyProp, Source={StaticResource Foo}}" />
```

You can create your own markup extension type by writing a class that derives from MarkupExtension. (You will need to introduce a namespace prefix using the techniques described earlier in the "Namespaces" section to make sure the XAML compiler can find your extension type.) To enable data to be passed to your extension, you can either provide one or more constructors that take strings, or define suitable properties. Your extension will be instantiated and its ProvideValue method called when the object tree corresponding to the relevant XAML is instantiated at runtime.

Built-in Markup Extensions

WPF supplies a number of useful built-in markup extensions. Some of them are defined in the XAML XML namespace, so by convention you access them using the x: prefix. Others are specific to WPF and are in the WPF namespace. The most commonly used built-in extensions are listed in Table A-1, and are described in the following sections. (The "Type" column follows the convention that the x: prefix denotes the XAML XML namespace and that the lack of a prefix denotes the WPF XML namespace.)

Table A-1. Commonly used markup extensions

Type	Usage
x:NullExtension	Used to indicate null (evaluated at compile time)
x:TypeExtension	Retrieves type object (evaluated at compile time)
x:ArrayExtension	Creates an array
x:StaticExtension	Retrieves static property value
StaticResourceExtension	Performs one-shot resource lookup
DynamicResourceExtension	Sets up resource binding
ComponentResourceKey	Creates a resource key for cross-component system resource references
Binding	Creates a data binding
RelativeSource	Creates a RelativeSource for use in a data binding
TemplateBinding	Connects a property in a control template to a property of the templated control

NullExtension

The NullExtension provides a way to set a property to null. In some cases, the distinction between not setting a property and setting it explicitly to null is important. For example, a Style might be setting the Background property on all elements of a particular value, and you might want to disable this on a specific element. If you wanted to remove the background entirely rather than setting it to some other color, you would do so by setting that element's Background explicitly to null.

This extension always evaluates to null, so it does not require any parameters. Example A-32 uses the NullExtension to set a button's background—this prevents the button from filling in its background.

Example A-32. Using the NullExtension

```
<Button Background="{x:Null}">Click</Button>
```

This is equivalent to the code in Example A-33.

Example A-33. Effect of NullExtension

```
Button b = new Button();
b.Background = null;
b.Content = "Click";
```

TypeExtension

TypeExtension returns a System.Type object for the named type. It always takes a single parameter: the type name. TypeExtension uses the IServiceProvider passed to its ProvideValue method to obtain information about the XAML parsing context in which it appears, enabling it to resolve type names in the same way that the XAML compiler does for element names. This means that you do not need to provide a fully qualified type name including the .NET namespace extension. Instead, you use it like this:

```
<Style TargetType="{x:Type Button}">...
```

The TypeExtension will resolve the string "Button" to a type in the same way the XAML compiler will—it will take into account the default XML namespace, and any namespace mappings that are present. The effect of this extension is equivalent to the code in Example A-34.

Example A-34. Effect of TypeExtension

```
Style s = new Style();
s.TargetType = typeof(Button);
```

Again, the reality is slightly more complex, as we showed in Example A-28. However, Example A-34 expresses the intent and effect of the extension.

ArrayExtension

ArrayExtension allows you to create an array of elements. This is a slightly unusual markup extension in that you do not use the brace syntax—you write it as a full element instead. This is because an array can contain multiple items, and with the ArrayExtension these are represented as children of the extension. (You could use the brace syntax if you wanted an empty array, though.)

Example A-35 uses ArrayExtension to create an array as a resource. It then uses this array as the data source for a ListBox. The ArrayExtension requires the array type to be specified through its Type property, for which we use the TypeExtension discussed previously. Here we are creating an array of type Brush.

Example A-35. Creating an array resource with ArrayExtension

```
<Grid>
  <Grid.Resources>
    <x:ArrayExtension Type="{x:Type Brush}" x:Key="brushes">
      <SolidColorBrush Color="Blue" />
      <LinearGradientBrush StartPoint="0,0" EndPoint="0.8,1.5">
        <LinearGradientBrush.GradientStops>
          <GradientStop Color="Green" Offset="0" />
          <GradientStop Color="Cyan" Offset="1" />
        </LinearGradientBrush.GradientStops>
      </LinearGradientBrush>
      <LinearGradientBrush StartPoint="0,0" EndPoint="0,1">
        <LinearGradientBrush.GradientStops>
          <GradientStop Color="Black" Offset="0" />
          <GradientStop Color="Red" Offset="1" />
        </LinearGradientBrush.GradientStops>
      </LinearGradientBrush>
    </x:ArrayExtension>
  </Grid.Resources>

  <ListBox ItemsSource="{StaticResource brushes}" Name="myListBox">
    <ListBox.ItemTemplate>
      <DataTemplate>
        <Rectangle Fill="{Binding}" Width="100" Height="40" Margin="2" />
      </DataTemplate>
    </ListBox.ItemTemplate>
  </ListBox>
</Grid>
```

This is effectively equivalent to the code in Example A-36.

Example A-36. Effect of ArrayExtension

```
Brush[] brushes = new Brush[3];
SolidColorBrush scb = new new SolidColorBrush();
scb.Color = Colors.Blue;
brushes[0] = scb;

LinearGradientBrush lgb = new LinearGradientBrush();
lgb.StartPoint = new Point(0,0);
lgb.EndPoint = new Point(0.8, 1.5);
GradientStop gs = new GradientStop();
gs.Offset = 0;
gs.Color = Colors.Green;
lgb.GradientStops.Add(gs);
gs = new GradientStop();
gs.Offset = 1;
gs.Color = Colors.Cyan;
lgb.GradientStops.Add(gs);
brushes[1] = lgb;
```

Example A-36. Effect of ArrayExtension (continued)

```
lgb = new LinearGradientBrush( );
lgb.StartPoint = new Point(0,0);
lgb.EndPoint = new Point(0, 1);
gs = new GradientStop( );
gs.Offset = 0;
gs.Color = Colors.Black;
lgb.GradientStops.Add(gs);
gs = new GradientStop( );
gs.Offset = 1;
gs.Color = Colors.Red;
lgb.GradientStops.Add(gs);
brushes[2] = lgb;

myGrid.Resources["brushes"] = brushes;
...
myListBox.ItemsSource = myListBox.Resources["brushes"];
```

Figure A-1 shows the results.

Figure A-1. Array of brushes presented by a ListBox (Color Plate 28)

Note that this is an example of where markup may not be the best choice. Example A-36 is a literal translation of the markup in Example A-35. However, it is possible to write much more succinct code to build an equivalent array:

```
Brush[] brushes = new Brush[3];
brushes[0] = Brushes.Blue;
brushes[1] = new LinearGradientBrush(Colors.Green, Colors.Cyan,
                           new Point(0, 0), new Point(0.8, 1.5));
brushes[2] = new LinearGradientBrush(Colors.Black, Colors.Red,
                           new Point(0, 0), new Point(0, 1));
```

If you have a choice between putting something in markup and putting it in code, code can often offer a more compact representation. The main reason ArrayExtension exists is for the benefit of XAML-based tools. It enables such tools to create an array without needing to be able to generate code.

StaticExtension

StaticExtension sets the target property to the value of a specified static property or field. This markup extension always takes a single parameter, which names the source property or field. The parameter is of the form *ClassName.MemberName*.

Example A-37 uses this extension to retrieve the value of one of the `SystemColors` properties.

Example A-37. Retrieving a static property

```
<TextBlock Background="{x:Static SystemColors.ActiveCaptionBrush}" Text="Foo" />
```

 You can retrieve properties defined in your own code with this extension. If you have introduced an XML namespace mapping for the namespace containing your custom type, you simply make the extension's parameter *myNamespace*:*ClassName*.*MemberName*, where *myNamespace* is your XML namespace prefix.

Note that in practice, you would not normally use the markup shown in this example. It does not integrate properly with the resource system, so if the application resources contained a brush overriding this system brush, this example would bypass that application-level resource. Also, Example A-37 does not update the property automatically when the property changes—`StaticExtension` takes a snapshot of the property value. Its effect is equivalent to the following code:

```
TextBlock tb = new TextBlock();
tb.Background = SystemColors.ActiveCaptionBrush;
tb.Text = "Foo";
```

However, you can use the `StaticExtension` in conjunction with the resource markup extensions described in the next two sections in order to overcome one or both of these issues.

StaticResourceExtension

`StaticResourceExtension` returns the value of the specified resource. It is equivalent to calling the `FindResource` method on the element with which you use the extension. (See Chapter 12 for more information on resource lookup.)

Example A-38 shows how to use this element to retrieve a named resource. Note that `StaticResource` must not be qualified with an `x:` prefix. This is because resource management is a WPF feature, rather than a generic XAML feature, so the resource markup extensions are in the WPF namespace.

Example A-38. Using a resource with StaticResource

```
<Grid>
  <Grid.Resources>
    <SolidColorBrush x:Key="fooBrush" Color="Yellow" />
  </Grid.Resources>

  <Button Background="{StaticResource fooBrush}" Name="myButton" />
</Grid>
```

The use of StaticResource in this markup is effectively equivalent to the following code:

```
myButton.Background = (Brush) myButton.FindResource("fooBrush");
```

This is a one-time resource lookup. The property value will be set to the resource value during initialization. If the value associated with the resource name changes, the property will not be updated automatically. For Example A-38, that might not be a problem, but consider Example A-39.

Example A-39. Using a system resource with StaticResource

```
<TextBlock Name="myText"
    Background="{StaticResource
        {x:Static SystemColors.ActiveCaptionBrushKey}}" />
```

This is similar to Example A-37, except this performs a resource lookup, enabling this resource's value to be overridden by an application skin. It is equivalent to the following code:

```
myText.Background = (Brush)
        myText.FindResource(SystemColors.ActiveCaptionBrushKey);
```

Although this uses the resource lookup system to retrieve the value, it still takes a snapshot—if the user changes the OS color scheme, this element's background will not be updated automatically. When using resources whose values might change, the DynamicResourceExtension is a better choice.

DynamicResourceExtension

DynamicResourceExtension associates the value of the property with the specified resource. This extension is similar to StaticResourceExtension, except that it tracks changes. Example A-40 shows the dynamic equivalent of Example A-39.

Example A-40. Using a system resource with DynamicResource

```
<TextBlock Name="myText"
    Background="{DynamicResource
        {x:Static SystemColors.ActiveCaptionBrushKey}}" />
```

This is equivalent to the following code:

```
myText.SetResourceReference(TextBlock.BackgroundProperty,
        SystemColors.ActiveCaptionBrushKey);
```

Instead of taking a snapshot of the resource, this tracks the value of the resource, and will update the text block's background automatically if the value changes. The resource system tracks changes the user makes to the OS color scheme, so this will automatically update if the user changes the relevant color. This tracking doesn't come for free, so if you know the resource will never change, the static resource extension is a better choice.

ComponentResourceKey

When using either the static or the dynamic resource markup extension, you can use any object as the key. Although this works well for resources defined within an application, there is an issue for resources defined at system scope by external assemblies. As described in Chapter 12, for cross-component system-scope resource references to work, the key must contain information about the target assembly. One option is to use a Type object as the key. For example, the default Style for a control uses the control's Type as the key. WPF can use the Type object to discover the assembly in which the control is defined, and it looks for system-scope resources in that assembly.

This works well when resources relate naturally to classes—each control type has an associated Style resource. But for some resources, suitable types may not exist. For example, a component might provide 30 drawings as system-scope resources to be used as icons on toolbars. These might not have any types directly associated with them. It would be tedious to define 30 types whose only purpose was to act as resource keys.

ComponentResourceKey solves this problem. It combines a type and a string identifier, enabling you to create many distinct resource key objects associated with a particular assembly without having to define a separate type for each key.

Although it is common practice to make ComponentResourceKey objects available through static properties—for example, the key properties offered by SystemColors—this is not the only option. ComponentResourceKey derives from MarkupExtension, enabling you to create instances directly from XAML. You can do this at the point where the resource is defined; for example, in your component's *themes\generic.xaml* file, as Example A-41 shows.

Example A-41. ComponentResourceKey

```
<ResourceDictionary
  xmlns="http://schemas.microsoft.com/winfx/2006/xaml/presentation"
  xmlns:local="clr-namespace:MyComponent">

  <SolidColorBrush x:Key="{ComponentResourceKey {x:Type local:MyType}, brush1}"
                   Color="Red" />
  <SolidColorBrush x:Key="{ComponentResourceKey {x:Type local:MyType}, brush2}"
                   Color="Green" />

</ResourceDictionary>
```

This is equivalent to the code shown in Example A-42.

Example A-42. ComponentResourceKey equivalent code

```
ResourceDictionary rd = new ResourceDictionary();
rd.Add(new ComponentResourceKey(typeof(MyType), "brush1"),
    new SolidColorBrush(Colors.Red));
```

Example A-42. ComponentResourceKey equivalent code (continued)

```
rd.Add(new ComponentResourceKey(typeof(MyType), "brush2"),
    new SolidColorBrush(Colors.Green));
```

You can also use the markup extension in Example A-43 at the point at which you refer to a resource.

Example A-43. Resource reference with ComponentResourceKey

```
<TextBlock Background="{DynamicResource
            {ComponentResourceKey {x:Type local:MyType}, brush1}}" />
```

This is equivalent to the code shown in Example A-44.

Example A-44. Resource reference with ComponentResourceKey equivalent code

```
TextBlock myText = new TextBlock();
myText.SetResourceReference(TextBlock.Background,
    new ComponentResourceKey(typeof(MyType), "brush1"));
```

Binding

The Binding markup extension is used for data binding. Example A-45 shows a very simple example.

Example A-45. Binding markup extension

```
<TextBlock Text="{Binding Foo}" Name="txt" />
```

This binds the Text property to the Foo property on whatever object is in the data context. It is effectively equivalent to the following code:

```
Binding b = new Binding("Foo");
BindingOperations.SetBinding(txt, TextBlock.TextProperty, b);
```

Chapters 6 and 7 provide a full explanation of how data binding works, and they describe the use of the Binding extension.

RelativeSource

The RelativeSource markup extension lets you set the RelativeSource property of a Binding. This allows a binding expression to choose an element as a data source based on the location of the binding expression rather than setting the binding's ElementName to the source element's name. Example A-46 uses this to bind a Rectangle element's Height to its own ActualWidth property, ensuring that the rectangle is always square.

Example A-46. RelativeSource

```
<Rectangle Fill="Red"
    Height="{Binding Path=ActualWidth,RelativeSource={RelativeSource Self}}" />
```

A RelativeSource can walk up the UI tree to locate its source. For example, instead of specifying Self, we can pass TemplatedParent to the markup extension. This is useful only for elements appearing inside a template, as it looks for the element to which the template has been applied.

Alternatively, you can search up the UI tree for an element of a particular type. Example A-47 uses RelativeSource with a mode of FindAncestor to find the nearest ancestor of type Grid.

Example A-47. FindAncestor mode

```
<TextBlock Text="{Binding Path=Margin,
    RelativeSource={RelativeSource FindAncestor,AncestorType={x:Type Grid}}}" />
```

Finally, the PreviousData mode allows you to choose the previous item in a list of data bound items as the source. Example A-48 shows the use of this in an ItemsControl data template.

Example A-48. PreviousData mode

```
<ItemsControl>
  <ItemsControl.ItemsSource>
    <x:Array xmlns:sys="clr-namespace:System;assembly=mscorlib"
            Type="{x:Type sys:String}">
      <sys:String>toe</sys:String>
      <sys:String>foot</sys:String>
      <sys:String>ankle</sys:String>
      <sys:String>knee</sys:String>
      <sys:String>thigh</sys:String>
    </x:Array>
  </ItemsControl.ItemsSource>

  <ItemsControl.ItemTemplate>
    <DataTemplate>
      <WrapPanel>
        <TextBlock Text="The " />
        <TextBlock Text="{Binding RelativeSource={RelativeSource PreviousData}}" />
        <TextBlock Text=" bone's connected to the " />
        <TextBlock Text="{Binding}" />
        <TextBlock Text=" bone" />
      </WrapPanel>
      <DataTemplate.Triggers>
        <DataTrigger Value="{x:Null}"
            Binding="{Binding RelativeSource={RelativeSource PreviousData}}">
          <Setter Property="Visibility" Value="Collapsed" />
        </DataTrigger>
      </DataTemplate.Triggers>
    </DataTemplate>
  </ItemsControl.ItemTemplate>

</ItemsControl>
```

Figure A-2 shows the results. Note that on the first row, there is no "previous" row, so a data trigger has been added to detect the first row and hide it. See Chapters 6 and 7 for more information on data bindings, templates, and triggers.

> The toe bone's connected to the foot bone
> The foot bone's connected to the ankle bone
> The ankle bone's connected to the knee bone
> The knee bone's connected to the thigh bone

Figure A-2. PreviousData

TemplateBindingExtension

TemplateBindingExtension is used in control templates to indicate where properties from the source object are to be mapped into properties of objects in the template. Example A-49 shows a simple example.

Example A-49. TemplateBinding markup extension

```
<ControlTemplate TargetType="{x:Type Button}">
  <Rectangle Width="100" Height="200" Fill="{TemplateBinding Background}" />
</ControlTemplate>
```

This binds the Rectangle element's Fill property to the underlying control's Background property. It is equivalent to the following:

```
ControlTemplate template = new ControlTemplate(typeof(Button));
FrameworkElementFactory factory = new FrameworkElementFactory(typeof(Rectangle));
factory.SetValue(Rectangle.WidthProperty, 100);
factory.SetValue(Rectangle.HeightProperty, 200);
TemplateBindingExtension tb =
                    new TemplateBindingExtension(Button.BackgroundProperty);
factory.SetValue(Rectangle.FillProperty, tb);
template.VisualTree = factory;
```

This code looks different from the previous examples of how XAML maps onto code, because a template element handles its child content differently than other elements. It generates a FrameworkElementFactory that is capable of building the content, rather than simply building the content. A factory is required because a template may be instantiated any number of times. We explained the use of control templates in Chapter 9.

 It is possible to use an ordinary data binding Binding expression to perform the same job as a TemplateBinding—just provide a RelativeSource set to TemplatedParent. TemplateBinding is considerably less verbose, and it's slightly more efficient—WPF handles template bindings using a different, less flexible but lighter weight mechanism than data bindings. However, there is one reason for using a full Binding instead of a TemplateBinding—only a Binding supports two-way binding. Some control templates require this. For example, a TreeViewItem needs two-way binding between the IsExpanded property and the ToggleButton that the user clicks on to expand or collapse the node.

Code Behind

Separate handling of appearance and behavior is an important design principle for keeping UI code manageable. To help with this separation, XAML supports the concept of *code behind*, where a XAML file has a corresponding source file containing executable code. The idea is that the XAML file defines the structure of the user interface, and the code-behind file provides its behavior.

 The exact definition of *behavior* can look a little different in WPF applications compared with what you may be used to. It is possible to use styling and event triggers to make a UI respond automatically to simple stimuli. In older UI technologies, you would typically have used code to achieve this, but in WPF we normally use markup. Although this is behavior in the sense that it is something the application does in response to input, it is essentially superficial behavior—it is part of the look and feel of the application, rather than the functionality. This superficial behavior usually lives in the control template, and you can therefore replace it without altering the underlying behavior of the control, as described in Chapter 9.

In the context of code behind, behavior usually means the application functionality invoked when you click a button, rather than what the button looks like when it is clicked.

Of course, you won't want to put much application logic in your code behind if you care about maintainability and testability. In practice, the code behind is likely to act as the glue between the UI and the code that implements the bulk of the application logic.

XAML supports code behind through the use of *partial classes*. Partial classes allow a class definition to be spread across multiple source files—each individual file contains only a partial definition of the class. At compile time, the compiler combines these to form the full class definition. The main purpose of partial classes is to allow generated code and handwritten code to share a class without having to share a source file.

When you add the x:Class attribute to the root element, the XAML compiler generates a partial class definition from the markup. You can then put your code behind in another partial definition for the same class. At compile time, the compiler will merge these two partial definitions into a single, complete class. This lets the XAML compiler add members into the class. These are internal members, making them inaccessible to code outside the component that defines the class, but they are directly accessible to your code.

If you have defined an element in XAML that you wish to use from the code behind, just set the Name attribute as in Example A-50.

Example A-50. Named element

```
<Button Name="myButton">Click</Button>
```

The XAML compiler will add a myButton field to the class, and will set this to refer to the button during initialization. This enables you to write code in the code behind that uses the element directly, such as Example A-51.

Example A-51. Using a named element from code behind

```
myButton.Background = Brushes.Green;
```

Not all types have a Name property. For example, the various brush types described in Chapter 13 do not. However, you can still generate a field for them in the code behind by using an x:Name attribute instead, with x: being the prefix for the XAML namespace, as Example A-52 shows.

Example A-52. x:Name attribute

```
<Button Content="Click">
  <Button.Background>
    <SolidColorBrush x:Name="bgBrush" Color="Yellow" />
  </Button.Background>
</Button>
```

In fact, you can use this x:Name style even on elements where Name is valid. Replacing Name with x:Name in Example A-50 would not change its behavior. This is because FrameworkElement identifies the Name property as mapping to the x:Name attribute. This is done using the RuntimeNamePropertyAttribute, as Example A-53 shows.

Example A-53. Mapping Name to x:Name

```
[RuntimeNameProperty("Name"),...]
public class FrameworkElement : UIElement, ...
```

If a type is annotated with this attribute, the named property is interchangeable with x:Name in XAML. But if the type does not have this custom attribute, you must use the x:Name attribute in XAML to generate a field in the code behind, even if the target type has a Name property.

 If you are using .NET 3.0 extensions for Visual Studio 2005, you will need to compile your project after adding an x:Name or Name attribute to an element in XAML before IntelliSense will work in the current WPF preview. This is because IntelliSense depends on being able to see the code that the XAML compiler generates in order to know that the field is present.

One of the main jobs of the code behind is to enact application functionality in response to user input. So, you will often need to attach event handlers to elements in the XAML. The preferred approach is to write code that attaches handlers during initialization in your code behind. (Chapter 4 discussed why this is the preferred technique.) However, XAML can attach event handlers for you, and this can be slightly more convenient for a simple UI where both the code and the XAML are maintained by the same individual. And, in some cases, you have little choice—if the element lives inside a template, the x:Name attribute doesn't create a field you can use to refer to the element from code behind, because the name is considered to be local to the template. You could still hook up events from the code behind, but you'd first have to call the template's FindName method to locate the element. It might be simpler just to use the XAML event syntax. The syntax is similar to that for properties—we use attributes in the XAML:

```
<Button x:Name="myButton" Click="ButtonClicked">Click</Button>
```

This is equivalent to attaching the handler in the code behind:

```
class MyWindow : Window {
    public MyWindow( ) {
        InitializeComponent( );
        myButton.Click += ButtonClicked;
    }
}
```

Although this looks similar to the property syntax, the XAML compiler will detect that the Click member is an event, not a property. It will expect your code behind to provide a function called ButtonClicked, and it will add that function as a handler for the button's Click event. You must make sure that the function has the correct signature—all .NET events expect a particular kind of function signature. Example A-54 shows a suitable method declaration for the Click event handler, and many event handlers will look something like this, but you should consult the documentation for the event you wish to handle to determine the exact signature required.

Example A-54. Event handler

```
void ButtonClicked(object sender, RoutedEventArgs e) { ... }
```

WPF's command handling architecture can often provide a more elegant and flexible way of responding to user input than handling events directly from elements, so you should consider using commands where possible. Chapter 4 describes handling input with events and commands in more detail.

The class generated by the XAML compiler clearly has a fair amount of work to do during initialization. It needs to create the tree of objects specified by elements in the XAML. It needs to assign values to properties. It needs to populate fields for named elements. It must attach any specified event handlers. All of this work is done by a method called `InitializeComponent`, which gets generated at compile time as a result of specifying the `x:Class` attribute. This is why when you create a new XAML page in Visual Studio, the class in the code behind always looks something like Example A-55.

Example A-55. Code behind and initialization

```
public partial class Window1 : Window {
    public Window1( ) {
        InitializeComponent( );
    }
}
```

You must not delete the call to `InitializeComponent`. This does all of the work the XAML document specifies. All of the fields referring to elements on the page will be null until you call this function, so you will normally want to leave it as the very first thing your constructor does. If you add overloaded constructors in order to allow parameters to be passed, make sure you call `InitializeComponent` from these, too.

Code in XAML

You will normally keep all of your source code in the code behind. This separation of code from UI structure usually makes code maintenance easier. However, it is possible to put code onto the XAML page, although there is rarely any reason to do so. The authors of this book aren't fans of this technique, which is described here only for completeness.

You can embed source into the XAML file by adding a `Code` element in the XAML XML namespace. Example A-56 shows an example.

Example A-56. Inline code

```
<Window x:Class="XamlProj.Window1"
    xmlns="http://schemas.microsoft.com/winfx/2006/xaml/presentation"
    xmlns:x="http://schemas.microsoft.com/winfx/2006/xaml"
    Title="XamlProj">

  <Grid>
    <Button Name="myButton" Click="InlineClickHandler">Click!</Button>

  </Grid>
  <x:Code><![CDATA[
    void InlineClickHandler(object sender, RoutedEventArgs e) {
      myButton.Background = Brushes.Blue;
    }
  ]]></x:Code>
</Window>
```

The XAML compiler takes any such `Code` elements and simply adds the content directly to the class it generates.

The XML CDATA section is a standard XML feature indicating that a section of non-XML content follows, and it saves us from adding escape sequences to prevent the code from being misinterpreted. You are not obliged to use CDATA—you could instead manually escape any characters that would otherwise be misinterpreted. But CDATA is usually easier—it allows blocks of non-XML text to be inserted verbatim.

If you try this yourself in Visual Studio, you will find this to be an unsatisfactory way of working. Because the file type is *.xaml*, the editor offers no syntax highlighting or IntelliSense for embedded C# code. And, because the code in question is simply injected into the partial class that the XAML compiler creates, it is equivalent to putting the same code into your code behind. This means you can use it only when XAML is being compiled—if you try this in a scenario where XAML is parsed at runtime, such as in the XamlPad utility, you will get an error. So, inline code offers no compelling benefits and some considerable disadvantages.

Why does this feature exist if it is of such limited value? Its only attractive feature is that it allows the UI structure and functionality to be combined into a single source file rather than being split across two. For very short example code, this simple packaging might look more attractive than splitting the code across two files. But in general, you should avoid this style of coding—for anything nontrivial it will just cause pain.

Loading XAML

If you use the x:Class attribute to generate a class from your XAML file, you can instantiate the tree of objects defined in the XAML by creating an instance of the relevant class. However, you are not required to generate a class.

If you do not generate a class, there are two ways in which you can get from XAML to a tree of objects. You can either parse the XAML at runtime, or you can precompile it at build time into a binary form called *BAML* and load that BAML at runtime. The precompiled approach performs better and offers the benefit of being able to use code behind. However, runtime XAML parsing gives you the freedom to decide at runtime what XAML to use. Tools such as XamlPad obviously need to use runtime parsing, but it could also be useful if you want to generate XAML by running an underlying XML data source through an XSLT (although data binding often provides better solutions than runtime XAML generation—see the section on data-driven UI in Chapter 7).

Parsing XAML at Runtime

The `System.Windows.Markup` namespace defines a `XamlReader` class. This has a `Load` method, which takes either a `Stream` or an `XmlReader`. Example A-57 passes an `XmlTextReader`, which derives from `XmlReader`.

Example A-57. Parsing XAML at runtime

```
StringReader sr = new StringReader(@"
    <Canvas xmlns='http://schemas.microsoft.com/winfx/2006/xaml/presentation'>
        <Rectangle Width='30' Height='100' Fill='Red' />
    </Canvas>");
XmlTextReader xr = new XmlTextReader(sr);

Canvas tree = (Canvas) XamlReader.Load(xr);
```

This is a slightly contrived example, as it loads the XAML as a string constant. It would have been simpler just to create the relevant objects from code. But you could load the XAML from elsewhere, at which point this becomes a much more powerful technique.

Note that if you put an `x:Class` attribute into XAML loaded in this way, you will get an error. You can generate a class for a XAML file only as part of a build process.

Loading Compiled XAML (BAML)

The `XamlReader.Load` method has to parse your XAML at runtime. This makes it flexible, but it is also expensive. If your XAML is not being dynamically generated, this overhead serves no useful purpose. Fortunately, you can precompile the XAML into a binary form called BAML by adding a XAML file to a Visual Studio project and setting its Build Action to Page. By parsing the XAML at compile time, you can minimize the runtime costs.

> As we saw in Chapter 12, this is exactly what happens by default when you add a XAML file to a project—Visual Studio runs the XAML compiler on it and adds the resulting BAML to your executable as an embedded resource.

If your compiled XAML file has a code-behind file, you can load the BAML by simply creating an instance of the corresponding class. But if you have a compiled XAML file without code behind in your project, you can load it by calling `Application.LoadComponent`. This takes a `Uri` object, which should contain a relative URI referring to the original XAML filename within the project, as Example A-58 shows.

Example A-58. Application.LoadComponent

```
Uri uri = new Uri("MyFlowDocument.xaml", UriKind.Relative);
FlowDocument doc = (FlowDocument) Application.LoadComponent(uri);
```

(Even though the compiled resource has a *.baml* extension, you must pass in the original *.xaml* name to this method.) This method works just like XamlReader.Load— it will build a tree of objects corresponding to the original XAML.

Interoperability

A few lucky souls have the luxury of building their applications using only WPF, ignoring the long history of Windows presentation frameworks that have come before. Unfortunately, the rest of us have presentation logic built up in Win32, Microsoft Foundation Classes (MFC), Windows Forms, ActiveX, and HTML that we'd like to keep, whether that means bringing new WPF-based controls into our existing application or bringing in existing controls built with other frameworks into our new WPF applications.

There are two gaps of interoperability that we have to worry about. The first is the core abstraction that defines the regions of functionality we'd like to use as a host or as a control: the HWND versus the WPF element. Raw Win32 applications are built in terms of HWNDs, as are MFC, Windows Forms, and ActiveX-based applications. HTML applications are built in terms of pages, which are served up with an instance of the Web Browser ActiveX control and which host other ActiveX controls as content. On the other side of this gap, we have the WPF element, which is a new thing that breaks the long tradition of Windows-based presentation stacks by not being HWND-based.

The second interoperability gap is characterized as native versus managed code. Raw Win32, MFC, and even HTML applications and controls are native whereas both Windows Forms and WPF are managed. Bridging the native/managed gap requires the Platform/Invoke (P/Invoke) capabilities of .NET.

Whether you have to cross one or both of these bridges depends on what techniques you need to bring to bear in hosting or being hosted. For example, moving between Windows Forms and WPF requires us to worry about HWNDs versus WPF elements, but the code for both of these presentation stacks is managed, which eases the journey. On the other hand, hosting a WPF control in an MFC dialog requires keeping in mind the coding conventions of both a specific managed library (WPF) and a specific native library (MFC), as well as the specifics of making them work together, most often with C++/CLI (the latest version of Microsoft's C++ that supports .NET).

WPF and HWNDs

Whether the existing code you're integrating with WPF is managed or not, it's going to be HWND-based if it was built on Windows. If you run a normal Windows application, like Calc, it will be composed of a parent window and several child windows. If you run the developer tool Spy++ and examine Calc, you'll see that the buttons and the calculation display are all windows, as shown in Figure B-1.

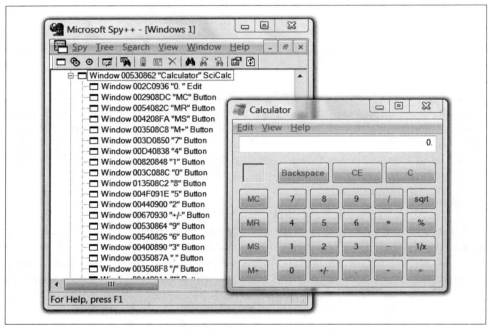

Figure B-1. Using Spy++ on Calc to see the HWNDs

Each window in Figure B-1 is an instance of the HWND type exposed by the User API, which is what has put the "windows" in Windows since 1985 (when Microsoft Windows version 1.0 was released). The top-level window, 00530862, is the parent window for the child button and the edit box windows that make up the calculator UI.

If you run Spy++ against the WPF calculator sample in the SDK, you'll see a very different picture, as shown in Figure B-2.

In Figure B-2, notice that there's a top-level window (001E0954), but no "+" to click on to drill into the WPF calculator's child windows because there is none. In fact, the only visible HWND in the entire application is the one provided for the main window. Every child on the main window is a Visual, not an HWND, and is managed directly by WPF. By default, only top-level window elements get HWNDs (this includes menus, pop ups, tool tips, and combo box drop downs so that they can extend past the main window's borders if necessary).

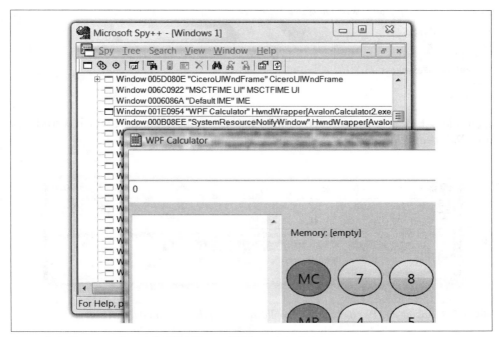

Figure B-2. Exposing the single HWND in a WPF version of Calc

The lack of HWNDs in WPF leads to somewhat of a problem for interoperability between WPF and the Windows applications that have come before it. If you want to host an HWND in WPF, whether it's the edit control provided by Win32 or the TextBox class provided by Windows Forms, you're going to first need to introduce an HWND into the WPF tree to serve as the control's parent, which is exactly what the HwndHost is for.

The HwndHost class is an abstract class that provides much of the functionality required to interop with HWND-based windowing, including message hooks, measuring, positioning, keyboard handling, and, of course, the ever-important window procedure (WndProc) into which all windowing messages come.

Hosting a Windows Form Control in WPF

On top of this core functionality of the HwndHost class, deriving classes handle details germane to their specific framework. As of this writing, WPF exposes only one such specialization: the WindowsFormsHost class from the System.Windows.Forms.Integration namespace and the WindowsFormsIntegration assembly. The WindowsFormsHost class has properties for background, font, and tab index properties to provide integration at those points with WPF. Example B-1 shows how to declaratively add a WindowsFormsHost element to a Window.

Example B-1. Adding an HWND host to a WPF tree

```
<!-- Window1.xaml -->
<Window ...>
  <Grid>
    <WindowsFormsHost />
  </Grid>
</Window>
```

Example B-1 creates an instance of the WindowsFormsHost control, which introduces an HWND into WPF's tree, as shown in Figure B-3.

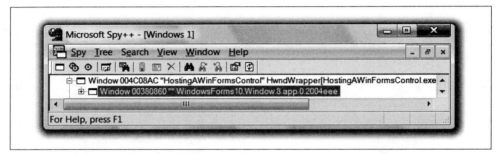

Figure B-3. Adding an HWND to a WPF application using the WindowsFormsHost

With an HWND injected into the WPF tree, we can now host a control from the HWND-based UI framework with which WPF integrates best: Windows Forms. For example, after adding a reference to the System.Windows.Forms assembly to the project, we can host a DataGridView control, as shown in Example B-2.

Example B-2. Hosting a Windows Forms DataGridView in WPF

```
<!-- Window1.xaml -->
<Window ...
  xmlns:wf="clr-namespace:System.Windows.Forms;assembly=System.Windows.Forms">
  <Grid>
    <WindowsFormsHost>
      <wf:DataGridView x:Name="gridView" />
    </WindowsFormsHost>
  </Grid>
</Window>
```

Here we've mapped in the System.Windows.Forms namespace so that we have access to the DataGridView control. We've also named the control in the same way that you would any element in WPF, which gives us programmatic access to the DataGridView from our code, as Example B-3 shows.

Example B-3. Populating the DataGridView from code

```
// Window1.xaml.cs
...
public class Person {...}
public class People : System.Collections.Generic.List<Person> { }
```

Example B-3. Populating the DataGridView from code (continued)

```
public partial class Window1 : Window {
  public Window1( ) {
    InitializeComponent( );

    gridView.DataSource = new Person[] {
      new Person("Tom", 11),
      new Person("John", 12),
      new Person("Melissa", 37)
    };
  }
}
```

In Example B-3, we're using normal Windows Forms data binding by setting the data source to a collection of Person objects. Because both WPF and Windows Forms are managed, we can call from one to the other without any special considerations. Figure B-4 shows the hosted DataGridView control in action.

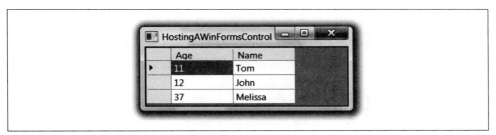

Figure B-4. Hosting a Windows Forms DataGridView in a WPF application

In the case of the DataGridView control, you can go even further when taking advantage of XAML, as Example B-4 illustrates.

Example B-4. Hosting and populating the DataGridView from XAML

```
<!-- Window1.xaml -->
<Window ...
  xmlns:wf="clr-namespace:System.Windows.Forms;assembly=System.Windows.Forms"
  xmlns:local="clr-namespace:HostingAWinFormsControl">
  <Grid>
    <Grid.Resources>
      <local:People x:Key="Family">
        <local:Person Name="Tom" Age="11" />
        <local:Person Name="John" Age="12" />
        <local:Person Name="Melissa" Age="37" />
      </local:People>
    </Grid.Resources>
    <WindowsFormsHost>
      <wf:DataGridView DataSource="{StaticResource Family}" />
    </WindowsFormsHost>
  </Grid>
</Window>
```

Notice that in Example B-4, we've mapped our local namespace into the XAML so that we could create our collection declaratively. With this in place, we can set the DataSource property of the DataGridView to this named resource with no special consideration for Windows Forms. In fact, as far as the DataSource property is concerned, it's just being handed a preinitialized collection, which is what it needs to drive its data binding implementation; it has no idea that the collection was declared in XAML and couldn't care less. It's not the case that every Windows Forms control "won't care" that it's being created in XAML, but sometimes you get lucky.

 The WindowsFormsHost can hold only a single child control, so if you want to host more than one Windows Forms control inside a single WindowsFormsHost, you can do so by creating a custom Windows Forms User Control and use that as a container for your Windows Forms controls. This allows you the benefits of the Windows Forms Designer for visual layout of the Windows Forms controls inside the User Control and separates you from the limitations of XAML when accessing Windows Forms controls.

You should know that there are a number of limitations with the integration between HWND-based Windows Forms and WPF, which we discuss at the end of this appendix. However, the ability to host an existing Windows Forms control in WPF can be a huge timesaver if you've got working code that you'd like to put to immediate use inside WPF. Still, hosting Windows Forms controls inside a WPF host is only half the story; you may also want to host WPF controls in a Windows Forms host, which is what we'll discuss next.

Hosting a WPF Control in Windows Forms

Hosting a WPF control in Windows Forms is much the same as hosting a Windows Forms Control in WPF: we need a host. In WPF, we needed a host that was an element that could fit into WPF, but that also provided an HWND for use by the Windows Forms control. In Windows Forms, we need a Windows Forms Control-derived class so that it can fit into a container's Controls collection. For that, we have the ElementHost class, also from the System.Windows.Forms.Integration namespace and the WindowsFormsIntegration assembly.

The ElementHost class derives from ContainerControl to enable hosting other Windows Forms controls. The element host knows about HWNDs, how to size and paint itself, and how to handle keystrokes and focus. As an example, let's say we've got a form all laid out in the Windows Forms Designer, as shown in Figure B-5.

In Figure B-5, we've got a form with two group boxes: one with a Windows Forms button laid out on the left using the Windows Forms Designer and one blank on the right, all ready for a WPF button to be added at runtime, which is what the code in Example B-5 does.

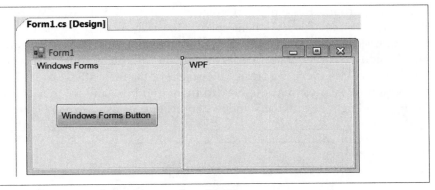

Figure B-5. A Windows Forms form with space for a WPF button

Example B-5. Creating a WPF button in a Windows Forms application

```
// Form1.cs
...
using System.Windows.Forms.Integration;

public partial class Form1 : Form {
  public Form1() {
    InitializeComponent(); // group boxes created in here

    // Create WPF button
    System.Windows.Controls.Button
      wpfButton = new System.Windows.Controls.Button();
    wpfButton.Content = "WPF Button";
    wpfButton.Click += wpfButton_Click;

    // Host the WPF button
    ElementHost host = new ElementHost();
    host.Left = 39;
    host.Top = 72;
    host.Width = 165;
    host.Height = 40;
    host.Child = wpfButton;

    // Add the element host to the groupbox
    rightGroup.Controls.Add(host);
  }

  // Handle the WPF button's Click event
  void wpfButton_Click(object sender, System.Windows.RoutedEventArgs e) {
    System.Windows.MessageBox.Show("Hello from WPF!", "Hello");
  }
}
```

To compile Windows Forms code with WPF added, you'll need to add the WPF assemblies to your project, including at least WindowsBase, PresentationCore, and PresentationFramework. Also, because you're integrating Windows Forms and WPF as before, you'll need to add a reference to the WindowsFormsIntegration assembly.

With the appropriate assemblies referenced, Example B-5 creates a WPF Button from the System.Windows.Controls namespace. However, as there's a Button class in the System.Windows.Forms namespace too, you'll have to be explicit when mixing WPF and Windows Forms code. After creating the button, setting its properties, and handling its Click event, we create an instance of the ElementHost class. Then we add the button to the host and the host to the group box, and we're all set to see our WPF button right next to the Windows Forms button, as shown in Figure B-6.

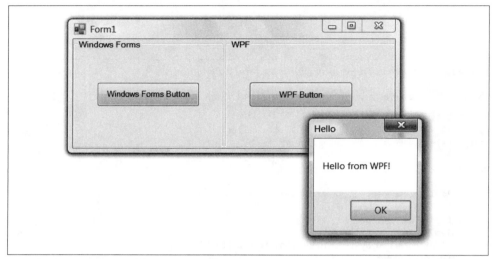

Figure B-6. A WPF control hosted on a Windows Forms form

Figure B-6 doesn't show much benefit from going to the trouble of hosting a WPF control in a Windows Forms application, but we could update the code to use one of the features that make WPF special, as we do in Example B-6.

Example B-6. Creating a fancier WPF button

```
System.Windows.Controls.Button wpfButton =
  new System.Windows.Controls.Button( );
...
wpfButton.Background =
  new System.Windows.Media.LinearGradientBrush(
    System.Windows.Media.Colors.White,
    System.Windows.Media.Colors.Red,
    new System.Windows.Point(0, 0),
    new System.Windows.Point(1, 1));
...
```

This gives us something a bit fancier, as Figure B-7 shows.

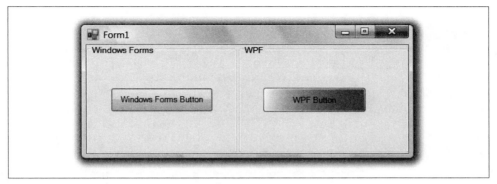

Figure B-7. A WPF button getting jiggy with it

Although there is not yet any designer support for hosting WPF elements in a Windows Forms form, the code-based basics are still the same (i.e., setting properties, calling methods, and handling events). In addition, notice that the font family, size, and weight are the same for both buttons, even though we didn't do anything font-specific in the creation of our WPF control. This is because the concept of ambient properties in Windows Forms is mapped to the concept of inherited properties in WPF, giving us a consistent look and feel (unless we choose to override it).

Hosting WPF in Native HWND Apps

Things can get a bit wackier when hosting a managed WPF control in a native Windows application, like a raw Win32 application or an MFC application. The first barrier to entry is that WPF is managed .NET code, whereas your non-Windows Forms HWND applications are likely written in native C/C++. There are various ways to interact programmatically between native and managed code (e.g., P/Invoke) and COM (the Component Object Model). For example, one way to use a WPF element in a native HWND-based application is to host the WPF element in a custom Windows Forms User Control and use the support in MFC 7.1+ for hosting Windows Forms controls.*

However, your smoothest interoperability experience is to use Visual Studio 2005's capability to switch your native C++ application to a managed one. For example, consider an MFC application, like the simple one shown in Figure B-8.

To compile this application as managed code, right-click on the project in the Solution Explorer, choose Configuration Properties → General, and set the "Common Language Runtime support" option to "Common Language Runtime Support /clr."

---

* Hosting a Windows Forms control in an MFC v7.1 application is described in "Windows Forms: .NET Framework 1.1 Provides Expanded Namespace, Security, and Language Support for Your Projects," written by Chris Sells and printed in *MSDN Magazine*, March 2003 (*http://msdn.microsoft.com/msdnmag/issues/03/03/WindowsForms/default.aspx* or *http://tinysells.com/87*).

Figure B-8. A managed MFC application

Compiling this sample MFC application and running it yields the same behavior as Figure B-8 (in fact, Figure B-8 is the managed version—fooled ya...). Once the application is compiled as a managed application, you can reference managed assemblies to bring in ADO.NET, System.XML, Indigo, Windows Forms, and of course, WPF.

For example, maybe we want the About box in our simple MFC sample to have some fancy WPF control in it. To start, you're going to need to add the WPF assemblies to your project. The simplest way to do that is to right-click on your MFC project in the Solution Explorer and choose References. This will bring up the project's property pages prenavigated to the Common Properties → References section, where you can add the WindowsBase, PresentationCore, PresentationFramework, and System assemblies, as shown in Figure B-9.

If this were a normal Win32 application, complete with a WinMain function, I'd tell you to add a managed attribute to it so that your main thread was marked as an STA thread, as shown in Example B-7.

Example B-7. Setting the UI thread to single-threaded mode

```
#include "stdafx.h"
...
[System::STAThreadAttribute]
int APIENTRY _tWinMain(...) { // MFC apps don't have these...
  ...
}
```

The STAThreadAttribute attribute is required on the UI thread for .NET-based UI stacks (i.e., Windows Forms and WPF). However, because MFC applications don't have a custom WinMain (MFC implements the WinMain method for you), that means you need to go another route to mark your entry point as STA-threaded. To do this, set the Configuration Properties → Linker → Advanced → CLR Thread Attribute property to "STA threading attribute (/CLRTHREADATTRIBUTE:STA)" in your project's properties.

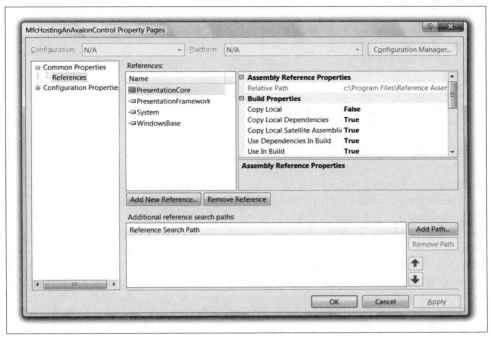

Figure B-9. Adding the appropriate .NET assemblies to interop with WPF

With the appropriate thread settings, we can now create a WPF control host suitable as an HWND child to host our WPF control. The host class is called HwndSource and is part of WPF in the System.Windows namespace. The C++/CLI code in Example B-8 creates a WPF button and hosts it in an instance of HwndSource.

Example B-8. Creating a WPF button in C++/CLI

```
HwndSource^ CreateWpfOkButton(
  HWND hwndParent, int x, int y, int width, int height) {

  // Create a fancy WPF OK button
  Button^ wpfButton = gcnew Button( );
  wpfButton->Content = "OK";
  wpfButton->Background =
    gcnew LinearGradientBrush(
      Colors::White, Colors::Red, Point(0, 0), Point(1, 1));

  // Host the button in the border to fill in the background
  Border^ wpfBorder = gcnew Border( );
  wpfBorder->SetResourceReference(Border::BackgroundProperty,
             System::Windows::SystemColors::ControlBrushKey);
  wpfBorder->Child = wpfButton;

  // Host the border in an HwndSource and return the host
  HwndSourceParameters params;
```

```
params.ParentWindow = IntPtr(hwndParent);
params.WindowStyle = WS_CHILD | WS_VISIBLE;
params.PositionX = x;
params.PositionY = y;
params.Width = width;
params.Height = height;
HwndSource^ src = gcnew HwndSource(params);
src->RootVisual = wpfBorder;

    return src;
}
```

Example B-8 shows a helper function that uses the C++/CLI syntax enabled by the CLR setting we enabled earlier.* The helper creates an instance of a WPF Button, and then creates an instance of a Border to host the button. The Border object's Background property is set to a resource reference to the brush for the dialog background color (called the "control" color for programmers and the "3D Object" color for Vista users†). With the resource reference set (which is the same as using a DynamicResource markup extension in XAML), if the user changes the color, the border around the button will update as appropriate. Without the border, the button will be surrounded with black, which ruins the whole "integration" experience we're going for. The border hosts the button, and the border in turn is hosted by an instance of the HwndSource via the RootVisual property. Using the helper function in the About box's OnInitDialog method, we replace the native OK button with our managed WPF button, as shown in Example B-9.

Example B-9. Hosting a WPF button in an MFC application

```
BOOL CAboutDlg::OnInitDialog() {
  // Get position of the native OK button relative to the About box
  HWND hwndParent = this->GetSafeHwnd();
  HWND hwndOkButton = ::GetDlgItem(hwndParent, IDOK);
  RECT rect = { 0 };
  ::GetWindowRect(hwndOkButton, &rect);
  // The violence inherent in the system...
  ::MapWindowPoints(0, hwndParent, (POINT*)&rect, 2);

  // Hide the native OK button
  ::ShowWindow(hwndOkButton, SW_HIDE);

  // Create and show the WPF button
  HwndSource^ srcWpfButton = CreateWpfOkButton(
    hwndParent,
```

---

* For more information on the C++/CLI syntax in VS2005, I recommend starting here: *http://msdn.microsoft.com/msdnmag/issues/06/00/PureC/default.aspx* (*http://tinysells.com/97*).

† Start → Control Panel → Personalization → Windows Color and Appearance → Open classic appearance properties for more color options → Advanced.

```
    rect.left,
    rect.top,
    rect.right - rect.left,
    rect.bottom - rect.top);

  // Handle the Click event
  Button^ wpfButton = (Button^)((Border^)srcWpfButton->RootVisual)->Child;
  wpfButton->Click += MAKE_DELEGATE(RoutedEventHandler, okButton_Clicked);

  ::ShowWindow((HWND)srcWpfButton->Handle.ToPointer( ), SW_SHOW);
  return TRUE;
}

void CAboutDlg::okButton_Clicked(Object^ sender, RoutedEventArgs^ e) {
  EndDialog(IDOK);
}
```

After doing some pedestrian Win32 dialog math to find the location of the native OK button relative to the client area of its parent and hiding it, we create our managed WPF button using the helper function and hook up its Click event to a member function of the CAboutDlg class that closes the dialog just like our native OK button was doing.

We construct the click handler with the MAKE_DELEGATE macro that VC++ provides to help map a native member function to a managed delegate. To make this work, we need to bring in the *msclr\event.h* header file and add a DELEGATE_MAP to our CAboutDlg class declaration, as Example B-10 illustrates.

Example B-10. Enabling the MAKE_DELEGATE macro

```
// stdafx.h
...
#include <msclr\event.h>

// MfcHostingAnWPFControl.cpp
...
class CAboutDlg : public CDialog {
  ...
public: // VS05b1 requires the delegate map to be public
  BEGIN_DELEGATE_MAP(CAboutDlg)
    EVENT_DELEGATE_ENTRY(okButton_Clicked, Object^, RoutedEventArgs^)
  END_DELEGATE_MAP( )
};
```

Figure B-10 shows the result.

One final note: although it's also possible to host HWND controls inside WPF applications, custom HWND controls have largely gone the way of the dodo in favor of ActiveX controls and Windows Forms controls (and hopefully, someday soon, WPF controls).

Figure B-10. Hosting a WPF button in a managed MFC application

WPF and ActiveX Controls

For hosting ActiveX controls, WPF relies completely on Windows Forms and its capability to host ActiveX controls. In other words, hosting ActiveX controls inside WPF is a matter of hosting a Windows Forms user control in your WPF element that itself hosts the ActiveX control of your dreams.

If you want to go the other way—that is, hosting WPF as an ActiveX control—you can do so by hosting a WPF control on a Windows Forms User Control as described earlier, because a Windows Forms control can be hosted as an ActiveX control, although this is technically supported only in MFC 7.1+.*

WPF and HTML

Unlike ActiveX or Windows Forms controls, WPF elements cannot be hosted directly on an HTML page (i.e., there's nothing to support this kind of thing in HTML), as shown in Example B-11.

Example B-11. WPF controls can't be hosted directly in HTML

```
<html>
  <body>
    <h1>WPF doesn't support anything like this!</h1>
    <object
      id="wpfctrl"
      classid="wpfctrl.dll#wpfctrl.MyWpfControl"
      width="100"
      height="100">
    </object>
  </body>
</html>
```

---

* If you need to explore this space, "Hosting Windows Forms Controls in COM Control Containers" at *http://www.ondotnet.com/pub/a/dotnet/2003/01/20/winformshosting.html* is a place to start (*http://tinysells.com/94*).

You can get around this issue again by hosting a WPF control on a custom Windows Forms User Control. Or, if you've got a WPF XBAP as described in Chapter 11, you can host it as a frame as shown in Example B-12.

Example B-12. WPF XBAP hosted in an HTML iframe

```html
<html>
  <body>
    <h1>WPF supports this!</h1>
    <iframe src="MyWpfApp.xbap"></iframe>
  </body>
</html>
```

The downside of this approach is that the WPF application cannot provide any programmatic interface (e.g., properties, methods, or events) to the surrounding HTML, like an ActiveX control would.

To go the other way and host HTML inside WPF is a matter of bringing either the COM or the Windows Forms Web Browser control into your WPF app and feeding it HTML. Or, if the HTML is available via a URL, you can navigate to it on a navigation host, as Example B-13 illustrates.

Example B-13. Navigating to an URL using a WPF navigation host

```
<Page ...>
  <Grid>
    <TextBlock>
      Check out
        <Hyperlink
          NavigateUri="http://sellsbrothers.com">sellsbrothers.com</Hyperlink>.
    </TextBlock>
  </Grid>
</Page>
```

Because the link references HTML, the WebBrowser control will be brought in automatically to host the content, as Figure B-11 shows.

For much more on the topic of navigation, see Chapter 11.

Limitations of WPF/HWND Interop

As useful as WPF's integration with other presentation technologies is, because WPF's approach to rendering and composition is radically different from the way Win32 UIs have previously worked, there are some limitations to how you can mix the two. Essentially, the new features that WPF offers do not translate back into the old world. The old UI technologies still have the same limitations they always did, even when being hosted by a WPF application.

Figure B-11. Navigation to HTML inside a navigation host

Airspace

The most important thing to understand is the principle of *airspace*: within any single top-level window, each pixel belongs to exactly one technology. So, a single pixel must belong either to WPF or to Win32.[*]

One of the upshots of the airspace principle is that the clip region of a UI element does not apply to any HWND-based children. This is a nonobvious restriction, and it applies because clipping is a composition feature. (Internally, it depends on a UI element and all its children being rendered, and then having the rendered output clipped. A Win32 element cannot render into the internal intermediate buffers that WPF uses to perform clipping.) For example, here we're nesting three Windows Forms controls inside a clipped WPF Grid:

```
<Grid ...>
  ...

  <Grid.Clip>
    <StreamGeometry>M174,0 348,174 174,348 0,174 z</StreamGeometry>
  </Grid.Clip>
```

[*] Or DirectX, but that's beyond the scope of this book.

```
<!-- properly clipped -->
<Rectangle ...>...</Rectangle>

<!-- properly clipped -->
<TextBlock ...>
  WPF<LineBreak />
  WPF<LineBreak />
  WPF
</TextBlock>

<!-- not clipped -->
<wfi:WindowsFormsHost ...>
  <wf:Label ... Text="Windows Forms" />
</wfi:WindowsFormsHost>

<wfi:WindowsFormsHost ...>
  <wf:Label ... Text="Windows Forms" />
</wfi:WindowsFormsHost>

<wfi:WindowsFormsHost ...>
  <wf:Label ... Text="Windows Forms" />
</wfi:WindowsFormsHost>

</Grid>
```

Figure B-12 shows a WPF Grid clipped to a diamond with three Windows Forms controls drawn inside, but they are not clipped.

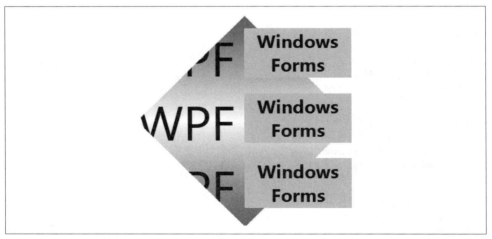

Figure B-12. HWND-based controls are not clipped to the clipping area set by their WPF parent

You could set the Region property of the Windows Forms controls so that they are clipped to the same shape as the WPF element. However, be careful with this—you might end up making the join between Win32 and WPF more visible. Win32 enables controls to be arbitrary shapes with its region facility, but this is accurate only to the nearest pixel—any given pixel in a window is either inside a particular control or not.

For certain shapes, this can give rise to visible "jaggies" around the edges of the shape. A WPF clip region, on the other hand, can be any Geometry, and Geometrys define shapes in a pixel-independent fashion. WPF renders the boundaries of clipped elements with anti-aliasing to reduce jaggies, so the boundary of the clip region would alternate between smooth and jagged as you went between WPF and Win32 elements.

Also, keeping a WPF clip in sync with a Win32 region isn't straightforward—you need to build the region yourself. Because this requires a lot of effort, and the results may be of disappointing quality, it's probably best to prevent this if you can. Try to avoid UI designs that require this.

Another consideration associated with airspace is that HWNDs always appear to be on top of WPF content. Consider Example B-14.

Example B-14. Airspace and HWNDs

```
<Grid ...>
  ...

  <!-- z-order = 0 -->
  <Rectangle ...>...</Rectangle>

  <!-- z-order = 1 -->
  <TextBlock ...>
    WPF<LineBreak />
    WPF<LineBreak />
    WPF
  </TextBlock>

  <!-- z-order = 2 -->
  <wfi:WindowsFormsHost ...>
    <wf:Label ... Text="Windows Forms" />
  </wfi:WindowsFormsHost>

  <!-- z-order = 3 -->
  <wfi:WindowsFormsHost ...>
    <wf:Label ... Text="Windows Forms" />
  </wfi:WindowsFormsHost>

  <!-- z-order = 4 -->
  <wfi:WindowsFormsHost ...>
    <wf:Label ... Text="Windows Forms" />
  </wfi:WindowsFormsHost>

  <!-- z-order = 5 -->
  <Ellipse ... />

  <!-- z-order = 6 -->
  <TextBlock ...>
    On Top
  </TextBlock>
</Grid>
```

As shown in Figure B-13, the red rectangle in Example B-14 contains the text "On Top" because it is at the top of the Z stack. The pink circle is directly behind it, and in front of everything else. The text labels on the left have been correctly obliterated because WPF rendered those. However, the Windows Forms controls on the right have rendered above the rectangle and the circle, despite the fact that in the XAML, they appeared beneath them in the Z order.

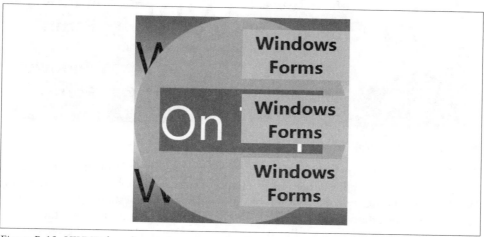

Figure B-13. HWND-based controls positioned in the background but rendered in the foreground

The Windows Forms controls are in front of the WPF controls, in spite of the Z order, because HWNDs use a strategy for dealing with Z order that's different than WPF. WPF uses the *painters algorithm*: all UI elements are (logically speaking) painted onto a single target canvas, starting from the elements at the back and working forward to the ones at the front. Win32, on the other hand, doesn't support transparency, nor does it support anti-aliasing at control boundaries, so it can use a much simpler approach: it assumes that for the region occupied by a particular HWND, the only control that needs to do any rendering is the one that owns the HWND. This causes two problems.

The first problem is that HWNDs tend to fill in their own background, so you can't see what's behind them (although there are ways around that, as we'll see). Second, you can't position WPF elements on top of HWNDs. This is a direct consequence of the airspace principle, combined with the different ways that WPF and Win32 deal with Z order.

Further, if an animated feature attempts to move in front of a Win32-based element, it will end up appearing behind it, as the ellipse disappearing behind the Windows Forms content shows in Figure B-14.

Figure B-14 is just another manifestation of the Z order problem that is shown in Figure B-13.

Figure B-14. WPF element animation improperly drawing behind the HWND-based controls

Another basic issue with WPF/HWND interop is that although WPF elements offer an Opacity property that allows them to be made partially or completely transparent, any Win32 elements that may be children of the UI element in question ignore this property. For example, the following constructs a checkerboard background, and then everything else is contained by a partially opaque Grid placed on top of the background:

```
<Page.Background>
  <DrawingBrush ...>...</DrawingBrush>
</Page.Background>

<Grid ... Opacity="0.8">
  ...
  <!-- opacity set by parent honored -->
  <Rectangle ...>...</Rectangle>
  <TextBlock FontSize="80" VerticalAlignment="Center">
    WPF<LineBreak />
    WPF<LineBreak />
    WPF
  </TextBlock>

  <!-- opacity set by parent ignored -->
  <wfi:WindowsFormsHost ...>
    <wf:Label ... Text="Windows Forms" />
  </wfi:WindowsFormsHost>

  <wfi:WindowsFormsHost ...>
    <wf:Label ... Text="Windows Forms" />
  </wfi:WindowsFormsHost>

  <wfi:WindowsFormsHost ...>
    <wf:Label ... Text="Windows Forms" />
  </wfi:WindowsFormsHost>

</Grid>
```

Figure B-15 shows the results.

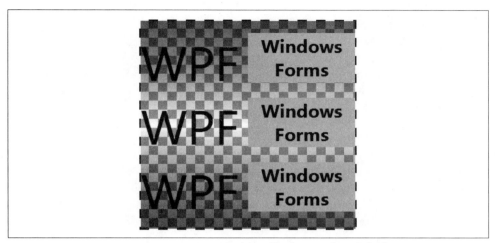

Figure B-15. Opacity property on WPF parent ignored by HWND-based children

This Grid has its Opacity set to 0.8. Consequently, all the WPF features—the gradient fill and the three lines of text—have rendered with partial transparency. However, the three Windows Forms controls, which are also elements of this same Grid, have rendered completely opaque.

Windows Forms has always offered a form of pseudotransparency, where a control could ask its parent to render itself into the child area before the child began to render. This allowed the appearance of transparency for simple designs (although it was fairly easy to construct a design for which this did not work correctly—anything with overlapping peer controls would produce wrong-looking results). The WindowsFormsHost element offers a similar feature:

```
<Grid Margin="2">
  ...

  <Rectangle Grid.ColumnSpan="2">...</Rectangle>

  <TextBlock FontSize="80" VerticalAlignment="Center">
    WPF<LineBreak />
    WPF<LineBreak />
    WPF
  </TextBlock>

  <wfi:WindowsFormsHost ... Background="Transparent">
    <wf:Label TextAlign="MiddleCenter"  Text="Windows Forms" />
  </wfi:WindowsFormsHost>

  <wfi:WindowsFormsHost ... Background="Transparent">
    <wf:Label TextAlign="MiddleCenter"  Text="Windows Forms" />
  </wfi:WindowsFormsHost>
```

```
<wfi:WindowsFormsHost ... Background="Transparent">
  <wf:Label TextAlign="MiddleCenter" Text="Windows Forms" />
</wfi:WindowsFormsHost>

<Ellipse Fill="#afaa" Grid.ColumnSpan="2" />
</Grid>
```

If you set the `WindowsFormsHost` object's `Background` to `Transparent`, it works out what WPF would have rendered where the Windows Forms control is, and then provides that as its background, as Figure B-16 shows.

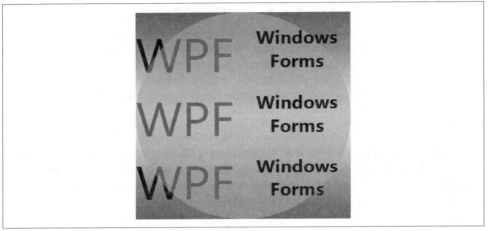

Figure B-16. Setting a transparent background on the WindowsFormsHost helps

Unfortunately, this is not a complete solution. In this example, the Windows Forms controls are at the same place in the Z order as the three lines of WPF text: they are in front of the background, but behind the semitransparent circle. But as you can see, the Windows Forms controls have been rendered in front of the circle, unlike the WPF text. Still, although the opaque appearance has now gone, there is a cost to this: this form of rendering runs noticeably slower than the normal style.

You can sidestep a number of these airspace issues by using multiple top-level windows, as each one gets its own HWND. WPF opens new top-level windows for pop ups of any kind, which avoids the "Win32 is always on top" issue we've seen in this appendix. Win32 elements appear at the top of the Z order of their containing top-level window, but because pop ups like `Menus` and `ToolTips` get their own top-level windows, they can appear above even these Win32 elements.

Also, because WPF supports use of a transparent client area in top-level windows, you can render shaped and/or partially transparent WPF features on top of Win32 elements by putting them in a second window that sits on top of the first one and has its `AllowsTransparency` property set to `True`. Such a window will be completely transparent in its client area except for areas containing a WPF element. You could even use this to run an animation that is overlaid on top of Win32 elements.

However, be aware that transparent top-level windows have performance issues: in Windows XP and Windows 2003, such windows will be rendered in software. Due to a limitation in DirectX on those versions of Windows, it is not possible for WPF to render a transparent window with hardware acceleration. And, although Windows Vista can use hardware acceleration with transparent windows, the results can still be substantially slower than with normal windows under both Windows XP and Windows Vista.[*]

Transforms, Events, and Nested Interop

In addition to airspace and Z-order issues, WPF's ability to apply transforms such as rotation and skews to any UI element does not apply to hosted Win32-based elements. Scaling is a special case: the Windows Forms host can apply scale transforms to its content, because Windows Forms itself has some scaling support built in. But because Win32-based components are generally intrinsically incapable of supporting such transforms, there's no way WPF can magically imbue them with such capabilities.

Also, the use of interop introduces some inconsistencies in the input events you see. When the mouse goes over a non-WPF element, you will stop seeing mouse events, and IsMouseOver for the containing element will return false, even though the mouse is inside a child of the element. Likewise, if a hosted Win32 element has the keyboard focus, you will not see keyboard or focus events bubbling out to the containing WPF element.

Finally, nested interop is not supported. This means that if you have, say, a Windows Forms control that uses interop to host WPF content, this Windows Forms control cannot be hosted via interop inside a WPF app. This would mean WPF wrapping Windows Forms wrapping more WPF, and this nesting is not supported.

For more information on the limitations of WPF interop, I recommend the SDK article "WPF and Win32 Interoperation Overview."[†]

---

[*] Hardware versus software rendering performance does depend on your hardware, however, as Seema Ramchandani points out at *http://blogs.msdn.com/seema/archive/2006/10/25/layered-windows-sw-is-sometimes-faster-than-hw.aspx* (*http://tinysells.com/98*).

[†] *http://msdn2.microsoft.com/en-us/library/ms742522.aspx* (*http://tinysells.com/93*).

Asynchronous and Multithreaded WPF Programming

If you like to write applications that annoy your users, a good way to do this is to make the user interface stop responding to input from time to time. For extra frustration, you can compound the problem by not giving any visible indication that work might be progressing, leaving the user to wonder whether the application is busy or has simply crashed. Because you'll get this behavior by default if you don't take certain steps to maintain responsiveness, you can stop reading now. Unless, that is, you'd prefer *not* to annoy your users.

Unfortunately, it's all too easy to write your application in such a way that it becomes unresponsive when it performs time-consuming work such as accessing a server over a network or reading files off disk. In Windows, all messages regarding user input for a particular window are delivered to the same thread. In general, this is a good thing, because it means your code has to deal with input events only one at a time, and does not have to worry about thread safety. The downside is that the application can respond to input only if this thread is available to process it.

Many APIs are *synchronous*—they do not return until they have completed the work you asked them to perform. (Such APIs are said to *block*.) If you write a handler for a button's Click event that makes a synchronous API call to retrieve data from a database, that call will not return until the database returns the data. The thread cannot do anything else until that synchronous call returns, so the application will be unable to respond to any other user input for the duration of the call.

Even if you avoid synchronous APIs, you could still cause sluggishness simply through slow code. Code risks being slow if it performs either CPU-intensive or memory-intensive work. Slow CPU-intensive work is fairly uncommon—computers are fast enough these days that you need to find a considerable amount of work for processing to seem anything less than instantaneous, and only a handful of applications do this. However, excessive memory use is much more common, and it can have a drastic effect on speed, particularly once paging to disk occurs. If the OS has to load a page off disk back into memory, the amount of time this takes is long enough to execute tens of millions of instructions. This has to happen only a couple of times before it adds up to a perceptible delay. Whether code is slow due to memory or CPU usage, running slow code on the same thread that handles user input will make the UI unresponsive.

There are two ways to solve this problem. One is to use *asynchronous* APIs. Some parts of the .NET Framework offer asynchronous invocation, where the API call returns immediately without waiting for the work to complete. For example, instead of using the Stream class's blocking Read method, you could call the nonblocking BeginRead, passing in a callback to be notified when the read operation completes. Alternatively, you can use multithreaded programming—if you execute code on some thread other than the thread that handles input, it doesn't matter whether this other thread executes slow code or calls synchronous APIs, because the input handling thread is free to respond to other user input.

Multithreaded programming in WPF works in the same way as in any other .NET application. Because this appendix deals only with multithreading issues specific to WPF applications, we won't be showing any of the general-purpose .NET threading techniques. For more general information on .NET's multithreading facilities, consult the "Managed Threading" topic in the SDK documentation at *http://msdn2.microsoft.com/library/3e8s7xdd.aspx* (*http://tinysells.com/80*).

Using asynchronous APIs often results in the use of multiple threads. Although you might not explicitly create any new threads, you may be notified of the completion of some asynchronous operation on a different thread from the one that started the work. So, regardless of whether you choose to use asynchronous APIs or multithreading to keep your application responsive, an understanding of WPF's threading model will be necessary.

The WPF Threading Model

Many WPF objects have *thread affinity*, meaning that they belong to a particular thread. Your code must always use a WPF user interface element on the same thread that created it. It is illegal to attempt to use any WPF element from any other thread.

If you are familiar with Windows Forms, you will be used to this threading model. If you are familiar with COM (the Component Object Model), you will recognize this as resembling the Single Threaded Apartment (STA) model.

WPF uses this model for various reasons. One is simplicity—the model is straightforward and does not introduce any complications for applications that have no need for multiple threads. This simplicity also makes it fairly straightforward for WPF to detect when you have broken the rules so that it can alert you to the problem with an exception. There are also performance benefits: thread affinity avoids locking, which is usually required with multithreaded models, and locks add both complexity and performance overhead.

Another important reason for using a single-threaded model is to support interop with Win32, which also has thread affinity requirements. (It is not quite as strict, in that it is possible to perform many operations from the "wrong" thread. However, such operations are often handled very differently than the same operations performed on the right thread, and numerous pitfalls are associated with cross-thread window usage.) By adopting a strict thread affinity model, you can mix WPF, Windows Forms, and Win32 user interface elements freely within a single application.

DispatcherObject

You might be wondering how you can be sure which types have thread affinity and which don't. Although all user interface elements have this requirement, it does not apply to every single type you use in a WPF application. For example, built-in types not specific to WPF, such as Int32, do not care which thread you use them on, as long as you use them from only one thread at a time.

But what about types that are specific to WPF but are not user interface elements, such as Brush, Color, and Geometry? How are we to tell which types have thread affinity requirements? The answer is to look at the base class. WPF types with thread affinity derive from the DispatcherObject base class. Brush and Geometry both derive from DispatcherObject, so usually you can use them only on the thread that created them.* Color does not, and therefore you can use it on a different thread from the one on which it was created.

> The DispatcherObject class defines a few members, all of which are exempt from the thread affinity rule—you can use them from any thread. Only the functionality added by classes that derive from DispatcherObject is subject to thread affinity.

DispatcherObject provides a couple of methods that let you check whether you are on the right thread for the object: CheckAccess and VerifyAccess. CheckAccess returns true if you are on the correct thread, false otherwise. VerifyAccess is intended for when you think you are already on the right thread, and it would be indicative of a problem in the program if you were not. It throws an exception if you are on the wrong thread. Example C-1 shows a method that uses this to ensure that it has been called on the right thread.

---

* It's slightly more complex than that for these particular types. Brush and Geometry derive from DispatcherObject indirectly via the Freezable base class. This means they can be frozen, which has the effect of detaching them from their dispatcher and removing the thread affinity requirement. We discuss freezing in more detail in Appendix D.

Example C-1. Use of VerifyAccess

```
public void Frobnicate(FrobLevel fl) {
    // Ensure we're on the UI thread
    VerifyAccess();

    ...
}
```

Many WPF types call VerifyAccess when you use them. They do not do this for every single public API, because such comprehensive checking would impose a significant performance overhead. However, it checks in enough places that you are unlikely to get very far on the wrong thread before the problem becomes apparent.

If your application causes multiple threads to be created, either through explicit thread creation or implicitly through the use of asynchronous APIs, you should avoid touching any user interface objects on those threads. If you need to update the user interface as a result of work done on a different thread, you must use the *dispatcher* to get back onto the UI thread.

The Dispatcher

Each thread that creates user interface objects needs a Dispatcher object. This effectively owns the thread, running a loop that dispatches input messages to the appropriate handlers. (It performs a similar role to a message pump in Win32.) As well as handling input, the dispatcher enables us to get calls directed through to the right thread.

 The Dispatcher class lives in the System.Windows.Threading namespace along with all other WPF-specific threading classes, including DispatcherObject.

Obtaining a Dispatcher

Recall that all WPF objects with thread affinity derive from the DispatcherObject base class. This class defines a Dispatcher property, which returns the Dispatcher object for the thread to which the object belongs.

You can also retrieve the Dispatcher for the current thread by using the Dispatcher.CurrentDispatcher static property.

Getting Onto the Right Thread with a Dispatcher

If you need to update the user interface after doing some work on a worker thread, you must make sure the update is done on the UI thread. The Dispatcher provides methods that let you invoke the code of your choice on the dispatcher's thread.

You can use either Invoke or BeginInvoke. Both of these accept any delegate and an optional list of parameters. They both invoke the delegate's target method on the dispatcher's thread, regardless of which thread you call them from. Invoke does not return until the method has been executed, whereas BeginInvoke queues the request to invoke the method, but returns straight away without waiting for the method to run.

Invoke can be simpler to understand, because you can be certain of the order in which things happen. However, it can lead to subtle problems—by making a worker thread wait for the UI thread, there is a risk of deadlock. The worker thread may be in possession of locks or other resources that the UI thread is waiting for, and each will wait for the other indefinitely, causing the application to freeze. BeginInvoke avoids this risk, but adds the complexity that the order of events is less predictable.

Example C-2 shows the use of the dispatcher's BeginInvoke method. This is a typical way of structuring code that is not running on the UI thread, but which needs to do something to the UI. In this case, the code sets the background color of the window. The RunsOnWorkerThread method in this example runs on a worker thread. (The mechanism by which that worker thread was created is not shown here, because the techniques used for creating worker threads in WPF applications are exactly the same as those used in any other .NET application.)

Example C-2. Using Dispatcher.BeginInvoke

```
partial class MyWindow : Window {
    ...
    public delegate void MyDelegateType( );

    void RunsOnWorkerThread( ){

        Color bgColor = CalculateBgColor( );
        MyDelegateType methodForUiThread = delegate {
            this.Background = new SolidColorBrush(bgColor);
        };
        this.Dispatcher.BeginInvoke(DispatcherPriority.Normal, methodForUiThread);
    }

    ...
}
```

We're using the C# anonymous delegate syntax here. You don't have to use this—you could just put the code in a separate method. However, anonymous delegates are often particularly convenient in this kind of scenario, because you can use any of the variables that are in scope in the containing method. In this case, we are setting the bgColor variable in the containing method, and then using that value in the nested anonymous method that will run on the UI thread. This sharing of lexical scope across two methods makes moving from one thread to another relatively painless.

The first parameter passed to BeginInvoke indicates the priority with which we would like the message to be handled. The Dispatcher does not operate a strict "first in first out" policy, because some messages need to be handled with higher priority than others. For example, suppose two work items are queued up with the dispatcher, where one is a message representing keyboard input and the other is a timer event that will poll some remote service for status. The remote polling is likely to take a while to complete, so delaying the poll a little won't have any visible effect. However, even fairly small delays in processing user input tend to make an application feel unresponsive, so you would normally want the key press to be handled before background tasks such as polling. The dispatcher therefore handles messages according to their specified priority to allow those that are sensitive to latency, such as input messages, to be handled ahead of less urgent tasks.

The Normal priority level is relatively high—it runs ahead of input processing and even rendering. For quick operations, this is not a problem, but in some cases you may want the work to run as a "background" operation—something that will run only when there is nothing more important to do. For this kind of processing, use either the ApplicationIdle or the SystemIdle priority level. ApplicationIdle will not process the message until the application has nothing else to do. SystemIdle considers activity across the whole machine, and processes the message only when a CPU would otherwise be idle.

The second parameter to BeginInvoke is the delegate. The Dispatcher will invoke this at some point in the future on the dispatcher thread. If we had used a delegate type that required parameters to be passed to the target function, we would have used one of the overloads of BeginInvoke that accepts extra parameters, as Example C-3 shows.

Example C-3. Passing parameters with BeginInvoke

```
delegate void UsesColor(Color c);
void SetBackgroundColor(Color c) {
    this.Background = new SolidColorBrush(c);
}

void RunsOnWorkerThread() {
    UsesColor methodForUiThread = SetBackgroundColor;
    this.Dispatcher.BeginInvoke(DispatcherPriority.Normal, methodForUiThread,
                        Colors.Blue);
}
```

Here we have defined a custom delegate type called UsesColor. It requires its target function to take a single parameter of type Color. The delegate was defined to match the signature of SetBackgroundColor, the method we want to call. This method sets the window background color, so it needs to run on the UI thread. We're assuming that the RunsOnWorkerThread method isn't on the right thread, so it uses the Dispatcher.BeginInvoke method to call SetBackgroundColor on the correct thread.

However, there are a couple of differences between Examples C-2 and C-3. One is cosmetic—we are no longer using the C# anonymous delegate syntax. The other is that we are now passing an extra parameter to BeginInvoke. You can pass as many extra parameters as you like—one of the BeginInvoke overloads accepts a variable length argument list. All of these parameters will be passed into the target function on the dispatcher thread.

If you are familiar with the .NET asynchronous pattern, you might be wondering whether there is an EndInvoke method. Typically, any call to a BeginXxx method has to be matched with a corresponding EndXxx call. But the Dispatcher does not use the standard asynchronous pattern. BeginInvoke has no corresponding EndInvoke method, nor does it provide a way of passing in a completion callback function to BeginInvoke as you would expect to see with a normal implementation of the .NET asynchronous pattern. However, it is possible to discover when an operation is executed by using the DispatcherOperation class. This class also supports cancellation, which is not available in the standard asynchronous pattern.

DispatcherOperation

The Dispatcher.BeginInvoke method returns a DispatcherOperation object. This represents the work item sent to the dispatcher. You can use it to determine the current status of the operation. Its Status property will be one of the values from the DispatcherOperationStatus enumeration, shown in Table C-1.

Table C-1. DispatcherOperationStatus values

Value	Meaning
Pending	The dispatcher has not yet called the method.
Executing	The method is currently executing on the dispatcher thread.
Completed	The method has finished executing.
Aborted	The operation was aborted.

You will see the Aborted status only if you cancel the operation. You can cancel an operation by calling the DispatcherOperation.Abort method. As long as the operation has not already started, this removes it from the dispatcher's queue. This method returns true if the operation was cancelled, and false if it had already started by the time you called abort.

You can wait for the operation to complete by calling the Wait method. This blocks the worker thread until the UI thread has executed the method. (This carries the same risk of deadlock as Invoke.) Alternatively, you can add a handler to the Completed event, which will be raised when the method completes. However, this is slightly tricky to use, because it's possible that the operation will already have run by the time you get around to adding the handler. It may be simpler just to write your code in a way that avoids using either of these. Remember that BeginInvoke calls the method you tell it to. If you need to do some work after the dispatcher has called your code, just add that to the method, as Example C-4 shows.

Example C-4. Avoiding Wait and Completed

```
MyDelegateType work = delegate {

    DoWorkOnUIThread();

    DoWhateverWeNeedToDoNowTheMainWorkHasBeenDone();
};
this.Dispatcher.BeginInvoke(DispatcherPriority.Normal, work);
```

Of course, both methods called in Example C-4 will run on the UI thread. If the second method is slow, just use a suitable multithreading or asynchronous invocation mechanism to move it back onto a worker thread.

When you call BeginInvoke, the dispatcher will run your method as soon as it is able to. If the UI thread is idle, this will happen immediately. This is not always desirable—it can be useful to be called back after a delay, which is what makes the dispatch timer useful.

DispatcherTimer

Applications often create timers in order to perform housekeeping tasks on a regular basis. You could use either of the Timer classes in the .NET class library, but both of these would notify you on a thread from the CLR thread pool, meaning you'd have to call Dispatcher.BeginInvoke to get back onto the right thread.

It is simpler to use the WPF-aware DispatcherTimer class. This raises timer notifications via the dispatcher, meaning your timer handler will always run on the correct thread automatically. This enables you to do things to the user interface directly from the handler, as Example C-5 shows.

Example C-5. Using a DispatcherTimer

```
partial class MyWindow : Window {

    DispatcherTimer dt;
    public MyWindow() {
        dt = new DispatcherTimer();
        dt.Tick += dt_Tick;
        dt.Interval = TimeSpan.FromSeconds(2);
        dt.Start();
    }

    Random rnd = new Random();
    void dt_Tick(object sender, EventArgs e) {
        byte[] vals = new byte[3];
        rnd.NextBytes(vals);
        Color c = Color.FromRgb(vals[0], vals[1], vals[2]);
```

Example C-5. Using a DispatcherTimer (continued)

```
        // OK to touch UI elements, as the DispatcherTimer
        // calls us back on the UI thread
        this.Background = new SolidColorBrush(c);
    }
}
```

By default, the `DispatcherTimer` uses the `Background` priority level to deliver notifications. If necessary, you can change this by passing in a value from the `DispatcherPriority` enumeration when you construct the timer. You can also pass in a `Dispatcher`, although by default it will use the `Dispatcher.CurrentDispatcher` property to retrieve the dispatcher for the current thread. However, you will need to pass the dispatcher explicitly if you are creating the timer from a different thread than the UI thread.

Multiple UI Threads and Dispatchers

It is not strictly necessary for there to be just one UI thread—it is possible for an application to create user interface objects on several threads. However, all of the elements in any given window must belong to the same thread. So, in practice, you can have at most one UI thread per top-level window.

> It is fairly rare to use more than one UI thread—the user can interact with only one window at a time, so there is normally no need for concurrent dispatchers. However, if for some reason, you cannot avoid blocking the UI thread, it might be appropriate to use multiple UI threads in order to localize the blocking to a single window. For example, suppose you need to host an unreliable or slow third-party UI component. Using one thread per top-level window would mean that if the component should freeze, it would take out only one window rather than the whole application. Internet Explorer uses multiple UI threads for this very reason. (Of course, IE isn't a WPF application, but the same principle applies to Win32 applications.)

Each thread that hosts UI objects needs a dispatcher in order for those UI objects to function. In a single-threaded application, you don't need to do anything special to create a dispatcher. The `Application` class creates one for you at startup, and shuts it down automatically on exit. However, if you create multiple user interface threads, you will need to start up and shut down the dispatcher for those manually. Example C-6 shows how to start a dispatcher.

Example C-6. Starting a dispatcher on a new UI thread

```
void StartDispatcher() {
    Thread thread = new Thread(MyDispatcherThreadProc);
    thread.SetApartmentState(ApartmentState.STA);
    thread.Start();
}
```

Example C-6. Starting a dispatcher on a new UI thread (continued)

```
void MyDispatcherThreadProc( ) {

    Window1 w = new Window1( );
    w.Show( );

    // Won't return until dispatcher shuts down
    System.Windows.Threading.Dispatcher.Run( );
}
```

The Dispatcher for a thread is created automatically the first time an object derived from the DispatcherObject base class is created. All WPF classes derive from this base class. So, the Dispatcher for the new thread will come into existence when the Window is created. All we have to do is call the static Dispatcher.Run method to ensure that messages are delivered to any UI objects created on the thread. This method will not return until you call InvokeShutdown or BeginInvokeShutdown on the dispatcher.

 WPF will call InvokeShutdown for you on the dispatcher it creates for the application's main thread. However, it is your responsibility to call this method for any other thread on which you call Dispatcher.Run. If you fail to do this, your application will continue to run even after the Application object shuts down the main thread.

The Dispatcher requires that you set the COM threading model to STA. Although a thread's COM threading model is used only in COM interop scenarios, many system features rely on COM interop under the covers. The Dispatcher therefore requires the model to be set even if your application does not use any COM components directly. The call to SetApartmentState in Example C-6 ensures that the correct model is used.

 Although WPF does support the use of multiple UI threads, it does not support UI in multiple AppDomains. All the UI threads in a given process must be in the same AppDomain.

The Event-Based Asynchronous Pattern

Some components allow you to perform asynchronous work without having to worry about the details of the dispatcher. This is possible thanks to the *event-based asynchronous pattern*, which was introduced in NET 2.0. Components that implement this pattern manage the necessary thread switching for you. They do so using the AsyncOperationManager family of classes,[*] which abstract away the details of UI threading requirements, supporting both Windows Forms and WPF through a common API.

---

[*] See *http://msdn2.microsoft.com/en-us/library/system.componentmodel.asyncoperationmanager.aspx* (*http://tinysells.com/91*) for details.

This means that classes designed for use in Windows Forms applications will also work correctly in WPF applications.

The event-based asynchronous pattern is fairly simple. A class will provide one or more methods whose names end in Async. For example, the WebClient class in the System.Net namespace offers an UploadFileAsync method. Each asynchronous method has a corresponding event to signal completion—UploadFileCompleted, in this case. There may optionally be other events to indicate partial progress, such as the UploadProgressChanged event offered by WebClient. The crucial feature of the event-based asynchronous pattern is that the events are raised on the UI thread. For example, if you call UploadFileAsync from the UI thread of a WPF application, the object will raise the UploadFileCompleted event on the same thread.

Not all components offer this pattern. Fortunately, .NET provides an implementation of the pattern that you can use to wrap slow, synchronous code: the BackgroundWorker class.

BackgroundWorker

The BackgroundWorker class is defined in the System.ComponentModel namespace. It makes it easy to move slow work onto a worker thread in order to avoid making the UI unresponsive. It also provides a very simple way of sending progress and completion notifications back to the UI thread. It uses the AsyncOperationManager internally to implement the event-based asynchronous pattern, so in a WPF application it will use the Dispatcher under the covers when raising events.

Example C-7 shows the BackgroundWorker class in use. We start by attaching a handler to the DoWork event. This event will be raised on a worker thread, so we can do slow work in this event handler without causing the UI to become unresponsive. This example also handles the ProgressChanged and RunWorkerCompleted events. Your code can cause these to be raised to indicate that the work is progressing or has completed. Note that you will not get ProgressChanged events automatically. First, you must enable them by setting the WorkerReportsProgress property to true. Having enabled them, they will be raised only if the DoWork handler calls the ReportProgress method from time to time.

Example C-7. Using a BackgroundWorker

```
partial class MyWindow : Window {

    BackgroundWorker bw;

    public MyWindow() {
        bw = new BackgroundWorker();
        bw.DoWork += new DoWorkEventHandler(bw_DoWork);
        bw.ProgressChanged += bw_ProgressChanged;
```

Example C-7. Using a BackgroundWorker (continued)

```csharp
    bw.RunWorkerCompleted += bw_RunWorkerCompleted;
    bw.WorkerReportsProgress = true;
    bw.RunWorkerAsync( );
}

void bw_DoWork(object sender, DoWorkEventArgs e) {

    // Running on a worker thread
    for (int i = 0; i < 10; ++i) {
        int percent = i * 10;
        bw.ReportProgress(percent);
        Thread.Sleep(1000);
    }

    // The BackgroundWorker will raise the RunWorkerCompleted
    // event when this method returns.
}

void bw_ProgressChanged(object sender, ProgressChangedEventArgs e) {
    // Running on a UI thread
    this.Title = "Working: " + e.ProgressPercentage + "%";
}

void bw_RunWorkerCompleted(object sender, RunWorkerCompletedEventArgs e) {
    // Running on a UI thread
    this.Title = "Finished";
}
```

When we call the RunWorkerAsync method, the BackgroundWorker raises the DoWork event on a worker thread. This means the DoWork handler can take as long as it likes, and will not cause the UI to freeze. Of course, it must not do anything to the user interface because it is not on the right thread. However, the ProgressChanged and RunWorkerCompleted events will always be raised on the UI thread, so it is always safe to use UI objects from these.

The RunWorkerCompleted handler is passed a RunWorkerCompletedEventArgs object. If there is a possibility that your DoWork method might throw an exception, you should check the Error property of this object. It will be null if the work completed successfully, and it will contain the exception otherwise.

WPF Base Types

WPF defines a large number of types, forming an extensive class hierarchy. This appendix describes the roles of the most important types. It does not provide a detailed description of each type—the MSDN documentation already does that. Instead, this is a high-level guide offering a broad view of how the various types fit together. Figure D-1 shows the inheritance relationships among the types described in this appendix.

DispatcherObject

System.Object

   System.Windows.Threading.DispatcherObject

DispatcherObject is the base class of any type associated with a Dispatcher. The dispatcher mechanism is WPF's message processing system. It underpins critical services including input handling, and certain aspects of layout and data binding. It is also at the heart of the WPF threading model. Threading and the dispatcher system are described in Appendix C.

All of the base types examined in this appendix derive from DispatcherObject, reflecting the dispatcher's central role. Although DispatcherObject is the most common base class in WPF, few classes derive from it directly. Most derive indirectly via DependencyObject.

DependencyObject

System.Object

   System.Windows.Threading.DispatcherObject

      System.Windows.DependencyObject

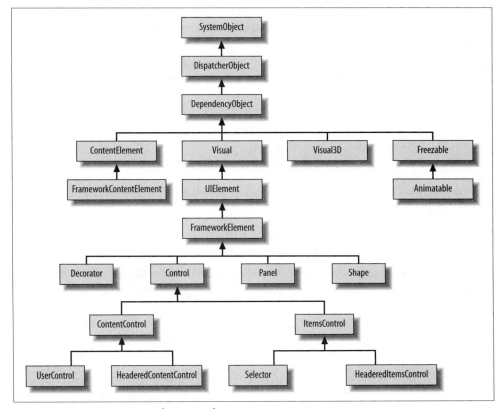

Figure D-1. WPF core types inheritance diagram

Classes derive from DependencyObject to employ WPF's *dependency property* (DP) system. The majority of WPF element types implement their properties using the GetValue and SetValue helper functions provided by DependencyObject. Chapter 18 illustrates this technique.

By handing control of a property to the dependency property system, we can take advantage of data binding, styling, animation, property value inheritance, default values, per-type metadata, and property change notifications.

It is fairly unusual to derive directly from DependencyObject—your classes will normally derive from one of the other classes described in this appendix, inheriting from DependencyObject indirectly. However, one scenario where deriving directly from this class can be useful is if you are writing a class whose only job is to act as a data binding source, with values that change on a regular basis. Although WPF supports ordinary CLR properties and can use the .NET Framework class library's INotifyPropertyChange interface to discover when properties change, it needs to use reflection to read ordinary properties. However, when binding to a dependency property, WPF provides the property implementation, so it does not need to use reflection to read properties, nor does it need to rely on property change events. This makes binding to a dependency property slightly more efficient than binding to an ordinary CLR property. However, the difference is slight, so you would typically use this approach only if you had identified performance problems in this area.

Visual

```
System.Object
    System.Windows.Threading.DispatcherObject
        System.Windows.DependencyObject
            System.Windows.Media.Visual
```

The Visual class is the abstract base class of all 2D elements in the visual tree. It provides rendering services, as well as transformation and hit testing support.

This class is not an extensibility point—you cannot usefully derive your own classes from it, because all the rendering services it provides are defined by members marked as internal. You must inherit from UIElement if you wish to exploit the rendering services. However, it is important to be aware of Visual because it crops up in various APIs. For example, the VisualBrush, which we describe in Chapter 13, lets you create a brush that can paint using a copy of the appearance of any object derived from Visual.

Most types derived from Visual derive from UIElement, which we describe later. One useful exception is the DrawingVisual class. This provides a lightweight way of hosting a drawing. We describe drawings in Chapter 13.

WPF provides a class called VisualTreeHelper. This provides methods for navigating the visual tree. Surprisingly, these are not defined in terms of the Visual class. This is because 3D elements have an independent branch of the class hierarchy, but are still considered part of the visual tree. VisualTreeHelper therefore works with both Visual and Visual3D objects. We describe the VisualTreeHelper class in Chapter 9.

Visual3D

```
System.Object
    System.Windows.Threading.DispatcherObject
        System.Windows.DependencyObject
            System.Windows.Media.Media3D.Visual3D
```

The abstract Visual3D class fulfills the same role for 3D content as Visual does in 2D. All 3D elements in the visual tree derive from Visual3D, which provides transformation and hit testing services.

In the current version of WPF, only one type is derived from Visual3D: ModelVisual3D. As with the 2D Visual class, you cannot usefully derive directly from Visual3D because the mechanisms by which content is rendered are internal. Nonetheless, you need to be aware of the class because it crops up in certain APIs, including the 3D hit testing APIs. We describe 3D hit testing in Chapter 17, along with the Visual3D and ModelVisual3D types.

UIElement

System.Object

  System.Windows.Threading.DispatcherObject

    System.Windows.DependencyObject

      System.Windows.Media.Visual

        System.Windows.UIElement

UIElement provides access to the rendering services implemented by Visual by offering protected wrappers around the relevant internal features of Visual. UIElement also implements input handling and WPF's routed event system. It provides the low-level aspects of the layout system, although this goes only as far as basic sizing and positioning—FrameworkElement extends this to provide the full layout system we describe in Chapter 3. Finally, UIElement provides basic animation support, although FrameworkElement builds on this to provide the full set of services we describe in Chapter 16.

UIElement may seem like a strange halfway house, providing an incomplete set of services to be finished off by FrameworkElement. This structure arises because WPF is built in layers—there is a split between the so-called *core* and *framework* parts. The core classes are defined in *PresentationCore.dll* and the framework classes are defined in *PresentationFramework.dll*. This split is designed to enable developers to use the low-level rendering and animation services of WPF without having to use the full framework. For example, it would technically be possible to write an HTML engine that uses the WPF core for rendering (although no such thing has been built at the time of this writing). That particular example would have no use for framework-level services—HTML defines its own layout rules; the API HTML presents to script is very different from WPF's, so it would be hard to map features of one to the other.

Most applications will not write classes that derive directly from UIElement, because it makes sense to do so only if you wish to use your own UI framework in place of WPF's.

This would be an unusual and radical choice, because a great deal of what WPF has to offer (and the bulk of what this book is about) is provided at the framework level, including layout, data binding, styling, templates, and most of the animation system. Most ordinary applications will therefore use UIElement via FrameworkElement.

FrameworkElement

System.Object

  System.Windows.Threading.DispatcherObject

   System.Windows.DependencyObject

    System.Windows.Media.Visual

     System.Windows.UIElement

      System.Windows.FrameworkElement

FrameworkElement is the base class of the majority of visible elements in WPF. It derives from UIElement, so types that derive from FrameworkElement are able to render their own appearance and respond to user input. FrameworkElement adds data binding, styling, and resource handling, and it builds the full set of layout and animation services on top of the primitive services provided by UIElement.

FrameworkElement also provides a great deal of the infrastructure for data templates and control templates, although you must use more specialized classes to exploit these features. Only a Control (or a type derived from Control) can have a control template. You can use data templates either from a ContentPresenter or from certain control types.*

FrameworkElement is arguably WPF's nearest equivalent to the Windows Forms Control class. WPF has a Control class too (which we describe later), but its role is more specialized.

 Types that derive directly from FrameworkElement are typically all-code affairs. Although you could create a XAML file for a FrameworkElement with a corresponding code-behind file, you can't use this to construct the appearance of the element. This is because adding child elements at this level requires code—you need to override the GetVisualChild method and the VisualChildrenCount properties so that WPF can discover and render these elements. XAML can only set properties. However, WPF offers various derived types such as Control, Decorator, and Panel, which provide the necessary code to let you define their content in markup.

---

* The control types in question are ContentControl, HeaderedContentControl, ItemsControl, and HeaderedItemsControl, or any type deriving from any of those classes. In fact, ContentPresenter is the key in all these cases, as these controls rely on ContentPresenter to instantiate data templates. ContentPresenter derives directly from FrameworkElement.

Decorator

System.Object

  System.Windows.Threading.DispatcherObject

   System.Windows.DependencyObject

    System.Windows.Media.Visual

     System.Windows.UIElement

      System.Windows.FrameworkElement

       System.Windows.Controls.Decorator

Decorator is the base class for elements that contain a single child, and which either apply some kind of effect or offer a service. For example, Border adds an outline and optional padding around an element. ViewBox scales its child to fit the space available. InkPresenter enables ink rendering on its child.

 Despite being defined in the System.Windows.Controls namespace, a Decorator is not technically a control, as it does not derive from the Control class. Indeed, many of the types in the System.Windows.Controls namespace are not controls. This namespace contains many utility types typically used in conjunction with controls in order to build a user interface.

Decorator is a very simple class—it just defines a public Child element and performs the necessary work to ensure that the child is added to the logical and visual trees. Its layout implementation simply defers to the child element. You should use either this or ContentControl when writing a custom element that wraps a single child. See the "ContentControl" section, later in this appendix, for a discussion on how to choose between these two types.

Panel

System.Object

  System.Windows.Threading.DispatcherObject

   System.Windows.DependencyObject

    System.Windows.Media.Visual

     System.Windows.UIElement

      System.Windows.FrameworkElement

       System.Windows.Controls.Panel

Panel is the abstract base class of elements that contain and arrange multiple child elements. Each derived type implements a particular layout strategy. For example, StackPanel arranges items in a single column or a row. We describe the panel types and their layout mechanisms in Chapter 3.

Shape

```
System.Object
   System.Windows.Threading.DispatcherObject
     System.Windows.DependencyObject
       System.Windows.Media.Visual
         System.Windows.UIElement
           System.Windows.FrameworkElement
             System.Windows.Shapes.Shape
```

Shape is the abstract base class of graphical shape elements that can be added to the UI tree. The derived types include Rectangle, Ellipse, and Path. WPF defines two sets of classes for working with graphical shapes: those derived from Shape and another set derived from Geometry. We describe both sets in Chapter 13. The distinction is that Shape-based elements derive from FrameworkElement and are therefore part of the UI tree, and can use data binding, handle input, raise events, employ styles, and participate in layout. Shape provides properties for controlling the fill and outline of a shape, so if you want to define your own custom shape types, you should derive from Shape to take advantage of these.

Control

```
System.Object
   System.Windows.Threading.DispatcherObject
     System.Windows.DependencyObject
       System.Windows.Media.Visual
         System.Windows.UIElement
           System.Windows.FrameworkElement
             System.Windows.Controls.Control
```

Control is the base class for elements that offer a particular interactive behavior. For example, a TextBox allows the user to enter and edit text; a ListBox presents a list of items, allowing the user to scroll through and select items.

Not all visual elements derive from Control. Elements with no intrinsic interactive behavior derive either directly from FrameworkElement or from one of the other non-control base classes described in this appendix.

 Controls are typically visible to the user as a single coherent interactive entity in the user interface. Elements that do not fit this mold tend not to be controls. For example, the Grid type is extremely useful to developers as a means of managing layout, but it is not something directly recognizable to a user, so it is not a control. Likewise, although a Border element will be visible on-screen, it has no interactive behavior and no standard appearance. Normal users don't recognize Border elements in the way that they will recognize and understand a Button, so Border is also not a control (but Button is).

Control defines a Template property. This contains a reference to a ControlTemplate that defines the appearance of the control. Most controls are *lookless*—they have no intrinsic appearance and rely entirely on their templates to provide their visuals. This further emphasizes that the role of a control is to define behavior, not appearance. Chapter 9 describes the use of control templates.

ContentControl

System.Object

  System.Windows.Threading.DispatcherObject

    System.Windows.DependencyObject

      System.Windows.Media.Visual

        System.Windows.UIElement

          System.Windows.FrameworkElement

            System.Windows.Controls.Control

              System.Windows.Controls.ContentControl

ContentControl is a specialization of Control. It's the base class for any control that can host a single piece of content, which goes in the Content property. The content can be plain text or a tree of user interface elements (e.g., a nested control, or a panel containing several child items). The content can also be any .NET object, in which case WPF will attempt to display it using a data template: if you set the ContentTemplate or ContentTemplateSelector property, WPF will use the template you supply, but otherwise it will attempt to locate a template automatically. If it can't find a template, it will display the value returned by the object's ToString method. We describe data templates in Chapter 6.

Some controls derive from ContentControl in order to offer a caption. For example, the various button types (e.g., Button, CheckBox, RadioButton; see Chapter 5 for details) typically contain either text or graphics. By deriving from ContentControl, these buttons are able to host any mixture of text and graphics.

An alternative reason to derive from ContentControl is to offer a service wrapped around arbitrary content. For example, ScrollViewer can host any content, providing scroll bars for when the content is larger than the available physical space. This wrapping scenario may seem like the same job for which Decorator was designed. However, there is one critical difference: ContentControl derives from Control. This means it should provide some interactive behavior (e.g., scrolling in the case of ScrollViewer). Also, a ContentControl can use a ControlTemplate to define its appearance. This makes it possible to define a custom appearance for a ScrollViewer, whereas you cannot replace the visuals of a Decorator such as a Border. ContentControl is therefore the base class for wrapper-like elements that provide a specific interactive behavior around their content, allowing the container's visuals to be customized, whereas Decorator is the base class for lower-level wrapper elements with no particular interactive behavior, and which either have no appearance or have a fixed appearance.

HeaderedContentControl

System.Object

  System.Windows.Threading.DispatcherObject

    System.Windows.DependencyObject

      System.Windows.Media.Visual

        System.Windows.UIElement

          System.Windows.FrameworkElement

            System.Windows.Controls.Control

              System.Windows.Controls.ContentControl

                System.Windows.Controls.HeaderedContentControl

Some controls offer two placeholders for content instead of just one. HeaderedContentControl supports this by adding a Header property alongside the ContentControl type's Content property. This is the base class of Expander, GroupBox, and TabItem, and it enables all three controls to host arbitrary content both in the main body of the control and as the header.

UserControl

```
System.Object

   System.Windows.Threading.DispatcherObject

     System.Windows.DependencyObject

       System.Windows.Media.Visual

         System.Windows.UIElement

           System.Windows.FrameworkElement

             System.Windows.Controls.Control

               System.Windows.Controls.ContentControl

                 System.Windows.Controls.UserControl
```

The UserControl class is designed to provide an easy way to build a custom control using the same techniques and tools you would use to create a window: the appearance is defined with markup, and the behavior is defined in a code-behind file. This provides an easy way to build a reusable chunk of user interface. It also offers a useful tool for managing complexity: if a window has become too complex, it may be easier to split its content into a set of user controls, allowing developers to work on individual pieces independently.

UserControl is almost identical to its base class, ContentControl. It adjusts the default values for a few properties. For example, a UserControl disables keyboard focus and tab stop navigation for itself, although not for its content—the assumption is that a UserControl will typically contain focus targets such as text boxes and buttons, so the containing control itself will usually not need to act as a distinct focus target.

UserControl is not strictly necessary for building elements through markup, composition, and code behind. You can also use this style if you derive directly from ContentControl, or any other element that accepts one or more children, such as Decorator or Grid. The main contribution of UserControl is to signal intent: it is clear to any developer looking at a control derived from UserControl that it is intended to be a chunk of UI that forms part of a window, designed to be used as is. This makes it clear that replacing the template is unlikely to be useful—user controls are typically not lookless, because their appearance is defined by their hardcoded content rather than by their template.

ItemsControl

System.Object

  System.Windows.Threading.DispatcherObject

    System.Windows.DependencyObject

      System.Windows.Media.Visual

        System.Windows.UIElement

          System.Windows.FrameworkElement

            System.Windows.Controls.Control

              System.Windows.Controls.ItemsControl

ItemsControl is the base class for all controls that present lists or trees of items, including ListBox, TreeView, and Menu. Because it is a concrete class, it can also be used in its own right. ItemsControl provides item presentation and data binding support, but does not offer item selection—this lets you present a list of items without being forced to make them selectable. Use the Selector base class if you require selection.

Chapter 5 describes how to use ItemsControl and the various list controls derived from it. Chapter 7 describes how to use data binding with these controls.

HeaderedItemsControl

System.Object

  System.Windows.Threading.DispatcherObject

    System.Windows.DependencyObject

      System.Windows.Media.Visual

        System.Windows.UIElement

          System.Windows.FrameworkElement

            System.Windows.Controls.Control

              System.Windows.Controls.ItemsControl

                System.Windows.Controls.HeaderedItemsControl

HeaderedItemsControl derives from ItemsControl, so it does everything that Control does, but it also adds a Header property designed to hold a single item of content. This works in the same way as the Content property of ContentControl.

Elements derive from `HeaderedItemsControl` if they need to present both a caption and a set of children. For example, both `MenuItem` and `TreeViewItem` derive from this class.

Selector

```
System.Object
    System.Windows.Threading.DispatcherObject
        System.Windows.DependencyObject
            System.Windows.Media.Visual
                System.Windows.UIElement
                    System.Windows.FrameworkElement
                        System.Windows.Controls.Control
                            System.Windows.Controls.ItemsControl
                                System.Windows.Controls.Primitives.Selector
```

`Selector` adds item selection functionality to its base class, `ItemsControl`. The selection management is designed to work with a single linear list of items, so although this is the base class of `ComboBox`, `ListBox`, and `ListView`, it is not the base class of `TreeView`. `TreeView` derives directly from `ItemsControl` and implements its own selection management.

ContentElement

```
System.Object
    System.Windows.Threading.DispatcherObject
        System.Windows.DependencyObject
            System.Windows.ContentElement
```

Text has distinctive layout requirements that are unlike those of the rest of the user interface. Consequently, there is a separate part of the class hierarchy for managing textual content. `ContentElement` is at the root of this hierarchy, and it derives directly from `DependencyObject`, not `Visual`.

`ContentElement` is the base class of `FrameworkContentElement`, which is the base class of all the types in WPF's text object model. The split between `ContentElement` and `FrameworkContentElement` exists for the same reason as the split between `UIElement` and `FrameworkElement`: `ContentElement` is part of WPF's core API, whereas

FrameworkContentElement is part of WPF's framework API. The separation of responsibilities is similar—ContentElement provides basic event handling and animation support, and FrameworkContentElement adds data binding and layout.

As with UIElement, you would derive directly from ContentElement only if you were writing your own UI framework on top of WPF's core services. Most WPF applications will only use types derived from FrameworkContentElement.

FrameworkContentElement

```
System.Object

   System.Windows.Threading.DispatcherObject

      System.Windows.DependencyObject

         System.Windows.ContentElement

            System.Windows.FrameworkContentElement
```

FrameworkContentElement is the base class of all types in WPF's text object model. Because this class does not derive from Visual, elements of this type do not generate their own appearance. Instead, a tree of content elements is merely a description of some textual content, and it requires some element derived from Visual to present the content. WPF provides four such elements. TextBlock presents simple textual content, whereas the three flow document readers—FlowDocumentScrollViewer, FlowDocumentPageViewer, and FlowDocumentReader—present larger bodies of text.

Chapter 14 describes the text object model and the visual elements that can present text.

Freezable

```
System.Object

   System.Windows.Threading.DispatcherObject

      System.Windows.DependencyObject

         System.Windows.Freezable
```

Many types in WPF describe features of the user interface rather than being UI elements in their own right. For example, the various brush types described in Chapter 13 describe how a particular UI feature should be colored; geometries describe shapes of graphical elements. Most of these descriptive classes derive from the common Freezable base class. You would not normally derive your own types from Freezable; it is an important class in the WPF class hierarchy because so many important types derive from it.

One of the most important characteristics of a freezable object is that you can use it in multiple places. Example D-1 contains a single description of an ellipse shape, which is shared by three UI elements.

Example D-1. Freezables and elements

```
<StackPanel Orientation="Horizontal">
  <StackPanel.Resources>
    <EllipseGeometry x:Key="pathDescription"
                     RadiusX="100" RadiusY="50" Center="100,50" />
  </StackPanel.Resources>

  <Path Data="{StaticResource pathDescription}" Fill="Green" />
  <Path Data="{StaticResource pathDescription}" Fill="Cyan" />
  <Path Data="{StaticResource pathDescription}" Fill="Black" />

</StackPanel>
```

As you can see from Figure D-2, this example has three distinct elements—the three ellipses correspond to the three Path elements. This highlights the fact that Path is more than just a description of a shape. The identity of a Path object is significant—each of the three shapes visible in the UI corresponds to exactly one of the three Shape objects created by Example D-1. However, all three share a single description of the shape: they all use the same EllipseGeometry object.

Figure D-2. One geometry shared by three elements

An EllipseGeometry does not belong to any part of the visual tree. On the contrary, this one instance is used from multiple places in the tree. All types that derive from Freezable, such as geometries and brushes, can be shared in this way.

The significance of the name *Freezable* is that it is possible to *freeze* such an object, preventing any further changes from occurring. By default, a newly created Freezable will not be frozen—it is possible to change the object.* For example, you could write code that modified the RadiusX of the EllipseGeometry in Example D-1. This would cause all three ellipses in Figure D-2 to change. WPF has to do a certain amount of tracking to enable such changes to work correctly, and this does not come for free.

---

* In early previews of WPF, this type was called Changeable. Confusingly, the old name is just as accurate a description as Freezable, despite seemingly having almost the opposite meaning. To clarify: these objects start life as changeable objects, but you can freeze them, preventing further changes.

If you don't need to be able to make such changes, you can opt out of the corresponding costs by freezing the object.

Freezing a Freezable in code is simple: just call the Freeze method. You can also freeze objects from markup. Example D-2 shows a version of Example D-1 modified to freeze the EllipseGeometry.

Example D-2. Freezing from XAML

```
<StackPanel Orientation="Horizontal"
    xmlns:po="http://schemas.microsoft.com/winfx/2006/xaml/presentation/options"
    xmlns:mc="http://schemas.openxmlformats.org/markup-compatibility/2006"
    mc:Ignorable="po">
  <StackPanel.Resources>
    <EllipseGeometry x:Key="pathDescription"
                     po:Freeze="True"
                     RadiusX="100" RadiusY="50" Center="100,50" />
  </StackPanel.Resources>

  <Path Data="{StaticResource pathDescription}" Fill="Green" />
  <Path Data="{StaticResource pathDescription}" Fill="Cyan" />
  <Path Data="{StaticResource pathDescription}" Fill="Black" />

</StackPanel>
```

Freezing a Freezable has three effects. First, any attempt to change a frozen object will cause an InvalidOperationException to be thrown. Second, WPF will no longer keep track of the relationship between the object and the places where it is used. This reduces the memory and CPU consumption of your application, and it may also enable WPF to perform some internal optimizations. Third, freezing detaches the Freezable from its Dispatcher, making it possible to use the object on a different thread than the one on which it was created.

Because freezing frees an object from thread affinity, this can help improve the responsiveness of an application that builds complex visualizations. If you are building a drawing, bitmap, or 3D model that is sufficiently complex that it takes a noticeable amount of time to create (e.g., anything more than 0.1 seconds), you should avoid doing this on the UI thread, because it will make the application unresponsive. Moving such work to a worker thread is the obvious response, but if you create objects derived from DispatcherObject on the wrong thread, they will be associated with the wrong dispatcher, and you will get an error when you try to use them in the UI thread. Freezing objects avoids this problem. You can use this technique with drawings, brushes, geometries, the various 3D model and geometry classes, and bitmaps, because the relevant classes, which we describe in Chapters 13 and 17, all derive from Freezable.

Sometimes it can be useful to obtain a modifiable copy of a frozen Freezable. Freezable offers a Clone method for this purpose. It performs a deep copy—it copies any nested objects. For example, consider a frozen GeometryDrawing object with a Brush property referring to a frozen SolidColorBrush. Calling Clone would make unfrozen copies of both the drawing and the brush.

Animatable

System.Object

   System.Windows.Threading.DispatcherObject

     System.Windows.DependencyObject

       System.Windows.Freezable

         System.Windows.Media.Animation.Animatable

Many of the Freezable types describe aspects of an element's appearance such as its shape or color, which makes them candidates for animation. Most Freezable types therefore derive from Freezable indirectly through the Animatable class. This class provides WPF's animation system with the hooks it needs to change properties over time.

If necessary, the animation system will call Clone to create an unfrozen copy of a value in order to animate the value.

Example D-2 shows the public types that derive from Animatable.

Table D-1. Public types derived from Animatable

BitmapEffect	GuidelineSet	Rotation3D
Brush	ImageSource	TextEffect
Camera	Material	TextDecoration
DashStyle	MediaPlayer	Timeline
Drawing	Model3D	Transform
Geometry	PathFigure	Transform3D
Geometry3D	PathSegment	
GradientStop	Pen	

Silverlight

WPF provides a rich model for creating user interfaces. At the core of WPF is the XAML markup language. The use of XAML to describe user interfaces as well as some interaction is a model that works well for developing desktop applications. Formerly known as WPF/E, Silverlight leverages XAML markup to create user interfaces for use as part of web application development. As you will see in this appendix, you will be able to take the skills learned here and apply them to create web content.

Why Silverlight?

The World Wide Web is growing up before our eyes. No, that is not quite correct. The *users* of the Web are growing up. They are no longer content to fly from one static page to another hoping to read some new tidbit of information. Today's users want a better Web.

When I received my first copy of WordPerfect many years ago, it came with a huge user manual. Before I could really work with it, I needed to be instructed in how it worked. Learning all the arcane key combinations to perform simple tasks like bolding words, printing, and saving files was unavoidable.

As operating systems have evolved into the graphical powerhouses that we use today, the need for user manuals has diminished but has not disappeared. Many applications (e.g., Microsoft Office, iTunes, and Acrobat Reader) supply user interfaces that are intuitive enough that users can dive right in to do most of what they want to do. This is possible because the mouse/keyboard combination, along with the near-standard elements of the graphical user interfaces that are part of current operating systems, make it clearer how to accomplish everyday tasks.

When the Web was formed, HTML was just fine. It presented a common markup that you could use to define content that a variety of browsers could consume. HTML was critical to the success of the Web. That was a long time ago. The difficulty with HTML today is that it uses markup that supports text and images well, but falls down on creating content such as video, animations, and complex user interaction.

Various alternatives are available for augmenting content in HTML. One of these alternatives is client-side script, but although scripting can get the job done, doing everything with scripts on the client is difficult, error-prone, and labor-intensive.

Another alternative to using raw HTML is to use custom programming, like Java applets or ActiveX controls. These technologies require the developer to write special code just to enable the applet or control to be embedded in the web browser. The appearance is determined entirely by the code. And, in the case of ActiveX controls, security is up to you. Further, because custom development relies on developers, there is no way for designers to take control of the user interface's appearance.

A popular solution for creating content has been plug-in-based solutions such as Adobe's Flash products. Web developers use these products to create everything from simple interactive content to animations and video. Flash allows you to create complex user interfaces, but creating Flash-based content requires skills that are specific to Flash and do not have much adaptability to other programming contexts.

Silverlight attempts to redress these limitations to empower developers and designers to build great content without the limitations of the other approaches. In Silverlight, the markup is XAML, which means you can describe complex and compelling content without the limitations inherent to HTML. The XAML markup is separate from the code, which makes it easier to build secure, dynamic content that is emitted either on the client or by servers. Lastly, Silverlight uses the same skills and tools that WPF uses, so when you work with Silverlight you can apply what you know from WPF to the new problem of web content.

What Is Silverlight?

Silverlight is a browser plug-in that allows rendering of elements described with XAML in a web browser. Currently, this browser plug-in supports several browsers and operating systems (Internet Explorer and Firefox on Windows; Firefox and Safari on Mac OS X). For example, Figures E-1 and E-2 show the same HTML and Silverlight code running in Internet Explorer and Firefox, respectively. Figure E-3 shows it in Safari on Mac OS X. Silverlight supports both JavaScript and managed code (e.g., C# and Visual Basic) to interact with the XAML. At this writing, JavaScript Silverlight support is in beta (referred to as Silverlight 1.0) and the managed support is in alpha (referred to as Silverlight 1.1). Because Silverlight 1.1 is only in alpha, our examples use the more mature Silverlight 1.0 (JavaScript model).

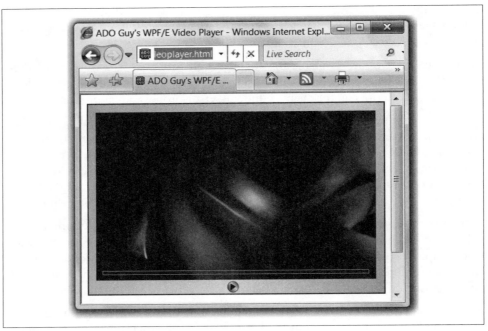

Figure E-1. Silverlight in Internet Explorer (on Windows Vista)

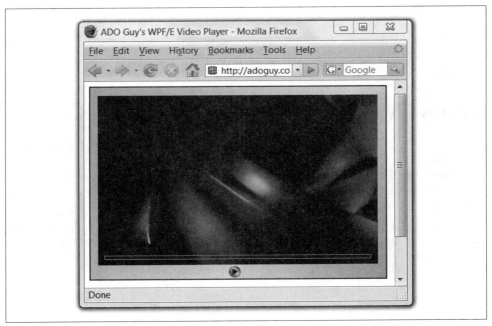

Figure E-2. Silverlight hosted in Firefox (on Windows Vista)

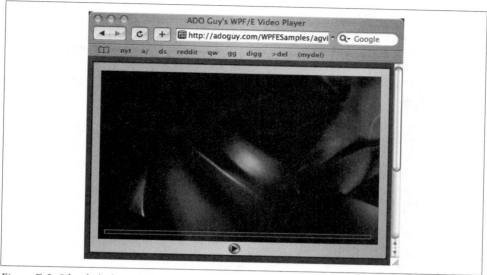

Figure E-3. Silverlight hosted in Safari (on Mac OS X)

Hello, Silverlight

Showing XAML-based content in a browser is not revolutionary (WPF supports this out of the box, as discussed in Chapter 11). What is revolutionary is that Silverlight does not require a Windows operating system (or even Windows Media Player for media functionality). One of the main capabilities of Silverlight is to make user interfaces for web sites. Silverlight's scope is not to replace HTML-based web sites, but instead to augment HTML. You should think of Silverlight as something that enables you to create content inside a web page, not something you would use to create replacement content for your existing web pages.

For instance, Example E-1 shows a simple XAML document that displays a smiley face, some text, and some shading.

Example E-1. Smiley face XAML

```
<!-- scene.xaml -->
<Canvas xmlns="http://schemas.microsoft.com/client/2007"
        xmlns:x="http://schemas.microsoft.com/winfx/2006/xaml">

  <!-- Background Rectangle -->
  <Rectangle Width="400" Height="400" Stroke="Black">
    <Rectangle.Fill>
      <LinearGradientBrush>
        <GradientStop Color="LightGray" Offset="0" />
        <GradientStop Color="Snow" Offset=".75" />
        <GradientStop Color="LightGray" Offset="1" />
      </LinearGradientBrush>
```

Example E-1. Smiley face XAML (continued)

```
    </Rectangle.Fill>
  </Rectangle>

  <!-- Smiley Face -->
  <Ellipse Canvas.Top="50" Canvas.Left="50"
           Width="300" Height="300"
           Fill="Yellow" Stroke="Black" />
  <Ellipse Canvas.Top="150" Canvas.Left="100"
           Width="50" Height="50"
           Fill="Black" />
  <Ellipse Canvas.Top="150" Canvas.Left="250"
           Width="50" Height="50"
           Fill="Black" />
  <Path Stroke="Black" StrokeThickness="5"
        Data="M 100,275 S 200,325 300,275" />

  <!-- Text Message (with Drop Shadow) -->
  <TextBlock Canvas.Top="352" Canvas.Left="152"
             FontFamily="Comic Sans MS"
             FontSize="36" Foreground="Gray"
             Text="Smile!" />
  <TextBlock Canvas.Top="350" Canvas.Left="150"
             FontFamily="Comic Sans MS"
             FontSize="36" Foreground="Black"
             Text="Smile!" />
</Canvas>
```

To show this XAML in an HTML page, we use a script file called *Silverlight.js*. This script file, the entry point into the Silverlight API, contains a JavaScript class called Sys.Silverlight that is used to create the Silverlight plug-in object in the browser. You can use the createObject function on the Sys.Silverlight object to load the Silverlight object into the HTML document. Example E-2 shows an HTML page that hosts our *scene.xaml* document.

Example E-2. Hello Silverlight default HTML

```
<html xmlns="http://www.w3.org/1999/xhtml">
<head>
  <title>Hello Silverlight</title>
  <!-- Load the Script that is used to
       show XAML in the browser -->
  <script type="text/JavaScript" src="silverlight.js"></script>
</head>
<body>
  <form>
    <div>
      <h3>Hello Silverlight</h3>
      <p>This is just plain HTML Code.</p>
      <p>Below you'll find XAML Hosted in the Browser:</p>
    </div>
```

Example E-2. Hello Silverlight default HTML (continued)

```
<div id="theHost">
  <script type="text/JavaScript">
    Sys.Silverlight.createObject(
    "Scene.xaml",                      // Url to the Xaml File
    document.getElementById("theHost"), // The Host element
    "SilverlightControl",              // Silverlight Object Name
    {                                  // Properties object
      width: "400",                    // Width of the Host
      height: "400",                   // Height of the Host
      version: "0.9"                   // Silverlight Plug-in
                                       // Version
    },
    {}                                 // Event to wire
                                       // (onLoad and onError)
                      );
  </script>
</div>
</form>
</body>
</html>
```

The createObject method of the Sys.Silverlight object is the key to showing XAML in the browser.* When you browse to the HTML page detailed in Example E-2, you will see our smiley face XAML on a web page (as shown in Figure E-4).

Silverlight XAML

Even though the XAML defined for use in Silverlight is not tied to WPF XAML, the Silverlight team has made an effort to use WPF XAML as a starting place for its XAML design. In this first release of Silverlight, all the XAML tags used in Silverlight are also compatible with WPF.

> Compatibility will be a priority in future releases. However, because WPF and Silverlight are evolving in parallel, you can expect that some innovations in the markup introduced on one platform may or may not appear on the other.

For the WPF developer, the most glaring omission is that it does not offer any built-in controls. Silverlight aims to provide the maximum functionality for the smallest download cost. Because of this design goal, no WPF controls are supported initially. This means no text boxes, no buttons, no combo boxes, and, in fact, nothing from WPF that derives from the Control base class at all.

---

* The version numbers used in the createObject method are a bit confusing. You would specify version 0.90 to use Silverlight 1.0 and Version 0.95 to use Silverlight 1.1. I hope that once the release versions are available the versions will become 1.0 and 1.1, respectively.

Figure E-4. Our first Silverlight page

As developers (and designers), it may seem that the exclusion of controls from the XAML is a show-stopper. Silverlight's goals are to have a small runtime and to be cross-platform-compatible. In this first release, Silverlight is attempting to fulfill some very specific web-related use cases:

- Video (e.g., sites like YouTube.com and Soapbox.msn.com)
- Animation (e.g., sites like Jibjab.com and Funnyflash.com)
- User interaction (e.g., sites like Gamespot.com)

These use cases mean that in addition to no control support, there is no 3D support or templates, and there is limited resource use, event support, layout modes, and text handling (e.g., no XPS support directly, although one can translate an XPS document's XAML to "Silverlight" XAML with some effort).

Layout Model

Silverlight applications normally contain a number of visual elements to display to a user. Being able to lay out these visual elements in a precise way is one benefit of using Silverlight (as opposed to HTML). That's where the Silverlight layout model fits in.

Unlike WPF, Silverlight supports only a single layout model: all elements have fixed positions. You specify positions by using Canvas elements as the only layout model supported. This means that the first tag in every Silverlight XAML document has to be a Canvas. For example:

```
<Canvas xmlns="http://schemas.microsoft.com/client/2007"
        xmlns:x="http://schemas.microsoft.com/winfx/2006/xaml">
  ...
</Canvas>
```

Within a Canvas, you can specify the position of any tag by using the Left and Top attached properties:

```
<Canvas ...>
   <Rectangle Canvas.Left="10"
              Canvas.Top="10"
              Width="100"
              Height="100"
              Fill="Blue" />
</Canvas>
```

You can also use the Canvas element to create groups of elements within the root Canvas. Because the Left and Top attached properties point to the parent Canvas, you can use the Canvas element to create sets of objects that are moved together. For instance, Example E-3 shows a simplified version of our *smileyface.xaml* from earlier.

Example E-3. Simplified smiley face

```
<!-- scene.xaml -->
<Canvas ... >

  <!-- Smiley Face -->
  <Ellipse Canvas.Top="50" Canvas.Left="50"
           Width="300" Height="300"
           Fill="Yellow" Stroke="Black" />
  <Ellipse Canvas.Top="150" Canvas.Left="100"
           Width="50" Height="50"
           Fill="Black" />
  <Ellipse Canvas.Top="150" Canvas.Left="250"
           Width="50" Height="50"
           Fill="Black" />
  <Path Stroke="Black" StrokeThickness="5"
       Data="M 100,275 S 200,325 300,275" />

  <!-- Some Text -->
  <TextBlock Canvas.Top="400" Canvas.Left="50">Smile!</TextBlock>
</Canvas>
```

We place each piece of the smiley face on our main canvas by specifying the Top and Left attached properties (or specific coordinates for drawing elements such as Path). This works well, except that when we want to move our smiley face, we need to change each of the Top and/or Left properties as well as the coordinates in the Path element individually, as shown in the following code:

```
<!-- scene.xaml -->
<Canvas ...>

    <!-- Smiley Face -->
    <Ellipse Canvas.Top="75" Canvas.Left="75"
            Width="300" Height="300"
            Fill="Yellow" Stroke="Black" />
    <Ellipse Canvas.Top="175" Canvas.Left="125"
            Width="50" Height="50"
            Fill="Black" />
    <Ellipse Canvas.Top="175" Canvas.Left="275"
            Width="50" Height="50"
            Fill="Black" />
    <Path Stroke="Black" StrokeThickness="5"
        Data="M 125,300 S 225,350 325,300" />

    <!-- Some Text -->
    <TextBlock Canvas.Top="400" Canvas.Left="50">Smile!</TextBlock>

</Canvas>
```

Instead of changing all the coordinate positions, we can use a Canvas to "group" the entire smiley face into one logical object, as shown in the following code:

```
<!-- scene.xaml -->
<Canvas ...>

    <!-- Smiley Face: coordinates relative to parent -->
    <Canvas Canvas.Top="50" Canvas.Left="50">
        <!-- nested elements positioned relative to parent -->
        <Ellipse Canvas.Top="0" Canvas.Left="0"
                Width="300" Height="300"
                Fill="Yellow" Stroke="Black" />
        <Ellipse Canvas.Top="100" Canvas.Left="50"
                Width="50" Height="50"
                Fill="Black" />
        <Ellipse Canvas.Top="100" Canvas.Left="200"
                Width="50" Height="50"
                Fill="Black" />
        <Path Stroke="Black" StrokeThickness="5"
            Data="M 50,225 S 150,275 250,225" />
    </Canvas>

    <!-- Some Text -->
    <TextBlock Canvas.Top="400" Canvas.Left="50">Smile!</TextBlock>

</Canvas>
```

Moving the smiley face becomes as simple as changing the Top and Left attached properties of the Canvas that holds the smiley face:

```
<!-- scene.xaml -->
<Canvas ... >

  <!-- Smiley Face -->
  <Canvas Canvas.Top="75" Canvas.Left="75">
    <!-- same as before, but now moved 25 right and 25 down -->
    ...
  </Canvas>

  <!-- Some Text -->
  <TextBlock Canvas.Top="400" Canvas.Left="50">Smile!</TextBlock>

</Canvas>
```

This grouping of objects into logical units becomes crucial as you start to work with objects as atomic units. In Silverlight, you will be creating objects that users will need to interact with logically as a single object. For example, you could create a play button for a video player, and even if that button comprises multiple objects (e.g., an Ellipse and a Polygon), you will want to handle mouse events as though the button were a single object (you'll see how to handle mouse events later).

Namespaces

You may have noticed that in all the examples so far, we are using a new namespace for Silverlight content:

```
<Canvas xmlns="http://schemas.microsoft.com/client/2007"
        xmlns:x="http://schemas.microsoft.com/winfx/2006/xaml">
</Canvas>
```

This new namespace is the official namespace, but the WPF namespace is supported as well:

```
<Canvas xmlns="http://schemas.microsoft.com/winfx/2006/xaml/presentation"
        xmlns:x="http://schemas.microsoft.com/winfx/2006/xaml">
</Canvas>
```

The reason for continuing to support the WPF namespace is less about technology and more about tool support. Tools are available for creating or converting XAML. By supporting the WPF namespace (at least in these early releases of Silverlight), you should be able to use a variety of XAML-powered tools to create Silverlight-compliant assets. We will list tools for Silverlight XAML creation later in this appendix.

Graphics

In Silverlight, drawing with XAML's graphics tags is important for creating visual elements that are not included by default. Although the breadth of the 2D graphics stack in Silverlight is on par with WPF, you will need to rely on it more often than you would in WPF. For example, the Button element does not exist in Silverlight XAML, so to create a button you will need to draw it manually. As an example, let's consider a simple button that looks like Figure E-5.

Figure E-5. A Silverlight button

First, we create a Canvas for our button:

```
<Canvas Canvas.Left="25" Canvas.Top="25">

</Canvas>
```

Next, we can add a Rectangle for our button:

```
<Canvas Canvas.Left="25" Canvas.Top="25">
  <Rectangle Height="32" Width="100"
             Stroke="LightGray" StrokeThickness="2">
  </Rectangle>
</Canvas>
```

To make the button a little more polished, we could round the corners subtly by setting the RadiusX and RadiusY attributes:

```
<Canvas Canvas.Left="25" Canvas.Top="25">
  <Rectangle Height="32" Width="100"
             Stroke="LightGray" StrokeThickness="2"
             RadiusX="25" RadiusY="25">
  </Rectangle>
</Canvas>
```

Now we can add a gradient fill to the background of our rectangle:

```
<Canvas Canvas.Left="25" Canvas.Top="25">
  <Rectangle Height="32" Width="100"
             Stroke="LightGray" StrokeThickness="2"
             RadiusX="25" RadiusY="25" >
    <Rectangle.Fill>
      <LinearGradientBrush StartPoint="0,0" EndPoint="1,1">
        <GradientStop Color="#EEEEEE" Offset="0"/>
        <GradientStop Color="#444444" Offset="1"/>
      </LinearGradientBrush>
    </Rectangle.Fill>
  </Rectangle>
</Canvas>
```

Lastly, we can add a TextBlock to provide the text in our button. Example E-4 shows our complete button.

Example E-4. The complete button

```
<Canvas Canvas.Left="25" Canvas.Top="25">
   <Rectangle Height="32" Width="100"
               Stroke="LightGray" StrokeThickness="2"
               RadiusX="25" RadiusY="25" >
      <Rectangle.Fill>
         <LinearGradientBrush StartPoint="0,0" EndPoint="1,1">
            <GradientStop Color="#EEEEEE" Offset="0"/>
            <GradientStop Color="#444444" Offset="1"/>
         </LinearGradientBrush>
      </Rectangle.Fill>
   </Rectangle>
   <TextBlock Canvas.Top="3" Canvas.Left="13"
               FontSize="18" Foreground="Black"
               Text="Press Me"/>
</Canvas>
```

Because of the limited palette of XAML tags in Silverlight, you will need to use the graphics tags to create the look and feel of objects that are not natively part of Silverlight XAML. Using the graphics tags usually requires that you implement behavior that is normally implicit in controls. For example, drawing the button in this example really requires that you handle not only when the button is clicked, but also when a mouse hovers over it and what the button looks like when you click on it. Later we will see how to add these features.

Mouse Cursors

Because Silverlight does not support common controls, it would be nice if we could indicate to the user that certain elements acting as controls are clickable. We can do this by using mouse cursors. The Canvas, MediaElement, TextBlock, Rectangle, Ellipse, Polygon, and PolyLine elements support a Cursor property that specifies which cursor to show while the mouse is over a particular element. The supported cursors are Arrow, Hand, Wait, IBeam, None, and Default. For example:

```
<Canvas xmlns="http://schemas.microsoft.com/client/2007"
        xmlns:x="http://schemas.microsoft.com/winfx/2006/xaml">
   <Canvas Width="100" Height="25"
            Cursor="Arrow"
            Canvas.Top="0" Canvas.Left="0"
            Background="Gray">
      <TextBlock Text="Arrow" />
   </Canvas>
</Canvas>
```

Measuring Text

Silverlight offers only coordinate-based layout (using the Canvas to lay out elements). Because of this, all text in our XAML documents is left-justified. To get around the limitation of not supporting the full text handling subsystem that is available in WPF, Silverlight enables you to measure the text so that you can do your own calculations to center or right-justify text. You measure text by using the actualWidth and actualHeight properties on the TextBlock element. For example, to center a piece of text within the Silverlight host, you could do this:

```
function root_Loaded(sender, args) {

    // Center Header
    var text = sender.findName("headerText");
    var host = sender.getHost();

    // Center it by measuring the text (with actualWidth)
    // and comparing to the host size
    text.setValue("Canvas.Left", (host.actualWidth - text.actualWidth)/2);
}
```

Transformations

Transformations allow users to manipulate the way parts of the visual tree are rendered. Like WPF, Silverlight XAML supports a number of transformations that you can use to manipulate the look of XAML elements. The RenderTransform property of every visual XAML element supports using transformations to change the way a tag (or a group of tags) is rendered. (There are no layout transforms because there is no real layout in Silverlight.) For instance, Example E-5 uses a ScaleTransform to stretch the button that we created in Example E-4.

Example E-5. Using RenderTransform

```
<Canvas xmlns="http://schemas.microsoft.com/winfx/2006/xaml/presentation"
        xmlns:x="http://schemas.microsoft.com/winfx/2006/xaml" >
  <Canvas.RenderTransform>
    <ScaleTransform ScaleX="1" ScaleY="2" />
  </Canvas.RenderTransform>
  <Canvas
Canvas.Left="25" Canvas.Top="25">
    <Rectangle Height="32" Width="175"
               Stroke="LightGray" StrokeThickness="2"
               RadiusX="25" RadiusY="25" >
      <Rectangle.Fill>
        <LinearGradientBrush StartPoint="0.5,2.109" EndPoint="0.5,-1.109">
          <GradientStop
Color="#EEEEEE" Offset="0"/>
          <GradientStop
Color="#444444" Offset="1"/>
        </LinearGradientBrush>
```

```
    </Rectangle.Fill>
  </Rectangle>
  <TextBlock Canvas.Top="3" Canvas.Left="13"
             FontSize="18" Foreground="Black"
             Text="Press Me"/>
</Canvas>
</Canvas>
```

By using a ScaleTransform to stretch our button to twice its size vertically (i.e., ScaleY), our button now looks like Figure E-6.

Figure E-6. Our button with a ScaleTransform

Silverlight XAML supports the same transformations that WPF does, as shown in Table E-1.

Table E-1. Transformations supported by Silverlight XAML

Transform class	Usage
MatrixTransform	An affine transformation (See Chapter 13 for more information)
RotateTransform	Rotates or spins an element
ScaleTransform	Resizes or stretches an element
SkewTransform	Tilts or slants an element
TransformGroup	Any mix of transformations
TranslateTranform	Moves an element

Animations

Animation support is a key component of Silverlight. Like WPF, Silverlight supports two styles of animations: simple and keyframe animations.

Simple animations include DoubleAnimation, ColorAnimation, and PointAnimation. These three animations support animating different types of properties on XAML elements. Unlike WPF XAML, the only number-based animation is the DoubleAnimation, as all numeric properties in Silverlight XAML are double values. The keyframe animations follow the pattern of the simple animations by supporting DoubleAnimationUsingKeyFrames, ColorAnimationUsingKeyFrames, and PointAnimationUsingKeyFrames. These keyframe animations are structured just like WPF keyframe animations.

For example, imagine that we want to fade an Ellipse into view when the Canvas loads. To do this, we add a new EventTrigger to our Canvas element's Triggers property.

EventTrigger is the only trigger supported in Silverlight. The EventTrigger allows you to specify a RoutedEvent to use as the triggering mechanism, but in this release of Silverlight, the only RoutedEvent supported for triggering is Canvas.Loaded. Here is a Canvas element with an EventTrigger added:

```
<Canvas xmlns="http://schemas.microsoft.com/winfx/2006/xaml/presentation"
        xmlns:x="http://schemas.microsoft.com/winfx/2006/xaml" >
  <Canvas.Triggers>
    <EventTrigger RoutedEvent="Canvas.Loaded">
      ...
    </EventTrigger>
  </Canvas.Triggers>
  <Ellipse x:Name="theCircle" Width="200" Height="200" Fill="Blue" />
</Canvas>
```

Inside an EventTrigger, you need an action that the event trigger fires. In Silverlight, the only action supported is a BeginStoryboard action. Inside the BeginStoryboard tag, we also need a Storyboard. The Storyboard is the container for any animations we want to show:

```
<Canvas xmlns="http://schemas.microsoft.com/winfx/2006/xaml/presentation"
        xmlns:x="http://schemas.microsoft.com/winfx/2006/xaml" >
  <Canvas.Triggers>
    <EventTrigger RoutedEvent="Canvas.Loaded">
      <BeginStoryboard>
        <Storyboard>
          ...
        </Storyboard>
      </BeginStoryboard>
    </EventTrigger>
  </Canvas.Triggers>
  <Ellipse x:Name="theCircle" Width="200" Height="200" Fill="Blue" />
</Canvas>
```

Last, we will need an animation to fade the opacity of the ellipse from zero to one (i.e., from invisible to visible):

```
<Canvas xmlns="http://schemas.microsoft.com/winfx/2006/xaml/presentation"
        xmlns:x="http://schemas.microsoft.com/winfx/2006/xaml" >
  <Canvas.Triggers>
    <EventTrigger RoutedEvent="Canvas.Loaded">
      <BeginStoryboard>
        <Storyboard>
          <DoubleAnimation
            Storyboard.TargetName="theCircle"
            Storyboard.TargetProperty="Opacity"
            From="0" To="1" Duration="0:0:2" />
        </Storyboard>
      </BeginStoryboard>
    </EventTrigger>
  </Canvas.Triggers>
  <Ellipse x:Name="theCircle" Width="200" Height="200" Fill="Blue" />
</Canvas>
```

Additionally, Storyboards can contain more than one animation:

```
<Canvas xmlns="http://schemas.microsoft.com/winfx/2006/xaml/presentation"
        xmlns:x="http://schemas.microsoft.com/winfx/2006/xaml" >
  <Canvas.Triggers>
    <EventTrigger RoutedEvent="Canvas.Loaded">
      <BeginStoryboard>
        <Storyboard>
          <DoubleAnimation
            Storyboard.TargetName="theCircle"
            Storyboard.TargetProperty="Opacity"
            From="0" To="1" Duration="0:0:2" />
          <DoubleAnimation
            Storyboard.TargetName="theCircle"
            Storyboard.TargetProperty="Width"
            From="100" To="200" Duration="0:0:5" />
        </Storyboard>
      </BeginStoryboard>
    </EventTrigger>
  </Canvas.Triggers>
  <Ellipse x:Name="theCircle" Width="200" Height="200" Fill="Blue" />
</Canvas>
```

Like WPF, Storyboards in Silverlight can exist in resources. As we will see later, we can delay an animation by placing it in the resources of one of our XAML elements. See the "Delaying storyboards" section, later in this appendix, for more information about how this works.

Silverlight and WPF

In .NET 3.0, XAML is used as an object graph serialization technology. For WPF, this allows XAML to be used as a user interface markup language that is then serialized into CLR objects. But it is important to note that WPF does not require XAML at all. You can create user interface objects by writing CLR code like so:

```
Canvas myCanvas = new Canvas( ); // You can't do this in Silverlight 1.0
```

Silverlight 1.0 is different in this respect, as it requires XAML. There is no way to create XAML objects from code without using XAML. Silverlight is about showing elements described with XAML on a web page. There are other differences between the two technologies, as detailed in Table E-2.

Table E-2. Silverlight and WPF

Silverlight	Windows Presentation Foundation
Web-based	Desktop applications, click-once deployment, or XBAP applications
Works across different operating systems (Windows and Mac OS X in the first release)	Requires Windows XP SP2, Windows Server 2003 SP1, or Windows Vista
Supports multiple web browsers (Internet Explorer and Firefox on Windows; Firefox and Safari on Mac OS X)	Internet Explorer 6+ for XBAP applications

Table E-2. Silverlight and WPF (continued)

Silverlight	Windows Presentation Foundation
No .NET Framework requirements	Requires .NET 3.0 Framework
No Windows Media Player required for media support	Requires Windows Media Player 10 for media support
Uses XAML for design markup, but the library of tags is smaller	Uses XAML for design markup, but supports a large library of tags
Supports JavaScript or managed languages (C#, Visual Basic, etc.) for Silverlight applications	Supports managed languages (C#, Visual Basic, etc.)
Plug-in download size approximately 4 MB (though on Mac OS X, size is slightly larger to accommodate Intel and PPC processors)	.NET 3.0 Framework size is fairly large (approximately 50 MB for x86, and 90 MB for x64)
Release of Silverlight 1.0 is scheduled for mid-2007, with Silverlight 1.1 slated for later than that (no dates had been announced as of this writing)	Released in November 2006

Development Model

Now that you have a sense of what Silverlight XAML is, we can look at how to use that XAML in a browser. Unlike WPF, with Silverlight 1.0 applications, you will add programmatic logic to your XAML in the JavaScript browser language.

Hosting in HTML

To show and interact with XAML in the browser, Silverlight loads a plug-in into the HTML document. An OBJECT tag is used in Internet Explorer and an EMBED tag in Firefox (on both Windows and Mac OS X). You can specify this tag manually, as shown in this code example:

```
<!-- Only works in IE6+ -->
<object
  id="WpfeControl"
  width="400"
  height="100"
  classid="CLSID:32C73088-76AE-40F7-AC40-81F62CB2C1DA"
  <param name="BackgroundColor" value="#ffebcd" />
  <param name="SourceElement" value=null />
  <param name="Source" value="HelloWorld.xaml" />
  <param name="WindowlessMode" value="true" />
  <param name="MaxFrameRate" value="30" />
  <param name="OnError" value="myErrorHandler" />
</object>
```

Although this works perfectly well for Internet Explorer, you want your XAML to work in every supported browser equally well. To address this, the Silverlight team has supplied a script called *Silverlight.js* that is used to host the XAML across all supported browsers, eliminating the need for you to use an OBJECT tag, an EMBED tag, or something dynamically generated according to server-side browser detection.* To take advantage of this script, you import it and use the Sys.Silverlight class to load your XAML:

```
<!-- Loading the script locally -->
<script type="text/JavaScript" src="silverlight.js"></script>
...
<div id="agContainer" >
  <script type="text/JavaScript">

    Sys.Silverlight.createObject(
      "Scene.xaml",                          // Url to the Xaml File
      document.getElementById("theHost"),    // The Host element
      "SilverlightControl",                  // Silverlight Object Name
      {                                      // Properties object
        width: "400",                        // Width of the Host
        height: "400",                       // Height of the Host
        version: "0.9"                       // Silverlight Plug-in
                                             // Version
      },
      {}                                     // Event to wire
                                             // (onLoad and onError)
    ); </script>
</div>
```

The newly created object hosts the XAML and attempts to display it. Note that either you can specify the XAML as a separate file (as shown in the previous example), or you can specify a source element name from which to get the XAML. When you specify the name of a source element, you would create an XML island inside the HTML page by adding a new script tag with a type of text/xaml:

```
<script type="text/xaml" id="myInlineXaml">
  <Canvas xmlns="http://schemas.microsoft.com/client/2007"
          xmlns:x="http://schemas.microsoft.com/winfx/2006/xaml">
    ...
  </Canvas>
</script>
```

When using inline XAML, you would change your call to createObject,† to specify passing XAML by using the hash symbol (#) and the name of the script tag, like so:

```
<div id="agContainer" >
  <script type="text/JavaScript">

    Sys.Silverlight.createObject(
      "#myInlineXaml",                       // The Inline XAML
      document.getElementById("theHost"),    // The Host element
      "SilverlightControl",                  // Silverlight Object Name
      {                                      // Properties object
```

---

* Although the current version of the Silverlight SDK includes the *Silverlight.js* script, the ASP.NET Futures Preview includes several ASP.NET controls that can eliminate this necessity.

† In all of the JavaScript examples, we are styling the code to conform to the convention of using camel casing for variables, functions, and method names. For example, use of the FindHost method of the plug-in object appears as findHost in the JavaScript example. JavaScript is not case-sensitive, so using this convention does not introduce any issues.

```
            width: "400",                   // Width of the Host
            height: "400",                  // Height of the Host
            version: "0.9"                  // Silverlight Plug-in
                                            // Version
        },
        {}                                  // Event to wire
                                            // (onLoad and onError)
                                  );
    </script>
</div>
```

The *Silverlight.js* file contains the JavaScript Sys.Silverlight class that generates the right HTML tags for the different browsers. For example, on Internet Explorer 6 and above, the Sys.Silverlight class generates an OBJECT tag. On Firefox and Safari browsers, it uses an EMBED tag.

End-User Installation

At this point in Silverlight development, when users go to a web page that contains an embedded Sys.Silverlight class, the browser will attempt to download the runtime like other ActiveX solutions (e.g., Flash), including support for upgrading the runtime as necessary.

Handling XAML Errors

As you work with XAML, errors are likely to occur from time to time. Many of these will be XAML parsing errors. By default, the *Silverlight.js* script file will show the error in an alert window. If you want more control over how to tell your users about this problem, you can specify the name of a function in the creation of the Sys.Silverlight class in your HTML markup:

```
Sys.Silverlight.createObject(
        "#myInlineXaml",                            // The Inline XAML
        document.getElementById("theHost"),         // The Host element
        "SilverlightControl",                       // Silverlight Object Name
        properties: {                               // Properties object
          width: "400",                             // Width of the Host
          height: "400",                            // Height of the Host
          version: "0.9"                            // Silverlight Plug-in
                                                    // Version
        },
        events: {onError:"myErrorHandler"}          // Events to wire
                                                    // (onLoad and onError)
```

By specifying in the events object the name of a function to use as the onError handler, you are telling Silverlight to call that function on any Silverlight error. The Silverlight host control passed several arguments to the error handler, including the line number, the column number, the error number, and a text message that explains the nature of the error.

The error handler is used only for Silverlight errors. Any script errors are handled by normal scripting error handling. Example E-6 shows a sample error handler.

Example E-6. Sample error handler

```
function myErrorHandler(line, col, errorNum, desc) {
  var str = "Silverlight Error: " + desc + "\n";
  str += "(line: " + line + ",  col: " + col + ")\n";
  str += "HRESULT: " + errorNum;
  alert(str);
}
```

Event Model

In Silverlight, all code interaction with the XAML elements revolves around using the events in the XAML object model. You wire events to JavaScript by specifying the name of the event, and the name of the handler function:

```
<Canvas xmlns="http://schemas.microsoft.com/client/2007"
        xmlns:x="http://schemas.microsoft.com/winfx/2006/xaml"
        Loaded="root_Loaded">
  <Ellipse x:Name="theCircle" Width="200" Height="200" Fill="Blue" />
</Canvas>
```

In this example, we are specifying that a JavaScript function called root_Loaded should be called when the Canvas has completed loading. For example, the root_Loaded function would look like Example E-7.

Example E-7. Event handling function

```
function root_Loaded(sender, args) {
  alert("Canvas has been loaded");
}
```

By convention, all event handling functions specify two parameters for the function signature: sender and args. The first parameter is the sender of the event and the second parameter is an optional object that contains data specific to the event.

Most UI elements (e.g., Canvas, Rectangle, Ellipse, etc.) support six common events, listed in Table E-3.

Table E-3. Events supported by UI elements

Event	Usage
Loaded	Fired after the element has completed loading, but before it is rendered
MouseEnter	Fired when the mouse moves from the outside to the inside of an element
MouseLeave	Fired when the mouse moves from the inside to the outside of an element
MouseMove	Fired as the mouse is moved within an element
MouseLeftButtonDown	Fired when the left mouse button is pressed while over an element
MouseLeftButtonUp	Fired when the left mouse button is released while over an element

In addition to these six common events, the root Canvas of any Silverlight document also supports keyboard handling events, listed in Table E-4.

Table E-4. Keyboard handling events supported by Canvas

Event	Usage
KeyDown	Fired when a keyboard key is pressed
KeyUp	Fired when a keyboard key is released
GotFocus	Fired when the Silverlight Canvas (or any of its children) receives keyboard focus
LostFocus	Fired when the Silverlight Canvas (or any of its children) loses keyboard focus

These events represent the primary methods for user interactivity with the XAML loaded in the browser.

Bubbling, Tunneling, and Direct Events

Like WPF, mouse events in Silverlight support bubbling up the object hierarchy. However, Silverlight does not support canceling bubbling. All other events are supported as direct events (e.g., Loaded). Also, unlike WPF, there are no tunneling events in Silverlight.

Working with XAML Properties

Once you have a reference to an individual XAML element in JavaScript, you can use simple property assignment to specify properties on the individual elements:

```
function root_Loaded(sender, args) {
  // Getting and setting Canvas properties
  if (sender.width == 200) {
    sender.width = 250;
  }
  sender.height = 300;
  sender.background = "#888888";
}
```

For attached properties, you use the getValue and setValue methods to get and set the values on the object:

```
sender.setValue("Canvas.Top", 5);
var top = sender.getValue("Canvas.Top");
```

You can register for events using the property syntax as well, by calling the addEventListener method of a XAML element. You call the method using the name of the event and the name of the function to call when the event is fired:

```
sender.addEventListener("mouseEnter", "canvas_MouseEnter");
sender.addEventListener("mouseLeave", "canvas_MouseLeave");
```

Once you register for events, you must have functions to handle events, such as the methods in Example E-8.

Example E-8. Event handlers

```
function canvas_MouseEnter(sender, args) {
  sender.background = "#FF0000";
}

function canvas_MouseLeave(sender, args) {
  sender.background = "#888888";
}
```

The Plug-in

Working with individual XAML elements is useful, but sometimes you will need to work directly with the Silverlight plug-in. Every XAML object has a getHost method that will return the Silverlight plug-in object, as Example E-9 illustrates.

Example E-9. Retrieving the host from a XAML element

```
function root_Loaded(sender, args) {
  var theHost = sender.getHost();
}
```

In addition, you can obtain the plug-in by calling the HTML document's getElementById method. When doing so, use the name you specified in the createObject function call that was used to instantiate the Silverlight object in the HTML, as shown in Example E-10.

Example E-10. Retrieving the host

```
function root_Loaded(sender, args) {
  var theHost = document.getElementById("SilverlightControl");
}
```

The Silverlight host has a number of properties that describe the plug-in object, listed in Table E-5.

Table E-5. Properties describing the plug-in object

Property	Meaning
background	The color of the background of the Silverlight host
source	A URL to a XAML document to load into the Silverlight host
windowlessMode	A Boolean value that indicates whether the Silverlight host should be windowless; windowless controls support alpha-channel colored backgrounds to enable HTML to display through the Silverlight control
enableFramerateCounter	Displays a number that reports the current frame rate

Table E-5. Properties describing the plug-in object (continued)

Property	Meaning
enableHtmlAccess	Allows the Silverlight object to interact with the HTML DOM
enableRedrawRegions	Displays colored regions on the plug-in that are currently being redrawn (for debugging of XAML performance)
initParams	A structure that contains the initialization properties, like height, width, and so on
isLoaded	Returns a Boolean value that reports whether the plug-in is completely loaded
maxFrameRate	The maximum frame rate to display content

In addition, the Silverlight host has properties that are available once the plug-in has loaded, listed in Table E-6.

Table E-6. Properties available once the plug-in has loaded

Property	Meaning
actualWidth	The actual computed width of the host
actualHeight	The actual computed height of the host
fullScreen	A Boolean that specifies whether the Silverlight host should be shown over the entire screen instead of embedded in the HTML object

The difference between the width and height values used in the initialization and their actual counterparts is how they are set initially. For example, if the width and height are set to static values (e.g., 400 × 400) the actual values will be identical. Alternatively, if you set the width and/or height to a percentage value (e.g., 50 percent), the actual height and/or width will be the actualWidth and actualHeight properties.

Silverlight allows you to display an asset over the entire screen. The fullscreen property is available only after the Silverlight host has loaded the XAML. For example, a mouse click on a canvas could cause the host to show itself full-screen, as shown in Example E-11.

Example E-11. Retrieving the host

```
function makeFullScreen_MouseLeftButtonUp(sender, args) {
  var theHost = sender.getHost();
  theHost.fullScreen = true;
}
```

In addition to the loaded event, the host also supports the events listed in Table E-7.

Table E-7. Supported events

Event	Usage
resized	Fired when the actual size (actualWidth and/or actualHeight) is changed
fullScreenChanged	Fired when the Silverlight host changes the state of the fullScreen property

When looking for objects in the HTML DOM, you normally use the document's getElementById method. Silverlight's findName method provides the same functionality, allowing you to find objects anywhere in the XAML document by name. The findName method exists on all Silverlight XAML elements as well as on the plug-in object. If you use it from a XAML element, you can call it directly. For example, we could use it in our root_Loaded function to find the ellipse and set its stroke (outline) to white, as shown in Example E-12.

Example E-12. Using findName

```
function root_Loaded(sender, args) {
  var theCircle = sender.findName("theCircle"); // from XAML DOM
  theCircle.stroke = "#000000";
}
```

If you want to use the findName method on the plug-in object, you will need to prefix the content property of the plug-in object:

```
// Check the entire XAML document
var theHost = sender.getHost();
var theCircle = theHost.content.findName("theCircle");
```

The findName method searches the entire document for the named element. An element's findName does not limit the search to just part of the document tree. In fact, the findName on a XAML element is a shortcut to the host's findName method. So, these two calls to findName are functionally identical:

```
// Check the entire XAML document
var theHost = sender.getHost();
var theCircle = theHost.content.findName("theCircle");

// Also check the entire XAML document
var theCircle = sender.findName("theCircle");
```

Working with the XAML Object Model

The XAML object model is a hierarchy built from the XAML loaded into the host. You can traverse this hierarchy using collections of contained objects. For the Canvas element, use its children property. To iterate through the collection, use the count property in conjunction with the getItem method of the children property, like so:

```
for (var x = 0; x < sender.children.count; ++x) {
  var child = sender.children.getItem(x);
  ...
}
```

XAML elements support a variety of collections. Table E-8 shows the parent elements and the collections they support.

Table E-8. Parent elements and supported collections

Parent element	Collection name
Canvas	Children
PathGeometry	Figures
LinearGradientBrush	GradientStops
RadialGradientBrush	GradientStops
ColorAnimationUsingKeyFrames	KeyFrames
DoubleAnimationUsingKeyFrames	KeyFrames
PointAnimationUsingKeyFrames	KeyFrames
PathFigure	Segments
Canvas	Triggers
EventTrigger	Actions

Each collection provides the methods listed in Table E-9.

Table E-9. Methods provided by each collection

Method	Usage
getItem	Retrieves a specific element in the collection by index
add	Adds an item to the end of the collection
insert	Adds an item to the collection at a specific position by index
remove	Removes a specific element from the collection
removeAt	Removes the element in the collection at a specific position by index

You can also use the getParent method of any XAML object to retrieve its container:

```
var parent = sender.getParent();
```

An Example: Creating a Button

Earlier in this appendix, we saw how we could create the beginnings of a button using XAML. With a little additional XAML, we can make it act like a real button:

```
<Canvas xmlns="..."
        xmlns:x="..."
        Loaded="root_Loaded">

    <!-- The button -->
    <Canvas x:Name="button1"
            Canvas.Left="25" Canvas.Top="25"
            Cursor="Hand">
        <Rectangle Height="32" Width="100"
                Stroke="LightGray" StrokeThickness="2"
                RadiusX="2" RadiusY="2" >
            <Rectangle.Fill>
                <LinearGradientBrush>
```

```
            <GradientStop x:Name="button1_gradientStop1"
                          Color="#EEEEEE" Offset="0"/>
            <GradientStop x:Name="button1_gradientStop2"
                          Color="#444444" Offset="1"/>
          </LinearGradientBrush>
        </Rectangle.Fill>
      </Rectangle>
      <TextBlock Canvas.Top="4" Canvas.Left="14"
                 FontSize="18" Foreground="#BBBBBB"
                 Text="Press Me"/>
      <TextBlock Canvas.Top="3" Canvas.Left="13"
                 FontSize="18" Foreground="#444444"
                 Text="Press Me"/>
    </Canvas>

  </Canvas>
```

Notice the root_Loaded event handler for the main Canvas, where we will set up our button's events. We have also given the button Canvas a name so that we can reference it with the findName method. Lastly, we have named the GradientStops so that we can manipulate them. The GradientStop names begin with the button name for a reason that will become apparent shortly.

The following setupButton function registers four event handlers for a button, and it is invoked by the root_Loaded function:

```
function setupButton(button) {
    button.addEventListener("mouseEnter", "handleMouseEnter");
    button.addEventListener("mouseLeave", "handleMouseLeave");
    button.addEventListener("mouseLeftButtonUp", "handleMouseUp");
    button.addEventListener("mouseLeftButtonDown", "handleMouseDown");
}

function root_Loaded(sender, args) {
    setupButton(sender.findName("button1"));
}
```

In each mouse event handler, we can change the offset for the gradient stop to make the button act like a real button (i.e., change the look when you move the mouse over the button as well as when the button is clicked and released). Notice that we are using the name of the sender of this event (the button's Canvas) to prefix our name to find the correct gradient stop for our button. In our MouseUp event handler, we will display an alert to show that the button was clicked:

```
function handleMouseEnter(sender, eventArgs) {
    var gradientStop1 = sender.findName(sender.Name +
                                        "_gradientStop1");
    var gradientStop2 = sender.findName(sender.Name +
                                        "_gradientStop2");
    gradientStop1.offset = 1;
    gradientStop2.offset = .203;
}
```

```
function handleMouseLeave(sender, eventArgs) {
  var gradientStop1 = sender.findName(sender.Name +
                                "_gradientStop1");
  var gradientStop2 = sender.findName(sender.Name +
                                "_gradientStop2");
  gradientStop1.offset = 0;
  gradientStop2.offset = 1;
}

function handleMouseUp(sender, eventArgs) {
  var gradientStop1 = sender.findName(sender.Name +
                                "_gradientStop1");
  var gradientStop2 = sender.findName(sender.Name +
                                "_gradientStop2");
  gradientStop1.offset = 1;
  gradientStop2.offset = .203;

  alert("clicked: " + sender.Name);
}

function handleMouseDown(sender, eventArgs) {
  var gradientStop1 = sender.findName(sender.Name +
                                "_gradientStop1");
  var gradientStop2 = sender.findName(sender.Name +
                                "_gradientStop2");
  gradientStop1.offset = 1;
  gradientStop2.offset = 1;
}
```

The mouse handlers retrieve the name of the button from the sender argument and use it to construct the names of that button's GradientStops. By using the same naming pattern for each button, the same event handlers can work for all of them. Because the mouse event handlers are generic enough to work for more than one button, we can add a new button to our XAML document, like so:

```
...
<!-- The second button -->
<Canvas x:Name="button2"
        Canvas.Left="25" Canvas.Top="75"
        Cursor="Hand">
  <Rectangle Height="32" Width="100"
             Stroke="LightGray" StrokeThickness="2"
             RadiusX="2" RadiusY="2" >
    <Rectangle.Fill>
      <LinearGradientBrush>
        <GradientStop x:Name="button2_gradientStop1"
                      Color="#EEEEEE" Offset="0"/>
        <GradientStop x:Name="button2_gradientStop2"
                      Color="#444444" Offset="1"/>
      </LinearGradientBrush>
    </Rectangle.Fill>
  </Rectangle>
```

```
        <TextBlock Canvas.Top="4" Canvas.Left="14"
                FontSize="18" Foreground="#BBBBBB"
                Text="Press Me"/>
        <TextBlock Canvas.Top="3" Canvas.Left="13"
                FontSize="18" Foreground="#444444"
                Text="Press Me"/>  </Canvas>
...
```

Finally, we can add code to the root_Loaded function to set up a new button:

```
function root_Loaded(sender, args) {
  setupButton(sender.findName("button1"));
  setupButton(sender.findName("button2"));
}
```

We can see the button's various states in Figures E-7, E-8, and E-9.

Figure E-7. Our button (normal state)

Figure E-8. Our button (MouseEnter state)

Figure E-9. Our button (MouseLeftButtonDown state)

Creating Dynamic XAML

So far, we have been working with largely static XAML, but Silverlight supports
dynamic XAML as well. You can use the host object to create elements from XAML
fragments. For example, we can create a new rectangle by using a string representation of the XAML fragment to call the createFromXaml method (on the host's content
property), as shown in the following code snippet:

```
function root_Loaded(sender, args) {
  // Get a reference to the Host
  var host = sender.getHost();

  // The XAML
  var xaml = '<Rectangle Fill="Blue" Width="100" Height="100" />';

  // Create a new object from the fragment
  var newRect = host.content.createFromXaml(xaml);

  // Add it to the children of our root Canvas
  sender.children.add(newRect);
}
```

Calling `createFromXaml` creates the element but does not add it to the document. Once the element is created, you can use the `Children` collection to add it to any children collection in the XAML object model. If you want to name an element, you must use the `Name` attribute prefix, as shown in the following fragment:

```
// The XAML
var xaml =
'<Rectangle
Name="aRect" Fill="Blue" Width="100" Height="100" />';
```

Silverlight does not include control templates or data templates; instead, we can use `createFromXaml` to create templates in JavaScript code. For example, if we were to create an HTML button that creates new rectangles every time it was clicked:

```
<input id="addButton" type="button"
       onclick="return addButton_click( )"
       value="Add Rectangle" />
```

the code to create the rectangles dynamically would look like Example E-13.

Example E-13. Dynamic XAML as templates

```
var currentTop = 0;
var currentLeft = 0;
var template = '<Rectangle Width="50" Height="50" ' +
               '              Canvas.Top="%1" Canvas.Left="%2" ' +
               '              Fill="Gray" Stroke="Black" />';

function addButton_click( ) {

    // Get the host and the root canvas
    var theHost = document.getElementById("theHost");
    var root = theHost.content.findName("theRoot");

    // Get a copy of the template and replace the
    // placeholders with the top and left values
    var newTemplate = template.replace("%1", currentTop);
    newTemplate = newTemplate.replace("%2", currentLeft);

    // Create the new rectangle from the template
    var newRect = theHost.content.createFromXaml(newTemplate);

    // Add it to the root canvas
    root.children.add(newRect);

    // Increment the top and left for the next rectangle
    currentTop += 10;
    currentLeft += 10;
}
```

By using a template, we can create any number of the objects we need at runtime using the host's `createFromXaml` method. When we run the page, we start with just

---

our button and no rectangles. Clicking the button a few times gives us multiple rectangles, as shown in Figure E-10.

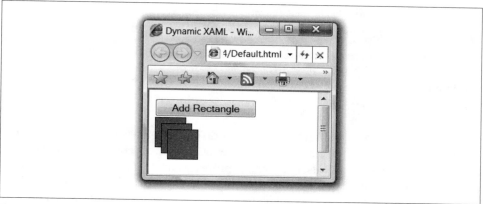

Figure E-10. Dynamic XAML—after

Controlling Media

Now that you are comfortable building your Silverlight XAML, you should learn how to use some of the more interesting tags. The first of these is the MediaElement tag. Using media (e.g., video and audio) is a key use case for Silverlight. To that end, Silverlight has rich support for media playback. The core of this support is the MediaElement tag. The MediaElement tag provides the following types of media:

- Windows Media Video (WMV)
- Windows Media Audio (WMA)
- MPEG-1 Audio Layer-3 (MP3)

To specify the media to be played you specify the URL from which to download the media, like so:

```
<MediaElement x:Name="theVideo"
              Width="450.222" Height="280"
              Source="xbox.wmv"/>
```

To control the flow of the media, the MediaElement provides three methods, listed in Table E-10.

Table E-10. Methods provided by the MediaElement

Method	Usage
play	Starts or restarts the media (if paused)
pause	Stops the media at the current position, allowing play to continue where it was paused
stop	Ends playing the video and resets its current position to the beginning of the media

`MediaElement` provides a number of events that are specific to playing media, listed in Table E-11.

Table E-11. Events provided by the MediaElement

Event	Usage
MediaOpened	Fired when the media has been opened and is about to play (which is normally after the `MediaElement` is loaded)
MediaEnded	Fired when the media has completed playing
MediaFailed	Fired if the media did not load correctly or could not be found

`MediaElement` can download and play prerecorded video and audio files from a web server, and it supports streaming media sources such as live webcasts. For downloads, `MediaElement` supports a `DownloadProgress` property and a `DownloadProgressChanged` event. You can use these to track a download's progress. `MediaElement` also provides a `BufferingProgress` property and a `BufferingProgressChanged` event to allow you to show the buffering progress of streamed media.

`MediaElement` allows access to media time through the `position` property. This allows you to get and set the current playing position (in seconds), as follows:

```
function root_Loaded(sender, args) {
    // Get a reference to the video
    var video = host.content.findName("theVideo");

    // Get the current Position
    var seconds = video.position.seconds;
    alert("Current Location: " + seconds);

    // Change the position to 2 minutes in
    video.position.seconds = 120;
}
```

`MediaElement` also provides the actual duration of the media by using the `naturalDuration` property. Similar to the `position` property, `naturalDuration` exposes the number of seconds, but the value is read-only. `naturalDuration` is useful for determining the difference between position and duration to see how much of the video has played. `naturalDuration` is valid only after the `MediaOpened` event has fired.

In addition to controlling the duration, `MediaElement` also provides volume control through the properties listed in Table E-12.

Table E-12. Volume control properties provided by the MediaElement

Property	Meaning
Volume	The current level of volume for the media.
Balance	The position in stereo space for the two audio channels (where −1 is left, 1 is right, and 0, the default, is the middle position).
IsMuted	A Boolean value that controls whether audio can be heard. Setting this property has no effect on the `Volume` property.

Controlling Animations

In addition to controlling media, Silverlight allows you to control animations. For example, here is a simple piece of XAML that displays a circle and then animates the opacity from visible to invisible, then back to visible:

```
<Canvas xmlns="http://schemas.microsoft.com/client/2007"
        xmlns:x="http://schemas.microsoft.com/winfx/2006/xaml"
        Width="480" Height="320"
        Loaded="root_Loaded">
  <Canvas.Triggers>
    <EventTrigger RoutedEvent="Canvas.Loaded">
      <EventTrigger.Actions>
        <BeginStoryboard>
          <Storyboard Completed="circleAnimation_Complete">
            <DoubleAnimation Storyboard.TargetName="theCircle"
                             Storyboard.TargetProperty="Opacity"
                             From="1" To="0"
                             Duration="0:0:2"
                             AutoReverse="True" />
          </Storyboard>
        </BeginStoryboard>
      </EventTrigger.Actions>
    </EventTrigger>
  </Canvas.Triggers>
  <Ellipse x:Name="theCircle"
           Canvas.Left="50" Canvas.Top="50"
           Width="100" Height="100"
           Fill="Blue" />
</Canvas>
```

The Storyboard element provides a Completed event that fires when the storyboard has finished. This allows us to alert the user when the circle animation has completed:

```
function circleAnimation_Complete(sender, args) {
  alert("Circle Animation done");
}
```

 A storyboard is not complete until all animations in a storyboard have finished.

Controlling animation execution

Storyboards provide a number of methods to allow you to control their playback. These methods are listed in Table E-13.

Table E-13. Storyboard playback methods

Method	Usage
begin	Starts an animation
stop	Stops an animation

Table E-13. Storyboard playback methods (continued)

Method	Usage
pause	Temporarily stops an animation at any point; allows `resume` to be called to continue the animation
resume	Continues an animation after calling `pause`
seek	Moves an animation to a particular position in time

For example, we can add an event handler for the mouse's left button on the `Ellipse` from our earlier example (allowing us to respond to a mouse click on the circle):

```
...
<Ellipse x:Name="theCircle"
         Canvas.Left="50" Canvas.Top="50"
         Width="100" Height="100"
         Fill="Blue"
         MouseLeftButtonUp="theCirle_MouseLeftButtonUp" />
...
```

To be able to stop the animation, we need to name the storyboard that contains the animation:

```
...
    <Storyboard x:Name="circleStoryboard">
      <DoubleAnimation Storyboard.TargetName="theCircle"
                       Storyboard.TargetProperty="Opacity"
                       From="1" To="0"
                       Duration="0:0:2"
                       AutoReverse="True" />
    </Storyboard>
...
```

Having named the storyboard, we can stop the animation in the mouse event:

```
function theCircle_MouseLeftButtonUp(sender, args) {
    var circleStoryboard = sender.findName("circleStoryboard");

    // Stop our Storyboard
    circleStoryboard.stop( );
}
```

Delaying storyboards

In our earlier examples, we showed only storyboards starting within a `Canvas` (when the `Canvas` is loaded, in fact). More often, we will want to delay the start of a storyboard until some user interaction (e.g., a mouse click). To accomplish this, Silverlight supports placing `Storyboards` inside a `Canvas.Resources` section. This prevents the storyboard from starting immediately:

```
...
    <Canvas.Resources>
      <Storyboard x:Name="circleStoryboard"
                  Completed="cirlceAnimation_Complete">
```

```
        <DoubleAnimation Storyboard.TargetName="theCircle"
                          Storyboard.TargetProperty="Opacity"
                          From="1" To="0"
                          Duration="0:0:2"
                          AutoReverse="True" />
      </Storyboard>
    </Storyboard>
  ...
```

Like our earlier example, we can get the storyboard (by name), but this time we can tell it to start in reaction to our mouse event:

```
function theCircle_MouseLeftButtonUp(sender, args) {
    var circleStoryboard = sender.findName("circleStoryboard");

    // Start our Storyboard
    circleStoryboard.begin( );
}
```

Mixing Silverlight and HTML

Although it is possible to create entire XAML-based user interfaces using Silverlight in your own projects, more likely you will want to use XAML and HTML together. For example, you might have an HTML button that starts a storyboard, as shown in Example E-14.

Example E-14. Mixing XAML and HTML

```
<html xmlns="http://www.w3.org/1999/xhtml">
<head>
  <script type="text/JavaScript" src="js/silverlight.js"></script>
  <script type="text/JavaScript">

    function startButton_Clicked( ) {
      var host = document.getElementById("theHost");
      var theStoryboard = host.content.findName("theStoryboard");
      theStoryboard.stop( );
      theStoryboard.begin( );
    }

  </script>
</head>
<body>
  <form>
    <input id="theButton" type="button" value="Click to Start"
           onclick="startButton_Clicked( );"></input>
    <div id="theContainer">
      <script type="text/JavaScript">
        Sys.Silverlight.createObject(
          "plugin.xaml",
          document.getElementById("theContainer"),
          "theHost",
```

Example E-14. Mixing XAML and HTML (continued)

```
        { width: "400", height: "400", version: "0.9"},
        {});
    </script>
  </div>
 </form>
</body>
</html>
```

Mixing HTML and Silverlight elements in the same page is the most likely model for adding Silverlight content to your web pages. You can host more than one piece of Silverlight content in a single HTML page by simply creating more than one host on your page. The containing HTML element and the host object must have unique names, but otherwise you can just add multiple elements to a single HTML page, as shown in the following example:

```
...
<div id="firstContainer">
  <script type="text/JavaScript">
    Sys.Silverlight.createObject(
        "first.xaml",
        document.getElementById("firstContainer"),
        "firstHost",
        { width: "400", height: "400", version: "0.9"},
        {});
  </script>
</div>
<div id="secondContainer">
  <script type="text/JavaScript">
    Sys.Silverlight.createObject(
        "second.xaml",
        document.getElementById("secondContainer"),
        "secondHost",
        { width: "400", height: "400", version: "0.9"},
        {});
  </script>
</div>
...
```

Although you can mix Silverlight into HTML simply by adding it to the markup of the page, you cannot mix HTML into XAML. Each XAML document must contain only XAML. For instance, the following does not work:

```
<Canvas xmlns="http://schemas.microsoft.com/client/2007"
        xmlns:x="http://schemas.microsoft.com/winfx/2006/xaml">
  <Rectangle Width="100" Height="100" Fill="Black" />
  <!-- THIS DOES NOT WORK -->
  <input type="button" value="Click to Start"></input>
</Canvas>
```

The Silverlight host contains the XAML object model. The Silverlight host is just another object within the HTML DOM. This allows us to use JavaScript to change both XAML and HTML objects from within the same script. For example, if we want to disable the HTML button in the page once we have used it to start our storyboard, we can use the HTML DOM:

```
...
function startButton_Clicked() {
  var host = document.getElementById("theHost");
  var theStoryboard = host.content.findName("theStoryboard");
  theStoryboard.stop();
  theStoryboard.begin();

  var button = document.getElementById("theButton");
  button.disabled = true;
}
...
```

In the real world, it is best to allow each technology to do what it does best. Attempting to create text layouts and flows using Silverlight XAML is just not feasible with the current state of Silverlight. Likewise, using HTML to create complex drawings is possible, but it is not the best tool for that job.

The Silverlight Downloader

A typical Silverlight application may comprise a number of different parts, including images, media, XAML, and code. Although Silverlight will typically download these pieces of the application for you, in some cases it is helpful to be able to control the download process (i.e., to give the user feedback regarding how long the download will take).

Silverlight provides a special type of object that gives you control over the downloading of content. This object is the Silverlight Downloader[*] (it works similarly to the XmlHttpRequest object). Before you can use the Downloader to make a request, you must create it with the Silverlight host object, like so:

```
function root_Loaded(sender, args) {
  var host = sender.getHost();
  var downloader = host.createObject("downloader");
  ... // do something with the downloader
}
```

The Downloader works by specifying a file to download. The Downloader then fires events both during the file's retrieval and at completion. For example:

```
// Setup some event handling
downloader.addEventListener("downloadProgressChanged",
                            "onDownloadProgressChanged");
downloader.addEventListener("completed", "onCompleted");
```

---

[*] Although Silverlight contains a Downloader, there is no corresponding object to facilitate uploading to the server.

To specify the file to retrieve, call the open method:

```
// Initialize the Downloader request.
downloader.open("GET", "addme.xaml");
```

To start the download, call the send method:

```
// Execute the Downloader request.
downloader.send();
```

Once downloading has started, the downloadProgressChanged event will fire periodically, allowing you to report progress to the user, as shown by the downloadProgress property:

```
function onDownloadProgressChanged(sender, args) {
    var progressText = sender.findName("progressText");
    progressText.Text = Math.floor(sender.downloadProgress * 100) + "%";
}
```

The completed event fires when the download is finished. You then use the responseText property to get the text of the downloaded file:

```
function onCompleted(sender, args) {
    // Get the result of our request
    var response = sender.responseText;

    // Use the host object to create our new XAML object
    var host = sender.getHost();
    var newObject = host.content.createFromXaml(response);

    // Find the root so we can add the new object
    var root = host.content.findName("root");
    root.children.add(newObject);
}
```

ASP.NET and Silverlight

Hosting Silverlight content in a plain HTML file is an interesting exercise, but most .NET web developers will want to be able to integrate Silverlight with their ASP. NET projects. Have no fear, Silverlight and ASP.NET work well together.

Commingling with ASP.NET

In the most basic case of integration between Silverlight and ASP.NET, you will want to add Silverlight content to existing *.aspx* pages. Because ASP.NET is a server-side technology and Silverlight is client-side, you can simply add the Silverlight to the markup of any *.aspx* page, as shown in Example E-15.

Example E-15. Silverlight on an ASP.NET page

```
<%@ Page Language="C#"
        AutoEventWireup="true"
        CodeFile="Default.aspx.cs"
        Inherits="_Default" %>
```

Example E-15. Silverlight on an ASP.NET page (continued)

```html
<html xmlns="http://www.w3.org/1999/xhtml" >
<head runat="server">
  <title>ASP.NET and Silverlight - Together!</title>
  <script type="text/JavaScript" src="js/silverlight.js"></script>
</head>
<body>
  <form id="form1" runat="server">
    <div>
      <h3>ASP.NET and Silverlight</h3>
      <p><asp:Button ID="clickMe" runat="server" Text="Click me!" /></p>
    </div>
    <div id="agContainer">
      <script type="text/JavaScript">
        Sys.Silverlight.createObject(
          "xaml/plugin.xaml",
          document.getElementById("agContainer"),
          "theHost",
          { width: "200", height: "200", version: "0.9"},
          {});
      </script>
    </div>
  </form>
</body>
</html>
```

The example shows a simple XAML document on an ASP.NET web page alongside HTML and server-side content. Much as you used the createFromXaml method of the Silverlight host to create dynamic XAML, ASP.NET allows you to create dynamic XAML on the server as well.

Dynamic XAML

HTML is markup. XAML is markup. If we can emit HTML dynamically with ASP.NET, we should be able to do the same with XAML. For example, we can create a new *.aspx* page that emits a new XAML document, as shown in Example E-16.

Example E-16. MyXAML.aspx

```
<!-- MyXAML.aspx -->
<%@ Page Language="C#"
        AutoEventWireup="true"
        CodeFile="MyXaml.aspx.cs"
        Inherits="MyXaml"
        ContentType="text/xaml" %>

<Canvas xmlns="http://schemas.microsoft.com/client/2007"
        xmlns:x="http://schemas.microsoft.com/winfx/2006/xaml"
        Width="400" Height="400">
  <%= GenerateCircles(10) %>
</Canvas>
```

Note that we change the content type to text/xaml to indicate the content we are generating. Also, note that we are calling a code-behind method called GenerateCircles, which creates a number of Ellipse elements and returns a string of all the circles. This method is shown in Example E-17.

Example E-17. GenerateCircles method

```
// MyXAML.aspx.cs
...

public partial class MyXAML : System.Web.UI.Page {
  ...
  protected string GenerateCircles(int numCircles) {
    StringBuilder bldr = new StringBuilder( );
    int left = 10;
    int top = 10;
    for (int x = 0; x < numCircles; ++x) {
      int size = top;
      bldr.AppendFormat("<Ellipse Width=\"{0}\" Height=\"{0}\" ", size);
      bldr.AppendFormat("Canvas.Top=\"{0}\" ", top);
      bldr.AppendFormat("Canvas.Left=\"{0}\" ", left);
      bldr.AppendFormat("Fill=\"#{0:X6}\" ", top * 100);
      bldr.Append(" />");

      top += 10;
      left += 10;
    }

    return bldr.ToString( );
  }
}
```

If you run this new page, it will display in the browser as an XML file, as shown in Figure E-11.

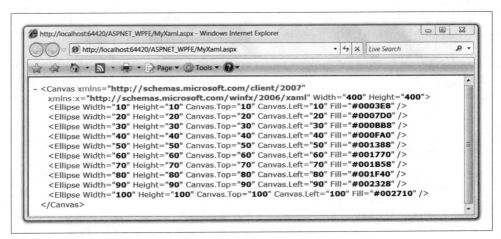

Figure E-11. MyXAML.aspx in the browser

We now have an ASP.NET page that generates the XAML we want to show in the browser. We can use that as the source of XAML on the original page:

```
<!-- MyXAML.aspx -->
...
    <div id="agContainer">
      <script type="text/JavaScript">
        Sys.Silverlight.createObject(
          "MyXAML.xaml",
          document.getElementById("theContainer"),
          "theHost",
          { width: "400", height: "400", version: "0.9"},
          {});
      </script>
    </div>
...
```

The *default.aspx* page now uses dynamic XAML to show the multiple circles, as shown in Figure E-12.

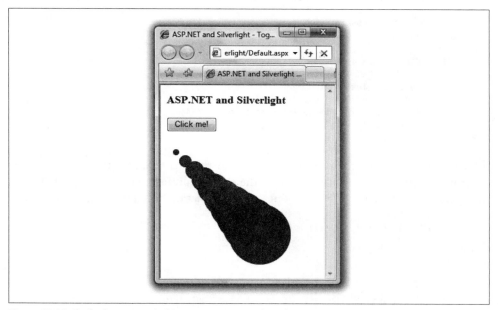

Figure E-12. Default.aspx with dynamic XAML (Color Plate 29)

XAML and User Controls

Just as we created an *.aspx* page that could create dynamic content, we can do the same for user controls. This allows us to create componentized XAML content, much as we do with HTML in ASP.NET today. To illustrate this, we can create a new ASP.NET user control to emit a XAML button (based on the earlier button examples). Example E-18 shows a simple user control that creates XAML representing our button.

Example E-18. XAML user control

```
<%-- XamlButton.ascx --%>
<%@ Control Language="C#"
           AutoEventWireup="true"
           CodeFile="XamlButton.ascx.cs"
           Inherits="XamlButton" %>
<Canvas x:Name="<%= Name %>"
        Canvas.Left="<%= Left %>"
        Canvas.Top="<%= Top %>"
        Loaded="root_Loaded"
        Cursor="Hand">
  <Rectangle Height="<%= Height %>" Width="<%= Width %>"
             Stroke="LightGray" StrokeThickness="2"
             RadiusX="25" RadiusY="25">
    <Rectangle.Fill>
      <LinearGradientBrush>
        <GradientStop x:Name="<%= Name %>_gradientStop1"
                      Color="#EEEEEE" Offset="0"/>
        <GradientStop x:Name="<%= Name %>_gradientStop2"
                      Color="#444444" Offset="1"/>
      </LinearGradientBrush>
    </Rectangle.Fill>
  </Rectangle>
  <TextBlock Canvas.Top="4" Canvas.Left="14"
             FontSize="<%= FontSize %>" Foreground="#BBBBBB"
             Text="<%= Text %>"/>
  <TextBlock Canvas.Top="3" Canvas.Left="13"
             FontSize="<%= FontSize %>" Foreground="#444444"
             Text="<%= Text %>"/>
</Canvas>
```

Notice that we're using the ASP.NET <%= %> construct to replace certain values in our control (e.g., Width, Height, Name, etc.). In the code behind shown in Example E-19, we can specify the different attributes of our control so that users can use simple attributes.

Example E-19. XAML user control code behind

```
// XAMLButton.ascx.cs

...

public partial class XamlButton : System.Web.UI.UserControl {
  string _name;
  int _width = 100;
  int _height = 25;
  int _top = 0;
  int _left = 0;
  string _text = "";
  int _fontSize = 14;

  public string Name {
    get { return _name; }
    set { _name = value; }
  }
```

```
public int Width {
  set { _width = value; }
  get { return _width; }
}

public int Height {
  set { _height = value; }
  get { return _height; }
}

public int Top {
  set { _top = value; }
  get { return _top; }
}

public int Left {
  set { _left = value; }
  get { return _left; }
}

public string Text {
  set { _text = value; }
  get { return _text; }
}

public int FontSize {
  set { _fontSize = value; }
  get { return _fontSize; }
}
}
```

Now that we have a user control, we can register it in our XAML page, like so:

```
<%-- UsingAscx.aspx --%>
<%@ Page ... >
<%@ Register Src="~/XamlButton.ascx"
             TagPrefix="myxaml"
             TagName="Button" %>
<html>
...
  <script type="text/xaml"id="theXaml"><?xml version="1.0"?>
    <Canvas xmlns="http://schemas.microsoft.com/client/2007"
            xmlns:x="http://schemas.microsoft.com/winfx/2006/xaml"
            Width="400" Height="400">
      <myxaml:Button Name="button1"
                     Text="Click Me"
                     runat="server" />
      <myxaml:Button Name="button2"
                     Text="Click me too"
                     Top="50" Left="50"
                     Width="175" Height="35"
                     FontSize="18"
                     runat="server" />
```

```
        </Canvas>
      </script>
  ...
    </html>
```

In this example, new buttons are created within a XAML script block in a standard ASP.NET page. This allows us to create dynamic, componentized XAML content on the server. Our resulting page looks like Figure E-13.

Figure E-13. XAML user control in action

Our new user control emits the right XAML to show our buttons, but we are not done. We will need to wire each button to mouse events to make them work as real buttons do. To do this, we need to add the following:

```
// XamlButton.js
function setupButton(button) {
    button.addEventListener("mouseEnter", "handleMouseEnter");
    button.addEventListener("mouseLeave", "handleMouseLeave");
    button.addEventListener("mouseLeftButtonUp", "handleMouseUp");
    button.addEventListener("mouseLeftButtonDown", "handleMouseDown");
}

function handleMouseEnter(sender, eventArgs) {
    var gradientStop1 = sender.findName(sender.Name +
                                        "_gradientStop1");
    var gradientStop2 = sender.findName(sender.Name +
                                        "_gradientStop2");
    gradientStop1.offset = 1;
    gradientStop2.offset = .203;
}

function handleMouseLeave(sender, eventArgs) {
    var gradientStop1 = sender.findName(sender.Name +
                                        "_gradientStop1");
    var gradientStop2 = sender.findName(sender.Name +
                                        "_gradientStop2");
```

```
      gradientStop1.offset = 0;
      gradientStop2.offset = 1;
  }

  function handleMouseUp(sender, eventArgs) {
    var gradientStop1 = sender.findName(sender.Name +
                                "_gradientStop1");
    var gradientStop2 = sender.findName(sender.Name +
                                "_gradientStop2");
    gradientStop1.offset = 1;
    gradientStop2.offset = .203;
  }

  function handleMouseDown(sender, eventArgs) {
    var gradientStop1 = sender.findName(sender.Name +
                                "_gradientStop1");
    var gradientStop2 = sender.findName(sender.Name +
                                "_gradientStop2");
    gradientStop1.offset = 1;
    gradientStop2.offset = 1;
  }
```

To make sure this script is included on each page that needs it, we can use the ASP.NET Page object's ClientScript property in the Page_Load event handler:

```
// XamlButton.ascx.cs
public partial class XamlButton : System.Web.UI.UserControl {
  ...

  protected void Page_Load(object sender, EventArgs e) {
    // Set up the shared XAML Script
    Page.ClientScript.RegisterClientScriptInclude(this.GetType(),
                                "XAMLBUTTON.JS",
                                "js/XamlButton.js");
  }
}
```

This call to RegisterClientScriptInclude ensures that every page that uses this control will have the *js/XamlButton.js* script included. If this is called with the same type and key (the first and second parameters), the script is not included more than once.

Now that the script is included, we also need a way to call the setup function in the script. We do this in several steps. In the XAML markup for the button's canvas, we target the event handler in the Loaded attribute:

```
<%--XamlButton.ascx--%>
<%@ Control ... %>
<Canvas x:Name="<%= Name %>"
        Canvas.Left="<%= Left %>"
        Canvas.Top="<%= Top %>"
        Loaded="<%= LoadedFunctionName %>"
        Cursor="Hand">
  ...
</Canvas>
```

Notice that we have replaced the name of the Loaded event handler with a control property called LoadedFunctionName. We now need to add this property to our user control:

```
// XamlButton.ascx.cs
public partial class XamlButton : System.Web.UI.UserControl {
  ...

  public string LoadedFunctionName {
    get { return string.Concat(Name, "_Loaded"); }
  }
}
```

This returns the button's name with _Loaded appended to it, so the button Canvas's Loaded event will look for an event handler with this tailor-made name.

For each button, we now need a handler with the name we have created. The following code, added to the button class's PageLoad method, will create (at runtime) a tailored script function for the button. Because this code uses the LoadedFunctionName property again, the function will receive the required custom name. Its purpose is simply to call the setupButton function we defined earlier, passing it a reference to the button. When setupButton is called, it hooks up the four mouse event handlers that were also defined earlier:

```
// XamlButton.ascx.cs
public partial class XamlButton : System.Web.UI.UserControl {
  ...

  protected void Page_Load(object sender, EventArgs e) {
    ...

    // Add Button Script
    string script =
      string.Format(@"
        function {0}(sender, args) {{
          setupButton(sender);
        }}",
        LoadedFunctionName);
    string key = string.Format("{0}_BUTTONSETUP", Name);
    Page.ClientScript.RegisterClientScriptBlock(
      this.GetType(), key, script, true);
  }
}
```

Now that we have all the mouse events wired up to each button, we're almost done. The only remaining task is to add support for a named function to call when the button is clicked. We can't simply add a MouseLeftButtonUp event handler, because one already exists in the button's JavaScript (to return the button's look and feel to normal once the button has been clicked). To get around this problem, we add a new function name that is optionally called when the button's MouseLeftButtonUp event is fired in the button. One solution to this is to modify the setupButton function to add a click event handler:*

---

* See the Silverlight SDK's "VideoLibrary" sample for an example of how to do this using classes and prototypes.

```
// XamlButton.js
var clickEvents = new Array();

function setupButton(button, clickHandler) {
  button.addEventListener("mouseEnter", "handleMouseEnter");
  button.addEventListener("mouseLeave", "handleMouseLeave");
  button.addEventListener("mouseLeftButtonUp", "handleMouseUp");
  button.addEventListener("mouseLeftButtonDown", "handleMouseDown");

  // If handler is specified, store the name to look up later
  if (clickHandler != null) {
    clickEvents.push(new Array(button.Name, clickHandler));
  }
}

...

function handleMouseUp(sender, eventArgs) {
  var gradientStop1 = sender.findName(sender.Name +
                                      "_gradientStop1");
  var gradientStop2 = sender.findName(sender.Name +
                                      "_gradientStop2");
  gradientStop1.offset = 1;
  gradientStop2.offset = .403;

  // Look for click event and fire it if necessary
  for (var x = 0; x < clickEvents.length; ++x) {
    var clickEvent = clickEvents[x];
    var buttonName = clickEvent[0];
    if (buttonName == sender.Name) { // This is our button
      var handler = clickEvent[1];
      handler.call(sender, eventArgs);
    }
  }
}

...
```

Because each button will have its own click handling function, we collect them all in an array (clickEvents). Then, in the shared handleMouseUp function, we search this collection to find the right function for the button that was clicked.

Now we need to pass the new parameter to setupButton. So, we add a ClickHandler property, which we will use to hold the name of the function. We then adapt the script-generating code in Page_Load to pass this to setupButton:

```
// XamlButton.ascx.cs
public partial class XamlButton : System.Web.UI.UserControl {
  protected void Page_Load(object sender, EventArgs e) {
    ...

    // Add Button Script
    string script =
      string.Format(
```

```
          @"function {0}(sender, args) {{
              setupButton(sender, {1});
          }}",
          LoadedFunctionName,
          ClickHandler.Length > 0 ? ClickHandler : "null");
      string key = string.Format("{0}_BUTTONSETUP", Name);
      Page.ClientScript.RegisterClientScriptBlock(this.GetType(), key, script, true);
    }

    string _clickHandler = "";
    public string ClickHandler {
      set { _clickHandler = value; }
      get { return _clickHandler; }
    }
  }
```

Lastly, we use the Page markup to fill in the ClickHandler property with the name of the function to be called:

```
<%-- UsingAscx.aspx --%>
<%@ Page ... %>
<%@ Register Src="~/XamlButton.ascx"
             TagPrefix="xaml"
             TagName="Button" %>
<html>
...
  <script type="text/xaml"id="theXaml"><?xml version="1.0"?>
    <Canvas xmlns="http://schemas.microsoft.com/client/2007"
            xmlns:x="http://schemas.microsoft.com/winfx/2006/xaml"
            Width="400" Height="400">
      <xaml:Button Name="button1"
                   Text="Click Me"
                   runat="server" />
      <xaml:Button Name="button2"
                   Text="Click me too"
                   Top="50" Left="50"
                   Width="175" Height="35"
                   FontSize="18"
                   ClickHandler="button2_Clicked"
                   runat="server" />
    </Canvas>
  </script>

  <script type="text/JavaScript">
  function button2_Clicked(sender, args) {
    alert("button2 was clicked");
  }
  </script>
...
</html>
```

The button2_Clicked function will now be called when a user clicks on our button, and it will carry out whatever actions are needed.

In most cases, when using ASP.NET controls to emit XAML, you will want to use inline XAML instead of external XAML resources. This is because when emitting XAML, you will likely want to emit JavaScript to the page as well. If you want to use ASP.NET controls that emit XAML on XAML-only pages (as shown in the dynamic XAML example earlier), you will not be able to emit the JavaScript to the page directly.

A Taste of Silverlight 1.1

Microsoft recently announced the availability of an alpha (think pre-CTP) version of Silverlight 1.1. This new version allows you to write your logic in .NET-compliant languages, including C#, Visual Basic, and IronPython. This new version supports a mini version of .NET. This means Silverlight 1.1 is still cross-platform and cross-browser and still uses a small runtime component.

Using Silverlight 1.1 is very similar to Silverlight 1.0. Hosting Silverlight in HTML still requires the *Silverlight.js*, but you specify the 0.95 version to specify Silverlight 1.1, as shown in Example E-20.

Example E-20. Silverlight 1.1 hosting

```
<html xmlns="http://www.w3.org/1999/xhtml">
<head>
  <title>Hello Silverlight 1.1</title>
  <script type="text/JavaScript" src="silverlight.js"></script>
</head>
<body>
  <form>
    <div id="theHost">
      <script type="text/JavaScript">
      Sys.Silverlight.createObject(
        "Scene.xaml",                      // Url to the Xaml File
        document.getElementById("theHost"), // The Host element
        "SilverlightControl",              // Silverlight Object Name
        {                                  // Properties object
          width: "400",                    // Width of the Host
          height: "400",                   // Height of the Host
          version: "0.95"                  // Silverlight Plug-in
                                           // Version
        },
        {}                                 // Event to wire
                                           // (onLoad and onError)
                           );
      </script>
    </div>
  </form>
</body>
</html>
```

Creating your XAML is also similar to Silverlight 1.0, except that you can specify the class that controls your particular XAML document. You specify the class by using the x:Class attribute of the root Canvas. This attribute includes both the name of the class (MyProject.Page) and the location of the assembly that contains the class (*ClientBin/MyProject.dll*). This assembly is downloaded to the client and run in a mini version of .NET:

```
<Canvas x:Name="parentCanvas"
        xmlns="http://schemas.microsoft.com/client/2007"
        xmlns:x="http://schemas.microsoft.com/winfx/2006/xaml"
        Loaded="Page_Loaded"
        x:Class="MyProject.Page;assembly=ClientBin/MyProject.dll"
        Width="640"
        Height="480"
        >
    <MediaElement x:Name="thePlayer" Width="400" Height="250" />
</Canvas>
```

If the x:Class attribute exists, all the event handlers must exist in the class you specify (instead of the name of the JavaScript functions as we saw earlier). As you saw in the preceding example, the Loaded event uses Page_Loaded as the event handler. This means our class must have a Page_Loaded method:

```
namespace SilverlightProject2 {
    public partial class Page : Canvas {
        public void Page_Loaded(object o, EventArgs e) {
            // Required to initialize variables
            InitializeComponent();
        }
    }
}
```

In addition, Silverlight 1.1 also provides automatic access to named elements in the managed code. For example, let's add a MediaElement (named thePlayer):

```
<Canvas ...>
    <MediaElement x:Name="thePlayer" Width="400" Height="250" />
</Canvas>
```

Our Page_Loaded event handler can now access the MediaElement by the local field (called thePlayer):

```
namespace SilverlightProject2 {
    public partial class Page : Canvas {
        public void Page_Loaded(object o, EventArgs e) {
            // Required to initialize variables
            InitializeComponent();

            thePlayer.Source = "bear.wmv";
            thePlayer.MediaEnded += new EventHandler(thePlayer_MediaEnded);

        }

        void thePlayer_MediaEnded(object sender, EventArgs e) {
            // Do Something...
```

```
            }
        }
    }
```

The .NET integration with Silverlight includes key features of both the CLR and the BCL to allow for a rich programming model. This includes key features in the BCL as well as support for writing custom controls to be hosted in your XAML. Much of the support is still in flux, and what Silverlight 1.1 ultimately delivers may be very different from this early alpha release. Understanding that a real .NET runtime is part of the Silverlight 1.1 story is the important piece of information. The specifics will change.

Tool Support

In most of the examples in this appendix, the XAML I have shown is fairly small and straightforward. The reality is that most interesting XAML is much more complex than what I can show you in a simple code example. Hand-coding complex XAML can be difficult, but that is where tools come in.

There are several tools to help you work with Silverlight XAML:

- The Expression Toolset (including Design and Blend)
- Visual Studio (including the Silverlight JavaScript Application Project)
- Third-party tools (e.g., Photoshop and Illustrator)

Expression Toolset

New to the Microsoft family of products is the Expression set of tools:

Expression Design
> An Adobe Illustrator-like tool for creating vector-based designs

Expression Blend
> A design tool that works directly against XAML and interoperates with developer-level tools (e.g., Visual Studio)

Expression Web
> A professional web design tool

Expression Media
> A multimedia asset management tool as well as a video/audio editing and transcoding tool

For the Silverlight developer, the three parts of Expression that are of most interest are Expression Design, Expression Media, and Expression Blend. Currently, Design and Media are compatible with Silverlight. A new version of Blend (Version 2) is also compatible with Silverlight. At the time of this writing, prerelease versions of Expression Media and Expression Blend Version 2 are available.[*]

---

[*] *http://microsoft.com/expression*

Expression Design

You use Design to mix vector and raster (i.e., bitmap) designs together. Expression Design allows you to create complex designs. The tool is geared primarily toward designers, rather than developers. Figure E-14 shows Expression Design (loaded with the Popcan sample).

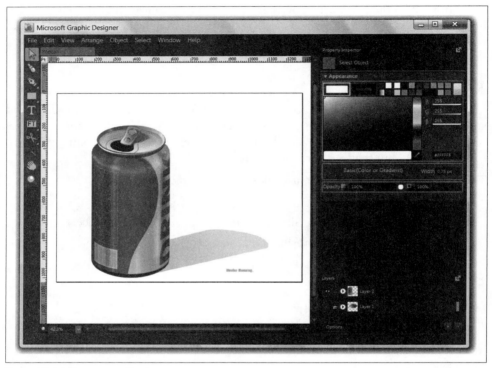

Figure E-14. Expression Design

Expression Design is a complex tool that we do not have the space to cover in depth. But for creating Silverlight XAML, it is necessary to be aware of one key Design capability.

Design can export files directly as Silverlight-compliant XAML. To take a Design file and export it for XAML, you would select File → Export → XAML from the main menu. When exporting from Design, open the Document Format drop down and select Silverlight, as shown in Figure E-15.

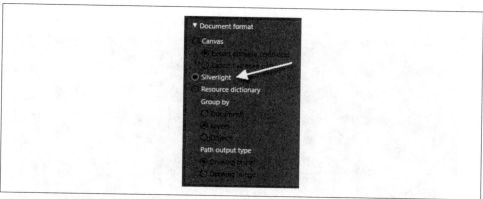

Figure E-15. Exporting for Silverlight from Expression Design

Expression Blend

Whereas Expression Design is the right tool for creating static designs, Expression Blend is a tool for working with native XAML. You use Blend for creating animations for Silverlight (as well as WPF). The Expression Blend window looks similar to the Expression Design window. Instead of working on an individual design file, Blend works with projects. Figure E-16 shows the Expression Blend user interface.

Expression Blend Version 2 fully supports the use of Silverlight for development. It creates new Silverlight projects and generates fully Silverlight-compatible XAML.

Expression Media

For applications that include video and audio streams, Expression Media is a tool for transcoding video and audio to the right format (cropping, trimming, adding metadata and alpha channels, and more). The preview version of Expression Media is also available now and supports encoding video packaged in several different Silverlight skins.

Visual Studio

The Silverlight 1.0 SDK includes an additional installer for adding a new project type in Visual Studio. You can find this installer in the *Tools* folder of the SDK (usually *C:\ Program Files\Microsoft SDKs\Silverlight*). Installing it will add a new project type to Visual Studio. Once you install the new project type, you can access it (it's called a Silverlight JavaScript Application) inside Visual Studio. You can find this project type under Visual C# projects. Figure E-17 shows you the New Project dialog with this project template.

Figure E-16. Expression Blend

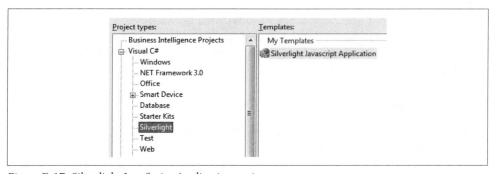

Figure E-17. Silverlight JavaScript Application project type

This new project type is a simple test bed for a XAML file hosted in HTML. Even though this project is hosted under the Visual C# project type, it creates a simple HTML page where you can specify and test your Silverlight assets before you integrate them into an ASP.NET project. When you run the project, it will run the HTML file hosting your XAML and allow you to set breakpoints to debug the JavaScript. Figure E-18 shows the Solution Explorer for a newly created project using the template.

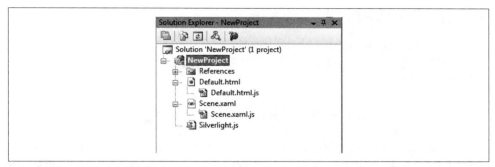

Figure E-18. Application project items

Other Tools

Designers are used to working with tools such as Adobe's Photoshop and Illustrator. To use the output from these tools, you need a way to create XAML files that are compatible with Silverlight. The key is to use Expression Design as the way to create XAML from these tools. Expression Design can import both Photoshop and Illustrator files. Once the files are imported into Design, it is simple to export them as Silverlight-compatible XAML (as we saw earlier in this appendix).

Examples in the World

Beyond the resources that are available from the Silverlight DevCenter[*] or the Silverlight web site,[†] there are several very good examples of Silverlight on the Web today. They include:

Mike Harsh's Lumines Hi-Score
> *http://blogs.msdn.com/mharsh/archive/2007/03/26/lumines-live-60-second-top-score-in-wpf-e.aspx (http://tinysells.com/82)*

ScreenEdit
> *http://www.screenedit.co.uk/sevideo/9992/9992.htm (http://tinysells.com/83)*

Airline Demo
> *http://blogs.msdn.com/delay/archive/2007/05/01/the-web-just-got-even-better-silverlight-announced-at-mix07.aspx (http://tinysells.com/84)*

---

[*] *http://www.microsoft.com/silverlight*
[†] *http://silverlight.net*

Where Are We?

Silverlight is a technology that allows use of XAML to design web content that works across different browsers and operating systems. By delivering XAML to the browser and using scripts to automate the XAML, we can create compelling content for a web audience.

Though named similarly, WPF and Silverlight are very different technologies. Silverlight's entire programming model is based on writing client-side scripts for use in a web browser. Although WPF XAML and Silverlight XAML have a lot in common, we still need to learn how to automate Silverlight's XAML assets in a completely different way.

One main question remains unanswered: when should I use WPF and when should I use Silverlight? You should use Silverlight when your intended audience is widely distributed across operating systems and web browsers. Because WPF requires Windows and the large .NET 3.0 runtime, it is perfect in scenarios where you have more control over your users' environment. Silverlight, on the other hand, is useful for true Internet applications. Although it does require a runtime, that runtime is very small in comparison and will be delivered in a way with which web users are comfortable (in the style of Adobe Flash's runtime).

—Shawn Wildermuth
Microsoft MVP (C#)

Index

Symbols

& (ampersand), 143
* (asterisk), 74
{...} (curly braces), 696
/ (forward slash), 252
_ (underscore), 143

Numbers

3D graphics, 34, 612
  3D data visualization, 642–647
  analogous 3D and 2D types, 629
  cameras, 613–618
    MatrixCamera, 618
    OrthographicCamera, 613, 617
    PerspectiveCamera, 613–617
  coordinate system, 618
  hit testing, 648–650
  lights (see lights)
  models, 618–629
    Geometry3D, 619–621
    Materials (see Materials)
    ModelVisual3D, 626–629
  textures, 635–637
  transforms, 637–642
    MatrixTransform3D, 641
    RotateTransform3D, 639
    ScaleTransform3D, 638
    Transform3DGroup, 641
    TranslateTransform3D, 638

A

AccelerationRatio and DecelerationRatio
    properties, 567
access keys, 142
  menus and, 163
AccessText element, 143
Activated event, 44
ActiveX controls and WPF, 728
AdornerDecorator, 680
adorners, 678–681
airspace, 730
ambient properties, 656
AmbientLight, 629
ampersand (&), 143
AnchoredBlock abstract base class, 510
Animatable class, 765
animation, 31, 563–566
  animating nested properties of
    properties, 577
  audio and video, 608
  clocks, controlling with, 604
    properties for monitoring clock
      progress, 605
  custom animations, 566
  dependency properties and, 565
  handoffs, 573
  IAnimatable interface, 568
  keyframe animations, 593–598
  path animations, 598–601
    DoubleAnimationUsingPath, 599
    MatrixAnimationUsingPath, 600
    PointAnimationUsingPath, 598

We'd like to hear your suggestions for improving our indexes. Send email to *index@oreilly.com*.

animation (*continued*)
  Silverlight, using for, 779
  storyboards, controlling with, 602–604
    methods for monitoring storyboard
      progress, 603
  timelines, 579–593
    duration, 583–584
    filling, 586–590
    hierarchies, 579–582
    repetition, 584
    speed, 591–593
    timeline properties, 579
  transition animations, 605–608
  triggers, 569–578
    action types and usage, 569
    DataTrigger and Trigger, 572
  types, 566–567
Application class, 4, 36, 386
application manifests, 52
Application object, 36
applications, 4–8, 36–60
  application lifetime, 36–48
    Activated and Deactivated events, 44
    application access, 37
    application events, 44–46
    application instancing, 46–48
    application instancing, desirable
      features, 47
    dispatcher events, 44
    Exit events, 45
    implicit creation, 38–40
    main windows, 41
    SessionEnding events, 45
    shutdown modes, 43
    single instance applications, 47
    Startup events, 44
    top-level windows, 41
  application settings, 55–59
    designing, 55
    integration with WPF, 59
    using, 57
  building, 2–4, 35
  content models, 16–18
  controls (see controls)
  data binding, 22–27
  dependency properties, 27
  deployment, 48–55
    publishing, 49
  excuse generator, 48–59
  layout, 19–22
  resources, 28
  styles, 30
  user experience, 52

ApplicationSettingsBase class, 55
ArcSegment, 420
arrange phase, layout, 105
ArrangeOverride method, 106
ArrayExtension, 699
ASP.NET and Silverlight, 802
  dynamic XAML, 803
Assembly class, 383
assembly manifest resources, 384
asterisk (*), 74
asynchronous APIs, 739
asynchronous printing, 542
AsyncOperationManager classes, 747
attached events, 116, 666
attached properties, 66, 67, 658, 693–695
  property element syntax and, 695
attached property syntax, 21

B

BackgroundWorker class, 748
BAML, 713
base classes, 652–655, 750–765
  Animatable class, 765
  ContentControl class, 757
  ContentElement class, 761
  Control class, 756
  core versus framework parts, 753
  Decorator class, 755
  DependencyObject class, 750
  DispatcherObject class, 750
  FrameworkContentElement class, 762
  FrameworkElement class, 754
  Freezable class, 762
  HeaderedContentControl class, 758
  HeaderedItemsControl class, 760
  ItemsControl class, 760
  Panel class, 755
  Selector class, 761
  Shape class, 756
  UIElement class, 753
  UserControl class, 759
  Visual class, 752
  Visual3D class, 752
BasedOn style attribute, 266
BaselineAlignment, 494
BeginAnimation method, 565
BeginInvoke method, 742
  lack of corresponding EndInvoke, 744
BeginStoryboard, 570
behavior, 708
Bézier curves, 423–425
binary resources, 383–389

Binding class properties, 178
Binding markup extension, 705
binding path syntax, 195
bindings, 177–180
bitmaps, 429–439
    BitmapEffects, 438
    creating, 433–436
    encoders and decoders, 437
    thumbnails and, 549–550
Block base class, 501–509
    BlockUIContainer, 508
    common block properties, 502
    List, 503–505
    Paragraph, 502
    Section, 508
    Table, 505–508
    TextAlignment, 477
blocking APIs, 738
Brimelow, Lee, xvii
bubbling routed events, 111
    code-behind file, 112
built-in markup extensions, 698–707
    ArrayExtension, 699
    Binding, 705
    ComponentResourceKey, 704
    DynamicResourceExtension, 703
    NullExtension, 698
    RelativeSource, 705
    StaticExtension, 701
    StaticResourceExtension, 702
    TemplateBindingExtension, 707
    TypeExtension, 699
bump maps, 636
ButtonBase base class, 118, 143
buttons, 141–144

C

C# minimal WPF application, 1
C1 and C2 continuity, 601
cameras, 613–618
Canvas, 19, 62, 84–86
    Silverlight, usage in, 773
Capture method, 119, 123
Captured property, 120
CellTemplate property, 156
certificates, 53
CharacterEllipsis, 475
CheckBox, 143
Cider, 12
classes, generating in XML, 687
Click events, 118

ClickOnce deployment, 48–55
    important features, 54–55
    locally installed and online only, 49
    user experience, 52
client-side script, 767
clock mode, 609
CLR events, 115
    CLR event wrappers, 115
    direct routed events, contrasted with, 112
code behind, 708–712
    behavior, 708
    code in XAML, 711
    partial classes, 708
code-behind files, 9
CodeProject, xvii
collection views, 203
ColumnDefinition elements, 71, 72
commands, 109, 124–137
    controls, use in, 141
ComponentResourceKey, 704
composition, 405
compression, 555
containers, 35
content models, 16–18
content presenters, 289–291
ContentControl class, 17, 150, 757
ContentElement class, 761
ContextMenu control, 160
Control class, 118, 756
control templates, 32, 285
    built-in templates, examining, 304
    content presenters, 289–291
    data-driven UIs, 308–313
    extending templates, 293–296
        custom dependency properties,
            defining, 294–296
        repurposing existing properties, 293
    graphics, 33
    logical and visual trees, 305–307
    lookless controls, 285, 296
    minimal control template, 285
    performance concerns, 290
    required features, 296–302
        content placeholders, 299–301
        controls with template parts, 298
        named parts, 297
        placeholders indicated by
            properties, 301
        property binding, 297
    special-purpose elements, 303
    styles and, 286–287
    template binding, 287–289
    template triggers, 292–293

controllable storyboards, 603
controls, 22, 35, 139–141
    access keys, 142
    buttons (see buttons)
    commands, use of, 141
    ContextMenu, 160
    control templates (see control templates)
    custom controls (see custom controls)
    events and, 141
    GridSplitter, 166
    GroupBox and Expander controls, 150
    list controls (see list controls)
    lookless controls, 285, 296
    menus, 160–164
    methods, use in, 141
    ProgressBar, 145
    properties, 141
    RichTextBox, 147
    slider and scroll controls, 144
    text controls (see text controls)
    toolbars, 164–166
    ToolTip control, 149
.csproj files, 3
cultures, 389
curly braces ({...}), 696
current item, 202
custom animations, 566
custom classes, 6
custom control templates, 668–674
    content placeholders, 671
    named parts, 669–671
    placeholders indicated by properties, 672
    property binding, 669
custom controls, 651
    adorners, 678–681
        AdornerDecorator, 680
    base classes, 652–655
    commands, 666
    default styles, 674
    design and storage management, 656
    design steps, 652
    events
        attached event handlers, 666
        custom RoutedEvent, 665
    FrameworkPropertyMetadataOptions,
        664
    functionality, 655–668
        attached events, 666
        change notifications for property
            consumers, 661
        events, 665
        property metadata options, 663

properties, 655–664
    attached properties, 658
    value change notification, 660
UserControl, 676–678
XAML, using properties from, 658

D

data binding, 22–27, 168, 177–180
    application example without data
        binding, 168–177
        object changes, 171
        UI changes, 174
    Binding class's properties, 178
    binding one element's property to another
        element's property, 184
    binding path syntax, 195
    binding target and binding source, 180
    bindings, 177–180
    data context, 180
    data islands, 182–183
    data templates, 26
    debugging, 198
    dialogs and, 331
    explicit data source, 184
    implicit data source, 180–182
    list data (see list data binding)
    relative sources, 197
    settings classes, 59
    text and, 514–517
    UpdateSourceTrigger, 197
    using in pages with KeepAlive, 352
    validation rules, 189–195
    value conversion, 185–189
    WPF, in, 25
    XAML markup extensions, 26
data islands, 183
data source providers, 228–245
    ObjectDataProvider, 229–232
        asynchronous data retrieval, 231
        passing parameters, 231
    relational data, binding to, 233–239
    XML data source providers, 239–245
        XML dat islands, 241
data templates, 210, 273
    DataContext and, 212
    styles and, 271–275
        setting data templates with, 275
    typed data templates, 212
data triggers, 278
data-centric UIs, 308
DataContext property, 180
data-driven UIs, 308–313

DataSourceProvider base class, 229
Deactivated event, 44
debugging and data binding, 198
DecelerationRatio and AccelerationRatio
 properties, 567
declarative sorting and grouping of list
 data, 227
decorations, 473
Decorator class, 755
 custom controls and, 654
 Viewbox element, 86–88
default collection views, list data, 219
default styles, 674
dependency properties, 27
 animation and, 565
dependency property system, 655
DependencyObject, 750
DependencyProperty object, 565
DependentUpon element, 11
device-independent pixels, 72, 76, 403
dialogs, 322
 common dialogs, 323–325
 custom dialogs, 325–340
  data exchange, 329–332
  data validation, 334–338
  look and feel, 328
  modeless dialogs, 337–340
  OK and Cancel, 332–334
  showing a custom dialog, 327
 data binding and, 331
direct routed events, 111
 CLR events, contrast with, 112
DirectionalLight, 630
discrete keyframes, 597
DiscreteObjectKeyFrame, 566
dispatchers, 741
 Dispatcher class, 741
 DispatcherObject, 740, 750
 DispatcherOperation object, 744
 DispatcherTimer class, 745
 getting onto the right thread, 741–744
 multiple UI threads and, 746
 obtaining, 741
DispatcherUnhandledExcexception
 events, 44
display members of data lists, 207
DisplayMemberBinding property, 156
DockPanel, 19, 62, 66–68
 DockPanel.Dock attribute, 66
DoubleAnimation, 564
DoubleAnimationUsingPath, 598

Downloader, 801
DrawGlyphRun method, 486
drawing object model, 399–401
 updating of images, 399
DrawingBrush class, 447, 454
DrawingContext drawing operations, 464
DynamicResourceExtension, 703

E

element-typed styles, 268–270
 derived types and, 269–270
 scoped below the Window, 269
 scoped to the application, 269
 scoped to the Window, 268
Ellipse, 411
Enhanced Meta File (EMF) format, 522
enter actions, 572
event handling, sender and args
 parameters, 785
event triggers, 281
 using in animation, 569
event-based asynchronous pattern, 747–749
 BackgroundWorker class, 748
events
 attached events, 666
 controls, raising in, 141
 custom controls and, 665
ExceptionValidationRule, 189, 190
exit actions, 572
Exit events, 45
Expander control, 150
explicit data source, 184
Expression toolset, 815–817
 Expression Blend, 817
 Expression Design, 816
 Expression Media, 817
extended buttons, 120
eXtensible Application Markup Language
 (see XAML)

F

FieldOfView, 616
Figure, 510
Fill property, 407
filtering list data, 220
findName method, 789
FindResource method, 367
FixedDocument class, 528
FixedDocumentSequence class, 525,
 526–528

FixedPage class, 529–533
    default size, 530
    fonts, bitmaps, and resources, 532
    page content limitations, 532
    page sizing, 530–532
Flash, 767
Floater, 510
flow documents, 481–484
FlowDirection property, 93–95
focus, 121
Focusable and IsFocused properties, 121
FolderBrowserDialog, 323
FontFamily class, 470
fonts
    font classes, 470
    FontSize, 471
    FontStretch, 471
    FontStyle, 472
    FontWeight, 472
    OpenType fonts, 519
forward slash(/), 252
fragment navigation, 347
frames, 359–360
FrameworkContentElement class, 261, 762
FrameworkElement base class, 261, 366, 754
    FindResource method, 367
    reference to element resources, 374
FrameworkElement base class properties, 89
FrameworkPropertyMetadataOptions, 664
FrameworkPropertyMetadataOptions.Journal
    flag, 351
Freezable class, 626, 762

G

Geometry types, 415
    PathGeometry, 418
Geometry3D, 619–621
GeometryGroup object, 416
GeometryModel3D, 618
GetAnimationBaseValue, 568
GetManifestResourceStream method, 383
GetNavigationService method, 344
GetPosition method, 119
global applications, 389–394
    satellite resource assemblies, 390
    XAML, building localizable applications
        with, 391–394
Glyphs element, 529
GlyphTypeface class, 470

graphics, 33, 395
    2D transformations, 461–463
    3D graphics, 34
        (see also 3D graphics)
    bitmaps (see bitmaps)
    brushes, 405, 439
        color, 440
        LinearGradientBrush, 442
        RadialGradientBrush, 445
        SolidColorBrush, 441
    composition, 405
    drawing object model, 399–401
        memory issues, 401
        updating of images, 399
    DrawingBrush class, 454
    ImageBrush class, 453
    integration, 395–399
        adding graphics to a button, 397
        drawing APIs and control APIs, 396
        XAML and code, 396
    Pen class, 459
    pens, 405
    rendering on demand, 463–467
    resolution independence, 401–404
        resolution, coordinates, and
            pixels, 403
        scaling and rotation, 402
    Shape Stroke properties and Pen
        equivalents, 408
    shapes, 404, 406–429
        Ellipse, 411
        Line, 412
        Path (see Path)
        Polygon, 413
        Polyline, 413
        Rectangle, 409–411
        Shape base class, 407
        shape objects versus geometrics, 407
    Silverlight, using for, 775
    TileBrush base class, 447
    visual layer programming, 463
    VisualBrush class, 456
Grid, 19, 62
    column widths and row heights, 72–76
        automatic sizing, 73
        proportional method, 74
    ColumnDefinition and RowDefinition
        elements, 71, 72
    consistency across multiple grids, 79–83

ShowGridLines property, 72
spanning multiple rows and
    columns, 76–79
UniformGrid, 83
Z order and element order, 71
zero-based numbering, 71
grid layout, 20
GridSplitter control, 166
GroupBox control, 150
grouping list data, 221–226
    custom group style, 223
    custom value converters, 224
    declarative sorting and grouping, 227
    default group style, 222
    establishing data groups, 222
    multiple groups, 226

H

Handled property, 114
handoffs, 573
HeaderedContentControl class, 150, 758
HeaderedItemsControl class, 760
Height property, 90
hierarchical binding of list data, 252–256
HierarchicalDataTemplate element, 254
hit testing, 118, 648–650
HorizontalAlignment property, 90
HTML, 766
    client-side script and, 767
    Java and ActiveX enhancements, 767
    navigation to, 363
    WPF and, 728
HWND applications
    hosting WPF in, 723–727
    interoperability limitations, 729–737
        airspace, 730
        transforms, events, and nested
            interoperability, 737
Hyperlink element, 343
hyperlinks, 551–555
hyphenation, 476
    language and, 477

I

IAnimatable interface, 568
ICollectionView interface, 203, 204
ICollectionView methods, 205
ICustomTypeDescriptor, 180

Image class, 430
ImageBrush class, 447, 453
images and the text object model, 514
ImageSource class, 432
implicit data source, 180–182
independent mode, 609
inherited properties, 469
InitializeComponent method, 315
ink, 109
ink input, 122
    stylus and ink events, 123
InkCanvas, 124
Inline base class, 473, 494
inline styles, 261
inline text, 494–501
    InlineUIContainer, 500–501
    LineBreak, 499
    Run, 495–497
    Span, 498
INotifyCollectionChanged interface, 215
INotifyPropertyChanged interface, 171, 181
input, 109
    code-based handling versus triggers, 137
    commands, 124–137
    extension openess, 116
integration, 395–399
interoperability, 715
    ActiveX controls, 728
    HTML, 728
    HWND limitations, 729–737
        airspace, 730
        transforms, events, and nested
            interoperability, 737
    HWNDs
        hosting WPF in, 723–727
        WPF and, 716
    Windows Form Controls, hosting in
        WPF, 717–720
    WPF controls, hosting in Windows
        Forms, 720–723
Invoke method, 742
IProvideCustomContentState interface, 351
IScrollInfo, 104
IsFocused and Focusable properties, 121
IsHitTestVisible property, 606
item container generation, 153
items panel templates, 300
ItemsControl base class, 152, 760
ItemsControl-derived controls, 207

J

Januszewski, Karsten, xvii
JPEG bitmap, creating, 549

K

KeepAlive switch, 351
  page functions and, 358
  XBAPS and, 363
keyboard input, 120–122
  keyboard input events, 121
  keyboard state, 122
keyframe animations, 593–598
  animation types, 597
  discrete style, 597
  Silverlight, usage in, 779

L

layout, 19–22, 61
  attached properties and, 67
  common layout properties, 89–99
    FlowDirection, 93–95
    HorizontalAlignment and
      VerticalAlignment, 90
    Margin, 91
    MinWidth, MaxWidth, MinHeight,
      and MaxHeight, 90
    Padding, 91
    Panel.ZIndex property, 95
    RenderTransform and
      LayoutTransform, 96–99
    Visibility, 92
    Width and Height, 90
  custom layout, 105–108
  measure and arrange, 105
  non-fitting content, 99–105
  panels (see panels)
  rotation of content, 98
  ScrollViewer control, 101–105
    IScrollInfo, 104
  Viewbox element, 86–88
layout model, Silverlight, 773
LayoutTransform property, 96–99, 402
Left property, 318
ligatures, 519
  standard and discretionary, 520
lights, 629–635
  AmbientLight, 629
  calculations, specular power and model
    detail, 623
  DirectionalLight, 630

PointLight, 631–633
SpotLight, 633
Line, 412
list controls, 152–159
  ListView, 155–158
  TreeView, 158
list data binding, 200
  adding items to data bound
    collections, 215
  binding list elements to list data
    sources, 205
  current item, 202
    getting the current item, 203
    navigating between items, 204
  data source providers (see data source
    providers)
  data templates, 210
    DataContext and, 212
    typed data templates, 212
  declarative sorting and grouping, 227
  default collection views, 219
  display members, value members, and
    look-up bindings, 207
  filtering, 220
  grouping, 221–226
    custom group style, 223
    custom value converters, 224
    default group style, 222
    establishing data groups, 222
    multiple groups, 226
  hierarchical binding, 252–256
  INotifyCollectionChanged interface, 215
  list changes, 215–217
  list data targets, 205
  ListBox control, 205
  look-up tables, binding to, 209
  master-detail binding, 245–252
  SelectedValue, 208
  sorting, 217–219
  ToString method and, 207
ListBox class, 207
locally installed applications, 49
logical focus, 121
logical trees, 305
LookDirection property, 615
lookless controls, 285, 296
look-up bindings, 207
look-up tables
  binding to selected values, 210
  data, binding to, 209
  helper for populating, 208
  suitable for binding, 209

M

Main entry point, 10
main windows, 41
Margin property, 91
markup extensions, 26, 696–707
  built-in markup extensions, 698–707
    ArrayExtension, 699
    Binding, 705
    ComponentResourceKey, 704
    DynamicResourceExtension, 703
    NullExtension, 698
    RelativeSource, 705
    StaticExtension, 701
    StaticResourceExtension, 702
    TemplateBindingExtension, 707
    TypeExtension, 699
master-detail binding, 245–252
  forward slash (/), 252
Materials
  DiffuseMaterial, 621
  EmissiveMaterial, 623
  MaterialGroup, 624–626
  SpecularMaterial, 622–623
MatrixAnimationUsingPath, 598
MatrixCamera, 618
MatrixTransform3D, 641
MaxHeight property, 90
MaxWidth property, 90
measure phase, layout, 105
MeasureOverride method, 106
measuring text, using Silverlight for, 778
media playback, 608
MediaElement, 608, 609
  clock mode, 609
    slipping, 610
MediaElement tag, 795
MediaTimeline, 579, 609
menus, 160–164
  access keys and, 163
MeshGeometry3D, 619, 642
methods, using controls in, 141
Microsoft Expression Blend and Microsoft
    Expression Design, 12
Microsoft WPF community site, xvii
MinHeight property, 90
MinWidth property, 90
mnemonics, 142
modal dialogs, 322
Model View Controller (MVC), 140
Model3D, 618
Model3DGroup, 618

modeless dialogs, 322
ModelVisual3D, 626–629, 643
Mouse class, 119, 120
mouse cursors, usage in Silverlight, 777
mouse input, 117–120
  hit testing and, 118
  mouse input events, 117
  mouse state, 119
  OverrideCursor property, 120
MoveCurrentTo methods, 204
msbuild tool, 3
multicondition data triggers, 280
multicondition property triggers, 277
multiple triggers, 277
MVC (Model View Controller), 140
MyApp.resources.dll file, 390

N

named styles, 262
namespaces, 684–686
  Silverlight, using for, 775
  XPS, for working with, 524
Navigate method, 342
NavigateUri property, 343
navigation hosts, 359
  frames (see frames)
  HTML, navigation to, 363
  navigation windows (see navigation
    windows)
  RootBrowserWindow (see
    RootBrowserWindow)
navigation services, 344
navigation windows, 341
  fragment navigation, 347
  loose XAML, 346
  pages (see pages)
  (see also frames)
NavigationService class, 344
NavigationWindow class, 341
nearest neighbor algorithm, 403
.NET Framework 3.0, xx
  Visual Studio 2005 extensions, 11
NullExtension, 698

O

ObjectDataProvider, 229
online only applications, 49
OnRender method, 463
Open Packaging Conventions (OPC), 523
OpenFileDialog, 323

OpenType fonts, 519
    standard and discretionary ligatures, 520
Orientation property, 66
OrthographicCamera, 613, 617
OverrideCursor property, 120
overriding style properties, 265
owner (windows), 320

P

pack URIs, 388
Padding property, 89, 91
Page class, 342
pages, 14, 342–345
    data binding and KeepAlive, 352
    page functions, 355–359
        KeepAlive switch and, 358
    page lifetime, 348–351
    passing data between pages, 351–355
    pop-up windows, 355
painters algorithm, 733
Panel class, 755
Panel.ZIndex, 95
panels, 19, 61
    panel types, 62–86
        Canvas, 84–86
        DockPanel, 66–68
        Grid, 69–84
        StackPanel, 62–65
        WrapPanel, 65
panning shots, 615
parallax, 616
ParallelTimeline, 580
partial classes, 708
partial keyword, 10
Path, 415–429
    Bézier curves, 423–425
    combining shapes, 425
    Geometry types, 415
    Path geometry text format, 427–429
    transparency, 418
path animations, 598–601
    DoubleAnimationUsingPath, 599
    MatrixAnimationUsingPath, 600
    PointAnimationUsingPath, 598
PathGeometry, 418
Pen class, 459
PerspectiveCamera, 613–617
pixels, 72, 76
    device-independent pixels, 72, 76, 403
    pixel doubling algorithm, 403
    resolution and, 403

PointAnimationUsingPath, 598
PointLight, 631–633
    attenuation, 632
Polygon, 413
Polyline, 413
pop-up windows, 355
presentation frameworks, 1
Preview, 112
PrintDialog, 323, 559
printing, 34
    asynchronous printing, 542
    FixedDocuments, 534–535
    visuals, 535–538
    with document paginators, 538–542
    (see also XPS)
PrintQueue, 555
PrintServer, 556
PrintSystemJobInfo, 557
PrintTicket and PrintCapabilities
        classes, 557–559
ProgressBar, 145
ProjectionMatrix, 618
properties, 141, 655–664
    ambient properties, 656
    attached properties, 693–695
        property element syntax and, 695
    inherited properties, 469
property element syntax, XAML, 18,
        692–695
    attached properties, 695
property triggers, 275
Publish Wizard, 51
publish.htm file, 51

R

RadioButton, 143
RangeBase class, 145, 146
relative sources, 197
RelativeSource markup extension, 705
RelativeSource property, 197
RemoveStoryboard and StopStoryboard, 571
rendering on demand, 463–467
RenderTargetBitmap, 433
RenderTransform property, 96–99, 778
RepeatBehavior property, 584
resolution independence, 401–404
    resolution, coordinates, and pixels, 403
    scaling and rotation, 402
ResourceDictionary class, 365
ResourceManager.GetStream method, 390

resources, 28, 365–367, 390
  binary resources, 383–389
    Application class and, 386–388
    assembly manifest resources, 384
    pack URIs, 388
  global applications, 389–394
    cultures, 389
    satellite resource assemblies, 390
    XAML, building localizable
      applications with, 391–394
  references, 372–374
    resources from markup, using, 373
    self-updating system resource
      reference, 373
  reusing drawings, 374–378
  scope, 367–372
    system-scope resources, defining, 369
    system-scope resources, using, 371
  styles and, 30, 378–383
    implicit use of styles, 379
    skins and themes, 380–383
retained mode rendering, 466
RichTextBox control, 147
right-handed coordinate system, 618
RootBrowserWindow, 361
RotateTransform class, 462
RotateTransform3D, 639
routed events, 109–117
  attached events, 116
  bubbling, tunneling, and direct routed
    events, 111
  CLR events and, 115
  halting event routing, 114
  normal events and, 115
  target, determining, 114
RowDefinition elements, 71, 72

S

satellite resource assemblies, 390
SaveFileDialog, 323
ScaleTransform, 462
ScaleTransform3D, 638
scroll controls, 144
ScrollViewer control, 101–105
  IScrollInfo, 104
SeekAlignedToLastTick, 602
segment types, 420
SelectedItem and SelectedIndex
    properties, 154
SelectedValue, 208

Selector class, 761
senders, 114
SessionEnding events, 45
Settings Designer, 55
Shape base class, 407, 408, 756
Show method, 316
ShowDialog method, 316, 324
ShowGridLines property, 72
ShowMeTheTemplate sample, 304
Silverlight, 766–771, 820
  animations, controlling, 797
    execution, 797
    storyboards, delaying, 798
  ASP.NET and, 802
    dynamic XAML, 803
  compatibility with WPF, 771
  controlling media, 795
  createObject function, 770
  development model, 782
    end-user installation, 784
    Event model, 785
    hosting in HTML, 782
    XAML errors, handling, 784
  dynamic XAML, 793–795
  event handling, 785
    bubbling, tunneling, and direct
      events, 786
  examples, 819
    creating a button, 790–793
  HTML, mixing with, 799
  plug-in, 787
  sample document, 769
  Silverlight downloader, 801
  supported transformations, 779
  tool support, 815
    Expression toolset, 815–817
    Photoshop and Illustrator files,
      importing, 819
    Visual Studio, 817
  Version 1.1 (alpha), 813–815
  WPF and, 767, 781
  WPF, contrasted with, 820
  XAML and user controls, 805–813
  XAML markup, 767, 771–781
    animations, 779
    graphics, 775
    layout model, 773
    measuring text, 778
    mouse cursors, 777
    namespaces, 775
    transformations, 778

Silverlight (*continued*)
    XAML object model, working with, 789
        parent elements and supported
            collections, 790
    XAML properties, working with, 786
simple animations, 779
SizeToContent property, 319
SkewTransform class, 462
slider controls, 144
    control templates and, 303
slipping, 610
smiley face XAML, 769
Sneath, Tim, xvii
sorting list data, 217–219
    declarative sorting and grouping, 227
SpecularPower, 623
SpeedRatio property, 591
spellchecking in TextBox and
        RichTextBox, 147
SpotLight, 633
STA thread, 37, 739, 747
StackPanel, 20, 62–65
star sizing, 74
Startup events, 44
StartupUri property, 345
STAThread attribute, 1
StaticExtension, 701
StaticResourceExtension, 702
StopStoryboard and RemoveStoryboard,
        compared, 571
Storyboard class, 602
Storyboard element, 797
Stretch property, 88
Stroke property, 407
Style element, 31
Style.Triggers element, 276
styles, 30, 257
    control templates and, 286–287
    data templates and, 271–275
        setting with styles, 275
    element-typed styles, 268–270
        derived types and, 269–270
        scoped below the Window, 269
        scoped to the application, 269
        scoped to the Window, 268
    extending, 265
    inline styles, 261
    named styles, 262
    programming example without
        styles, 257–260
        control properties, setting
            individually, 260

    reusing, 263–264
    setting programmatically, 266–267
    style properties, overriding, 265
    TargetType attribute, 262
    triggers, 275–282
        data triggers, 278
        event triggers, 281
        multicondition data triggers, 280
        multicondition property triggers, 277
        multiple triggers, 277
        property triggers, 276
Stylus class, 123
stylus events, 123
Swanson, Michael, 12
synchronous APIs, 738
System.Boolean setting, 55
System.IO.Packaging namespace, 525
System.Printing namespace, 555
System.String setting, 55
System.Windows.Controls.Primitives
        namespace, 303
System.Windows.Documents, 525
System.Windows.Shapes namespace, 406
SystemColors, SystemFonts, and System
        Parameters classes, 368

T

TabControl, 152
TargetType attribute, 262
template binding, 287
Template property, 32
TemplateBindingExtension, 707
templated parent, 288
templates
    control templates (see control templates)
    custom control templates (see custom
        control templates)
    data templates (see data templates)
    item panel templates, 300
text, 468
    common text properties, 469
    decorations, 473
    flow documents, 481–484
    FlowDirection property and, 93–95
    fonts, 470
        FontSize, 471
        FontStretch, 471
        FontStyle, 472
        FontWeight, 472
    Glyphs class, 491–493
    hyphenation, 476
        language and, 477

text alignment, 477
text controls, 146–149
text object model (see text object model)
text wrapping, 475
   WrapWithOverflow, 476
TextBlock element, 478–481
   Label and AccessText, 480
   text with mixed content, 479
trimming, 474
typography, 519
underlines and strikethroughs, 473
user interface and, 478
visual layer text, 484–490
   FormattedText, 487–490
   GlyphRuns, 485–487
text controls, 146–149
  Label, 148
text object model, 493–519
  Block, 501–509
   BlockUIContainer, 508
   common block properties, 502
   List, 503–505
   Paragraph, 502
   Section, 508
   Table, 505–508
  coding with, 517–519
  Figures and Floaters, 510–514
  images, 514
  inline text, 494–501
   InlineUIContainer, 500–501
   LineBreak, 499
   Run, 495–497
   Span, 498
  text and data binding, 514–517
TextBlock style, 31
TextDecorations property, 473
TextElement class, 469
  inherited properties, 470
TextInput events, 121
textures, 635–637
themes/generic.xaml files, 674
thirteen23, xvii
thread affinity, 739
thumbnails, 549–550
TileBrush base class, 447
timelines, 579–593
  duration, 583–584
  filling, 586–590
  hierarchies, 579–582
  ParallelTimeline, 580
  repetition, 584

  speed, 591–593
  timeline properties, 579
ToggleButton class, 143
toolbars, 164–166
ToolTip control, 149
  top-level windows of, 150
Top property, 318
top-level windows, 41
TopMost property, 318
ToString method and list data binding, 207
Track controls and control templates, 303
tracking shots, 615
TransformGroup class, 462
transforms, 96
  2D graphics, 401, 461–463
   transform types, 462
   TranslateTransform class, 462
  3D graphics, 637–642
   MatrixTransform3D, 641
   RotateTransform3D class, 639
   ScaleTransform3D class, 638
   Transform3DGroup class, 641
   TranslateTransform3D class, 638
tree binding, 252
TreeView control, 158
  data binding and, 159
TriangleIndices property, 620
triggers, 275–282
  animation, in, 569–578
  control template triggers, 292–293
  data triggers, 278
  event triggers, 281
  multicondition data triggers, 280
  multicondition property triggers, 277
  multiple triggers, 277
  property triggers, 276
tunneling routed events, 111
  code-behind file, 112
type conversion versus value conversion, 188
typed dataset designer, 233
TypeExtension, 699
Typeface class, 470

U

UI elements, 62
  content and size, 64
  content space and properties, 63
UIElement base class, 753
  command bindings, 132
  focus properties, 121
  mouse input events, 117

UIs (user interfaces)
  data-driven UIs, 308–313
    Windows Forms UI framework,
      compared to, 313
  description in XAML, 8
  input (see input)
  layout (see layout)
  text and, 478
underscore (_), 143
Unicode and text flow, 93
UniformGrid, 20, 62, 83
UpdateSourceTrigger, 197
UpDirection property, 616
UserControl class, 676–678, 759

V

validation, 189–195
ValidationError, 191
ValidationResult class, 193
ValidationRule base class, 189, 192
value conversion, 185–189
  editable value conversion, 188
  type conversion, versus, 188
value members of data lists, 207
VerticalAlignment property, 90
VerticalAnchor property, 512
Viewbox element, 86–88
  Stretch property, 88
viewer controls and flow documents, 481
ViewMatrix property, 618
Viewport3D element, 612
Viewport3D, Camera property, 613
VirtualizingStackPanel, 104
Visibility property, 92, 321
Visual class, 752
visual layer programming, 463
visual layer text, 484–490
  FormattedText, 487–490
  GlyphRuns, 485–487
Visual Studio, xx, 817
  binary resource streams, embedding into
    applications, 383
  custom windows, defining in XAML, 315
  DependentUpon element and, 11
  file format, 3
  getting a Page class skeleton, 343

getting an XBAP application
    skeleton, 361
  interoperability, 723
  lack of WPF localization support, 391
  .NET Framework 3.0 extensions, 11
  Silverlight project type installer, 817
  typed dataset designer, 233
  WPF applications settings mechanism, 55
  WPF extensions and .NET Framework
    3.0, download sites, xx
  XBAP execution, 362
  XBAP publication, 51
visual trees, 305
Visual3D class, 752
VisualBrush class, 447, 456
visuals, printing, 535–538

W

Width property, 90
Window class, 314
Window1 class, 6
windows, 314–322
  lifetime, 315–318
    associated events, 317
  location and size, 318–319
  look and feel, 314
  modal and modeless showing, 316
  navigation windows (see navigation
    windows)
  owners, 320
  resize modes, 319
  visibility and state, 321–322
Windows Application (WPF) project
    template, 11
Windows form controls, hosting in
    WPF, 717–720
Windows Forms compared to data-driven UI
    frameworks, 313
WindowStartupLocation property, 318
WindowState property, 321
WordEllipsis, 475
WPF assemblies, 2
WPF Designer, 12
WrapPanel, 20, 62, 65
  Orientation property, 66
WrapWithOverflow, 476

X

x:Class property, 316
XAML, 8–16, 683
  attached property syntax, 21
  code behind, 708–712
  code in XAML, 711
  collections, declaring in, 201
  custom controls, using properties in, 658
  editing, 11–14
  example file, 683–690
    children, 688–690
    classes, generating, 687
    namespaces, 684–686
    properties, 687
  examples, 63
  loading, 712
    loading compiled XAML (BAML), 713
    parsing at runtime, 713
  loose XAML, 346
  markup extensions, 26, 696–707
    built-in markup extensions, 698–707
  namespace mapping syntax, 29
  navigation windows and, 346
  properties, 690–695
    attached properties, 693–695
  property element syntax, 18, 692
  ResourceDictionary, populating, 366
  Silverlight and, 767, 771–781
    smiley face, 769
  user controls and, 805–813
  WPF and, 683
  XBAPs (XAML Browser
    Applications), 14–16
.xaml.cs files, 9
XamlPad tool, 13
XBAPs (XAML Browser Applications), 361
  KeepAlive switch and, 363
  NavigationWindow and, 345
  publication and deployment, 362
XML
  namespace prefixes, 685
  Office Open XML standards suite, 523
  XML data binding, 239
    programmatic binding, 244

XML data source providers, 239–245
  XML data islands, 241
XML Paper Specification (see XPS)
XmlDataProvider, 229
XmlnsDefinitionAttribute, 684
XPS (XML Paper Specification), 522,
    522–524
  displaying fixed documents, 561
  file structure, 525
  FixedDocument class, 528
  FixedDocumentSequence, 526–528
  FixedPage, 529–533
  FixedPage class
    fonts, bitmaps, and resources, 532
    page content limitations, 532
    page sizing, 530–532
  namespaces for working with, 524
  outputting to files, 533
  XPS document classes, 524–533
  XPS file generation features, 543–555
    compression, 555
    core document properties, 547–549
    hyperlinks, 551–555
    package-level XPS API, 544–547
    thumbnails, 549–550
  XPS output, generating, 533–543
  XPS viewer application, 561
  XpsDocumentWriter class, 533–535
    (see also printing)
XPS, System.Printing namespace, 555–560
  media description, 560
  PrintDialog, 559
  PrintQueue, 555
  PrintServer, 556
  PrintSystemJobInfo, 557
  PrintTicket and
    PrintCapabilities, 557–559

Z

Z order, 71
ZAM 3D, 12

About the Authors

Chris Sells is a Program Manager for the Connected Systems Division at Microsoft. He's written several books, including the first edition of *Programming WPF* as well as *Windows Forms 2.0 Programming* and *ATL Internals* (both Addison-Wesley). In his free time, Chris hosts various conferences and makes a pest of himself on Microsoft internal product team discussion lists. More information about Chris, and his various projects, is available at *http://www.sellsbrothers.com.*

Ian Griffiths is a WPF course author and instructor with Pluralsight, and a widely recognized expert on the subject. He also works as an independent consultant and is coauthor of *.NET Windows Forms in a Nutshell* and of *Mastering Visual Studio .NET* (both O'Reilly). He maintains a popular blog at *http://www.interact-sw.co.uk/iangblog/.*

Colophon

The animal on the cover of *Programming WPF*, Second Edition, is a kudu. Not to be confused with kudzu (a purple-flowered vine indigenous to East Asia), the kudu, native to East Africa, comprises 2 of the 90 species of antelope: lesser kudu (*Tragelaphus imberbis*) and greater kudu (*Tragelaphus strepsiceros*). Both species have coats of a brownish hue, adorned with white stripes and spots, and a crest of long hair along the spine. Their coloring and markings help camouflage them from predators including big cats, wild dogs, eagles, hyenas, and pythons. If alarmed, kudus will stand very still, making them virtually impossible to spot.

Kudu males are easily distinguished from their distaff counterparts by their twisted horns, whose myriad traditional applications among African cultures include serving as musical instruments, honey receptacles, and ritual symbols of male potency. Males sometimes form small bachelor groups but more often remain solitary and widely dispersed. Dominance is usually established quickly and peacefully by means of a lateral display, in which one male kudu stands sideways in front of another, making himself look as large as possible. Males only join females during mating season. Female kudus leave their newborns for four or five weeks after birth, but the calves eventually accompany their mothers, forming small groups of 6–10 females and offspring. Calves grow rapidly and are fairly independent by six months of age.

The cover image is from the Dover Pictorial Archive. The cover font is Adobe ITC Garamond. The text font is Linotype Birka; the heading font is Adobe Myriad Condensed; and the code font is LucasFont's TheSans Mono Condensed.